The Gold Hill Mining District of Utah

by US Department of Interior

with an introduction by Kerby Jackson

This work contains material that was originally published in 1935.

Introduction

It has been years since the Us Department of Interior released their important publication "The Gold Hill Mining District of Utah". First released in 1935, this work has been unavailable to the mining community since those days, with the exception of expensive original collector's copies and poorly produced digital editions.

It has often been said that "*gold is where you find it*", but even beginning prospectors understand that their chances for finding something of value in the earth or in the streams of the Golden West are dramatically increased by going back to those places where gold and other minerals were once mined by our forerunners. Despite this, much of the contemporary information on local mining history that is currently available is mostly a result of mere local folklore and persistent rumors of major strikes, the details and facts of which, have long been distorted. Long gone are the old timers and with them, the days of first hand knowledge of the mines of the area and how they operated. Also long gone are most of their notes, their assay reports, their mine maps and personal scrapbooks, along with most of the surveys and reports that were performed for them by private and government geologists. Even published books such as this one are often retired to the local landfill or backyard burn pile by the descendents of those old timers and disappear at an alarming rate. Despite the fact that we live in the so-called "Information Age" where information is supposedly only the push of a button on a keyboard away, true insight into mining properties remains illusive and hard to come by, even to those of us who seek out this sort of information as if our lives depend upon it. Without this type of information readily available to the average independent miner, there is little hope that our metal mining industry will ever recover.

This important volume and others like it, are being presented in their entirety again, in the hope that the average prospector will no longer stumble through the overgrown hills and the tailing strewn creeks without being well informed enough to have a chance to succeed at his ventures.

Please note that at times it is necessary to rearrange illustration plates in these texts. Any illustrations not found in their original sequence may be found following the index.

Kerby Jackson
Josephine County, Oregon
March 2015

www.goldminingbooks.com

CONTENTS

	Page
Abstract	VII
Introduction	1
Location and accessibility	1
Geography	1
Physical features	1
Climate and vegetation	2
Field work and acknowledgments	3
Previous work	3
Present work	4
Geologic formations	4
Cambrian system	4
Prospect Mountain quartzite	4
Cabin shale	6
Busby quartzite	7
Abercrombie formation	8
Young Peak dolomite	10
Trippe limestone	11
Lamb dolomite	12
Hicks formation	14
Unconformity at top of Upper Cambrian	14
Ordovician system	15
Chokecherry dolomite	15
Unconformity at base of Upper Ordovician	16
Fish Haven dolomite	16
Unconformity at top of Upper Ordovician	17
Silurian system	17
Laketown dolomite	17
Unconformity between Silurian and Devonian	18
Devonian system	18
Sevy dolomite	18
Simonson dolomite	19
Guilmette formation	20
Unconformity at base of Carboniferous	21
Origin of the pre-Carboniferous dolomitic formations	22
Correlation of pre-Carboniferous sedimentary rocks in eastern Nevada and western Utah	23
Carboniferous system	23
Madison limestone	24
Woodman formation	27
Ochre Mountain limestone	29
Manning Canyon formation	31
Mississippian-Pennsylvanian contact	33
Oquirrh formation	33
Gerster formation	39
Correlation of the Carboniferous formations	41
Lower Triassic limestones	42
Unconformity at the base of the Eocene (?)	42
Tertiary system	42
White Sage formation	42
Unconformity above White Sage formation	43
Older igneous rocks	43
General features	43
Quartz monzonite	43
Geologic formations—Continued.	
Tertiary system—Continued.	
Older igneous rocks—Continued.	
Porphyry dikes	46
Aplite dikes	48
Age of the older igneous rocks	48
Pliocene(?) sediments	48
Younger igneous rocks	49
Distribution and relations	49
Petrography	49
Biotite and hornblende andesites or latites	50
Hypersthene-augite latite	50
Trachyte	51
Rhyolites	51
Alkali basalt	52
Pyroclastic rocks	52
Alteration of the volcanic rocks	53
Age of the volcanic rocks	53
Gravel and clay	53
Older gravel and clay	54
Younger gravel and clay	54
Lake Bonneville beds	54
Geologic structure	55
Structural cycles	55
First cycle	55
Second cycle	55
Third cycle	56
Fourth cycle	58
Fifth cycle and faults related to the quartz monzonite intrusion	60
Progressive variation in the character of deformation	60
Late normal faulting and its relation to the present topography	61
Age of the structural features	63
Local descriptions	64
Deep Creek Mountain block	66
Uiyabi Canyon block	69
Ochre Mountain block	72
Dutch Mountain block	78
Northwestern block	85
Quartz monzonite block	88
Igneous metamorphism	91
Alteration of the sedimentary rocks	91
Recrystallization	91
Alteration to silicate minerals	92
Alteration to jasperoids	93
Dolomitization	94
Alteration of the quartz monzonite	94
Diopside-orthoclase alteration	94
Sericitization and chloritization	95
Silicification	95

Page

Igneous metamorphism—Continued.
Comparison of the alteration of the sedimentary rocks and the quartz monzonite 96
Ore deposits 97
Classification 97
Pipelike deposits 97
Veins with silicate minerals in the gangue 99
Veins containing chiefly quartz and metallic sulphides 101
Veins with carbonate or sulphate minerals in the gangue 101
Arsenic replacement bodies 102
Copper-lead-silver replacement bodies 103
Superficial alteration of the ores 104
Relation of the water table to superficial alteration 104
Relation of the physical and chemical character of the ores to superficial alteration 105
Areal relations of the ore deposits 107
Influence of zoning on the distribution of the ore deposits 107
Influence of the Ochre Mountain thrust on the distribution of the ore deposits 108
Genesis of the ore deposits 108
Future of the district 109
Tungsten-bearing pipes and veins 109
Veins with silicate minerals in the gangue 109
Quartz-sulphide veins 110
Carbonate-sulphate veins 110
Arsenic replacement bodies 110
Copper-lead-silver replacement bodies 110
Summary 110
Minerals of the metamorphosed rocks and the ore deposits 110
Native elements 110
Sulphides, selenides, tellurides, arsenides, and antimonides 111
Sulphosalts 111
Haloids 112
Oxides 112
Carbonates 112
Silicates 113
Titanosilicates 116
Phosphates, arsenates, vanadates, and antimonates 116
Sulphates, chromates, and tellurates 117
Tungstates and molybdates 117
Mines and prospects 118
Clifton district 118
History of mining and production 118
Mines and prospects 119
Pipelike deposits 119
Reaper 119
Yellow Hammer 122
Doctor 122
Centennial and Enterprise 122
Veins with silicate minerals in the gangue 123
Frankie 123
Calaveras 124
Pole Star Copper Co 124
Copperopolis (Ida Lull) 125
Napoleon Mining Co 125
Gold Bond 125
Copper Bloom 127
Victory No. 1 127
Minnehaha 127
Ozark 128
Copper Hill 128
Alvarado 128

Page

Mines and prospects—Continued.
Clifton district—Continued.
Mines and prospects—Continued.
Veins with silicate minerals in the gangue—Continued.
Cane Springs 131
Midas 134
Bonnemort 135
Rube 136
Wilson Consolidated 138
Veins containing chiefly quartz and metallic sulphides 140
Lucy L 140
Boston 143
New York 143
Silver & Gold Mining Co 143
Mascot 143
Monte del Rey 144
Fortuna 144
Bonanza 144
Cyclone 144
Success 145
Spotted Fawn 145
Western Utah Extension Copper Co 146
Climax 147
Southern Confederate 147
Red Jacket 148
Copper Queen Midland Mining Co 148
Cash Boy (Mammoth) 148
New Baltimore 149
Bird 149
Shay 149
Gold Hill Standard Mining Co 149
Gold Belt 149
Pay Rock 150
Undine 150
Rea 150
Christmas Mining Co 151
Veins with carbonate or sulphate minerals in the gangue 151
Troy 151
Immense 151
Arsenic replacement bodies 151
Gold Hill mine of Western Utah Copper Co 151
Gold Hill mine of United States Smelting, Refining & Mining Co 156
Oregon 162
Herat 162
Copper-lead-silver replacement bodies 162
Monocco 162
Silver King 163
Mohawk 163
Walla Walla 164
Garrison Monster Mining Co 164
Consolidated claim 164
New Year claim 166
Uncle Sam claim 166
Evans 166
Willow Springs district 167
History and production 167
Prospects 167
Dewey 167
Sunday 167
Lead-Carbonate 167
Silver 168
Other prospects 168
Index 169

ILLUSTRATIONS

	Page
PLATE 1. Geologic map and sections of the Gold Hill quadrangle, Utah	In pocket
2. Geologic map and sections of Gold Hill and vicinity	In pocket
3. Fault map of the Gold Hill quadrangle	In pocket
4. *A*, Bonneville beach and spit, southeast of Dutch Mountain; *B*, Dutch Mountain from the southeast; *C*, Clifton Flat from the southwest	8
5. *A*, Mottled Young Peak dolomite; *B*, Laminated Trippe limestone; *C*, Pisolitic dolomite from the Hicks formation; *D*, "Marble cake" dolomite near the base of the Laketown dolomite; *E*, Laminated Simonson dolomite; *F*, Chert-pebble conglomerate with oolitic matrix from Oquirrh formation	8
6. *A*, East slope of Ochre Mountain; *B*, Dissection on west slope of Ochre Mountain; *C*, *D*, Dissected postmature erosion surface	64
7. *A*, Crumpling beneath nearly flat fault on the west side of Ochre Mountain; *B*, Plunging minor anticline in the Manning Canyon formation; *C*, Variable dip of fault between the Madison limestone and the Woodman formation in Accident Canyon; *D*, Minor thrust in the Woodman formation north of the Garrison Monster new camp	64
8. *A*, Wollastonite replacing garnet in metamorphosed Ochre Mountain limestone; *B*, Jasperoid from the U.S. mine, with inclusions of opal in quartz; *C*, Wollastonite replaced by spadaite; *D*, Preservation of calcite cleavage lines in jasperoid	96
9. *A*, Elongated quartz grains in silicified quartz monzonite; *B*, Successive replacements in a specimen from the tungsten-bearing pipe on the Reaper claim; *C*, Apatite and molybdenite in amphibole	96
10. *A*, Replacement of specularite by danburite and fluorite, Gold Bond claim; *B*, Replacement of tourmaline by specularite, Gold Bond claim; *C*, Quartz carbonate vein, 7,000 feet east of Clifton; *D*, Quartz and orthoclase replacing calcite, Wilson Consolidated mine; *E*, Polished section showing arsenopyrite fragments cemented by other sulphides and quartz, Cyclone mine	104
11. *A*, Bladed arsenopyrite, Tunnel level, U.S. mine; *B*, Polished section showing brecciated arsenopyrite veined by pyrite, quartz, sphalerite, and galena, U.S. mine; *C*, Polished section showing replacement of arsenopyrite fragments by quartz and sericite, Western Utah mine; *D*, Thin section showing barite replacing sulphides, Garrison Monster mine	104
PLATE 12. *A*, Dense white scorodite with associated crystalline green scorodite, Western Utah mine; *B*, Brown scorodite, Western Utah mine; *C*, Crystalline scorodite forming from metacolloid	104
13. Plan of workings, Lucy L mine	140
14. Block diagram of Gold Hill mine of Western Utah Copper Co.	152
15. Level map of Gold Hill mine of Western Utah Copper Co.	152
FIGURE 1. Index map of Utah showing location of Gold Hill quadrangle	1
2. Sections of the Young Peak dolomite, showing the interfingering northward of limestone	10
3. Correlation of pre-Carboniferous rocks in eastern Nevada and western Utah from west to east	24
4. Correlation of pre-Carboniferous rocks in eastern Nevada and western Utah from north to south	25
5. Relations between the three facies of the Carboniferous rocks	26
6. Correlation of Carboniferous formation in an east-west belt from Eureka, Nev., to the Cottonwood-Park City area, Utah	40
7. Correlation of Carboniferous formations in a northeast-southwest belt from Pioche, Nev., to the Randolph quadrangle, Utah	41
8. Block diagram showing the generalized structure along the Garrison Monster transverse fault	60
9. Crumpling of Guilmette formation north of Lincoln Highway	70
10. Sketch map showing folding of a bed in the Oquirrh formation on the northwest side of Dutch Mountain	85
11. Generalized section showing supposed original relations between the Twin Peaks recumbent anticline and the Dutch Mountain thrust	86
12. Strikes and dips of various types of fractures in the quartz monzonite	90
13. Plan of main workings, Reaper claim	120
14. Prospect pits and mineralization adjacent to Reaper open cut	121
15. Plan of adit tunnel, Copperopolis group	126
16. Plan of Alvarado mine workings	129
17. Geologic cross section through Alvarado shaft	129
18. Stope projection on plane through shaft, Alvarado mine	130
19. Plan of Cane Springs mine workings	132
20. Composite section through Cane Springs mine	133
21. Stope projection, Cane Springs mine	133
22. Plan of tunnel level, Midas mine	134
23. Plan of mine workings, Rube mine	137

ILLUSTRATIONS

	Page
FIGURE 24. Longitudinal section through Rube mine	137
25. Sketch plan and section of W lson Consolidated mine	139
26. Cross section of Lucy L mine	141
27. Plan of tunnel and surface workings on north side of gulch, Spotted Fawn mine	145
FIGURE 28. Plan of tunnel level, Western Utah Extension Copper Co	146
29. Plan of workings, U.S. mine	157
30. Section through adit tunnel, U.S. mine	159
31. Mine workings on Consolidated claim, Garrison Monster mine	165

ABSTRACT

Introduction.—The Gold Hill quadrangle is in west central Utah and is limited by parallels 40° and 40°15′ and meridians 113°45′ and 114°. This area includes the north end of the Deep Creek Mountains, one of the ranges in the Great Basin. The climate of the region, like that of the major province, is relatively arid, the average annual rainfall being about 13 inches.

Geologic formations.—The following stratigraphic sequence is described:

System	Series	Formation	Thickness (feet)
Quaternary and Tertiary.	Recent to Pliocene?	Gravel and clay	
	Unconformity.		
	Pliocene (?)	Gravel and marl	+100
	Unconformity.		
	Eocene (?)	White Sage formation	600
	Unconformity.		
Triassic	Lower Triassic	Limestone	50
Carboniferous	Permian	Gerster formation	600
	Permian and Pennsylvanian.	Oquirrh formation	±8,000
	Pennsylvanian (Pottsville) and Mississippian (?).	Manning Canyon formation.	±500
	Mississippian	Ochre Mountain limestone.	±4,500
		Woodman formation	±1,500
		Madison limestone	0–400
	Unconformity.		
Devonian	Middle Devonian	Guilmette formation	900–1,200
		Simonson dolomite	1,000
		Sevy dolomite	450
	Unconformity.		
Silurian		Laketown dolomite	±1,000
Ordovician	Upper Ordovician	Fish Haven dolomite	250
	Unconformity.		
	Lower Ordovician	Chokecherry dolomite	±0–1,000
	Unconformity.		
Cambrian	Upper Cambrian	Hicks formation	600–1,200
		Lamb dolomite	1,050
	Middle Cambrian	Trippe limestone	725
		Young Peak dolomite	0–600
		Abercrombie formation	2,700
		Busby quartzite	450
	Lower Cambrian	Cabin shale	510
		Prospect Mountain quartzite.	±3,000–4,750

The considerable thickness of dolomites found in the pre-Carboniferous sequence is noted, and it is suggested that much of the dolomite in the area has been formed by the alteration of an original limestone shortly after its deposition in shallow waters in which little or no additional deposition was possible.

Three facies of Carboniferous rocks were recognized, which are separated from each other by two major thrust faults. The three facies differ from one another in lithology and in the thickness of certain of the formations.

An intrusive stock of quartz monzonite is of early Tertiary age. Variations in composition ranging from that of granite to one approaching diorite can be recognized, but no sharp boundary was found between these different phases. The boundaries of the stock in several places show a dependence upon preexistent faults, but the intrusion itself appears to have caused essentially no deformation in the invaded rocks. The limitation of the stock to the region between two major transverse faults that also limit one of the major overthrusts may be due to the more thorough shattering of the area thus enclosed and the consequent greater ease in the emplacement of the magma.

Numerous porphyry dikes associated with the intrusion show an almost complete gradation between granite porphyries in which the groundmass has an allotriomorphic texture to basalt dikes in which the groundmass is characterized by an intergranular texture. Aplite dikes in the quartz monzonite are younger than the porphyry dikes.

A younger series of igneous rocks is composed almost entirely of flows and pyroclastic rocks. The bulk of the material is andesitic in appearance, but chemical analysis of typical specimens proved them to be of latitic or trachytic composition. One flow, partly glassy, contained 8.90 percent of K_2O, although no potash-bearing feldspar was recognized under the microscope. Small outcrops of basaltic-appearing rocks also proved to be notably high in potash. These rocks are thought to be of late Pliocene age.

Geologic structure.—The structural history of the quadrangle is characterized by at least four and possibly five cycles of folding and faulting, each cycle composed of an initial stage in which compressive forces were active and a final stage in which normal faulting was dominant.

The structural features of the first cycle are naturally obscure, but there appears to have been an early stage of relatively minor thrusting, succeeded by rather intense normal faulting. During the first stage of the second cycle numerous folds, of which at least one was recumbent, and minor thrusts were formed, apparently under a moderately thick cover. The second stage of the second cycle is represented by a small number of normal faults, the throws along which are generally several thousands of feet. The third cycle was initiated, after a prolonged period of erosion, by a long phase of thrusting and transverse faulting, which must have occurred under a very light load. One of the two major thrusts of this stage was originally limited between two transverse faults, and associated with both of the thrusts are relatively narrow thrust sheets. Considerable evidence is available that these thrusts, in the regions now exposed, moved over the then existing surface. The normal faulting at the end of this cycle was relatively slight, and much of it appears to have taken place along preexistent faults. The early stage of the fourth cycle was characterized by numerous transverse faults with an almost complete lack of folding and thrust faulting. Unusually complex minor structural features are associated with some of the larger transverse faults. Normal faults that should belong to the final stage of this cycle appear to be almost completely lacking. These four cycles antedate the intrusion of the quartz monzonite, and a possible fifth cycle is indicated by minor thrust faults that cut the intrusive.

It is suggested that the successive dominance of folding, thrusting, and transverse faulting in the initial stages of progressively younger cycles is genetically connected with the fact that these structural processes occurred under a constantly decreasing load. If it may be assumed that normal faults are the result of relaxational movements after excess compression, the apparent decrease in the importance of normal faulting throughout the period of deformation may be attributed to the progressively greater resistance of the rocks within the quadrangle as a result of the successive periods of compression.

Recent normal faults displace an old postmature erosion surface that bevels all the older structural features. Evidence is presented that these faults are not all strictly contemporaneous, that the faulting tended to utilize older fault lines, and that both walls of individual faults have been active.

The structural features of the third cycle appear to be more or less contemporaneous with the deposition of the Eocene White Sage formation. The two previous cycles are considerably older, because a period of erosion must have intervened between them and the third cycle, and a Cretaceous age is therefore suggested for them. The relatively recent normal faults are probably of late Pliocene age.

Igneous metamorphism.—The sedimentary rocks near the quartz monzonite have been more or less affected by the intrusion. Four kinds of alteration were recognized—one involving recrystallization, one in which silicate minerals were introduced, one in which silicification occurred, and one in which limestones were dolomitized. These represent successive stages in the alteration. Similarly, three major stages of alteration were recognized as having occurred in the quartz monzonite, after its consolidation—a diopside-orthoclase alteration, sericitization and chloritization, and silicification—each successively younger. The obvious similarities between the metamorphism of the sedimentary and intrusive rocks point to a common origin, at a stage that must have followed the consolidation of the portions of the intrusive now exposed. Differences in the metamorphism are explained chiefly by the different physical and chemical conditions existing in the two kinds of rock at the time of the alteration.

Ore deposits.—The ore deposits show a very considerable range in character. For purposes of description the veinlike deposits have been divided into pipes, characterized by tungsten minerals in a pegmatitic gangue of hornblende, orthoclase, and other silicates; veins with silicate minerals in the gangue, in which copper and gold are the valuable constituents and in which the content of the silicate minerals in the gangue may range from almost 100 percent to nearly zero; veins containing chiefly quartz and metallic sulphides, in which arsenic, lead, and silver are the chief metals found; and veins with carbonate or sulphate minerals in the gangue, which are at present of little or no economic importance. There are no very sharp boundaries between the successive members of this series of deposits, and veins that show gradations between two members of the series are abundant. In regions underlain by limestone, replacement bodies of arsenic ore and copper-lead-silver ore are found; and two of the arsenic ore bodies are unusually large. Surficial alteration of the ore bodies has been relatively slight in the ore bodies with silicate minerals in the gangue, but is widespread in the other deposits. The arsenic replacement ore bodies have been particularly affected, the process resulting in the conversion of the primary arsenopyrite to scorodite. The bottom of the zone of complete alteration is considerably above the present water table, corroborating the other evidence of relatively recent faulting.

It is suggested that the lack of zonal distribution of the ore bodies is chiefly the result of recurrent fracturing in the intrusive throughout the period of ore deposition. A further factor that has inhibited the development of a zonal pattern in the ore deposits is the presence of one of the major overthrusts within the mineralized area. The rocks above the thrust are essentially barren, and it is thought that this is due to the inability of the ore-bearing fractures to penetrate the wide crushed zone that marks the fault.

The several kinds of altered rock and of ore deposits and the relations that are exhibited between them lead to the suggestion that the fluids that cause igneous metamorphism and ore deposition pass through a long series of changes that are comparable in degree to the changes produced by differentiation in many large intrusive masses. In this district many of these steps have been preserved by the recurrent fracturing to which the quartz monzonite has been subjected, and to this factor is ascribed the disappointingly small size of so many of the ore bodies. Only the gold lodes and arsenic replacement bodies are thought to have any great future importance.

Brief notes are given on the 100 minerals recognized in the metamorphosed rocks and in the ore bodies.

Mines and prospects.—The Clifton mining district, which lies within the quadrangle, is one of the oldest mining districts of Utah, having been organized in 1869. The value of its output of gold, silver, copper, lead, and zinc from 1901 to 1927, is more than $2,000,000, and in addition it is estimated that about 9,000 tons of metallic arsenic was contained in the ores shipped from the district during the period from 1920 to 1925. The northern part of the Willow Springs district is also included within the quadrangle, but the production from this source is almost negligible.

THE GOLD HILL MINING DISTRICT, UTAH

By T. B. Nolan

INTRODUCTION

LOCATION AND ACCESSIBILITY

The Gold Hill quadrangle, in western Utah (fig. 1), is an area of 228 square miles enclosed between parallels 40° and 40°15′ and meridians 113°45′ and 114°. The area has weekly train service over the Deep Creek Railroad to Wendover, a division point on the Western Pacific Railroad. Gold Hill, the principal town in the area, with a population of about 50, is the southern terminus of the branch line. The Lincoln Highway passes through both Gold Hill and Ibapah, a small agricultural community in the southwest corner of the quadrangle. This highway, however, is relatively little used and in many places is in rather poor condition. About 40 miles of equally poor highway connects both towns with the Victory Highway at Wendover.

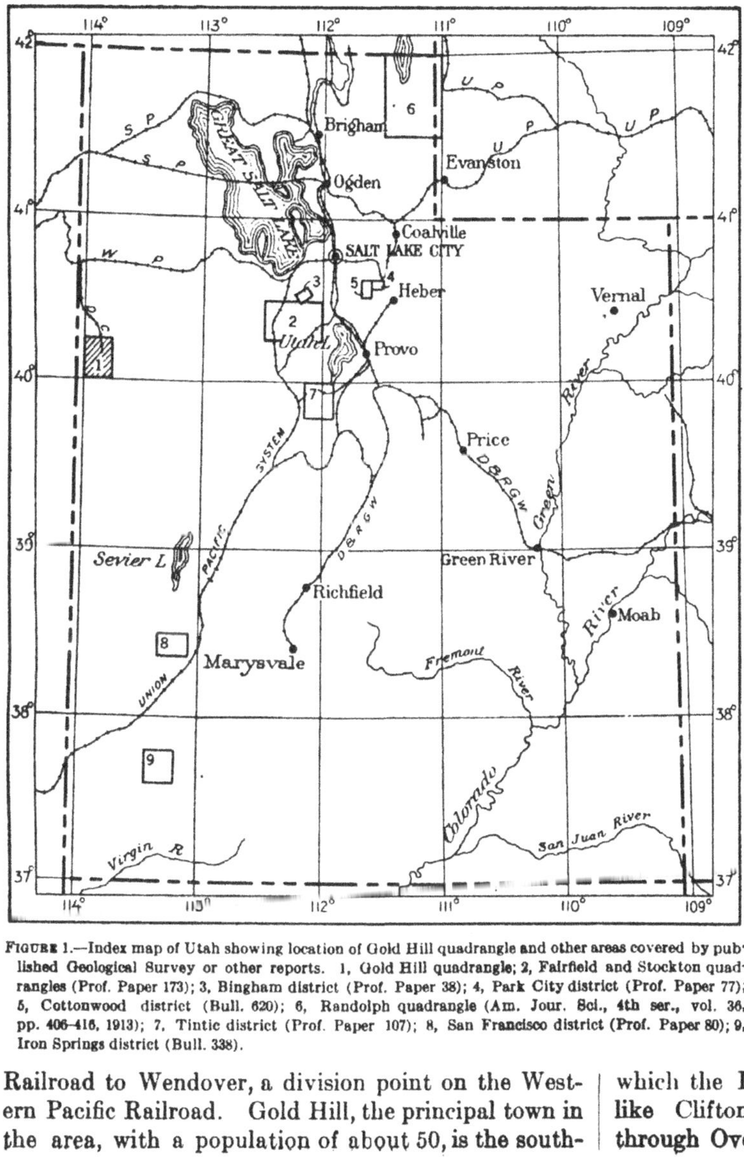

Figure 1.—Index map of Utah showing location of Gold Hill quadrangle and other areas covered by published Geological Survey or other reports. 1, Gold Hill quadrangle; 2, Fairfield and Stockton quadrangles (Prof. Paper 173); 3, Bingham district (Prof. Paper 38); 4, Park City district (Prof. Paper 77); 5, Cottonwood district (Bull. 620); 6, Randolph quadrangle (Am. Jour. Sci., 4th ser., vol. 36, pp. 406–416, 1913); 7, Tintic district (Prof. Paper 107); 8, San Francisco district (Prof. Paper 80); 9, Iron Springs district (Bull. 338).

GEOGRAPHY

PHYSICAL FEATURES

The quadrangle includes the north end of the Deep Creek Mountains, one of the nearly north-south ranges that are common in the Great Basin. On the east and north the mountain area is separated by gravel slopes from the flat plain of the Great Salt Lake Desert, and on the west it is bounded by Deep Creek Valley and groups of irregular low hills.

South of the southern edge of the quadrangle the Deep Creek Mountains have remarkably straight escarpments both on the east and the west. These persist for about 3 miles north of the quadrangle boundary. The distance between the two escarpments in this region is about 4 miles, and the area thus enclosed will be referred to in this report as the Deep Creek Mountains.

The eastern escarpment becomes less distinct to the north and in the latitude of Blood Mountain disappears entirely. The western escarpment is more persistent and forms the western limit of the mountain region for nearly 12 miles within the quadrangle. To the north this escarpment forms the western border of a nearly rectangular elevated block known as Ochre Mountain, which is separated from the Deep Creek Mountains on the south by a westward-draining open valley through which the Lincoln Highway passes and by the basin-like Clifton Flat, which drains to the southeast through Overland Canyon (pl. 4, *C*).

Overland Canyon may be taken as the boundary between the Deep Creek Mountains and the well-dissected country to the north, which has been called the Clifton Hills. This region, whose highest summit is Montezuma Peak, lies east of Clifton Flat and is limited on the east by a poorly defined but distinctly linear escarpment that is less than a mile west of the eastern border of the quadrangle. East of the escarpment gravel-covered slopes lead down to the Great Salt Lake Desert. To the north the Clifton Hills merge westward with the Ochre Mountain mass and extend eastward beyond the escarpment in a series of low hills to the edge of the desert.

At about the latitude of the town of Gold Hill the Clifton Hills by a gradual decrease in altitude pass northward into a wide belt of low-lying country which drains to the east. Farther north lies the rugged mass of Dutch Mountain (pl. 4, *B*), which rises abruptly from the Great Salt Lake Desert, in the northeast corner of the quadrangle. In this region also are some of the best exposures of the shore phenomena of the ancient Lake Bonneville (pl. 4, *A*).

To the west Dutch Mountain decreases in altitude through a series of rude steps and merges with a hilly tract of country that lies north and northwest of Ochre Mountain. The escarpment that separates Ochre Mountain and the Deep Creek Mountains from Deep Creek Valley cannot be recognized in this region, which therefore marks the northern limit of the open and locally flat-floored portion of Deep Creek Valley.

The only perennial stream within the area is the southern part of Deep Creek, which rises in the high mountains south of the quadrangle and flows northward through Deep Creek Valley along a course that closely parallels the 114th meridian. Owing to the demands of irrigation the stream is intermittent north of the Sheridan ranch. The ranches north of the Sheridan obtain water either from dug wells or from artesian wells. Several good-sized springs along the east side of Deep Creek Valley provide water for stock and for the irrigation of a small area. The remainder of the quadrangle is very poorly supplied with water, the small quantities available being obtained from a few shallow wells and numerous small springs. The largest springs are the Ochre Springs, about 2 miles southwest of the town of Gold Hill, which furnish water for both the town and the mining operations. The water from these springs, like that from the other springs and wells in the mineralized area, has a high percentage of dissolved salts and is rather unpalatable.

CLIMATE AND VEGETATION

The Gold Hill quadrangle lies well within the region of interior drainage that includes western Utah and most of Nevada, and, like the rest of that province, it has an arid climate. Pronounced differences in temperature between night and day are characteristic, but the dryness of the air mitigates the high temperatures that often prevail during the summer afternoons.

The annual precipitation averages somewhat more than 12 inches, about half of which falls in the 4 months from February to May. The rainfall of the summer and early fall is commonly in the form of severe thunderstorms or cloudbursts. Snowstorms may be expected from October to May.

The following tables present climatic data for Ibapah, in the southwest corner of the quadrangle, furnished by the United States Weather Bureau. The conditions at the town of Gold Hill are similar, except that the extremes of temperature are somewhat less pronounced.

Monthly and annual mean temperature at Ibapah, Utah (° F.)

Year	Jan.	Feb.	Mar.	Apr.	May	June
1903–18	24. 7	27. 9	35. 6	44. 7	48. 5	56. 7
1919	27. 7	30. 6	36. 1	45. 8	56. 2	61. 2
1920	24. 2	31. 8	33. 6	38. 6	50. 8	58. 4
1921	29. 2	33. 2	40. 5	40. 3	54. 1	61. 2
1922	15. 6	25. 1	32. 4	38. 6	50. 8	63. 8
1923	31. 0	16. 4	31. 8	40. 4	51. 2	54. 8
1924	19. 7	36. 8	31. 6	44. 6	50. 4	62. 4
1925	25. 4	36. 3	40. 2	45. 8	56. 3	60. 6
1926	23. 8	34. 4	39. 0	49. 7	54. 2	64. 6
1927	27. 4	32. 8	38. 4	43. 3	51. 5	62. 0
1928	24. 0	30. 0	42. 5	44. 2	56. 9	60. 4
1929	22. 9	25. 9	38. 6	46. 0	52. 6	57. 7

Year	July	Aug.	Sept.	Oct.	Nov.	Dec.	Annual
1903–18	65. 8	65. 9	56. 6	44. 7	34. 5	24. 4	44. 2
1919	70. 1	69. 0	59. 7	37. 7	32. 5	20. 2	45. 6
1920	68. 2	65. 6	58. 1	43. 5	33. 2	24. 6	44. 2
1921	68. 6	66. 3	54. 1	51. 0	39. 4	31. 0	47. 4
1922	68. 8	67. 4	60. 8	47. 6	31. 0	29. 0	44. 2
1923	70. 7	64. 9	59. 3	43. 4	36. 9	21. 2	43. 5
1924	68. 5	65. 3	56. 8	46. 0	34. 9	20. 9	44. 8
1925	71. 2	(a)	56. 0	46. 4	35. 8	29. 8	------
1926	68. 6	68. 0	54. 8	47. 2	41. 4	24. 6	47. 5
1927	70. 6	65. 3	56. 0	48. 6	43. 5	22. 3	46. 8
1928	69. 6	67. 2	59. 8	49. 5	37. 0	18. 9	46. 7
1929	71. 7	70. 5	60. 8	53. 0	35. 8	37. 4	47. 7

a No record.

Monthly and annual precipitation at Ibapah, Utah (inches)

Year	Jan.	Feb.	Mar.	Apr.	May	June
1903–18	1. 04	1. 33	1. 31	0. 89	1. 98	0. 97
1919	. 00	1. 91	1. 46	1. 07	. 26	. 00
1920	. 82	. 58	2. 66	2. 74	3. 20	. 40
1921	. 50	. 40	. 91	3. 51	3. 51	. 24
1922	1. 16	1. 46	1. 01	2. 32	. 76	. 23
1923	1. 03	. 50	. 67	1. 86	2. 12	. 74
1924	. 09	. 12	1. 35	1. 68	. 29	Trace
1925	. 28	. 48	. 95	. 96	1. 08	2. 63
1926	. 89	1. 24	. 86	. 68	. 83	. 70
1927	. 56	1. 01	1. 61	2. 19	1. 09	1. 02
1928	. 65	1. 52	3. 14	1. 10	1. 40	2. 84
1929	. 59	. 77	1. 10	2. 31	. 70	. 95

Monthly and annual precipitation at Ibapah, Utah (inches)—Continued.

Year	July	Aug.	Sept.	Oct.	Nov.	Dec.	Annual
1903–18	0. 91	0. 86	0. 69	0. 96	0. 67	0. 66	12. 27
1919	. 14	. 66	1. 02	1. 21	1. 04	. 34	9. 11
1920	1. 79	1. 37	. 88	2. 04	. 65	. 74	17. 87
1921	. 78	2. 69	. 37	. 32	. 25	1. 50	14 98
1922	. 93	3. 00	. 00	. 67	1. 71	. 99	14. 24
1923	. 84	. 83	1. 83	2. 21	. 50	1. 40	14. 53
1924	. 34	. 69	. 52	1. 32	. 80	1. 24	8. 44
1925	1. 45	. 72	. 94	. 66	. 67	. 11	10. 93
1926	2. 03	1. 33	. 14	. 33	1. 55	1. 45	12. 03
1927	. 36	. 67	1. 14	. 40	1. 54	. 89	12. 48
1928	. 66	. 25	. 00	1. 54	. 60	1. 38	15. 08
1929	. 10	2. 15	1. 45	. 00	. 00	. 27	10. 39

Miscellaneous climatic data for Ibapah, Utah, 1925–29

Year	Highest temperature		Lowest temperature	
	° F.	Date	° F.	Date
1925	104	July 14	−2	Jan. 7
1926	99	June 26	−16	Dec. 27
1927	98	July 19	−20	Jan. 22
1928	100	July 27	−19	Dec. 22
1929	102	July 25	−20	Jan. 24

Year	Snowfall (inches)	Number of days			
		Clear	Partly cloudy	Cloudy	With 0.01 inch of precipitation
1925	24. 4	178	138	49	74
1926	51. 2	185	128	50	59
1927	54. 2	160	155	50	59
1928	70. 0	181	147	38	60
1929	35. 5	192	128	45	46

The higher portions of the Deep Creek Range and small areas near the summits of Ochre Mountain and Dutch Mountain support a fairly heavy growth of yellow pine, small quantities of which are cut for local use. The lower slopes of these higher tracts have a sparse covering of juniper and piñon trees, few of which reach a height of 15 feet. On the lower hills and on the gravel slopes surrounding them these stunted trees give way to the group of shrubs characterized by the sagebrush, and the irregular and scattered distribution of these plants provides the "spotty" appearance that is so characteristic of the lower altitudes of this portion of the Great Basin.

The floor of Deep Creek Valley is cultivated in several places where water for irrigation is available, and the green fields provide a striking contrast to the more somber coloring of the surrounding slopes. The floor of the Great Salt Lake Desert in the northeast corner of the quadrangle, on the other hand, is almost completely barren of vegetation.

FIELD WORK AND ACKNOWLEDGMENTS

PREVIOUS WORK

The first published record of exploration within the quadrangle is found in the report of Lt. E. G. Beckwith.[1] His party, after crossing the Great Salt Lake Desert, camped at what is now known as Redding Springs, just beyond the southeast corner of the area. His report suggests that there had been no previous travel through this part of the country, for the presence of Overland Canyon, which was later in general use, was unknown either to him or to his Indian guides. He discovered the pass through the canyon, however by following the crest line of the range northward and noted the presence of "metamorphic [quartzite?] shale, and limestone."

By 1866 much of the travel between San Francisco and Salt Lake City had become concentrated on the overland stage route that passed through Redding Springs, Overland Canyon (then known as Uiyabi Pass), and Deep Creek, where a settlement had been established.[2] Ruins of the old corrals may still be seen at Ibapah and south of Clifton. The first transcontinental telegraph line also followed this route.

The geologists of the Wheeler and Fortieth Parallel Surveys followed the overland route, and reports of both contain notes on the general geology.[3] Neither recognized the intrusive character of the granitic rocks, considering them the Archean basement upon which the sediments were deposited.

Gilbert visited the area again in the course of his field work on Lake Bonneville and recorded post-Bonneville disturbances on the east side of the range.[4]

In 1892 Blake [5] noted the intrusive character of the granitic rock and the attendant contact metamorphism. In the same year Kemp [6] described several rocks from the region, one of them an andalusite hornfels from a point near the Cane Springs mine.

Kemp visited the region himself in 1908 and later published his observations in a joint paper with Billingsley,[7] who had studied the ore deposits in 1913. In 1912 Butler [8] made a rapid reconnaissance through the district.

[1] Beckwith, E. G., U.S. Pacific R.R. Expl. Rept.: 33d Cong., 1st sess., H.Ex.Doc. 129, vol. 18, pt. 2, p. 24, 1855.

[2] Browne, J. R., Mineral resources of the States and Territories west of the Rocky Mountains for 1866, p. 267, 1867.

[3] Gilbert, G. K., U.S. Geog. and Geol. Surveys W. 100th Mer. Rept., vol. 3, pp. 30, 123, 182, 1875. Hague, Arnold, and Emmons, S. F., U.S. Geol. Expl. 40th Par. Rept., vol. 2, pp. 472–476, 1877.

[4] Gilbert, G. K., Lake Bonneville: U.S. Geol. Survey Mon. 1, p. 353, 1890.

[5] Blake, W. P., Age of the limestone strata of Deep Creek, Utah, and the occurrence of gold in the crystalline portions of the formation: Am. Geologist, vol. 9, pp. 47–48, 1892; Eng. and Min. Jour., vol. 53, p. 253, 1892.

[6] Kemp, J. F., Notes on several rocks collected by E. E. Olcott, E. M., near Gold Hill, Tooele County, Utah: New York Acad. Sci. Trans., vol. 11, pp. 127–128, 1892.

[7] Kemp, J. F., and Billingsley, Paul, Notes on Gold Hill and vicinity, Tooele County, western Utah: Econ. Geology, vol. 13 pp. 247–274, 1918.

[8] Butler, B. S., and others, The ore deposits of Utah: U.S. Geol. Survey Prof. Paper 111, pp. 469–485, 1920.

Since the completion of the railroad in 1917 several short articles have appeared, dealing mainly with the mines and prospects.

PRESENT WORK

The reconnaissance work of B. S. Butler in 1912 showed that it was desirable to make a more detailed study of the Clifton district, but it was not until 1924 that conditions permitted the initiation of the work by the Geological Survey. Topographic mapping was started in that year by a party under R. T. Evans and was completed the following year by W. J. Lloyd and E. S. Rickard. The general excellence of the topographic map produced greatly facilitated the geologic field work, which was started by the writer July 12, 1925. Work continued that season through September 28 but was several times interrupted by another assignment. The field work was resumed April 26, 1926, and continued until November 6. During most of this season Frank A. Melton also participated in the field work. Dr. Melton is responsible for the greater part of the mapping of the southern and western flanks of Ochre Mountain and also collaborated in the mapping of the southern third of the quadrangle. The geologic mapping was completed during the season of 1927, which extended from April 25 to August 7. During this period the writer was ably assisted by William D. Mark, who mapped in detail the numerous dikes southeast of Dutch Mountain.

The writer is glad to acknowledge the whole-hearted cooperation and hospitality of the people of the district, all of whom assisted the work freely. Particular thanks are due to Messrs. Rowley, Greenwood, and Tiffany, of the Western Utah mine; Mr. Leffler Palmer, of the Rube mine; Mr. James Busby, of the U.S. mine; and Messrs. Gerster and Ollie Young, whose knowledge of the earlier history of the district was very helpful. Mr. V. C. Heikes, formerly of the Geological Survey and later of the Bureau of Mines, assisted the work in every way and provided considerable material that would not otherwise have been available.

During the course of the field work Edwin Kirk and G. H. Girty made short visits to the quadrangle and were of the utmost assistance in the determination of the stratigraphy of the pre-Carboniferous formations. The writer was also greatly benefited by the visits of G. F. Loughlin, made each season, during which his helpful criticisms and advice greatly facilitated the geologic mapping.

The preparation of the present report has been influenced throughout by the discussions and criticisms of the writer's colleagues on the Geological Survey, especially James Gilluly, and he wishes to express his appreciation, particularly to H. G. Ferguson, D. F. Hewett, M. N. Short, and G. F. Loughlin, who have read and criticized the final manuscript. Many of the mineralogic determinations were made by W. T. Schaller, C. S. Ross, M. N. Short, and E. P. Henderson, and the chemical analyses of the volcanic rocks are the work of J. G. Fairchild. The photomicrographs are in large part the result of Mr. Short's unusual skill with the microscope and camera.

GEOLOGIC FORMATIONS

In the following sections are described in their proper chronologic order the 28 geologic formations that are distinguished on the geologic maps (pls. 1 and 2). Of these formations 24 are composed of sedimentary rocks and 4 of igneous rocks.

Of the sedimentary formations 20 are of Paleozoic age—8 in the Cambrian, 2 in the Ordovician, 1 in the Silurian, 3 in the Devonian, and 6 in the Carboniferous. Only 1 formation is assigned to the Mesozoic, a limestone of Lower Triassic age. The remaining 7 formations are thought to belong in the Tertiary. One of these is considered to be probably Eocene; an intrusive stock of quartz monzonite and two kinds of allied dike rocks are placed in the late Eocene or early Oligocene; a series of gravel deposits are questionably assigned to the Pliocene; and a group of volcanic rocks are tentatively put in the late Pliocene. The youngest formation in the quadrangle, composed of gravel and lake beds, is of Pliocene (?) to Recent age.

CAMBRIAN SYSTEM

PROSPECT MOUNTAIN QUARTZITE (LOWER CAMBRIAN)

Distribution.—The Prospect Mountain quartzite is the oldest formation exposed within the quadrangle. The two largest outcrops are bands of varying width on the east sides of Dutch Mountain and the Deep Creek Mountains.

The exposure in the Deep Creek Mountains is nearly 3 miles long and narrows from 4,000 feet in width at the 40th parallel to less than 500 feet at Bagley Gulch, where the formation ends against a transverse fault. The quartzite forms the east base of the mountains, its resistant beds rising abruptly from the gravel slopes to the east.

The outcrop on the east side of Dutch Mountain is also about 3 miles long and is bounded on the east by recent gravel. It varies considerably in width, owing to encroachment of gravel on the east and to faulting on the west. The width ranges from a few hundred feet at the mouth of Tribune Gulch to more than 1½ miles along the ridge 2 miles to the north. A transverse fault just south of the Garrison Monster mine marks the northern limit of the formation.

In addition to these principal exposures there are several smaller outcrops north and east of the Gold Hill mine. These are either completely or partly surrounded by gravel and are in all probability continuous beneath the gravel. The largest of these areas of quartzite forms the prominent summit at an altitude of 5,556 feet east of the Rube mine.

Another small outcrop of the Prospect Mountain quartzite surrounded by gravel is found near the edge of the Great Salt Lake Desert, 1 mile east of benchmark 4552 on the Deep Creek Railroad.

Lithology.—The Prospect Mountain quartzite is composed chiefly of light-gray to dark-brown quartzite, but near the base of the exposed section on Dutch Mountain there are one or more zones containing a large proportion of shaly material. These zones are distinguished on the geologic map as shale members.

The apparent homogeneity of the quartzite portion of the formation is due largely to the general presence of a brownish stain of iron oxides on the weathered surfaces, but close examination shows several distinct varieties of rock. Of these the most widely distributed is a fine to medium grained quartzite which is pale pinkish on fresh fracture. The grains are partly rounded and closely packed, the quartz cement between grains forming a very small portion of the total rock. A second variety has similar grain but is rather dark purplish on fresh fracture, owing to the presence of iron oxides in the cementing material. This variety is usually found interlaminated with the lighter-colored variety, and the difference in color reveals cross lamination throughout. The laminae meet at low angles (generally 10° or less) and may be truncated by others both above and below. Where the rock consists of only one variety this cross lamination is not visible, even on weathered surfaces. At no place was the cross lamination found to depend on varying size of grain. On the contrary, it seemed to be confined to the finer-grained quartzites just described.

In addition to the fine-grained quartzites, many beds are composed largely of quartz grains from 5 to 10 millimeters in diameter. The larger grains are less rounded than the smaller ones and locally consist of altered feldspars instead of the usual quartz. The larger grains lie in a matrix of smaller quartz grains, and by an increase in the amount of these smaller grains the rock grades into typical fine-grained quartzite. In general these coarser-grained quartzites are light-colored on fresh fracture. Within both coarse-grained and fine-grained quartzites there are beds of conglomerate as much as 2 feet thick. The pebbles in these beds are predominantly of white vein quartz, with a minor proportion of rose quartz and a very few of red jasper. The maximum size of pebble observed was about 75 millimeters and the average size about 25 millimeters. Such conglomerate beds are lenticular and cannot be traced for any great distance along the strike. They were found extremely useful, however, in proving the identity of the rocks in the scattered and metamorphosed exposures east of the Rube mine, where the Prospect Mountain quartzite has been faulted against the Oquirrh formation, which there consists largely of fine-grained sandstone without conglomerate layers.

In many places the bedding is marked by thin shale zones, in others by the change from a dominantly colored bed to one almost colorless, and in still others by an abrupt change in grain size. Wherever areas of such bedding planes have been exposed by erosion any sedimentary structural features, such as ripple marks, that may have been present have been destroyed by later movements parallel to the bedding surface.

The upper 75 to 100 feet of the quartzite differs from the beds beneath in several respects. The most noticeable difference is in the thickness of the individual beds, which ranges from 10 to 30 feet, in contrast to 1 to 5 feet in the remainder of the formation. The color on fresh fracture is a medium gray, but weathered surfaces are of a uniform dark brownish red, which results from the leaching and subsequent deposition of iron from numerous pyrite cubes scattered throughout the rock. The size of grain (1 to 2 millimeters) is somewhat larger than in many of the lower beds, and cross lamination is apparently absent.

A conglomerate occurs just beneath this upper part of the quartzite. It is best exposed south of Dry Canyon but may also be found for a mile or so to the north, usually as float. It is a dark rock that commonly forms a bench, with the result that its relations in most croppings are obscure. Its chief feature of interest is that its pebbles represent several different kinds of rock and thus differ markedly from those of the quartz-pebble conglomerates described above. The pebbles are angular to subangular and are as much as 6 inches in maximum diameter. Many are tabular or slaty. They include quartzite, schists, especially a quartz-biotite schist, slate, and various altered igneous rocks, one pebble of a granitic rock being noted. With these are smaller quartz grains, such as are found in the quartzites below. The matrix is in most places a slate, in which abundant specular hematite has been developed, but locally it is a fine-grained quartzite. Along the strike, to the north of Dry Canyon, the bed contains but few pebbles and is not unlike other shale beds in the formation, except for its greater thickness. Similar beds of shale are present at several other horizons in the formation. These are generally only a fraction of an inch thick but locally are as much as a foot. In the thicker beds slaty cleavage has been developed.

In all exposures the Prospect Mountain quartzite is cut by numerous joints. As a rule, these are parallel in strike and dip to nearby major or minor faults. On Dutch Mountain the formation is so thoroughly jointed that it has weathered into angular blocks which conceal bedrock exposures over wide areas. Along the fault planes the quartzite, in addition to being brecciated, has been bleached to a dull white color. Discontinuous thin veinlets of white quartz are found everywhere. No general course for the veinlets was ascertained, other than that many follow the bedding planes.

Shale members.—On the lower slopes of the east side of Dutch Mountain, there are several exposures of slaty shales and rather thin-bedded dark quartzites. These have been distinguished on the geologic maps (pls. 1 and 2) as shale members. Exposures on Basin Creek, in the Deep Creek Mountains south of the quadrangle, show that they are conformably interbedded with the normal light-colored Prospect Mountain quartzites at the bottom of the section exposed there. These beds are similar in lithology and position to the poorly exposed beds on Dutch Mountain. The shales are generally a dark grayish blue or greenish blue, though locally shades of khaki color are observed. Many beds are distinctly sandy, and in almost all of them a pronounced slaty cleavage, essentially parallel to the bedding, has been developed. The quartzite beds are mostly 6 inches or less in thickness. They are much darker than the quartzites that make up the greater part of the formation, owing to a larger content of impurities.

Thickness.—No complete section of the Prospect Mountain quartzite was observed. In the southern part of the quadrangle a maximum thickness of about 800 feet is exposed, and on Dutch Mountain the beds probably exceed 3,000 feet, although the exposures there are much too poor for measurement. A rapid and very rough measurement of the exposed portion of the formation was made on Basin Creek, about 7 miles south of the 40th parallel. This amounted to 4,750 feet and may be summarized as follows:

Section of Prospect Mountain quartzite on Basin Creek

	Feet
Cabin shale.	
Massive, dominantly light-colored quartzite	2, 500
Slate and quartzite (shale member)	300
Light-colored quartzite	500
Slate and quartzite (shale member)	600
Light-colored quartzite	200
Shale and quartzite (shale member)	100
Light-colored quartzite	500
Shale	50
Base not exposed.	
	4, 750

Age and correlation.—No fossils have been found in the Prospect Mountain quartzite, but as there is no apparent break of importance between it and the overlying Cabin shale, which contains Lower Cambrian fossils, the formation is considered to be of Lower Cambrian age.

A quartzite series of varying thickness, occurring beneath the lowest fossiliferous Cambrian, which usually is a shale, is widespread over western Utah and eastern and southern Nevada. In the Nevada localities that have been described the formation is over 1,000 feet in thickness and is overlain by Lower Cambrian sediments. The name Prospect Mountain [9] quartzite has been generally applied to the formation. For Utah Butler [10] suggested the name Tintic quartzite, from the Tintic Mountains, for this formation. However, as the overlying shale has been determined to be Middle Cambrian at some localities in Utah (as at Tintic [11] and Blacksmith Fork [12]), thus suggesting that the top of the quartzite may here be Middle Cambrian, and to be Lower Cambrian at others (Oquirrh Range [13]), and also as the Nevada name has priority, the formation is here called Prospect Mouns tain quartzite rather than Tintic quartzite.

Several investigators in the Wasatch Range in recent years have shown the presence of an unconformity in the thick nonfossiliferous and predominantly siliceous sediments below the fossiliferous Cambrian and have considered it to mark the boundary between the Cambrian and the Algonkian.[14] This unconformity is marked by a thin conglomerate, containing pebbles of the underlying rocks. Because of this discovery it was at first thought that the conglomerate near the top of the formation in the Gold Hill region might mark the Cambrian-Algonkian contact, as it contains boulders of different kinds of rock, and in some exposures its lower contact is discordant. But further field work and comparisons with the published descriptions of the unconformity in the Wasatch Range have led to the conclusion that the conglomerate in the Gold Hill region is of only local significance. This conclusion is based chiefly on its slight extent, its gradation northward into shale similar in appearance to other shale beds both above and below, and the dissimilarity of the quartzites below it to any of the known Algonkian beds in the Wasatch Range.

CABIN SHALE (LOWER CAMBRIAN)

Distribution.—The Cabin shale, named from Cabin Gulch, between North Pass and Sheep Canyons, crops out as a narrow band above the Prospect Mountain quartzite on the east side of both the Deep Creek Mountains and Dutch Mountain. On the southeast flank of Dutch Mountain the shale is concealed by faulting, and the Prospect Mountain quartzite is in contact with higher beds. The formation is much less resistant to erosion than the quartzites above and below and in most localities forms a narrow brush-covered bench.

Lithology.—The formation is dominantly shaly, the typical rock being a dark-green to khaki-colored shale,

[9] Hague, Arnold, Abstract of the report on the geology of the Eureka district, Nevada: U.S. Geol. Survey Third Ann. Rept., p. 254, 1883.

[10] Butler, B. S., Ore deposits of Utah: U.S. Geol. Survey Prof. Paper 111, p. 78, 1920.

[11] Loughlin, G. F., Geology and ore deposits of the Tintic mining district, Utah: U.S. Geol. Survey Prof. Paper 107, p. 25, 1919.

[12] Walcott, C. D., Cambrian sections of the Cordilleran area: Smithsonian Misc. Coll., vol. 53, no. 5, p. 171, 1908.

[13] Emmons, S. F., in Spurr, J. E., Economic geology of the Mercur mining district, Utah: U.S. Geol. Survey Eighteenth Ann. Rept., pt. 2, p. 362, 1895.

[14] Blackwelder, Eliot, New light on the geology of the Wasatch Mountains, Utah: Geol. Soc. America Bull., vol. 20, pp. 520–523, 1910. Hintze, F. F., A contribution to the geology of the Wasatch Mountains, Utah: New York Acad. Sci. Annals, vol. 23, p. 103, 1913. Calkins, F. C., Ore deposits of Utah: U.S. Geol. Survey Prof. Paper 111, p. 235, 1920.

with little sandy material and almost no calcium carbonate. Weathered surfaces are lighter in color and in most places are shades of brownish red. Slaty cleavage is developed in much of the formation, as a rule nearly parallel to the bedding, though in several places it cuts the bedding at a small angle. The slaty cleavages are generally marked by the development of flakes of white or golden-colored mica. In many beds, especially those near the base of the formation, cubes of limonite pseudomorphous after pyrite are present.

There are several variants from the typical rock just described. One of these is a light-gray finely laminated shale, generally 2 feet or less thick, found at the base of the formation, both in the Deep Creek Mountains and on Dutch Mountain. Near the middle of the section the shale locally contains small amounts of calcite, as shown by a weak effervescence with dilute hydrochloric acid. This limy variety is of a lighter color than the rest of the rock. On fresh fractures it is a light greenish gray, and on weathered surfaces brownish or reddish yellow. Both near the base and near the top of the section thin lenticular laminae of sandstone are found. These are 1 millimeter or so thick and are of lighter shades than the thicker interbedded shale.

Just beneath the top of the formation there is a persistent and, for this formation, unique concretionary bed. The numerous concretions are about the size of a silver dollar and lie parallel to the bedding planes. They differ from the remainder of the rock in having a slightly darker color, a somewhat finer grain of the mica, and a larger proportion of sand.

The lower contact of the shale is notably sharp. The light-gray shale mentioned above rests upon thick-bedded Prospect Mountain quartzite with no observable transition. There is, however, no indication of anything other than a purely lithologic break. The upper contact is not so well defined. The line has been drawn at the top of a 15-foot zone of interbedded sandy shale and shaly quartzite. Many of the quartzite beds are flecked with iron oxides. Above the 15-foot interval are the basal thicker-bedded Busby quartzites.

Thickness.—Two measurements of the thickness of the Cabin shale gave 493 and 530 feet. The first was made on the ridge south of Sheep Canyon and the second on the north side of Cabin Gulch. A third section, measured on the south side of Dry Canyon, was only 114 feet thick; and a fourth, half-way between the Spotted Fawn mine and the Garrison Monster mine, 381 feet. The first two figures are thought to approximate the true thickness. The diminution in thickness indicated by the other measurements was probably effected by local overriding within the shale along strike faults, but exposures are generally too poor to permit exact proof. Such variations in thickness are numerous on Dutch Mountain, and some are also found in the Deep Creek Mountains.

Age and correlation.—A single fragmentary trilobite was found by Edwin Kirk in the Cabin shale at a horizon somewhat above the middle of the formation. It was submitted for identification to Dr. C. E. Resser, of the Smithsonian Institution, who reported as follows: "The thoracic segment from Sheep Canyon, because of the sharp angle on its anterior side, seems pretty definitely to belong to a mesonacid, which would make it Lower Cambrian in the present usage of that term in the West."

It is rather difficult to determine the exact correlation of the Cabin shale in the published sections from areas in Utah and Nevada. The sequence quartzite, shale, and limestone is common to most of these sections, but fossil collections from the shale zones in areas in Utah and Nevada indicate a lack of contemporaneity in deposition. For this reason, the local name Cabin shale has been applied to the shale found at Gold Hill, rather than Pioche shale or Ophir shale, which have been widely used in Nevada and Utah, respectively.

It is probable that the formation closest in age to the Cabin shale is the lowest shale belt in the House Range, which was called Pioche by Walcott.[15] The Pioche shale, in its type locality,[16] differs from the Cabin shale in being over twice as thick and in containing several limestone beds. It probably includes in the lower part beds older than those present in the shale at Gold Hill.

The shale zones in the Tintic,[17] Ophir,[18] and Cottonwood-American Fork [19] areas, however, are, on the whole, younger. These shales, known generally as the Ophir shale, contain Middle Cambrian fossils through the greater part of their extent, but in the Ophir and Cottonwood districts Lower Cambrian fossils have been reported from the basal portions. The Cabin shale is perhaps equivalent in age to the lower portion of the shale and the upper beds of the underlying quartzite at these localities.

BUSBY QUARTZITE (MIDDLE CAMBRIAN)

Distribution.—In the Deep Creek Mountains the Busby quartzite is terminated on the south side of North Pass Canyon by the same transverse fault that cuts off the outcrops of the Cabin shale and Prospect Mountain quartzite. The quartzitic beds of the Busby are fairly resistant to erosion and form a series of low cliffs above the weak shale beds beneath. The formation is exposed also on Dutch Mountain in a band of extremely irregular width from a point half a mile south of the Spotted Fawn mine to the transverse

[15] Walcott, C. D., Cambrian sections of the Cordilleran area: Smithsonian Misc. Coll., vol. 53, no. 5, p. 184, 1908.

[16] Westgate, L. G., Geology and ore deposits of the Pioche district, Nev.: U.S. Geol. Survey Prof. Paper 171, pp. 8-10, 1932.

[17] Loughlin, G. F., Geology and ore deposits of the Tintic mining district, Utah: U.S. Geol. Survey Prof. Paper 107, p. 29, 1919.

[18] Gilluly, James, Geology and ore deposits of the Stockton and Fairfield quadrangles, Utah: U.S. Geol. Survey Prof. Paper 173, pp. 9-12, 1932.

[19] Calkins, F. C., The ore deposits of Utah: U.S. Geol. Survey Prof. Paper 111, p. 237, 1920.

fault south of the Garrison Monster mine. Another small outcrop is found in the foothills west of Garrison siding on the Deep Creek Railroad. The formation is poorly exposed on Dutch Mountain, because of the numerous faults which cut it and cause either duplication or elimination of individual beds. The name is taken from Busby Canyon, on the east slope of Dutch Mountain, in which the formation is exposed.

Lithology.—The basal portion of the Busby quartzite, 50 to 75 feet thick, is a fairly coarse grained rock, gray-brown on fresh fracture and weathering to shades of reddish brown. Many of the grains are more than 1 millimeter in diameter and a few are as much as 5 millimeters. Most of the grains are of quartz, and the remainder are of rock fragments, so that this rock locally resembles a graywacke. Shale partings are present and in places show mud cracks, which are filled by the coarser sands that make up the main portion of the rock. Iron oxide flecks are abundant.

A rather distinctive variety is found near the base of the formation in the Dutch Mountain exposures. This is a white quartzite containing irregular dark-brown patches. Thin sections of it show that the brown portions of the rock differ from the white portions only in the presence of abundant interstitial iron oxide. The quartz in this as well as in other quartzitic parts of the formation is crowded with microscopic fluid inclusions, in many of which gas bubbles are present.

Above the basal, coarse-grained quartzite there is little uniformity or continuity in the strata. Fine-grained sandy and shaly material are the principal components and are present in varying proportions in the individual beds. The most abundant varieties are thin-bedded pink to purplish fine-grained quartzites and thin-bedded gray quartzitic sandstones which are in many places micaceous. Green sandy shales are less abundant than the quartzite and sandstone except near the top of the formation, where they predominate.

The top of the formation has been placed at the base of the lowest limestone bed. The contact is not sharp, as there are a few thin quartzite beds above the boundary as thus drawn. It is also rather certain that the lowest limestone is not a continuous bed. But the zone including the lowest limestone and highest quartzite, which probably does not exceed 25 feet in thickness, makes a distinct lithologic break from beds of distinctly sandy and shaly character to beds characteristically calcareous.

Thickness.—Sections of the Busby quartzite measured on the south and north sides of Dry Canyon and the north side of Sheep Canyon gave thicknesses of 519, 433, and 452 feet, respectively. A fourth measurement about halfway between the Spotted Fawn and Garrison Monster mines showed 314 feet. The first figure possibly includes some duplication caused by undetected normal faulting; and the fourth is probably much too small for the same reason. The second and third figures are believed to be fairly close to the true thickness.

Age and correlation.—In addition to numerous annelid (?) trails a single fragmentary trilobite was found in the Busby quartzite, but unfortunately it was lost before being identified. The overlying Abercrombie formation contains abundant remains of a Middle Cambrian fauna, whereas the shale beneath the Busby is of Lower Cambrian age. Because of the presence of coarser material at the base of the formation, the lack of a sharp contact between the Busby and the Abercrombie, and the evidence of shallow-water conditions indicated by mud cracks, the Busby quartzite is thought to be best considered the initial deposit of the Middle Cambrian rather than the final deposit of the Lower Cambrian. No evidence of an angular unconformity at the base was seen, however, and it is indeed negatived by the continuity of the concretionary bed of the Cabin shale, which lies immediately beneath the base of the quartzite, and the presence of 15 feet of gradational beds.

In stratigraphic position the Busby is probably equivalent to the Langston (?) formation in the House Range [20], which lies above a sandy shale and is furthermore described as being almost a sandstone at the base. The correlation of the formation with other Utah sections is not certain except that it may represent that part of the Ophir shale, as exposed in Cottonwood Canyon [21] and the Oquirrh Mountains,[22] lying above the Lower Cambrian portion.

ABERCROMBIE FORMATION (MIDDLE CAMBRIAN)

Distribution.—The Abercrombie formation, named from Abercrombie Peak, on the ridge south of Dry Canyon, is completely exposed only in the southern third of the quadrangle, where it crops out as a wide band along the eastern part of the Deep Creek Mountains. This band is terminated on the north side of North Pass Canyon, in part by the overriding of younger formations adjacent to a transverse fault, but chiefly by burial beneath gravel. Incomplete and badly faulted sections are found on the east and northeast sides of Dutch Mountain from a point south of the Spotted Fawn mine northward nearly to the northern limit of the quadrangle.

Lithology.—The Abercrombie formation is composed dominantly of thin-bedded argillaceous limestone, interbedded with which are a few beds of more massive limestone and considerable amounts of shale. Except for the more massive limestone beds the formation is in general poorly exposed. The shale in particular

[20] Walcott, C. D., Cambrian sections of the Cordilleran area: Smithsonian Misc. Coll., vol. 53, no. 5, p. 183, 1908.

[21] Calkins, F. C., Ore deposits of Utah: U.S. Geol. Survey Prof. Paper 111, pp. 235-236, 1919.

[22] Gilluly, James, Geology and ore deposits of the Stockton and Fairfield quadrangles, Utah: U.S. Geol. Survey Prof. Paper 173, pp. 11-12, 1932.

crops out in but few places, usually forming a bench between steeper slopes underlain by more resistant limestone.

The rock most characteristic of the series is a blue-gray dense limestone whose thin bedding is caused by thin partings of shale, most of which are yellow or buff, though locally pink or light-gray colors are found. The limestone portions are from a quarter to half an inch thick and leave a large residue of clay when dissolved in hydrochloric acid. The shale partings contain minor amounts of calcite and quartz but are dominantly made up of a clay mineral of low birefringence. The thickness of the shale partings averages about 1 millimeter but is extremely variable. Along many of the bedding planes the shaly material is present only locally, resulting in a mottling by splotches of yellow or reddish shale. Less commonly splotches that are not parallel to the bedding may be found within the limestone. This variety is best developed near the top of the section in North Pass Canyon, where the shaly splotches are light gray.

With increase in the amount of clay the rock passes into a khaki-colored or light-greenish shale containing but little calcite. On weathered surfaces the shale shows the reddish or yellowish tints found in the shaly partings in limestone. Fossils are much more abundant in the shale than in any other portion of the formation, and nearly every bed contains at least a few phosphatic brachiopods of the genus *Obolus*.

Boundaries between the thin-bedded limestone and the more massive limestone are also gradational. The shaly partings and splotches become fewer, and the resultant rock is a resistant fine-grained to dense blue-gray limestone with local small inclusions of shale. The more massive beds contain very little material that is insoluble in dilute acid. Included in the more massively bedded limestone are beds of darker-colored limestone containing abundant oval algal or concretionary growths. These beds are in some places finely oolitic and in others contain thin intraformational conglomerates with small fossil fragments, but such beds are neither abundant nor persistent.

As might be expected from such gradations between the different lithologic varieties included in the formation, there is but little persistence of individual beds along the strike. Three sections about a mile apart showed only a very generalized agreement in the succession of beds. This variation is especially true of the upper boundary of the formation. South of North Pass Canyon the base of the lowest massive dolomite in the overlying Young Peak dolomite has been considered to mark the upper limit. But the dolomite beds pinch out to the north, and on the north side of North Pass Canyon the top of the formation has been considered to be the base of thick-bedded limestones resembling in texture the dolomite beds of the Young Peak dolomite.

The following section, measured on the south side of Dry Canyon, is similar to the other sections measured, but it should be understood that the individual beds are not persistent.

Section of Abercrombie formation on south side of Dry Canyon

	Feet
Young Peak dolomite.	
Abercrombie formation:	
Thin-bedded limestone, gray mottled	188
Shale	46
Thin-bedded limestone; thin shale beds at 96 and 126 feet from top	626
Shale, calcareous at top	180
Laminated gray limestone	154
Shale, calcareous at top	180
Thin-bedded limestone	61
Massive limestone, concretionary, oolitic, and with local conglomerates	13
Thin-bedded limestone	88
Massive limestone, concretionary and oolitic	39
Thin-bedded limestone	17
Shale	90
Thin-bedded limestone	30
Calcareous shale	90
Thin-bedded limestone	21
Massive limestone, dolomitized	14
Thin-bedded limestone	93
Massive limestone, dolomitized	48
Shale, calcareous at base	173
Thin-bedded limestone	71
Shale, calcareous at base	119
Massive limestone, dolomitized	62
Thin-bedded limestone	148
Shale, calcareous at top; a few thin beds of quartzite at base	147
Limestone, dolomitized	10
Sandy shale (top of Busby quartzite).	
	2, 708

Most of the massive limestone beds, as indicated in the section, have been partly dolomitized. The altered rock weathers to a light-brown color that sharply distinguishes it from the unaltered blue-gray limestone. The dolomite is coarser-grained and more resistant to weathering than the limestone. The dolomitized portions show no relations to bedding planes or to any depositional features but are localized along joints or minor faults, which strike in a general east-west direction and are in places accompanied by minor deposits of lead and silver. The alteration is clearly much later than the original formation of the sediments.

Thickness.—Three measurements of the formation on the south and north sides of Dry Canyon and the north side of Sheep Canyon gave thicknesses, respectively, of 2,708, 2,080, and 2,680 feet. The first and third figures probably correspond closely with the true thickness of the formation. The second figure is much too low and is the result of overriding along a strike fault, which, on the ridge line, cuts the formation about 850 feet above the base.

Age and correlation.—Fossils collected from several of the shale zones show that the Abercrombie formation is of Middle Cambrian age. Dr. C. E. Resser, of the Smithsonian Institution, reports as follows upon the collections:

12. At fork in Dry Canyon, 1 mile west of spring:
    Bathyuriscus productus (Hall and Whitfield).
    Obolus sp.
    Hyolithes sp.
16. Ridge line on south side of Dry Canyon at altitude of about 7,900 feet:
    Zacanthoides sp.
    Bathyuriscus productus.
    Lingulella sp.
    This seems to represent the lowest horizon among the collections. The fauna corresponds with the Chisholm and Ophir.
18. Just east of the 7,300-foot closed contour on the north side of Sheep Canyon:
    Paterina cf. P. utahensis.
    Elrathia sp.
19. Just west of the 8,200-foot closed contour on the south side of Dry Canyon:
    Micromitra sp.
17. Saddle west of peak 8182, on south side of Dry Canyon:
    Obolus sp.
    Fucoids.
    Elrathia sp.

All these are Middle Cambrian and apparently about the same horizon somewhere in the lower part.

The formation is possibly equivalent to the Chisholm shale and the lower portions of the Highland Peak limestone at Pioche,[23] the Teutonic, Dagmar, and Herkimer limestones at Tintic,[24] and the Hartmann and Bowman limestones at Ophir.[25] These correlations are based almost solely on position in the stratigraphic column, as variations in lithology are characteristic of the Middle Cambrian in this portion of Utah.

YOUNG PEAK DOLOMITE (MIDDLE CAMBRIAN)

Distribution.—The Young Peak dolomite is named from Young Peak, on the north side of Dry Canyon, the summit of which is underlain by the formation. It crops out only in the southern part of the quadrangle in the Deep Creek Mountains. It forms a north-south band, somewhat interrupted by faulting, extending from the southern boundary to the north side of North Pass Canyon, where it curves to the east before disappearing beneath an overthrust plate. Half a mile to the east it reappears from beneath the plate and continues eastward for half a mile before being covered by later gravel.

Lithology.—The Young Peak dolomite changes almost completely in lithologic character in the 4 miles along which it is exposed. At the southern boundary it is composed almost entirely of dolomite, but in North Pass Canyon the same horizon is marked by limestone beds with only a few thin interbedded dolomite layers. This variation does not occur abruptly but is caused by a gradual interfingering northward of limestone at both the top and the bottom of the formation, until finally on the north side of North Pass Canyon only one dolomite bed about 5 feet thick is exposed.

The base of the formation as mapped is neither synchronous nor continuous. As far north as the head of Bagley Gulch it is mapped at the lowest locally exposed bed of massive gray dolomite. Owing to the successive lensing out of the lower beds northward, however, as indicated in the preceding paragraph and in figure 2, the base is represented not by one continuous bed but rather by higher and higher beds. Northward from Bagley Gulch, the dolomite beds thin out so rapidly that it was thought best to continue the boundary at the base of a series of massive limestones containing rodlike markings similar to those in the typical dolomite to the south. Although this is admittedly a compromise between lithologic mapping and synchronous mapping, it seemed to be the best course available. Mapping the continuation of the lowest dolomite bed northward would be impossible, because the interfingering limestone beds are indistinguishable, and poor exposures and numerous displacements by both major and minor faults preclude continuous tracing. To continue the mapping of the lowest dolomite bed as the base in the vicinity of North Pass Canyon would not only be difficult on

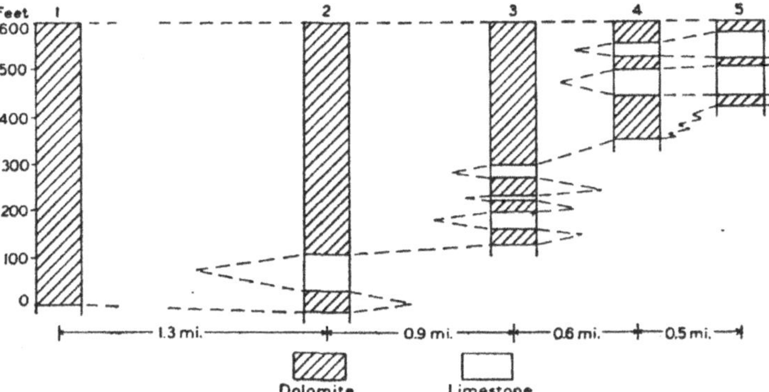

FIGURE 2.—Sections of the Young Peak dolomite, showing the interfingering northward of limestone. 1, South side of Dry Canyon; 2, north side of Dry Canyon; 3, north side of Sheep Canyon; 4, ridge between Bagley and Trippe Gulches; 5, ridge between Trippe Gulch and North Pass Canyon.

[23] Westgate, L. G., Geology and ore deposits of the Pioche district, Nev.: U.S. Geol. Survey Prof. Paper 171, pp. 11–13, 1932.

[24] Loughlin, G. F., Geology and ore deposits of the Tintic mining district, Utah: U.S. Geol. Survey Prof. Paper 107, pp. 27–28, 1919.

[25] Gilluly, James, Geology and ore deposits of the Stockton and Fairfield quadrangles, Utah: U.S. Geol. Survey Prof. Paper 173, pp. 12–15, 1932.

the scale of this map but would give a false suggestion of an overlap. The mapping adopted shows the horizon continuing conformably, as it does, and facilitates the delineation of the somewhat complex structure on the north side of North Pass Canyon.

The upper contact of the formation, on the other hand, is sharp. It has been taken as the base of a dark-gray dolomite containing abundant nodules of black chert, which are as much as a meter in maximum diameter. This bed is overlain by a cream-colored, finely laminated dolomite. This sequence persists throughout the outcrop of the formation, and there are no beds containing such chert nodules lower in the section and none above until the upper portion of the Chokecherry dolomite is reached, about 3,000 feet higher, and here the characteristic laminated dolomite is missing. The beds above the upper boundary are essentially all limestones, many of them similar to beds in the Abercrombie formation.

No section for the north side of North Pass Canyon is available because extreme crushing and minor faulting prohibit accurate measurement, but the base of the formation there is the same as that shown in section 5 of figure 2. The dolomite present in such a section would be limited to a 5-foot bed somewhat above the middle of the thickness shown.

The typical rock of the dolomitic portion of the formation is a dark-gray to black dolomite spangled with short white rods of dolomite. The rods have an average length of about 10 millimeters and an average diameter of about 1 millimeter. They contain a little calcite, as shown by slight effervescence with dilute hydrochloric acid. The dolomite matrix in which the rods occur is finely crystalline, the grains being 0.5 millimeter or less in diameter. The rods are composed of grains of slightly larger size. The grains of both rods and matrix are readily distinguished by the naked eye, the rock thus differing from the dense limestones found beneath in the Abercrombie formation. Locally the spangled rock shows a mottling caused by irregular splotches of darker and lighter dolomite (pl. 5, *A*). The rods in such varieties are generally localized in the darker splotches. The mottled rock is generally found near the top of the formation and is thinner-bedded than the rock below. Much of the thinner-bedded rock contains but few of the rods, and in many beds they may be entirely lacking. The lighter-colored portions of the mottled dolomite generally effervesce weakly with dilute hydrochloric acid, showing that they contain some calcite.

The limestone of the formation includes several varieties. A gray mottled limestone similar to that found in the Abercrombie formation makes up the greater part of the limestones interbedded with dolomite at the top and bottom of the formation. It is particularly abundant north of the road in North Pass Canyon. The massive limestone that takes the place of the dolomite in the middle of the formation is medium gray and extremely dense. Many of the beds contain white rods similar to those in the dolomite but composed of calcite. This fact is of some interest in that the rods have been thought to be fossil remnants, whose structure has been destroyed by subsequent dolomitization; but the structure of the rods where both they and the matrix are of calcite is as obscure as where both are of dolomite. If they represent organic remains of some sort, it is apparent that the lack of structure observed is due to some other factor than dolomitization. A few of the beds show bedding surfaces covered by a network of what appear to be fossil worm tracks. In many places these now consist of dolomite and are of lighter color than the rest of the rock.

Age and correlation.—No determinable fossils have been found in the Young Peak dolomite. Because of its gradation into the underlying Abercrombie formation, whose age is known, it is thought to be Middle Cambrian. Similar lithology has been found in the Bluebird dolomite, of Middle Cambrian age, in the Tintic district,[26] but a positive correlation with that formation is not made, because of the known lack of continuity in the lithology in the Gold Hill quadrangle. Correlation with formations in other districts in which this texture has not been noted must be limited to the suggestion that the Young Peak dolomite is equivalent to the beds in the upper part of the Middle Cambrian sequence.

TRIPPE LIMESTONE (MIDDLE CAMBRIAN)

Distribution.—The Trippe limestone, named from Trippe Gulch on the south side of North Pass Canyon, crops out as a northward-trending band about 1,000 feet wide, at an average distance of a mile east of the main divide of the Deep Creek Mountains. The outcrop extends northward from the southern border of the quadrangle to North Pass Canyon, on the north side of which the strike changes to northeast. About a quarter of a mile farther along the strike the formation disappears beneath a plate of overthrust rocks, and three-quarters of a mile east-northeast of this point it reappears with a strike of nearly due east, which changes to southeast before the beds are covered beneath the gravel that flanks the range. The formation has not been recognized on Dutch Mountain.

Lithology.—The Trippe limestone is composed largely of thin-bedded limestones but includes also more massive limestones, a few dolomite beds, and one thin shale.

Three sections were measured which show considerable variation in the lithologic succession, indicating that individual beds are generally lenticular. The

[26] Loughlin, G. F., Geology and ore deposits of the Tintic mining district, Utah: U.S. Geol. Survey Prof. Paper 107, p. 28, 1919.

following section was measured on the ridge line on the south side of Dry Canyon.

Section of Trippe limestone on ridge south of Dry Canyon

Light-gray oolitic, cross-bedded dolomite (base of Lamb dolomite).

Trippe limestone:	Feet
1. Thin-bedded limestone with gray mottlings	43
2. Dark dolomite	19
3. Thin-bedded limestone with pink and yellow mottlings	98
4. Oolitic limestone with local intraformational conglomerates and cross-bedding	13
5. Thin-bedded limestone like no. 3. Thin shale near base	75
6. Cream-colored, finely laminated dolomite	1
7. Thin-bedded limestone like no. 3 with local massive limestone	46
8. Coarsely crystalline massive light-gray limestone	19
9. Laminated medium gray limestone	65
10. Thin-bedded limestone like no. 3	133
11. Gray dolomite	17
12. Thin-bedded limestone like no. 1, massive dark-gray dolomite 20 feet above base	79
13. Finely laminated light-gray dolomite	22
14. Thin-bedded limestone like no. 1	30
15. Thin-bedded gray dolomitic limestone	40
16. Thin-bedded limestone like no. 1	22
17. Gray dolomitic limestone	10
18. Laminated cream-colored dolomite	5
19. Dark-gray dolomite with black chert nodules	8
Young Peak dolomite.	745

Division 8 of this section is one of the few persistent beds and crops out as a low cliff throughout the exposure of the formation. Its presence is of assistance in determining the presence or absence of faults on the brush-covered side slopes of the canyons.

Mottled limestone makes up the bulk of the formation and is similar in character to the mottled limestone of the two lower formations. The dolomite beds are dark gray, massive, and without the texture and markings characterizing those of the Young Peak dolomite.

The most striking parts of the formation are the finely laminated white or cream-colored beds. These may be composed of either limestone or dolomite, although in no place was a single bed found to grade from limestone to dolomite. Locally these beds show phenomena that probably have resulted from the generation of gas in the carbonate mud prior to consolidation. In the specimen illustrated in plate 5, *B*, rupture was linear rather than through a vent of small cross section. The essential contemporaneity of such disturbances is proved by other specimens that show bedding continuing undistorted over the jumbled zone. One specimen was collected in which such a zone is seen to originate in a thin layer composed of tiny dolomite fragments in a limestone matrix.

The base of the formation is taken at the base of a dark dolomite containing large lenses and nodules of black chert. This bed, though unusually continuous, apparently does not indicate any significant time break, for the limestone beds above are similar to those which are found interbedded with the dolomite beds of the Young Peak dolomite, below.

The upper boundary of the formation has been placed at the base of a series of massive light-gray dolomites, many of which are oolitic and cross-bedded. The lithologic change is abrupt, but no other evidence of unconformity was determined.

Thickness.—A section measured on the ridge line south of Dry Canyon gave a thickness of 745 feet, and one on the ridge south of Sheep Canyon 765 feet. On the ridge south of North Pass Canyon, however, the thickness measured was only 660 feet.

Age and correlation.—No fossils have been found in the Trippe limestone, but it is thought to be of Middle Cambrian age. This opinion is based on the lithologic resemblance of the mottled limestone members to those in the two underlying formations and on the lithologic break between it and the overlying Lamb dolomite which is believed to be of Upper Cambrian age. Whether the variations in thickness shown by the measured sections indicate an unconformity at the top of the formation or are due simply to minor faulting or concealed changes in dip is not known. An unconformity between the Middle and Upper Cambrian has not been previously reported in Utah, and the evidence in this area is not sufficient to consider that one exists. Walcott [27] believed that sedimentary barriers and local warpings are sufficient to explain the faunal change.

The Cole Canyon dolomite in the Tintic district [28] is possibly equivalent to the Trippe limestone. Each overlies a dolomite formation of similar texture, and the Cole Canyon contains laminated cream-colored dolomite beds resembling those found in the Gold Hill quadrangle. Any further correlation is not warranted, owing to the lack of fossils and the known lithologic variations.

LAMB DOLOMITE (UPPER CAMBRIAN)

Distribution.—The Lamb dolomite is exposed as a faulted band, about a quarter of a mile wide, at various distances east of the divide in the Deep Creek Mountains. It extends in a general northerly direction from the southern boundary of the quadrangle to North Pass Canyon. North of this canyon the trend of the outcrop changes to northeast and then to east, and the width of the exposure ranges from a hundred yards to over half a mile. The formation in this area is highly shattered, owing to the fact that it overrides three of the lower formations and is itself overridden

[27] Walcott, C. D., The Cambrian and its problems, in Problems of American Geology, p. 191, Yale University Press, 1915.

[28] Loughlin, G. F., Geology and ore deposits of the Tintic district, Utah: U.S. Geol. Survey Prof. Paper 107, p. 28, 1919.

by a higher formation. To the north a fault separates the formation from the Pennsylvanian Oquirrh formation. Beds included in the Lamb dolomite are found at several places on Dutch Mountain, but as it was not practicable to separate them from similar beds in the overlying Hicks formation, the two formations were mapped together as Upper Cambrian.

The name is taken from Lamb Gulch, on the north side of Dry Canyon, which is underlain by the formation.

Lithology.—The base of the Lamb dolomite is marked by massive beds of light-gray dolomite. These are commonly composed of small rounded grains of darker dolomite in a matrix of much lighter colored dolomite. The size of the grains ranges between 0.5 and 1 millimeter, and they are thought to have been originally oolites, although no concentric structure is now discernible. Local concentrations of the darker grains in rude lenses essentially parallel to the bedding give a characteristically streaked appearance to many of the beds. Cross-bedding is commonly shown by the supposed oolitic beds.

Interbedded are layers of pisolitic dolomite. The pisolites are rarely circular but usually elliptical in section and range in size from 1 to 10 millimeters. The larger ones show a poorly defined concentric structure, which, with the apparent gradation in size, makes it appear probable that the oolitic rocks described in the previous paragraph are really of that origin. Locally the pisolites show asymmetric outgrowths, which, according to W. H. Bradley,[29] of the Geological Survey, are similar in size and shape to algal growths found by him in pisolitic rocks occurring in the Green River formation in Wyoming. The matrix is a light-colored dolomite that is, in many places, recrystallized and shows shining cleavage faces. The pisolites are usually oriented with the longer axis parallel to the bedding. The pisolitic and oolitic rocks make up the basal 500 feet or so of the formation and recur as thinner zones throughout it.

The bulk of the formation, however, is composed of a light to medium gray dolomite mottled by patches of darker dolomite containing white rods, resembling closely parts of the Young Peak dolomite. In many places the darker dolomite appears to occur as boulders in the lighter-colored matrix, but in others the contact between the two varieties is indefinite and apparently the result of a replacement of the darker variety by the lighter. That this is the probable explanation is supported by the presence in several places of continuous beds of the dark, rod-speckled dolomite.

Throughout the exposure in the Deep Creek Mountains the greater part of the formation has been recrystallized and bleached to a white resistant dolomite containing numerous vugs lined with dolomite crystals. Locally, the old texture may be faintly discerned on the weathered surfaces, but in most places no traces of it remain.

The top 150 feet of the formation is quite different in character from the lower part. Thin-bedded dolomite with partings of yellow or red sandy shale, together with a few massive dolomite beds, compose the lower 100 feet or so of this zone. The change from the more massive beds is not abrupt. Locally, the thin-bedded rocks are dolomitic limestones, and in a few places they are essentially limestones. The limestone beds resemble somewhat the thin-bedded mottled limestones of the Middle Cambrian, except that the partings are rather more sandy than shaly. The top 25 to 50 feet of this zone is made up of a reddish-weathering fine-grained sandstone, which is yellowish on fresh fracture. It is rather impure, containing moderate amounts of mica and dolomite, and is not sharply set off from the dolomites below. The sandy partings increase in thickness until they form the bulk of the rock. The top of this sandstone has been taken as the top of the formation. The sandstone is probably continuous from the south boundary of the quadrangle as far north as the ridge on the north side of Sheep Canyon. On the north slope of this ridge, however, the bed apparently lenses out and is replaced by another sandstone about 100 feet higher stratigraphically. This higher bed has been mapped as the top of the formation for the remainder of the exposure of the formation in the Deep Creek Mountains.

Thickness.—Three measurements of the Lamb dolomite in the Deep Creek Mountains gave thicknesses of 1,080, 1,035, and 1,020 feet. These variations may be easily explained by changes in strike and dip that are concealed owing to poor exposures and by minor faulting. The true thickness is probably not far from 1,050 feet.

Age and correlation.—As no fossils have been found in the formation, its age is not definitely known. It is, however, similar in lithology to the overlying formation, and the sandstone beds used to delimit the two are probably lenticular. This, combined with the sharp change in lithology at the base of the formation, makes it probable that the age of the Lamb dolomite is the same as that of the overlying Hicks formation—Upper Cambrian. Because of the lack of fossils the Lamb is difficult to correlate with any degree of certainty, but it is probably equivalent in age to the lower 800 feet of the Mendha formation at Pioche[30] and the Opex dolomite at Tintic.[31] Beds of similar lithology are lacking at the base of the Upper Cambrian in both the Eureka and the House Range sections.

[29] Personal communication.

[30] Westgate, L. G., Geology and ore deposits of the Pioche district, Nev.: U.S. Geol. Survey Prof. Paper 171, pp. 13-14, 1932.

[31] Loughlin, G. F., Geology and ore deposits of the Tintic mining district, Utah: U.S. Geol. Survey Prof. Paper 107, p. 29, 1919.

HICKS FORMATION (UPPER CAMBRIAN)

Distribution.—The Hicks formation takes its name from Hicks Gulch, in North Pass Canyon. This locality is near the northern limit of the chief exposure of the formation, which extends as a band, made discontinuous by transverse faults, east of the divide of the Deep Creek Mountains. A small wedge of the formation is exposed on the north side of North Pass Canyon, north of the fault that limits northward the main outcrop. Beds belonging to the formation are also found at several places on Dutch Mountain, but these beds have been included with the underlying Lamb dolomite and mapped as undifferentiated Upper Cambrian.

Lithology.—The lithology of the Hicks formation is in part similar to that of the Lamb dolomite. Oolitic, streaked, pisolitic, and mottled dolomites make up a large portion of the formation. A specimen of the pisolitic type, obtained near the base of the formation, is illustrated in plate 5, *C*. Some of these beds contain tiny nodules of white chert, which are neither abundant nor conspicuous.

In addition to the dolomites, there are several lenticular beds of sandstone and of limestone, and in one place a thin bed of shale was noted. The presence of the several rock types and the fact that the limestones are abundantly fossiliferous were the main factors in separating the formation from the one below.

The following section, measured on the ridge on the north side of Sheep Canyon, is fairly characteristic of the formation:

Section of Hicks formation on north side of Sheep Canyon

	Feet
Base of Chokecherry dolomite: Mottled dolomite with nodules of black chert, local conglomerates, and cross-bedding.	
Hicks formation:	
1. Mottled dolomite, locally calcareous	90
2. Bleached and recrystallized massive dolomite	33
3. Sandy shale	38
4. Bleached and recrystallized massive dolomite	73
5. Massive oolitic gray dolomite	129
6. Thin-bedded sandy limestone and calcareous sandstone	79
7. Thin-bedded sandy dolomite	34
8. Massive oolitic, pisolitic, and rod-speckled dolomite	38
9. Thin-bedded oolitic sandy dolomite	24
10. Massive oolitic gray dolomite	14
11. Thin-bedded oolitic sandy dolomite; weathers to shades of tan	28
12. Medium to dark gray cross-bedded streaked oolitic dolomite; many pisolitic layers at base; near the top are a number of beds of dark dolomite with numerous small white rods	173
Sandstone at top of Lamb dolomite.	
	753

Three other sections were measured in the Deep Creek Mountains. They are of the same general character as the one given above but show that the individual beds are extremely lenticular. For example, the limestone zone (no. 6 of the section) on the north side of Sheep Canyon is 311 feet above the base of the formation and 79 feet thick, whereas half a mile to the north it is 171 feet thick and starts 215 feet above the base, and a little more than a mile to the south it was not found at all.

No sections of the formation were found that were free from recrystallized and bleached members such as nos. 2 and 4 in the section given above. These occur at very different horizons and in varying amounts. On the south side of Sheep Canyon, for example, the upper 315 feet has been thus altered. Like similar beds in the Lamb dolomite, these show throughout indistinct remnants of the original texture.

The upper limit of the formation has been taken as the base of the lowest dolomites containing nodules and bands of black chert. This zone usually includes local dolomite conglomerates and cross-bedded layers. The exact contact is difficult to find because of poor exposures and rather general recrystallization.

Thickness.—The thicknesses measured were variable, ranging from 1,200 feet on the south side of Dry Canyon through 890 and 750 feet on the south and north sides of Sheep Canyon, respectively, to 590 feet at the head of North Pass Canyon.

Age and correlation.—Fossils found in one of the limestone members at the head of North Pass Canyon have been reported upon by Dr. C. E. Resser, of the Smithsonian Institution, as follows:

M-3. Half a mile east of peak 8135, in North Pass Canyon:
- Pseudagnostus sp.
- Dunderbergia sp.
- Obolus sp.

20. Ridge line on north side of Dry Canyon:
- Acrotreta sp.

These suggest a possible correlation with the Secret Canyon shale. It represents a lower Upper Cambrian horizon, at any rate.

This horizon is probably unrepresented in the Tintic district, where there are less than 400 feet of Upper Cambrian beds. The upper part of the Mendha formation at Pioche [32] is probably of equivalent age.

UNCONFORMITY AT TOP OF UPPER CAMBRIAN

The progressive northward thinning of the Hicks formation from 1,200 feet to less than 600 feet in a distance of 3½ miles indicates a pronounced unconformity at its top. The basal Ordovician beds show local dolomite conglomerates and abundant shallow-water phenomena, such as cross-bedding. No sandstone, however, has been recognized as being at the contact. The only criterion that was found of assistance in the mapping is the universal occurrence of dark chert in the Ordovician sediments.

[32] Westgate, L. G., Geology and ore deposits of the Pioche district, Nev.: U.S. Geol. Survey Prof. Paper 171, pp. 13-14, 1932.

The presence of an erosional unconformity at the base of the Ordovician has not been generally recognized in the Great Basin region. In the Tintic district [33] one was recognized but considered to be of only local significance. Earlier Richardson [34] had described an unconformity at this horizon in the Randolph quadrangle, in northern Utah, resulting in the removal of over 800 feet of Upper Cambrian beds. In the House Range and at Eureka, Nev., however, Walcott has considered the Ordovician to overlie the Upper Cambrian conformably, and in a general review of the subject [35] he notes that the Upper Cambrian formations in the Cordilleran region pass into the overlying beds without apparent stratigraphic break.

The proof of a definite erosional unconformity at the top of the Upper Cambrian in three localities so widely separated as the Tintic district, northern Utah, and Gold Hill, however, seems to indicate that it is more than a local occurrence, and it is probable that future work, with carefully measured sections, will show that the unconformity is of wider extent than is now recognized.

ORDOVICIAN SYSTEM

CHOKECHERRY DOLOMITE (LOWER ORDOVICIAN)

Distribution.—The Chokecherry dolomite, named after Chokecherry Canyon, just beyond the south edge of the quadrangle, crops out in the Deep Creek Mountains, where it is exposed as a discontinuous band, of variable width, as far north as North Pass Canyon. South of the pass at the head of Dry Canyon, where the base of the formation is just east of the crest of the range, its width is about three-quarters of a mile, owing to the fact that the surface slope is nearly equal to the dip of the beds. The wide outcrop, most of which lies west of the crest, is terminated by a transverse fault in Dry Canyon. North of the fault the outcrop lies east of the crest and is much narrower, a quarter of a mile being the maximum width. A few transverse faults offset its northerly course, and it is finally terminated by a large transverse fault in North Pass Canyon. The formation is absent on Dutch Mountain, where Upper Ordovician dolomite rests upon beds of Upper Cambrian age.

Lithology.—The Chokecherry dolomite is characterized by the presence of considerable silica, found both as nodules and as layers of chert, usually dark-gray to black, and as sandy laminae between thin beds of dolomite. The lower beds are, as a rule, rather massive dark mottled dolomite, locally oolitic and cross-bedded and containing thin lenses of dolomite conglomerate. Small black chert nodules are found throughout. These beds are supplanted higher in the formation by thinner-bedded dolomite with sandy laminae, or locally by bands of dark chert. In a few places the laminae become sufficiently thick to form lenses of sandstone. One bed, near the top of the formation, that has been found to be continuous in the southern part of the exposure in the Deep Creek Mountains is a light-gray dolomite filled with siliceous concretions about the size and shape of a gooseberry.

The formation has been particularly susceptible to the bleaching and recrystallization that has affected the two lower formations, described above. In most of the sections examined between a third and a half of the formation has been thus altered.

This alteration, combined with poor exposures of the thin-bedded dolomites at the top of the formation, makes the determination of the upper boundary uncertain. Where best exposed the basal beds of the overlying Fish Haven dolomite are seen to be medium thick bedded dolomites, free from the sandy laminae of the lower dolomites and containing but little chert. In mapping, therefore, the boundary was placed at the top of the highest sandy or cherty float.

Thickness.—The formation shows a rather notable variation in thickness from the southern part of the quadrangle northward. On the south side of Dry Canyon at least 1,000 feet is exposed; on the north side of Sheep Canyon, 890 feet; and at the head of North Pass Canyon, 850 feet. On Dutch Mountain the Chokecherry dolomite is absent, and dolomite of Upper Ordovician age rests upon Upper Cambrian dolomite.

Age and correlation.—Scanty fossil collections made by Edwin Kirk, of the Geological Survey, have been determined by him as follows:

TN–26 37. East of saddle on ridge between peaks 8550 and 8350, on north side of Dry Canyon, and also on ridge line of peak 8491, at head of Dry Canyon. *Scaevogyra?* sp.

The few gastropods in this lot do not permit exact age determination, and as yet we know of no other horizon with which it may be correlated. It may safely be considered early Lower Ordovician, however.

Rocks of Lower Ordovician age are found in many places in the Great Basin. In each area, however, the lithology is, as a rule, markedly different from that of neighboring areas, and the only reliable method of correlation is by means of the contained fossils. The fossil evidence indicates that the Chokecherry dolomite represents only a portion of Lower Ordovician time. As in other districts higher beds may be present, exact equivalents are difficult to determine, but in general the Chokecherry dolomite may be considered of about the same age as the Ajax and Opohonga limestones at Tintic,[36] the Garden City limestone in the

[33] Loughlin, G. F., Geology and ore deposits of the Tintic mining district, Utah: U.S. Geol. Survey Prof. Paper 107, p. 80, 1919.

[34] Richardson, G. B., The Paleozoic section in northern Utah: Am. Jour. Sci., 4th ser., vol. 36, p. 408, 1913.

[35] Walcott, C. D., The Cambrian and its problems, in Problems of American geology, p. 191, Yale University Press, 1915.

[36] Loughlin, G. F., Geology and ore deposits of the Tintic mining district, Utah; U.S. Geol. Survey Prof. Paper 107, pp. 31–33, 1919.

Randolph quadrangle,[37] the Yellow Hill limestone at Pioche,[38] part of the Grampian limestone in the San Francisco region,[39] and the basal part of the Pogonip limestone of the Eureka district.[40]

UNCONFORMITY AT BASE OF UPPER ORDOVICIAN

The variable thickness of the Chokecherry dolomite in the Deep Creek Mountains and its apparent absence on Dutch Mountain indicate an unconformity between it and the overlying Fish Haven dolomite, of Upper Ordovician age. Further evidence of an unconformity is indicated by the presence in the southern part of the range of a Lower Ordovician fauna that resembles that of a higher formation than the beds found within the quadrangle;[41] and on the reported presence to the south of a quartzite that is apparently equivalent to the Eureka quartzite found in the Middle (?) Ordovician of Nevada.[42]

This unconformity has been reported from three other localities—Eureka, Nev.,[43] northern Utah,[44] and southeastern Idaho.[45] In all three the unconformity is shown by the varying thickness of an underlying quartzite, which is, in the Utah and Idaho localities, of Chazy (?) age. The quartzite in Nevada is probably of about the same age. The hiatus represented by the unconformity is thus much greater at Gold Hill than it is to the north or south, but whether the absence of the high Lower Ordovician beds is due to erosion or to nondeposition is not clear. The latter hypothesis is perhaps more probable, in view of the lack of conglomerate or other clastic rocks at the base of the Upper Ordovician sediments.

At Eureka and in the northern Utah area the unconformity is shown by the varying thickness of an underlying quartzite which is of Chazy (?) age in the Utah locality but is unfossiliferous at Eureka. In southeastern Idaho the quartzite of Chazy (?) age appears to lie conformably beneath the Fish Haven, but a considerable time break is required by the absence of beds containing faunas that in other localities intervene between the rocks of Chazy age and those of Fish Haven age.

[37] Richardson, G. B., The Paleozoic section in northern Utah: Am. Jour. Sci., 4th ser., vol. 36, p. 408, 1913.

[38] Westgate, L. G., Geology and ore deposits of the Pioche district, Nev.: U.S. Geol. Survey Prof. Paper 171, p. 14, 1932.

[39] Butler, B. S., Geology and ore deposits of the San Francisco region, Utah: U.S. Geol. Survey Prof. Paper 80, p. 30, 1913.

[40] Hague, Arnold, Geology of the Eureka district, Nev.: U.S. Geol. Survey Mon. 20, p. 13, 1892.

[41] Butler, B. S., Ore deposits of Utah: U.S. Geol. Survey Prof. Paper 111, p. 471, 1920.

[42] Reagan, A. B., Geology of the Deep Creek region, Utah: Salt Lake Min. Rev., vol. 19, June 30, 1917, p. 25.

[43] Hague, Arnold, Geology of the Eureka district, Nev.: U.S. Geol. Survey Mon. 20, p. 56, 1892.

[44] Richardson, G. B., The Paleozoic section in northern Utah: Am. Jour. Sci., 4th ser., vol. 36, p. 408, 1913.

[45] Mansfield, G. R., Geology and geography of southeastern Idaho: U.S. Geol. Survey Prof. Paper 152, p. 58, 1927.

FISH HAVEN DOLOMITE (UPPER ORDOVICIAN)

Distribution.—The Fish Haven dolomite crops out as a narrow band underlying the massive Laketown dolomite in the Deep Creek Mountains as far north as North Pass Canyon. In this region it is in general poorly exposed, being covered by the debris from the resistant formation above. Outcrops of the formation also occur at three places on Dutch Mountain—on the southeast flank, from Pool Canyon to the south side of the canyon in which the Spotted Fawn mine is located; on the north flank, in Royal Gulch; and on the northwest flank, in the lower foothills. In these three localities the formation, although cut by numerous faults, is much better exposed than in the southern part of the quadrangle.

The name "Fish Haven" is that given by Richardson[46] to rocks of similar age and lithology in northern Utah.

Lithology.—The Fish Haven dolomite is composed of moderately thick to thick-bedded dolomite, usually dark gray, with but little chert. On Dutch Mountain lighter-colored beds are found in the middle part of the formation, but the color is, in part at least, due to bleaching. In general the mottling and other textural features so abundant in the formations above and below are lacking, but several beds show lighter gray splotches in a matrix of dark gray. Some beds also, near the top of the formation, contain vugs filled with white crystalline dolomite. On Dutch Mountain the basal bed is characterized by numerous small silicified brachiopods (*Rhynchotrema argenturbica*), which greatly simplify the mapping of the boundary. This bed was not found in the Deep Creek Mountains.

The lower contact is well exposed on Dutch Mountain and at a few places in the Deep Creek Mountains. This contact is irregular in detail, but nowhere could it be shown that any notable amount of the Hicks formation had been removed before the deposition of the Fish Haven. Locally the basal beds of the overlying Laketown dolomite are dolomite conglomerates, but in most places they are dolomite sands, with wavy bedding planes and numerous fragments of Silurian corals and brachiopods.

Thickness.—The thickness of the formation is surprisingly constant over the whole area. On Dutch Mountain 278 feet was found, on the ridge between Dry Canyon and Sheep Canyon 253 feet, and at two other poorly exposed localities in the Deep Creek Mountains about 250 feet.

Age and correlation.—Fossil collections were made both on Dutch Mountain and in the Deep Creek Mountains. They have been identified by Edwin

[46] Richardson, G. B., The Paleozoic section in northern Utah: Am. Jour. Sci., 4th ser., vol. 36, pp. 409–410, 1913.

Kirk, who assigns them to the Upper Ordovician. His report is as follows:

TN-26 33. 1 mile south of peak 7800 of Dutch Mountain, about 3 miles north of Gold Hill:

Halysites gracilis (Hall).
Streptelasma trilobatum Whiteaves.
Calapoecia cf. C. anticostiensis Billings.
Rhynchotrema capax Conrad.
Rhynchotrema argenturbica (White).
Dinorthis subquadrata Hall.
Zygospira recurvirostris (Hall).

TN-26 36. Just west of saddle between peaks 8550 and 8359 on ridge on north side of Dry Canyon near head:

Streptelasma trilobatum Whiteaves.
Streptelasma sp.
Columnaria sp.

This horizon is correlative with the upper portion of the Montoya limestone of Texas and New Mexico, the Fish Haven limestone of northern Utah, and the upper portion of the Bighorn dolomite of Wyoming. Rocks of equivalent age occur in the lower part of the Lone Mountain limestone of the Eureka district.

The upper part of the Bluebell dolomite at Tintic [47] is also of this age, as is the Ely Springs formation at Pioche, Nev.[48]

UNCONFORMITY AT TOP OF UPPER ORDOVICIAN

In the Gold Hill quadrangle there is little physical evidence of an unconformity between the Fish Haven dolomite and the overlying Laketown dolomite. The Fish Haven is remarkably constant in thickness throughout the area, and the dolomite conglomerate and wavy contact found at the base of the Laketown dolomite are no better defined than similar features within many of the lower Paleozoic formations. Further, the regional variation in thickness of Upper Ordovician sections that are overlain by Silurian beds is relatively slight. For example, the thickness at Pioche, Nev., is 525 feet; at Gold Hill, 260 feet; and in the Randolph quandrangle, Utah, 500 feet. In no one of these localities, moreover, does there seem to have been any notable amount of erosion before middle Silurian time. The absence of late Upper Ordovician and early Silurian faunas at all these localities, however, implies that there has been a considerable hiatus in sedimentation throughout this region.

SILURIAN SYSTEM

LAKETOWN DOLOMITE

Distribution.—The Laketown dolomite crops out prominently in the Deep Creek Mountains, forming the crest of the range from Dry Canyon north to North Pass Canyon. The width of this outcrop varies greatly, owing in part to the approximate coincidence of the dip of the beds and the slope of the surface west of the crest. South of Dry Canyon the formation is found entirely on the western flank of the range, where it forms the 7,662-foot hill between the forks of Simonson Canyon. A narrow band is present on the north side of North Pass Canyon. It is terminated both to the north and south by faults. Two small outcrops partly surrounded by gravel are also exposed on the southern flanks of Blood Mountain.

On Dutch Mountain the formation is exposed overlying the Fish Haven dolomite from Pool Canyon on the south to Spotted Fawn Canyon on the north. It is also present in Royal Gulch and in the foothills of the northwestern slope of Dutch Mountain.

The name of the formation is the same as that used by Richardson [49] for rocks of similar age in northeastern Utah.

Lithology.—The lower half of the Laketown dolomite is dark gray, rather massively bedded, and notably fossiliferous. Much of the rock is mottled or laminated, and such beds contain intraformational conglomerates. The appearance of these conglomerates was so striking that in the field they were distinguished by the name "marble cake" dolomite (pl. 5, *D*). Sections of a pentameroid brachiopod (*Virgiana* sp.) may be found throughout this zone, and one persistent bed, about 100 feet above the base, is largely made up of this fossil.

Above this dark dolomite is 350 to 400 feet of medium-gray massive dolomite. This zone is almost lacking in fossils and has none of the textural features so abundant in the lower beds. Most of the beds are rather coarsely crystalline, and a few contain vugs filled with white, well-crystallized dolomite.

This zone is overlain by another of massively bedded dark-gray to black dolomite, which also shows no unusual textural features except local thin chert stringers. It contains abundant fossil corals, which are locally silicified. This zone is about 150 to 200 feet thick. Above it from Sheep Canyon southward is a medium to light gray coarsely crystalline dolomite, which locally contains a bed crowded with large brachiopods of the genus *Trimerella*. This dolomite is not found to the north.

The upper contact of the formation is unconformable, the basal beds of the overlying Sevy dolomite clearly occupying depressions in the Laketown dolomite and resting upon successively lower beds of the Silurian northward. The top light-gray member, as noted above, is not present in the northern exposures of the formation in the Deep Creek Mountains.

Thickness.—A section of the formation measured on the ridge between Dry Canyon and Sheep Canyon was 970 feet thick. No other satisfactory measurements of the thickness were made, because of the presence of strike faults or because of poor exposure; but it is

[47] Loughlin, G. F., Geology and ore deposits of the Tintic mining district, Utah: U.S. Geol. Survey Prof. Paper 107, p. 35, 1919.

[48] Westgate, L. G., Geology and ore deposits of the Pioche district, Nev.: U.S. Geol. Survey Prof. Paper 171, p. 16, 1932.

[49] Richardson, G. B., Paleozoic section in northern Utah: Am. Jour. Sci., 4th ser., vol. 36, p. 410, 1913.

thought that the limits for the thickness in the Deep Creek Mountains within the quadrangle are 1,200 and 850 feet. No estimate of thickness on Dutch Mountain can be made, for the top is nowhere exposed, a fault contact with the Mississippian being found at all points.

Age and correlation.—The Laketown dolomite is abundantly fossiliferous throughout. Collections were made at various horizons, and these have been reported upon by Edwin Kirk as follows:

M4. About 100 yards due east of peak 8135, on south side of North Pass Canyon. 544 feet above base of formation:

Halysites catenularia (Linnaeus).	Zaphrentis sp. Favosites sp.

M13. Near head of Sheep Canyon, on north side, about 150 feet below top of formation:

Sections of brachiopod, probably Trimerella sp.

TN-26 22. Three-quarters of a mile north of peak 8550, Sheep Canyon, near base of formation:

Virgiana? sp.

TN-26 32. Crest of peak 8135, at head of North Pass Canyon:

Halysites catenularia (Linnaeus). Halysites, 2 sp. Coenites sp.	Syringopora, 2 sp. Zaphrentis sp. Favosites sp.

TN-26 34. Slope half a mile south of peak 8291, on north side of Sheep Canyon:

Halysites catenularia (Linnaeus).	Trimerella sp.

TN-26 35. South slope of peak 8550 on north side of Dry Canyon, near head:

Halysites catenularia (Linnaeus). Halysites sp. Syringopora, 2 sp.	Zaphrentis, 2 sp. Favosites sp. Virgiana? sp.

TN-26 39. 1 mile south-southeast of peak 7800, Dutch Mountain:

Favosites sp. (digitate form). Zaphrentis sp.	Amplexus sp. Heliolites sp.

TN-26 40. 4,500 feet east-northeast of peak 8135, North Pass Canyon:

Favosites sp. (digitate form). Zaphrentis sp.	Heliolites sp.

Gray dolomite above typical Silurian on ridge at head of south branch of Sheep Canyon, half a mile northwest of peak 8550:

Huronia sp.

This formation may be considered of Niagaran age. It is correlative in part with the Fusselman limestone of Texas and New Mexico, the Laketown dolomite of northern Utah, and probably the upper portion of the Lone Mountain limestone of the Eureka district.

UNCONFORMITY BETWEEN SILURIAN AND DEVONIAN

The truncation of beds at the top of the Laketown dolomite, as shown by the disappearance northward of the upper light-gray, coarsely crystalline member, and the local presence, in the basal Devonian formation, of conglomerate containing pebbles of the underlying Silurian formation, leave little doubt that there is a pronounced unconformity between the Laketown dolomite and the Sevy dolomite. An unconformity at this point has not previously been reported from the Great Basin or adjacent regions, chiefly because sediments of either Silurian or Devonian age or both are commonly lacking. Both series have been reported from three localities in Utah and Nevada—the Randolph quadrangle, Utah,[50] Pioche, Nev.,[51] and Eureka, Nev.[52] In the Randolph quadrangle the succession is said to be apparently conformable; at Pioche the two are not in contact; and at Eureka the contact is gradational. It would thus appear that the unconformity in the Gold Hill quadrangle is local in extent, but it is perhaps significant that no late Silurian faunas have been reported from either Eureka or the Randolph quadrangle.

DEVONIAN SYSTEM

SEVY DOLOMITE (MIDDLE DEVONIAN)

Distribution.—The Sevy dolomite, named from Sevy Canyon, is exposed only in the Deep Creek Mountains, generally being found on the west flank of the range. The most southerly exposure is in the south branch of Simonson Canyon, on the southern boundary of the quadrangle. This is of small extent and is separated on the north from the Laketown dolomite by a northwestward-striking fault. Outcrops occur also in the north branch of Simonson Canyon, on the north side of the Dry Canyon transverse fault. From this place the formation extends, with only minor interruption by faulting, in a direction a little east of north.

Lithology.—The Sevy dolomite is remarkably homogeneous throughout the area of outcrop. The typical rock is a well-bedded mouse-gray dolomite in layers 6 to 12 inches thick and weathers to a very light gray. It is of extremely dense texture and has a conchoidal fracture. In most of the beds a faint lamination parallel to the bedding is visible, in part at least, because of slight differences in color in adjoining laminae. A few beds of darker dolomite occur near the top of the formation, and locally there are present beds containing tiny nodules of light-colored chert.

The basal beds show the only notable variations in character from the main mass of the formation. The lower 30 feet includes in most places lenticular beds from 1 to 5 feet thick of medium gray, rather coarse grained dolomite sand, which is similar in color and texture to the top member of the Laketown dolomite. Some of these lenses contain numerous pebbles or boulders of dolomite. Some of the boulders are subangular in outline and consist of dark dolomite similar in lithology to various beds of the Laketown dolomite. The greater number, however, are sharply angular

[50] Richardson, G. B., Paleozoic section in northern Utah: Am. Jour. Sci., 4th ser., vol. 36, p. 411, 1913.

[51] Westgate, L. G., Geology and ore deposits of the Pioche district, Nev.: U.S. Geol. Survey Prof. Paper 171, pp. 16–19, 1932.

[52] Hague, Arnold, Geology of the Eureka district, Nev.: U.S. Geol. Survey Mon. 20, p. 63, 1892.

thin wedges or blocks of a light-gray dolomite identical with the enclosing beds. The lamination of the pebbles shows that they have been considerably rotated. The apparent anomaly of a conglomerate containing boulders of the younger rock in a matrix of material from the older rock may perhaps be explained as follows: The waters in which the Sevy dolomite was deposited were part of an advancing shallow sea, which was, at the locality and time represented by these sediments, just beginning to spread over the older rocks. Occasional severe storms broke up the partly consolidated sediments just deposited and at the same time swept in abundant fine-grained debris and a few larger boulders from the nearby shore composed of Silurian rocks. On the cessation of the storm, the material was deposited, and the resulting rock was similar to the material here described.

Thickness.—On the north side of Sevy Canyon the formation is 450 feet thick. The rocks here are well exposed and apparently not faulted. On the north side of Simonson Canyon 600 feet of beds were measured. The formation at this place is poorly exposed, however, and there may be some repetition of beds by faulting. Some variations in thickness are to be expected in an overlapping formation such as the Sevy dolomite, and the difference of 150 feet between the two measurements may be a difference in original deposition.

Age and correlation.—The only fossils found in the Sevy dolomite were small crinoid stems at a few horizons and several poorly preserved gastropods near the base. None of these, according to Edwin Kirk, who examined the formation in the field, are sufficiently diagnostic for determination of age. The formation grades into the overlying Simonson dolomite, which contains a Middle Devonian fauna. The Sevy dolomite is therefore considered to be Devonian and probably Middle Devonian.

SIMONSON DOLOMITE (MIDDLE DEVONIAN)

Distribution.—The Simonson dolomite, named from Simonson Canyon, on the west side of the Deep Creek Mountains near the southern boundary of the quadrangle, is exposed chiefly in these mountains. The only complete sections are found on the west side of the range, where the formation overlies the Sevy dolomite and is of similar extent. Smaller outcrops composed of portions of the formation occur at three other places. The largest of these is on the north side of North Pass Canyon, where, south of a large fault separating lower Paleozoic from Pennsylvanian rocks, a few hundred feet of the Simonson dolomite rests, with fault contact, upon beds of the Laketown dolomite. A smaller area of the formation is located in North Pass Canyon a quarter of a mile west of the branch road leading up Bagley Gulch. This is surrounded by gravel. A small exposure is also found on the north side of Dutch Mountain.

Lithology.—The base of the formation was placed at a dark crystalline dolomite, on the weathered surfaces of which may be seen thin discontinuous laminae of brown sandy material. The bed is strikingly laminated, a feature which is characteristic of the whole formation. Below this horizon there are a few dark-gray dolomites, and above it there are a few light-gray dolomites similar to those characteristic of the Sevy dolomite. The contact between the two formations is merely a change in the proportions of light and dark gray dolomites and does not indicate any time break.

The typical rock of the Simonson is a dark to medium gray dolomite in which the individual grains are large enough to be distinguished by the unaided eye. Individual beds are from 1 to 2 feet thick. The most striking feature is the very general presence of a fine lamination, caused chiefly by variations in the amount of darker pigment present in the laminae and to a much less degree by variations in the grain size. The laminae are in general extremely irregular in detail, much of this irregularity being clearly the result of original variations in deposition. Locally the irregularities are even more pronounced (pl. 5, *E*), and these are thought to have been caused by subsurface solution and subsequent slumping during the time the formation was being deposited.

The following section of the formation was measured on the north side of Sevy Canyon and is typical of the formation in the area.

Section of Simonson dolomite on north side of Sevy Canyon

	Feet
Dolomite conglomerate (base of Guilmette formation).	
Simonson dolomite:	
Medium- and dark-gray laminated dolomite, in beds 1 to 2 feet thick, locally coarsely crystalline	329
Light-gray sandy laminated dolomite; includes two thin layers of dark-gray dolomite and a 3-foot bed of dolomite conglomerate 75 feet above the base	96
Dark-gray laminated dolomite	56
Medium- and light-gray sandy dolomite	52
Dolomite conglomerate	6
Covered; probably largely laminated dolomite	170
Medium- and dark-gray laminated dolomite with a few thin light-gray beds near base; at base dark dolomite 3 feet thick containing thin laminae of brown sandstone	254
Light-gray dolomite of Sevy dolomite.	
	963

The two dolomite conglomerates in the above section apparently have little significance, as they cannot be found everywhere in the area. A similar conglomerate which is continuous, however, has been used to designate the base of the next higher formation. Its continuity is proved by the fact that it is found at the same distance below a distinctive fossiliferous bed throughout the area. Above this conglomerate the lithology is distinctly different from that of the Simonson dolomite, although the fossil evidence indicates that but little time difference is represented.

Thickness.—In addition to the measurement obtained in Sevy Canyon, a second measurement was made on the north side of Kelly Canyon, where the thickness was found to be 1,030 feet. The difference of 70 feet between the two probably represents errors in measurement due to poor exposures and minor faulting rather than to original variations of deposition.

Age and correlation.—Fossils are not abundant in the Simonson dolomite, except for small spherical *Stromatopora*-like corals. These are usually not more than an inch in diameter and are found in large numbers in certain beds. Three small lots were collected, upon which Mr. Kirk reports as follows:

Three-quarters mile north-northwest of South Peak, on north side of Sevy Canyon:
- Favosites (digitate form).
- Bellerophon sp.
- Stringocephalus burtoni Defrance.
- Martinia cf. M. meristoides Meek.
- Atrypa reticularis Linnaeus.

M4C. North side of Simonson Canyon near mouth:
- Atrypa reticularis Linnaeus.

TN-26 21. Half a mile north of Dewey prospect, on north side of Sevy Canyon:
- Favosites (digitate form).

The formation is probably correlative with the Nevada limestone of the Eureka district in part. The horizon, by virtue of the *Stringocephalus*, may accurately be placed as high as Middle Devonian.

GUILMETTE FORMATION (MIDDLE DEVONIAN)

Distribution.—The Guilmette formation, named after Guilmette Gulch, on the west side of the Deep Creek Mountains, forms the westernmost exposures of the range from Simonson Canyon northward to Sheridan Gulch, except for a few small areas occupied by the younger Woodman formation. The best exposure of the formation is on the north side of Sevy Canyon. The area covered by the formation is not continuous, being interrupted by three large transverse faults; and in the north it is further affected by warping and minor folding. In addition several small areas along the Lincoln Highway in the pass between the Deep Creek Mountains and Ochre Mountain are underlain by crumpled and crushed beds similar to those of the Guilmette. Another exposure that is thought to belong to this formation occurs on the north side of North Pass Canyon about half a mile east of the junction of the road from Bagley Gulch with the main road up the canyon. On the east edge of the quadrangle near the southern boundary there are outcrops of highly brecciated rock similar to this formation in lithology and, in some places, in fossil content. Some scattered outcrops on the north side of Dutch Mountain are also believed to belong in the Guilmette formation.

Lithology.—The Guilmette formation is composed chiefly of dolomite but contains also some thick limestone beds and several lenticular sandstones. The dolomites for the most part differ in character from those found in the Simonson dolomite, although a few laminated beds are present near the bottom of the formation. The most abundant variety is a fine-grained dolomite, dark to medium gray on fresh fracture and weathering to lighter shades of gray, that contains numerous vugs almost completely filled with white coarsely crystalline dolomite. Less abundant but far more striking in character is a dark dolomite filled with fragments of tubular corals. Most of these beds contain a coral of small diameter (*Cladopora* sp.), but some are filled with a larger, branching variety (*Striatopora* sp.). So far as known these coralline beds are limited to this formation.

The limestones are different from any found lower in the section. They are massively bedded, dense rocks that are light brownish gray on fresh fracture but weather to shades of bluish gray. The weathered surface is characteristically splotched with a tan discoloration. Fossils have not been found in such beds. The sandstone beds form a comparatively small portion of the formation, but the brownish color they assume on weathering makes them conspicuous. They are fine-grained and are thoroughly cemented by dolomite or calcite.

The following section, measured on the north side of Sevy Canyon, illustrates the interbedding of the various lithologic types:

Section of Guilmette formation on the north side of Sevy Canyon

	Feet
Sandstone and limestone of Woodman formation.	
Guilmette formation:	
1. Limestone, massively bedded; weathers to a light bluish gray splotched with tan	20
2. Dolomite, dark gray, coralline	2
3. Limestone, like no. 1	10
4. Sandstone, light gray on fresh fracture; weathers brown	15
5. Limestone, like no. 1	30
6. Dolomite, dark and medium gray, fine-grained; contains numerous vugs almost completely filled with white coarsely crystalline dolomite	31
7. Sandstone, like no. 4	6
8. Dolomite, like no. 6; includes a few thin layers like no. 2	46
9. Dolomite, dark gray, filled with *Striatopora*	3
10. Dolomite, like no. 6	25
11. Dolomite, like no. 9	6
12. Dolomite, like no. 6	28
13. Sandstone, like no. 4	6
14. Dolomite, like no. 6	14
15. Sandstone; weathers brown, dolomitic	3
16. Sandy dolomite, medium gray; poorly exposed	29
17. Dolomite, dark and medium gray, mottled; a few vugs filled with white coarsely crystalline dolomite; poorly exposed	34
18. Limestone, like no. 1	10
19. Limestone, thinner-bedded, including a few thin layers of dark-gray dolomite	26
20. Limestone, light gray, mottled with dark-gray dolomite splotches	27

Section of Guilmette formation on the north side of Sevy Canyon—Continued

	Feet
21. Dolomite, dark gray; includes lighter-gray dolomite conglomerate	21
22. Dolomite, medium gray, finely laminated	26
23. Dolomite, like no. 17	6
24. Limestone, like no. 1	10
25. Dolomite, like no. 17	63
26. Dolomite, bleached and brecciated	60
27. Limestone, like no. 1, poorly exposed	78
28. Dolomite, like no. 17	32
29. Limestone, like no. 1	9
30. Limestone, dolomitic; poorly exposed	22
31. Dolomite, like no. 22	3
32. Limestone, like no. 1; poorly exposed	9
33. Sandstone, like no. 4	14
34. Dolomite, like no. 22	58
35. Dolomite, medium gray, full of sections of *Stringocephalus burtoni*	4
36. Dolomite, like no. 17, with thin zone like no. 9, 30 feet above base	78
37. Dolomite conglomerate	24
Laminated dolomite of Simonson dolomite.	
	888

The upper contact of the formation is well exposed on the north side of Sevy Canyon, where a thin bed of bluish-gray limestone containing abundant Carboniferous fossils overlies massive unfossiliferous limestone similar to those found throughout the Guilmette formation. No angular discordance or clastic beds were distinguished at the contact.

Thickness.—Three measurements of the thickness of the formation were made. One on the north side of Simonson Canyon showed 1,400 feet and did not include the uppermost beds. A second, on the south side of Sevy Canyon, showed 1,200 feet; and a third, given in detail in the preceding section, 888 feet. All three of the sections measured are cut by numerous small faults. Allowance was made for the displacements caused by many of these faults, but it is not improbable that some escaped detection. The greater part of the variation in thickness, however, is due to an unconformity at the top of the formation.

Age and correlation.—Fossil collections were made at different horizons in the formation. Edwin Kirk, who participated in the collecting, reports on them as follows:

TN–26 25. One mile east of southeast corner of sec. 13, T. 9 S., R. 19 W.:

Stringocephalus burtoni Defrance.

TN–26 38. Three-fourths of a mile north-northwest of South Peak:

Stringocephalus burtoni Defrance.
Atrypa reticularis Linnaeus.

M–5. South side of Sevy Canyon:

Stringocephalus burtoni Defrance.

These three lots came from beds equivalent to no. 35 in the section above. The two following lots are somewhat higher.

M–4B. North side of Simonson Canyon, about 2 miles southeast of Simonson ranch:

Favosites (digitate form).
Syringopora sp.
Atrypa reticularis Linnaeus.

M–6. South side of Sevy Canyon:

Atrypa reticularis Linnaeus.
Martinia meristoides Meek.

The next two lots were obtained from limestone beds near the top of the formation.

TN–26 31. About 1 mile southwest of hill 6634, on west side of Ochre Mountain:

Pycinodesma? sp.

North side of Sevy Canyon:

Platyschisma? cf. P. mccoyi Walcott.
Cyclonema? sp.
Pycinodesma? sp.

Mr. Kirk further reports:

In the formation occur large numbers of *Cladopora* sp., which has a very widespread distribution throughout the Western States, being found in the Jefferson limestone of Montana and ranging south into Nevada. It is readily recognized by its small size, seldom being over 2 millimeters in diameter. Associated with this is a branching coral probably referable to *Striatopora*, which often forms a network on some of the surfaces. Occasional heads of "Stromatopora", ranging in size up to 3 or 4 inches in diameter, are found.

The formation is probably correlative with the Nevada limestone of the Eureka district in part. The horizon by virtue of the *Stringocephalus* may accurately be placed as high as Middle Devonian.

UNCONFORMITY AT BASE OF CARBONIFEROUS

The only exposures of the contact between the Mississippian and the Devonian that are not complicated by faulting are north and south of Sevy Canyon. There is little physical evidence in either of these places for the presence of an unconformity. Three bits of indirect evidence, however, indicate that there is a marked unconformity at this horizon. The first is the variation in thickness of the Devonian Guilmette formation from 1,400 feet to 890 feet within a distance of about 3 miles. Second, in the Deep Creek Mountains upper Mississippian rocks belonging to the Woodman formation overlie the Devonian directly, but on Dutch Mountain several hundred feet of the lower Mississippian Madison limestone is found beneath beds of the Woodman formation that are equivalent to those immediately above the Devonian to the south. The third bit of evidence is the absence of upper Devonian sediments at Gold Hill. Beds of this age are found at Pioche, Nev.,[53] and in the San Francisco district, Utah,[54] to the south; in the Eureka district, Nev.,[55] to the west; in the Tintic district,

[53] Westgate, L. G., Geology and ore deposits of the Pioche district, Nev.: U.S. Geol. Survey Prof. Paper 171, pp. 16–19, 1932.

[54] Butler, B. S., Geology and ore deposits of the San Francisco district, Utah: U.S. Geol. Survey Prof. Paper 80, pp. 34–35, 1913.

[55] Hague, Arnold, Geology of the Eureka district, Nev.: U.S. Geol. Survey Mon. 20, pp. 81–84, 1892.

Utah,[56] to the east; and in the Randolph quadrangle, Utah,[57] to the northeast.

Loughlin [58] has summarized evidence for an unconformity between the Devonian and Mississippian for several places in central Utah. Since Loughlin wrote his report Calkins [59] has noted a break at this horizon in the Cottonwood district, and Gilluly [60] found one in the Oquirrh Range. At the last-named locality Madison limestone overlies Devonian (?). This, combined with the several unconformities found at Gold Hill, suggests that the unconformity is somewhat less significant than was thought by Loughlin, and that the break he observed at various places in central Utah is a summation of several periods of erosion, of which the pre-Mississippian period was perhaps the longest.

ORIGIN OF THE PRE-CARBONIFEROUS DOLOMITIC FORMATIONS

The method of formation of dolomite and dolomitic limestones has been a matter of debate for a number of years. The evidence afforded by the thick dolomite formations in the Gold Hill quadrangle is thought to be of sufficient scientific interest to warrant presentation at this place.

The theories of origin that have been advanced are numerous, but the causes assigned may be classed under three general headings—(1) primary deposition, the dolomite having been laid down either as a chemical or organic precipitate, or as a clastic deposit; (2) alteration, an original limestone deposit having been altered to dolomite either before or after its elevation above sea level; (3) leaching, magnesium carbonate having been concentrated in a deposit that originally contained only a small amount of it by the removal of calcium carbonate in solution, either above or below sea level.[61] At the present time the view most generally held is that dolomite is formed by the alteration of an original limestone deposit before it is elevated above the sea.

Dolomites formed by two different methods have been described in the sections on the Abercrombie formation and the Sevy dolomite—those in the Abercrombie formation, as a result of alteration along fractures after elevation above sea level; and the dolomite matrix in the conglomerates near the base of the Sevy dolomite, as a result of clastic deposition. The remainder and great bulk of the dolomite in the Gold Hill quadrangle is thought to have been formed by the alteration of an original limestone deposit before the rock was elevated above sea level. Furthermore, it is thought that most, if not all, of the alteration occurred very shortly after the deposition of the limestone, for the most part in shallow water, and probably at times of little or no deposition. Raymond [62] and Twenhofel [63] have recently noted briefly the possible importance of the last-named factor. The writer considers it to have been probably the most important one in the formation of the dolomites exposed at Gold Hill.

The evidence indicating that dolomitization was accomplished by the alteration of an original limestone before it was elevated above sea level is similar to that which has been advanced by many investigators and need not be repeated here. The coincidence of dolomitization with texture and structure characteristic of shallow water has been pointed out by several writers [64] in recent years. Such features occur throughout the dolomitic formations at Gold Hill and are illustrated in plate 5, *C*, *D*, *E*. They include cross-bedding, oolites and pisolites, intraformational conglomerates, local unconformities, and lenticular beds. It is perhaps significant that many of the beds not possessing these features are mottled dolomites, in which the mottling is due to areas of less complete dolomitization. Near many of these mottled dolomites beds of relatively pure limestone are found.

The evidence for the theory that dolomitization is related to periods of nondeposition on the sea bottom is less direct. It is based largely on the following reasoning: A thick section of sediments that shows shallow-water phenomena throughout implies continual sinking of the sea floor. This sinking must have progressed at the same rate as the deposition of sediment, or more slowly; otherwise the higher beds would show characteristics of deeper water. Sinking at the same rate as deposition would almost certainly imply a dependence of sinking upon sedimentation, which Barrell [65] has shown is not warranted by the evidence afforded by the deltas of the Nile and other great rivers. But if the rate of sinking is slower than the rate of deposition, there must, of necessity, be many periods during which there is no deposition of sediment, and any material deposited will be above the baselevel of wave or current action and will be swept away to regions that are below wave base. Calcareous muds will thus be subject to reworking and alteration by the sea water for some time, and it is thought that in this fact is the chief explanation of dolomitization. The analyses assembled by Steidtmann show that

[56] Loughlin, G. F., Geology and ore deposits of the Tintic mining district, Utah: U.S. Geol. Survey Prof. Paper 107, p. 36, 1919.

[57] Richardson, G. B., The Paleozoic section in northern Utah: Am. Jour. Sci., 4th ser., vol. 36, pp. 411–412, 1913.

[58] Loughlin, G. F., op. cit., pp. 36–38.

[59] Calkins, F. C., Ore deposits of Utah: U.S. Geol. Survey Prof. Paper 111, pp. 237–238, 1919.

[60] Gilluly, James, Geology and ore deposits of the Stockton and Fairfield quadrangles, Utah: U.S. Geol. Survey Prof. Paper 173, p. 22, 1932.

[61] The evidence in favor of and opposed to the various theories, together with a historical summary, may be found in either Steidtmann, Edward, The evolution of limestone and dolomite: Jour. Geology, vol. 19, pp. 323–345, 392–428, 1911; or Van Tuyl, F. M., The origin of dolomite: Iowa Geol. Survey, vol. 25, pp. 251–421, 1916.

[62] Raymond, P. E., A possible factor in the formation of dolomite: Geol. Soc. America Bull., vol. 36, p. 168, 1925.

[63] Twenhofel, W. H., A treatise on sedimentation, p. 262, Baltimore, 1926.

[64] Skeats, E. W., The formation of dolomite: Am. Jour. Sci., 4th ser., vol. 45, pp. 194–199, 1918. Van Tuyl, F. M., The depth of dolomitization: Science, new ser., vol. 48, pp. 350–352, 1918. Tarr, W. A., A possible factor in the origin of dolomite: Science, new ser., vol. 51, p. 521, 1920.

[65] Barrell, Joseph, The strength of the earth's crust: Jour. Geology, vol. 22, pp. 36–48, 1914.

Almost all limestones contain a small amount of magnesium carbonate, which might be interpreted as a measure of the amount of replacement or alteration that occurs during continuous sedimentation. A prolonged exposure of the same calcareous mud to wave and current action would also permit selective leaching of calcium carbonate by sea water, a phenomenon which is known to occur in nature.[66]

The hypothesis outlined in the preceding paragraph seems to explain most of the characteristics of the dolomitic formations in the Gold Hill quadrangle. Beds showing shallow-water texture, wherever more than a few feet thick, are very thoroughly dolomitized, yielding no effervescence whatever with dilute acid. Dolomitic beds without this texture are mottled by patches higher in calcium carbonate and are in many places interbedded with limestone. It is thought that these represent periods when sedimentation was slightly slower than downwarping, or in which downwarping was somewhat spasmodic, allowing rather thick beds to be deposited before baselevel was reached, and then sinking was again initiated before dolomitization was complete.

Similar dolomitic rocks at Tintic have been explained by Loughlin[67] as the result of alteration of porous sediment in shallow water continuing for long periods after deposition but inhibited at certain times and places by the deposition of impervious argillaceous sediment or limestone mud. This explanation implies conditions similar to those inferred by the writer but is too restricted to be applicable at Gold Hill, because of the many places in which coarsely crystalline limestone and dolomite are in contact without intervening shaly material or dense limestone, as in the Trippe limestone and the Guilmette formation. Shaly material is, however, far more abundant in limestone zones than elsewhere, but it is thought that this is due rather to more rapid sedimentation in areas that had not yet reached the baselevel of deposition. Blackwelder[68] has considered the formation of the Bighorn dolomite in Wyoming the result of an abundance of magnesia-rich algae. There is no evidence at Gold Hill that algae have exerted any influence in the formation of dolomite. Daly[69] has suggested that many of the pre-Cambrian and early Paleozoic dolomites in the Rocky Mountain region at the international boundary are the result of direct precipitation. The evidence that has been presented in the foregoing descriptions is opposed to such an origin at Gold Hill, and it is not believed to be of any quantitative importance there.

[66] Clarke, F. W., The data of geochemistry, 5th ed.: U.S. Geol. Survey Bull. 770, p. 574, 1924.

[67] Loughlin, G. F., Geology and ore deposits of the Tintic mining district, Utah: U.S. Geol. Survey Prof. Paper 107, pp. 91–93, 1919.

[68] Blackwelder, Eliot, Origin of the Bighorn dolomite of Wyoming: Geol. Soc. America Bull., vol. 24, pp. 607, 624, 1913.

[69] Daly, R. A., First calcareous fossils and the evolution of the limestones: Geol. Soc. America Bull., vol. 20, pp. 153–170, 1909.

It is not at all probable that the theory that has been outlined here will be everywhere applicable, for the many diverse hypotheses that have been put forward indicate that the conditions of dolomitization differ in different places. Furthermore, it may be that the basic cause of dolomitization has not yet been determined and that the many theories of origin simply reflect the various environmental conditions in which this unknown cause is effective.

CORRELATION OF PRE-CARBONIFEROUS SEDIMENTARY ROCKS IN EASTERN NEVADA AND WESTERN UTAH

The correlations made for the pre-Carboniferous formations are given in tabular form in figures 3 and 4. Many of the correlations are extremely tentative, because of the common paucity of fossils and the notable variations in lithology in nearby areas. These figures bring out rather clearly the several unconformities present and, to a less extent, the variations in the kind of sediment deposited. The latter feature is somewhat masked by the failure of some of the earlier reports to differentiate dolomite and limestone.

Of chief interest, however, are the striking differences between the north-south and east-west sections. In the former the thicknesses of formations of the same age are roughly equivalent, and except for the absence of Middle Ordovician and Upper Devonian at Gold Hill, the time and extent of intersystemic and intrasystemic erosion are shown to have been nearly the same in all sections. In the east-west sections, however, there is an abrupt thickening of all formations from east to west and also a different succession.[70]

CARBONIFEROUS SYSTEM

Rocks of Carboniferous age are by far the most widespread of the Paleozoic sedimentary rocks in the quadrangle. They have been divided into 6 formations—3 Mississippian, 2 Pennsylvanian, and 1 Permian. Three facies of the Carboniferous have been distinguished and designated the eastern, central, and western facies. They have been brought into more or less close contact with one another by two large thrust faults, although originally they were probably several miles apart. The eastern facies is represented by rather scanty outcrops of only one formation, the Woodman, which overlies the older Paleozoic rocks with slight unconformity and is overridden by the lower of the two thrusts. The central facies, which includes the Ochre Mountain limestone and the Manning Canyon and Oquirrh formations, lies between the two thrusts. The western facies, which contains representatives of all six formations, lies above the upper thrust. The lithologic differences between the Manning Canyon and Oquirrh formations in both the

[70] Nolan, T. B., A late Paleozoic positive area in Nevada: Am. Jour. Sci., 5th ser., vol. 16, pp. 154–161, 1928.

western and central facies are striking. The relations between the three facies are summarized by figure 5.

MADISON LIMESTONE (LOWER MISSISSIPPIAN)

Distribution.—The Madison limestone is found only on Dutch Mountain. Outcrops occur on all sides of the mountain at altitudes between 6,000 and 7,000 feet. On the south and east sides this limestone forms a fairly continuous belt, broken by two large faults, one in Tribune Gulch and one south of the Spotted Fawn mine. On the northwest and west sides the formation is found only in the bottoms of valleys, where it is exposed in inliers, eroded through younger rocks. The largest of these outcrops is in Royal Gulch, and two smaller ones are in Accident Canyon and near the head of Trail Gulch. There are two small outcrops on the north side of Dutch Mountain, one near the mouth of Accident Canyon and one near the summit of the hill above the Garrison Monster mine.

The small area of limestone near the town of Clifton contains a few poorly preserved fossils, which, according to G. H. Girty, somewhat resemble those found in the Madison limestone. Lithologically, however, the beds resemble the Ochre Mountain limestone, and this apparent relationship is heightened by the presence of an interbedded belt of black shale, apparently the Herat shale member of the Ochre Mountain. The

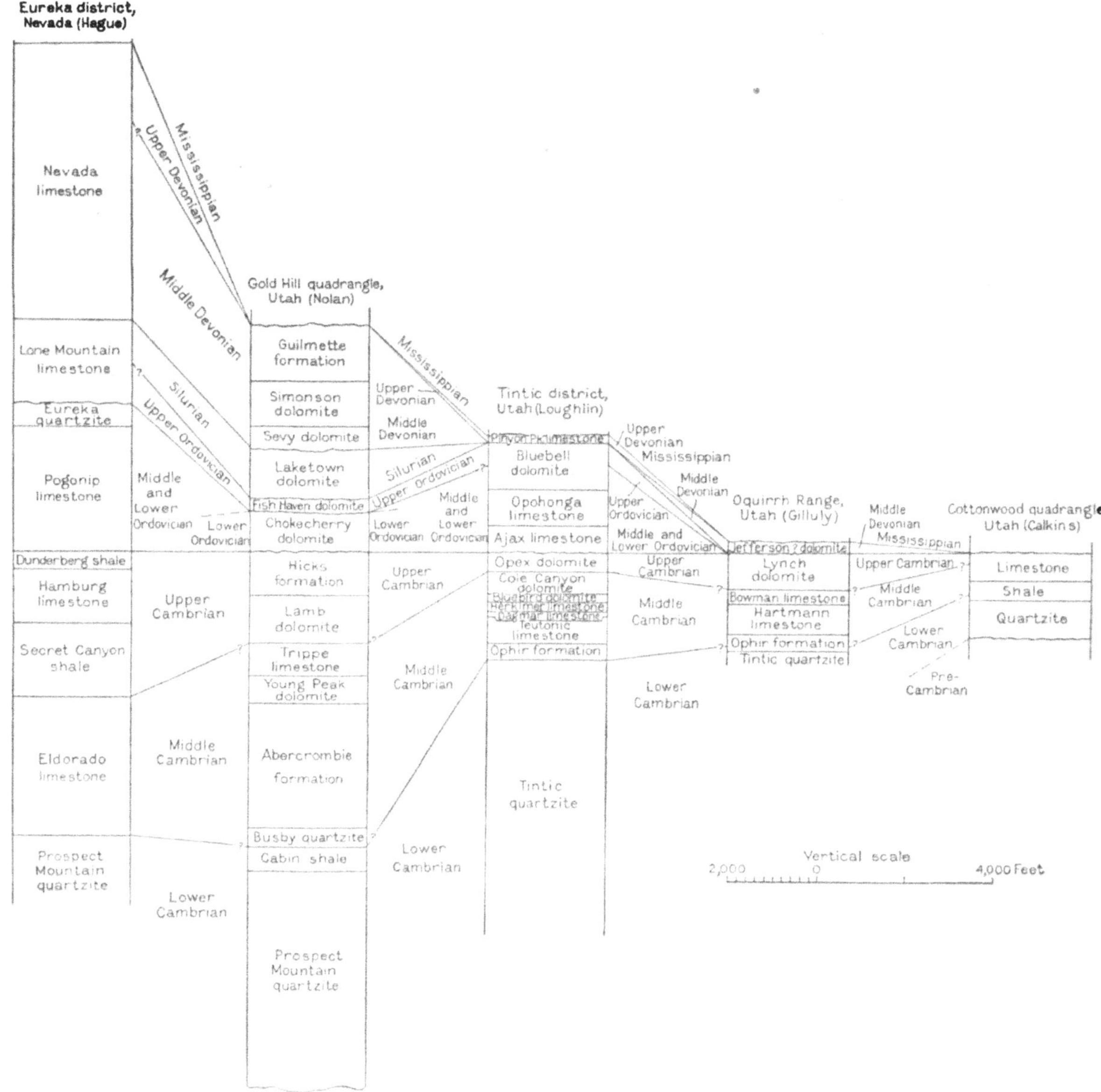

FIGURE 3.—Correlation of pre-Carboniferous rocks in eastern Nevada and western Utah from west to east

outcrop has therefore been mapped as the Ochre Mountain limestone.

All the outcrops of the Madison belong to the western facies of the Carboniferous. No beds of this age are found in the eastern facies, in which upper Mississippian rocks rest directly upon the Devonian. It is not known whether the formation is present in the central facies, as the oldest beds of this group exposed within the quadrangle belong to the Ochre Mountain limestone, of upper Mississippian age.

stone is a dull dark-gray on fresh fracture and weathers to a distinctly lighter-gray. It is normally very dense but includes a great number of crinoid stems made up of coarsely crystalline calcite.

In the greater part of the formation as exposed the beds are moderately thin, ranging from 3 inches to 1 foot in thickness. The bedding is marked in many places by a concentration of pink or less commonly yellowish clay. Small amounts of similarly colored clay are also found within individual beds in some

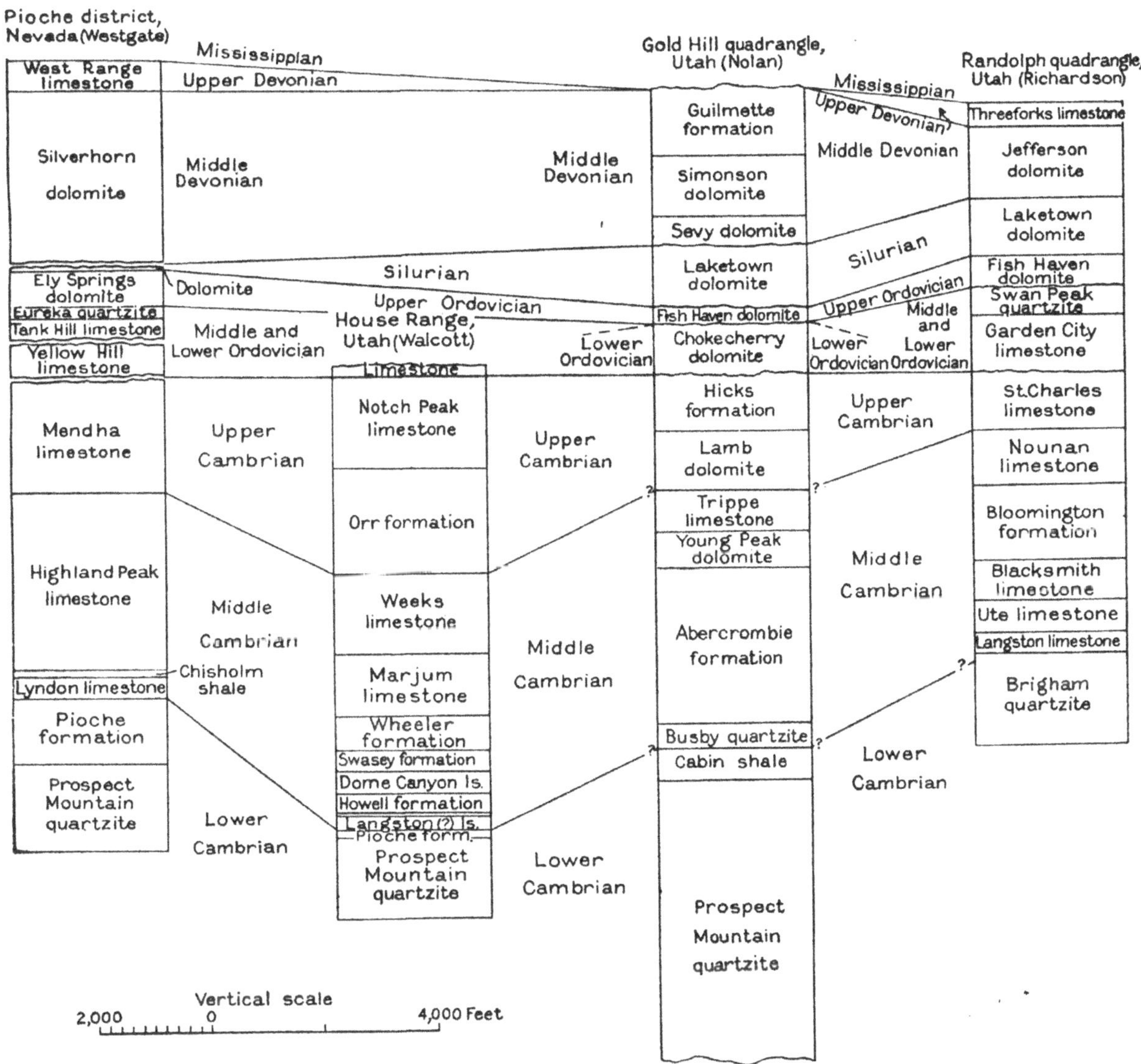

FIGURE 4.—Correlation of pre-Carboniferous rocks in eastern Nevada and western Utah from north to south.

The name is taken from the Madison Range, in south-central Montana, where rocks of this age were described by Peale.

Lithology.—The Madison limestone is best exposed on the north side of Pool Canyon, where, in places distant from the quartz monzonite, it forms cliffy slopes beneath less resistant sandstones. The lime-

places, and the weathered surfaces of such beds have a faint pinkish mottling.

Many beds are crowded with crinoid stems and small cup corals. In a few places these fossils are partly silicified and weather out in relief from the usual smooth surface. Fossils other than the two kinds mentioned are not easily found. This is probably due to the rather general fracturing to which the formation has been subjected and which has resulted in an abundance of veinlets and splotches of white calcite.

At the top of the formation there are about 10 or 15 feet of more massively bedded limestone, which contains numerous nodules of dark chert, some as much as a foot in largest diameter. Above these beds, apparently conformable, are sandstones of the Woodman formation.

The faunas are not very extensive, and the specimens are very poorly preserved, but there can be little doubt of the geologic age as lower Carboniferous and the correlation as with the Madison limestone.

6052 and 6329. North side of Tribune Gulch on ridge line:

Zaphrentis sp.	Spirifer centronatus.
Amplexus aff. A. fragilis.	Straparollus ophirensis.
Syringopora surcularia.	Euomphalus utahensis.
Triplophyllum excavatum.	Euomphalus luxus?
Lithostrotion sp.	Nautilus? sp.
Chonetes loganensis.	Phillipsia peroccidens.

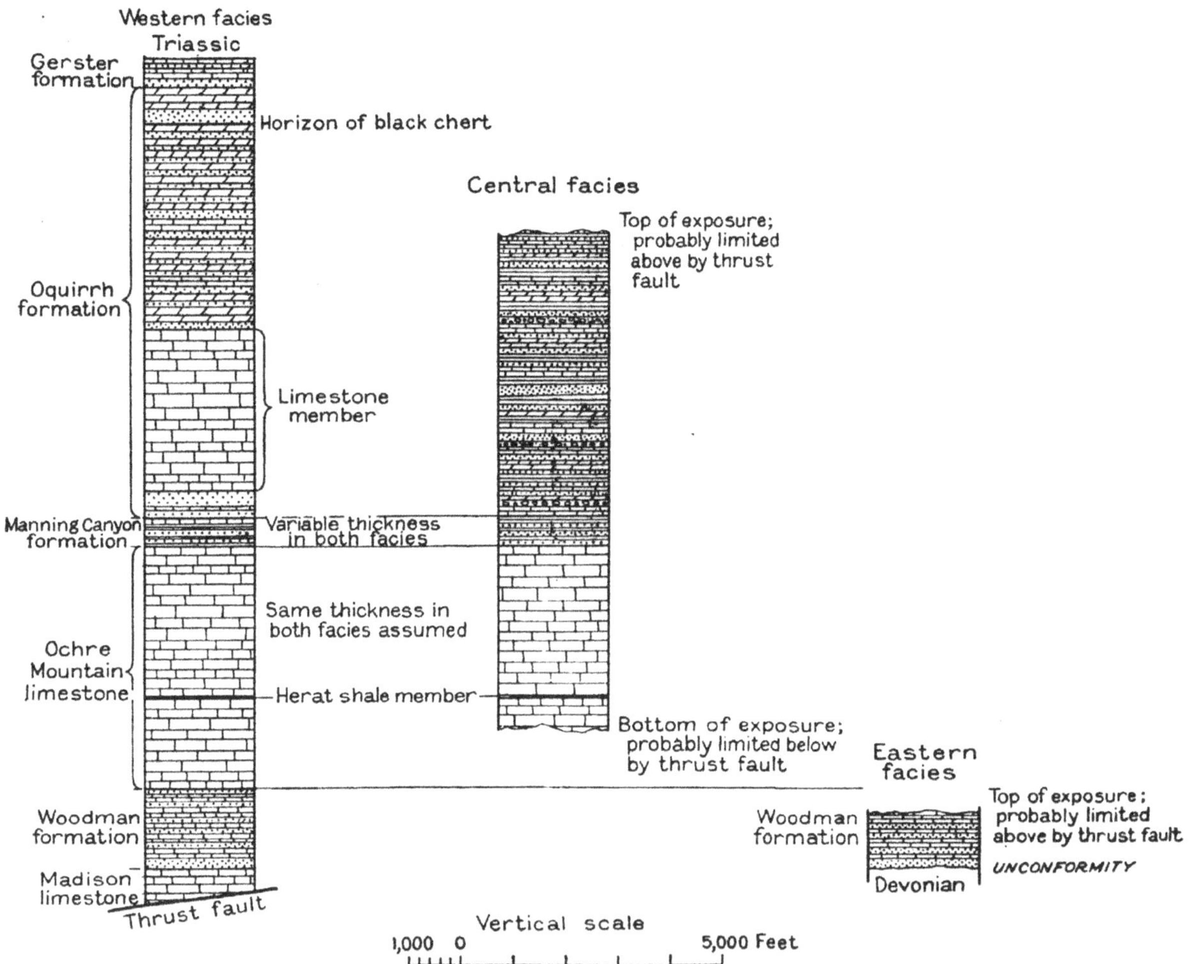

FIGURE 5.—Relations between the three facies of the Carboniferous rocks.

Thickness.—The maximum thickness of the Madison limestone was found in Pool Canyon, where it is about 400 feet. Here, however, as elsewhere on Dutch Mountain, the lower contact is a thrust fault, and as a result the observed thickness varies considerably. In the Deep Creek Mountains the formation was not found, the next higher (Woodman) formation resting directly upon the Guilmette formation.

Age and correlation.—Fossils from the Madison limestone were examined by G. H. Girty, who says:

6323. North side of Royal Gulch 2,000 feet southeast of cabin:

Triplophyllum sp.	Composita sp.
Syringopora surcularia?	Euomphalus utahensis?
Spirifer centronatus?	Platyceras sp.

Two collections from this formation were made by L. D. Burling during a reconnaissance trip through Utah and Nevada in August 1905. Lists of these have not previously been published and are therefore included here.

98. North side of Pool Canyon, southeast side of Dutch Mountain, about 1½ miles up the canyon and 200 to 300 feet above the canyon bottom:

Syringopora? sp.	Euomphalus sp.
Triplophyllum sp.	Platyceras sp.

This collection was made about 150 feet below the top of the formation.

99. North side of Pool Canyon, southeast side of Dutch Mountain [label incomplete]:

Cladochonus sp.	Productus galeanus?
Triplophyllum sp.	Dielasma? sp.
Crinoid columnals.	Spirifer aff. S. grimesi.
Spirorbis sp.	Spirifer aff. S. vernonensis.
Fenestella, several sp.	Spiriferina subelliptica?
Pinnatopora sp.	Spiriferina solidirostris?
Cystodictya sp.	Reticularia cooperensis.
Schizophoria? sp.	Cleiothyridina sp.
Pustula sp.	

This collection was made at the top of the formation near the contact with the Woodman formation.

Mr. Girty states that "both lots appear to be Madison."

The Madison limestone in the Oquirrh Range[71] is of lower Mississippian age, as are the Victoria quartzite, the Gardner dolomite, and the lower portion of the Pine Canyon limestone in the Tintic district.[72]

WOODMAN FORMATION (UPPER MISSISSIPPIAN)

Distribution.—The Woodman formation, named from Woodman Peak, on the south side of Dutch Mountain, is exposed at several places within the quadrangle. In the Deep Creek Mountains there are four outcrops north and south of Sevy Canyon. These belong to the eastern facies; the remaining areas belong to the western facies. Beds higher in the formation are present on the west and south sides of Ochre Mountain. The most extensive exposures of the formation, however, are found on Dutch Mountain, particularly on the higher parts of the western slope. Smaller exposures occur in several places along the north side of Dutch Mountain.

There are two other areas in which the Woodman formation may be present. One of these is the large block of sedimentary rocks surrounded by quartz monzonite north of Clifton. A small collection of poorly preserved fossils from this locality was regarded by Mr. Girty as resembling the Woodman fauna more closely than any other. Lithologically, however, the beds resemble those of the overlying Ochre Mountain limestone, and because of their association with a black shale, thought to be the Herat shale member, they have been mapped as the higher formation. The other region for which some doubt exists is at the 6,267-foot hill on the south side of North Pass Canyon. Two poor fossil collections were made here. The lower one was referred somewhat doubtfully to the Woodman formation, and the upper one with similar reservations to the Ochre Mountain limestone. However, on the north side of the canyon similar beds that are apparently continuous with these are definitely of Pennsylvanian age, and the beds in question have therefore been mapped as a part of the Oquirrh formation.

Lithology.—The Woodman formation consists of a lower division of dominant calcareous sandstone and an upper division consisting chiefly of sandy limestone. These two units are found in both the eastern facies and the western facies.

The sandstone portion at the base is roughly 200 feet thick. The beds are purplish or reddish brown, are fine-grained, and contain a variable though small proportion of calcium carbonate as cement. Locally nodules of black chert, an inch or so in maximum diameter, are found in the sandstone. Several thin beds of sandy limestone, which are probably lenticular, and a minor amount of shale are usually present. This part of the formation is everywhere poorly exposed, as the sandstone breaks down into small rectangular blocks, which not only cover the surface underlain by the formation but form extensive areas of talus that conceal the adjoining formations.

The upper and thicker calcareous division comprises rocks of several varieties. The most abundant is a sandy limestone which is dark gray to almost black on fresh fracture but which weathers light brown to pinkish. It leaves a large residue of sandy material when dissolved in hydrochloric acid. Most beds of this character contain nodules of dark-gray or black chert. These nodules are generally 6 inches or so in diameter but may be as much as a foot. They include casts of fossils in many places. There is, as a rule, no sharp boundary between the chert and the limestone, the contact being formed by alternate irregular laminations of dark chert and tan-weathering sandy limestone. Interbedded with the sandy limestones are calcareous sandstones. The boundary between the two kinds of rock is not sharp, and one passes into the other with increase or decrease in the amount of sand. The sandy limestones are much more abundant.

Two other varieties of limestones may be noted. One is a platy fine-grained limestone which is dark-gray on fresh fracture and a very light gray on weathered surfaces. It contains only a small amount of insoluble material. The other variety is found locally in thin beds. It is a coarsely crystalline medium-gray limestone, crowded with fossils, chiefly large crinoid stems. The fossils are silicified in many outcrops of these beds.

The following section of the formation was measured on the south side of Sevy Canyon, in the Deep Creek Mountains. It is incomplete, as the top of the formation is not exposed, but is the thickest of all the outcrops of the formation examined.

[71] Gilluly, James, Geology and ore deposits of the Stockton and Fairfield quadrangles, Utah: U.S. Geol. Survey Prof. Paper 173, pp. 23–25, 1932.

[72] Loughlin, G. F., Geology and ore deposits of the Tintic mining district, Utah: U.S. Geol. Survey Prof. Paper 107, pp. 38–41, 1919.

Incomplete section of Woodman formation on south side of Sevy Canyon

	Feet
Thin-bedded sandy and cherty limestone	77
Calcareous sandstone	59
Thin-bedded blue-gray cherty limestone	76
Thin-bedded sandy limestone	30
Calcareous sandstone	46
Thin-bedded sandy limestone	63
Blue-gray massively bedded cherty limestone	15
Thin-bedded sandy and cherty limestone	166
Thin-bedded sandy limestone with some calcareous sandstone	137
Thin-bedded sandy and cherty limestone	62
Thin-bedded sandy limestone	86
Calcareous sandstone with a few beds of sandy limestone	209
Limestone	1
Limestone of Guilmette formation.	
	1, 027

Thickness.—The total thickness of the formation is unknown, as nowhere in the quadrangle is a complete section exposed. The lower 1,000 feet is exposed on the Deep Creek Mountains, and the upper 700 or 800 feet on Ochre Mountain. A varying thickness of the formation is shown on Dutch Mountain, but at every exposure there the upper beds have been eliminated by faulting at the contact with the overlying Ochre Mountain limestone. Although no satisfactory correlation could be made between the lower beds on Ochre Mountain and the upper beds in the Deep Creek Mountains, they are thought to indicate a total thickness for the formation of about 1,500 feet. There is no evidence to indicate any striking difference in thickness between the various facies.

Age and correlation.—The Woodman formation is of upper Mississippian age. The overlying Ochre Mountain limestone is also of this age, and Mr. Girty reports that "the Woodman and Ochre Mountain faunas are not sharply distinguished in my mind; or better, many of the collections are too small, or too poorly preserved, or too nondescript in character to be amenable to the distinctions that I do make." The formation may be correlated directly with the Deseret limestone and Humbug formation of the Oquirrh Range, [73] the Humbug formation of the Tintic district,[74] and the lower portion of the widespread Brazer limestone,[75] to the northeast.

The fossil collections from the formation have been studied by Mr. Girty, whose determinations are as follows:

Collections from the eastern facies

6046. 2,200 feet east-southeast of southeast corner of sec. 13, T. 9 S., R. 19 W.:

Fenestella sp.
Productus aff. P. burlingtonensis.
Productus ovatus.
Pustula aff. P. alternata.
Rhynchopora? sp.
Coelonautilus? sp.

6053 and 6324. North side of Sevy Canyon, 2,300 feet west-southwest of point at 7,164 feet:

Triplophyllum sp.
Cladochonus sp.
Crinoid? indet.
Fenestella, several sp.
Pinnatopora sp.
Cystodictya sp.
Orbiculoidea sp.
Chonetes aff. C. oklahomensis.
Productus aff. P. burlingtonensis.
Pustula aff. P. alternata.
Pugnax n. sp.
Spirifer aff. S. grimesi.
Spirifer sp.
Brachythyris suborbicularis.
Spiriferella? sp.

6069. 1.7 miles north of east from Simonson ranch:

Pustula aff. P. concentrica?
Productus aff. P. burlingtonensis.
Spirifer aff. S. imbrex.
Brachythyris suborbicularis.
Cleiothyridina sublamellosa?
Proetus n. sp.

The preceding three collections were taken from the base of the formation.

6051 and 6382. Near southeast corner of sec. 13, T. 9 S., R. 19 W.:

Amplexus aff. A. fragilis.
Triplophyllum sp.
Fenestella sp.
Orbiculoidea sp.
Rhipidomella sp.
Schizophoria aff. S. swallowi.
Chonetes aff. C. ornatus.
Chonetes aff. C. platynotus.
Productus ovatus.
Productus semireticulatus.
Productus aff. P. parvus.
Productus aff. P. setiger.
Productus aff. P. keokuk.
Productus aff. P. gallatinensis.
Pustula aff. P. alternata.
Pustula aff. P. subsulcata.
Pustula aff. P. oklahomensis.
Pustula aff. P. patula.
Pustula aff. P. millespinosa.
Pustula aff. P. biseriata?
Pustula n. sp.
Pustula? sp.
Rhynchopora? aff. R. cooperensis.
Rhynchopora sp.
Cranaena aff. C. globosa.
Spirifer aff. S. rostellatus.
Spirifer sp.
Brachythyris suborbicularis.
Reticularia aff. R. pseudolineata.
Spiriferina aff. S. solidirostris.
Syringothyris sp.
Composita sp.
Eumetria verneuiliana.
Hustedia aff. H. mormoni.
Solenomya? sp.
Streblopteria? sp.
Deltopecten sp.
Worthenia? sp.
Pleurotomaria sp.
Platyceras aff. P. capax.

This collection came from a horizon about 1,050 feet above the base of the formation.

Collections from the western facies

6274. Accident Canyon, east of cabin:

Productella hirsutiformis.
Leiorhynchus carboniferum var. polypleurum.

This lot came from the sandstone at the base of the formation and seems to contain the fauna of the Herat shale member. It is quite possible that this occurs at several horizons.

6366. South side of Ochre Mountain, 2,500 feet east of 6,886-foot hill:

Triplophyllum aff. T. centrale.
Stenopora aff. S. ramosa.
Rhipidomella? sp.
Productus aff. P. burlingtonensis.
Productus aff. P. setiger.
Productus sp.
Pustula aff. P. alternata.
Pustula aff. P. subsulcata.
Pustula? sp.
Spirifer aff. S. rostellatus.
Brachythyris suborbicularis.

[73] Gilluly, James, Geology and ore deposits of the Stockton and Fairfield quadrangles, Utah: U.S. Geol. Survey Prof. Paper 173, pp. 25–29, 1932.

[74] Loughlin, G. F., Geology and ore deposits of the Tintic mining district, Utah: U.S. Geol. Survey Prof. Paper 107, pp. 41–42, 1919.

[75] Mansfield, G. R., Geography, geology, and mineral resources of part of southeastern Idaho: U.S. Geol. Survey Prof. Paper 152, pp. 63–71, 1927.

6367. 250 feet north of 6366:

Triplophyllum sp.
Chonetes aff. C. platynotus.
Productus ovatus.
Productus ovatus var. latior?
Productus aff. P. mesialis.
Productus sp.
Productus aff. P. setiger.
Pustula alternata.
Pustula aff. P. biseriata.
Pustula aff. P. concentrica.
Pustula aff. P. subsulcata.
Pustula aff. P. moorefieldana.
Pustula aff. P. oklahomensis.
Spirifer aff. S. increbescens.
Reticularia aff. R. pseudolineata.
Spirifer aff. S. rostellatus.
Spiriferella sp.

6368. 250 feet north of 6367:

Favosites sp.
Triplophyllum sp.
Echinocrinus sp.
Productus ovatus.
Productus aff. P. mesialis.
Brachythyris aff. B. suborbicularis.
Spiriferina aff. S. subelliptica.
Composita sp.
Cleiothyridina sublamellosa var.
Hustedia aff. H. multicostata.

6369. 100 feet north of 6368:

Echinocrinus sp.
Chonetes aff. C. oklahomensis.
Productus aff. P. mesialis.
Productus sp.
Cranaena aff. C. subglobosa.
Composita sp.
Cleiothyridina sublamellosa.
Leptodesma sp.

6065. 2,100 feet south-southeast of hill 7150, south side of Ochre Mountain:

Triplophyllum aff. T. centrale.
Schizophoria aff. S. swallowi.
Chonetes aff. C. oklahomensis.
Productus ovatus.
Productus aff. P. mesialis.
Pustula aff. P. subsulcata.
Spirifer aff. S. increbescens.
Spirifer aff. S. grimesi.
Spiriferella? sp.

This lot was taken near the top of the formation.

6319. 1,000 feet west of 6,964-foot point on southwest side of Dutch Mountain:

Zaphrentis aff. Z. excentrica.
Crinoidal fragments.
Fenestella sp.
Productus ovatus?

6322. 1,000 feet north of cabin in Royal Gulch:

Michelinia aff. M. meekana.
Triplophyllum aff. T. centrale.
Zaphrentis aff. Z. excentrica.
Stenopora? sp.
Fenestella sp.
Productus aff. P. inflatus.
Productus aff. P. semireticulatus.
Spirifer sp.
Orthoceras? sp.

These two collections were taken from beds rather high in the formation. They present an aspect rather different from the other collections and one that resembles some of the collections from the Oquirrh formation.

OCHRE MOUNTAIN LIMESTONE (UPPER MISSISSIPPIAN)

Distribution.—The Ochre Mountain limestone is exposed in several places within the quadrangle. The largest exposure is on Ochre Mountain, which is in large part underlain by the formation and from which it takes its name. Dutch Mountain is also capped by this limestone, and there are other outcrops along the northern border of the quadrangle and in a belt along Trail Gulch. Smaller areas of the formation are found at the borders of the quartz monzonite stock and as roof pendants within it from Pool Canyon and the Rube mine south to Clifton. Still another locality is north and south of Overland Canyon from the Midas mine westward into Blood Canyon.

Although the association of these outcrops with distinctive areas of the Manning Canyon and Oquirrh formations shows that some of them must represent a central and some a western facies, no lithologic distinction can be drawn between exposures definitely belonging to the one or the other. Isolated outcrops or those in fault contact with the surrounding sedimentary rocks therefore cannot readily be placed in their proper facies, except by reason of their relations to nearby outcrops or to structural features such as the thrusts. The outcrops in the vicinity of Overland Canyon, together with those in which the Western Utah, United States, and Cane Springs mines are located, have been referred to the central facies, and the remainder to the western facies.

The area of limestone near Clifton may possibly be Madison limestone, and the portion of the roof pendant north of Clifton mapped as Ochre Mountain limestone may belong rather to the Woodman formation, but for the reasons previously given they are regarded as belonging to the Ochre Mountain limestone. On the other hand, a fossil collection from hill 6267, on the south side of North Pass Canyon, was doubtfully referred by Mr. Girty to the Ochre Mountain limestone but for the reasons given in the description of the Woodman formation, to which another collection from this locality was referred, it seems more probable that these beds are part of the Oquirrh formation.

Lithology.—The Ochre Mountain limestone is composed chiefly of rather thick bedded limestone. Near the base the limestone contains a considerable amount of chert, and near the top a smaller amount. About 1,700 feet above the base of the western facies is a thin bed of black shale, which has been mapped separately as the Herat shale member. This is also present in the central facies.

The contact of the formation with the underlying Woodman formation was seen only on the south and west sides of Ochre Mountain. Here laminae of sandy limestone, similar to that in the Woodman, are found several hundred feet above the lowest bed of massive limestone, which was chosen as the base of the Ochre Mountain limestone.

The limestone beds are similar in appearance throughout the formation. They are commonly brownish gray on freshly broken surfaces and weather to light bluish gray. They are usually fine-grained, but coarser-grained beds occur locally. Individual beds may be as much as 10 feet in thickness, and almost all are more than 1 foot thick. In a few places thinner-bedded limestones are found. These contain a much larger proportion of insoluble material than the normal pure limestones and weather to hues of yellow and pink.

The basal few hundred feet of the formation includes beds that contain large amounts of chert, in some beds considerably more than half. The chert is generally light gray but weathers to a characteristic tan. The chert lenses and masses are everywhere highly shattered. In the upper cherty zone, which is less pronounced, the chert is present in the form of small nodules and stringers. The limestone beds included in the upper zone contain more sand than is generally present elsewhere.

Near the intrusive rock the formation has been bleached and recrystallized, and in some beds silicate minerals have replaced the calcium carbonate in varying amounts. In other places not visibly related to areas of intrusive rocks the limestone has been changed to dolomite, the alteration causing a change in the color of the weathered surface to a dull gray. These alterations are described in more detail on pages 91–94.

Herat shale member.—The Herat shale member has been mapped at several places on the south side of Ochre Mountain, in Blood Canyon, and north and west of Clifton. The name is taken from the Herat mine near Clifton. Outcrops of the shale are rare, and it may be present at several places not shown on the map. The member is made up of black shale with thin lenses of sandstone. In most outcrops it has been the site of movements parallel to the bedding, with the result that its thickness is extremely variable, ranging from almost nothing to about 50 feet. In two of the exposures on Ochre Mountain the limestone beneath the shale, which is normally only slightly sandy, has been rather thoroughly silicified. In many respects the Herat shale member is similar to the stratigraphically higher Manning Canyon formation, and in the absence of fossils it is often difficult to distinguish the two.

Thickness.—A complete section of the Ochre Mountain limestone was not found within the quadrangle. An approximation to the true thickness may be obtained by assuming that the central and western facies have the same thickness and that the Herat shale member has the same position in both facies. Both assumptions are probably open to question, and the result must be regarded merely as indicating the order of magnitude of the thickness. It is based upon an estimate of the thickness from the base of the western facies of the formation up to the Herat shale member, made at two places on the south side of Ochre Mountain; and an estimate of the thickness from the shale to the top of the central facies of the formation, made along Overland Canyon. These estimates were, respectively, 1,700 feet and 2,800 feet, indicating a total thickness of 4,500 feet. The figures were obtained by scaling the thickness from the geologic cross sections and are therefore only rough approximations, but more refined measurements did not seem justified in view of the assumptions made.

Age and correlation.—The Ochre Mountain limestone, like the Woodman formation, is of upper Mississippian age. Mr. Girty's notes on the difficulties in distinguishing between the faunas of the two formations were quoted under the Woodman formation (p. 28) and need not be repeated here. The formation most nearly equivalent to the Ochre Mountain limestone is the "Great Blue" limestone in the Oquirrh Range.[76] The formation is probably also more or less equivalent to the upper portions of the Brazer limestone of northeastern Utah [77] and southeastern Idaho.[78]

Mr. Girty's determinations of the fossils in the collections are as follows:

Collection from the central facies

6325. Blood Canyon, north of spring:

Triplophyllum sp.	Girtyella indianensis?
Campophyllum sp.	Composita sp.
Fenestella sp.	Cleiothyridina sublamellosa?
Schizophoria aff. S. swallowi?	Cleiothyridina? n. sp.
Orthotetes sp.	Bellerophon sp.
Productus aff. P. parvus.	

This is the only collection from the central facies. Metamorphism by the quartz monzonite stock appears to have destroyed most of the fossils originally present in it.

Collections from the western facies

Because of the difficulties in determining the throws of the numerous faults that cut the Ochre Mountain limestone, no attempt is made to list the collections in their proper stratigraphic order. The collections from the Herat shale, which is distinctive lithologically, are listed separately.

5865. 3,300 feet N. 60° W. from summit above Garrison Monster mine:

Crinoid columnals.	Bellerophon? sp.
Levidentalium? sp.	

5866. West side of Ochre Mountain at base of ridge on south side of northernmost canyon:

Crinoid columnals.	Productus ovatus.
Stenopora sp.	Productus aff. P. parvus.
Rhombopora? sp.	Diaphragmus elegans?
Fenestella, several sp.	Spirifer aff. S. pellensis.
Schizophoria sp.	Cleiothyridina sublamellosa.

5866a. Same canyon as 5866, halfway up ridge:

Productus brazerianus.

5866b. Same canyon as 5866, just below summit:

Campophyllum? sp.

5866c. Same canyon as 5866, at head of canyon:

Euphemus aff. E. randolphensis.	Holopea? sp.
	Orthoceras aff. O. choctawense.

5866d. Same canyon as 5866, divide at head of north branch:

Syringopora sp.

5866e. Same canyon as 5866, 400 feet above gravel on northern ridge:

Spiriferella? sp.

---

[76] Gilluly, James, Geology and ore deposits of the Stockton and Fairfield quadrangles, Utah: U.S. Geol. Survey Prof. Paper 173, pp. 29–31, 1932.

[77] Richardson, G. B., The Paleozoic section in northern Utah: Am. Jour. Sci. 4th ser., vol. 36, p. 413, 1913.

[78] Mansfield, G. R., Geography, geology, and mineral resources of part of southeastern Idaho: U.S. Geol. Survey Prof. Paper 152, pp. 63–71, 1927.

6044. 1,000 feet southwest of hill [illegible], on southwest side of Ochre Mountain:

Stenopora aff. S. mutabilis.
Stenopora sp.
Meekopora? sp.
Chonetes sp.
Productus semireticulatus.
Productus ovatus?
Productus inflatus?
Spirifer aff. S. pellensis.
Spirifer aff. S. brazerianus.
Spiriferella? n. sp.
Hustedia multicostata?
Griffithides sp.

This collection was obtained near the base of the formation.

6045. Due south of peak 6886, on south side of Ochre Mountain, at an altitude of 6,750 feet:

Productus aff. P. parvus.
Dielasma sp.
Spirifer aff. S. pellensis.
Composita sulcata?

6059. 1,500 feet east-southeast of 6,975-foot closed contour on south side of Ochre Mountain:

Productus inflatus.
Pustula aff. P. moorefieldana.
Spirifer aff. S. pellensis.
Spiriferella? n. sp.

6060. Just west of hill 6634, on southwest side of Ochre Mountain:

Productus gallatinensis?
Pustula aff. P. genevievensis.
Composita sulcata?
Cleiothyridina sublamellosa.

6062. 1,200 feet north of peak 7182, on ridge line of Ochre Mountain:

Productus ovatus.
Diaphragmus elegans?
Dielasma n. sp.

6063. 1,500 feet west of 7,150-foot peak on south side of Ochre Mountain:

Productella hirsutiformis.
Pustula aff. P. subsulcata.
Deltopecten aff. D. batesvillensis.
Brachymetopus sp.

This collection came from the limestone immediately beneath the Herat shale.

6067. West of mouth of Accident Canyon, on north side of Dutch Mountain:

Lithostrotionella sp.

6072. 1,000 feet south-southeast of peak 7150, on south side of Ochre Mountain:

Amplexus sp.
Echinocrinus sp.
Fenestella, several sp.

This collection was obtained near the base of the formation.

6075. 200 yards southeast of spring at Clifton:

Syringopora surcularia.
Cladochonus sp.
Campophyllum sp.
Triplophyllum sp.
Lithostrotionella sp.
Amplexus sp.
Fenestella sp.
Cystodictya sp.
Schizophoria aff. S. swallowi.
Euomphalus utahensis?

[Mr. Girty regards this as possibly of Madison age, but, for the reason given above, the exposure has been mapped as Ochre Mountain limestone.]

6277. 1,000 feet north of Clifton:

Fistulipora sp.
Fenestella sp.
Productus ovatus.
Productus aff. P. setiger.
Pustula aff. P. concentrica.
Pustula aff. P. biseriata.
Productella hirsutiformis?
Spirifer aff. S. pellensis.
Spiriferina transversa.
Reticularia sp.
Cleiothyridina sublamellosa.
Aviculipecten aff. A. spinulifer.
Platyceras sp.
Griffithides sp.

[Mr. Girty states that this collection would suit him better as Woodman, but for the reasons noted above it is here included in the Ochre Mountain limestone.]

6373. 6,475-foot hill on southeast side of Ochre Mountain:

Productus ovatus.
Diaphragmus elegans?
Camarotoechia aff. C. mutata.
Camarotoechia sp.

[Mr. Girty notes that this lot "is in its very meager way sui generis. It does not look like Ochre Mountain, but then I do not know what it does look like."]

6391. Southwest of highest summit of Ochre Mountain:

Fistulipora sp.
Stenopora sp.
Rhombopora sp.
Chonetes oklahomensis.
Productus semireticulatus.
Avonia arkansana?
Girtyella indianensis.
Spirifer arkansanus?
Spirifer aff. S. tenuimarginatus.
Reticularia sp.
Spiriferina transversa.
Spiriferina spinosa.
Ambocoelia fayettevillensis?
Composita subquadrata var. lateralis.
Composita n. sp.
Cleiothyridina sublamellosa.
Pectinopsis squamula?
Pectinopsis jenneyi.
Griffithides sp.
Paraparchites sp.

This collection came from a horizon above the Herat shale.

6045 and 6365. Same locality as 6063:

Lingula aff. L. halli.
Orbiculoidea aff. O. batesvillensis.
Crania? sp.
Productella hirsutiformis.
Pustula moorefieldana var. pusilla.
Pustula subsulcata.
Diaphragmus elegans.
Leiorhynchus carboniferum.
Cleiothyridina sublamellosa.
Deltopecten catactus.
Deltopecten n. sp.
Pectinopsis squamula.
Pleurotomaria? sp.
Euomphalus? sp.
Ostracoda.

6370. About 50 feet up the slope to summit above bench at an altitude of about 7,000 feet on south side of Ochre Mountain:

Cladochonus sp.
Triplophyllum sp.
Pustula aff. P. subsulcata?
Leiorhynchus carboniferum.
Deltopecten catactus?
Brachymetopus? sp.
Ostracoda.

The two preceding collections are from the Herat shale member. The fauna is clearly the fauna of the White Pine shale of the Eureka district, Nev. A similar fauna was found near the base of the Woodman formation.

MANNING CANYON FORMATION (UPPER MISSISSIPPIAN? AND PENNSYLVANIAN)

Distribution.—The Manning Canyon formation was named by Gilluly [79] in the Oquirrh Range, Utah, where rocks of similar lithology have essentially the same stratigraphic position as those so designated in the Gold Hill region.

The chief group of exposures of the Manning Canyon formation are found in a belt 2 miles in maximum width that extends from the head of Gold Hill Wash northward to the south side of Dutch Mountain. Most of these exposures have been assigned, on the basis either of lithology or of relations to the overlying formation, to the central facies. Several of the more westerly outcrops, however, belong to the western facies. These include the exposures above the Ochre Mountain thrust in the vicinity of the Ochre Springs, the small areas beneath the two down-faulted blocks of the Oquirrh formation on Ochre Mountain, and the ex-

[79] Gilluly, James, Geology and ore deposits of the Stockton and Fairfield quadrangles, Utah: U.S. Geol. Survey Prof. Paper 173, pp. 31-34, 1932.

posure on the southwest flank of Dutch Mountain northwest of hill 6566.

Smaller outcrops occur on the northwest side of Dutch Mountain; just east of the Western Utah Copper Co.'s mine on Gold Hill; and at several places in Blood Canyon, in Overland Canyon, and near the Midas mine. The outcrop on the northwest side of Dutch Mountain belongs to the western facies of the formation; the remainder to the central facies.

Lithology.—The two facies of the Manning Canyon formation are composed almost entirely of quartzite, sandy shale, and black shale. The quartzite is dark gray to black on fresh fracture, fine-grained, and in many places finely laminated. These beds generally weather to rusty or brownish colors. Many of the beds appear to be lenticular. The black shale is similar to that in the Herat shale member of the Ochre Mountain limestone. In all the exposures of the formation seen there was either considerable alteration due to nearby intrusive masses or abundant crushing and slipping as a result of faulting. Beds of reddish-weathering dark limestone a foot or so thick are present sparingly.

The central facies contains somewhat more quartzite than the western facies, but its chief distinction lies in the scarcity of limestone. In most outcrops of this facies limestone is entirely absent and the top of the formation has been drawn at the base of the lowest limestone. This line also approximately marks the upper limit of black-shale beds more than an inch or so in thickness. Some thin limestone beds, however, were observed in the exposures just west of the town of Gold Hill and on the east slope of Gold Hill, both of which are thought to belong in the central facies. In the western facies several thin beds of limestone occur in the upper part of the formation, and the upper boundary was placed at the top of the highest black shale.

In both facies the thickness of the quartzite beds is variable. Locally, as in the exposures of the central facies east and north of the northern Ochre Spring, quartzite appears to make up the greater part of the formation, but in the much thinner section exposed on the south side of Pool Canyon, which is of the same facies, quartzite beds are comparatively rare.

Thickness.—The thickness of the formation is variable, and nowhere was a section found that was thought to represent the true thickness. South of Pool Canyon on Dutch Mountain the apparent thickness in places is 50 feet or less, but to the south of the Ferber Road about 2 miles west of Gold Hill it is nearer 1,000 feet. Near the Midas mine, where the beds are considerably metamorphosed but seem to have suffered only minor faulting, the thickness is about 450 feet. The figures given are all for the central facies. The western facies appears to show less variation, but this is probably because there are fewer exposures.

Age and correlation.—Two faunas were obtained from the Manning Canyon formation. One of these is represented by the three following collections, identified by G. H. Girty:

6327. 4,500 feet northwest of spring in Blood Canyon:

Solenomya? n. sp. aff. S. anodontoides.
Nucula? sp.
Yoldia aff. Y. levistriata.
Goniatites? sp.

6348. 2,000 feet southeast of benchmark 5885 on Ferber Road:

Naiadites? sp.

6381. Dump from northern Ochre Spring:

Nucula aff. N. anodontoides.
Leda sp.
Phanerotrema? sp.

The first two lots represent the central facies of the formation. The third lot is from a locality where outcrops of the two facies are brought into contact by the Ochre Mountain thrust, and its proper assignment is somewhat doubtful. An assignment to the western facies, however, seems more probable. Mr. Girty has prepared the following note on these collections:

> Insofar as faunas limited to so few species can be said to have a faunal facies each of these collections is almost unique. Lot 6381 might not be exceptional if the usual quota of brachiopods and bryozoans were present and if the extremely ill-preserved fossils did not prove to belong to alien species. All the ordinary Pottsville brachiopods are missing also from lot 6327, and in addition we have the large and striking form listed as *Solenomya?* and the large coiled shell that probably belongs in one of the goniatite genera. Lot 6348 is still different. Aside from the pinnule of a fern, this collection contains only a small pelecypod together with fragments of a somewhat larger one. The larger fragments suggest the form so common in the nonmarine Pottsville of the Applachian region, which is usually cited as *Naiadites elongatus*. The smaller but also ill-preserved specimens can scarcely be *N. elongatus* unless they are immature as well as somewhat distorted, which is quite possible. On the other hand, it is possible that none of the specimens belongs to *N. elongatus* or even to the genus *Naiadites*. Other genera, such as *Myalina*, give us species very similar in appearance, and specimens rarely afford any evidence as to their true generic position. These facts are important, inasmuch as *Naiadites* is supposed to be a fresh-water or at least a nonmarine genus, whereas *Myalina* is distinctly marine. Instead of themselves affording evidence of the marine or nonmarine origin of deposits by their generic characters, these forms often have to be given a generic assignment on the strength of the marine or nonmarine origin of the deposits as determined on other evidence. When we were making this collection (lot 6348) I remember suggesting that it might be of nonmarine origin because of a certain parallel with the nonmarine Pottsville of the East. In the East, however, the evidence of one collection is corroborated by hundreds of others, indicating nonmarine conditions that extended over wide areas and persisted through long periods of time. Here, on the other hand, the evidence of one collection is contradicted by that of others, for lot 6327 can scarcely be nonmarine and still less lot 6381. The peculiarities of these three lots are probably to be attributed rather to the character of the bottom and to distance from shore than to the fresh or brackish condition of the waters.

The second fauna is found both in the upper portion of the Manning Canyon formation and in the basal portion of the overlying Oquirrh formation. It is considered by Mr. Girty to indicate a lower Pennsylvanian age and to be approximately equivalent to the Pottsville formation of the eastern United States. With one exception, collections of this fauna from the Manning Canyon formation were found in the western facies of the formation. Mr. Girty has made the following identifications:

6281. 600 feet northwest of old smelter west of Gold Hill:

Orbiculoidea sp.	Composita ozarkana?
Crania modesta.	Leda bellistriata?
Schizophoria texana.	Myalina perniformis.
Derbya robusta.	Astartella aff. A. compacta.
Productus ovatus?	Pleurophorus tropidophorus.
Productus ovatus var. minor.	Bacanopsis aff. B. meekana.
Productus aff. P. gallatinensis.	Griffithides morrowensis?

This collection is from the central facies.

6276. 1,000 feet west of hill 6337, northeast side of Ochre Mountain:

Streblotrypa sp.	Spiriferina spinosa.
Lingula carbonaria?	Composita subquadrata var. lateralis.
Productus n. sp.	Edmondia aff. E. mortonensis.
Productus ovatus var. minor.	Deltopecten occidentalis.
Pugnoides osagensis?	Pectinopsis n. sp.
Dielasma? sp.	Pectinopsis n. sp.
Spirifer opimus var. occidentalis.	Griffithides morrowensis?

6374. 1,000 feet north of hill 6256, at head of Gold Hill Wash:

Triplophyllum sp.	Spirifer opimus var. occidentalis.
Leioclema sp. b.	Spiriferina transversa.
Lingula carbonaria?	Composita ozarkana.
Orbiculoides meekana?	Cleiothyridina pecosi.
Rhipidomella aff. R. penniana.	Myalina perniformis.
Derbya robusta.	Myalina aff. M. arkansana.
Productus cora.	Modiola subelliptica.
Productus ovatus var. minor.	Deltopecten occidentalis.
Productus n. sp.	Pterinopecten? sp.
Pustula? sp.	Pectinopsis n. sp.
Avonia aff. A. arkansana.	Pectinopsis n. sp.
Pugnoides n. sp.	Pleurophorus aff. P. oblongus.
Pugnoides osagensis var. percostata?	Platyceras n. sp.
Spirifer opimus.	Griffithides morrowensis?

6377. 1,000 feet northeast of benchmark 5723 on Lincoln Highway south of Gold Hill:

Triplophyllum sp.	Parallelodon aff. P. pergibbosum.
Polypora sp. b.	Aviculipecten sp.
Cystodictya sp. b.	Astartella aff. A. compacta.
Productus ovatus var. minor.	Pleurophorus? sp.
Avonia aff. A. arkansana?	Phanerotrema? sp.
Spirifer opimus var. occidentalis.	Bulimorpha aff. B. chrysalis.
Spiriferina transversa.	Eotrochus? sp.
Composita ozarkana.	Griffithides morrowensis?
Cleiothyridina pecosi?	

6378. 1,000 feet west-northwest of benchmark 5723 on Lincoln Highway south of Gold Hill:

Rhipidomella aff. R. penniana.	Spirifer opimus.
Derbya robusta.	Composita ozarkana.
Productus cora?	Cleiothyridina pecosi.
Productus ovatus var. minor.	Deltopecten occidentalis.
Productus n. sp.	Modiola subelliptica?
Productus sp. b.	Bellerophon aff. B. sublevis.

6380. From dump of southern Ochre Spring:

Echinocrinus sp.	Chonetes arkansanus.
Fistulipora sp. b.	Pustula globosa var.
Stenopora sp. a.	Spirifer opimus.
Batostomella sp.	Spirifer sp.
Fenestella sp.	Composita sp.
Polypora sp. a.	Cleiothyridina pecosi.
Ptilopora? sp.	Deltopecten occidentalis?
Cystodictya sp. a.	Griffithides morrowensis?
Rhipidomella aff. R. penniana.	Ostracoda indet.

The preceding five collections are from the western facies.

MISSISSIPPIAN-PENNSYLVANIAN CONTACT

The contact between the Mississippian and Pennsylvanian in several places in Utah and Idaho has been described as unconformable.[80] In the Gold Hill quadrangle the presence of Pennsylvanian fossils in the Manning Canyon formation and Mississippian fossils in the underlying Ochre Mountain limestone, the variations in thickness of the Manning Canyon, and the peculiar character of the faunas found in three of the Manning Canyon collections would seem, in the absence of other evidence, to indicate that such an unconformity exists here at the base of the Manning Canyon. The contact between the Ochre Mountain and the Manning Canyon is well exposed only on the bottom level of the Cane Springs mine, but here the contact seems clearly to be gradational rather than unconformable. The explanation of this somewhat conflicting evidence may perhaps be furnished by the type locality of the Manning Canyon in the Oquirrh Mountains,[81] which contains late Mississippian fossils at its base and Pennsylvanian fossils near the top, the break occurring within the formation.

OQUIRRH FORMATION (PENNSYLVANIAN AND PERMIAN)

The Oquirrh formation was named by Gilluly[82] for the Oquirrh Range, in Utah, where there is an unusually thick series of Pennsylvanian rocks, similar stratigraphically to the rocks in Gold Hill.

Distribution.—The Oquirrh formation has a wider distribution within the quadrangle than any other of the Paleozoic formations. Two large areas and several smaller ones are underlain chiefly by it. The southern of the two large areas extends from North Pass and Christiansen Canyons northward to the south side of Ochre Mountain and to Clifton. The northern area extends from Trail Gulch on Dutch Mountain to the western border of the quadrangle. Smaller areas are found near the eastern border of the quadrangle south of the continuation of Overland Canyon, immediately south and west of the town of Gold Hill; east of the Napoleon mine; and on the south side of Dutch Mountain.

[80] Blackwelder, Eliot, New light on the geology of the Wasatch Mountains, Utah: Geol. Soc. America Bull., vol. 21, pp. 530-533, 1910. Richardson, G. B., The Paleozoic section in northern Utah: Am. Jour. Sci., 4th ser., vol. 36, p. 413, 1913. Mansfield, G. R., Geography, geology, and mineral resources of part of southeastern Idaho: U.S. Geol. Survey Prof. Paper 152, p. 73, 1927.

[81] Gilluly, James, Geology and ore deposits of the Stockton and Fairfield quadrangles, Utah: U.S. Geol. Survey Prof. Paper 173, pp. 32–34, 1932.

[82] Idem, p. 34.

Lithology.—The Oquirrh formation, like the Manning Canyon, has two facies, which, however, are much more distinct than those in the Manning Canyon formation. The southern of the two large areas underlain by the formation and the areas around the town of Gold Hill are composed chiefly of the central facies; the areas west of Dutch Mountain, of the western facies. The exposures of the formation on the south side of Ochre Mountain, on the north and northeast borders of Clifton Flat, and in Rodenhouse Wash are also of the western facies.

The central facies is made up of several different kinds of rocks, and each rock type represented is repeated over and over again throughout the section, although individual beds are generally lenticular. This makes it impossible to break up the formation into subdivisions, a course that would have made the study of the geologic structure much more simple.

This facies is prevailingly sandy. Sandstones form perhaps half of the section, and sandy limestones and shales a large part of the remainder. Interbedded with these are numerous beds of limestone and dolomite and a few lenses of conglomerate.

The sandstones are generally fine-grained rocks, rather dark gray on fresh fracture and deep reddish brown on weathered surfaces. They are not at all resistant to erosion, and in places where they are abundant there are few outcrops, the surface being mostly covered by a sandy soil or by small blocks of rock. Many of these beds contain varying amounts of shaly material or of calcite. Near the base of the formation the sandstones in some places show a distinct lamination, which is in part due to the presence of thin films of carbonaceous matter similar to that which is so abundant in the underlying Manning Canyon formation. Near the quartz monzonite the sandstones are bleached to a dull white color and are notably harder.

The limestone beds vary greatly in appearance. Many are fine-grained, dark bluish gray on fresh fracture and light bluish gray on the weathered surface. Such beds usually contain silica, either in the form of sandy laminae or as chert nodules or lenses. Locally, especially on the east side of Blood Canyon and in the low hills south and southeast of the Midas mine, there is a great deal of thin-bedded platy limestone which is nearly black on fresh fracture and purplish on weathering. Such beds are commonly very fossiliferous, containing especially large numbers of the characteristic Pennsylvanian fossil *Fusulina*. In many places ½-inch layers of this limestone alternate with equally thin layers of brown sandstone and black chert. Near the intrusions the limestones, like the sandstones, are thoroughly bleached; and many beds have been completely replaced by silicate minerals.

Dolomite beds are also found in many places. Some of these are clearly the result of a much later alteration of limestone; but others are, without much doubt, primary, in the sense that dolomitization occurred as a result of sedimentary processes. One of the most widespread of such dolomites is fine-grained bluish-gray rock, filled with round or spindle-shaped white dots, which, in part at least, represent poorly preserved Fusulinas. Other dolomites are similar to the beds of cherty limestone mentioned in the preceding paragraph, except for a slightly duller appearance.

Locally the limestones and dolomites are conglomeratic and contain pebbles as much as 6 inches in diameter. The pebbles are in part limestone or dolomite, but the greater proportion are chert. A specimen of such a rock in which the chert fragments are unusually small is illustrated in plate 5, F. This specimen is rather unusual in having an oolitic matrix, whereas generally the matrix is either fine-grained limestone or dolomite. Individual beds when traced along the strike may show a limestone matrix in one place and dolomite in another. Many of the conglomerate beds were found to pass into normal limestone or dolomite within a short distance, but others were traced along the strike for as much as 3 miles.

Because of the angularity of the chert pebbles and also because of the presence of pebbles of limestone and dolomite, it would seem almost certain that the chert pebbles were deposited as such. If so, there are two possible sources for the pebbles—either from older chert-bearing rocks that were undergoing erosion at the time the conglomerates were being deposited or from a silica-rich layer deposited in essentially the same locality as the conglomerates and broken up by storm waves or currents, or perhaps by subaerial agencies brought into play by a temporary emergence before being covered by younger beds. In spite of the fact that the presence of limestone and dolomite pebbles is more easily explained by the first hypothesis, the second hypothesis seems the more attractive, because of the restriction of the pebbles to individual beds and because of the extremely slight extent of some of the beds. If this is the true explanation, it indicates that the siliceous ooze from which some cherts are thought to form [83] may harden rather soon after deposition.

The western facies shows very little resemblance to the central. The amount of sandy material present is much smaller, and the chert-pebble and other conglomerates are lacking.

At the base of this facies is a moderate thickness of light-colored sandstone, similar to that in the eastern facies. This appears to thin toward the north, as the amount present in the northwestern part of Dutch Mountain is less than that found south of the 7,262-foot peak at the head of Pool Canyon.

Above the sandstone is a succession of thick-bedded limestones, nearly 3,000 feet thick. These limestones are similar to those in the Ochre Mountain limestone.

[83] Tarr, W. A., in Twenhofel, W. H., A treatise on sedimentation, p. 384, 1926.

Thin beds of sandstone are usually associated with them and help to distinquish the two formations, as does the abundance of *Fusulina* in the Pennsylvanian limestone. Locally these small fossils are so numerous as to make up an entire bed. The distribution of chert throughout the limestone series is erratic rather than limited to two rather distinct horizons, as in the Ochre Mountain limestone. In some places the limestones have been dolomitized. The dolomitization shows no relation to the bedding or other features of sedimentary structure but rather has occurred near faults or minor folds. It has given the rock a duller and grayer aspect than normal.

Above the massively bedded limestone is about 4,500 feet of dolomite and sandstone, with only minor amounts of limestone. The dolomite is rather light gray and medium-grained. Many beds contain dark-gray chert nodules and stringers. Unlike the dolomites mentioned in the preceding paragraph, these beds are thought to be formed by sedimentary processes, as their distribution shows no relation to structural features and as the interbedded limestones where dolomitized have an altogether different appearance.

The sandstones are for the most part medium-grained gray rocks which weather to tints of light reddish-brown. Almost all have a moderately large content of calcite as a cement. In one specimen of cross-bedded sandstone obtained near the base of this portion of the formation the quartz grains, together with a very few of plagioclase, were surprisingly angular, especially when it is considered that the nearest shore of the Pennsylvanian sea is supposed to have been at least 100 miles away. In the upper 1,500 feet of the formation as exposed on each side of Deep Creek sandstones are much more abundant. These beds weather to vivid hues of red and yellow, but a large part of the coloring material is thought to be derived from the weathering of nearby volcanic rocks.

The limestones that are found in the upper division are similar to those making up the lower division.

One characteristic zone is found about 3,800 feet above the base of the upper division. This was one of the two distinctive horizon markers on the western facies, the upper contact of the limestone series being the other. It is a poorly exposed zone of extremely cherty and sandy limestone and usually appears at the surface as a bench covered with fragments of black chert. This bed occurs at several places in the area westward from the low-lying hills west of Dutch Mountain.

Thickness.—No accurate measurement of the thickness of the Oquirrh formation was made, because of the difficulty of correlating precisely the various short sections unaffected by folding or faulting. The total thickness of the central facies could not be determined even if this were done, because the contact of this facies with the Permian was nowhere seen. Estimates from cross sections indicate a minimum thickness for this facies of 5,300 feet. The bottom and top of the western facies are both exposed in the northwestern portion of the area. A result which was obtained by piecing together estimates of thickness of the two divisions and which is believed to allow for the greater part of the folding and faulting points to a figure between 7,500 and 8,000 feet for the total thickness of this facies.

Age and correlation.—Mr. Girty has divided the fossil collections from the Oquirrh formation into three groups, representing three different ages. Near the base of the formation in both the central and western facies, the fossils indicate a Pottsville or lower Pennsylvanian age. The remainder of the central facies and the greater part of the western facies contain fossils characteristic of the higher Pennsylvanian. Finally, near the top of the western facies, the fossils are similar to those found in the overlying formation, which is of Permian age. Mr. Girty has kindly provided the following notes:

A sharp demarcation exists between the higher Pennsylvanian faunas and the Permian faunas of the Gold Hill district. It is true that specific distinctions among the Compositas do not amount to much, so that *C. mira* closely resembles *C. subtilita*, and that *Pustula subhorrida* resembles, more or less closely, the species cited in these lists as *Pustula* aff. *P. wallaciana*, but either fauna, given a collection of reasonable size, can be recognized with ease and certainty.

Naturally enough, this is less true of the faunas that occur in the higher Pennsylvanian and in the Pottsville. The fossils in the much disturbed strata of the Gold Hill district are not as a rule in a good state of preservation, so that specific differences, if not lost entirely, may have been overlooked. With a better understanding of individual species and a more complete knowledge of their range in the section, a more accurate distinction between the Pottsville and post-Pottsville faunas could probably be drawn. As it is, small collections of poorly preserved shells cannot be referred with any confidence. Considered in a broad way, with the stratigraphic data and the paleontologic data supplementing each other, one rather well marked distinction appears to exist between these two faunas. Most of the collections from the higher Pennsylvanian contain *Fusulina* in more or less abundance, whereas not one of the Pottsville collections contains any of these shells. Of course there are other differences between the faunas, but this is the most obvious one and so far as facts are available the most practical one. The distinction thus suggested works only one way, however. All the collections that contain *Fusulina* can be classed as higher Pennsylvanian, but not all the collections that fail to contain *Fusulina* can be classed as Pottsville, and of these, as already noted, certain small and nondescript collections must be assigned largely on the basis of their stratigraphic occurrence rather than upon the fossils which they contain.

You are, I believe, recognizing a central and a western facies in the rock characters of the Pennsylvanian of the Gold Hill district. I am unable to make a like distinction in the faunas, though here again a nicer discrimination of species and closer attention to forms like the Bryozoa, to which I have been able to give only a summary treatment, might show differences that I have failed to recognize. It is true that in checking up the faunas that represent the two lithologic phases a number of species occur in one list and not in the other and especially a large number of species have been found in the central facies, that appear to be absent from the western facies, but on the other hand the central collections outnumber the western collections almost 2 to 1. Besides this, several of the western faunas possess striking and individual peculiarities which distinguish them as much from other western faunas as from any of the central faunas. In comparisons of this sort a species to be significant should occur repeatedly in one fauna and not at all in the other. In the present series of collections a single occurrence, let us say, in the central fauna might stand against about 22 nonoccurrences in the same fauna and about 15 nonoccurrences in the western fauna, so that it would not mean very much. The only striking instance of such a difference that would seem to be significant is invested in the form listed as *Rhynchopora* sp., which has been found only in the central fauna and which has been noted in five collections. In the present state of our knowledge, then, the central and western faunas do not differ recognizably, though differences that are now obscure may actually exist.

Collections of Pottsville age

6079. About one-third mile southeast of hill 6837, on west side of Blood Canyon:

Derbya robusta.
Productus n. sp.
Productus ovatus var. minor.
Spirifer opimus var. occidentalis.
Spiriferina spinosa.
Composita ozarkana.
Cleiothyridina pecosi.
Aviculipecten? sp.
Lima? sp.
Griffithides morrowensis?

6326. Blood Canyon, 2,500 feet north-northwest of spring:

Echinocrinus sp.
Fistulipora sp.
Derbya robusta?
Productus semireticulatus.
Avonia aff. A. arkansana.
Spirifer opimus.
Composita ozarkana.
Cleiothyridina pecosi.
Conocardium sp.

6328. Blood Canyon, 5,000 feet west-northwest of spring:

Derbya robusta?
Productus n. sp.
Spirifer opimus var. occidentalis.
Spirifer sp.
Spiriferina spinosa.
Composita ozarkana.
Cleiothyridina pecosi.

The preceding three lots came from the central facies. The following lots represent the western facies.

6064, 6070, 6372. 3,100 feet southeast of benchmark 6163, at north end of Clifton Flat:

Sponge spicules.
Fistulipora sp. b.?
Stenopora sp. c.
Rhombopora lepidodendroides.
Leioclema sp. b.
Fenestella aff. F. tenax.
Orbiculoidea meekana?
Derbya robusta.
Chonetes choteauensis.
Productus n. sp.
Productus ovatus var. minor.
Productus cora.
Avonia aff. A. arkansana?
Pustula sp.
Dielasma sp.
Spirifer opimus.
Spirifer opimus var. occidentalis?
Spiriferina transversa.
Composita ozarkana.
Cleiothyridina pecosi.
Hustedia sp.
Schizodus? sp.
Deltopecten occidentalis.
Deltopecten occidentalis var.
Deltopecten n. sp.
Streblopteria n. sp.
Pterinopecten? sp.
Pectinopsis jennyi?
Pectinopsis n. sp.

6333. Just west of saddle west of 7,262-foot summit on south side of Dutch Mountain:

Cryptozoon?
Favosites n. sp.
Fistulipora sp. b.?
Stenopora sp. b.
Anisotrypa sp.
Leioclema sp. b.
Schizophoria texana.
Derbya robusta.
Productus n. sp.
Productus sp. a.
Productus ovatus var. minor.
Avonia aff. A. arkansana.
Pustula semipunctata.
Pugnoides n. sp.
Dielasma aff. D. bovidens.
Spirifer opimus.
Spirifer opimus var. occidentalis.
Spiriferina spinosa.
Composita ozarkana.
Composita subquadrata var. lateralis?
Cleiothyridina pecosi.
Hustedia sp.
Edmondia? sp.
Pleurophorus? sp.

6334. South of 6333, near sill of quartz monzonite porphyry:

Orbiculoidea meekana?
Spirifer opimus var. occidentalis.
Spiriferina spinosa.
Composita ozarkana.
Acanthopecten carboniferus.
Pectinopsis n. sp.
Deltopecten occidentalis.
Myalina perniformis.
Griffithides morrowensis?

6335. About same horizon as 6334 and a few hundred feet west of it:

Leioclema sp. a.
Schizophoria texana.
Derbya robusta.
Productus ovatus var. minor.
Avonia aff. A. arkansana.
Spirifer opimus var. occidentalis.
Composita ozarkana.
Cleiothyridina pecosi.
Acanthopecten carboniferus.
Pinna aff. P. peracuta.
Griffithides morrowensis?

6336. About 100 feet stratigraphically above 6335:

Orbiculoidea meekana?
Crania modesta.
Derbya robusta.
Productus n. sp.
Productus aff. P. gallatinensis.
Pugnoides osagensis var. percostata.
Dielasma sp.
Spirifer opimus var. occidentalis.
Spiriferina spinosa.
Composita ozarkana.
Composita subquadrata var. lateralis.
Cleiothyridina pecosi.
Myalina perniformis.
Griffithides morrowensis?

6337. About 50 feet stratigraphically above 6336:

Echinocrinus sp.
Derbya robusta.
Productus n. sp.
Productus cora.
Productus ovatus var. minor.
Productus aff. P. gallatinensis.
Avonia aff. A. arkansana.
Pugnoides n. sp.
Spirifer opimus var. occidentalis.
Spiriferina spinosa.
Composita ozarkana.
Composita subquadrata var. lateralis?
Cleiothyridina pecosi.
Hustedia mormoni?
Parallelodon? sp.
Aviculipecten sp.
Pterinopecten sp.
Deltopecten occidentalis.
Euomphalus? sp.
Griffithides morrowensis?
Fish tooth.

6338. About 50 feet stratigraphically above 6337:

Syringopora sp.
Spirorbis carbonaria.
Ortonia sp.
Hederella sp.
Stenopora sp. b.
Rhombopora lepidodendroides.
Derbya robusta.
Chonetes platynotus?
Productus cora.
Productus nolani.
Productus sp. a.
Avonia aff. A. arkansana.
Dielasma aff. D. bovidens.
Spirifer opimus var. occidentalis.
Composita ozarkana.
Cleiothyridina pecosi.
Griffithides morrowensis?

6349. West side of Dutch Mountain near base, 3,500 feet east-southeast of benchmark 5369 on Ferber Road:

Productus n. sp.
Spirifer opimus var. occidentalis.
Spirifer sp.
Spiriferina spinosa.
Composita ozarkana.
Cleiothyridina pecosi?
Myalina perniformis.
Modiola? sp.
Bucanopsis n. sp.
Naticopsis n. sp.
Pleurotomaria aff. P. beckwithana.
Schizostoma catilloides?
Platyceras sp.
Griffithides morrowensis?
Paraparchites sp.

6078. South side of Dutch Mountain, 1,050 feet north-northwest of benchmark 6149 on Lincoln Highway:

Schizophoria texana.
Productus ovatus var. minor.
Avonia aff. A. arkansana.
Pustula globosa var.
Spiriferina spinosa.
Composita ozarkana.

6273. 1,000 feet north of hill 5688, at northwest tip of Dutch Mountain:

Schizophoria texana.
Productus nolani var.
Productus ovatus var. minor.
Spirifer opimus.
Spiriferina spinosa.
Spiriferina transversa.
Composita ozarkana.
Cleiothyridina pecosi?
Pleurophorus sp.

6316. About half a mile east-northeast of New York claim, on southwest side of Dutch Mountain:

Lingula carbonaria?
Orbiculoidea meekana?
Productus n. sp.
Productus cora.
Spirifer opimus.
Spiriferina spinosa.
Composita ozarkana.
Cleiothyridina pecosi.
Myalina perniformis.
Deltopecten occidentalis.
Platyceras sp.
Griffithides morrowensis?

6350. About 500 feet east of 6316:

Productus semireticulatus.
Spirifer opimus var. occidentalis.

6353. West side of Dutch Mountain, 2,000 feet northeast of hill 6518:

Productus n. sp.
Spirifer opimus var. occidentalis.
Spirifer sp.
Composita ozarkana.

6375. Same locality as 6374 (Manning Canyon formation) but just above road:

Lingula carbonaria?
Derbya robusta.
Productus n. sp.
Productus ovatus var. minor.
Productus sp. b.
Avonia aff. A. arkansana.
Avonia aff. A. arkansana var.
Spirifer opimus.
Spirifer opimus var. occidentalis?
Spiriferina transversa.
Spiriferina spinosa.
Composita ozarkana.
Cleiothyridina pecosi.
Hustedia sp.
Edmondia aff. E. mortonensis.
Edmondia aff. E. circularis.
Deltopecten occidentalis.
Pectinopsis n. sp.
Bellerophon aff. B. sublevis.
Griffithides morrowensis?

6376. About 75 feet higher than 6375:

Fistulipora sp. a.
Derbya robusta.
Chonetes choteauensis?
Productus n. sp.
Productus cora.
Productus ovatus var. minor.
Avonia aff. A. arkansana.
Spirifer opimus var. occidentalis.

Collections of higher Pennsylvanian species

The following 24 lots came from the central facies.

6047. One-fourth mile northwest of peak 7660, in saddle on divide between Overland Canyon and North Pass Canyon:

Campophyllum torquium?
Rhombopora sp.
Chonetes aff. C. granulifer.
Marginifera? sp.
Composita? sp.
Griffithides? sp.

6048. East-west spur west of 7,300-foot closed contour on main ridge line of Deep Creek Mountains, about 200 feet stratigraphically below westernmost outcrops:

Stenopora sp.
Derbya? sp.
Spirifer opimus.
Spiriferina spinosa.
Composita subtilita.

6049. Same as 6048, about 100 feet stratigraphically below 6058:

Fusulina sp.
Sponge?
Campophyllum torquium.
Polypora sp.
Rhombopora lepidodendroides.
Marginifera splendens?
Hustedia mormoni.

6050. 1,000 feet north of 6058:

Fenestella sp.
Rhombopora sp.
Spirifer rockymontanus.
Spiriferina kentuckyensis.
Composita subtilita.

6055. Same spur as 6048 but about 400 feet stratigraphically lower:

Fusulina sp.
Campophyllum kansasense?
Echinocrinus sp.
Stenopora sp.
Polypora sp.
Composita subtilita.
Griffithides major?

6056. 800 feet west-southwest of peak 7472, on main ridge line of Deep Creek Mountains:

Fusulina sp.
Rhombopora sp.

6057. Same spur as 6056 but about 200 feet stratigraphically lower:

Syringopora n. sp.

6058. Same spur as 6056 but about 500 feet stratigraphically lower:

Syringopora sp.
Campophyllum torquium.
Plagioglypta? sp.

6066. 3,100 feet southeast of benchmark 6163 on Lincoln Highway:

Echinocrinus sp.
Spirifer opimus.
Spiriferina kentuckyensis.
Composita subtilita.

6071. 700 feet north-northwest of benchmark 5855 on Lincoln Highway:

Campophyllum sp.
Crinoid stems.

6073 and 6077. Near southeast corner of sec. 17, T. 9 S., R. 19 W. (unsurveyed):

Triplophyllum sp.
Michelinia sp.
Echinocrinus sp.
Fenestella aff. F. tenax.
Productus cora.
Pustula aff. P. biseriata.
Girtyella? sp.
Spirifer opimus.
Cleiothyridina pecosi.
Aviculipecten aff. A. coloradoensis.
Pinna? peracuta.
Paraparchites sp.
Kirkbya sp.

6074. About three-quarters of a mile west-southwest of Montezuma Peak:

Rhombopora sp.
Marginifera splendens?
Rhynchopora sp.
Spiriferina? sp.

6076. Summit of peak 5800, half a mile southwest of U.S. Mineral Monument no. 7:

Fusulina sp.
Syringopora sp.
Syringopora? (n. gen.?) sp.
Campophyllum? sp.
Echinocrinus sp.
Productus cora.
Pleurotomaria? sp.

6290. South of mouth of Uiyabi Canyon:

Fusulina sp.
Syringopora sp.
Zaphrentis sp.
Productus cora.
Productus semireticulatus.

6330. Southeast flank of Montezuma Peak, near mouth of gulch in which road leads westward to Midas mine:

Fusulina sp.
Schwagerina? sp.

6357. Lower slopes of center spur in Sheridan Canyon:

Stenopora sp.
Derbya robusta?
Spirifer opimus var. occidentalis.
Composita subtilita.

6358. About 200 feet stratigraphically lower than 6357:

Syringopora multattenuata.	Productus semireticulatus.
Campophyllum kansasense?	Spirifer sp.
Stenopora aff. S. ramosa.	Composita subtilita.
Rhombopora sp.	

6359. About 100 feet stratigraphically lower than 6358:

Lophophyllum profundum?	Rhynchopora sp.
Productus semireticulatus.	Squamularia perplexa?
Pustula aff. P. semipunctata.	Cleiothyridina pecosi.
Pustula n. sp. aff. P. wallaciana.	

6360. About 100 feet stratigraphically lower than 6359:

Fusulina sp.	Marginifera splendens.
Syringopora sp.	Marginifera lasallensis?
Campophyllum kansasense?	Rhynchopora sp.
Rhombopora sp.	Spiriferina spinosa?
Productus cora.	Pleurotomaria sp.
Productus semireticulatus.	Omphalotrochus? sp.

6361. About 300 feet stratigraphically lower than 6360:

Syringopora aff. S. multattenuata.	Productus cora.
Rhombopora sp.	Pustula semipunctata var.

6362. Just west of intersection of the spur of 6357 with main ridge line:

Fusulina sp.	Rhipidomella aff. R. carbonaria.
Syringopora aff. S. multattenuata.	Chonetes sp.
Campophyllum torquium.	Rhynchopora sp.
Fenestella sp.	Spiriferina spinosa.
Polypora sp.	Omphalotrochus sp.
Rhombopora sp.	

6363. About a quarter of a mile south of 6362:

Syringopora? sp.	Spirifer n. sp.?
Echinocrinus sp.	Spiriferina spinosa.
Enteletes? n. sp.	Ambocoelia planiconvexa var.
Derbya aff. D. multistriata.	Composita subtilita.
Próductus? sp.	Pleurotomaria sp.

6364. North of road leading to cabin just northeast of benchmark 5855, at southeast corner of Clifton Flat:

Fusulina sp.	Schizophoria n. sp.
Syringopora aff. S. multattenuata.	Meekella? sp.
Campophyllum torquium?	Chonetes aff. C. geinitzianus.
Cyathophyllum subcaespitosum?	Productus cora.
Echinocrinus sp.	Productus n. sp.
Polypora sp.	Productus semireticulatus.
Acanthocladia sp.	Pustula aff. P. semipunctata.
Rhombopora lepidodendroides.	Rhynchopora sp.
Rhombopora sp.	Dielasma bovidens?
Cystodictya aff. C. inaequimarginata.	Spiriferina spinosa var.

The next 15 lots came from the western facies of the formation.

6317. 3,000 feet south of benchmark 5963 on Ferber Road:

Productus semireticulatus.	Avonia? sp.

6318. 4,250 feet southwest of benchmark 5963 on Ferber Road:

Productus sp.	Spirifer aff. S. triplicatus.

6320. Southwest side of Dutch Mountain, 1,250 feet west of 5,964-foot point:

Schizophoria? sp.	Spirifer opimus var. occidentalis.
Productus cora.	Composita subtilita.
Productus semireticulatus.	
Avonia? sp.	

6321. West side of Dutch Mountain 4,000 feet due west of 6320:

Stenopora sp.	Productus sp.
Rhombopora sp.	Spirifer sp.
Rhipidomella aff. R. carbonaria.	

6331. A quarter of a mile north-northeast of A B claim, west side of Dutch Mountain:

Fusulina sp.	Rhombopora sp.
Favosites? sp.	Productus cora.
Triplophyllum sp.	

6332. A quarter of a mile east of 6331:

Fusulina sp.	Productus semireticulatus.
Syringopora sp.	Productus n. sp.?
Campophyllum torquium.	Dielasma aff. D. bovidens.
Fistulipora sp.	Spirifer triplicatus.
Stenopora aff. S. carbonaria.	Composita subtilita.
Rhombopora sp.	Omphalotrochus sp.
Derbya? sp.	

6344. 1 mile southwest of hill 6060 (southern one of Twin Peaks) west of Dutch Mountain:

Fusulina sp.	Cyathophyllum subcaespitosum?

6345. About 250 feet stratigraphically below 6344:

Cladochonus sp.	Marginifera splendens?
Rhombopora sp.	Spiriferina spinosa?
Derbya? sp.	

6346. In gulch north of 6344 and 6345 and stratigraphically between them:

Syringopora sp.	Campophyllum sp.

6351. Near hill 6360, on west side of Dutch Mountain:

Streblotrypa sp.	Marginifera splendens.
Rhombopora sp.	Spiriferina spinosa?
Polypora sp.	

6352. 2,000 feet north-northeast of hill 6518, on west side of Dutch Mountain:

Fistulipora sp.	Pustula n. sp. aff. P. wallaciana.
Stenopora sp.	Spirifer opimus var. occidentalis.
Rhombopora sp.	
Productus semireticulatus.	
Productus cora.	

6354 and 6354a. 1,000 feet west of hill 6518, on west side of Dutch Mountain:

Crinoid columnals.	Astartella n. sp.
Echinocrinus sp.	Goniospira? sp.
Lingula carbonaria.	Zygopleura? sp.
Tegulifera? sp.	

6379. Same locality as 6378, of Pottsville age, but about 75 feet stratigraphically higher:

Fistulipora sp.	Avonia sp
Rhombopora sp.	Pustula n. sp. aff. P. wallaciana.
Derbya robusta?	Spirifer aff. S. triplicatus.
Productus cora.	Squamularia perplexa.
Productus semireticulatus.	Composita subtilita.
Productus sp.	

6583. North side of gulch from 6346:

Fusulina sp.	Productus semireticulatus.
Productus cora.	

In addition to these lots two others were collected on the south side of North Pass Canyon in rocks thought to be of this age, for the reasons given in the section on the Ochre Mountain limestone. It is entirely possible that these rocks are of Mississippian rather than Pennsylvanian age, but in the absence of the further field investigations that would be necessary to prove their correct assignment the two lots are listed here.

6383. Lower eastern slopes of hill 6267, on south side of North Pass Canyon:

Triplophyllum sp.	Productus aff. P. arcuatus.
Productus ovatus.	Spirifer aff. S. increbescens.
Productus semireticulatus.	Composita? sp.

6384. Same as 6383 but just below summit:

Echinocrinus sp.	Pustula aff. P. biseriata.
Fenestella sp.	Pugnoides, several sp. indet.
Chonetes aff. C. oklahomensis.	Cranaena aff. C. globosa.
Productus ovatus.	Spirifer aff. S. grimesi.
Pustula aff. P. millespinosa.	Composita? sp.
Pustula aff. P. concentrica.	Griffithides n. sp.
Pustula n. sp.	

Mr. Girty writes as follows regarding these two collections:

The fauna of lot 6383, which was included among the Ochre Mountain collections, is noncommittal. It might be Pennsylvanian; the faunal evidence is concessive but not confirmatory. The same question was raised with reference to lot 6384. Though the fauna comprised in this lot is peculiar, it fits in reasonably well with the Woodman fauna and very badly with the Pottsville or post-Pottsville as those faunas are at present known in the Gold Hill district.

Collections of Permian age

These lots all came from the western facies.

6339. Half a mile south-southeast of benchmark 5544, in Tank Wash:

Derbya sp.	Camarotoechia? sp.
Pustula aff. P. signata.	Heterelasma? sp.
Pustula subhorrida.	Spiriferina pulchra?
Pustula subhorrida var. rugatula.	Composita sp.
	Cleiothyridina n. sp.

6340. Just west of benchmark 5544 on Ferber Road:

Leioclema? sp.	Pustula subhorrida.
Derbya aff. D. multistriata.	Strophalosia? n. sp.
Pustula nevadensis.	Dielasma? sp.
Pustula aff. P. montpelierensis.	Cleiothyridina n. sp.

6341. A quarter of a mile west of 6340, about 50 feet stratigraphically lower:

Derbya aff. D. robusta.	Pustula subhorrida var. rugatula?
Pustula nevadensis?	
Pustula subhorrida.	

6342. Near peak 5850, west of 6341:

Leioclema? sp.	Pustula subhorrida var. rugatula?
Pustula nevadensis.	Spiriferina pulchra.
Pustula subhorrida.	

6343. 1,000 feet west of 6342:

Pustula subhorrida?	Composita subtilita.

6356. 1,000 feet west of benchmark 5097 on Deep Creek, on north side of gulch:

Pustula subhorrida?	Composita subtilita?

The collections here referred to the Permian are cited with varying degrees of confidence. Some of the collections are small or poorly preserved or both. Some also fail to contain the most characteristic species of the *Spiriferina pulchra* fauna and present a facies that is appreciably different though related. However, all the collections that possess individual or distinctive characters show a closer relationship to the Permian than to the Pennsylvanian faunas of the region.

The formation as a whole is difficult to correlate with formations found in other districts. It is most closely comparable to the Oquirrh formation in the Stockton and Fairfield quadrangles [84] but appears to contain older beds at the base and younger ones at the top. It is less confidently correlated with the Weber quartzite [85] in the Wasatch Range and with the Ely limestone [86] of Nevada.

GERSTER FORMATION (PERMIAN)

Distribution.—The Gerster formation crops out within the Gold Hill quadrangle only in the narrow area west of Deep Creek. There is a small exposure on the south end of the hill west of benchmark 4984, but the largest outcrop occurs on the south side of Gerster Gulch, from which the formation is named. Another small area partly covered by volcanic rocks was found west of benchmark 5097, about a quarter of a mile beyond the western border of the quadrangle. All these outcrops are placed without hesitation in the western facies of the Carboniferous.

Lithology.—The Gerster formation is made up largely of thin-bedded sandy and shaly limestones, which are brownish gray on fresh surfaces and weather to yellowish brown or pink. The beds are from 2 inches to 1 foot thick and generally have a concentration of sandy or shaly material along the bedding planes. These beds are richly fossiliferous in all the exposures seen. Locally thin beds of sandstone may be found, and in most exposures moderately thick beds of cherty limestone are also present.

These beds are sharply set off from the underlying sandstones and dolomites of the Oquirrh formation by their lithology and especially by their abundant fossil content, which was the basis for mapping the contact between the two. In most places there is a thin bed of sandstone at this contact, but no other evidence of discordance was found, and Mr. Girty's determination of a Permian age for some of the fossil collections in the upper portion of the Oquirrh formation suggests that the lithologic break is of minor importance.

Thickness.—East of Deep Creek the Gerster formation has been removed by pre-Eocene (?) erosion, and to the west all but one of the outcrops are overlain by the Eocene (?) or by volcanic rocks. In the gulch south of that leading to Ferber, however, a closer measure of the original thickness may be obtained, as here

[84] Gilluly, James, Geology and ore deposits of the Stockton and Fairfield quadrangles, Utah: U.S. Geol. Survey Prof. Paper 173, pp. 34-38, 1932.

[85] Boutwell, J. M., Geology and ore deposits of the Park City district, Utah: U.S. Geol. Survey Prof. Paper 77, pp. 45-49, 1912.

[86] Spencer, A. C., Geology and ore deposits of Ely, Nev.: U.S. Geol. Survey Prof

a small remnant of Lower Triassic limestone is found above the Gerster formation. In this place the thickness is about 600 feet.

Age and correlation.—Four fossil collections from the Gerster formation have been referred by Mr. Girty to the *Spiriferina pulchra* zone of the Permian. His identifications are as follows:

6061 and 6355. Half a mile west-northwest of benchmark 5097 on Ibapah-Wendover road:

Sponge.
Clionolithus? sp.
Fistulipora n. sp.
Leioclema sp.
Polypora sp.
Derbya aff. D. multistriata.
Chonetes n. sp. aff. C. geinitzianus.
Productus longus.
Pustula subhorrida var. rugatula?
Strophalosia? sp.
Strophalosia? n. sp.
Spirifer pseudocameratus.
Spiriferina pulchra.
Spiriferina aff. S. kentuckyensis.
Productus multistriatus.
Pustula nevadensis?
Pustula nevadensis var.
Pustula subhorrida.
Pustula subhorrida var.
Composita mira.
Hustedia mormoni?
Deltopecten n. sp.
Deltopecten sp.
Deltopecten sp.
Pteria? sp.

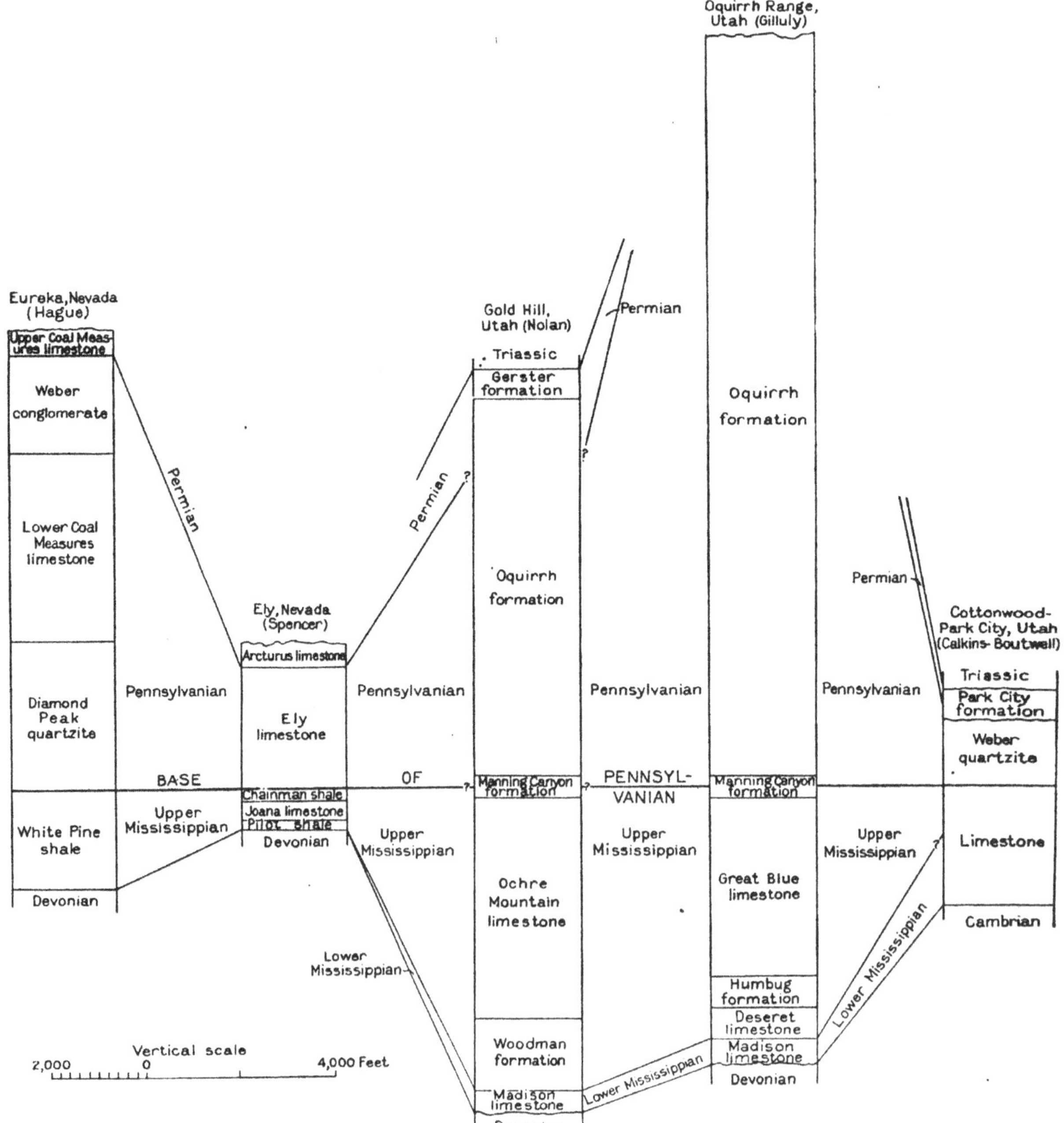

FIGURE 6.—Correlation of Carboniferous formations in an east-west belt from Eureka, Nev., to the Cottonwood-Park City area, Utah.

6278. 3,000 feet west-northwest of benchmark 4984 on Ibapah-Wendover road:

Derbya aff. D. multistriata.	Hustedia? sp.
Pustula subhorrida?	Deltopecten n. sp.
Spiriferina pulchra.	Bellerophon? sp.
Spiriferina aff. S. kentuckyensis.	Euphemus? sp.

6279. 1,500 feet south of 6278:

Leioclema sp.	Pustula subhorrida.
Domopora? sp.	Pustula subhorrida var. rugatula.
Chonetes n. sp. aff. C. geinitzianus.	Spiriferina pulchra.
Productus multistriatus.	Composita mira.
Pustula nevadensis.	Acanthopecten? coloradoensis?

of the Ely district, Nev.[89] Rocks of this age appear to have been rather generally removed by erosion in the region west of the Wasatch Mountains.

CORRELATION OF THE CARBONIFEROUS FORMATIONS

Figures 6 and 7 summarize the correlations that have been made for the Carboniferous formations in the Gold Hill area. Figure 6 includes districts in an east-west belt through Gold Hill, and figure 7 districts in a northeasterly belt, but the variations shown by the Carboniferous formations are quite unlike those shown by the pre-Carboniferous formations in the same belt (figs. 3 and 4). In the east-west belt, for example,

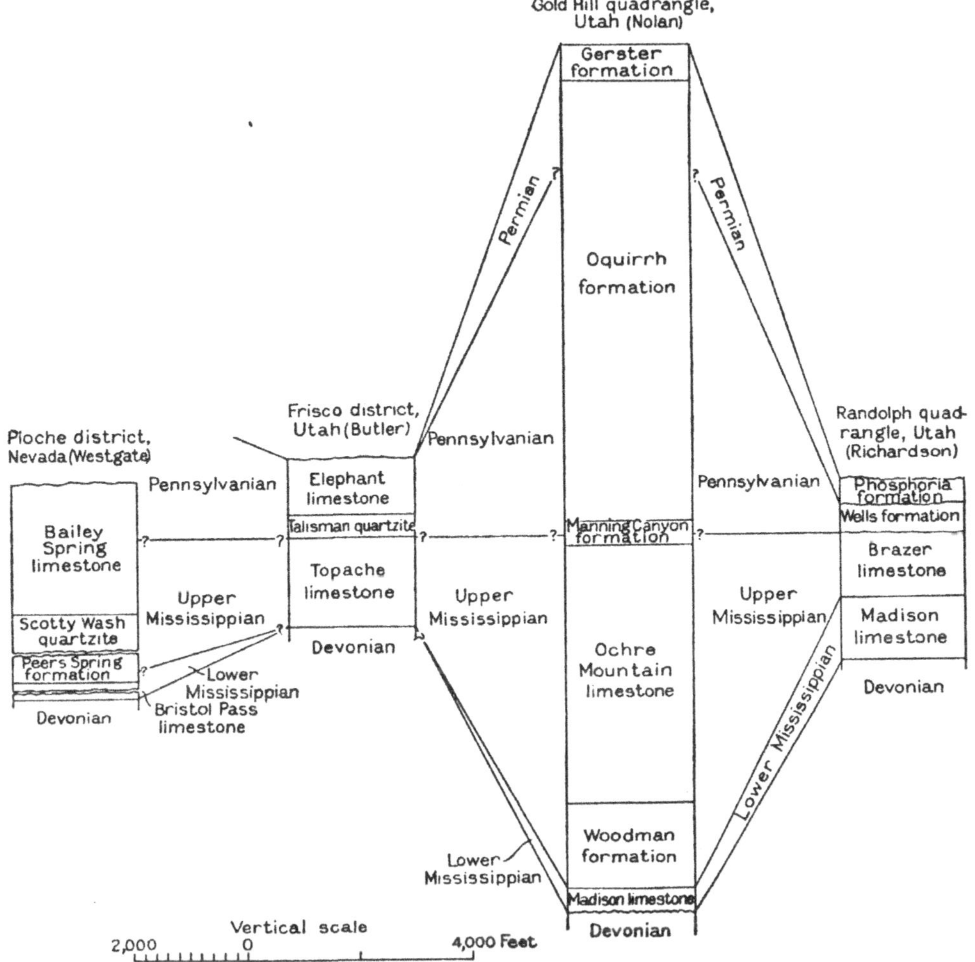

FIGURE 7.—Correlation of Carboniferous formations in a northeast-southwest belt from Pioche, Nev., to the Randolph quadrangle, Utah.

The *Spiriferina pulchra* fauna is found in the Park City formation of the Wasatch Mountains [87] and the Phosphoria formation of southeastern Idaho.[88] A similar fauna was also found in the Arcturus limestone

the thickness of the pre-Carboniferous formations increases rather regularly from east to west, whereas the Carboniferous formations show a pronounced thickening from the Cottonwood-Park City area to the Oquirrh Range, a thinning thence westward to Ely, and another thickening at Eureka. This change is

[87] Boutwell, J. M., Geology and ore deposits of the Park City district, Utah: U.S. Geol. Survey Prof. Paper 77, pp. 49–52, 1912.

[88] Mansfield, G. R., Geography, geology, and mineral resources of part of southeastern Idaho: U.S. Geol. Survey Prof. Paper 152, pp. 75–81, 1927.

[89] Spencer, A. C., Geology and ore deposits of the Ely district, Nev.: U.S. Geol. Survey Prof. Paper 96, p. 28, 1917.

thought to be the result of the formation of a land area in western Nevada in late Paleozoic time about on the site of maximum sedimentation in pre-Carboniferous time, which resulted in the shifting of this area of maximum sedimentation eastward into Utah.[90]

The figure for the northeast belt of Carboniferous formations is also quite different from the corresponding figure for the pre-Carboniferous, owing in part to the substitution of the relatively easterly Frisco section for that of the House Range, which contains no Carboniferous beds, and in part to the incompleteness of the Pioche section. The thinness of the section in the Randolph quadrangle, however, suggests that if more complete data were available the regularity shown by the pre-Carboniferous formations in this zone would not be found.

LOWER TRIASSIC LIMESTONES

About 3,000 feet west of benchmark 4984 on Deep Creek, on the south side of the gulch, there is a small outcrop of brown-weathering limestone that contains numerous specimens of an ammonite related to *Meekoceras*. This outcrop is just west of the Gold Hill quadrangle. Its thickness is less than 50 feet. The contact of these limestones with the Gerster formation is concealed by gravel in the gulch, but the two are essentially conformable in strike and dip. In the report on the Park City district,[91] to the east, the Triassic is stated to overlie the Permian conformably, although one of the cross sections given by Boutwell (B–B′, pl. 27) shows an unconformity at this horizon. In the Frisco district no unconformity was recognized in the field, although it is suggested that one may be present.[92] Mr. Girty has provided the following notes upon the fossils collected:

> This collection contains fossils of two types—small gastropods and large ammonites. Specimens are abundant but badly preserved. Very few of the gastropods show even the most general features of configuration. Some of them are apparently naticoid shells and suggest *Natica lelia*, but nothing more definite can be said of them. Of the ammonites also but little can be said save what is very general in character. Most if not all of them are discoidal in shape and more or less strongly evolute. Some have plicated sides; others are plain. Some have a narrowly rounded venter; others a venter truncated by a groove. The suture is shown by but few specimens and not completely and in detail by any of them. One shows the suture in detail but only in small part. The saddles are simple and rounded; the lobes fimbriated—evidently the suture is of the *Meekoceras* type. Inasmuch as a fairly complete knowledge of the suture is required for a close generic identification, even the best of these specimens cannot be classified generically, and it has seemed futile to attempt specific identifications. Of these specimens, however, it may fairly be said that most if not all of them are probably ammonites of the *Meekoceras* group and that they probably represent several related genera or subgenera and an equal or larger number of species. This conclusion is closely connected with the stratigraphic occurrence of the fauna, with its utter unlikeness to the Permian fauna of the underlying beds, and with its close resemblance in type and preservation to the Lower Triassic faunas of this general region, which abound in shells of the *Meekoceras* group, many of them closely resembling in configuration the shells in this collection.

UNCONFORMITY AT THE BASE OF THE EOCENE (?)

Sedimentary rocks belonging to the Jurassic and Cretaceous periods were not found in the quadrangle, and the area was presumably being eroded during at least part of the time between the Triassic and the Tertiary. This erosion is shown by the unconformity between the Eocene (?) and older rocks. A conglomerate containing boulders of the older rocks is found at the base of the Eocene (?), and the conglomerate itself in various places rests upon the Triassic limestones, the Gerster formation, and the Oquirrh formation.

TERTIARY SYSTEM

WHITE SAGE FORMATION (EOCENE?)

Distribution.—The deposit to which the name White Sage formation is herein applied is found only in the northwestern part of the quadrangle. Most of the outcrops are on one or the other side of Deep Creek between benchmarks 5120 and 4984. The two most extensive are those east of benchmarks 5045 and 5062. Another area underlain by the formation is found about a mile north of peak 6266; and still farther east there are two additional areas, both of them, however, being west of the road between Gold Hill and Ferber.

The name is taken from White Sage Flat, which is just west of the most southerly outcrop.

Lithology.—The White Sage formation consists of a basal conglomerate of variable thickness overlain by fresh-water, rather impure limestones. The conglomerate ranges in thickness from 1 foot to more than 50 feet. The included pebbles are mostly less than 6 inches in diameter. They are derived from Pennsylvanian and Permian sediments and are considerably less altered in appearance than the bedded rocks of those formations now in place. Sand lenses are abundant in the conglomerate. Most of the exposures weather to a deep red and contrast strongly with the lighter-colored rocks beneath them. In some places thin layers of similar conglomerate are interbedded with the overlying limestone.

The limestones are very fine grained rocks which are generally brownish on fresh fracture but weather to a dead white or chalk color. Individual beds are a foot or more in thickness, and a few are as much as 6 feet thick. All the beds examined contain a rather large amount of extremely fine clay and varying amounts of quartz. In some beds grains of quartz or chert 1 millimeter or more in diameter are scattered throughout.

---

[90] Nolan, T. B., A late Paleozoic positive area in Nevada: Am. Jour. Sci., 5th ser., vol. 16, pp. 153-161, 1928.

[91] Boutwell, J. M., Geology and ore deposits of the Park City district, Utah: U.S. Geol. Survey Prof. Paper 77, pp. 51-52, 1912.

[92] Butler, B. S., Geology and ore deposits of the San Francisco and adjacent districts, Utah: U.S. Geol. Survey Prof. Paper 80, p. 37, 1913.

A few beds contain thin brown-weathering chert stringers and some beds show a characteristic wavy or concentric banding on weathered surfaces, not unlike some banding that has been attributed to algal action.

About a mile west of benchmark 4984 on Deep Creek, beyond the limits of the quadrangle, beds of limestone belonging to the White Sage formation show noteworthy discordances in dip among themselves and with the conglomerate of the formation. It is thought that these may be the result of earth movements that were active during the time the beds were deposited.

Thickness.—The original thickness of the White Sage formation is not known, for it is everywhere unconformably overlain by lava or by recent gravel. The maximum thickness observed was in the isolated hill east of benchmark 5045 on Deep Creek, where about 600 feet is present.

Age and correlation.—Two collections of fossils were made from the White Sage formation. These were reported upon by J. B. Reeside, Jr., as follows:

TN-27 125. About 4,000 feet east-southeast of benchmark 5045, Deep Creek: I have been unable, by chemical or mechanical means, to get anything but cross sections of the abundant gastropods in this lot. The genus *Physa* is represented by species very similar in form to those known in the Eocene of the region; and a high-spired species that probably belongs in the genus *Goniobasis* is also abundant and might well belong to one of several Eocene forms. These alone would not be sufficient for an age assignment, but the widespread occurrence of an identical fresh-water limestone in the Wasatch and Green River formations of central Utah, coupled with the fossils, makes it highly probable that the present material is also Eocene.

TN-27 124. About 2,500 feet southeast of benchmark 5097 on Deep Creek: This lot is smaller than the first, but it appears to contain the same fauna, and the same remarks apply to it.

Eocene beds have been found in western or central Utah in only a few places, almost all some distance to he south and southeast of Gold Hill. About 125 miles o the east-southeast are rather extensive exposures f limestone underlain by conglomerate, which are re-rred to the Wasatch epoch of the Eocene by Richard-on[93] and Loughlin.[94] These rest upon different Paleo-ic and Mesozoic formations. A thick series of lime-ones with some conglomerate and sandstone beds in e Iron Springs district, 175 miles to the south, was apped by Leith and Harder[95] as the Claron limestone, Eocene age. It rests unconformably upon Creta-ous rocks with little discordance of dip. The near-t area in which rocks of supposed Eocene age have en recognized is near the north end of the Pilot ange, 75 miles north of Gold Hill. Hague[96] has rrelated these rocks with the Green River Eocene. ese dip 45° E., but their relations to the underlying cks are not described.

There is no trustworthy evidence to indicate which if any of these three areas of Eocene rocks is equivalent to the White Sage formation.

UNCONFORMITY ABOVE WHITE SAGE FORMATION

The unconformity separating the White Sage formation from younger rocks, either volcanic rocks or gravel, is a pronounced stratigraphic break. The younger rocks are either horizontal or have low depositional dips, in contrast to dips as high as 55° in the White Sage formation. The volcanic rocks are the next younger of the rocks found in contact with the Eocene (?) beds, and the surface of contact is approximately as rough as that of the present topography. The significance of the unconformity is touched upon in the consideration of the age of the intrusions and of the major structural features (pp. 63-64).

OLDER IGNEOUS ROCKS (EOCENE OR OLIGOCENE)

GENERAL FEATURES

About one-tenth of the quadrangle is underlain by a group of intrusive igneous rocks. By far the most extensive member of this group is a stock of quartz monzonite. Locally the stock has quartz dioritic or granitic facies, but these cannot be sharply differentiated from the quartz monzonite.

Two groups of somewhat younger dike rocks, shown as porphyry dikes and aplites on plates 1 and 2, are associated with the stock. The porphyry dikes are generally dark gray and commonly contain conspicuous phenocrysts in a dense groundmass, but there are some varieties that are only slightly porphyritic. They show an almost complete gradation in composition from granite porphyries to basalts. The aplites are characterized by a pale-pink or white color, due to the almost complete absence of dark minerals, and an equigranular texture. Two varieties of aplites were recognized.

QUARTZ MONZONITE

Areal extent.—The quartz monzonite crops out as a stock in the east-central part of the quadrangle. The main body extends about 8 miles from north to south and about 4½ miles from west to east within the quadrangle. Beyond the eastern border it is exposed at intervals for an additional 1½ miles before disappearing beneath Lake Bonneville beds. The town of Gold Hill is near the northwest corner of this main body. Extending westward from the town and underlying most of the valley through which the Ferber Road passes is a wedge-shaped outcrop of the quartz monzonite about 3 miles long and about 1½ miles wide at its junction with the main body. Projections of the sedimentary rocks into the stock are numerous. South of Clifton, on Montezuma Peak, two such projections nearly divide the quartz monzonite into two separate bodies, and the outcrop of quartz monzonite on the ridge at the summit is only 300 feet wide.

Richardson, G. B., Underground water in San Pete and central Sevier Valleys, ah: U.S. Geol. Survey Water-Supply Paper 199, p. 10, 1907.

Loughlin, G. F., Ore deposits of Utah: U.S. Geol. Survey Prof. Paper 111, 326, 421, 1920.

Leith, C. K., and Harder, E. C., The iron ores of the Iron Springs district, thern Utah: U.S. Geol. Survey Bull. 338, pp. 41-44, pl. 2, 1908.

Hague, Arnold, U.S. Geol. Expl. 40th Par. Rept., vol. 2, p. 498, 1877.

There are also several areas of sediments, or "roof pendants", entirely enclosed within the quartz monzonite which further reduce its area of outcrop. Several small exposures of the intrusive that are without surface connection with the main body occur in the adjacent sedimentary rocks. The largest of these is at the head of Overland Canyon and has an area of about a quarter of a square mile. Smaller ones appear in Barney Reevey Gulch, in Hopkins Gulch below the Midas mine, and near the Ozark prospect. Many other smaller bodies have been mapped within the roof pendants or the projecting areas of sedimentary rocks. Outcrops of the quartz monzonite cover an aggregate area within the quadrangle of over 24 square miles.

In Dry and Sheep Canyons, in the Deep Creek Mountains, there are exposures of highly sheared and altered igneous rock that are probably to be correlated with the quartz monzonite. In both places the amount of such rock exposed is small.

Petrographic and chemical character.—The unaltered quartz monzonite, though it all has the same general appearance, varies rather widely in both composition and texture from place to place. The greater part of the stock falls within the limits assigned to quartz monzonite by Lindgren,[97] but locally specimens are found that have the composition of granite, granodiorite, or even quartz diorite. In a few places quartz is sufficiently scarce to permit the rock to be classified as a monzonite. Similarly, the bulk of the stock is nonporphyritic, but porphyritic facies are not uncommon. No sharp contact was found between any of these varieties, and the transition, whenever observed, was gradual in respect to either the proportion of the feldspars to each other or the number of phenocrysts present.

The variety that is perhaps the most abundant and is also medial in character between various extremes may be considered typical of the stock as a whole. This is a medium-grained rock, which assumes on weathered surfaces a purple-gray or brownish-gray color. Scattered through it are a few crystals of reddish orthoclase as much as 2 inches long. Smaller crystals of orthoclase are also present but are not as abundant as those of white plagioclase, which show fine twinning striae on their cleavage faces. The crystals of the two feldspars are generally larger than those of the other constituents. Dark minerals make up about a quarter of the rock. Both hornblende and biotite are present, the former as greenish-black prisms with a good cleavage and the latter as small black hexagonal plates. Quartz is not readily apparent but on close examination may be recognized as small interstitial grains.

Thin sections studied with the microscope show these minerals and in addition minor amounts of magnetite, titanite, apatite, and zircon. Plagioclase is the most abundant of the major constituents. In most specimens it is more or less strikingly zoned. The zoning is not progressive, although there is a general tendency for the more calcic zones to form the central portion of the crystal. The zones determined range in composition from a sodic oligoclase to a calcic labradorite. By far the bulk of the plagioclase is andesine, for the most part rather sodic. The potash feldspar is orthoclase and in most sections is perthitic. Quartz is interstitial to the other minerals. Hornblende in most specimens of this variety of rock is more abundant than biotite. It is notably pleochroic, ranging from a pale yellow-green to green. The biotite is also pleochroic from yellow-brown or greenish brown to deep brownish black. Locally it replaces hornblende but in most places it has euhedral outlines. Apatite is particularly abundant. The larger crystals show a faint purplish-gray pleochroism. The amount of titanite present is variable. Most of the crystals are irregular in outline and are associated with hornblende that has been altered to actinolite. It is probable that such titanite is secondary. Much of the magnetite is also probably secondary, as it is largely localized in partly or wholly altered crystals of biotite and hornblende. In a few sections zircon crystals are included in biotite and are surrounded by pleochroic haloes.

The following chemical analysis, quoted from Butler,[98] represents a specimen of this variety of quartz monzonite obtained west of the Western Utah Copper Co.'s Gold Hill mine:

Analysis of quartz monzonite west of Gold Hill mine of Western Utah Copper Co.

[R. C. Wells, analyst]

SiO_2	62. 84	TiO_2	0. 42
Al_2O_3	14. 21	ZrO	Trace
Fe_2O_3	. 91	CO_2	. 38
FeO	3. 75	P_2O_5	. 41
MgO	3. 04	S	. 01
CaO	4. 72	MnO	. 06
Na_2O	2. 85	BaO	. 03
K_2O	4. 60		
H_2O-	. 26		99. 72
H_2O+	1. 23		

The mineral composition calculated from the above analysis is as follows:

Quartz	17. 46	Biotite	5. 58
Orthoclase	23. 35	Apatite	1. 01
Albite molecule	23. 06	Calcite	. 30
Anorthite molecule	8. 90		
Hornblende	19. 21		98. 87

In the calculation the relative proportions of hornblende and biotite were arbitrarily assumed, and an average of analyses of these minerals from similar rocks was assumed to represent their composition. After apportioning the oxides to the different minerals

[97] Lindgren, Waldemar, Granodiorite and other intermediate rocks: Am. Jour. Sci., 4th ser., vol. 9, p. 279, 1900.

[98] Butler, B. S., Ore deposits of Utah: U.S. Geol. Survey Prof. Paper 111, p. 96, 1919.

there remained a small excess of FeO and a rather large one of H_2O+ which probably indicates that the specimen analyzed was partly sericitized. Specimens collected by the writer near the Gold Hill mine all showed this alteration more or less advanced. It is of some interest to note that both Fe_2O_3 and TiO_2 are completely used up in the calculation of hornblende and biotite, leaving none for magnetite and titanite. This is in accord with the observation that the magnetite and titanite, as observed in the sections, are more or less restricted to large crystals of hornblende and biotite and in some places at least have been formed at their expense.

An examination of specimens taken from the wedge-shaped area of the intrusive south of Dutch Mountain indicates that they are close to the dividing line between granite and quartz monzonite. Biotite is more abundant than hornblende, and the plagioclase is slightly more sodic and is apparently a calcic oligoclase, although rather thorough sericitization in the slides examined prevented accurate measurement. There are no other differences from the more common variety.

At the other extreme is a specimen taken from the main body of the intrusive near the east border of the quadrangle, in which the content of orthoclase has decreased to 10 or 15 percent. This rock is without the large phenocrysts of orthoclase and has a larger proportion of darker minerals. The ratio of the feldspars places the rock in the group of granodiorites. A similar rock is found as a dike cutting the Ochre Mountain limestone a few hundred feet north of the Overland Road half a mile southeast of the junction of roads from Ibapah and Gold Hill. The quartz content of this rock is rather less than normal but is large enough for the rock to be classed as a granodiorite.

The quartz monzonite is porphyritic in places, particularly at its contacts, with phenocrysts of both orthoclase and plagioclase. In this variety there are all gradations in size between the phenocrysts and the crystals of the same minerals in the groundmass. The smaller grains are of about the same size as that in the nonporphyritic rock. Such a facies may be classed as porphyritic quartz monzonite.

The porphyritic habit is particularly pronounced in the exposures of the intrusive south and southwest of Dutch Mountain and west of Gold Hill. Thin sections of specimens from this region show that there is apparently a gradation between the porphyritic quartz monzonite and rock that is more properly termed quartz monzonite porphyry. In the latter variety the phenocrysts of quartz, feldspars, and the dark minerals may be several millimeters long, but the crystals in the groundmass are only a fraction of a millimeter in diameter and are for the most part of quartz and feldspar, chiefly orthoclase. In texture and composition these rocks are not unlike some of the lighter colored porphyry dikes that cut the main mass of the intrusive to the east.

Darker nodules or basic segregations are found scattered throughout the normal quartz monzonite. They range from an inch to a foot in diameter and may be much more abundant in one place than another. The nodules are characterized by a concentration of hornblende, a diminution of feldspars, and an absence of quartz and biotite. A thin section of one of them shows a large amount of euhedral magnetite, some titanite, apatite, and much green hornblende, similar to that of the quartz monzonites. Andesine and orthoclase are present in about equal amounts and are later than the hornblende, which is frayed and embayed by them.

Another kind of inclusion, usually of dark color, which is found near the contacts of the quartz monzonite, is metamorphosed sedimentary rock. These are fine-grained to dense and are commonly less than 2 or 3 inches in maximum diameter. They are not so uniform in texture and appearance as the basic segregations and furthermore show a border of different color and texture at the contact with the normal quartz monzonite. Thin sections show a mineral composition quite unlike that of the segregations, and different specimens differ from one another. One specimen obtained near Gold Hill, for example, showed a fine-grained aggregate of quartz, plagioclase, biotite, magnetite, and a green isotropic mineral that is probably pleonaste, the magnesia-iron spinel. The inclusion is separated from the normal igneous rock by a border of sericite. The restriction of such inclusions to the contact, their mineral composition, and the presence of borders or "reaction rims" of different composition indicate that they are highly altered fragments from the Oquirrh formation that have been engulfed in the igneous rock during its intrusion.

Factors influencing the localization of the quartz monzonite.—Preexistent faults appear to have played an important part in determining the location of the quartz monzonite stock. The influence in a minor way of such older faults is extremely well shown in several places on the south side of Montezuma Peak, where the quartz monzonite contact follows faults that must have existed prior to the intrusion. In these places the quartz monzonite apparently utilized the old fracture lines as a means of ingress but caused no additional deformation.

A more definite relation between old faults and the intrusion is suggested by the essentially complete restriction of the intrusion between two large transverse faults, the Blood Canyon fault on the south and the Pool Canyon fault on the north. These two faults are thought to limit also an extensive thrust fault. In view of the dependence of the intrusion upon preexistent faults noted in the preceding paragraph, it seems probable that there may be a similar relation between these major faults and the intrusive body. The thrust fault limited by the transverse faults must have caused a high degree of fracturing in the affected rocks, and this in turn provided the necessary lines of weakness that were apparently required for the emplacement of the stock.

This suggestion implies that the intrusion came into place without causing any great deformation of the invaded rocks, and the implication is confirmed by the absence of any discernible doming in the sedimentary rocks bordering the stock. The only evidence that there were any pronounced earth movements during the intrusion of the quartz monzonite is found along the western border of the main mass of the intrusive, where there are several faults of large throw. For several reasons (see p. 89) these faults are considered to have been caused by the intrusion and to mark the location of the primary channel through which the quartz monzonite was intruded.

PORPHYRY DIKES

Distribution and size.—Porphyry dikes are rather widely distributed throughout the quartz monzonite area and also over much of Dutch Mountain. They are most abundant in the region about 2 miles east of Clifton, where an area of nearly a square mile is more than half underlain by porphyries.

The ratio between the length and breadth of the dikes is rather variable. The quartz monzonite porphyry dike cutting through the claims of the Western Utah Copper Co. at Gold Hill, for example, may be traced for nearly 2 miles and for the greater part of this distance is less than 20 feet wide. Some other dikes that were 10 feet or less in width were followed for distances close to half a mile. On the other hand, several of the dikes in the locality east of Clifton are 250 feet or more wide and are less than half a mile long. A similar rather thick lens occurs on the north side of Dutch Mountain half a mile south of the Garrison Monster mine, and another just north of the town of Gold Hill. In several places dikes less than a foot wide could not be traced beyond the rock outcrop in which they were found.

Appearance.—As these dikes have a considerable range in composition, it is not surprising that there is a corresponding variation in their appearance. Two general varieties may be distinguished. One is a highly porphyritic rock, whose prevailing color is a greenish or pinkish gray, or even white in places where alteration has been especially intense. The phenocrysts consist chiefly of rounded quartz crystals and dull feldspars, with locally some of ferromagnesian minerals, particularly biotite. The groundmass is invariably too fine-grained for any of its constituent minerals to be recognized.

The other variety has characteristically a dark greenish-gray color, that contrasts strongly with the lighter color of the quartz monzonite. Its phenocrysts are commonly neither abundant nor conspicuous and are for the most part of the ferromagnesian minerals, but in several specimens they are similar in numbers and in character to those in the lighter-colored rocks. Locally also, particularly east of Clifton, scattered phenocrysts as much as an inch in length may be found. In some of the rocks rounded quartz phenocrysts about an eighth of an inch in diameter are present in small quantities and are conspicuous because of the dark color of the rest of the rock. The matrix in this variety also is much too fine-grained to be determinable megascopically.

Only one equigranular dike was noted during the field work. This was the thick dike south of the Garrison Monster mine. It has a pepper-and-salt appearance due to the presence in nearly equal quantities of dark-greenish hornblende and other dark minerals and white feldspathic minerals. Some of the hornblende is in the form of needles or poorly defined platy aggregates nearly a quarter of an inch long, but they are not sufficiently distinct to give the rock a porphyritic aspect.

Microscopic features.—Two varieties of the porphyry dikes may be distinguished on the basis of their composition and texture as disclosed by microscopic examination. These two varieties correspond roughly with the two megascopic divisions, in that the lighter-colored dikes contain a higher proportion of quartz and feldspars and their groundmass has an allotriomorphic texture, whereas the darker dikes contain a higher proportion of dark minerals and their groundmass includes laths of plagioclase, whose relations to the other minerals in the groundmass are characteristic of what has been named an "intergranular" texture. Several specimens, however, appear to bridge the gap between the two extremes of composition and texture, and the distinction between them is chiefly valuable for purposes of description.

The dikes characterized by predominance of the light-colored minerals and allotriomorphic texture of the groundmass contain phenocrysts of quartz, orthoclase, plagioclase, biotite, and rarely hornblende, in a groundmass of the same minerals. The quartz phenocrysts are strikingly corroded and embayed by the groundmass. In many places the tabular feldspars are too altered for satisfactory determination, even where those in the surrounding quartz monzonite are relatively fresh. Where they can be identified, however, it is generally possible to prove that both orthoclase and plagioclase are present; the composition of the plagioclase ranges in different dikes from albite to andesine. Biotite in small quantities is a common constituent and occurs as hexagonal prisms that are about a sixteenth of an inch across, from a half to a quarter of the diameter of the phenocrysts of quartz and feldspar. Hornblende is an uncommon phenocryst in the more siliceous rocks. The groundmass is composed of a very fine grained aggregate of quartz, feldspar, and, locally, shreds of biotite, although in many specimens it is so thoroughly altered that the original composition is uncertain. The minerals in the groundmass, unlike the phenocrysts, do not show crystal outlines, and the resultant xenomorphic texture is markedly different from that shown by the groundmass of many of the darker dike rocks.

In this variety the proportions of quartz and the two kinds of feldspars vary greatly in different dikes. The dike that forms the footwall of the Cyclone vein, for example, is a granite porphyry. On the other hand, a dike in Tribune Gulch, on the southeast side of Dutch Mountain, is close to a diorite porphyry. Between these two extremes are dikes that contain more or less quartz and both orthoclase and plagioclase and are classified as quartz monzonite porphyries, of which the prominent dike that cuts through Gold Hill is an example.

The porphyry dikes of the second variety contain phenocrysts of augite, hornblende, biotite, plagioclase, and quartz. Augite is abundant in a few of the dikes but in several is partly altered to green hornblende. The hornblende, generally accompanied by biotite, also occurs in some of the dikes that contain no augite. The phenocrysts of these dark minerals are generally from a sixteenth to an eighth of an inch in diameter, but in a few places phenocrysts of augite as much as an inch in length have been noted. The plagioclase phenocrysts may be as much as half an inch in diameter but are generally a quarter of an inch or less and have a composition ranging from sodic andesine to sodic labradorite. Corroded and embayed quartz phenocrysts are found sparingly in almost all the dikes. The most abundant mineral in the groundmass is microscopic plagioclase, which, where determinable, is somewhat more sodic than that of the phenocrysts. It has a striking tabular habit. The laths, however, do not show a uniform orientation but are haphazard or, locally, in the form of rosettes. Between the laths are tiny grains of augite (in dikes that contain augite phenocrysts), hornblende, biotite, and locally quartz and orthoclase. This texture is similar to that called intergranular in basalts and andesites, and many of these dikes may be accurately termed augite or hornblende andesite or basalt.

There is a considerable variation in composition in the rocks of this variety, as in the lighter-colored dikes. All the dikes in this group, however, show the intergranular texture of the groundmass. Some of them contain sufficient quartz to be called dacites, and others are clearly basaltic.

Several dikes were found that have in part the characteristics of the first variety and in part those of the second variety. These rocks commonly contain phenocrysts of quartz, orthoclase, plagioclase (oligoclase or andesine), and locally biotite, but phenocrysts of hornblende or augite are either scarce or completely absent, the rocks thus resembling the more siliceous, light-colored dikes. The groundmass of such rocks is largely made up of laths of plagioclase, and the intergranular texture thus formed is similar to that of the darker-colored dikes. A dike of this class that crops out just east of the old Garrison Monster camp has a groundmass in part xenomorphic and in part composed of radiating laths of plagioclase, similar in appearance to those found in rocks whose groundmass is wholly intergranular.

Several of the porphyry dike rocks show a local development of granophyric texture in the groundmass. This microscopic intergrowth of quartz and feldspar was found chiefly in the lighter-colored siliceous dikes, but it is also present in the nearly equigranular thick dike south of the Garrison Monster mine. Its significance in these dikes is not understood, but the conditions favoring its development were evidently nearly independent of the composition of the dike.

All the dikes are more or less altered, and almost invariably the degree of alteration in the dikes intrusive into the stock is greater than that of the surrounding quartz monzonite. Sericite, calcite, chlorite, and quartz are the chief secondary minerals, as they are in most of the altered quartz monzonite.

Relations to other rocks.—The porphyry dikes intrude both the quartz monzonite and the sedimentary rocks and are in many places localized along minor faults. At least two of the dikes in the quartz monzonite differ from those in the sediments in that they are discontinuous. One of these dikes is on the east side of the northward-draining gulch east of the summit of Gold Hill, and the other is about a quarter of a mile east of the Success mine. The exposures of the second dike show clearly that the discontinuity is not the result of later faulting but is an original feature. Preexistent joint planes or fractures in the quartz monzonite appear to have played an important part in the determination of the course of the dike, and where they were not sufficiently well developed, the dike did not enter.

In several places on the southeast side of Dutch Mountain aplite dikes are in contact with the porphyry dikes, and in all such occurrences the aplites are found to be younger. Quartz-sulphide veins are also younger than the dikes, as is shown by the developments at the Cyclone mine and elsewhere. In the locality east of Clifton the dikes are cut by several carbonate veins, which are thought to represent the latest of the series of events initiated by the intrusion of the quartz monzonite.

Relations of the porphyry dikes to one another.—In a few places different varieties of the porphyry dikes are in contact with each other, by reason of the formation of compound dikes. Examples of such dikes are found about 2,000 feet west of the Western Utah mine and also in the area of dike concentration east of

Clifton. At both localities the lighter-colored, more siliceous dikes are younger than the darker ones. On the eastern slope of hill 5675, near the mouth of Rodenhouse Wash, however, a light-colored quartz monzonite porphyry is clearly cut by a more basic dike, which strikes nearly at right angles to it. It appears, therefore, that although the lighter-colored dikes are in general younger, there are local exceptions to the rule.

APLITE DIKES

Distribution and character.—Two varieties of aplite dikes may be distinguished. One of these is a pale-pinkish to white rock that occurs as small lenticular or cylindrical masses in the quartz monzonite. Its boundaries with the main intrusive are gradational, there being a zone between the two in which a coarsening of the grain and an increase in dark minerals from the aplite to the quartz monzonite may be discerned. Almost all the occurrences of aplite of this kind may be measured in inches or feet; a few extend for 10 feet or so; and exceptionally some of the cylindrical masses may have a diameter of 30 or 40 feet. This variety of aplite is widely distributed throughout the main outcrop of the quartz monzonite stock, but because of the small size of the individual bodies they are not shown on the geologic map.

The second variety of aplite is limited to the quartz monzonite area on the southeast side of Dutch Mountain north and northwest of the town of Gold Hill. These dikes are shown on the geologic map. They are light-colored rocks that are generally more resistant to erosion than the surrounding rocks and can be readily traced by reason of their color and superior relief. Most of the exposures are relatively narrow dikes that are only exceptionally wider than 20 feet and are generally only 10 feet or less. Several of them have been traced for at least 2,000 feet. A few of the outcrops, notably one about three-quarters of a mile northwest of the town of Gold Hill, have a bulbous outline, from which thin dikes extend for some distance.

Quartz and feldspar make up almost all of this variety of aplite, and many of the feldspar crystals have a tabular habit. Crystals of biotite can be distinguished in several of the dikes but are absent in others. Tiny irregular splotches of blue tourmaline are also present in some specimens.

Microscopic features.—The minerals found in the first variety of aplite are quartz, calcic oligoclase, perthitic orthoclase, rare biotite, and the accessories apatite, titanite, zircon, and iron ores. They do not differ in any respect from the same minerals found in the quartz monzonite—in fact, the only differences from the main intrusive shown by this variety of aplite are the slightly smaller grain size and the nearly complete absence of the dark minerals.

The second variety of aplite is much finer grained than the first, individual crystals having an average diameter of 1 to 2 millimeters. Nearly equal quantities of quartz, perthitic orthoclase, and calcic oligoclase make up almost the entire rock. Zircon is present as an accessory mineral, but apatite, titanite, and iron ores are almost completely absent. In some specimens biotite is present in small crystals. The texture of the rock is panidiomorphic in that many of the feldspar grains are euhedral, with quartz filling the interstices. Where tourmaline is present it replaces the other constituents in irregular splotches. Its pleochroism in thin section is ω = deep greenish blue, ϵ = pale yellow-green.

Relations to other rocks.—The aplite dikes were not recognized as cutting sedimentary rocks and are apparently restricted to the quartz monzonite. Those of the second variety are clearly younger than the porphyry dikes exposed in that area, and the aplites of the first variety have been noted in the wall rocks of some of the quartz sulphide veins. If the two varieties are of the same age, the combined evidence would make them later than the period of porphyry dike intrusion and earlier than much of the ore deposition. The difference in habit and occurrence of the two varieties, however, makes any assumption of contemporaneity between them rather doubtful.

AGE OF THE OLDER IGNEOUS ROCKS

Although the White Sage formation, of Eocene (?) age, is not itself intruded by either the quartz monzonite or the dike rocks within the quadrangle, it is locally metamorphosed and is therefore believed to be older than the intrusive. This conclusion is checked by the structural history of the quadrangle. (See p. 64.) On the other hand, volcanic rocks thought to be of late Pliocene age overlie the quartz monzonite unconformably. The emplacement of the stock must therefore have occurred at some time between these two epochs. As a long period of erosion must have been required to expose the quartz monzonite before the volcanic rocks could be deposited upon it, it would appear that the intrusion probably took place between the late Eocene and early Oligocene.

In other parts of Utah similar igneous rocks have been reported to be either of late Cretaceous or early Eocene age[99] or of late Eocene or post-Eocene age.[1] The Gold Hill intrusion must be of the latter age.

PLIOCENE (?) SEDIMENTS

About a mile west-southwest of Ibapah, on the west edge of the quadrangle, a small area is covered by a series of marl, sandstone, and gravel. These materials are exposed much more extensively to the west.

The beds have a white or light brownish-gray color that contrasts with the darker color of the younger

[99] Gilluly, James, Basin Range faulting along the Oquirrh Range, Utah: Geol. Soc. America Bull., vol. 39, pp. 1117-1118, 1928.

[1] Loughlin, G. F., Geology and ore deposits of the Tintic mining district, Utah: U.S. Geol. Survey Prof. Paper 107, p. 104, 1919.

gravel marl. The most common rock is a coarse grit or sandstone, fairly well cemented by calcium carbonate. Locally these pass into beds containing pebbles that must have come from the west or south, as shown by bedrock exposures in those directions. The grits are composed chiefly of quartz grains, but there are also numerous flakes of biotite. Some of the grits are perceptibly cross-bedded.

A few beds of marl are included. These are 2 or 3 feet thick and are more resistant to weathering than the other members of the series. They are filled with casts of tiny tubes, which may represent plant rootlets or stems. A few grains of quartz 1 or 2 millimeters in maximum diameter can usually be found within the marl.

About 100 feet of these beds is exposed within the quadrangle, but the total thickness exposed to the west is much larger.

No diagnostic fossils were found in these rocks. A few fragments of bones were found and submitted to Dr. J. W. Gidley, of the United States National Museum, but the material was too poor to be identified even generically. The beds are essentially flat-lying but are well dissected and overlain in some places by gravel containing pebbles of volcanic rocks. They are therefore thought to be of prevolcanic age, and, as they are not disturbed, of post-Eocene age. It is thought that they were deposited shortly before the volcanic rocks were erupted, and because of this belief they have been assigned tentatively to the Pliocene.

YOUNGER IGNEOUS ROCKS (LATE PLIOCENE?)

At several places in the quadrangle there are small areas covered by igneous rocks whose relations make them easily recognized as being much younger than the Gold Hill stock and its associated dikes. The greater number of these outcrops are either lavas or pyroclastic rocks but in several places small intrusive bodies were found. The composition ranges from rhyolite to basalt, with rocks of intermediate composition and rich in potassium greatly predominating.

Because of the small size of most of the outcrops of these rocks, and because of the impossibility of establishing the correct chronologic sequence between such isolated occurrences, the whole group is shown on the map under the same symbol.

DISTRIBUTION AND RELATIONS

The bulk of the volcanic rocks are found in the northwestern part of the quadrangle, particularly on both sides of Deep Creek. In the canyon of Deep Creek itself from benchmark 5045 south there are five small necks, and to the east and west flows and pyroclastic rocks occur. The largest area covered by the volcanic rocks within the quadrangle is that about 2 miles east of Deep Creek on the western and southern slopes of peak 6147. There are also some fair-sized exposures in the area of low relief between the Ferber Road and the wagon road between the Erickson ranch and Gold Hill. These are chiefly lavas but include some tuffaceous rocks.

These volcanic rocks were erupted before the cutting of the present Deep Creek Valley, as is shown by the lack of outcrops other than necks in the flat-bottomed portion of the valley, and by the restriction of the flows to mature valleys in the higher land on each side. The recent cutting of the lateral gulches east and west of benchmark 5062 on Deep Creek has exhibited small hanging valleys filled by the lavas. The pyroclastic rocks appear to have been erupted first, for they are overlain by lavas or cut by necks wherever observed. Erosion was active during the extrusion of the lavas in this region, for a widespread flow of hypersthene-augite latite rests unconformably upon the other lavas and locally lies directly upon the filling of the necks through which these older flows were erupted.

Small exposures are found at a number of places in the south-central and southeastern parts of the area. There are several patches on the Lincoln Highway south of Gold Hill and similar occurrences on the northern and northeastern parts of Clifton Flat. These are chiefly lavas. In Rodenhouse Wash about 1½ miles north of Clifton a small area is covered by both lavas and pyroclastic rocks. An exposure of moderate size was found in Blood Canyon, and smaller residual patches are present here and there along the lower part of Overland Canyon and among the Lake Bonneville deposits through which the stream has cut.

The volcanic rocks in these more easterly localities commonly occur in valleys cut in the quartz monzonite or in the sedimentary rocks intruded by it. Their eruption appears to have been more or less contemporaneous with the deposition of the gravel that fills some of the valleys in this region. At the mouth of North Pass Canyon, for example, a dike of alkali basalt is exposed within the gravel and is thought to be younger, for otherwise it would be necessary to believe that the dike must have stood as a narrow wall over 20 feet high while coarse gravel was being deposited around it—a view that is difficult to accept, because the dike is much less resistant to weathering than the Pennsylvanian rocks that would have originally formed its walls. Some of the outcrops of lava in Blood Canyon also appear to be younger than the gravel. On the other hand, many of the exposures of volcanic rocks in this region are overlain by gravel, which is now being eroded.

PETROGRAPHY

The younger volcanic rocks have a considerable diversity in composition, the silica in the five specimens analyzed ranging from 47.36 to 70.30 percent. Rocks containing about 60 percent of silica are by far the most abundant. In the field, and even in the microscopic study of the lavas, the rocks appear to represent a normal series of basalts, andesites, and rhyolites. The chemical analyses, however, show that they are all rich in potassium and that the series includes alkali basalts, latites, trachytes, and rhyolites.

The abundance of such potassium-rich volcanic rocks in Utah and New Mexico has been noted and commented upon by Butler[2] and by Lindgren, Graton, and Gordon.[3]

Biotite and hornblende andesites or latites.—By far the most abundant volcanic rocks in the quadrangle are biotite and hornblende andesites or latites. Most of the flows and necks found on both sides of Deep Creek are of this composition, as are those in Blood Canyon and in Clifton Flat. These are all porphyritic rocks that commonly weather to shades of brownish gray but are greenish to purplish gray on fresh fracture.

Plagioclase, biotite, hornblende, and augite are the only abundant phenocrysts and are embedded in a groundmass that may be almost entirely glassy in many of the flows or nearly holocrystalline in some specimens from the necks. All the rocks show some alteration, but this is most marked in the necks, which are in places so affected that only traces of the original minerals remain.

The zoned plagioclase phenocrysts range in composition from sodic andesines to calcic labradorite. The more calcic varieties particularly contain numerous glass inclusions. In most of the specimens either hornblende or biotite is the dominant dark mineral, but in one specimen from Blood Canyon the two are present in nearly equal amounts. They are commonly bordered by thick rims of magnetite. Both green and brown hornblende were recognized, but the former appears to be limited to varieties in which biotite is abundant. Sparse phenocrysts of augite are present in both the biotite-rich and hornblende-rich lavas and sporadic crystals of quartz are even less common. Apatite and, in one specimen, titanite are accessories.

The groundmass of these rocks is commonly composed of glass in which are embedded tiny laths of plagioclase and dots of magnetite. The plagioclase laths appear to be somewhat less calcic than the phenocrysts, most of those determined being sodic to medium andesines. Trichites and globulites were found in the glass in some specimens, and perlitic cracks are also present. Both the color of the glass and its index of refraction are different in different rocks, the index ranging from less than 1.50 to slightly less than that of balsam. In many specimens, particularly those from the necks, the glass has been devitrified, and poorly defined areas of quartz and feldspar replace it. In several of the glassy flows oriented plagioclase laths are distributed in wavy bands that are locally interrupted by and in part flow around nodules containing much glass.

An analysis of a specimen of this group of lavas collected west of benchmark 5030 on Deep Creek gave the following result:

Analysis of biotite-augite latite

[J. G. Fairchild, analyst]

SiO_2	57.94	K_2O	8.90
Al_2O_3	16.66	TiO_2	1.00
Fe_2O_3	2.73	P_2O_5	.11
FeO	.57	H_2O+	1.66
MgO	.60	H_2O-	3.82
CaO	4.91		
Na_2O	1.29		100.19

I(II).″5.2.″2, vulsinose.

The high content of K_2O was totally unexpected, for the microscopic examination had indicated no potash-bearing mineral except a relatively minor amount of biotite. A comparison of the norm of the rock with the mode makes it evident that the glassy groundmass must consist almost entirely of potash feldspar with a small amount of quartz. The propriety of terming this rock a latite may perhaps be questioned, but the relatively low silica and alumina and relatively high lime made it seem preferable to use this name rather than trachyte, in spite of the preponderance of potash over soda. The rock is somewhat similar in chemical composition to a trachyte from the Iron Springs district described by Leith and Harder[4] but is higher in lime and lower in silica.

No other analyses were made of members of this group of rocks, and their reference to "andesites or latites" reflects the uncertainty as to their true nature that results from the lack of additional analyses.

Hypersthene-augite latite.—Rocks of the composition of hypersthene-augite latite are exposed in many localities in the northwestern part of the area from the western slopes of Dutch Mountain to the western border of the quadrangle. All these exposures appear to be a part of the same flow or of closely related flows, as they all have the same relations to the other volcanic rocks. Only one vent through which these rocks could have reached the surface was found. This is a small elliptical neck about 2,500 feet north-northwest of benchmark 5062 on Deep Creek.

In hand specimens the rock is dark gray to grayish black. Phenocrysts of yellowish or white plagioclase and greenish-black pyroxene are abundant and make up one-third to one-half of the rock. The groundmass is dense black and in some places has a conchoidal fracture. Locally there are tiny vesicles, which may be filled with a chloritic mineral, but these are not abundant.

Thin sections show that the abundant plagioclase phenocrysts have an average composition of $Ab_{45}An_{55}$.

[2] Butler, B. S., Ore deposits of Utah: U.S. Geol. Survey Prof. Paper 111, p. 89, 1920.

[3] Lindgren, Waldemar, Graton, L. C., and Gordon, C. H., Ore deposits of New Mexico: U.S. Geol. Survey Prof. Paper 68, pp. 43–44, 1910.

[4] Leith, C. K., and Harder, E. C., The iron ores of the Iron Springs district, southern Utah: U.S. Geol. Survey Bull. 338, p. 58, 1908.

They commonly show an oscillatory zoning, however, and portions may be as sodic as $Ab_{60}An_{40}$ or as calcic as $Ab_{25}An_{75}$. Glass inclusions are present locally. Hypersthene and augite phenocrysts are found in about equal amount. The hypersthene is pleochroic in shades of light reddish brown and greenish gray. Sparse phenocrysts of brown hornblende were recognized in a few specimens. Magnetite and apatite are accessory minerals. In several of the specimens the groundmass is composed entirely of brown glass, which locally showed perlitic cracks, trichites, and globulites. Other specimens show numerous labradorite laths in the groundmass and, with increasing crystallinity, small pyroxene crystals. In the latter specimens the texture is typically hyalopilitic.

A specimen of this rock taken a quarter of a mile west of benchmark 5045 on Deep Creek was analyzed with the following results:

Analysis of hypersthene-augite latite

[J. G. Fairchild, analyst]

SiO_2	61.52	K_2O	3.02
Al_2O_3	15.25	TiO_2	1.00
Fe_2O_3	2.20	P_2O_5	.16
FeO	3.97	H_2O+	2.23
MgO	2.59	H_2O-	.36
CaO	5.72		
Na_2O	2.31		100.33

''II.4.3.3, harzose.

The analysis shows that the rock falls into the latite group. It is rather similar to a latite from the Tintic district described by Loughlin,[5] which also is hypersthene-bearing. In the Rosenbusch classification a volcanic rock of this composition would be termed a trachyandesite. A rock of this name from Col d'Oreccia, Corsica, is chemically similar.[6]

The norm was calculated from the analysis and compared with a mode roughly estimated by the Rosiwal method. The result indicated that the glassy base, if it were crystalline, would be composed of about 2 parts of quartz, 2 of orthoclase, and 1 of sodic andesine.

Trachyte.—Just east of the small knob in the gulch east of benchmark 5120 on Deep Creek there is a small area of rock which is notably different in appearance from the latite lavas. This is a light-pink rock, locally splotched by pale-green areas. Small laths of feldspar are scattered through the rock, and there are a very few crystals of black hornblende. A thin section shows that about a third of the rock is composed of phenocrysts, chiefly albite-oligoclase, with much less abundant sanidine. Green hornblende and augite are of minor importance. Apatite needles, magnetite, and zircon were identified as accessory minerals. The remaining two-thirds of the rock was originally of glass, but much of it, together with almost all of the augite crystals, has been replaced by calcite. In a few places there are areas of a colorless, almost isotropic chloritic mineral fringed with calcite. A partial analysis of this rock gave the following result:

Partial analysis of trachyte

[J. G. Fairchild, analyst]

SiO_2	65.00	Na_2O	2.23
Al_2O_3	14.28	K_2O	5.19

The rock is over 4 percent higher in silica than the average trachyte listed by Daly [7] and lower in alumina and soda. It is even more discordant with the average rhyolite, however, and the fact that no quartz was recognized in the thin section, while sanidine, which as a rule crystallizes later than quartz, is present, makes the assignment to the trachyte group fairly certain.

Rhyolites.—Two occurrences of rhyolite were found, one about a mile southwest of benchmark 5045 on Deep Creek and the other in the northern part of Rodenhouse Wash. The Deep Creek exposure is part of an old neck, and to the south there are lavas that are related to it. The rock is greenish gray and contains a few phenocrysts of biotite and a sodic andesine that is almost completely altered to thompsonite. Small laths of plagioclase are enclosed in a glassy matrix, which has an index of refraction slightly less than 1.50 where unaltered. In most places the glass has been devitrified and consists of quartz, oligoclase, and orthoclase. A partial analysis shows clearly that this rock is most closely related to rhyolite:

Partial analysis of rhyolite

[J. G. Fairchild, analyst]

SiO_2	70.30	Na_2O	2.66
Al_2O_3	14.92	K_2O	4.37

The Swansea rhyolite of the Tintic district [8] has a similar chemical composition but is quite different in mineralogic habit, being an intrusive rock.

The rhyolite in Rodenhouse Wash is very different in appearance and texture from the rock described above. It is a poorly banded fine-grained purple rock that originally consisted of sparse plagioclase phenocrysts in a spherulitic matrix. It has undergone a rather complete recrystallization, however, and the phenocrysts are now composed of a finely crystalline aggregate that is probably oligoclase, in a matrix consisting of irregular and poorly defined areas of quartz and oligoclase. The boundaries of these two minerals show no relation to the outlines of the old spherulites. Megascopic crystals of a red garnet and microscopic laths of tourmaline are also present.

[5] Loughlin, G. F., Geology and ore deposits of the Tintic mining district, Utah: U.S. Geol. Survey Prof. Paper 107, p. 62, 1919.

[6] Rosenbusch, Harry, Elemente der Gesteinslehre, 4th ed., by A. Osann, p. 416, Stuttgart, 1923.

[7] Daly, R. A., Igneous rocks and their origin, p. 21, New York, 1914.

[8] Loughlin, G. F., Geology and ore deposits of the Tintic mining district, Utah: U.S. Geol. Survey Prof. Paper 107, p. 52, 1919.

Alkali basalt.—Small outcrops of alkali basalt are exposed on both sides of Overland Canyon from about the mouth of Blood Canyon to the eastern border of the quadrangle. The rock is also found near the mouth of North Pass Canyon and in Rodenhouse Wash. The North Pass Canyon exposure appears to be a dike, but the others are flows. The small size and wide distribution of the present outcrops indicate that the rock formerly had a much greater extent.

The rock is dark gray in all exposures and is characterized by the presence of numerous small reddish-brown grains of iddingsite. All but the dike are vesicular, and the vesicles locally have a calcite filling. Phenocrysts of glassy pyroxene and of feldspar as much as an inch in length are found in the dike and in the more easterly outcrops.

The sections show that the chief constituents are olivine, largely altered to iddingsite, augite, and plagioclase. Magnetite, apatite, and amygdular calcite are present in minor amounts. Most of the iddingsite is deep reddish brown, but a little is distinctly yellowish. Its optical properties are similar to those of an iddingsite from Gatos Creek, Colorado, described by Ross and Shannon.[9] Augite is present in notable quantities. In a specimen taken from the outcrop south of the Midas mine one large group of augite crystals has a spherulitic habit. Both andesine and oligoclase are present in the rock. Andesine occurs as larger lath-shaped crystals, and the sodic oligoclase as small anhedrons. Olivine, iddingsite, augite, and andesine make up the bulk of the rock, with only a small amount of interstitial material. This, however, instead of being glassy, as in the typical intersertal texture, is holocrystalline and is composed of small crystals of iddingsite, augite, and oligoclase. In this material most of the apatite is concentrated as long, slender needles.

The strikingly porphyritic varieties from the eastern border of the quadrangle contain in addition to these minerals phenocrysts an inch or less in length of augite, andesine, quartz, and a potash-soda feldspar. The quartz phenocrysts are not abundant, and all show rather extreme resorption. The potash-soda feldspar is biaxial negative and has an optic angle (2V) estimated by C. S. Ross to be about 20°. Its indices of refraction are those of sanidine, α being 1.518 ± 0.003. The extinction angle on cleavage plates parallel to 010 are 4°–5° and on plates parallel to 001 up to 9°, indicating that the mineral must be triclinic. It shows no twinning. These properties are similar to those found by Iddings for a feldspar occurring in lithophysae in Yellowstone National Park, which analysis proved to contain 5.08 percent of Na_2O and 8.36 percent of K_2O.[10]

[9] Ross, C. S., and Shannon, E. V., The origin, occurrence, composition, and physical properties of the mineral iddingsite: U.S. Nat. Mus. Proc., vol. 67, p. 14, 1925.

[10] Iddings, J. P., Obsidian Cliff, Yellowstone National Park: U.S. Geol. Survey Seventh Ann. Rept., p. 268, 1888.

The presence of phenocrysts of this highly alkaline feldspar and quartz in certain of the lavas and its absence in others is thought to be the result of the rapidity with which the porphyries apparently consolidated. The lava on the eastern border of the quadrangle is much finer grained than the nonporphyritic varieties, and, although it is filled with vesicles, these are much smaller than normal, suggesting a cooling so rapid that the expelled volatile matter had no opportunity to collect. The result of so rapid a cooling would be the preservation of such phenocrysts as would otherwise be resorbed were the solidification more gradual.

These rocks closely resemble in mineralogic composition those grouped by Rosenbusch under the name alkali basalt, in his family of trachydolerites.[11] The texture is that of basaltic rocks, and the abundance of soda-rich plagioclase feldspar is indicative of their alkaline affinities.

A partial analysis of the rock indicates that the silica percentage is somewhat higher and the soda percentage somewhat lower than in the typical analyses of alkali basalts quoted by Rosenbusch, but the potash content is much higher than in the normal basalt. The specimen analyzed was obtained 1,200 feet northeast of benchmark 5509 in Overland Canyon. The rock here does not contain any of the large phenocrysts of potash-soda feldspar, and no potash mineral was recognized in the thin section, although the rock is holocrystalline. It is possible that the potash found by the analysis is present as a potassium-aluminum silicate in isomorphous combination with the plagioclase, but there is no evidence for this view other than the apparent absence of a potassium-bearing mineral in the mode.

Partial analysis of alkali basalt

[J. G. Fairchild, analyst]

SiO_2	47.36	K_2O	2.66
Na_2O	2.80		

Pyroclastic rocks.—Tuffs and breccias are exposed in the vicinity of Deep Creek, in Rodenhouse Wash, and in Blood Canyon.

The tuffaceous rocks west of Deep Creek and in Rodenhouse Wash are dark-purplish or reddish well-bedded rocks that contain larger fragments of andesine or labradorite, hornblende, and locally augite set in a matrix of glass fragments, which are locally devitrified, particularly near bedding planes. Most of the specimens examined are considerably altered. Another variety of tuff, which is poorly cemented, was found on the southwest slope of Twin Peaks. Except for a few small crystals of quartz, it is composed entirely of glass fragments, whose index of refraction is 1.495.

The breccias in the Deep Creek region are of small extent and, in part at least, fill old volcanic necks.

[11] Rosenbusch, Harry, Elemente der Gesteinslehre, 4th ed., by A. Osann, pp. 454–458, Stuttgart, 1923.

The rock fragments contained are entirely of the surrounding andesites or latites. The breccias in Rodenhouse Wash and Blood Canyon differ from those in the Deep Creek region in containing numerous fragments both of sedimentary rocks and of the quartz monzonite. The Rodenhouse Wash exposures are mostly well bedded and probably represent surface accumulations, but those in Blood Canyon are thoroughly altered and are thought to mark centers of eruption.

ALTERATION OF THE VOLCANIC ROCKS

Three kinds of alteration of the volcanic rocks have been recognized. One of these is thought to have been the result of reactions occurring before the complete consolidation of the lava. The other two, which affected the minerals in the groundmass as well as the phenocrysts, were considerably later. Of these an alteration characterized by a series of silica minerals with calcite was restricted to volcanic necks or their vicinity, but the other, in which zeolites were abundantly developed, had no apparent relation to the necks.

Some of the hornblende and magnetite and all of the iddingsite found in these lavas are clearly reaction products of the earlier-crystallized minerals with the still molten lava. A variety of chlorite with the optical properties of delessite seems to furnish a connecting link between these minerals and those produced by the other kinds of alteration, as it replaces augite, hornblende, biotite, and plagioclase phenocrysts and cuts the groundmass of various rocks in veinlets and in more irregular areas. In some places it has apparently been developed with magnetite in the alteration of biotite or hornblende, and in others it is associated with calcite, which as a rule is found with the later minerals. The conditions under which delessite forms seemingly have a wide range. A colorless chlorite whose index of refraction is much less than that of delessite has essentially the same habit as delessite but is not nearly as abundant. A mineral thought to be leverrierite was found with delessite in Blood Canyon, where it is locally abundant.

Evidence of the alteration characterized by silica minerals was found only in specimens from volcanic necks or in rocks adjacent to the necks. The silica minerals are locally associated with calcite and occur as veinlets ranging from those of microscopic size to some that are nearly a foot in width. In places the veinlets show enlargements with rather irregular outlines. Tridymite, opal, chalcedony, quartz, and calcite are found in the veinlets, and where the age relations can be determined the order of formation is that given, with tridymite earliest and calcite last.

The zeolitic alteration was rather widespread and affected both flows and pyroclastic rocks with no apparent relation to the sites of extrusion, although there are important exceptions in that two necks east of Deep Creek show a nearly complete replacement of plagioclase by thompsonite. The zeolites have replaced the feldspar phenocrysts and form irregular areas in the groundmass. Veinlets of the minerals are of minor extent. The minerals recognized are stilbite, analcite, thompsonite, and calcite. Locally these minerals are enclosed in veinlets of the silica minerals.

The differences in habit and occurrence of the minerals of the two groups prompt the suggestion that the silica series represents a concentration from a larger body of cooling rock than the zeolite series. The wide-spread occurrence of the zeolitic minerals indicates that the solutions which caused their formation were obtained from adjacent portions of the lava.

AGE OF THE VOLCANIC ROCKS

The volcanic rocks cannot be directly dated. So far as their relations to other rocks go, they are clearly younger than the Eocene (?) White Sage formation and the quartz monzonite, on both of which they rest unconformably. They are also thought to be younger than the Pliocene (?) sediments, which contain no pebbles of volcanic rock, although overlain by gravel which contains such pebbles. On the other hand, they are older than the Lake Bonneville sediments, from which they are separated by a period of considerable erosion. The Pliocene age of the prevolcanic sediments, however, is based (see p. 49) on their relations to the volcanic rocks. As far as stratigraphic evidence goes, therefore, the volcanic rocks are later than Eocene (?) and earlier than the Lake Bonneville Pleistocene. Geomorphic evidence, however, permits a somewhat closer dating. The volcanic rocks rest upon a surface which is very similar to the present one and which is clearly later than the normal faulting of the Basin Range type. The position of lavas and breccias in Rodenhouse Wash and Blood Canyon shows indisputably that they were erupted in valleys cut in an old topographic surface, the dissection of which was initiated by Basin Range faulting. The large area east of Deep Creek, moreover, apparently lies along the course of one of the Basin Range faults. Finally, the dike of alkali basalt in North Pass Canyon is thought to cut the gravel developed as a result of the faulting. The age of the Basin Range faulting is discussed on page 64, where it is shown that a Pliocene date is probable. With allowance for the prevolcanic erosion that has been noted, the date of eruption probably was in the later part of the Pliocene.

GRAVEL AND CLAY (PLIOCENE (?) TO RECENT)

About one-third of the area of the quadrangle is underlain by partly or completely unconsolidated sediments derived from the older rocks by weathering and erosion. They include gravel and clay deposited in the Pleistocene Lake Bonneville [12] in addition to

[12] Gilbert, G. K., Lake Bonneville: U.S. Geol. Survey Mon. 1, 1890.

terrestrial gravel and clay that are both older and younger than the lake beds. Locally these deposits may be readily distinguished from one another, but in many places the assignment of an exposure to a definite chronologic position is impossible, either because it is isolated or because there is no sharp line of division between beds which in one place were clearly deposited at one time and in a second placo at another. For the purposes of this report the beds will be arbitrarily grouped into three divisions—(1) older gravel and clay, (2) younger gravel and clay, (3) Lake Bonneville beds.

OLDER GRAVEL AND CLAY

At several places in the quadrangle there are exposures of gravel and clay which are clearly out of adjustment with regard to the present topography. These are thought to be remnants of deposits that were formed before the most recent faulting in the area. One area in which such gravel is displayed extends from North Pass Canyon north and east to the Midas mine. One almost continuous exposure of gravel in this area extends from the low ridge west of hill 6267, near the mouth of North Pass Canyon, northward to the divide between North Pass and Blood Canyons. Between these two places outcrops of bedrock are found at several points in the bottoms of gulches. The gravel lies as much as 450 feet above the present drainage channels. Here there appears to be almost no cementation of the beds. Pebbles and boulders as much as several feet in diameter lie in a matrix of smaller rock fragments and sand. The pebbles and boulders consist of rocks derived from formations exposed some distance to the west and north of the gravel outcrops, the formations adjacent to the gravel being almost entirely unrepresented. In Blood Canyon there are also gravel deposits on the higher slopes which are thought to be contemporaneous with those to the south. Still another area is south and southwest of the Midas mine, where the gravel is well cemented by calcium carbonate and contains almost no boulders of quartz monzonite, although there are extensive exposures of that rock immediately to the north. In all these localities there is some evidence to indicate that the gravel had been deposited before the volcanic rocks were erupted. (See p. 49.)

Clifton Flat is also underlain by material now being actively dissected. The beds consist chiefly of clay, with only a minor amount of coarser material. Near the road leading to Clifton they overlie volcanic rocks and may therefore be in part younger than the gravel near North Pass Canyon.

Another area in which old gravel is exposed is on the west side of Dutch Mountain in a belt that roughly parallels Trail Gulch. This gravel is apparently unconsolidated and in places, as in the isolated patch east of hill 6518, contains a great deal of clay. The rocks represented by the boulders are those exposed to the east. The gravel was clearly deposited under conditions differing from those of the present time. The isolated patch mentioned above, for example, is found at the head of a canyon that drops 400 feet in a horizontal distance of 3,000 feet. In Woodman Canyon ridges made up of gravel rise over 200 feet above the canyon bottom, which, in many places, is cut in solid rock.

These are the only areas in which the early age of the gravel or clay is definitely indicated. There are probably others, particularly north and northwest of Ochre Mountain and on the southeast side of Dutch Mountain, but in these the evidence is not clear.

YOUNGER GRAVEL AND CLAY

Several different kinds of sediment are included in the group of younger gravel and clay. The most extensive are the gravel deposits that flank all the highlands. These are poorly sorted, poorly stratified, and uncemented and do not differ materially from the gravel found throughout the Great Basin region. At least three stages of fairly recent deposition of the gravel was recognized. Less extensive are the sand and clay deposits in Deep Creek Valley, which lie above the level of Lake Bonneville. These occur not only along the present course of Deep Creek but also in a linear zone in the eastern parts of secs. 3, 10, 15, and 22, T. 9 S., R. 19 W. The younger gravel also includes the areas of talus mapped on the higher part of Dutch Mountain. These are limited to places in which the basal part of the Woodman formation is exposed. The sandstones which are so numerous at that horizon break up on weathering into small fragments and form talus slopes that conceal not only the beds of the Woodman but of the formation beneath.

LAKE BONNEVILLE BEDS

At the time of maximum extent of Lake Bonneville nearly one-fifth of the quadrangle was under water. For the most part the flooding by the lake waters resulted only in a reworking of previously deposited gravel. In two areas, however, lacustrine clay was deposited. These were in the Deep Creek Valley and in the northeast corner of the quadrangle.

In many places the reworking of the older gravel was slight and is expressed chiefly in distinct beach lines. Locally, however, especially where outcrops of hard rock influenced the shore currents, impressive shore features were developed. One of the most striking of these is the large hooked spit on the east side of Dutch Mountain. This is over a mile long and for much of this distance rises 600 feet above the gravel slope to the east. There is a smaller similar spit to the south on the north side of Tribune Gulch, and another on the south side of the prominent quartzite hill east of the Rube mine. All three of these were built up to the highest level of the lake, an altitude of about 5,200 feet.

Another prominent feature resulting from the reworking of older gravel by the Lake Bonneville waters is the bar half a mile south of the dry lake in Bar Creek. This narrow, even-topped ridge approaches the regularity of a railroad grade.

The clay deposits in the localities mentioned above are light-colored and calcareous and are similar to those found throughout the area formerly covered by the lake.[13]

GEOLOGIC STRUCTURE

The accompanying geologic maps (pls. 1 and 2) show a notable lack of continuity in the older sedimentary formations that is in large part the result of a protracted period of crustal unrest, during which these older rocks were warped and complexly faulted. By means of the mutual relations of the faults and, to a less extent, the folds, a structural history of the quadrangle was deciphered that appears to be unique for this portion of the Great Basin.

The determined sequence of events indicates that the deformation was cyclic in character, in that an initial stage in which compressive forces were active was followed by one in which normal faulting took place. (See p. 65.) Five cycles of this character were distinguished; the first two are thought to have been of Cretaceous or early Eocene age, the third was contemporaneous with the Eocene (?) White Sage formation, and the fourth and fifth are considered to have been of about the same age as the quartz monzonite intrusion.

There is a progressive variation in the character of the structural features developed during the successive cycles. Folding appears to have been dominant in the compressive stage of early cycles, low-angle thrust faults of large throw characterize this stage of the third cycle, and transverse or tear faults are particularly abundant in the later cycles. It is suggested that the change in character through the five cycles is the reflection of a progressively lighter load and that transverse faults have optimum conditions for their formation at or near the surface.

The normal faults that were formed in the second stage of each of the five cycles show a decrease in both number and intensity in the successive cycles. A possible explanation for this decrease is considered to be that the additional strength or rigidity imparted by the successive periods of compression made relaxational movements, as typified by the normal faults, less and less necessary.

A later period of normal faulting followed the development of a post-mature erosion surface over the older structural features. This later faulting is thought to have begun in late Pliocene time. The faults are not all strictly contemporaneous, and many of them utilized earlier fault planes.

[13] Gilbert, G. K., Lake Bonneville: U.S. Geol. Survey Mon. 1, p. 190, 1890. Nolan, T. B., Potash brines in the Great Salt Lake Desert, Utah: U.S. Geol.

STRUCTURAL CYCLES

In a region that is structurally as complex as the Gold Hill quadrangle, a detailed geographic description of folds and faults tends to conceal the succession of events and to becloud the correlation of related features that are widely separated areally. The following section gives a chronologic account of the major structural features and outlines their relations to one another. The detailed observations upon which this section is based are given on pages 66–91, where the structural features in each of the six structural blocks into which the quadrangle is divided are described geographically. The fault map of the quadrangle (pl. 3) and the geologic structure sections on plates 1 and 2 will be found useful in the reading of both discussions.

FIRST CYCLE

First stage.—Structural features assignable to the first stage of the first cycle were not widely recognized. This may be due in part to the impossibility of making age assignments for isolated features and in part to the probability of renewed movement along faults that first became active at this time. Two rather minor low-angle faults, thought to be thrusts, and local folds are found on the southwest flank of Ochre Mountain, and as they are cut by normal faults that definitely belong to the second stage of this cycle, they are considered to record an initial stage of compression.

The meager evidence available provides scant information as to the character of the compressive forces. Transverse faults appear to be absent, but the folds and reverse faults are so few and small that their relative importance is not known.

Second stage.—Several normal faults with relatively small throw on Ochre Mountain are clearly older than the minor thrusts that belong to the second cycle. There is also a group of small normal faults on Dutch Mountain of similar strike that are cut by faults of the second cycle. Both of these groups are therefore believed to represent a period of rather wide-spread normal faulting that followed the minor thrusting and folding of the first stage.

SECOND CYCLE

First stage.—Folds, thrusts, and transverse faults were formed during the first stage of the second cycle, but folding was far more intense than faulting. The continuity of the folds has been largely destroyed by the disturbances of later cycles, but the portions that can be examined leave no doubt that they were of considerable magnitude.

The Deep Creek Mountains south of North Pass Canyon appear to represent the western half of a major anticline whose axis coincides approximately with the eastern border of the mountains, as easterly dips are found in the Prospect Mountain quartzite south of Dry Canyon. In North Pass Canyon itself the Cam-

canyon show an anticlinal structure that is thought to be a continuation of that found farther south.

North of this anticline an equally large but unrelated anticline in Mississippian and Pennsylvanian rocks is exposed around the borders of the south half of Clifton Flat. A much-faulted core of Ochre Mountain limestone is overlain on each side by a large thickness of the Oquirrh formation. The beds of the Oquirrh on the west flank show some minor superposed folds that were probably formed during a later cycle.

A third large fold, a recumbent anticline, is best exposed on the southern flank of Twin Peaks in the northwestern part of the quadrangle, and its axis may be traced for some distance. The axial plane of the fold strikes about N. 15° E. over this area, but in detail it varies considerably because of later warping.

All three of these major folds are cut by normal faults that are older than the thrust faults formed during the succeeding cycle, and it is believed that they are therefore essentially contemporaneous. Their present close association is fortuitous, as each now lies in a separate thrust plate.

The thrusts that are contemporaneous with these folds are for the most part of minor importance. The only recognized large thrust of this age is found on Dutch Mountain. This has been called the Dutch Mountain thrust, as it has a nearly continuous outcrop around the crest of the mountain. Stratigraphically the thrust is not striking, because it has Ochre Mountain limestone above and the Woodman formation below—the normal sequence. The bedding of both formations is discordant to the contact, however, and the thickness of the underlying Woodman formation varies notably from place to place.

Continuations of the thrust are found to the south on peak 7011, on the south side of Pool Canyon, and, at a much lower altitude, on the west side of Accident Canyon. At both localities the relations are the same, the Ochre Mountain limestone resting upon the Woodman formations, but in these exposures the Woodman is considerably crumpled.

The segment near the mouth of Accident Canyon has a rather low dip, comparable to that shown by the thrust below the summit of Dutch Mountain. As the fault is traced south along Accident Canyon, however, the dip steepens and is as high as 60° at the point where it is cut off by a later normal fault. This zone of steeper dip between two portions with relatively flat dip must be an original feature of the thrust, as its origin by a later warping is precluded by the lack of similar warping in the adjacent beds. The absence of such warping is shown rather conclusively by the inliers of Madison limestone near the south end of the steeply dipping portion of the fault.

Some transverse faulting also occurred during this stage. The west-northwest fault in North Pass Canyon and the parallel Pool Canyon fault on Dutch Mountain appear to have been formed at this time. Other faults with similar strike became active in the third cycle, however, and locally it is difficult to distinguish between the two ages.

The dominant structural features of this stage of the second cycle are folds of considerable magnitude. Thrust faults are rather numerous but have relatively small displacements; and transverse faulting appears to have been of even less magnitude. The thrust faults appear to have been formed by the sliding of more resistant stratigraphic units over less resistant underlying beds, which yielded to the compression by crumpling. Their character, as well as the size of the folds, suggests that the deformation took place under a relatively heavy load. The strike of the transverse faults and the strike of the axis of the recumbent fold indicates that the compressive forces were directed from the west-northwest.

Second stage.—Normal faults that were formed during the second stage of the second cycle are found throughout the quadrangle. They do not appear to be quite as numerous as the faults of this character developed in the preceding cycle, but many of them have unusually large throws. Several of them are also characterized by the fact that they mark lines of weakness that persisted throughout several cycles.

The fault along the east base of the Deep Creek Mountains, for example, has a throw of 6,000 feet, of which 4,000 feet may be assigned to this cycle, as a thrust formed in the next cycle is displaced only 2,000 feet. Similarly the Spotted Fawn fault, on the east side of Dutch Mountain, has a throw of 2,000 feet, of which 1,500 feet, as shown by its relations to a thrust of the next cycle, can be assigned to this stage. The Trail Gulch fault, on the west side of Dutch Mountain, has had a comparable history. The Tank Wash and Bar Creek faults, in the northwestern part of the quadrangle, are also of this class, with total throws of about 4,000 and 5,000 feet respectively, of which the greater part took place during this stage.

THIRD CYCLE

First stage.—In the first stage of the third cycle large-scale overthrusting was accompanied by relatively minor transverse faulting and slight folding. Two large overthrusts were formed during this stage—an earlier one, which appears to have been limited between two transverse faults, and a later one, which has overridden the earlier structure. A long period of erosion is thought to have separated the beginning of this cycle from the last stage of the preceding one. Although the total movement along either of the thrusts cannot be determined from the evidence provided within the quadrangle, it must have been rather large, because distinctive facies of the Carboniferous formations are found above each of the thrusts (p. 23 and fig. 5).

The earlier or North Pass thrust is exposed in only a few places, but the distribution of the central facies of the Carboniferous rocks makes it fairly certain that the thrust extends as far north as the Pool Canyon transverse fault, on the south side of Dutch Mountain.

In North Pass Canyon the thrust is exposed in only one small outcrop. Minor structural features accompanying the thrust are locally well exposed, however, and by piecing these together a fairly adequate picture of the structural conditions may be obtained. The most striking of these minor features are found on the west flank of the anticline and north of the transverse fault along the floor of the valley, both of which were formed in the preceding cycle. They consist of thrust plates of the more resistant pre-Carboniferous formations that have overridden the axis of the anticline. The plates decrease in number and in thickness eastward, and at the mouth of the canyon, north of hill 6267, only one 100-foot plate, which is composed of Laketown dolomite, remains. This plate is overlain by beds of the Oquirrh formation that are essentially continuous with the large outcrop that nearly surrounds Clifton Flat. The contact between the shattered Laketown dolomite and the Oquirrh formation is the plane of the North Pass thrust.

The minor thrusts very clearly are limited southward by the older transverse fault, and it seems rather certain that the main North Pass thrust was also so limited, as it is nowhere exposed to the south, although many places along the ridge lines reach sufficiently high altitudes to have been cut by the thrust if it had originally extended that far.

The relations of the thrust plates beneath the main thrust to the older anticline are those that would result had the anticline been deeply eroded and then subjected to compression from the west, the more competent beds on the western limb of the fold riding forward over the eroded core and extending for short distances farther east. This in turn implies that the main thrust at this locality was also moving over a surface of erosion. A measure of the amount of erosion is given by the normal fault along the eastern front of the Deep Creek Mountains, which had a pre-thrust throw of 4,000 feet. By the time of the thrusting, however, erosion must have completely beveled across the fault, for the thin plate of Laketown dolomite crossed it without interruption.

The North Pass thrust may also be located rather closely at two other localities—along the Lincoln Highway south of Ochre Mountain and in the southeast corner of the quadrangle. These provide a measure of the minimum movement along the thrust, for they are about 9 miles apart in a direction approximately at right angles to the strike of the thrust.

The North Pass thrust appears to be limited northward by the Pool Canyon transverse fault, as the Carboniferous formations of the central facies that overlie the thrust are cut off by the transverse fault; north of the fault lower Paleozoic formations are exposed that are thought to be the continuation of those exposed south of the parallel transverse fault in North Pass Canyon. The North Pass thrust cannot be recognized north of the Pool Canyon fault, and evidence is provided by a nearly contemporaneous thrust that it was never present in that region.

The limitation of the North Pass thrust between two transverse faults that are, in part at least, older than the thrust is thought to be the result of the erosion that took place between the second and third cycles, which appears to have exposed the resistant Prospect Mountain quartzite both to the north and south of the transverse faults and thus prevented the overriding that is found between the faults, where the quartzite was deeply buried.

The second major thrust, the Ochre Mountain thrust, has a wider extent and is well exposed on both Ochre Mountain and Dutch Mountain. On the south side of Ochre Mountain this thrust abuts against a younger transverse fault, beyond which it has been almost entirely removed by erosion, and on the north it disappears beneath the gravel flanking Dutch Mountain.

The Ochre Mountain thrust, like the North Pass thrust, is thought to be an "erosion thrust" in the sense that the overriding block moved over the then existent surface. The chief evidence for this belief is found in the behavior of the overriding block where the thrust crosses the Pool Canyon transverse fault. Although there has been an intrusion of quartz monzonite along the transverse fault, the major relations between the two faults are readily seen. The thrust is clearly the younger, as there is no sign of the transverse fault in the beds above the thrust. North of the transverse fault a gently dipping sequence of beds with Madison limestone at the base lies above the thrust. South of the transverse fault, however, the beds are considerably disturbed and are even locally overturned, and beds high in the Woodman formation lie immediately above the thrust. South of the transverse fault, also, the thrust is about 300 feet higher than it is to the north. The relations outlined indicate that the overriding thrust plate was considerably hindered in its forward movement at this place, and it seems probable that the structural features in the overridden beds would prove to be an obstacle only if they were exposed at the surface at the time of thrusting. The occurrence of thin thrust plates of a single formation below the main thrust on both Dutch Mountain and the north slope of Ochre Mountain also imply, as in the North Pass thrust, that the Ochre Mountain thrust reached the surface.

In addition to the nearly continuous outcrops of the Ochre Mountain thrust on Ochre Mountain and Dutch Mountain, the thrust is exposed in several places in roof pendants within the quartz monzonite stock and also in "windows" on the northwest slope of Dutch Mountain and within Ochre Mountain. The minimum movement along the thrust as indicated by these exposures may be placed at 4 miles, but obviously the total amount is much more, as the lithologic differences between the two facies of the Carboniferous formations persist throughout this distance.

The Ochre Mountain thrust and the North Pass thrust have been placed in the same structural cycle, because each of them has the same relations to the faults and folds of other cycles. In Pool Canyon the Ochre Mountain thrust is clearly shown to be the younger of the two, although there is some evidence at that place to indicate that the age difference is not great. The thin-bedded limestones and sandstones of the Oquirrh formation beneath the thrust south of the Pool Canyon transverse fault are much less resistant to erosion than the massive lower Paleozoic dolomites north of it. The weaker beds now stand at a higher altitude, however, and as the Ochre Mountain thrust appears to have moved over the surface at this point, it follows that they must also have been at a higher altitude at the time that thrust was active. This in turn implies that but little time could have elapsed between the Ochre Mountain thrust and the North Pass thrust, which brought the weaker beds into the position they now have.

The slight difference in age between the two thrusts provides additional evidence that the North Pass thrust was limited northward by the Pool Canyon transverse fault, for north of that fault the Ochre Mountain thrust plate rests upon lower Paleozoic formations without the intervening mass of Carboniferous rocks that forms the North Pass thrust plate. As the two thrusts were almost contemporaneous there was obviously no time for the North Pass thrust plate to be eroded north of the Pool Canyon fault before the Ochre Mountain thrust was formed, and it must therefore never have extended that far.

The two major thrust faults were accompanied by many small thrusts, and in addition there appears to have been a reversal of movement along at least one of the older normal faults during this stage. On the western or hanging-wall side of the Trail Gulch fault, for example, the Oquirrh formation shows several small folds that in places are overturned; similar folds are absent in the footwall. Furthermore, neither this fault nor the beds on its hanging wall have been affected by the deformation shown by the Ochre Mountain thrust and the Mississippian beds above the thrust in the region where the thrust crosses the Pool Canyon transverse fault. Both of these features are most readily explained by the assumption of renewed movement along the Trail Gulch fault, by which beds on one side of the fault could be deformed independently of those on the other side.

Folding during this stage was confined to the relatively small drag folds that are associated with the thrusts and with the renewed movement along the Trail Gulch fault. Some gentle broad warping may have taken place, such as the warping of the axial plane of the recumbent anticline of the second cycle, but it appears to have been of minor intensity.

Several west-northwest transverse faults also appear to be of this age, as they have the same relations as the major thrusts to other faults. Some transverse faults of this strike became active during the second cycle, however, and others, such as the Pool Canyon fault, must have been active during both cycles.

This stage of the third cycle appears to have been initiated, after a protracted period of erosion that followed the second cycle, by a long period of thrusting. The two most extensive overthrust masses in this region both moved over the then existing surface. Transverse faults were formed in moderate abundance, but only minor folds. All these features are thought to indicate that the deformation took place under a relatively light load. As the transverse faults correspond in strike to those of the preceding cycle, it is thought that the compression came from the west-northwest.

Second stage.—The normal faults of the second stage are neither abundant nor of large throw. On Dutch Mountain and Ochre Mountain much of the normal faulting of this stage took place along older faults. In both areas most of the faults of this age cut the Ochre Mountain thrust, and the difference in throw of the thrust and of the rocks below the thrust provides a measure of the later movement, which in all the examples known has been relatively small.

FOURTH CYCLE

First stage.—The principal structural features of the first stage of the fourth cycle are four nearly east-west transverse faults, along which the horizontal movement may have been a mile or more. Minor steep thrusting and a small amount of gentle warping accompanied the transverse faulting, and two series of faults that are thought to have conjugate relations are associated with the most northerly transverse fault (pp. 83–84).

These transverse faults cut both the major overthrusts of the preceding cycle and the normal faults that followed the overthrusting. For this reason as well as the change in the strike of the transverse faulting, they are considered to represent a new structural cycle.

The most southerly of the transverse faults is the Dry Canyon fault. It appears to have a nearly vertical dip throughout its exposed extent of 4 miles. The beds on the north side of the fault have been shifted about 1,000 feet to the east.

The other three faults have somewhat more complex relations. The Blood Canyon transverse fault may be traced for nearly 8 miles and over much of this distance has a steep dip similar to that of the Dry Canyon fault. To the east, however, its dip is notably flatter, and the thin-bedded members of the Oquirrh formation adjacent to it show complex crumplings that are absent away from the fault. A measurement of the movement along this fault is difficult, because for a considerable distance it separates the overriding block of the North Pass thrust from the overridden block. However, on the basis of the correlation of two older west-northwest transverse faults that are found on the two sides of the Blood Canyon fault, the south side is thought to have moved about a mile to the east.

The transverse fault on the south slope of Ochre Mountain also flattens notably eastward. The change in dip here appears to coincide with the presence of the Ochre Mountain thrust in the block south of the fault. The throw along the transverse fault cannot be exactly determined but must be large, because the Oquirrh formation overlies the Ochre Mountain thrust south of the fault, whereas to the north the Ochre Mountain limestone is above the thrust. If the block south of the transverse fault has moved to the east, as would seem probable from the fact that the thrust is at a higher altitude on this side, a minimum movement of 3 miles appears necessary. The thrust has been considerably warped adjacent to the transverse fault, however, and the north side may therefore have moved to the east; in that case the movement may be nearer to 1 mile.

The remaining major transverse fault of this stage, the Garrison Monster fault, is the most complex of the group. Its exposures are for the most part at or near the altitudes at which the Ochre Mountain thrust crops out, and the structural complexities observed appear to be the result of this coincidence, for to the east, at altitudes well below the thrust, the transverse fault is a simple steep fracture. To the west, near the thrust, the simple fault is replaced by a zone of moderately northward-dipping faults, which effect the same displacement as the single fault to the east. The strike of some of the faults in this zone changes to northeast and east-northeast as they extend westward and southward. Such continuations may show either normal or reverse faulting, but because of their relations to the faults in the transverse fault zone itself it seems certain that the dominant movement along them has been horizontal.

The amount of horizontal movement along the transverse fault in the vicinity of the Garrison Monster mine must have been about 1½ miles, the rocks north of the fault moving to the east. Westward in the fault zone, however, both the number of faults in the zone and the amount of displacement decrease, and in the low hills that end the northwesterly spur of Dutch Mountain the fault zone can no longer be recognized.

The behavior of the Ochre Mountain thrust on both sides of the transverse fault appears to throw some light on the mechanics of faults of this type. North of the transverse fault exposures are few but are sufficient to show that the thrust surface cannot be greatly deformed but must rise with a relatively gentle slope to the east. South of the transverse fault, however, the numerous outcrops indicate that the thrust plane has been folded into a shallow syncline whose axis roughly parallels Accident Canyon and a marked anticline that coincides more or less closely with the crest of Dutch Mountain. The anticlinal axis appears to die out southwestward.

The block north of the transverse fault, which has apparently undergone no folding, has moved eastward relative to the folded block to the south, suggesting that the true movement may have been westward by the southern block. There are several objections to this supposition, however—one being that in the previous cycles the true direction of movement, wherever determinable, has been eastward. A more weighty objection lies in the fact that the Garrison Monster fault must curve to the north beyond its present most easterly outcrop, as it is clearly absent in the exposures of Prospect Mountain quartzite east and south of its projected continuation. The change in strike to the northeast is difficult to reconcile with a westward movement of the southern block.

An eastward movement of the block north of the transverse fault, combined with the lack of contemporaneous folding in the block, suggests that the crustal shortening required by the movement was accomplished by thrusting, and the change in strike of the transverse fault eastward may be interpreted as marking the line of overriding. The folding and minor reverse faulting in the block south of the transverse fault is of sufficient magnitude to account for the shortening required on that side, and the fact that the folding dies out southward appears to confirm the conclusion that the northern block was the active one.

The general relations of the Garrison Monster transverse fault are shown diagrammatically in figure 8. It is not known how widely applicable these relations are to the other transverse faults in the quadrangle, but the lack of outcrops east of the similar transverse fault on the south side of Ochre Mountain suggest strongly that it also passes into a thrust. The flattening of the Blood Canyon fault eastward may also indicate that the same relations hold for it.

The compressive forces of this stage seem to have been relieved by movements that were accomplished under a very light load, for the dominance of faulting over folding is extreme, faults on the north side of Dutch Mountain even appearing to replace some of the drag effects that would normally be expected to accompany transverse faults of this magnitude.

Second stage.—There appears to have been essentially no normal faulting in the fourth cycle. In the Ochre Mountain and Dutch Mountain blocks there are a few faults that may belong to the second stage of this cycle, but it is difficult to distinguish them from the conjugate faults of the first stage.

FIFTH CYCLE AND FAULTS RELATED TO THE QUARTZ MONZONITE INTRUSION

The structural features developed in the first four cycles are all earlier than the quartz monzonite intrusion, for at different places features of each cycle are terminated by the intrusive contact. In some places, however, the intrusive rocks are affected by small thrust faults, notably east of hill 5675, on the north side of Rodenhouse Wash, and in a tunnel on the northeast side of Ochre Mountain, and these are thought to indicate a relatively minor recurrence of the compressive forces that were so active in the preceding cycles.

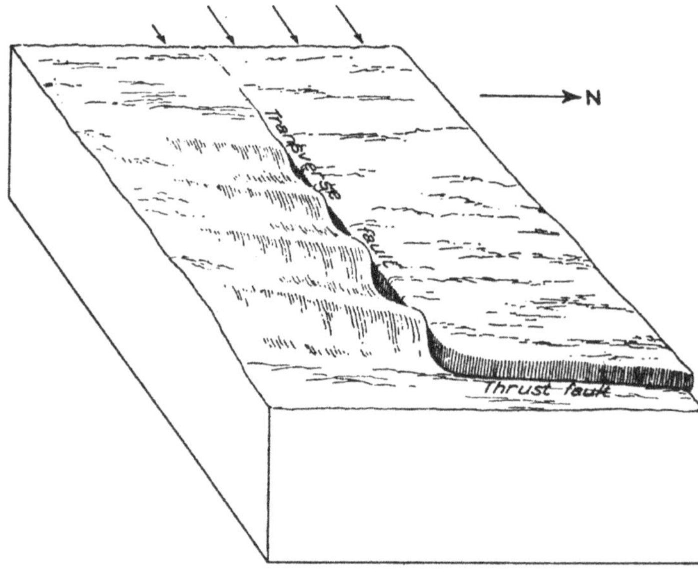

FIGURE 8.—Block diagram showing the generalized structure along the Garrison Monster transverse fault.

In addition to these faults, there are several other faults in or adjacent to the quartz monzonite stock that are thought to have a causal relation to it. One group of these faults is localized along and is parallel to the western border of the intrusion and has caused very large displacements in the Ochre Mountain thrust plane. Partly because faults of this magnitude do not cut the thrust at other localities and partly because the zone coincides with a belt of ore deposits that are characterized by high-temperature minerals, the fault zone is thought to mark the location of the primary channel through which the stock was intruded.

A much larger group of faults is distributed throughout the intrusive area. These faults have everywhere a small throw, but have very diverse orientation as well as time relations. They are thought to have resulted from the stresses set up at intervals during the slow cooling of the stock.

PROGRESSIVE VARIATION IN THE CHARACTER OF DEFORMATION

In the summary account of the five cycles in the preceding pages, mention was made of an apparent dominance in each cycle of certain types of structure. Thus the first cycle was characterized by an abundance of normal faults; the second by folds, with only a minor amount of thrusting and transverse faulting, followed by a few normal faults of large throw; the third, by predominant thrusting succeeded by minor normal faulting; and the fourth, by transverse faults accompanied by faults along which the chief movement appears to have been horizontal. The fourth cycle also appears to have had but little normal faulting.

Because of the dominance of folding and the character of the thrusting in the second cycle, it was deduced that the deformation proceeded under a moderately heavy load. The absence of folding and the abundance and character of the thrusts and transverse faults in the third and fourth cycles prompted the suggestion that the load was considerably lighter during these times.

The fact that the load appears to have been less in the more recent cycles of deformation is not in itself surprising, for it would appear to be the natural result of a progressively greater sum total of erosion during a long-continued period of diastrophism. The interesting feature, however, is the implication that transverse faults, which overshadow in importance other structural forms in the fourth cycle, have optimum conditions for their formation at a time when the overlying cover is at a minimum.

This relation cannot of course be regarded as proved from the evidence in the Gold Hill quadrangle. It might be considered, for example, that as transverse faults were formed in both the second and the third cycles their apparent dominance in the fourth cycle is not real and is a result of incomplete exposures. Furthermore, the change in strike of the transverse faults of the fourth cycle, which indicates a change in the direction of the causative force, might be taken to mean that the conditions accompanying the compression also changed in a way to favor transverse faulting rather than folding or thrusting. Although neither of these objections can be successfully refuted from the evidence at hand, the relations displayed by some of these faults, particularly the Garrison Monster transverse fault, suggest strongly that there is a causal relation between transverse faulting and a relatively light load.

The apparent decrease in the amount and intensity of normal faulting in the successive cycles cannot be readily explained by a progressive decrease in load. A widely accepted theory to explain the sequence of folding or thrusting followed by normal faulting assumes that the normal faults are in the nature of relaxational movements to restore equilibrium after excess compressional movements that originated through a lack of immediate resistance in the earth's crust. Although there are some objections to this theory, it appears to provide an explanation for the progressive variation in the normal faulting. It would appear that during the initial period of compression, in the first cycle, the crust in this area was notably deficient in its resistance to compressive movements in excess of those necessary to relieve the stress; on the relief of the compression, therefore, a large amount of normal faulting occurred. When the compressive forces of the second cycle became effective, however, the local crust may have become sufficiently strengthened or rigid during the preceding compression, perhaps by reduction of pore space or by recrystallization or some similar process, to resist the compressive forces much more effectively, and therefore it underwent much less subsequent normal faulting. Each successive period of compression would thus strengthen the crust, so that in the fourth cycle relatively little excess movement occurred during compression, and, as a result, practically no normal faulting was necessary at the end of the cycle.

LATE NORMAL FAULTING AND ITS RELATION TO THE PRESENT TOPOGRAPHY

In addition to the folds and faults developed during the five structural cycles and during the intrusion of the quartz monzonite, there are several normal faults that are considered to be of relatively recent age, because of their topographic relations. In the present section these faults, which are shown on plate 3, will be considered as a group and their supposed influence on the development of the present topography described.

A feature whose recognition leads to a considerably increased knowledge of these late faults is a dissected erosion surface that has been partly preserved in certain areas in the quadrangle. The surface, judged from these remnants, must have been well past maturity and have approached the condition of a peneplain. It is best exposed southeast and southwest of the town of Gold Hill (pl. 6, *C*, *D*), where it is represented by a group of closely spaced hills and ridges, all of which have an altitude close to 6,000 feet. The drainage pattern of this area is also that of postmaturity, contrasting strongly with the youthful drainage found on the west side of Ochre Mountain and in the Deep Creek Mountains.

It seems improbable that a surface such as this could have been originally limited to an area as small as the present one. Therefore, when remnants of a postmature surface in other parts of the quadrangle were recognized, they were correlated with this one, and the differences in altitude were considered to give a measure of the movement along the late normal faults that separate these remnants.

The fault most directly connected with the old erosion surface is that along the west sides of Ochre Mountain and the Deep Creek Mountains. Although there is no direct stratigraphic evidence for it, the convergence of several kinds of reasoning leaves little doubt as to its presence. First of all, the remarkably linear boundary between the mountains and the gravel-filled valley is extremely suggestive of faulting, as it transgresses the geologic structure to a notable degree. The rock-floored pass on the south side of Ochre Mountain through which the Lincoln Highway enters the Deep Creek Valley, together with the youthful character of the drainage all along the mountain front, also implies recent uplift. Additional evidence is provided by the fact that the eastern slope of Ochre Mountain is a tilted continuation of the old erosion surface southeast of the town of Gold Hill. The close relationship between the two surfaces is shown by the absence of any distinct topographic break between them, by the presence on the eastern slope of the mountain of a partly entrenched drainage system that is approximately equivalent in maturity to that in the region near the town, and by the presence of a moderately deep soil on the ridges of this portion of the mountain. This tilted surface on the eastern slope of Ochre Mountain (pl. 6, *A*) contrasts strongly with the abrupt western front, with its excellent exposures and youthful drainage pattern (pl. 6, *B*).

The fault must terminate rather abruptly northward about at its intersection with the trail from Gold Hill to the Erickson ranch, because to the north the old surface continues across the line of the fault unaffected. Southward the fault continues for several miles beyond the southern border of the quadrangle. The throw along the fault cannot be definitely determined. From the evidence of tilting on Ochre Mountain it is apparent that the block east of the fault must have moved upward about 1,500 feet. The block west of the fault is covered by gravel, but it must have been depressed at least 1,000 feet, as shown by the altitude of the gravel. It is rather strongly indicated, therefore, that the movement along the fault has been accomplished by a combination of elevation in the footwall block and depression in the hanging-wall block.

The fault just described is matched on the east side of the mountain area by two major and probably several minor faults of relatively recent age. The more southerly of the two major faults is indicated by stratigraphic as well as physiographic evidence. This is the fault along the eastern front of the Deep Creek Mountains south of Overland Canyon. There has been a 2,000-foot throw along this fault subsequent to the North Pass thrust (see p. 68), which is thought to be of relatively recent date. This figure corresponds with the difference in altitude between the low hills east of the fault and the long east-west ridges on each side of North Pass Canyon, both of which are considered to be remnants of the old erosion surface.

The surface represented by the low hills east of the fault may be continued through Blood Canyon to Clifton Flat and thence north to the type area south of Gold Hill. The correlation of the east-west ridges is less evident. In the first place, the ridge lines on both sides of Dry, Sheep, and North Pass Canyons reach altitudes on their east ends that are about the same as those found throughout the ridge. This, combined with the youthful, essentially unforked drainage, seems to require an original relatively flat surface that has been recently uplifted and has undergone relatively little erosion except along the master streams. This view appears to be confirmed by several areas characterized by poor exposures, owing to deep weathering and slight relief along the ridge lines, as at the head of the south fork of Dry Canyon and at the head of Sheep Canyon.

The ridge lines have progressively lower altitudes from south to north. The higher areas surrounding Uiyabi Canyon continue the trend still farther northward. The region about the canyon, however, is topographically the continuation of the east side of Ochre Mountain and therefore provides the connecting link between the nearly flat but elevated portion of the surface to the south with the tilted portion on Ochre Mountain. This rather devious attempt to establish the topographic throw along the fault would not be particularly convincing were it not for the coincidence of the topographic displacement with the stratigraphic throw at the mouth of the North Pass Canyon.

The fault has been traced northward to the south edge of Clifton Flat. Both the topographic and the stratigraphic throws decrease in this direction, but the latter cannot be quantitatively evaluated here. The fault cannot be recognized on the north side of the flat and presumably dies out beneath it. South of the quadrangle the fault must continue for many miles along the eastern front of the Deep Creek Mountains.

The southern part of the Deep Creek Mountains as included within the quadrangle is thus composed of an uplifted block bounded on each side by a depressed block. Northward this structure passes into a tilted block by the dying out of the eastern boundary fault. The uplifted block to the south is, in one sense, a horst. Strictly considered, however, it is not, for the two faults on its sides are very probably of different ages, the eastern fault being the older. This conclusion is reached by a consideration of the position of the divide, which is more than 3 miles from the eastern fault and less than 2 miles from the western fault. On the east side, moreover, the range is fronted by the resistant Prospect Mountain quartzite. It is therefore rather certain that the eastern fault was the earlier, because there must have been time for the consequent drainage along it to cut back through harder rocks, nearly twice the distance that the streams have cut across the western fault.

The second of the two major faults on the east side of the mountain area that balance the fault on the west side must follow the eastern boundary of the quadrangle closely. There is no stratigraphic evidence for this fault, but there are two physiographic features that seem to require it. One is the linear character of the mountain front south of benchmark 4767 on the Lincoln Highway, which is continued, south of the hilly region, by the line of outcrops in the southeast corner of the quadrangle and beyond. The other is a deformation of the old erosion surface west of the supposed fault. As this is traced southward from its exposures around Gold Hill, it is seen to be gradually tilted to the west. The tilting must have been accomplished by an elevation of the east side while the west side, as represented by the surfaces bordering Clifton Flat, remained stationary. The maximum tilt appears to have been in the latitude of Montezuma Peak, which rises more than 1,000 feet above the undeformed surface. The course of Rodenhouse Wash offers strong confirmatory evidence for such a tilting. The decrease in tilting to the south corresponds to the approximate point of termination of the fault south of Overland Canyon, which therefore is en échelon with the one now being discussed.

The basinlike depression of Clifton Flat appears to have resulted from the movements along the three faults just described. The flat is bordered on the east, south, and west by high lands; on the north, however, it is continuous with the much dissected old erosion surface. Apparently the border faults east of Montezuma Peak and west of Ochre Mountain were so far apart that the tilting of the surface which accompanied the faulting affected only slightly or not at all the region now occupied by the depression.

The old surface to the south was uplifted by means of the southern of the two eastern border faults. The present outlines of the basin are apparently due to the difference in age between the eastern and western border faults. The southern of the two eastern faults is clearly older than the western one, and, as the northern fault has en échelon relations with the southern, it too is presumably older than the western fault. As a result of this earlier faulting, a drainage channel appears to have formed extending westward from Montezuma Peak.

With the initiation of movement along the western border fault, this drainage channel kept pace with the gradual elevation of the block east of the fault by an equally rapid excavation of its bed, before the process was terminated by the headward erosion of Overland Canyon. Before this event happened, however, about 1,000 feet of rock must have been removed at the site of the present pass through which the Lincoln Highway descends into the valley of Deep Creek. The net result was to give the depression its present roughly triangular shape rather than the linear shape with northward drainage that it would have possessed if the three faults had been exactly contemporaneous.

The recent normal faulting in the northern third of the quadrangle is entirely distinct from that just described. This is indicated by the presence in the latitude of the Gold Hill town site of remnants of the old surface at accordant altitudes from the eastern border of the quadrangle almost to the western border. North of this zone several of these faults have been recognized.

Movement along the most easterly fault of the northern group shown on plate 3 is thought to be the cause of the present altitude of Dutch Mountain. This fault is wholly concealed by alluvium, and the chief evidence of its presence, aside from the drainage pattern along the east side of the mountain, is the difference of nearly 2,000 feet in altitude that separates the old erosion surface around the town of Gold Hill from the summit of Dutch Mountain. The considerable dissection of the east side of Dutch Mountain suggests that the fault must be somewhat older than that on the east side of the Deep Creek Mountains, which also has the Prospect Mountain quartzite on the uplifted side.

The two faults on the west side of Dutch Mountain can be shown with more certainty. The more westerly, along the western base of the mountain, bends from a southeasterly to an easterly course and appears to coincide with an older transverse fault. Remnants of the old erosion surface are preserved on the ridges east of the fault, and their altitude as compared with the altitude of similar remnants on the hanging-wall side of the fault near its south end indicate that the east side has been elevated about 500 feet.

The eastern fault represents renewed movement along a portion of the Trail Gulch fault. Several bits of evidence testify to its presence—the topographic discordance, its influence upon the drainage pattern, and the high-level gravel immediately west of the fault. The displacement along the fault cannot be exactly determined, because the position of the old erosion surface in the uplifted block cannot be determined, but the throw must be at least 800 feet.

The fault in the northwestern part of the quadrangle is also thought to follow a line of older faulting. The total throw of this fault as determined stratigraphically is much too great to account for the present distribution of the White Sage formation, and it is suggested that there has been renewed movement whose magnitude may be estimated from the topography on each side as from 600 to 800 feet. This suggestion is based on the presence, west of the fault, of a postmature erosion surface at an altitude of about 5,600 feet, in which Deep Creek and its tributaries are entrenched. East of the fault the country is considerably dissected, but there appears to be no topographic break between it and the type area of the old surface around Gold Hill. Several of the summits near the fault reach an altitude of 6,200 feet, however, and it is thought that, in addition to the required depression of about 400 feet west of the fault, there must have been an elevation of at least 200 feet in the block east of it. The sum of these two agrees fairly well with the figures indicated by the observed distribution of the White Sage formation.

Gilbert [14] has described even more recent normal faulting in the Lake Bonneville beds on the east side of the range. This locality was not examined by the writer, and the extent of the faulting of this age is not known.

The relatively recent normal faulting shown in the Gold Hill quadrangle is not as spectacular as that in many other regions in the Great Basin, but the mechanics of the process is seemingly well illustrated. The characteristics of the faulting in this quadrangle may be summarized as follows:

1. The faults are by no means contemporaneous.
2. They exhibit a strong tendency to utilize earlier fault lines.
3. Displacements along them were accomplished by movements of both the hanging-wall and footwall blocks.
4. Both elevation and depression appear to have been accomplished by tilting of the affected blocks. At relatively short distances away from the fault the tilt is no longer discernible.
5. They were initiated after a long period of stability, during which the surface was reduced to a state of postmaturity.
6. The faults may terminate abruptly.
7. En échelon relations among the faults are found.
8. Both curving and straight faults were formed.
9. Apparent horsts, and presumably also graben, may result from two faults of somewhat different ages.
10. The faults have no obvious relation to the igneous rocks exposed within the quadrangle, being much younger than the intrusive quartz monzonite and older than the volcanic rocks.

During the field work scant attention was given to the minor topographic changes that followed the normal faulting of this age. Casual observations indicated, however, that the quadrangle contains a wealth of material bearing upon the postfault history, and that detailed work would produce a great deal of information concerning the climatic changes that have occurred not only since Lake Bonneville time but also in the earlier stages of the lake.

AGE OF THE STRUCTURAL FEATURES

The age of the faults and folds formed during the five structural cycles can best be determined by their relations to the Lower Triassic limestone, the Eocene (?) White Sage formation, and the quartz monzonite stock, which was probably intruded in late Eocene or

[14] Gilbert, G. K., Lake Bonneville: U.S. Geol. Survey Mon. 1, p. 353, 1890.

early Oligocene time (p. 48). All the cycles are younger than the Triassic, as the Triassic limestone is a unit of the nearly conformable stratigraphic column affected by the structural disturbances.

The first and second cycles are older than the White Sage formation, as the beds of this formation unconformably overlie both the recumbent anticline that was formed in the first stage of the second cycle and the normal faults that were active in the second stage. As there are no recorded periods of orogeny during early Mesozoic time in the eastern Great Basin, the structural features of the first and second cycles may be tentatively classed as of Cretaceous or early Eocene age.

Normal faults that are considered to belong in the second stage of the third cycle cut the White Sage formation at several places in the northwestern part of the quadrangle, and in at least one locality (p. 43) there are considerable discordances in dip between beds within the formation. These features are thought to indicate that the formation was deposited during the final stages of the compression that caused the first stage of the third cycle, and the faults and folds of this cycle are considered to be of Eocene age.

The structural features of the fourth cycle are younger than the White Sage formation but are cut off by the quartz monzonite intrusion and must therefore date from late Eocene or early Oligocene time. The similarity in strike of the transverse faults of this cycle to the minor transverse faults of the fifth cycle, which cut the intrusive, suggests that the time interval between these two cycles was small.

In a recent review of the thrust faults previously described in the northern Rocky Mountains, Mansfield [15] notes that "these faults were in all probability not synchronous but some occurred later than others. This fact indicates that the compressive stresses that produced the overthrusts were maintained over a considerable period and that they found relief at more or less distinct successive intervals—a conclusion that should naturally be expected in view of the greatness of the region affected and of the tremendous stresses involved."

The Gold Hill quadrangle appears to be unique among those so far mapped in that it exhibits several of the successive thrusts. The reason for such a localization of thrusts of different ages in one area instead of the ideal sequence of successively younger thrusts from west to east postulated by Thom,[16] is not clear. In contrast to other regions of thrusting, Gold Hill is not at or particularly near the limits of earlier sedimentation, and therefore the localization of thrusts within the quadrangle cannot be ascribed to the influence of "initial dip," as has been done in other areas. A possible explanation of this sort might be considered to lie in the presence immediately to the east of Schuchert's positive area, "Utah." [17]

The writer, however, is more inclined to regard the thick Pennsylvanian sedimentary prism in the Oquirrh Mountains [18] as the most important factor. Rocks of this age are so much thinner within short distances both to the east and west that there must have been a marked original depositional syncline. Initiation of compression from the west would tend to increase the synclinal fold and permit overriding by the thinner sedimentary column to the west. Successive periods of compression would only accentuate the syncline, and thrusting would thus be localized in the zone immediately to the west.

The age of the relatively recent normal faulting cannot be definitely fixed. Gilluly [19] has recently summarized the evidence at hand regarding the age of faulting of this type in the Great Basin region. He notes that the initiation of faulting appears to differ in different regions. He concludes that in the Oquirrh Range the faults now expressed by the present topography probably became active at some time between the Oligocene and the upper Pliocene. In the Gold Hill quadrangle the direct evidence consists in the observations that the faulting is younger than a mature erosion surface developed upon both the sedimentary rocks and the quartz monzonite and is older than the volcanic rocks and is also probably older than the Pliocene (?) sediments. As the age of the Pliocene (?) formation is purely speculative, it has no immediate bearing upon the age of the faulting. The writer prefers the younger of the two ages set by Gilluly for the inception of the Gold Hill faulting, because of the fact that time must be allowed for the exposure of the late Eocene or post-Eocene quartz monzonite by erosion and the development upon it of a mature erosion surface.

LOCAL DESCRIPTIONS

To facilitate the description of individual features, the quadrangle has been divided into six structural blocks. The extent of these blocks is indicated on plate 3, where it may be seen that the dividing lines between blocks, except those outlining the quartz monzonite, are major structural features. The accompanying correlation table summarizes the structural history of each of the blocks and indicates the contemporaneous features.

[15] Mansfield, G. R., Geography, geology, and mineral resources of part of southeastern Idaho: U.S. Geol. Survey Prof. Paper 152, p. 383, 1927.

[16] Thom, W. T., Jr., The relation of deep-seated faults to the surface structural features of central Montana: Am. Assoc. Petroleum Geologists Bull., vol. 7, pp. 1-13, 1923.

[17] Schuchert, Charles, Paleogeography of North America: Geol. Soc. America Bull., vol. 20, p. 474, 1910.

[18] Gilluly, James, Geology and ore deposits of the Stockton and Fairfield quadrangles, Utah: U.S. Geol. Survey Prof. Paper 173, pp. 34-38, 1932.

[19] Gilluly, James, Basin Range faulting along the Oquirrh Range, Utah: Geol. Soc. America Bull., vol. 39, pp. 1118-1120, 1928.

Correlation of structural features in Gold Hill quadrangle

Cycle and stage		Deep Creek Mountain block	Uiyabi Canyon block	Ochre Mountain block	Dutch Mountain block	Northwestern block	Quartz monzonite block
First.	First stage.	Not represented?	Not represented?	Minor thrusts and folds.	Not represented?	Not represented?	
	Second stage.	Not represented?	Tilted fault in Uiyabi Canyon?	Normal faulting. Abundant.	North-south normal faults.	Not represented?	
Second.	First stage.	Major anticline. West-northwest transverse faulting.	Major anticline. West-northwest transverse faulting.	Major folding? Transverse faulting.	Major folding. Dutch Mountain thrust and minor thrusts.	Recumbent anticline and other folds.	
	Second stage.	Normal faulting. Early movement on eastern border fault.	Normal faulting.	Normal faulting.	Normal faulting. Trail Gulch fault and northwest faults.	Trail Gulch and Bar Creek normal faults.	
Third.	First stage.	North Pass thrust and subsidiary thrusts. West-northwest transverse faulting.	North Pass thrust.	Transverse faulting. Ochre Mountain thrust and subsidiary thrusts.	Pool Canyon transverse fault. Ochre Mountain thrust and subsidiary thrusts. Reversal of movement on Trail Gulch fault.	Minor thrusts? Warping of axial plane of recumbent anticline?	
	Second stage.	Normal faulting. Northeasterly fault on Blood Mountain.	Normal faulting east of benchmark 5868.	Normal faulting, especially along older faults.	Normal faulting rare.	Normal faulting of northerly strike?	
Fourth.	First stage.	East-west Blood Canyon and Dry Canyon faults. Minor thrusts and reverse faults.	Blood Canyon transverse fault. Minor reserve faults. Warping of North Pass thrust.	East-west transverse faults. East northeast faults.	Garrison Monster transverse fault and related conjugate faulting.	Conjugate faults.	
	Second stage.	Not represented?	Not represented?	Not represented?	Small normal faults?	Not represented?	
Fifth cycle and faulting related to the quartz monzonite.		Not represented?	Not represented?	Faults related to the quartz monzonite.	Not represented?	Not represented?	Normal faults related to intrusion. East-west transverse faults and minor thrusts. Small faults related to cooling of intrusive.
Late normal faulting.		East and west border faults.	East and west border faults.	West border fault.	Normal faulting in part along older faults.	Renewed movement along north-south fault.	

Evidence for the separation of the structural history into five epochs is given in the following pages. It is far from being as conclusive as might be desired, and future more detailed study may result either in the elimination of some of the five epochs or in the addition of others. Some of the structural features could not be definitely assigned to specific epochs, because their relations to features of known age could not be determined, and on plate 3 it was necessary to correlate them on the basis of their similarities to features for which more definite information was available. The difficulty of correlation is increased by the evidence of recurrent movements along some of the faults and by the impression that such movements may have been widespread; however, in spite of the uncertainties regarding individual features and the exact correlation of structural epochs, it is clear that deformation in this region has taken place in recurrent cycles and has continued over a long period of time.

DEEP CREEK MOUNTAIN BLOCK

The Deep Creek Mountain block includes that portion of the quadrangle south of the Blood Canyon transverse fault and thus includes the southern extension of the Clifton Hills as well as the Deep Creek Mountains.

The structure in this block is simpler than in any other part of the quadrangle. The pre-Carboniferous beds make up the westward-dipping limb of an anticline formed during the second structural cycle and bounded both on the east and west by recent normal faults. The continuity of the beds is broken by three rather large transverse faults of different ages, in addition to the one that limits the block on the north. Several minor normal and transverse faults and several small thrust faults have been recognized. Section *P–P′* on plate 1 illustrates the monoclinal character and shows two of the minor thrust faults. Near the northern boundary fault simplicity of structure is replaced by complexity, and several thrust plates that underlie the North Pass thrust may be recognized. These features are illustrated in the eastern part of section *J–J′–J″*. Overturning along low-angle transverse faults is found in the Carboniferous area to the northeast (sec. *H–H′*).

Dry Canyon transverse fault.—The southernmost transverse fault follows more or less closely the course of Dry Canyon on the east side of the mountains and Simonson Canyon on the west side. Its dip was not measured directly, but subsidiary parallel fractures dip 80°–85° N. The fault is poorly exposed throughout its extent. Where it cuts through shale and thin-bedded limestone the fault plane is covered by talus, and in its course through the more resistant dolomite and quartzite these rocks are so shattered, bleached, and recrystallized that in most places it is impossible to recognize the actual fault contact. The bleaching and recrystallization are probably in part, at least, the result of igneous metamorphism, for a small body of a sheared intrusive igneous rock was found along the fault just west of the spring near the mouth of Dry Canyon. The apparent displacement is somewhat variable, because of variations in dip on the two sides of the fault. The presence of thrust faults on both sides and the character of the drag shown on the south side of the fault on the divide render it probable that the greater part of the displacement was horizontal, the north side moving toward the east. The amount of horizontal movement was close to 1,000 feet. Outcrops west of the ridge line are offset more than twice this distance, owing to the combination of west dips and the steep slope.

Minor faults south of Dry Canyon transverse fault.—In the prospect tunnel south of the mouth of Dry Canyon a fault zone is exposed that strikes nearly north and dips 65°–90° W. Prospect Mountain quartzite forms both walls, but on the east the quartzite dips to the east at moderately high angles, and on the west it is slightly inclined to the west. The fault has normal relations, as the thickness of the eastward-dipping quartzite is in excess of that exposed to the west. There is a parallel shear zone about 100 yards to the west.

Half a mile west of these normal faults there are two rather similar faults that strike west of north and dip to the east. The eastern one strikes N. 16° W. and dips 50° E. It drops the upper contact of the Prospect Mountain quartzite about 75 feet. The throw decreases northward along the two branches of the fault in the gulch south of Willow Spring. The Dry Canyon fault is offset by both branches. The western fault has about the same strike and dip, but its displacement is considerably greater, probably being more than 400 feet where it crosses the ridge. This fault also offsets the Dry Canyon fault, but north of the intersection the normal fault can be recognized for only a short distance, beyond which the beds of the Busby quartzite are sharply warped, the more easterly outcrops being thus relatively depressed.

There must be additional faulting on the Cabin shale in this region, for exposures of the formation not affected by either of the two normal faults are only 100 feet or less in thickness. Locally also the bedding strikes at right angles to the underlying quartzite. These features are thought to indicate the presence within the shale of a low-angle fault, which is probably related to the transverse fault.

A minor fault in the southern branch of North Pass Canyon is indicated by a displacement of 200 to 300 feet of the outcrops of the resistant Lamb and Hicks dolomites. It was probably formed at the same time as the large transverse fault in Dry Canyon, but it could not be traced into that fault through the poorly exposed beds of the Abercrombie formation. Subsidiary fractures parallel to it strike N. 70° E. and dip 75° S. This is probably the strike and dip of the fault itself, but the fault plane was not exposed.

Two other faults were found south of the main transverse fault. These are on the west side of the range, in the southern branch of Simonson Canyon. The easterly fault strikes about N. 45° W. and dips steeply to the southwest. It brings various beds of the Laketown dolomite into contact with the Fish Haven dolomite and the Chokecherry dolomite. The western fault brings the Sevy dolomite into contact with the Laketown dolomite. The two faults are exposed for only a short distance within the quadrangle. Their continuation to the north is covered by the gravel in the canyon bottom, but they must be cut off by the Dry Canyon fault.

Sevy Canyon transverse fault.—The transverse fault in Sevy Canyon has a west-northwesterly strike, in distinction to the nearly east-west strike of the Dry Canyon fault to the south. As a result the two are only a mile apart on the east side of the range and over 2 miles apart on the west side. The Sevy Canyon fault has a pronounced northerly dip over much of its course, as may be seen on the steep slopes on the south side of North Pass Canyon. Parallel fractures dip 60° NNE. The drag shown by thinner-bedded formations cut by the fault, especially the Cabin shale, and the distribution of fragments in shatter zones indicate that the movement was chiefly horizontal, the south side moving relatively to the east. The offsetting of formations along the fault increases rather regularly westward. Thus outcrops of the Cabin shale are shifted about 600 feet, the Young Peak dolomite about 1,200 feet, the Fish Haven dolomite about 2,000 feet, and the Guilmette formation about 4,000 feet. This variation is in part the result of subsidiary thrust faults and in part the result of a steepening in the westward dip of the bedding on the south side of the fault but not on the north side. A minor fault of similar strike occurs a short distance to the north and was probably formed at the same time.

Relation of Sevy Canyon fault to Dry Canyon fault.—The age of the Sevy Canyon fault relative to the Dry Canyon fault is not obvious. It is probable that the northwestward-striking Sevy Canyon fault is the older, for faults of similar strike apparently terminate against the east-west Dry Canyon fault and against the parallel Blood Canyon fault, to the north. Contemporaneity of the two faults cannot be disproved, however, as the contact between them is not exposed, but, inasmuch as crumpling in the rocks between the two faults to the east might be expected if they were of the same age, the absence of crumpling suggests that the Sevy Canyon fault is of similar age to the other northwesterly transverse faults.

Minor faults between the Dry Canyon and Sevy Canyon faults.—On the ridge between Dry Canyon and Sheep Canyon the Abercrombie formation is 700 feet thinner than on the ridges to the north or south. A zone of disturbed strikes and dips in the saddle west of peak 7423 on this ridge is thought to be the site of the fault movement. The beds are thought to have been cut out by overriding rather than by normal faulting, because the beds east of the pass dip more steeply (40°–50° W.) than normal, whereas those to the west dip less steeply (25°–30° W.). Such drag effects are not characteristic of normal faulting but may be the result of thrust faulting. The fault was not traced to the north or south because of poor exposures on the hillsides, but it must die out to the north, for on the ridge north of Sheep Canyon the Abercrombie formation has its normal thickness. It probably terminates southward against the Dry Canyon fault. This inferred thrust fault is shown on section *P–P′*, plate 1.

The northwesterly fault that is cut off by the Dry Canyon fault near the head of Dry Canyon is traceable with difficulty, because of shattering and recrystallization for some distance from the main fault. Its presence is required by an offset in the outcrop of a characteristic bed near the top of the Choke-cherry dolomite. It is apparently terminated on the west by a thrust fault exposed on the divide. The thrust fault strikes about north and dips rather steeply to the west. It has caused beds near the middle of the Laketown dolomite to override the lower beds of the Sevy dolomite, involving a repetition of about 600 feet stratigraphically. (See sec. *P–P′*.) Toward the north, the strike of the thrust changes to northwest, the dip steepens and inclines to the southwest, and the fault is indistinguishable from other minor transverse faults.

A somewhat similar thrust fault is found about a mile to the north, on the south slope of peak 8291. Here, however, the thrust has not caused a duplication of strata but has eliminated more than half of the normal thickness of the Laketown dolomite. The line of the fault is marked by a zone of crushed dolomite and poor exposures near the base of the formation. The fault must die out to the south, for it was not recognized south of the head of the canyon, where the Laketown dolomite has its full thickness. To the north the strike swings to the northwest, the dip steepens, and the apparent displacement increases, as Sevy dolomite and Simonson dolomite south of the fault are successively brought into contact with beds of Laketown dolomite north of the fault. At an altitude of about 7,000 feet in Sevy Canyon this fault meets the Sevy Canyon fault. The increased apparent displacement is probably an actual increase, because overriding by massive beds in the Simonson dolomite may be observed in the region where the fault changes its strike to northwest.

Blood Canyon transverse fault.—The transverse fault in Blood Canyon, which limits the Deep Creek Mountain block to the north, has a rather sinuous course, which averages close to east-west and thus makes an angle of about 25° with the older northwesterly transverse faults. Its dip is also variable. West of Blood Canyon it is steep either to the north or south, but to the east the fault has a moderately low south dip. East of Overland Canyon the fault cuts through an area in which metamorphism has partly or completely concealed many of the minor structural features connected with the fault. Adjacent to the more easterly mile of exposure of the fault the Oquirrh formation to the south is complexly folded on a small scale, although away from the fault the formation has a rather uniform eastward dip.

Structure in Sevy Canyon south of the Blood Canyon fault.—The most striking structural feature in this region is the pronounced northeasterly strike of the formations near the Blood Canyon fault. Very little crumpling or folding is observed in the beds except on the extreme western flank of the range, where beds of the Guilmette formation are compressed into several small close folds. Beds on each side of the Blood Canyon fault are badly shattered, and in most places the fault cannot be exactly located, but where it forms the northern boundary of the large outcrop of the Woodman formation a thick breccia zone is exposed, dipping almost vertically.

North Pass transverse fault.—The North Pass transverse fault, striking northwest, terminates the linear outcrops of Prospect Mountain quartzite, Cabin shale, and Busby quartzite that extend to the south boundary of the quadrangle. North of the fault are exposed Middle and Upper Cambrian formations that are folded into a plunging anticline. Westward along the fault the Young Peak dolomite and Trippe limestone are but little offset. This portion of the fault, therefore, marks a rather local line of differential movement, the beds south of the fault showing a more or less uniform westward dip, and those to the north being folded to form an anticline. The westward continuation of the North Pass fault again shows a considerable displacement, as the fault in this region marks the southern limit of a number of thin overthrust plates. The fault is cut off to the northwest by the Blood Canyon fault. It may be traced beneath gravel some distance to the east, however, by reason of the isolated outcrops east of the main range.

Major anticline along east front of range.—The plunging anticline in North Pass Canyon that is terminated southward by the transverse fault is thought to be a continuation of a major anticline whose axis appears to be nearly coincident with the eastern front of the range. The axis is covered by gravel in most places, but eastward dips in the Prospect Mountain quartzite south of Dry Canyon and nearly horizontal bedding in a down-faulted exposure of higher Cambrian beds half a mile north of the mouth of Sheep Canyon allow it to be located with moderate accuracy.

If the two anticlines are the same, their present positions imply that the south side of the eastern segment of the North Pass transverse fault has moved relatively eastward and upward.

Thrust plates on the north side of North Pass Canyon.—The anticline in North Pass Canyon has affected only the Middle Cambrian portion of the section. The Upper Cambrian Lamb dolomite is not folded but extends across the anticlinal axis without regard for the underlying structure. The lower contact of the dolomite is a thrust fault, whose plane is irregular and which shows a strong tendency to be at a higher altitude where the underlying strata are resistant and at a lower altitude where they are weak. The dolomite beds, although they retain their characteristic lithology, are thoroughly shattered in the whole overriding mass, but the underlying beds are comparatively little affected. The map shows clearly the disappearance beneath the thrust plate on the west and the emergence on the east of the folded Young Peak dolomite and the Trippe limestone, and this feature is easily recognized in the field. The occurrence of a small patch of dolomite undoubtedly belonging to the Lamb dolomite above the Trippe limestone on the eastern flank of the anticline suggests that this overriding plate had only a small extent, and this is borne out by features farther east.

There are several other thrust plates above that of the Lamb dolomite. The small patches of the Hicks formation and the

Chokecherry dolomite extending northward from North Pass Canyon are not easily delimited but are certainly present because of their characteristic lithology and, in the Hicks, characteristic fossils. Their boundaries to the east and west are thought to be thrust faults. To the west is a somewhat larger thrust plate of Laketown dolomite, which contains recognizable and characteristic fossils. This plate is offset by a transverse fault, which is fairly well exposed on the south slope of peak 7660. North of the transverse fault the overthrust plate of Laketown dolomite extends nearly 2,500 feet farther east and rests upon the overriding plate of Lamb dolomite. It is in turn overlain by dolomites similar in lithology to those in the Simonson dolomite.

North Pass thrust and minor related thrusts east of North Pass Canyon.—The North Pass thrust crops out at only one locality in the block east of North Pass Canyon. At two other places it may be located rather closely, however, and a true measure of its extent may be obtained from the exposures of the central facies of the Carboniferous rocks that lie above it.

The only exposure of the thrust is found half a mile north of hill 6267, southwest of Blood Mountain. Here thin-bedded strata of the Oquirrh formation rest upon thoroughly brecciated fossiliferous Laketown dolomite. The contact between the two is a thrust dipping about 10° N., which is exposed for only a short distance before being terminated to the west by gravel and to the east by a younger normal fault.

The Laketown dolomite beneath the thrust is only 100 feet thick and rests upon limestones lithologically identical with those of the Guilmette formation. The fault contact between the two parallels the North Pass thrust above. This 100-foot slice of Laketown dolomite is considered to be the eastward continuation of the thrust plate of the same formation that was found in North Pass Canyon, where it rests upon a similar thrust plate of Lamb dolomite.

The main thrust may also be located rather closely on the south side of Blood Mountain. Just south of the road fork at an altitude of 5,854 feet there is an outcrop of brecciated fossiliferous Laketown dolomite, identical with that underlying the thrust half a mile to the northwest. Outcrops of the Oquirrh formation are found to the east, north, and west; and the North Pass thrust almost certainly is concealed by the intervening gravel. The thrust may also be approximately located for nearly a mile south of this region, for the six small outcrops of the Oquirrh formation south of hill 6267, as well as the beds at the base of the hill, are shattered, brecciated, and in some places dolomitized, suggesting that the thrust is not far beneath.

The remaining region in which the thrust may be recognized is in the southeast corner of the quadrangle, where there are several outcrops entirely surrounded by gravel. The largest and most westerly of these outcrops is composed of brecciated beds of the Oquirrh formation, which have been extensively silicified and dolomitized. The three small eastern outcrops are equally brecciated but are made up of dark dolomites similar to those in the Guilmette formation and the Simonson dolomite. In the northern outcrop were found unbroken fragments that contained the large brachiopod *Stringocephalus burtoni*, which is characteristic of these formations. On the map the three exposures are shown under the symbol for the Guilmette formation, but it is not improbable that beds belonging to the Simonson dolomite are present. The contact between the Devonian and Pennsylvanian strata is concealed, but it seems certain, because of the extensive brecciation and the stratigraphic relations, that this contact is a continuation of the North Pass thrust.

Eastern border fault.—There is evidence from several sources that a normal fault of considerable throw must parallel the east front of the Deep Creek Mountains. The physiographic evidence of faulting has been noted on pages 61–62 and indicates a throw of about 2,000 feet. The stratigraphic evidence is conflicting: in part it indicates a throw of 2,000 feet, checking the physiographic evidence, and in part it suggests a displacement of 6,000 feet. These contradictory results are explained by the fact that the 2,000-foot throw is based on beds above the North Pass thrust, and the 6,000-foot throw on beds beneath the thrust. There have therefore been two periods of activity along the fault, the first preceding the thrust and the second following the thrust.

Two groups of outcrops provide a measure of the movement preceding the thrust. One of these is about half a mile north of the entrance to Sheep Canyon, where a crescent-shaped outcrop of thoroughly brecciated limestones and dolomites is found only 1,000 feet east of the mountain front. These beds have been mapped as the Abercrombie formation and the Young Peak dolomite, respectively, because their lithology is characteristic of those formations. The contact between the limestone and the dolomite has a very gentle dip and apparently is close to the axis of the major anticline. The stratigraphic interval between these beds and the Prospect Mountain quartzite immediately to the west is 6,000 feet.

The second group of outcrops includes those in North Pass Canyon northwest of hill 6267. These are composed of gray and black laminated dolomites that are identical with beds in the Simonson dolomite. The two northwesterly outcrops dip 25°–90° E. and are less than a quarter of a mile from beds of the Abercrombie formation that have gentle eastward dips. The stratigraphic interval between the two formations is again 6,000 feet, and the only fault that could reasonably come between them is the eastern border fault. Incidentally, the difference in stratigraphy on the east side of the fault between this region and that to the south shows that the North Pass Canyon transverse fault continues east of the border fault.

The best stratigraphic measure of the movement along the eastern border fault after the thrust is provided by the 100-foot slice of Laketown dolomite lying beneath the North Pass thrust. This was correlated with the similar thrust plate west of the border fault, and by projecting both plates to the fault line, the throw is seen to be 2,000 feet (sec. *J′–J″*), thus checking the physiographic evidence.

The fault plane itself is exposed only along the divide between North Pass Canyon and Blood Canyon. In this region the fault splits into two branches, both of which offset the Blood Canyon transverse fault. The throw along the westerly branch is comparatively small, amounting to about 300 feet; the easterly branch has a greater throw, but it cannot be directly measured in the vicinity of the outcrops, as the North Pass thrust underlies the beds to the east but has been eroded west of the fault.

Minor structural features on Blood Mountain.—A normal fault following the west side of Blood Mountain offsets the Blood Canyon transverse fault about 1,200 feet. The transverse fault has a considerably lower dip at this point than in the region to the west, and it is believed that the large offset reflects this low dip. The normal fault must die out southward if the inferred position of the North Pass thrust southeast of hill 6267 is correct.

The northeasterly fault cutting through the crest of Blood Mountain has a throw of about 400 feet, measured by the position of a thick limestone bed on each side. This fault branches to the north, and the western branch is cut off by the Blood Canyon fault. A fault with similar strike to the southwest, which terminates the exposure of the North Pass thrust, must have a throw of about the same magnitude, to judge from the altitude of the thrust on each side of it.

The Pennsylvanian sandstones and limestones that underlie Blood Mountain show numerous discontinuous folds. In section *J′–J″* a syncline is shown just east of the fault, but this feature cannot be traced much beyond the line of the section, and in fact it is replaced by a minor anticline to the north. The irregular folding is probably due to the North Pass thrust, which underlies the mountain at no great depth.

Faults east of Overland Canyon.—South of the eastern portion of the Blood Canyon transverse fault several faults have been recognized. Most of these are of minor importance, and only two seem to warrant special description. These are the two faults with west-northwesterly strike at the south end of the Clifton Hills. Both have low dips to the south—the northern one, less than 30°; the southern, about 45°. (See sec. *H–H'*.) In both faults the beds on the southern or hanging-wall side are bent into local overturned folds. They are thus similar to the eastern portion of the Blood Canyon fault and are considered to represent older transverse faults. The northern of these two faults is both cut by and cuts off minor normal faults.

Mutual relations of the structural features.—The first recorded structural event in the Deep Creek Mountain region was the initiation of compressive forces from the west-northwest. These forces resulted in the formation of the transverse faults striking in that direction and in the anticlinal fold along the east front of the range. Then came a period of relaxation, expressed by 4,000 feet of the 6,000 feet total throw along the eastern border fault. These features are believed to belong to the second structural cycle. Renewed compression from the same direction as before resulted in the formation of the North Pass thrust and the associated thrust plates exposed in North Pass Canyon. After the second compressive movement a second period of normal faulting ensued, as shown by the northeasterly fault on Blood Mountain, which cuts the thrust plates and is cut off by the Blood Canyon transverse fault. These thrusts and normal faults are correlated with the third structural cycle.

A third renewal of compression, considered to mark the fourth cycle, is indicated by the Blood Canyon and related east-west transverse faults. It seems probable that minor thrusting occurred in this period also, for minor thrust faults are apparently associated with the Dry Canyon fault, which belongs to this period.

The final episode in the structural history of this block resulted in the late normal faulting that has largely produced the present topography. The eastern border fault is the most readily studied of these faults and shows that some of them at least have had a rather complex history.

UIYABI CANYON BLOCK

The southern boundary of the Uiyabi Canyon block is the Blood Canyon transverse fault, already described. The northern boundary, west of Clifton Flat, follows the parallel transverse fault on the south side of Ochre Mountain. East of Clifton Flat this fault continues for only a short distance, and the boundary in this region is marked by three large faults, as shown on plate 3.

The block is underlain almost entirely by Carboniferous rocks, chiefly of the central facies of the Oquirrh formation. In the pass through which the Lincoln Highway descends to the Deep Creek Valley these rocks are thrust over contorted Devonian limestones and dolomites, and it is probable that this relation holds true for the whole block. The thrust is considered to be the North Pass thrust (sec. *J–J''–J'*). Along the western margin of the mountains, on the other hand, Devonian strata are locally thrust upon the Pennsylvanian along faults that are thought to be younger than the main thrust (sec. *O–O'*). The Carboniferous beds are folded into a broad anticline whose axis is probably close to the west side of Blood Canyon. West of the anticlinal axis the Pennsylvanian beds have been bent into discontinuous folds, but east of the axis the beds have a uniform eastward dip averaging about 25°. Normal faults of several ages are found throughout the block. A transverse fault at the northern border of the block (sec. *J–J''*) is accom modified by warping, and a higher thrust plate is exposed in one of the downwarped portions (secs. *L–L'* and *I–I'*).

Minor structural features between Christiansen and Sheridan Gulches.—On the north side of Christiansen Canyon a reverse fault striking nearly due north and dipping steeply to the west has thrust Devonian beds over the Oquirrh formation (sec. *O–O'*). West of the main thrust are two minor faults that strike northwest and are marked by wide breccia zones. The Devonian rocks are closely folded and are locally overturned, as is clearly shown by the contact between the Guilmette formation and the Simonson dolomite near the western extremity of the spur.

A northwesterly transverse fault east of this area of folded and thrust Devonian rocks separates beds belonging to the central facies of the Oquirrh formation from gently folded beds of the Guilmette formation, upon which rests a small patch of the Woodman formation that belongs to the eastern facies. The fault is terminated at the southeast by the Blood Canyon transverse fault, which, east of the intersection, forms the boundary between the two facies. As the central facies of the Carboniferous rocks are found in the plate above the North Pass thrust and the eastern facies in the overridden mass, this transverse fault in Christiansen Gulch marks the southern boundary of the North Pass thrust plate. The North Pass transverse fault (p. 67) has similar relations and a parallel strike, and it is therefore suggested that the two northwesterly transverse faults are segments of the same fault which have been offset by the Blood Canyon fault.

Direction and amount of movement along the Blood Canyon fault.—The correlation of the transverse fault in Christiansen Gulch with the North Pass transverse fault provides a measure of the amount of movement along the Blood Canyon fault. The two segments indicate that the rocks south of the Blood Canyon fault have moved about a mile eastward, relative to those on the north side. Several features appear to corroborate this conclusion. The direction of the movement appears to be confirmed by the drag effects along the Blood Canyon fault, particularly as shown by the fault east of hill 6526, north of Blood Canyon, and by the drag folds along the most easterly exposures of the Blood Canyon fault.

The eastern limit of minor folding in the Oquirrh formation on both sides of the Blood Canyon fault is also offset in the same direction and in roughly the same amount. North of the fault the minor folding dies out east of hill 7511, at the head of Blood Canyon; to the south, it dies out on Blood Mountain.

The fact that many of the other structural features found north of the fault cannot be recognized in the proper positions to the south appears to be a serious objection to the suggested displacement. This may be due, however, to either of two factors. One is that the late normal faults which cut the Blood Canyon fault are so placed that north of the transverse fault they duplicate the major earlier normal fault in Blood Canyon, and south of the transverse fault, according to the probable projections, they conceal it. The second factor is that to the north the normal faults are readily apparent by reason of their cutting distinctive formations, such as the Ochre Mountain limestone and the Manning Canyon formation, but to the south the poorly exposed beds are all of the Oquirrh formation, in which the detection of faults is difficult, and the evaluation of of their displacement, when found, almost impossible.

Minor thrust east of benchmark 5684 on Lincoln Highway.—A second area of Devonian thrust over Pennsylvanian rocks is found about 2 miles north of the locality above described and just south of the Lincoln Highway. Here beds of massive limestone and dark dolomite containing *Cladopora* sp. clearly overlie the Oquirrh formation above a fault that dips about 30° NW. The fault is thought to continue north of the highway and to lie between the isolated hills of the Oquirrh formation and the main southern spur of Ochre Mountain. The limestone is considerably deformed, as are also the thinner-bedded rocks in the spur to the east. The thrust apparently terminates against the transverse fault that forms the northern boundary of the block. The transgression of this thrust along its strike from the Guilmette formation into the Oquirrh formation is thought to indicate that the displacement along it is small, and that it, as well as the thrust to the south, represent minor thrusts that have cut through the underlying North Pass thrust and brought up rocks that normally lie beneath the major thrust.

North Pass thrust.—The North Pass thrust, which must underlie the whole Uiyabi Canyon block, crops out at two places in the northwestern portion of the block. In both exposures, which are along the Lincoln Highway west of benchmark 6149, brecciated dolomites and yellow sandstones of the Oquirrh formation rest upon highly crumpled beds of the Guilmette formation (fig. 9). These Devonian beds below the North Pass thrust are almost certainly the equivalents of the beds of the same age exposed by the minor thrusts described in the preceding paragraphs.

The North Pass thrust plane must be considerably folded or warped, because at a number of places beds of the Oquirrh formation crop out at lower altitudes than those at which the fault is exposed along the Lincoln Highway. This later deformation is probably the result of the stresses that caused the east-west transverse fault that bounds the block on the north.

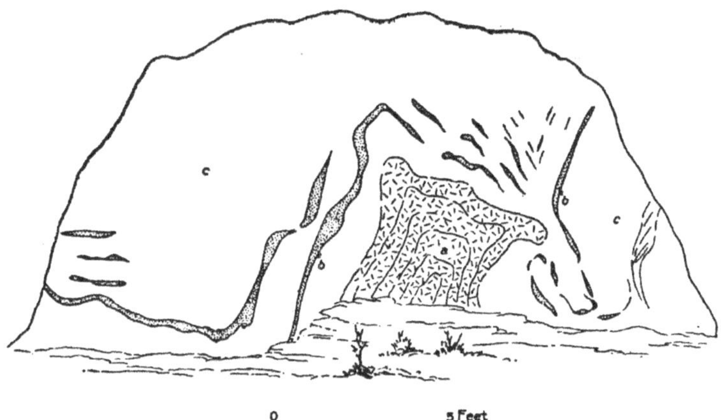

FIGURE 9.—Crumpling of Guilmette formation 1 mile west of benchmark 6149, north of Lincoln Highway. *a*, Dolomite; *b*, sandstone; *c*, limestone.

Minor folds in Uiyabi Canyon.—Several rather discontinuous folds are found in the Oquirrh formation in the western portion of Uiyabi Canyon. Two anticlines and a syncline were distinguished, but only one—the western anticline—can be traced for much more than a mile. The axis of this fold strikes west of north and follows a course that corresponds roughly with the ridge line between Uiyabi Canyon and the Deep Creek Valley. The western limb of the fold extends down to the valley gravel with increasingly steep dips, but the eastern limb has moderately low dips and is succeeded eastward by a shallow syncline. The syncline cannot be traced northward, and the structure there seems to be that of a single broad anticline which plunges to the north. The second anticlinal axis is about a quarter of a mile east of hill 7009 within Uiyabi Canyon. This fold also cannot be traced to the north, and its place is taken by the region of confused dips and minor faults near hill 6831. East of the second anticline, nearly east-west strikes and northerly dips are dominant for more than a mile and are succeeded eastward gradually by the north-south strikes and easterly dips that characterize the remainder of the district. A generalized idea of the folding is given by section *O–O'* and the left-hand portion of section *J'–J''*.

Minor faults west and southwest of Clifton Flat.—Minor faults of several ages and characters are found in the belt of minor folding. In almost every one the throw is unknown, because of the poor exposures and the lenticular nature of the Oquirrh formation. Along the west side of the Deep Creek Mountains there is a rather distinctive contact between massively bedded limestone and dolomite and underlying thinner-bedded rocks. By means of this contact the presence of numerous faults can be proved. Only one of these faults, along which there is a shift of the contact amounting to several hundred feet, has a sufficient displacement to be shown on the geologic map. This is the eastward-striking fault that ends near hill 7472. The short north-northwesterly fault about half a mile southeast of this hill is a small reverse fault with a throw of less than 100 feet.

The fault of low dip just east of hill 7194 along the northern boundary of Uiyabi Canyon is probably an old normal fault, tilted to its present position by later deformation, as it appears to have normal relations. It is cut off on the east by a younger normal fault, but the faulted segment may be represented by an obscure fault near hill 6831.

The younger normal fault is probably a continuation of a fault of similar strike that cuts the North Pass thrust along the Lincoln Highway. The thrust is about 100 feet lower west of this fault.

Major anticline south of Clifton Flat.—A major anticline affects all the Carboniferous rocks that lie in the block above the North Pass thrust. Its axis is difficult to trace because of younger structural features but appears to trend nearly north and to pass beneath the gravel of Clifton Flat just east of the entrance to Uiyabi Canyon. Several younger normal faults cut the anticline, and as a result the oldest formation involved in the fold, the Ochre Mountain limestone, is exposed on the eastern flank rather than at the core. East of the axis there is a rather constant eastward dip, but west of it the minor folds in Uiyabi Canyon are superposed on the older fold, although even here the more westerly beds are the higher stratigraphically (sec. *O–O'*).

Normal faulting in Blood Canyon.—On the western flank of the major anticline the Oquirrh formation has been brought into contact at two places with the Ochre Mountain limestone by faults dipping 30° W. These are believed to be parts of the same fault, as the recent movement of 2,000 feet along the eastern border fault (p. 68), which is exposed between them, is of the correct amount to cause the repetition (sec. *O–O'*). In both of the exposures of the westward-dipping fault the normal eastward dip of the Ochre Mountain limestone is reversed for a distance of 100 feet or so from the fault. Along the eastern exposure a considerable thickness of the Manning Canyon formation is found beneath the Oquirrh, but along the western exposure these beds are missing over much of the distance.

Transverse fault north of Overland Canyon.—The best exposure of the transverse fault north of Overland Canyon is about 1,600 feet northeast of benchmark 5768. Here dark quartzites and black micaceous schists that are metamorphosed members of the Manning Canyon formation abut against massively bedded Ochre Mountain limestone. In most places, however, the beds northeast of the fault have been engulfed by the quartz monzonite, and the limestone beds to the south are almost untouched. This is but one of several examples of the preference shown by the intrusive for following fault contacts during its emplacement. The eastward extension of the fault may be approximately located by a belt of jasperoid that almost certainly represents a silicification of the fault breccia. The transverse fault appears to be cut off by a younger normal fault about at its intersection with the road to the Midas mine, but the presence in this vicinity of several small areas of monzonite makes the exact relations uncertain. The normal fault is itself terminated by the Blood Canyon transverse fault.

Normal faults north of Overland Canyon.—The normal faults north of Overland Canyon have exerted an even more striking influence upon the quartz monzonite intrusion than the northwesterly transverse fault. Four faults have been recognized, and all of them, in at least parts of their courses, form the contact between the intrusive and the sedimentary rocks.

The most northwesterly of these faults' forms the linear boundary of the isolated area of quartz monzonite east of benchmark 5855 at the head of Overland Canyon. Its course is east-northeast, and its dip is to the northwest. A quartz-carbonate vein follows the fault. A minimum estimate of the displacement is given by the upper contact of the Manning Canyon formation, which is cut off by the fault about 1,000 feet west of hill 6807. As the Manning Canyon is nowhere exposed on the hanging-wall side of the fault, the displacement must amount to at least 2,000 feet (sec. *G–G′*). The age of this fault with respect to the transverse fault is not known.

The next fault to the southeast is perhaps open to question, because it is, throughout its exposure, bounded by quartz monzonite on the southeast. A quartz-carbonate vein is also found along this contact. There is little doubt that the monzonite was intruded along a fault, for, as shown in section *G–G′*, there is a displacement of about 2,500 feet between the outcrops of the Manning Canyon formation at the Midas mine and those northwest of the monzonite. The greater part of the throw must have taken place along this fault, but a small part may be represented by the third fault of this group. This is exposed on the west side of the ridge about a mile north of the Midas mine; its throw is probably comparatively small, so far as can be determined by the members of the Oquirrh formation on its two sides. The age of the third fault relative to the northwesterly transverse fault is unknown; the second one is clearly older, as it cannot be recognized southwest of the transverse fault.

The fourth fault is that at the Midas mine. The displacement here also is relatively small, amounting to about 350 feet. This fault must cut the northwesterly transverse fault, but the contact between the two has been destroyed by the intrusion.

Just south of the Midas mine there is a fault of similar strike but with a low dip to the southeast. It is cut off by the Blood Canyon transverse fault, but beyond this its relations to the other faults are not known.

Minor faults are abundant throughout this region, but the displacements rarely amount to more than 10 feet and on many are measured in inches. To the east the minor faulting is clearly shown by thin limestone beds. It was perhaps more abundant here because of the probable closer approach at this point to the underlying North Pass thrust.

Ochre Mountain thrust.—The exposures of the Oquirrh formation that underlie hill 6519, on the northwest side of Clifton Flat, and the low hills north of the road to the Monocca mine, on the northeast side of Clifton Flat, belong to the western facies of the formation and must therefore lie above the Ochre Mountain thrust (secs. *I–I′* and *L–L′*). The beds exposed are rather thick-bedded cherty and chert-free limestones and dolomites, with only minor sandstones. Some of them are identical with beds in the northwest quarter of the quadrangle, which are definitely a part of the western facies. The thrust plane is everywhere concealed by gravel within this block and may be located closely only on the southwest side of hill 6519, where the two facies of the Oquirrh formation are only a few hundred feet apart.

Warping of the North Pass and Ochre Mountain thrusts.—The two major thrusts have both been considerably deformed in this block. This is shown not only by the outcrops of the North Pass thrust at altitudes considerably higher than in regions where the Oquirrh formation above the thrust is exposed, and by the younger reverse faults that cut through the thrust, but also by the close proximity of the two major thrusts in Clifton Flat. The warping is most intense adjacent to the east-west transverse fault that bounds the block on the north. An anticlinal warping has brought the North Pass thrust to the surface in this region, and a syncline to the east has preserved a portion of the plate above the Ochre Mountain thrust. Similar warping is associated with the Garrison Monster transverse fault to the north (p. 83), where the two features are considered to be genetically related.

The close proximity of the two major thrusts in Clifton Flat permits a rough estimate of the thickness of the plate between them. The original eastward dip of the common limb between the anticline to the west and the syncline to the east has, however, been increased by two other factors. One of these is the eastward tilt imparted to the footwall block of the western border fault (p. 61); the other is that the northern continuation of the eastern border fault extends beneath this part of Clifton Flat, and although it cannot be recognized on the north side of the flat, it must be represented in the central part either by an actual fracture or by a pronounced downwarp to the east, as its throw on the south edge of the flat is still 2,000 feet. Neither of these factors can be accurately determined, but rough estimates indicate that the North Pass thrust plate was probably about 2,000 to 2,500 feet thick at this point.

Transverse fault on the south side of Ochre Mountain.—A transverse fault is continuously exposed for more than a mile about half a mile south of hill 6886, south of Ochre Mountain, and is marked by a zone of silicified and crushed dolomite several hundred feet in width (sec. *J–J′*). In this portion of the fault the dip is steep, and the fault separates the western facies of the Carboniferous to the north and the central facies of the Carboniferous to the south. These relations hold for the exposures of the fault in two gravel-surrounded outcrops to the east, but the breccia zone is considerably narrower. Still farther east the fault curves around the north end of hill 6519 and the dip flattens notably. This pronounced change in the course of the fault corresponds with its intersection with the older Ochre Mountain thrust (sec. *L–L′*). The presence of the low-angle thrust fault at this point was probably the major factor in causing the change from steep to flat dip in the transverse fault, as the related Garrison Monster transverse fault to the north (p. 83) behaves in a similar manner where it cuts through an older thrust.

It is highly improbable that the gently dipping portion of the fault represents a later thrust that has concealed the steeply dipping transverse fault, for there are no other exposures of such a fault in the higher areas to the northeast.

East of hill 6519 the transverse fault is concealed by the gravel of Clifton Flat. It is thought to be represented east of the gravel by a wide crushed zone south of hill 6256, half a mile east of the road intersection at an altitude of 6,089 feet. This fault separates Ochre Mountain limestone on the north from the western facies of the Oquirrh formation on the south—relations similar to those shown by the transverse fault on hill 6519, on the northwest side of the flat. The exposure of the fault extends only a short distance to the east, however, where it is terminated by a large normal fault that forms a part of the boundary of this structural block.

The amount of movement along the transverse fault is not known. If an analogy may be drawn from the similar Garrison Monster fault, the pronounced warping south of the fault implies that the rocks on the north side moved relatively eastward. If that assumption is correct, there must have been a minimum movement of a mile in this direction. If the south side moved relatively eastward, however, the amount of movement must have been much greater. Both of these estimates are based on exposures of the Oquirrh formation north of the fault.

Normal faults bordering the block east of Clifton Flat.—The normal fault that terminates the transverse fault described in the preceding paragraphs brings the central facies of the Oquirrh formation on the east into contact with the western facies of the same formation. The throw must therefore be large, but it cannot be estimated in this region, for the altitude of the Ochre Mountain thrust separating the two facies cannot be determined on either side of the fault. The normal fault is considered related to the intrusion of the quartz monzonite, as shown by its relations in the block to the north (p. 76).

The northeasterly fault three-quarters of a mile northwest of Montezuma Peak is poorly exposed throughout but is marked by a zone of shattering and erratic dips. The central facies of the Oquirrh formation forms both walls, and as no distinctive beds were recognized, its throw is unknown. The fault is perhaps related to the normal faults of similar strike on the southern slope of Montezuma Peak.

Mutual relations of the structural features.—The Uiyabi Canyon block presents a sequence of structural events similar to that found in the Deep Creek Mountain block, to the south. Tilted normal faults in Uiyabi Canyon are probably older than the major anticline on the south side of Clifton Flat. The anticline itself and some of the normal faults on the south side of Montezuma Peak in turn antedate the North Pass thrust and related features that were formed in the third structural cycle. Normal faults that cut these features are in turn cut off by the great transverse faults, or by their associated faults which characterize the fourth cycle. The transverse fault on the south side of Ochre Mountain is itself cut by a normal fault related to the intrusion. Finally, the late normal faults are found on the south side of Clifton Flat and along the western border of the block.

OCHRE MOUNTAIN BLOCK

The Ochre Mountain block includes not only Ochre Mountain but also the low-lying hills to the north. Its northern boundary is marked by the wedge-shaped tongue of quartz monzonite that extends westward from the town of Gold Hill along the south side of Dutch Mountain. To the west the block is limited for several miles by the western border fault, but this fault appears to die out at about the northwest point of Ochre Mountain, and from this point to the western tip of the quartz monzonite wedge the boundary of the block follows gravel-filled valleys that have no structural significance. The main body of quartz monzonite lies east of the block. It includes several roof pendants of sedimentary rocks, whose structure is considered in this section.

The Ochre Mountain thrust is the dominant structural feature in the block (sec. $K-K'$, $M-M'$). A nearly continuous exposure of this fault extends in a north-northwesterly direction from the quartz monzonite stock to the northern boundary of the block. The thrust is also exposed in a "window" west of the thrust, and in several of the roof pendants. Several transverse faults with low north dips are exposed on Ochre Mountain that are thought to be contemporaneous with the major thrust (sec. $J-J'$). There are in addition several others, chiefly normal faults, whose relations both to one another and to the thrusts provide the most complete chronologic sequence found in the whole quadrangle (sec. $K-K'$).

Over much of the block the rocks are poorly exposed, owing to the fact that the present surface closely parallels the old post-mature surface (p. 61) and faults are difficult to trace. The absence of distinctive beds in the Ochre Mountain limestone, which underlies much of the area, adds to the difficulty and prevents accurate measurement of fault throws in many places. On the western face of Ochre Mountain rock exposures are unusually good, and several distinctive beds are present. As a result, many faults were recognized, and their abundance in this region probably provides a measure of the amount of faulting in the remainder of the block.

Main outcrop of the Ochre Mountain thrust.—The most southeasterly outcrop of the Ochre Mountain thrust is just west of the Lincoln Highway about a quarter of a mile north of benchmark 5723. At this point, north of and below the thrust, are sandstones and black shales belonging to the central facies of the Manning Canyon formation. These beds are badly crumpled and show marked variations in strike and dip. To the south and above the thrust are poorly exposed black shales with a few interbedded fossiliferous limestones that belong to the western facies of the same formation. They are overlain by cherty dolomites and limestones of the Oquirrh formation. The thrust is poorly exposed here, and were it not for the difference in lithology between the two facies of the Oquirrh formation overlying the two areas of the Manning Canyon, it might easily pass unrecognized. To the southeast the termination of the thrust by the quartz monzonite stock is concealed by gravel.

To the west and north the thrust is also concealed by gravel for some distance. The beds at the base of the ridge above the northern Ochre Spring are the Ochre Mountain limestone and the western facies of both the Manning Canyon and Oquirrh formations. They show rather variable strikes and dips, and this variation is illustrated by the irregularity of the outcrops of the three formations. Hill 5919, between the two springs, is covered largely by quartzite float, but the tunnel at the northern spring indicates that the quartzite is present as thin beds in less resistant black shale. East of these beds and surrounded by gravel are several low hills composed of the central facies of the Manning Canyon formation. The thrust must be concealed by the gravel between the outcrops of the two facies.

About a quarter of a mile west of the point at an altitude of 5,658 feet shown on the map the concealed thrust is cut by an eastward-dipping normal fault. West of the normal fault, whose post-thrust throw is about 150 feet, the thrust is shown by eastward-dipping thick-bedded Ochre Mountain limestone resting upon the central facies of the Manning Canyon formation. The stratigraphic displacement along the normal fault in the beds above the thrust amounts to several thousand feet. The normal fault has clearly been active at least twice, therefore, the bulk of the movement being earlier than the thrust. The normal fault has also caused the exposure of the thrust southwest of hill 5919 between the two Ochre Springs. The relations here are similar to those west of the fault to the north.

Northwest of this normal fault there are two lines of outcrop of the thrust, as a result of an east-west normal fault whose throw is about 50 feet. To the north another normal fault, of northwesterly strike, displaces the thrust 100 feet. A small "klippe" or thrust outlier occurs on peak 5959, northeast of this region, Ochre Mountain limestone above the thrust resting upon beds low in the Oquirrh formation. The salient of the thrust due west of the "klippe" conceals the Manning Canyon and Oquirrh contact in the overridden rocks for nearly half a mile. Locally the Ochre Mountain limestone above the thrust shows zones of disturbed dips parallel to the thrust that appear to represent minor sympathetic thrusts. These are commonly reflected in the topography by pronounced benches.

Just north of the intersection of the thrust with the trail from Gold Hill to the Erickson ranch, the western facies of the Oquirrh formation replaces the Ochre Mountain limestone as the formation above the thrust. This is the result of an east-northeast fault earlier than the thrusting. The east-northeast fault is exposed for only a short distance along the divide between the Gold Hill and Deep Creek drainage basins, but its persistence for nearly [illegible] miles westward is proved by the continued presence of the Oquirrh formation to the north of the trail and of the Ochre Mountain limestone to the south. The age relations of this fault seem to ally it with the north-northwest transverse faults, in spite of its divergent strike, which may be the result either of a low dip or of warping accompanying the thrusting.

North of its intersection with the transverse fault the overthrust can be traced continuously for more than half a mile. Its outcrop is sinuous, owing chiefly to the effect of the topography, although variations in dip play some part. The western facies of the Oquirrh formation continues to overlie the thrust and beneath it are found Ochre Mountain limestone and the central facies of both the Manning Canyon and the Oquirrh. The appearance of the Ochre Mountain limestone immediately below the thrust coincides with an increase in complexity in the structure of the overridden rocks. Two minor thrusts in the rocks below the thrust were recognized in this region in addition to minor folds (sec. *N–N'*). The more southerly of the minor thrusts is exposed just north of the road to the Erickson ranch and east of the outcrop of the main thrust. It has resulted in the Ochre Mountain limestone overriding the Manning Canyon formation. The strike of the minor thrust is nearly at right angles to the strike of the bedding. Because of this it involves, in addition to the Ochre Mountain limestone, both the Manning Canyon and Oquirrh formations. The relatively small displacement suffered by the Manning Canyon and Oquirrh contact on the northeastern extension of the fault indicates that the fault dies out within a rather short distance in this direction. The changes in strike of this contact in the overridden beds are considered to have been developed as a result of the thrust. The behavior of the minor thrust described in the next paragraph indicates that the dip of this fault probably steepens notably along its southwestern extension and that, coincident with the change in dip, the strike swings to nearly east-west.

These two features are clearly shown by the second of the minor thrusts, which is found just beneath the Ochre Mountain thrust east of peak 6125. Here, in the east-west draw north of hill 5925 both the minor thrust and the major thrust are well exposed. The minor thrust strikes nearly due east and dips 60° N. Ochre Mountain limestone is found above the fault, and the Manning Canyon formation below. Toward the east the strike of the thrust swings to the north and the dip flattens notably, as is shown by the trace of its outcrop. Only a small width of the thrust plate of Ochre Mountain limestone is exposed, owing to overlapping by the main thrust.

The complexity in structure shown by the overridden rocks in this region contrasts with the simple structure to the southeast, where the contact between the Manning Canyon and Oquirrh formations shows that there has been little deformation of the rocks beneath the thrust. It seems probable that the change in structure is due to the presence of the resistant Ochre Mountain limestone immediately below the thrust in the northern area, in that the competent limestone is much more readily fractured and that a break in the limestone would involve breaking in the immediately adjacent nonresistant beds.

The outcrop of the Ochre Mountain thrust is terminated less than a quarter of a mile north of the second of the minor thrusts by a northwesterly normal fault. This normal fault forms the contact between beds above the thrust to the west and beds below the thrust to the east, northward from the intersection to the northern boundary of the block. The throw along the normal fault amounts to about 300 feet (p. 77).

"Window" west of the main outcrop of the Ochre Mountain thrust.—Another isolated and poor outcrop of the thrust is in a "window" in the open valley about three-quarters of a mile west of the [illegible] Springs (sec. *M–M'*). The presence of the thrust here is shown by outcrops, in the floor of the valley and near its edges, of beds of the Ochre Mountain limestone and the Manning Canyon and Oquirrh formations, in striking unconformity with the eastward-dipping Ochre Mountain limestones on each side. This relation is most clearly shown in the southeast corner of the valley, where there are small outcrops of the Manning Canyon and Oquirrh formations. The beds of the Ochre Mountain limestone immediately above the fault have irregular strikes and dips, in striking contrast to the uniformity of their attitude higher on the ridge. The thrust has caused an erratic distribution of the three formations that are here beneath it, but the lack of an adequate number of outcrops prevents the determination of the character of this deformation. In the left-hand portion of section *M–M'* it is extremely generalized.

Ochre Mountain thrust east of the Lincoln Highway.—Although the main outcrop of the Ochre Mountain thrust is terminated on the southeast by the quartz monzonite, there is ample evidence that the thrust plate originally extended much farther eastward, over the region now underlain by the intrusive rock. This is shown by the occurrence of the western facies of the Carboniferous formations in roof pendants and locally by small exposures of the thrust itself. In this region, however, the thrust plane has been affected by faulting related to the intrusive.

The exposures of the Oquirrh formation on the east side of the Lincoln Highway and south of the point where the thrust crosses the road belong to the western facies of the formation and are the continuation of beds west of the road that occur above the thrust. These beds are west of a north-south tongue of the quartz monzonite, which has apparently followed a preexistent north-south fault, as to the east Ochre Mountain limestone is exposed. The limestone is now separated by rather narrow belts of quartz monzonite on the north, east, and south from other masses of Ochre Mountain limestone and was probably continuous with them before the intrusion. The limestone masses are those in the vicinity of the Lucy L mine, the large roof pendant north-northeast of Clifton, which includes also beds of the western facies of the Oquirrh formation, and the block of limestone upon which Clifton itself is built.

All these exposures are considered to be above the Ochre Mountain thrust, for at several places the limestone is in contact with either the Manning Canyon or the Oquirrh formation, in relations that can be explained only by thrusting. This is definitely proved at the Lucy L mine, where mine workings expose the thrust and also show that beds belonging to the central facies of the Oquirrh formation extend beneath a hill capped with Ochre Mountain limestone. (See p. 141 and fig. 26.) The localities at which the thrust was recognized in this region are shown on plate 3.

The distribution of the small exposures of the thrust show that it has suffered deformation in this region as compared to its relatively undisturbed condition to the west and north. Two normal faults seem to have been the chief factors in the deformation. One of these is the northern continuation of a fault that displaced the thrust in the Uiyabi Canyon block (p. 72) and has dropped the beds to the west at least 1,000 feet. The second fault terminates on the west the exposures of the thrust and the rocks above it just west of the Lucy L mine. Its throw cannot be accurately measured but must be of the same magnitude as that of the parallel fault to the west, although in the opposite direction.

The restriction of these large post-thrust disturbances to the vicinity of the quartz monzonite suggests that the faulting is genetically connected with the intrusion, and this view seems to be somewhat confirmed by features of the ore deposits observed near the faults (pp. 88–89).

Magnitude of the Ochre Mountain thrust.—The amount of movement along the thrust cannot be accurately determined. The force causing the thrust must have come from the west, and a minimum estimate may therefore be obtained from the distance between the easternmost and westernmost outcrops of the thrust, or of rocks known to overlie the thrust. This distance amounts to more than 5 miles. It must, however, be far short of the true figure, for the lithologic distinction between the westernmost outcrop of the central facies of the Oquirrh formation beneath the thrust and the easternmost outcrop of the western facies is everywhere evident. A figure approximating 20 miles would seem to be nearer the true amount but has, of course, no basis in field observations.

Northward-dipping transverse faults on Ochre Mountain.—Three faults with rather low north dips and east strikes occur on Ochre Mountain in the rocks above the Ochre Mountain thrust. They are in general poorly exposed and are therefore difficult to trace. All these faults are probably contemporaneous with the main thrust, for their relations to normal faults appear to be the same as those shown by the thrust. The movement along two of the faults appears to have been dominantly horizontal, and, as the other is closely related to them, they are all considered to be rather flat portions of transverse faults.

The southern of the three faults was recognized at several places south and east of the summit of Ochre Mountain but was not traced definitely between these points. The longest of these recognized outcrops was found at the head of Gold Hill Wash, where the fault crosses the Lincoln Highway 500 or 600 feet southwest of benchmark 5972. In this region the Ochre Mountain limestone is north of the fault and the western facies of the Manning Canyon and Oquirrh formations to the south. The fault is cut off on the east by the same normal fault that cuts the Ochre Mountain fault near Ochre Springs (p. 72). East of the normal fault the continuation of the transverse fault is uncertain because of faulting related to the quartz monzonite intrusion, but segments of faults that may represent portions of it are shown on plate 3. West of the highway the fault may be traced for nearly a mile because of discordant stratigraphic relations. Two small outcrops are readily found farther west by reason of the relations between the Ochre Mountain limestone and the Woodman formation. The most westerly exposure occurs along the northeast side of the pronounced bench at an altitude of about 6,800 feet that lies between summits 7233 and 6886, on the south side of Ochre Mountain. The Herat shale member of the Ochre Mountain limestone caps the bench and lies below (south of) the fault. The same member is also exposed above the fault just south of the summit of Ochre Mountain. The fault was not traced west of the bench, but it may continue along the west face of the mountain and join the second of the transverse faults, as no offsetting that can be attributed to it alone was recognized. The fault has its highest altitude and lowest dip at the 6,800 foot bench, and it decreases in altitude markedly to the east, where the dip appears to be considerably steeper. If it joins the other transverse fault at the west, it must decrease its altitude in that direction also. This variation in altitude is considered to be partly the result of original variations in dip and partly the result of later deformation, the eastward tilt caused by the western border fault (p. 61) being one of the most influential factors.

The movement along the fault is estimated at about 2,500 to 3,000 feet, the beds north of and above the fault moving eastward. This measurement is based upon the correlation of structural features on the two sides of the fault. The large normal fault that forms the western boundary of the exposures of the Oquirrh formation along the Lincoln Highway east of Ochre Springs is correlated with a fault south of the fault with rather similar relations 1,000 feet west of benchmark 6163 at the north end of Clifton Flat; the faults bounding the graben of Oquirrh formation composing hill 6439, north of the fault, are correlated with the faults that compose the graben of Ochre Mountain limestone north of hill 6519, south of the fault; and the fault 2,000 feet west of hill 7150, which limits the Woodman formation on the west, is correlated with the similar fault west of the bench at 6,800 feet. The stratigraphic throw shown by the Herat shale member of the Ochre Mountain limestone is also satisfied by a displacement of this magnitude.

A second fault with low north dip crops out 1,500 feet south of the highest point on Ochre Mountain. It terminates on the west a band of Herat shale, and farther east in the amphitheater-like valley below the summit it is recognized by considerable crumpling in the massive beds of the Ochre Mountain limestone. On the western flank of the mountain it may be recognized at several places as a result of the relatively recent extensive erosion (pl. 7, *A*) and also by its termination of the belt of Woodman formation and the fault that bounds that formation. The amount of movement along this fault could not be determined, as the beds above it are all of the Ochre Mountain limestone. The altitude of the outcrops of the fault ranges from about 6,650 to 7,250 feet. The highest point is on the bench north of peak 7233.

The last of the group of low-angle faults whose outcrops have a dominantly east-west trend is found on the north slope of Ochre Mountain. The chief outcrop of this fault is north of hill 6439, on the east side of the mountain. Here the fault strikes west-northwest and dips at a moderately low angle to the north. The footwall side is marked by extensive silicification. A down-faulted block of Pennsylvanian rocks is cut by the fault, and these beds south of the fault are shifted about 1,700 feet relatively east. A probable westward continuation of the fault was found about a mile to the west, just north of peak 7000. Other outcrops thought to represent this fault occur a mile still farther west, where, however, there are two faults with the same approximate strike as in the other outcrops but with a nearly vertical dip. Although these three outcrops were not traced into one another, it is thought that they are parts of the same fault, whose dip flattens eastward and upward.

Southward-dipping transverse faults on Ochre Mountain.—A fault striking west-northwest and dipping at a moderate angle to the south is exposed on the south side of Ochre Mountain south of the bench at an altitude of 6,800 feet. To the northwest the fault abuts against a younger normal fault, and to the southeast it is covered by gravel, although it must be cut by the east-west transverse fault that bounds the block on the south. Several normal faults exposed north of the fault are clearly terminated by the transverse fault.

An apparent measure of the throw along the fault is given by the positions of the Herat shale member of the Ochre Mountain limestone and the Woodman and Ochre Mountain contact on both sides of the fault. These show that the beds south of the fault have dropped vertically about 700 feet. A simple vertical movement, however, is impossible, because of the lack of correspondence of structure on the two sides of the fault, and particularly because of the absence, to the south, of any fault that might correspond with the normal fault east of the 6,800-foot bench that forms the western boundary of the Woodman formation. This, together with the erratic northeasterly strikes found at many places adjacent to the fault, suggest that it is a transverse fault. Its termination to the west by a normal fault that is in turn cut off by the northward-dipping transverse faults implies that it belongs to a different structural cycle from the other transverse faults on Ochre Mountain.

A second parallel fault crops out 1,000 feet east of hill 6634, on the southwest spur of Ochre Mountain. The vertical component of its throw amounts to 250 feet, as shown by the Woodman and Ochre Mountain contact on both sides of the fault, but a purely vertical movement is improbable because the displacements of two older normal faults require the movement along the fault to have been dominantly horizontal, the north side moving relatively eastward about 1,000 feet.

Minor thrusts and fold on south side of Ochre Mountain.—Two minor thrusts and a small anticline are exposed on the southwestern spur of Ochre Mountain that are thought to have been formed during the first structural cycle. The more westerly thrust crops out just east of the point at an altitude of 5,613 feet on the road along the west side of Ochre Mountain and is terminated eastward by a younger normal fault. The displacement of the thrust is unknown, as it is within the Ochre Mountain limestone.

About half a mile to the southeast, another minor thrust is exposed. This fault separates beds high in the Guilmette formation, as shown by the lithology and by the presence of the large clam, *Pycinodesma* sp., from beds high in the Woodman formation. The stratigraphic throw thus amounts to nearly the thickness of the Woodman formation (about 1,500 feet), but the total movement along the fault is larger than this, as the low east dip of the fault nearly coincides with the dip of the bedding. The thrust is terminated at the northwest by a normal fault and at the southeast by the transverse fault that forms the southern boundary of the block.

A minor anticlinal fold is exposed on the west side of hill 6886, south of the summit of Ochre Mountain. It is terminated on the north by a transverse fault of the second cycle.

Normal faults on Ochre Mountain.—By means of their relations to the thrusts and transverse faults, the normal faults on Ochre Mountain are seen to belong to three different chronologic groups, corresponding to the first three structural cycles. Those of the first cycle are probably the most abundant.

The two most westerly normal faults belong to the oldest group, as they are offset by a transverse fault of the second cycle. Both dip about 45° W. The throw along the western fault is unknown, but the eastern one drops the beds on its hanging-wall side about 2,000 feet.

About 1,500 feet east of hill 6634, on the southwest spur of the mountain, another westward-dipping normal fault crops out. This belongs to the second structural cycle, however, as it cuts a transverse fault of the second cycle and is cut off by one of the third cycle. The throw along this fault amounts to about 2,000 feet also, as is shown by the position of the upper contact of the Woodman formation on each side. In the gulch that heads between peaks 7102 and 7182, on the ridge line of Ochre Mountain, the fault is cut by one of the northward-dipping transverse faults. Beneath the transverse fault, which has a very low dip at this point, the strike of the normal fault swings to east of north, its dip flattens and the beds on each side are crumpled. The compressive forces that caused the flat fault evidently were also partly relieved by some movement along the older fault. North of the intersection a north-south fault is exposed that appears to be a continuation of the normal fault to the south, but the known displacement along the transverse fault (about 2,000 feet) makes a correlation impossible. At the north end of the mountain, along the continuation of this line of faulting, still another westward-dipping normal fault is found. The throw along the fault cannot be exactly determined but must be considerable, because the beds on the footwall side are near the base of the Ochre Mountain limestone, and those on the hanging-wall side are rather high in the formation. This fault is terminated on the south by the northern of two northwestward-striking transverse faults. Adjacent to the transverse fault the strike of the normal fault swings to the southwest, and its dip is notably flatter—phenomena similar to those exhibited by the normal fault to the south at its intersection with a younger transverse fault. As the displacements along the branching transverse fault to the north and the flat transverse fault to the south are roughly compensatory, it is possible that the most northerly and southerly normal faults are segments of the same fault.

Two north-south normal faults east of the 6,800-foot bench on the south side of the mountain are similar in the character of their displacement as well as in strike. Both are older than the transverse fault of the second cycle that is exposed in this region. The western of the two normal faults has a throw of nearly 2,000 feet; the eastern, about 500 feet. North of the third-cycle transverse fault that cuts these faults on the north only one north-south fault of large throw was recognized. This crops out about 2,000 feet east of the southward-trending ridge whose altitude is 7,150 feet. It is the continuation of the more westerly of the two normal faults south of the transverse fault, as it corresponds to that fault in stratigraphic relations. The more easterly of the two normal faults to the south is perhaps represented north of the transverse fault by a poorly exposed fault in the valley east of summit 7130.

Three more normal faults are present north and northwest of hill 6519, on the southeast spur of Ochre Mountain. The westernmost one has a small downthrow to the east, as shown by the presence in the hanging wall of beds low in the Ochre Mountain limestone. The two more easterly faults are exposed on both sides of hill 6475, which is 2,000 feet north of hill 6519. These two faults form the boundaries of a graben of beds high in the Ochre Mountain limestone, the Woodman formation being exposed east of the graben and basal beds of the Ochre Mountain limestone west of it.

These two normal faults are cut by the most southerly of the northward-dipping transverse faults and north of the intersection are shifted about 2,500 feet to the east. The depressed block between the faults (hill 6439) in the region to the north is made up of beds low in the Oquirrh formation, as shown by a small exposure of the Manning Canyon formation to the north. The graben is also cut by a second transverse fault farther north and shifted 1,750 feet westward. The beds in this segment of the graben are also basal members of the Oquirrh formation and the upper portion of the Manning Canyon formation. The bounding faults of the graben converge northward in this region and are very nearly united where they are cut off by the Ochre Mountain thrust along the south side of the "window" described on page 73. They were not recognized on the north side of the "window."

The faults that bound the graben are clearly older than the northward-dipping transverse faults and Ochre Mountain thrust of the third cycle. They appear to be unaffected, however, by a minor transverse fault which is exposed 2,000 feet northwest of bench mark 6163 at the north end of Clifton Flat, and which was probably formed in the first stage of the second cycle. The two normal faults, therefore probably represent the normal faulting of the second cycle.

Another normal fault of the second cycle with a northerly strike is exposed 1,000 feet west of bench mark 6163. This fault dips eastward and has a throw about equal to the thickness of the Ochre Mountain limestone, for beds of the Manning Canyon formation are found on the hanging wall and beds near the base of the Ochre Mountain limestone make up the footwall. The fault is not affected by the second-cycle transverse fault shown on the ridge to the west but is cut by the southern of the third-cycle transverse faults. The faulted segment is 3,000 feet to the east on the north side of the transverse fault, where it forms the western boundary of the mass of Oquirrh formation exposed along the Lincoln Highway. There has been renewed movement amounting to about 150 feet along this segment, as shown by the offsetting of the Ochre Mountain thrust (p. 72).

Structural features east of the Lincoln Highway and south of the U.S. mine.—The most striking structural feature in the region east of the Lincoln Highway is a horst affecting the Ochre

Mountain thrust, which is probably genetically related to the intrusion of the quartz monzonite stock. The fault that bounds the horst on the west extends northward from hill 6455, about 1⅓ miles northwest of the town of Clifton and is a northern continuation of the fault described on page 72. In this vicinity the fault appears to have at least three branches. A small mass of quartz monzonite has followed the fault zone for more than a mile, north of the branched portion, but a northern continuation appears to be represented by the fault 1,000 feet east of the highway in the region east of Ochre Springs. The beds on the footwall side of the block have been elevated relative to those on the hanging-wall side. Both to the north and to the south the beds of the central facies of the Oquirrh formation are exposed in the footwall and have been raised to altitudes several hundred feet higher than the Ochre Mountain thrust plane, which they normally underlie. North of hill 6455 beds above the thrust are found on the footwall side of the fault, but even here the thrust is considerably higher than west of the normal fault.

This fault zone must also have been the site of movement before the Ochre Mountain thrust, for west of it the western facies of the Oquirrh formation is above the thrust, but to the east the Ochre Mountain limestone has this position. The pre-thrust throw must have been large but cannot be closely estimated as the horizon in the Ochre Mountain limestone east of the fault is unknown. The post-thrust movement may have been somewhat smaller but certainly has amounted to at least several hundred feet and to the south may have been more than 1,000 feet. The relations north of hill 6455 suggest that the post-thrust throw may have been variable along the strike.

Several more or less east-west faults in the vicinity of hill 6455 are cut by the normal fault zone, but their short extent and the considerable metamorphism of the adjacent beds make their true nature uncertain. They perhaps represent faulted segments of either the Ochre Mountain thrust or the northward-dipping transverse faults of the same age.

The fault that bounds the horst on the east is exposed at two places. Near the Lucy L mine the central facies of the Oquirrh formation is brought into contact with Ochre Mountain limestone that lies above the Ochre Mountain thrust. The second exposure of the fault is west of the town of Clifton. Here the fault dips about 30° E. and has similar relations, except that the Ochre Mountain thrust is not exposed below the Ochre Mountain limestone in the hanging wall (sec. *I–I'*). The limestone, however, appears to have been originally continuous with the beds in the roof pendant northeast of the town, which definitely overlie the thrust.

Two large faults cut the roof pendant northeast of Clifton. One of them strikes east of north and separates fossiliferous beds of the western facies of the Oquirrh formation on the east from Ochre Mountain limestone on the west. The fault is similar in relations to the normal faults of the second cycle on Ochre Mountain and is probably of that age.

Both the normal fault and the outcrop of the Oquirrh formation are terminated on the south by a fault striking east-northeast and dipping, in its western portion, 60° N. This fault is difficult to trace toward the west in the Ochre Mountain limestone but seems to be marked by a zone of crumpling and minor overturned folds along the projected strike. These features suggest that the fault is one of the group of northward-dipping transverse faults that are exposed on Ochre Mountain.

The Ochre Mountain limestone in the roof pendant has undergone minor folding. Section *K–K'* shows a shallow syncline that appears to be limited to the northwestern part of the pendant, but an asymmetric anticline to the east is more continuous.

The exposures of the central facies of the Carboniferous formation immediately east of the Lincoln Highway and west of the westerly normal fault related to the intrusion lie immediately beneath the Ochre Mountain thrust. Although metamorphism and local gravel capping mask their structure considerably, it is clear that they are irregularly warped. The outcrop of Ochre Mountain limestone near the north end of the exposure of these rocks requires a local doming in the overridden rocks at that point.

Minor faults are probably rather abundant in the beds near the quartz monzonite but are readily recognized only where prospect pits or mine workings provide suitable exposures. Thus several faults were recognized at the Lucy L mine (p. 141 and pl. 13) and at the Wilson Consolidated mine (p. 139 and fig. 25).

Faults near the U.S. mine.—Three faults are exposed in the vicinity of the U.S. mine. One of these, just south of the mine office, offsets the Ochre Mountain and Manning Canyon contact about 200 feet and is clearly earlier than the intrusion. The second fault, which strikes east-northeast and dips 60° S., crops out 250 feet south of the portal of the main tunnel of the mine. It has beds low in the Oquirrh formation on its hanging wall and cuts across the Ochre Mountain and Manning Canyon contact in the footwall, indicating a throw of about 1,000 feet. The fault is rather poorly exposed at the surface and is seen underground only at the face of the most southerly working on the tunnel level. Beyond the fact that the fault is earlier than the intrusion its relative age is unknown. It is shown on plate 3 as a normal fault of the first cycle but this is purely conjectural. As shown in section *M–M'* the fault appears to be nearly horizontal, but this is the result of the essential parallelism between the line of section and the strike of the fault.

The third fault is northwest of the mine workings and forms the contact between the intrusive and sedimentary rocks. It cannot be recognized at the surface as the contact is covered by talus from the sediments above. Underground, however, the contact is exposed in the workings on the 234-foot level northeast of the shaft, where it is seen to be a fault striking about northwest and dipping 35° SW. On section *M–M'* the fault is shown as a normal fault, but the low dip perhaps makes this interpretation questionable. If the fault is considered to be normal, the throw may be about 200 to 300 feet; but if it is a reverse fault, the throw would necessarily be much greater. As no sign of the fault was observed along its projected course on the west side of Gold Hill Wash, it must die out in that direction; and therefore the smaller throw required by the normal fault makes that interpretation preferable. Several minor faults or shear planes were observed underground in the U.S. mine and are described on pages 158–160.

Transverse fault north of Ochre Springs.—The structure in the flat west of the Lincoln Highway and northeast of Ochre Springs is obscure, as the outcrops of the Manning Canyon formation are low mounds covered by angular blocks of dark quartzite. The bedding is presumably nearly horizontal, as the exposures are found over a wide area. On the north side of the flat the low hills are composed of eastward-dipping beds of the Oquirrh formation. The discordance between the observed dip here and the inferred dip of the Manning Canyon outcrops in the flat suggests an east-west fault between them, and this suggestion is confirmed by the continuous exposures to the west, where a transverse fault forms the contact between the two formations. This fault is clearly older than the Ochre Mountain thrust, which is not affected by it.

Northwesterly normal faults west of the Lincoln Highway and east of the main outcrop of the Ochre Mountain thrust.—There are probably several northwestward-striking normal faults in the region west of the Lincoln Highway that are not shown on plate 2, but the rather poor exposures and the lack of distinctive beds in the central facies of the Oquirrh formation prevent accurate mapping.

The most westerly of the recognized faults of this group may be traced with minor interruptions from the north side of the

east north of Dolan Springs to the northern boundary of the block. The fault dips to the west, one exposure of the fault plane showing a dip of 70°. Over much of its outcrop the Manning Canyon formation is exposed in the footwall and beds low in the Oquirrh formation in the hanging wall. Farther north the relations are not so simple, as a result of intersections with other faults, and for the most northerly half mile of outcrop in this region, the fault forms the boundary between the overriding and overridden rocks of the Ochre Mountain thrust. This portion of the fault is cut by younger northeasterly faults. The throw along the fault is about 300 feet.

Two parallel faults to the northeast have both been traced for more than a mile by means of zones of disturbed strikes and dips. Both faults dip to the northeast, however. Their throw is between 200 and 300 feet, as nearly as can be estimated. Neither of these faults can be traced confidently much north of the road from Gold Hill to the Erickson ranch.

Another fault with northwesterly strike may be traced from Gold Hill Wash just south of the town of Gold Hill to the northern boundary of the block. It dips to the southwest and appears to have its maximum throw of about 1,000 feet in the vicinity of the Cane Springs mine. The throw probably decreases to the north.

Northeasterly faults west and northwest of Gold Hill.—Several northeastward-striking faults may be recognized in the region west of Gold Hill. Most of them are the youngest structural features in that region, as they cut the northwesterly normal faults, some of which in turn are younger than the Ochre Mountain thrust. The amount of displacement along these faults is small, but many of them are reverse faults.

Locally the northeasterly faults appear to die out to the southwest. This feature is best shown about three-quarters of a mile west of Gold Hill. Here a northeasterly fault, which to the northeast clearly offsets a northwesterly fault, has merely warped a second northwesterly fault, and still farther to the southwest its influence cannot be recognized at all.

Although the larger number of these faults are younger than the other structural features, some must represent an older generation of faulting. This is shown about three-quarters of a mile south of bench mark 5885 on the Ferber Road, where one of these northeasterly faults is cut off sharply by a northwesterly fault. A parallel northeasterly fault a short distance to the north offsets the northwesterly fault, however. The northeasterly faults at this locality also show that there are two generations of northwesterly faults, as both of the northeasterly faults are younger than a northwesterly fault whose dip is 45° SW. and whose throw is about 250 feet.

Transverse fault at the northern border of the block.—Exposures immediately north and west of benchmark 5885 on the Ferber Road show that there must be a nearly east-west transverse fault in this region. The fault is now concealed through much of its course, however, by the tongue of quartz monzonite, or, locally, by gravel. In view of the known relation between the intrusion and preexistent faults in other parts of the quadrangle, it seems probable that this transverse fault may have controlled the intrusion of the tongue along the northern border of the block.

The areal association of a nearly east-west transverse fault and northeasterly faults, both of which are relatively young, is similar to conditions near the Garrison Monster mine.

Structural features in the vicinity of the Western Utah mine.—The most striking fault near the Western Utah mine is that marked by a linear outcrop of jasperoid replacement of fault breccia that passes through Gold Hill. Over most of its length the fault forms the contact between the Ochre Mountain limestone and the Manning Canyon formation. Its dip is about 60° E. This is almost the same as the dip of the beds on each side of the fault in the vicinity of the mine, and it is only when beds of the Ochre Mountain limestone are traced to the north and found to change their strike to nearly east-west that the considerable throw of the fault is realized. The throw along the fault is unknown, but a minimum estimate, based on the thickness of Ochre Mountain beds terminated by the fault, is about 1,000 feet.

On the eastern slope of the hill the relations of the Ochre Mountain limestone and the Manning Canyon formation indicate the presence of a synclinal fold. Owing probably in large part to the fault described above, the dips on the western limb are much steeper than those on the eastern (sec. *M–M'*). The fold is cut by a fault striking N. 30° W. and dipping 65° W., whose throw is about 200 feet at its most southeasterly exposure but apparently increases to the northwest, as the displacement of the Ochre Mountain and Manning Canyon contact in that direction is obviously greater. The fault is cut by the eastward-dipping fault that passes through Gold Hill, and it cannot be identified on the footwall side of that fault. A smaller fault to the north strikes N. 35° W. and dips 70° W. Its throw is roughly 150 feet. Both of these faults are older than the quartz monzonite intrusion.

The remaining fault in this region is that which forms the contact between the sediments and the intrusive on the east side of the southern tip of the roof pendant. This fault cannot be recognized at the surface but was found in the tunnel 500 feet south of the portal of the Copperopolis (Ida Lull) mine. In this tunnel the fault contact is exposed 75 feet from the portal and here strikes N. 12° W. and dips 60° W. The sediments on the hanging-wall side are brecciated for 25 feet away from the fault, and the quartz monzonite is intensely crushed throughout most of its exposure in the tunnel. It is uncertain how far north the fault forms the contact, because of the lack of exposures, and for this reason it is difficult to give even a minimum figure for the throw.

Mutual relations of the structural features.—The Ochre Mountain block furnishes the most complete record of the structural history of the quadrangle.

The first stage of the first cycle is represented by the minor thrusts and folds on the south side of Ochre Mountain and by the folds in the roof pendant north of Clifton. These localities are the only ones in which structural features of this age have been recognized. Normal faults belonging to the second stage are definitely present on the south side of Ochre Mountain, where they are cut by faults of the second cycle. The assignment of other normal faults in the block to this group is less certain.

No major folds that were formed in the second cycle are shown in the block, but the prevailing easterly dip suggests that the region forms the western limb of a major anticline. Several minor transverse faults of this age were also recognized. The normal faults formed during the second stage of the cycle seem to be characterized by large throws. On the south side of Ochre Mountain two of them form a graben.

The Ochre Mountain thrust is the major structural feature of the third cycle. The North Pass thrust of this age is not exposed in the block, but the beds of the central facies of the Carboniferous, which are above that thrust, are widely exposed, and the North Pass thrust must therefore underlie the region. Several low-angle transverse faults of this age are exposed on Ochre Mountain and offset some of the older faults. The normal faults of the second stage of the third cycle are neither numerous nor of large throw.

East-west transverse faults of the fourth cycle are found at both the north and south boundaries of the block. The northern transverse fault is coextensive with a number of northeastward-striking faults, some of which are reverse faults, and the two kinds of faults are considered to be contemporaneous, on the basis of evidence from the vicinity of the Garrison Monster mine, to the north. These faults cut off all the older ones.

Some large normal faults that affect the sedimentary rocks of this block along the Lincoln Highway south of Gold Hill are younger than the structural features of the fourth cycle and are thought to be related to the quartz monzonite intrusion. They have no influence upon the present topography, however, and are therefore older than the western border fault along the west base of Ochre Mountain.

DUTCH MOUNTAIN BLOCK

The geographically more or less isolated mass of Dutch Mountain is bounded on the west by a gravel-filled valley that conceals a normal fault of large throw and on the south by a wedge of quartz monzonite that separates it from the Ochre Mountain block.

The most pronounced structural feature in the Dutch Mountain block is the northern continuation of the Ochre Mountain thrust, which can be traced, with only two interruptions, for the length of the block. North of Pool Canyon the thrust forms the contact between Carboniferous formations and earlier Paleozoic rocks (secs. *C–C′* and *D–D′*), but south of the canyon the central facies of the Carboniferous lies beneath the fault (sec. *E–E′*). A transverse fault earlier than the thrust is the cause of the change in the overridden formations. Both the Carboniferous and the earlier Paleozoic rocks beneath the thrust are cut by numerous normal faults that are also earlier than the thrust. A few normal faults, however, are later, but some of these have utilized the lines of earlier faulting. At the north end of the block the thrust is also displaced by an east-west transverse fault. A group of faults striking east-northeast with either reverse or normal relations are associated with this transverse fault, and faults of similar strike are found to the south, where they also cut the thrust fault (secs. *A–A′* and *B–B′*). Relatively few notable faults have been found in the overriding block of Carboniferous rocks on the west slope of Dutch Mountain. Those that are present, however, give evidence of a complex history, in that the same fault has been the site of renewed movements of both reverse and normal character. The beds between the faults are generally folded on a small scale (sec. *F–F′*).

Ochre Mountain thrust south of Pool Canyon.—The segment of the Ochre Mountain thrust east of the normal fault that terminated on the north the exposures of the thrust in the Ochre Mountain block (p. 73) must be concealed by the gravel west of the divide south of Dutch Mountain. The central facies of the Oquirrh formation crops out on hill 6286, north of the divide, and the western facies is exposed to the northwest and west. The exact position of the thrust in the intervening gravel-covered area is uncertain. The thrust outcrop is shifted at least a mile eastward by a northwesterly fault that crops out about 1,000 feet north of hill 6286.

The offset segment north of the fault is the most southerly exposure of the thrust in the Dutch Mountain block. On the east side of hill 6566, three quarters of a mile northeast of bench-mark 5885 on the Ferber Road the thrust appears to be of minor throw, as Ochre Mountain limestone forms both walls. The only difference apparent between the limestones on the two sides of the fault is the noticeably greater metamorphism of the beds below the thrust. The magnitude of the fault is shown, however, by the fact that the Ochre Mountain limestone above the thrust is conformably overlain by the western facies of the Pennsylvanian formations, but below the fault it is associated with the central facies. Sandstone beds belonging to the basal portion of the central facies of the Oquirrh formation occur beneath the thrust less than 1,000 feet north of the most southerly exposure of the thrust, and the Woodman formation takes the place of the Ochre Mountain limestone immediately above the thrust. These relations continue northward for about a third of a mile, to a point where the outcrop of the thrust is interrupted by the mass of quartz monzonite at the head of Pool Canyon.

Ochre Mountain thrust in Pool Canyon.—The thrust is also exposed northeast of the quartz monzonite mass in Pool Canyon, where the Madison limestone lies above the thrust, and metamorphosed dolomites, thought to belong to the Laketown dolomite, below it. The altitude of the thrust also differs on the two sides of the intrusive, being about 300 feet lower to the northeast. A transverse fault that follows Pool Canyon and may be called the Pool Canyon transverse fault appears to have produced these changes in the relations of the thrust. The contact between this transverse fault and the thrust is concealed by the quartz monzonite, but it seems certain that the transverse fault is older, for it cannot be found in the beds overlying the thrust northwest of the quartz monzonite area.

The way by which a change in the formations above the thrust was accomplished is shown by the exposures of the Woodman formation that surround the quartz monzonite. Northeast of the intrusion the Woodman formation conformably overlies the Madison limestone and dips at low angles to the north and west. At the northwestern tip of the intrusion, which is in line with the prolongation of the transverse fault, the beds of the Woodman show abundant minor faulting and shattering and have locally erratic dips. To the southeast, along the border of the intrusion, the bedding is concealed in most places but is clearly vertical at the summit of Woodman Peak. From this point southeastward the dip changes to steep southeast and the Ochre Mountain limestone is found above the Woodman. In the Ochre Mountain the dip continues to decrease to the southeast and passes through horizontality to a low northwesterly dip where the contact of the Ochre Mountain and the Woodman is again exposed on the ridge south of Pool Canyon. There are thus a sharp anticline and a low syncline southwest of the intrusive and a gentle monocline northeast of it.

These relations indicate that the overriding thrust plate suffered a considerable disturbance where it crossed the older transverse fault. There must have been some rupturing in the thrust plate along the line of the older fault to account for the difference in structure shown on the two sides of Pool Canyon, but the absence of a major fracture in the Woodman formation along the prolongation of the transverse fault suggests strongly that the greater part of the variation was accomplished by warping.

It seems improbable that the Pool Canyon transverse fault could have exerted so strong an influence upon the thrust unless the thrust plate were moving over a surface whose topography had been influenced by the transverse fault. This conclusion appears to be confirmed by the fact that the greater disturbance in the beds above the thrust is found southwest of the transverse fault, the side that is about 300 feet higher. As the sandstones and limestones making up the Oquirrh formation southwest of the transverse fault are much less resistant to erosion than the massively bedded dolomites to the northeast, it would appear that relatively little time could have elapsed between the formation of the transverse fault and the Ochre Mountain thrust.

Ochre Mountain thrust between Pool Canyon and the Garrison Monster mine.—North of Pool Canyon the thrust may be readily traced without serious interruption to the north side of Dutch Mountain. The Madison limestone overlies the thrust in this series of exposures, but various formations of pre-Devonian age underlie it. From Pool Canyon to the south side of Tribune Gulch the outcrop of the thrust changes its trend from east to northeast, and in this distance it is cut by several faults whose throws are less than 100 feet and which are not shown on plate 3. On the south side of Tribune Gulch the thrust is cut by two faults with northeasterly strikes. The more southeasterly of these has caused the repetition of the thrust outcrop on the ridge at an altitude of 6,555 feet.

A northwesterly fault that follows Tribune Gulch offsets the thrust about [illegible] feet to the northwest. The vertical movement along this fault required to accomplish the observed offset of the thrust is only 300 feet, but the displacement shown by the beds beneath the thrust requires a vertical drop of more than 600 feet. This discordance suggests that there were two stages of movement along the fault, but the observed relations might equally well be explained by a dominant horizontal movement. This explanation is probably the correct one, as exposures of the fault in Royal Gulch, to the north, exhibit pronounced horizontal striae (p. 82).

Another large offset in the thrust outcrop is found in the vicinity of the Spotted Fawn mine. In this region several branches of the Spotted Fawn normal fault cut the thrust. The vertical displacements of the thrust along these faults are small, but some of them have throws of 2,000 feet or more in the overridden rocks. These faults are unlike the fault described in the preceding paragraph, however, in that the discordances cannot be reconciled by postulating horizontal movement along the faults, and they must therefore have been active at more than one period.

North of the Spotted Fawn mine the thrust is interrupted at only a few places by minor faults and may be readily traced to a point within a short distance west of the old camp of the Garrison Monster mine, where it is cut off by one of the faults in the Garrison Monster transverse fault zone. Throughout this distance Madison limestone lies above the thrust and Upper Cambrian dolomite below it.

The Madison limestone above the thrust throughout this region dips at very nearly the same angle as the thrust. The progressive thinning of the limestone northward, however, shows that there is a slight discordance. The only place where a notable discordance was observed is near the north end of the main outcrop of the thrust, in the region between it and the exposures of the thrust in Royal Gulch. In this region, which is considerably faulted, there is a sharp asymmetric anticline in the Madison limestone that has resulted in a considerably greater thickness of the limestone than normal being present above the thrust.

Ochre Mountain thrust near Garrison Monster mine.—North of the Garrison Monster transverse fault a thrust that is probably the continuation of the Ochre Mountain thrust is exposed a short distance west of the new Garrison Monster camp. In this region the Woodman formation lies above the thrust and Upper Cambrian dolomites beneath it. The thrust may be traced northward for more than a mile, beyond which it is concealed by gravel.

"Window" in Royal Gulch.—The erosion of Royal Gulch on the north slope of Dutch Mountain has provided additional exposures of the Ochre Mountain thrust a short distance west of the main outcrop (secs. *B–B′* and *C–C′*). In this region the thrust is cut by northwesterly faults that appear to be continuations of the faults that cut the thrust in the vicinity of the Spotted Fawn mine. These faults cause offsets of the thrust outcrop of a few hundred feet, but like their probable continuations near the Spotted Fawn mine, have very different effects in the overridden formations. At least two northeasterly faults related to the Garrison Monster transverse fault also cut the thrust in this region.

Either the Fish Haven dolomite or the Laketown dolomite underlies the thrust throughout a greater part of the "window." In several places the contact between these two formations is transgressed by the thrust. Madison limestone lies immediately above the thrust throughout the exposure.

Ochre Mountain thrust along north edge of Dutch Mountain.—At several places west of the mouth of Accident Canyon, on the north side of Dutch Mountain, a low-angle fault is exposed separating lower Paleozoic formations, ranging from Cambrian to Devonian, from the overlying Woodman formation. The gravel that covers much of the area enclosing the exposures of the fault conceals its outcrop for considerable distances. The fault is thought to be a westward continuation of the Ochre Mountain thrust, as its stratigraphic relations are the same as those shown along the east side of Dutch Mountain, and just east of the mouth of Accident Canyon the probable continuation of the fault is less than half a mile from outcrops of the thrust in the "window" in Royal Gulch. The thrust has a pronounced northerly dip in this region, which is probably due to the close proximity of the westward extension of the Garrison Monster transverse fault, as the dip appears to be steepest in those outcrops nearest the transverse fault (sec. *F–F′*). Several normal faults cut the thrust to the northwest, and one of them terminates the series of exposures on the west.

Thrust plates associated with Ochre Mountain thrust.—Locally relatively thin thrust plates are associated with the Ochre Mountain thrust. They are in some respects similar to those found on Ochre Mountain (p. 73) and to those related to the North Pass thrust in North Pass Canyon (pp. 67–68). One of these plates, composed of Upper Cambrian dolomite, lies beneath the easternmost exposure of the main thrust north of the Spotted Fawn mine. Bedding planes are preserved in many places in the plate, and their discordance not only with the bedding in the Middle Cambrian beneath but also with both the upper and lower contacts of the plate shows conclusively that the block has a tectonic origin. The plate has a thickness of about 300 feet on the steep slope north of the 7,333-foot point on the ridge line of Dutch Mountain and near the Garrison Monster mine, but elsewhere it is much thinner. It appears to have a rather slight areal extent, as it was not recognized in the "window" of Royal Gulch. In Royal Gulch, however, the Upper Cambrian is beneath the thrust in its normal stratigraphic position on the west limb of a northeastward-trending anticline. It seems probable that the thrust plate of dolomite is a continuation of these beds which has overridden the less resistant underlying Middle Cambrian during the period of overthrusting. The relations are closely similar to those in North Pass Canyon, where the presence of plates of resistant rocks beneath the main North Pass thrust is considered to indicate that both the main thrust and the plates moved forward over an older erosion surface (p. 57).

Several minor thrusts in the rocks above the Ochre Mountain thrust are exposed in the vicinity of the Garrison Monster mine. Some of these thrusts in the Woodman formation can be seen along the Lake Bonneville beach at 5,200 feet, west of the portal of the tunnel (altitude 4,894 feet) at the new camp. One of these thrusts (pl. 7, *D*) clearly reveals minor folds in the overridden beds. Another thrust, which encircles the summit between the old and the new Garrison Monster workings, brings Madison limestone over the Woodman formation. It may be a continuation of one of the minor thrusts exposed to the north.

Appearance of Ochre Mountain thrust.—In almost all places it is difficult to determine the precise horizon of the thrust, and the location shown on the map represents a halfway point between beds that may be recognized as belonging to formations above and below it. The intervening rock, which in many places reaches a thickness of 20 feet and is rarely less than 10 feet, is so thoroughly recrystallized that it is impossible either to distinguish characteristic sedimentary structure or to choose a dividing plane. Angular fragments of any size, or a fault breccia, can be distinguished megascopically in only a few places, although there is, in many places, a slight streakiness parallel to the thrust. A typical specimen from Royal Gulch is a light grayish-brown rock in which thin bands and lenses of a white coarser-grained calcite alternate with thicker bands of grayish-brown fine-grained carbonate. The cleavage planes of the white calcite reach an eighth of an inch in diameter, and locally tiny remnants of a bluish calcite may be distinguished within them. Optical tests on crushed fragments of the finer-grained material indicate that it is in large part dolomite. Under the microscope the coarsely crystalline calcite is seen to be the older mineral. Individual crystals are rather turbid and are commonly twinned. Curving cleavage planes are strongly developed and are characteristic of this stage. The white calcite is embayed and veined by a clear, unstrained carbonate mineral, most of which, as noted above, is probably dolomite. This is the material that is grayish brown in the hand specimen, and the microscope shows that the color is due to the presence of a brown mineral, probably iron oxide, around the borders of the dolomite crystals. Similar brown material surrounds fragments of the older calcite where it is in contact with the younger crystals. A few laths of sericite are present in some places with the iron oxides. Small blebs and stringers of fine-grained quartz show intense shearing and undulose extinction. The relation of the quartz to the white calcite is not clear, but it is clearly veined by the dolomite.

The features observed in this specimen are interpreted as follows: The white calcite crystals are thought to be sheared and enlarged crystals of the original limestone. Enlargement seems required, as they are of larger diameter than any seen in any of the unaltered limestones. The quartz stringers and lenses are considered to have formed as a result of the shearing of cherty and sandy portions of the limestone. Partial recrystallization of the quartz and enlargement of the white calcite crystals resulted in their having somewhat anomalous relations to each other. These two components of the rock mark the initial stages of the thrusting. As the movement continued, shearing became localized along planes parallel to the fault, and on these planes recrystallization accompanied by expulsion of the impurities in the original grains occurred, resulting in the formation of the clear unstrained crystals with their boundaries of iron oxides and sericite. The presence of so much dolomite apparently indicates that there must have been some transfer of material during recrystallization, the magnesium being derived from the overridden dolomites. Such a transfer was probably accomplished by circulating solutions, as the absence of extensive cataclastic structure argues against anhydrous conditions during the thrusting.

Folding of Ochre Mountain thrust.—Variations in the altitude of the thrust outcrop that are independent of later faulting indicate that it has been warped into several minor folds. A well-defined anticline is shown by the thrust north of the Spotted Fawn mine, the altitude of the thrust outcrop increasing from 6,600 feet or less to about 7,200 feet on the divide between Spotted Fawn Gulch and Busby Gulch, and decreasing west of the divide, as shown by the "window" in Royal Gulch and the Madison limestone outcrops in the gulches to the south. The anticlinal axis must strike about northeast and be located approximately along the ridge line of Dutch Mountain.

Beneath Accident Canyon the thrust must have an altitude of 4,500 feet or less, as shown by the absence of exposures of Madison limestone south of the east-west fault that extends along the north side of the mountain here. Farther west, however, the thrust is again exposed at an altitude of about 5,100 feet, showing that a synclinal fold must occur in the vicinity of Accident Canyon.

The folds in the thrust are thought to be related to the Garrison Monster transverse fault (p. 59).

Magnitude of the thrust.—The distance between the easternmost and westernmost exposures of the thrust is about 4 miles, slightly less than was found in the Ochre Mountain block (p. 74). This is a minimum figure for the amount of movement along the thrust, however, and the total throw must be much larger.

Pool Canyon transverse fault.—The existence of a large fault in Pool Canyon is shown by the occurrence of lower Paleozoic formations beneath the Ochre Mountain thrust on the north side of the canyon and of Carboniferous formations on the south side. Exposures of the fault, which has been called the Pool Canyon transverse fault, are poor and of small extent, most of its projected course being concealed either by gravel or by younger intrusive rocks.

The fault does not cut the rocks above the thrust, but its intersection with the thrust in the northwestern part of Pool Canyon is concealed by a mass of quartz monzonite. The fault is exposed for a distance of about 2,000 feet in the central part of the canyon, but the extensive metamorphism of sediments on each side makes it difficult to distinguish the fault plane. A small intrusion is present along the fault in this region, and its linear northern boundary is thought to coincide with the fault plane. A prospect pit at this locality shows that the contact dips steeply to the south. In the lower reaches of Pool Canyon another body of quartz monzonite has been intruded along the fault, but its continuation is shown by the beds exposed on each side of the canyon.

Another group of outcrops is found in the vicinity of the Rube mine. The westernmost outcrop of the fault in this region is just north of hill 5057. Here the Prospect Mountain quartzite north of the fault is in contact with Ochre Mountain limestone. A prospect tunnel on the northwest side of the low ridge apparently parallels the fault immediately to the south. The tunnel shows thoroughly crushed rock but does not give any definite indication of the dip of the fault at this point.

A small outcrop of Ochre Mountain limestone about 1,200 feet to the northwest, which is surrounded by gravel, indicates that the transverse fault must be offset to the north at least 700 feet. The fault causing the offset is shown on the map with a north-south strike, but there is no evidence to prove that it may not strike northeast. Another offset of about the same amount is required by exposures of the transverse fault west of the Rube mine. This offset is thought to be the result of a westward-dipping fault exposed in the Ochre Mountain limestone on the Ruby claim, to the south. If this fault really is the one causing the offset and the movement along it is of the normal type, the transverse fault must dip to the south, as it does in Pool Canyon. It is possible, however, that the offsetting fault may have a northeast strike; if so, it would crop out beneath the gravel of Gold Hill Wash.

Another offsetting fault must be present in the gravel-covered slope west of hill 5556, east of the Rube mine. This fault must be older than the intrusion of quartz monzonite, as no trace of it was found to the south. East of the offset the transverse fault cannot be exactly located for some distance, but its approximate position is shown southeast of hill 5556 by an isolated outcrop of Pennsylvanian limestone in close proximity to one of Prospect Mountain quartzite. There are probably no further offsets concealed by the gravel in the area to the east. The easternmost exposure within the quadrangle is found about half a mile west of the Christmas mine. Here the transverse fault is cut off by a fault trending nearly due north, but the amount of displacement is not known.

There is no evidence by which the amount of movement along the Pool Canyon transverse fault can be determined. The stratigraphic throw ranges from 10,000 to 20,000 feet, as shown by the formations on each side. These figures, however, do not take into account the facts that the Carboniferous rocks south of the fault belong to the central facies and lie above the North Pass thrust, and that the lower Paleozoic formations to the north appear to be a continuation of the similar beds south of North Pass Canyon that are below the North Pass thrust.

Relation of Pool Canyon transverse fault to North Pass thrust.—The occurrence of the central facies of the Carboniferous formations on the south side of the Pool Canyon transverse fault shows that the North Pass thrust must have extended into this structural block, but the quartz monzonite intrusion and the gravel that occurs along the eastern portion of the block combine to conceal its outcrop. As the rocks north of the transverse fault are similar to those that were overridden by the North Pass thrust, the transverse fault marks the northern limit of the present exposures of the North Pass thrust plate.

If the suggestions made on page 78 are correct—that the Ochre Mountain thrust moved over the then existing surface and is only slightly younger than the Pool Canyon transverse fault—the transverse fault must have limited the thrust plate on the north at the time of thrusting, for otherwise the segment of the North Pass thrust plate north of the Pool Canyon fault would have been preserved beneath the Ochre Mountain thrust. This conclusion, together with the apparent limitation of the North Pass thrust on the south by a parallel transverse fault (p. 57), indicates that the North Pass thrust had a relatively slight extent along its strike in comparison with the amount of horizontal movement that took place along it.

Folding in rocks beneath Ochre Mountain thrust.—The lower Paleozoic rocks along the eastern front of Dutch Mountain form the western limb of a major anticline. The axis of the fold probably roughly coincides with the eastern base of the mountain, to judge from the prevailing flat dips and local east dips found there. The scattered exposures of the rocks beneath the thrust along the northern base of the mountain suggest that a minor anticline and syncline are superposed on the major fold in this region. These folds appear to be independent of the warping shown by the Ochre Mountain thrust.

Faulting below Ochre Mountain thrust south of Pool Canyon fault.—South of Pool Canyon the rocks underlying the Ochre Mountain thrust belong to the central facies of the Carboniferous. The two most prominent faults in this region, which strike west-northwest, have acted to enclose a band of the Oquirrh formation between two bands of the Ochre Mountain limestone. Minor faults, striking west of north, are made apparent in the central belt by offsets of the lower contact of the Oquirrh formation and are, in part at least, younger than the west-northwest fault, which they displace. In the central belt the Oquirrh formation and the Ochre Mountain limestone are separated by less than 100 feet of black shale that has been referred to the Manning Canyon formation. Such a thickness is much less than that normally shown by the Manning Canyon, and it seems probable that here, as in some other places, it has been thinned by overriding during thrusting. The thinning at this place may perhaps be correlated with a marked thickening to the southwest, just south of the Ferber Road. The two west-northwest faults are parallel in strike to the large transverse fault in Pool Canyon and are probably subsidiary fractures developed at the same time as the main fault. The northern of the two faults has been the site of movement sufficient to give an apparent vertical throw of at least 4,000 feet.

Spotted Fawn normal-fault zone.—A branching normal fault, which separates Lower and Middle Cambrian beds on the northeast from younger formations on the southwest, extends in a southwesterly direction from the vicinity of the Spotted Fawn mine. It may be traced to the north side of Tribune Gulch, beyond which it is concealed by gravel.

At the most southeasterly exposures, near the mouth of Tribune Gulch, the fault separates Prospect Mountain quartzite on the northeast from Upper Cambrian dolomite on the southwest. Though poorly exposed, it is, without much doubt, a single fracture. On the small 5,384-foot hill a 40-foot lenticular dike of quartz monzonite has been intruded along the fault, and a prospect pit on the southwest side shows the dip of the contact to be 58° SW. It is probable that this figure approximates the dip of the fault plane in this region. The fault continues as a single fracture without change in stratigraphic relations for more than 4,000 feet to the northwest. It is offset from 100 to 400 feet by four northeastward-striking faults that dip to the southeast. In all these places the outcrop of the fault is shifted to the southwest in the hanging wall of the younger faults, indicating a reverse movement along them.

North of the fourth offset, at a point where the fault is crossed by latitude 40°12′30″, it splits into two branches—a minor one separating the Prospect Mountain quartzite from the Cabin shale and the Busby quartzite and a main branch separating those two formations from the Upper Cambrian. The contact between the shale and the Busby quartzite in the block between the two branches is clearly the result of overriding by the quartzite, as shown by the discordance in dip between the two formations and also by the absence of the characteristic concretionary bed that normally occurs at the top of the shale.

About 500 feet north of the junction both branches are shifted about 100 feet to the west by the northeasterly reverse fault that causes a repetition of the outcrop of the Ochre Mountain thrust (p. 78). Two more branches are found north of the offsetting fault—one relatively small, within the Busby quartzite, and one that brings in a wedge of Middle Cambrian limestone between the Busby quartzite and the Upper Cambrian. The latter branch and the main branch are, a short distance father north, shifted about 300 feet to the east by still another northeasterly fault, along which, however, the displacement is apparently of the normal type. The two eastern branches cannot be confidently distinguished north of the intersecting fault, but there are two nearly parallel faults to the west, which are, in all probability, new branches. The throw on both of them is small, as is shown by the displacement of the Fish Haven dolomite.

Several of the branches cut the Ochre Mountain thrust. Along three of them the displacement of the thrust is notably at variance with the displacement of the beds beneath the thrust, indicating that the Spotted Fawn fault zone has been active during more than one structural cycle. Thus the most southwesterly branch that cuts the thrust drops the thrust several hundred feet to the southwest and drops the beds beneath the thrust an approximately equal amount to the northeast. The main branch of the fault that crops out a few hundred feet west of the Spotted Fawn shaft at 6,543 feet has a throw of 200 feet or less as measured by the thrust and at least 2,000 feet as measured beneath the thrust. The most easterly fault has similar relations. It offsets the thrust less than 100 feet, but in the beds beneath the thrust it separates Middle Cambrian limestone from Cabin shale and Busby quartzite—relations indicating a much larger throw.

The total throw along the Spotted Fawn fault zone in the beds beneath the thrust amounts to about 4,000 feet.

Faults in Royal Gulch "window."—The branches of the northwesterly Spotted Fawn fault are also exposed in Royal Gulch. Here, as on the east side of Dutch Mountain, they have been the sites of post-thrust as well as pre-thrust movement. There are in addition several northeastward-striking faults younger than the thrust. Some of these cut the post-thrust portions of the northwesterly faults, but others are cut by them.

The northwesterly continuation of the main branch of the Spotted Fawn normal fault illustrates most of the complexities of the faulting. Near the head of Royal Gulch it cuts the Ochre Mountain thrust and drops the portion to the southwest several hundred feet. It also offsets the Madison limestone above the thrust in such a way as to exhibit the local flexure in that formation (p. 79). Near the prospects on the north side of Royal Gulch it is cut and offset by a northeasterly fault with a low northwestward dip. The faulted segment causes a repetition of the Ochre Mountain thrust outcrop, which is 100 to 200 feet lower on the southwest side. Beneath the thrust, however, the beds on the northeast side have been dropped; Upper Cambrian dolomite is exposed on the northeast immediately below the thrust, and Laketown dolomite on the southwest, showing a pre-thrust throw that amounts to 1,000 feet or more. Near the mouth of the gulch the fault shifts a northeasterly fault several hundred feet. The northeasterly fault is similar in strike and dip to the one that cuts the Spotted Fawn fault to the southwest.

The probable continuation of the fault in Tribune Gulch whose movement is thought to have been dominantly horizontal (p. 79) is exposed in Royal Gulch. The tunnel at 5,593 feet cuts this fault and follows it for several feet. Throughout this distance the polished fault plane shows deep horizontal grooving.

Minor faults between Spotted Fawn and Pool Canyon faults.—The triangular area of rocks ranging from Upper Cambrian to Silurian between the Spotted Fawn normal fault, the Pool Canyon transverse fault, and the Ochre Mountain thrust show widespread minor faulting. Such faulting is apparently concentrated in the regions in which the Fish Haven dolomite crops out (pl. 2), for this dolomite is one of the few reliable horizon markers by which faults may be distinguished from zones of shattering. It is probable that more intensive field work would show the presence of additional outcrops of the Fish Haven dolomite in this region, especially in the strip of country between the two northeasterly faults on the two sides of hill 6279, on the south side of Tribune Gulch.

The faults in this triangular area strike in three general directions. The northeasterly faults are the youngest and include both reverse and normal faults. The other faults strike either north or west of north. The relations between these two groups are not conclusive, but farther north those striking west of north appear to be the younger. They are for the most part older than the thrust, however, but along some of them there has been renewed movement after the thrusting. These faults are essentially parallel in strike to the large normal fault just described and may have been formed at the same time. The alternate hypothesis, however, that some of the faulting was the direct result of the overthrusting whereby original slight elevations of the overridden surface were eliminated by being downfaulted, is suggested by the position of the outcrops of the Fish Haven dolomite on the south side of Tribune Gulch.

Faults beneath the thrust north of the Spotted Fawn fault.—The rocks beneath the thrust on the footwall side of the Spotted Fawn fault are all of Cambrian age, chiefly Lower and Middle Cambrian. The Prospect Mountain quartzite forms a large part of these rocks, and its uniform character and poor exposures prevent any attempt to correlate the faults exposed at its upper contact with those along the east base of Dutch Mountain in the places where shale members crop out. The exposures of the shale are relatively few, and are all partly concealed by gravel, but they show the same kinds of faults as are found along the upper contact of the quartzite. One of the largest of the faults along the east base of Dutch Mountain terminates on the south the exposure of the shale member north of the road to the Spotted Fawn mine. The shale member was not recognized south of the road, and the throw along this fault must therefore be about 1,000 feet.

In the interval between the upper boundary of the Prospect Mountain quartzite and the Ochre Mountain thrust several faults have been recognized by means of the distribution of the Cabin shale and Busby quartzite. To the north, in the wide outcrop of undifferentiated Middle Cambrian rocks, exposures are poor and faults are difficult to trace.

Several faults are exposed in the vicinity of the Spotted Fawn mine in addition to the Spotted Fawn normal faults. One of these is parallel to and on the north side of the canyon bottom southeast of the mine workings. It is unusual in that it is one of the few faults on Dutch Mountain that dips to the northeast. The fault drops the thrust 150 feet on the east side and causes a somewhat smaller but similar displacement of the upper contact of the Prospect Mountain quartzite beneath the thrust. Between these two points, however, the Cabin shale forms the footwall of the fault, and in the hanging wall are found successively Cabin shale, Busby quartzite, and a portion of the Abercrombie formation, representing vertical displacements ranging from 0 to about 1,000 feet. This, combined with the presence of Middle Cambrian limestones beneath the thrust on the footwall side of the fault, implies that there must have been some pre-thrust movement along this fault, in spite of the apparent concordance in throw at its intersections with the thrust and with the upper contact of the Prospect Mountain quartzite.

The exposures in the main tunnel of the Spotted Fawn mine indicate the presence of a minor thrust that is not readily recognized on the surface. The rocks exposed are highly metamorphosed beds of the Busby quartzite. The exposures on the surface and in two shallow shafts above the tunnel (see fig. 27), however, are Middle Cambrian limestones. The attitude of the two sets of exposures, together with the details of their distribution, show that they must be separated by a nearly horizontal fault. This fault is probably represented by 6 feet of breccia exposed at the top of the vertical raise in the northern branch of the tunnel, and its outcrop is probably just below the dump 100 feet north of the tunnel portal. The flat fault appears to offset the most easterly branch of the Spotted Fawn normal fault about 100 feet. No such offset was found along the eastward-dipping fault, and it is possible that the minor thrust is earlier.

Other evidences of horizontal movement in this region are abundant. In the tunnel the individual beds of quartzite are truncated by minor flat faults. Even more striking is the local overriding of the Cabin shale by the thin strip of Busby quartzite exposed in the footwall of the east branch of the Spotted Fawn fault. The best example of this feature was found about 1,400 feet east of south from the cabin at the Spotted Fawn.

There are undoubtedly many other nearly flat faults in the overridden formations between the Spotted Fawn and Garrison Monster mines, but extremely detailed work would be necessary to recognize and trace them. The unusually small thickness of the Busby quartzite and Cabin shale in Busby Canyon (pp. 7–8) points to this conclusion, as does the difficulty that was met in attempting to reconcile contradictory evidence as to the amount of displacement along many of the minor faults.

Only two other faults in the overridden block, south of the Garrison Monster mine, merit detailed description. One of these is the northwesterly normal fault about 1,000 feet south of the point at 6,785 feet and 2,500 feet northeast of the Spotted Fawn mine. This fault is relatively small, for the throw corresponds to a vertical drop of only 100 feet on the southwest side. Its chief interest lies in the fact that it cuts three nearly north-south normal faults, indicating that there is represented on Dutch Mountain a period of normal faulting definitely earlier than that of the prevailing northwesterly faults.

The second fault, or rather fault zone, strikes northwestward from peak 6264, on the north side of Busby Gulch. This zone is cut by several northeasterly faults, the largest of which is a reverse fault with a throw of about 100 feet. The fault zone has dropped the beds on the southwest side at least 500 feet and is the only one of this group comparable in size with the fault that terminates the shale member of the Prospect Mountain quartzite north of the road leading to the Spotted Fawn mine. If, as seems likely, the two faults are the same, they might serve as starting points to determine the fault pattern in the Prospect Mountain quartzite, should a more detailed study of the geology be undertaken.

The eastern portions of sections *C–C′* and *D–D′* show the more striking features of the overridden rocks. They are somewhat diagrammatic, however, particularly in the almost complete omission of the nearly horizontal minor thrusts that are probably rather widespread.

Garrison Monster transverse fault zone.—The fault zone near the Garrison Monster mine illustrates the mechanism of transverse faulting better than any of the other faults of this type in the quadrangle. It appears to represent a line of differential movement, north of which shortening was accomplished by thrusting and to the south by folding (p. 59 and fig. 8). The fault zone varies in character from a single steep fracture to a group of faults with relatively low dip.

The simple, steep portion of the fault is best seen south of the Garrison Monster inclined shaft, where it separates Prospect Mountain quartzite on the south from dolomitized Middle Cambrian limestones on the north (sec. $A-A'$). Eastward from this point the poor exposures indicate a swing in strike toward the northeast, and east of the tunnel at 4,834 feet, the strike, as shown by the scattered outcrops surrounded by gravel, must be very close to that direction. At the triple-peaked hill 2,000 feet southwest of bench mark 4382 on the railroad, the eastward continuation of the fault appears to be cut by a fault striking west-northwest.

West of the Garrison Monster incline, on the south side of the fault, the Prospect Mountain quartzite is overlain by the Cabin shale and the Busby quartzite. The shale shows pronounced drag effects near the fault, its strike swinging to nearly east-west and its dip steepening to more than 40° N. The Busby quartzite, however, shows no notable drag but has overridden the shale along a low-angle westward-dipping fault, which is exposed only close to the transverse fault. On the north side of the transverse fault the outcrop of Middle Cambrian beds wedges out westward, and the thrust plate of Upper Cambrian dolomite above it is adjacent to the fault. The thrust plate of dolomite in turn wedges out within a short distance, and at the bottom of the gulch leading to the Garrison Monster camp the Ochre Mountain limestone is next to the fault. The contact between the limestone and the dolomite must represent the Ochre Mountain thrust. Gravel flooring the gulch interrupts the outcrops for a few hundred feet. The dip of this section of the fault cannot be directly measured, but both the dips in the beds on each side and the effect of the topography upon its outcrop indicate that it must dip steeply to the north.

On the west wall of the gulch the Ochre Mountain limestone is in fault contact with Middle Cambrian beds, but the fault dips at a moderately low angle (about 40°) to the north. This fault has several branches with somewhat lower dips, which bring in, with various relations, all the formations that intervene between the Ochre Mountain limestone and the Middle Cambrian in the region to the south, where the thrust is essentially undeformed. The single steep fracture to the east has thus been replaced westward by a fault zone of low dip. The change in character coincides with the intersection of the transverse fault with the Ochre Mountain thrust. A similar coincidence was noted on the south side of Ochre Mountain (p. 71), and it was suggested that the low dip of the thrust had caused the change in dip of the transverse fault.

About 1,000 feet east of the mouth of Royal Gulch the northernmost of the series of branch faults disappears beneath the piedmont gravel. West of this point the projected course of the transverse fault is covered by gravel until the west side of the gravel-filled area in Accident Canyon is reached. In this distance, however, east-west strikes in the Woodman formation to the south and local nearly east-west fracture zones, particularly in the two eastern isolated outcrops in Accident Canyon, suggest strongly that the fault is not far distant. On the west side of Accident Canyon the projected line of the fault corresponds with a fault separating Madison limestone on the north and the Woodman formation on the south. The Woodman beds are poorly exposed but are thought to be rather closely folded, and the Madison limestone shows rather pronounced drag effects.

West of another gravel-covered interval the fault is again exposed along the base of the linear steep slope west of Accident Canyon. Here the Ochre Mountain thrust appears on the north side, the Woodman formation resting upon the Laketown dolomite. At the point where the steep slope curves northward, however, the fault does not cross the spur, as is shown by the continuous exposure of the Ochre Mountain thrust. There must, however, be some warping along this general line still farther west, because the Ochre Mountain thrust as exposed in the isolated outcrops to the north is at a much lower altitude than to the south (sec. $F-F'$).

Nature and amount of movement along Garrison Monster fault zone.—In the vicinity of the Garrison Monster mine the rocks north of the transverse fault are believed to have moved relatively eastward about 1½ miles. This belief is based upon the assumption that the westward-dipping fault separating the Woodman formation from the Ochre Mountain limestone exposed west of the Garrison Monster workings is the same as the steeply dipping portion of the Dutch Mountain fault (p. 84), to the south. This figure is roughly checked by the position of the Ochre Mountain thrust on both sides of the transverse fault.

It is probable that the transverse fault represents a line of differential movement, north of which crustal shortening took place along a thrust fault, and south of which shortening was accomplished by folding (fig. 8). The evidence for this belief is as follows: Thrusting of some sort seems required north of the thrust, for the Ochre Mountain thrust, which may be used as a horizon marker, is relatively undeformed north of the thrust except for a gentle westward dip. As the north side has apparently moved eastward, the crustal shortening must therefore have been effected by faulting. The northeastward curvature in strike shown by the transverse fault as it is followed eastward suggests that the transverse fault itself is passing into a thrust, but the absence of adequate exposures in that direction makes it impossible to prove the suggestion.

The folding of the Ochre Mountain thrust south of the transverse fault (p. 80) appears to provide the required amount of shortening to the south. The scaled distance along the folded thrust in a section nearly 2 miles south of the transverse fault showed that there had been half a mile of shortening along this line. This amount is only a third of the probable movement along the transverse fault and suggests that the amount of compression decreased southward, a suggestion that appears to be confirmed by the absence of comparable folding of the thrust in Pool Canyon, where the thrust is exposed for some distance in an east-west direction, and by the northeast strike of the axis of the fold, rather than the northerly strike that would be expected if the compression were of equal magnitude to the south.

Probable conjugate faulting related to Garrison Monster fault.—Two groups of faults that are younger than the Ochre Mountain thrust are present on Dutch Mountain, chiefly south of the Garrison Monster fault zone. The faults of one of these groups strike northeast and dip northwest. Many of them show an apparent reverse movement. The faults of the other group strike northwest and dip southwest. They commonly follow lines of pre-thrust faulting in the beds below the thrust. On some of them the movement has been largely horizontal. Although the northeasterly faults commonly cut the northwesterly ones, locally, as in Royal Gulch, the reverse is true. These relations suggest that the two groups of faults are essentially contemporaneous and form a set of conjugate faults. As some of the northeasterly faults appear to change their strike to east as they approach the Garrison Monster fault zone and to become a part of that zone, it seems probable that the conjugate faulting was genetically related to the transverse faulting.

Similar conjugate faults adjacent to the contemporaneous transverse faults to the south are apparently lacking. A possible explanation for the difference in relations may lie in the fact that the Garrison Monster fault has a much smaller strike length than the other faults of this character, and that for this reason the necessary readjustments in the passive block south of the fault were accomplished by both folding and faulting, whereas in the longer transverse faults the necessary shortening in the passive block could be accomplished by folding alone.

Because of their abundance, some of the conjugate faults are not shown on plate 3. Where the northwesterly faults of the system do not cut the Ochre Mountain thrust, it is uncertain whether or not the fault was active in pre-thrust or post-thrust time or in both. For this reason many of the faults shown on plate 3 are marked with the symbol for two different structural cycles, although most of them were probably active at only one time.

One of the most persistent of the northeasterly faults has a low northwestward dip throughout most of the exposures in Royal Gulch and Accident Canyon, but at the floor of Accident Canyon its dip is almost vertical (pl. 7, *C*).

Dutch Mountain thrust.—The contact between the Ochre Mountain limestone and the Woodman formation throughout the block is a thrust fault. In most of the region the thrust has a low dip, and its presence is shown either by a minor discordance in dip between the two formations and rather considerable variations in the thickness of the underlying Woodman formation in the higher portion of Dutch Mountain, or by the close folding of the Woodman formation below the thrust on the west side of Accident Canyon. The thrust dips steeply westward, however, in the southern part of Accident Canyon. This steeply dipping portion almost certainly connects a flatter portion whose outcrop encircles the summit of the mountain and another flatter portion exposed west of Accident Canyon, for no other faults were recognized that could bring about the observed relations.

The steep portion of the thrust must be an original feature and not due to later folding. This is definitely proved by the absence of such folding in the beds beneath the thrust, as is shown particularly by small outcrops of Madison limestone close to the steep portion of the thrust at altitudes that closely approximate those obtained by projecting the outcrops on the east side of Dutch Mountain.

In the exposures of the Dutch Mountain thrust along the northwestern edge of the mountain the interval between this thrust and the Ochre Mountain thrust is much smaller than to the southeast, beneath the higher parts of Dutch Mountain. This is due chiefly to the occurrence of the steeper part of the Dutch Mountain thrust between the two localities, but in addition there appears to have been some minor warping of the Dutch Mountain thrust that is not shown by the Ochre Mountain thrust. The Dutch Mountain thrust must therefore be the older of the two. This conclusion is confirmed by the relations of the two thrusts to the Trail Gulch fault, described below. The Dutch Mountain thrust is cut off by this fault, but the Ochre Mountain thrust is not affected by it.

In addition to the two major exposures of the thrust, there are two smaller isolated outcrops that are considered to be continuations of it. One of these is on the south side of Pool Canyon southeast of peak 7262, where the Ochre Mountain limestone rests with fault contact upon the Woodman formation. The thrust here dips notably to the east as a result of the disturbance in the beds above the Ochre Mountain thrust by the Pool Canyon transverse fault. The second small outcrop is in the vicinity of the Garrison Monster mine. Here a westward-dipping fault that separates Ochre Mountain limestone from the Woodman formation is believed to be a continuation of the steeper part of the Dutch Mountain thrust offset eastward by the Garrison Monster transverse fault.

Trail Gulch fault.—The fault in Trail Gulch, on the west slope of Dutch Mountain, shows rather noteworthy variations in strike, ranging from nearly north in the south-central portion through northwest to nearly west in the northern portion. It has been traced for about 4 miles and through most of this distance forms the boundary between the Oquirrh formation on the west and Mississippian formations on the east. The dip is also somewhat variable but is in general steep to the west or south.

The total throw along the fault cannot be measured with any confidence, because of the lack of definite horizon markers on either side, and also because to the south it includes the throw of the steep portion of the Dutch Mountain thrust. Immediately north of its intersection with the thrust, the throw must be equivalent to about 1,000 feet or more of the Pennsylvanian plus at least 1,500 feet of the Ochre Mountain limestone. The throw appears to be considerably less farther north, however. At the extreme south end the total throw is about equal to the thickness of the Ochre Mountain limestone, but here the throw along the Dutch Mountain thrust is included.

The chief interest of this fault lies in the fact it has been active at least three times. The greater part of the movement clearly occurred before the formation of the Ochre Mountain thrust, because at its south end it is cut off by the thrust. This movement was normal. A second normal movement along the central portion of the fault appears to have occurred at a comparatively recent time, to judge from the topographic discordance at the fault, the notable influence of the fault upon the drainage pattern, and the presence of gravels resting upon the mature surface adjoining the fault east of knoll 6518. The amount of the later movement, as estimated from the topography, is thought to be about 800 feet (sec. *D–D'*).

In addition to these two periods of activity, both of which resulted in normal faulting, the fault also appears to have been the site of reverse movement at the time the Ochre Mountain thrust was formed, but it was not possible to obtain a quantitative idea of the amount, as the evidence is indirect. One indication is the abundance of minor folds in the Oquirrh formation immediately west of the Trail Gulch fault and the absence of such features to the east (sec. *D–D'*). This appears to show that the fault acted as a plane of relief along which movement took place while the beds to the west were being folded, thus protecting the beds to the east from similar deformation. Another indication is that in the region west of Pool Canyon neither the fault itself nor the Oquirrh formation in its hanging wall have been affected by the notable deformation shown by the thrust and the overlying Mississippian beds at the point where the Pool Canyon transverse fault was overridden by the thrust. These relations strongly suggest renewed movement along the fault, either of a reverse or transverse character, by the beds on its hanging wall.

In summary, the fault appears to have been first formed as a normal fault of large throw after the period of thrusting represented by the Dutch Mountain thrust but before the Ochre Mountain thrust. During the formation of the Ochre Mountain thrust it was again active, but the direction of movement was reversed. Finally, renewed normal faulting occurred at a relatively recent time.

Minor structural features in the rocks above the Ochre Mountain thrust.—In addition to the minor faults that cut the rocks both above and below the Ochre Mountain thrust, there are a few minor faults that occur only in rocks above the thrust. One of these is a small reverse fault south-southwest of Woodman Peak and west of the Trail Gulch fault. This fault dips 45° W. and has caused the lower beds of the Oquirrh formation to override several hundred feet of the Manning Canyon formation. Its relation to the Trail Gulch fault could not be determined, and whether it is of the same age as the Ochre Mountain thrust or the Dutch Mountain thrust is therefore not known. It is terminated on the southwest by a younger fault.

Folding in this area was largely confined to the beds west of the Trail Gulch fault. Gentle folds are also found east of the fault, as is shown in section *D–D'*, but are of much less intensity. Two well-defined folds occur west of the fault—a syncline near the fault and an anticline farther west. The synclinal axis strikes a little east of north, passing about 500 feet east of summit 6518. Dips on the east limb are in general steeper than those on the limb common to both the syncline and the anticline.

The anticlinal axis strikes nearly north through a point 1,000 feet east of Summit 6130. On the north the axis appears to split into several minor folds, one of which is shown in plate 7, *B*. On this fold the steeper dips are on the west limb, where locally vertical beds are found. West of the anticline the folding apparently increased in intensity but decreased in regularity, and no continuous folds could be recognized in the low hills that form the northwest spur of Dutch Mountain (sec. *F–F'*). In the minor and discontinuous folds in this region overturned beds are locally found. Figure 10 shows the course of a cross-bedded dolomitic sandstone west of the anticlinal axis which illustrates these points. The position of three summits shown on the topographic map is added to aid in the location of the bed.

It is probable that two stages of folding are represented west of the Trail Gulch fault. The two larger and more persistent folds are believed to have been formed before the Trail Gulch fault became active, as they do not affect the fault and there are no comparable folds east of the fault. The smaller, locally overturned folds to the north, however, are considered to have

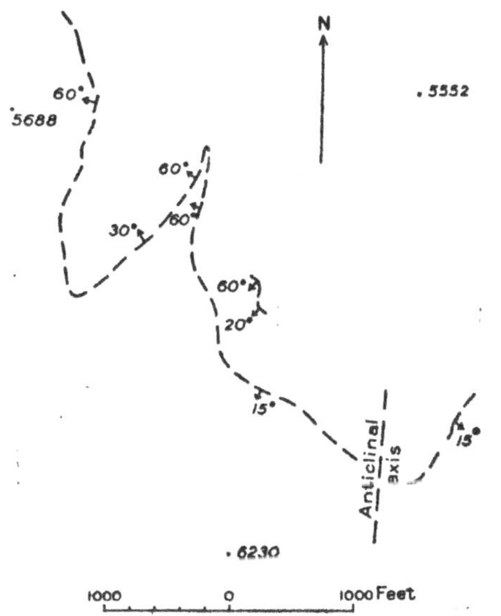

FIGURE 10.—Sketch map showing folding of a bed in the Oquirrh formation on the northwest side of Dutch Mountain. Elevations are summits shown on plate 2.

been superposed on the older folds at the time of the reverse movement along the Trail Gulch fault. The steep dips on the east limb of the larger syncline may also have originated at this time, as in the rest of the folded belt the intensity of folding increases westward.

Fault along west side of Dutch Mountain.—The notably straight west side of Dutch Mountain, which transgresses the structure at a considerable angle, suggests strongly that there has been relatively recent faulting here. Locally the tips of the spurs along this line exhibit slickensided surfaces. The throw along the supposed fault cannot be determined stratigraphically, but there is a difference in altitude of about 500 feet between the linear flat ridges east of the fault and the flat-topped isolated outcrops to the west. To the south the fault line changes its strike from southeast to east-southeast. The topographic discordance persists into this region, but to a somewhat less degree. Rock exposures on both sides of the fault, however, show that the movement along this part of it has been more complex. The distribution of the central facies of the Oquirrh formation on both sides of the fault and the presence of the Ochre Mountain thrust on the northeast side indicate that the movement was reverse. This conflicting evidence is believed to indicate that movement along the fault has occurred at two different times—an earlier one, in which the movement was probably transverse, resulting in the relative depression of the thrust northeast of the fault, and a recent one, in which the apparent movement was in the opposite direction but was not of sufficient magnitude to conceal the older movement.

Mutual relations of the structural features.—The relations of the structural features exposed in the Dutch Mountain block to one another are not as clear as in the blocks to the south. A group of north-south normal faults on the east side of Dutch Mountain appear to be the oldest features that were recognized. They are cut by a series of northwesterly normal faults, the greater part of whose activity must have preceded the Ochre Mountain thrust, and for this reason they are considered to have been formed in the second stage of the first cycle. None of these faults were found in contact with structural features assigned to the first stage of the second cycle, however, and their age is therefore in some doubt.

The initial stage of the second cycle is clearly represented by the Dutch Mountain thrust, whose age relative to the Ochre Mountain thrust is definitely shown by the intersections of the two thrusts with the Trail Gulch fault. This stage appears to have been characterized chiefly by folding, however, and at least five of the larger folds in the block were formed at this time. Normal faults of the second stage of the cycle are abundant. The bulk of the movement along the Trail Gulch and Spotted Fawn faults was accomplished before the development of the Ochre Mountain thrust, and several parallel faults of less magnitude are of the same age.

The dominant structural feature of the block—the Ochre Mountain thrust—was formed in the first stage of the third cycle. The relatively thin thrust plates beneath it north of the Spotted Fawn mine are contemporaneous. A number of transverse faults, of which the Pool Canyon fault is the largest, appear to be only slightly older than the Ochre Mountain thrust and to be of the same age as the North Pass thrust. Renewed activity along the Trail Gulch fault and minor drag folding adjacent to the fault also occurred at this time. Normal faulting in the second stage of the third cycle appears to have been very slight in amount, only one fault being assigned to this stage.

The fourth cycle was marked by the formation of the Garrison Monster transverse fault and its associated warping and conjugate faulting. Several of the northwesterly conjugate faults appear to have followed normal faults that first became active in the second cycle.

The youngest faults are the relatively recent normal faults to which the elevation of the block is largely due. The two faults of this age on the west have utilized older fault lines along at least parts of their courses.

NORTHWESTERN BLOCK

The northwestern block is west of the Dutch Mountain block and northwest of the Ochre Mountain block. Its southern boundary is the northern limit of the wide part of the Deep Creek Valley. The boundary between this block and the Dutch Mountain block coincides with a normal fault of rather large throw. There is, however, no structural break between this block and the Ochre Mountain block.

Geologically, the block is one of the simplest so far considered. The dominant structural feature in its east half is a recumbent anticline, whose axis appears to lie roughly parallel to and 2,500 to 3,000 feet higher than the Ochre Mountain thrust (secs. *F''–F*, *D''–D*, and *N''–N*). The fold is older than the White Sage formation, but both are cut by two groups of faults, one striking northeast and one northwest.

The portion of the block west of Bar Creek is separated from the eastern portion by a nearly north-south zone, which is to the north a gravel-filled valley, and to the south a linear outcrop of volcanic rocks. This zone marks the line of a fault or group of faults along which the beds to the west have probably been dropped 5,000 feet. There is some evidence to indicate that a small part of this throw may have occurred in rather recent time. The region west of the fault zone is characterized by an open anticlinal fold and abundant small normal faults. Along the extreme west edge, however, there are locally rather close folds and minor overthrusts.

Tank Wash fault.—The fault along the boundary between the northwestern block and the Dutch Mountain block is nowhere exposed, but one is obviously required in Tank Wash between the eastward-dipping White Sage formation at an altitude of 5,610 feet and the fossiliferous beds high in the Oquirrh formation near benchmark 5544, on the one hand, and the beds low in the Oquirrh formation to the east, on the other. The total throw along the fault in this region must amount to about 4,000 feet, which was probably accomplished in stages, as indicated by the relations of the fault to the Ochre Mountain thrust.

To the north the strike of the fault appears to swing to the northwest, as is suggested by the fracturing seen in the exposures at the road fork southwest of benchmark 5068 on the Ferber Road. A fault with similar strike and westward dip in the Ochre Mountain block (pp. 76–77) is thought to be a continuation of the Tank Wash fault. This fault is clearly later than the overthrust and has a throw estimated at 300 feet. In both of these respects it differs from the northerly outcrops of the Tank Wash fault. The large throw along the fault is clearly of pre-thrust age, as the nearly continuous exposures south of Dutch Mountain show that the thrust has nowhere been cut by normal faults that cause more than a few hundred feet of vertical displacement. The main movement along the Tank Wash fault must therefore have occurred before the development of the Ochre Mountain thrust, and the post-thrust throw of 300 feet represents renewed movement along the older fault.

Twin Peaks recumbent anticline.—The recumbent anticline that is so prominent a feature of the east half of the block is best exposed just south of the southern summit of Twin Peaks. Exposures on the south side of peak 6147, 4 miles to the south, are also convincing and serve to justify the extension of the axis of the fold between the two points into regions where it can be located less easily. As shown on the map and structure sections $D''-D$, $F''-F$, and $N''-N$, the axial plane of the fold has a low and somewhat irregular northerly dip. At both Twin Peaks and peak 6147 the beds involved in the fold are the massive rather pure limestones that belong in the lower part of the western facies of the Oquirrh formation. This indicates that the original strike of the axis of the fold was about N. 15° E. The present low northward dip of the axial plane is probably a later development.

The fold is clearly older than the Eocene (?) White Sage formation, for beds belonging to that formation overlap the axis of the fold about a mile west of a point in Tank Wash on the Ferber Road at an altitude of 5,610 feet. It is also, of course, older than the northeasterly and northwesterly faults that cut that formation. It is believed to be older than the Ochre Mountain thrust for the following reasons: The fold is clearly older than the latest movement along the Tank Wash fault, along which the bulk of the throw must be of pre-thrust age, although some 300 feet may represent post-thrust movement. It is also probably older than the pre-thrust component of the normal fault. If it were younger, some trace of the fold should appear on the high ridges on Dutch Mountain west of the Trail Gulch fault, but none has been found. Moreover, if the fold were younger than the earliest movement along the fault, the fault could scarcely have the linear outcrop it now shows, nor could there have been renewed movement along it. If these two features can be relied upon, the fold must be considerably older than the Ochre Mountain thrust, and the folding must have been separated from the thrusting by a period of normal faulting.

Relations of recumbent anticline to structural features on Dutch Mountain.—The Dutch Mountain thrust and the larger folds west of the Trail Gulch fault on Dutch Mountain, like the Twin Peaks recumbent anticline, are older than the Ochre Mountain thrust. These features are also older than two westward-dipping normal faults of rather large throw, and it is believed that they were all formed during the same cycle of deformation. If this view is correct, the more easterly exposures represent the features formed at greater depths, for the two younger normal faults, the Trail Gulch fault and the Tank Wash fault, have the down-thrown side on the west. The most intensive folding, however, is found in the westerly exposures, where the recumbent anticline occurs. Folding in the Oquirrh formation west of the Trail Gulch fault decreased in intensity eastward, and east of the fault folds are essentially absent. The strongest folding, therefore, was originally at the higher altitudes. Figure 11 shows the supposed relations between these features before the initiation of movement along the Trail Gulch and Tank Wash faults.

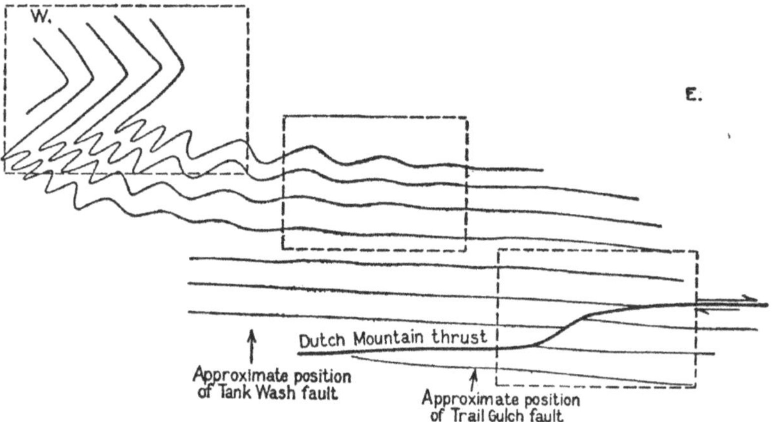

FIGURE 11.—Generalized section showing supposed original relations between the Twin Peaks recumbent anticline and the Dutch Mountain thrust. The areas enclosed by dashed lines represent in a general way the present exposures on both sides of the two normal faults.

The concentration of the close folding at higher altitudes suggests that a thrust fault, now removed by erosion, once existed above the highest of the present exposures. The observed structure and stratigraphy west of Bar Creek (p. 88) to some extent support this view.

The close folds of relatively small scale and the variations in the thickness of individual beds that are thought to lie immediately below the main recumbent fold (fig. 11) appear to be rather poorly exposed in the vicinity of hill 5850, west of benchmark 5544, and in the region south and west of the hill toward summit 6266.

Minor faulting east of Bar Creek.—Four faults of relatively small throw cut the recumbent fold and also the White Sage formation. Two of these faults strike northwest and are offset by two northeasterly faults. One of the northwesterly faults is readily recognized on the southwest side of Twin Peaks, where the anticlinal axis is dropped on the southwest side. The vertical throw amounts to about 800 feet and may be measured rather accurately by the offset shown by the upper contact of the series of limestones that form Twin Peaks. Just north of peak 5876 this fault is offset about a quarter of a mile to the east by a northeasterly fault. South of this point the offset segment is readily traced by reason of the fact that it limits on the east a narrow outcrop of the White Sage formation. Still farther to the south the fault is concealed by volcanic rocks.

The second of the two northwesterly faults crops out northeast of the 5,850-foot hill that lies on the north flank of peak 6266. This fault forms the western boundary of another exposure of the White Sage formation. The positions of the axial plane of the fold on both sides of the fault indicate that the maximum throw along it does not exceed 400 feet. The fault is terminated on the south by one of the northeasterly faults. The offset portion was not recognized in the lava-capped region to the south.

The northeasterly fault south of Twin Peaks can be definitely recognized only on the north side of peak 5876, where it offsets the northwesterly fault. The throw of the fault must be rather large at this point, with downthrow to the southeast, because of the stratigraphic differences on the two sides and also because of the amount of offset of the older fault. The displacement must die out within a short distance to the southwest, however, for individual beds that cross its projected strike less than a mile southwest of peak 5876 show no offset. The relation of the fault to the northwesterly fault along the east boundary of the block is unknown, the gravel cover in this region preventing any direct observations.

The second of the two northeasterly faults is on the north and northwest sides of peak 6266, where its presence is indicated by the difference in structure on the two sides. To the northwest the axial plane of the fold crops out at an altitude of about 5,700 feet, and to the southeast the structure observed at the summit of hill 6266 shows that the axial plane must have been several hundred feet higher still. The throw along the fault at this point must therefore approach 1,000 feet. To the northeast the course of the fault is apparently marked by a region of silicification east of hill 5850. Beyond this point the fault was not recognized, and the fact that individual beds continue unbroken across its projected strike seems to indicate that it dies out within a rather short distance in this direction.

The age of these four faults is not known. On plate 3 they are all assigned to the fourth cycle, as they correspond in strike with the conjugate faults related to the Garrison Monster transverse fault. The apparent throws are somewhat larger than those along the other conjugate faults, and the faults may therefore represent two unrelated stages of faulting, the northwesterly faults being the older.

Bar Creek fault.—West of peak 6147 there is a strip of volcanic rocks about three-quarters of a mile in width. This is succeeded northward by a somewhat wider valley filled with gravel. The gravel and volcanic rocks in this belt must conceal a considerable fault or fault zone, because of the differences in structure and stratigraphy on the two sides. On peak 6147, where prevolcanic rocks crop out nearest to the supposed fault, here called the Bar Creek fault, the rocks belong to the thick limestone member that occurs near the base of the western facies of the Oquirrh formation. At this point, too, the axial plane of the recumbent fold is exposed at an altitude of about 5,600 feet. West of the concealed zone, however, the beds belong to the highest portion of the Oquirrh formation and are overlain by the White Sage formation. Furthermore, the structure observed on the west side cannot be correlated with the recumbent fold, although the altitudes are such that the axis of this fold should be exposed if it continued westward unbroken. These two features make it seem certain that the belt is the site of notable displacement with north-south strike and with downthrow to the west. The apparent throw along the fault is about 5,000 feet, as it includes the thickness of the Oquirrh formation above the limestone member (4,500 feet) plus about 500 feet of that member. If, however, the region west of the fault is underlain by a thrust fault, as there is some reason to believe (p. 88), the actual throw may depart widely from this estimate. The present distribution of the White Sage formation on both sides of the fault is such that a much smaller throw is necessary than any that would reasonably explain the structure shown by the underlying Carboniferous rocks and suggests that the Bar Creek fault, like many others in the quadrangle, has been the site of recurrent movement. A rough measure of the later movement is suggested by the difference in altitude of the old postmature erosion surface on the two sides of the fault, which amounts to about 600 to 800 feet, the region west of the fault being the lower. This figure is ample to explain the present distribution of the White Sage formation if it was, as supposed, deposited in relatively small basins.

Anticline west of Bar Creek.—West of the Bar Creek fault the Carboniferous formations are folded in a poorly defined anticline, which is most readily recognized to the south. About a mile east of that portion of Deep Creek between benchmarks 5097 and 5045 the Oquirrh formation strikes west of north and dips to the east. Farther north and west the strike swings to the northwest. On the west side of Deep Creek the strike is somewhat more westerly, and still farther west it changes to west with northerly dips. Finally, the most westerly outcrops of the Carboniferous formations strike a little east of north and dip to the west, completing the fold (sec. *D″–D*).

The axis of the fold in this region strikes about N. 15° E. through benchmark 5045 and plunges gently to the north. North of the hills west of the 5,122-foot depression the projected axis passes beneath gravel and could not be further traced. At this point the axis is poorly defined and is obscured by faulting. Several minor folds and thrusts exposed near the northern boundary of the quadrangle may replace the single major fold to the north.

Minor folds west of Bar Creek.—The most striking of the several minor folds west of Bar Creek is an anticline with moderately steep dips on both limbs, which is exposed in the isolated hill in the Deep Creek Valley half a mile east of north of altitude 4,992 feet on the Deep Creek road. Just beyond the northern border of the quadrangle dips as high as 85° were observed. A syncline must be present in the alluvium-filled valley between these outcrops and the hills to the east.

Southeast of the anticline the erratic east and southeast dips north of hill 5434 may indicate the presence of another subsidiary fold on the west limb of the main anticline, but the extensive faulting in this region prevents any satisfactory interpretation.

Two small overturned folds are exposed beneath a minor thrust fault in the hills along the western border of the quadrangle west and northwest of altitude 4,984 feet on the Deep Creek road. The presence of the folds is shown by the repetition of outcrops of the dark cherty beds in the upper portion of the Oquirrh formation, which dips 60°–75° W. on both limbs of the folds. The more westerly of the two folds is an anticline. It is cut off on the south by a fault striking north of west, which just east of the quadrangle boundary swings in strike to nearly south and decreases notably in dip. The unfolded beds above the fault dip rather gently to the south and include the basal beds of the Gerster formation. The stratigraphic hiatus between this horizon and the black chert zone is about 2,500 feet. The curving fault seems to be best explained as a transverse fault that passes eastward into a thrust, a relation that was also found in several places in the Deep Creek Mountains (p. 67). Although these faults are shown on plate 3 as being of the same age as the large anticline, it is equally possible that they were formed in a later structural cycle.

There is apparently another fold on the west side of Deep Creek. This is an east-west synclinal warp that is indicated by the northerly dips in the hills west of altitude 5,045 feet and southerly dips in the region west of altitude 4,984 feet. The intervening low-lying area is covered by volcanic rocks and gravel, which conceal the structure of the Carboniferous rocks beneath them. The syncline cannot be recognized on the east side of Deep Creek. The strike of the axis of this fold does not correspond to any of the other structural features that have been found in the district, and the apparent limitation of the fold to the west side of Deep Creek suggests that it may be causally connected with the volcanic rocks that now occupy its axial portion. Two intrusive plugs were found in this volcanic area, and a careful search might disclose others. The syncline might therefore be interpreted as a downwarp resulting from the extrusion of volcanic matter from a source immediately beneath.

Faulting west of Bar Creek.—Three groups of faults are found in the region. A group of northeasterly faults appear to be the youngest of the three and are widely distributed. A group of northwesterly faults are also found throughout this part of the block; they are everywhere cut by the northeasterly faults. Two nearly north-south faults northwest of altitude 5,062 feet on the Deep Creek road are thought to belong to a third group. They are terminated on the south by one of the northwesterly faults.

Two of the northwesterly faults and one northeasterly fault have rather large throws. The northeasterly fault cuts the northwesterly faults and is believed to shift them three-quarters of a mile, the offset being to the northeast on the northwest side of the younger fault.

The two northwesterly faults are both exposed on the east side of Deep Creek. The more southwesterly one crops out east of benchmark 5097 and has brought the White Sage formation on the southwest into contact with the Oquirrh formation on the northeast. By projecting the contact between the two formations as exposed on both sides of the fault, the throw is seen to be about 1,200 feet. The more northeasterly of the two faults is parallel in strike and about three-quarters of a mile distant. The relations are similar, but the throw is about 1,800 feet.

On the west side of Deep Creek northwesterly faults with comparable throws are found some distance to the north. Thus just west of benchmark 5062 on the Deep Creek road there is a northwesterly fault whose throw is about 1,000 feet and which appears to correspond with the more southwesterly of the two faults east of the creek. The second northwesterly fault appears to be concealed by the gravel north of altitude 5,045 feet on the Deep Creek road. The throw along this fault is about 2,000 feet, as measured by exposures of the White Sage formation on each side of the fault, and it is therefore comparable to the throw along the more northeasterly of the two faults east of Deep Creek.

The northeasterly fault that is believed to have caused this shifting of the northwesterly faults is concealed by the gravel and clay that floor the Deep Creek Valley throughout most of its course. The exposures on the east side of Deep Creek, east of altitude 5,045 feet, permit it to be located rather closely, however, as beds in the White Sage formation southeast of the fault strike directly into beds well below the top of the Oquirrh formation on the northwest. The throw along this fault appears to be chiefly horizontal and to amount to about three-quarters of a mile. The vertical component of the throw is comparatively small and varies not only in amount but in direction at different places along the fault.

All three faults are shown on plate 3 as having been formed in the fourth structural cycle, in the belief that they are a part of the conjugate fault system exhibited on Dutch Mountain. The throws along these faults are much larger than were observed on Dutch Mountain, however, and these faults may therefore be of different age.

Concealed thrust fault west of Bar Creek.—If, as seems certain, the down-faulted continuation of the Twin Peaks recumbent anticline underlies the region west of the Bar Creek fault, any attempt to project the surface structure downward to connect with that fold fails, because of the impossibility of correlating the progressively older beds encountered in the core of the fold as it is followed westward with the progressively younger formations exposed at the surface westward from the Bar Creek fault. The only apparent method by which these conflicting features may be reconciled lies in the assumption that a nearly horizontal thrust fault must intervene between the recumbent fold and the structural features exposed at the surface. East of the Bar Creek fault this hypothetical thrust has been removed by erosion, but it provides an explanation of the curious relation of the recumbent anticline to the observed structure on Dutch Mountain.

Mutual relations of the structural features.—The faults and folds in the northwestern block are not easily dated with relation to those in the remainder of the quadrangle. The folding of the Twin Peaks recumbent anticline and the major part of the movement along the Tank Wash fault are the only two events whose chronologic position is certain, and both belong in the second structural cycle. The early movement along the Bar Creek fault is also thought to have occurred during this cycle, as all the other normal faults of large throw found in the quadrangle were formed at that time. If that assignment is correct, the large anticline west of the fault was also formed at least as early as the second cycle, for it is cut by the fault. The minor folds and thrusts associated with the anticline were perhaps also formed at this time, but it is equally possible that they were developed at some later date.

The third structural cycle, which produced so many changes in other parts of the quadrangle, is very poorly represented in this block. The warping of the axial plane of the recumbent anticline may have occurred at this time, as may some of the minor folds and thrusts shown on plate 3 as belonging to the second cycle. The north-south normal faults west of Deep Creek are believed to represent the second stage of the third cycle.

The abundant northeasterly and northwesterly faults found throughout the block have been assigned to the fourth cycle, in the belief that they are similar to the conjugate faults of this age on Dutch Mountain.

The recent movement along the Bar Creek fault and the east-west synclinal warping west of Deep Creek are the latest events recognized.

QUARTZ MONZONITE BLOCK

The quartz monzonite block differs from the other structural blocks in the quadrangle in that the faults it contains either affect only the quartz monzonite or have a causal relation to the quartz monzonite. Three groups of faults appear to be included by this description. The first group is composed of faults that are thought to have formed contemporaneously with the emplacement of the intrusive; the second is made up of faults of small throw and diverse age that probably are related to the cooling igneous mass; and the third includes faults that seem to require the action of external forces for their formation.

Faults related to the emplacement of the quartz monzonite.—The faults of the first group cannot be proved to be directly connected with the intrusion, for they do not themselves cut the quartz monzonite. The faults that are placed in this group are those that displace the Ochre Mountain thrust in the roof pendants, or in the sedimentary rocks adjoining the stock along or near its western boundary. The location and character of the two largest faults in this group are described on pages 75–76, where these faults are correlated with the intrusion on the grounds that elsewhere in the district faults of this magnitude did not cut the thrust.

The distribution of these faults seems to have some significance. They show a localization along the western border of the stock, to which they are roughly parallel. Similar faults appear to be absent both in the roof pendants to the east and in the exposures of sedimentary rocks along the southern and northern borders. These spatial relations are the same as those of a group of ore deposits that contain considerable quantities of such minerals as tourmaline, humite, axinite, danburite, and scheelite, the formation of which is commonly thought to require relatively high temperatures.

The coincidence of the belt of faulting with the belt of high-temperature mineralization is thought to indicate that this belt marks the location of the primary channel through which the quartz monzonite was intruded, the faulting being a secondary consequence of the upwelling magma. As the faulting occurred before the intrusive solidified and the faults were utilized by the magma in its ascent, there would be no displacement of the igneous contacts, and thus there is no direct evidence of the relation between the two.

In several other places the quartz monzonite has used faults during its emplacement, but in all of them, so far as can be ascertained, the relation is a passive one, the faults being much older than the intrusive and undergoing no renewal of movement during the process. This is certainly the case on the south side of Montezuma Peak, where the influence of earlier faulting upon the boundaries of the igneous rock is most marked; and also in Pool Canyon, where the older Pool Canyon transverse fault has served to localize a tongue of the intrusion.

There is a considerable body of evidence indicating that the intrusive did not exert any doming effect on the invaded rocks except for the relatively slight uplift in the zone described in the preceding paragraphs. This is best shown by the exposure of the Ochre Mountain thrust plane in roof pendants at altitudes rather closely concordant with those of the thrust in areas distant from the intrusion. On the southern slopes of Montezuma Peak, moreover, the intrusion has broken through an eastward-dipping monoclinal sequence without any apparent effect on the preintrusive strike and dip of the invaded rocks. The same lack of concordance between the boundary of the intrusive and the structure of the invaded rocks is shown along the northern and western contacts but somewhat less clearly because of the more complex structure of the sedimentary rocks at these places.

Structural features related to the solidification of the quartz monzonite.—The structural features of the second group are numerous and wide-spread. They include faults and shear zones whose throws can be definitely measured, as well as fractures followed by dikes and veins, along some of which also faulting can be definitely proved. The joints that occur in the quartz monzonite may also be included, for the evidence is clear that at least some of them were formed during the same period as the other structural features of this group.

An attempt was made to classify these features according to their strikes and dips and to correlate such groups either with an areal distribution or with the type of dike or vein that filled them or was faulted by them—an indirect and approximate measure of the age. In this attempt nearly 100 strikes and dips were chosen at random, about one half from quartz-sulphide veins and the remainder from other ore-bearing veins, from dikes, and from unmineralized faults.

The only conclusion that was reached from this study was that unmineralized faults or shear zones showed a strong tendency to strike either nearly east or nearly north. For the other groups there was no uniformity in strike or dip within a group, nor was any pronounced areal pattern of fracturing discernible. A graphic compilation of the strikes and dips upon which this conclusion is based is shown in figure 12.

These fractures appear to be of diverse age and throw, as well as of diverse orientation, although they were all formed after the solidification of the quartz monzonite and before the introduction of the material that now fills them. Only a few preserve any evidence whatever of the amount of movement along them.

Intersecting dikes of different kinds within the stock indicate fissuring at different times. They are found particularly northwest of Gold Hill, and also immediately east of hill 5675, on the north side of Rodenhouse Wash. There appears to have been little or no movement along any of these fractures.

The relatively early formation of some of the joints in the igneous rock is shown by two different sets of phenomena. One is the coating of joints by black tourmaline or green epidote, both minerals characteristic of what are thought to be the earliest of the ore deposits. The other is the transgression of the joints at a large angle by quartz-sulphide veins on the old Mammoth claim and also at several prospects on the south side of Rodenhouse Wash.

Less conclusive evidence for different times of fracturing is furnished by compound dikes and by the occurrence in the same fracture either of two different kinds of veins or of a dike and a vein. Compound dikes are not uncommon, and in the Monocca mine a carbonate vein follows the same fissure that had been filled earlier by a copper-lead sulphide deposit. The presence of a quartz-sulphide vein along the wall of a granite porphyry dike in the Cyclone mine proves that this particular fracture must have been opened at two widely separated times, for quartz-sulphide veins were formed relatively late in the sequence of mineralization, all of which took place later than the intrusion of the dike.

There are only a few fractures along which the throw can be determined. One of these is exposed on the property of the Silver & Gold Mining Co., southeast of Calico Hill. Here an unbrecciated quartz vein occupies a fissure that displaces the contact of the quartz monzonite and the sedimentary rocks 10 feet. An even more striking example is shown on the Helmet claim of the Western Utah Extension Copper Co., where a mineralized fissure striking north cuts an augite porphyry dike striking east of north and displaces it about 50 feet. The individual mine descriptions include additional information on this group of fractures.

The differences shown by these fractures in strike and dip, and in age, seem rather definitely to eliminate any directed horizontal force as being instrumental in their formation. As they are essentially limited to the intrusive, they have evidently resulted from the stresses set up at intervals in the slowly cooling stock.

Structural features not related to the emplacement or cooling of the quartz monzonite.—In addition to the structural features of the two groups just described, there appears to be some evidence for faulting that requires a cause outside of the stock itself. One of the most significant pieces of evidence in this respect was observed in a tunnel on the northeast side of Ochre Mountain, which cuts the crushed rocks immediately beneath the Ochre Mountain thrust. East of the tunnel an uncrushed dike of quartz monzonite porphyry is exposed cutting the overridden rocks. The dike is about a mile west of the stock—clearly well beyond the range of any movements emanating from the igneous rocks. What is apparently a continuation of the dike in the tunnel, however, is thoroughly crushed, apparently as the result of movement along the major thrust. As several of the roof pendants included within the quartz monzonite show that the Ochre Mountain thrust is older than the intrusion, the crushed dike in the tunnel can only be interpreted to mean that there has been renewed movement along the thrust after the emplacement of the stock and beyond its range of influence.

Evidence to the same effect appears to be afforded by the intersecting dikes east of hill 5675, on the north side of Rodenhouse Wash. At the summit of the hill and extending westward are several quartz and quartz-carbonate veins that dip at a rather low angle to the west and are exposed at intervals for more than 2 miles to the south. One of the dikes on the east side of the hill strikes south of east, almost normal to the strike of the veins. The other dike, a composite one, strikes south of east and is clearly the younger, as it can be traced continuously through the first. It has, however, been sheared sufficiently to develop a rude cleavage, a feature that is lacking in the older dike. Both dikes are cut off by the most easterly quartz-carbonate vein. West of the zone of veins the quartz monzonite has been thoroughly chloritized and is seamed by a network of thin quartz veinlets.

evidence of compression movements. Among the most notable are two faults exposed a short distance south of the Western Utah Copper Co.'s open cut on Gold Hill. Both strike about N. 20° E., and one at least definitely dips to the west. The more westerly of the two cuts the vein on the Helmet claim of the Western Utah Extension Copper Co. in such a way that it must either be a reverse fault or a normal fault in which the horizontal component of movement is large. The dip on the eastern fault was not observed, but its relations to the westward-dipping porphyry dike that extends southward from the summit of Gold Hill are the same. Although neither of these faults can

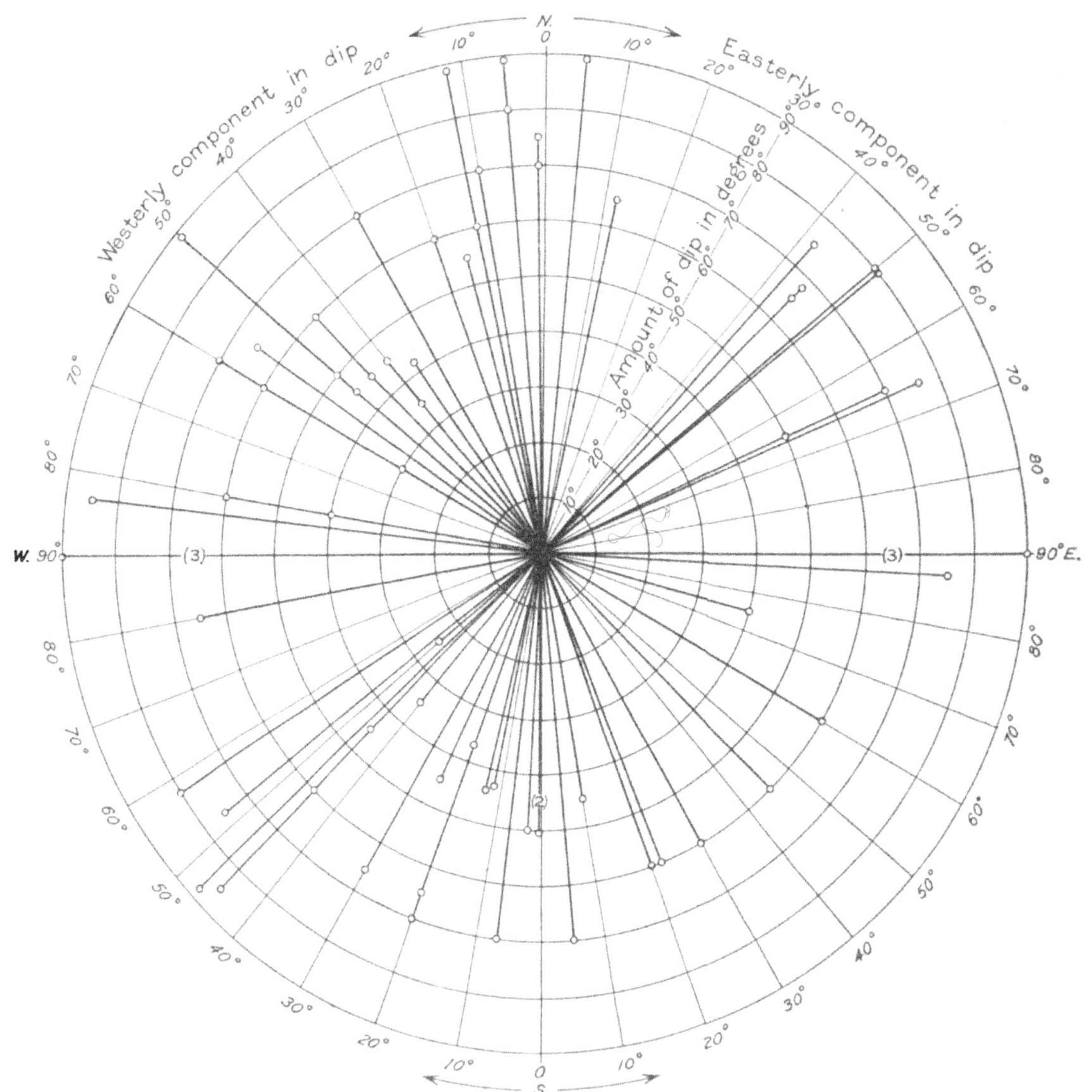

FIGURE 12.—Strikes and dips of various types of fractures in the quartz monzonite. Fractures having dips with an easterly component shown at the right, those with a westerly component at the left. Strike direction measured along the circumference of the circle; amount of dip measured by distance outward from center of circle.

These observations, particularly the selective shearing shown by the dikes, suggest that the zone now occupied by the veins represents a zone of faulting that resulted from compression. The faulting must have occurred after the intrusion of the dikes on the east side of hill 5675 and before the formation of the quartz and quartz-carbonate veins.

With the evidence from these two localities in mind, other phenomena observed in the intrusive area appear to present be definitely said to be a reverse fault, their parallelism in strike with the zone to the south would seem to make this the most probable explanation.

Similarly, the fact that all the veins in the district with a nearly north-south strike show gouge, in which crushed ore minerals are present, on either or both walls, although veins with a nearly east-west strike do not, is also suggestive of a directed pressure. It is also possible that the numerous small faults of east-west strike and nearly vertical dip that cut both veins (as on the Copper Queen Midland group) and dikes (as best shown east of the Success workings) may be considered to represent minor transverse faults that accompanied the reverse faulting.

The normal faults that form the boundaries between sedimentary and igneous rock east of the U.S. mine (p. 76) and the Western Utah mine (p. 77) may represent a stage of normal faulting that followed the reverse faulting. Both the normal and reverse faults at the U.S. mine are clearly later than the ore. The throws along the normal faults—200 to 300 feet at the U.S. mine and probably an equal amount or more at the Western Utah mine—are much larger than any determined for the faults belonging to the second group, and this, with their postmineral age, makes it difficult to consider that they have formed as a result of the cooling of the intrusion.

IGNEOUS METAMORPHISM

Throughout the greater part of the quadrangle the quartz monzonite stock and the sedimentary rocks which it invades have changed in composition or texture in varying degrees as a result of the after effects of the intrusion. In part these changes may be correlated with differences in the original composition of the rocks affected, but for the greater part they are clearly the result of the addition of material to the rock. In both igneous and sedimentary rocks a single rock type may have several different altered facies, each of which is characterized by some distinct mineral or group of minerals. In many places rocks containing minerals of different groups were found, but microscopic study of such occurrences indicated that different groups were not contemporaneous but that one set replaced or was replaced by another. Recognition of a series of such progressive replacements in both the altered sedimentary rocks and the igneous rocks led to the conclusion that the processes causing the alteration extended over a considerable time, during which they were continuously changing.

Ores of gold, silver, copper, lead, zinc, arsenic, tungsten, bismuth, and molybdenum are also widely distributed throughout the quartz monzonite area and in the bordering sediments. These are associated with the metamorphosed rocks mentioned in the preceding paragraph, and in many of the occurrences it is apparent that some, if not all, of the ore minerals closely approximate in age certain of the mineral groups that characterize the igneous metamorphism. There thus appears to exist a parallelism between the progress of the rock alteration and the formation of the ore minerals. Additional factors, however, prevent a close correlation between the distribution of a particular facies of rock alteration and the ore bodies, which are the result of concentrations of ore minerals. Perhaps the most effective of these factors is the presence of crustal movements during the time interval in which the alteration and ore deposition took place. In localities where no crustal movement has occurred the correlation is possible. There is some evidence to indicate that in this region fracturing and minor faulting proceeded hand in hand with the processes of alteration and to this may perhaps be attributed the numerous but disappointingly small concentrations of ore minerals in the district.

ALTERATION OF THE SEDIMENTARY ROCKS

The metamorphism of the sedimentary rocks as considered here is of four classes—recrystallization, alterations resulting in the formation of silicate minerals, alteration to jasperoids, and dolomitization. This grouping is in some respects unsatisfactory, for it does not permit separate consideration for the effect of the original composition of the rock. It lends itself more readily to a comparison with the changes undergone by the quartz monzonite, however, and has been adopted for this reason. Moreover, the greater part of the rock affected is made up of limestone.

Recrystallization.—The most widely distributed type of alteration within the quadrangle is recrystallization, and the greater part of the metamorphosed area shown on plate 2 is underlain by rocks that have been recrystallized rather than changed by the introduction of additional material. This appears to have been the earliest of the several types of metamorphism, for minerals characteristic of the other types have been found replacing all varieties of the recrystallized sediments. The distribution of the recrystallized rocks and especially the failure to find much evidence of alteration of this kind in some of the masses of Ochre Mountain limestone occurring as roof pendants within the quartz monzonite area appear to require some causative agency in addition to the heat given off by the intrusive rock. The fact that the essentially unaffected limestones lie above the Ochre Mountain thrust and are separated by it from highly altered sediments beneath would seem to support the theory that the recrystallization was induced by circulating waters, either connate or magmatic, that had been started in motion by the magma.

Both limestones and quartzites affected by the recrystallization show an increased grain size, which was accompanied by the development of an allotriomorphic texture and a marked bleaching. In addition, the strain phenomena found in both the unaltered calcite and the quartz have disappeared. In the rocks made up of calcite and quartz there appears to have been practically no reaction between these two minerals during the period of recrystallization. For example, in specimens of strikingly recrystallized limestone from the Western Utah Copper Co.'s Gold Hill mine no silicate minerals were noted, although solution of the rock in dilute acid showed the presence of a small percentage of quartz.

This feature does not seem to be true for the argillaceous rocks, of which the black shales of the Manning Canyon formation are the most abundant examples. These rocks have been altered to andalusite hornfels, in which biotite and sericite have been formed in abundance, in addition to the andalusite. The several stages in the development of the andalusite, which have been illustrated and described by Kemp,[20] may be observed in a single thin section and, to the writer, appear to furnish clear evidence that these minerals were formed without the introduction of any new material.

Alteration to silicate minerals.—The type of metamorphism consisting of alteration to silicate minerals is frequently referred to as "contact" metamorphism. The writer has refrained from the use of this term because of the two most striking features in the distribution of rock of this kind in the Gold Hill quadrangle. One of these features is that the silicate-mineral alteration has been effected with very little regard for the actual igneous contact. Perhaps one of the best localities to show this lack of relationship is on the southern boundary of the quartz monzonite body on the south slope of Montezuma Peak. Just east of the road leading up Barney Reevey Gulch the rocks in contact with the quartz monzonite are members of the central facies of the Oquirrh formation. They have been only slightly affected by the igneous rock, and in one place a limestone bed that appeared to have escaped even the usual bleaching was found essentially at the contact. The same beds as those just described are also in contact with the quartz monzonite about half a mile to the east, in the vicinity of the Midas mine. There appears to be no difference in physical conditions at these two localities, but at the more easterly outcrops the limestone beds have been almost completely replaced by silicate minerals.

Alteration of this type was also noted at two localities in Spotted Fawn Canyon, both more than a mile from any outcrops of the quartz monzonite. These localities may, of course, be underlain by igneous rock at no great depth, but the fact remains that alteration of this type has occurred here, where there is no contact, and no evidence of it has been found at many places along the contact.

The second feature in the distribution of this alteration is the fact that the rocks lying above the Ochre Mountain thrust have suffered essentially no alteration. In several places, particularly in the vicinity of the Lucy L mine, there are roof pendants in which nearly unaltered Ochre Mountain limestone rests upon highly altered members of the Oquirrh formation. The sides of the pendants are steep, and both formations are in equal proximity to the intrusive.

This lack of relation between the so-called "contact" metamorphism and the igneous contact has been emphasized by many authors, and the only excuse that is offered for bringing up the matter here is that the term is still used for alteration of this type, even though it is recognized that the term is inappropriate. It hardly seems desirable to use so descriptive a term in this region where its lack of pertinence is so obvious.

Individual occurrences of this alteration have several different habits. The most wide-spread of these is probably the localization of the silicate minerals to a single bed, between others that have been affected to only a very minor degree. This habit is well shown in the 760-foot level of the Western Utah Copper Co.'s Gold Hill mine, where two beds of limestone have been almost entirely converted to a mixture of silicates but are separated by a coarsely crystalline limestone, which yielded practically no insoluble matter on testing with dilute acid. In the Midas, Alvarado, and Cane Springs mines limestone beds that have been altered to silicate minerals have been developed in the search for ore; and in all three of these mines the altered bed has been the site of minor slipping that parallels the strike and dip of the bed. In other localities the silicate minerals are found as small irregular masses. At least some of these masses appear to have been localized by intersecting fractures, but whether or not all of these occurrences can be so explained is somewhat questionable. Finally, on the fourth level of the Cane Springs mine a tabular mass of silicate rock about 1 foot thick was found cutting across the bedding of the enclosing rocks nearly at right angles.

In all these types of occurrence there is, in some localities, a suggestion that the alteration has been guided by preexistent minor fractures. Something of this nature is required in view of the lack of relation to the igneous contact.

Mineralogically, there tend to be two main types of rock that are formed by the silicate alteration of the limestone beds. One of these is dark-colored and heavy and is composed almost entirely of green diopside and a brown garnet, probably near grossularite in composition. The other is a strikingly light-colored type in which white bladed wollastonite predominates. In general the wollastonite-rich rock is more wide-spread than the garnet-diopside mixture, which appears to be more or less confined to regions in which the intensity of metamorphism has been at a maximum, as indicated by the nearly complete destruction of original minerals and texture in the sedimentary rocks and the adjacent quartz monzonite and by the occurrence in these places of tungsten, bismuth, and molybdenum minerals. Several specimens were collected in which the three silicate minerals occur together. In these specimens the colored minerals occur as rounded areas or as bands in the wollastonite, and thin sections cut from such areas indicate that the wollastonite was the latest mineral to form (pl. 8, *A*).

Variations from these two types of alteration are rather numerous but are quantitatively of distinctly minor importance. Perhaps the most interesting of these unusual facies are found in the immediate vicinity of ore bodies. Microscopic examination of garnet-

[20] Kemp, J. F., Notes on Gold Hill and vicinity, Tooele County, western Utah: Econ. Geology, vol. 13, pp. 255-256, 1918.

diopside rocks from such localities shows that locally [illegible], humite, and an amphibole near actinolite have partly replaced the garnet and diopside. In such specimens also microscopic crystals of titanite and apatite may be also present. The wollastonite rock was not found to contain these later minerals. In several of the gold mines, however, wollastonite has been replaced almost completely by the hydrated magnesium silicate, spadaite ($MgO \cdot SiO_2 \cdot 2H_2O$). (See pl. 8, *C*.)

A more wide-spread variation, which, however, seems to be most abundantly represented near the ore bodies, consists of a chloritic replacement of the other silicate minerals. Both the garnet-diopside facies and the wollastonite facies appear to have been subject to such a replacement. Both green and colorless chlorite were noted, generally accompanied by either quartz or calcite. In many of the specimens the chlorite is in the form of microscopic rosettes, which in some places are embedded within quartz areas and in others embayed by the quartz.

The silicate alteration of rocks that originally contained minerals other than calcite is an additional facies of metamorphism. The sandstone members of the Woodman and Oquirrh formations, which have only a relatively small content of calcite, characteristically change to a light-colored, heavy rock that is composed of diopside and quartz. The brown color shown by weathered surfaces of the unaltered rock is absent from the metamorphosed equivalent, suggesting that the small amount of iron normally present was incorporated into the newly formed diopside.

Many of the metamorphosed quartz-rich rocks were also found to contain orthoclase in amounts ranging from scattered tiny grains, which had developed in quartz near the diopside areas, to aggregates that included only small amounts of other minerals. Biotite was found in moderate amounts in some of these quartz-rich rocks, and garnet and wollastonite were noted in specimens that probably were originally rather calcareous sandstones. Sericite and chlorite were also found in some specimens, but, as in the garnet-diopside and wollastonite rocks, they appear to have formed at the expense of the earlier silicates.

Tourmaline was recognized in only two specimens. Both of these rocks were originally sandy shales—one from the Cambrian in Spotted Fawn Canyon and the other from the Manning Canyon formation near the head of Overland Canyon.

Alteration to jasperoids.—Alteration of the sedimentary rocks to jasperoids has been rather wide-spread. This phase of the metamorphism occurred, in general, rather near the contact with the quartz monzonite. (See pl. 2, on which areas of jasperoid are shown.) Its occurrence at the igneous contact is particularly striking east of Clifton, in the vicinity of the Minnehaha group of claims, where the interbedded sandstones and limestones of the Oquirrh formation have been almost completely altered for distances of more than 100 feet from the contact.

In other places faults older than the quartz monzonite have localized the formation of jasperoid. One of the most striking occurrences of this sort is the linear ridge composed of brownish-weathering jasperoid that extends north and south from the summit of Gold Hill. This mass marks a fault that separates the Ochre Mountain limestone and the Manning Canyon formation. The workings in the Western Utah Copper Co.'s mine have exposed this jasperoid on both the 300-foot and 700-foot levels. The low jasperoid hill west of the Yellow Hammer mine, northwest of Clifton, is also clearly the result of alteration along the lines of two intersecting faults.

Bodies of jasperoid probably were also formed in the Ochre Mountain limestone where the limestone is directly overlain by flat-lying beds of the Manning Canyon formation. This is particularly clear near the mouth of Barney Reevey Gulch and was probably also a contributive factor in the development of the abundant jasperoid found in the vicinity of the U.S. mine, south of the town of Gold Hill.

The jasperoids are dense siliceous rocks, which have, in general, the appearance of cemented siliceous breccias, owing to the presence of several generations of quartz. In many specimens gray quartz is cemented by veinlets of white quartz, in the centers of which are sporadic vugs lined with terminated quartz crystals, but in other specimens white quartz fragments are set in a matrix of darker quartz. The cementing veinlets, when examined closely, are seen not to cut the older quartz sharply but to have gradational contacts, marked by a gradual change in color and a slight coarsening of grain outward. Locally similar changes may be observed within the older quartz areas around small vugs. White, glistening barite is in many places abundant in the jasperoids, especially where remnants of unreplaced limestone are present. Near the south end of the jasperoid mass forming Gold Hill plates of this mineral more than an inch in length were observed set in a matrix of green chalcedony. Small quantities of sulphides, probably chiefly pyrite, are present in most of the occurrences, and weathered surfaces of the rock as a result have a deep reddish-brown coloration.

Under the microscope the jasperoids present many interesting features. Quartz forms the great bulk of the material, and with it are associated small amounts of barite, sericite, calcite, a colorless chlorite (?), chalcedony, and opal. In most of the specimens a very finely crystalline quartz predominates. Within it are small inclusions of the colorless chlorite or sericite, splotches or bands of barite, and locally tiny blebs of opal (pl. 8, *B*). Remnants of replaced calcite are present in many of the specimens, and in one slide cleavage lines of calcite characteristic of the recrystallized limestones have been preserved (pl. 8, *D*). The fine-grained quartz in some places shows features that might be interpreted as desiccation cracks, and these appear to have partly controlled localization of the veinlets of later quartz that give the rock its brecciated appearance. The later quartz veinlets are more coarsely crystalline than the earlier quartz. In plain parallel light individual crystals appear to have developed normal to the walls of the veinlets, and lines of inclusions mark several stages in the growth of each grain. With crossed nicols, however, it may be seen that the present grain boundaries do not conform to the outlines marked by the inclusions. This recrystallization has apparently also extended into the areas of older quartz adjacent to the veinlets and accounts for the blurred outlines of the veinlets noted in the hand specimens.

The time of formation of the jasperoid was clearly later than the initial recrystallization of the sedimentary rock, as the quartz has been found to replace the recrystallized limestones. Its relations at the U.S. mine indicate that it is also later than the silicate alteration. There the ore minerals are limited in their distribution by the silicate rock and are later than that rock. Some of the sulphide minerals, however, particularly arsenopyrite, are shattered and veined by the jasperoid, whose age must therefore be relatively late in the metamorphic sequence.

The texture disclosed by the microscope indicates that the initial replacement of the limestone by silica resulted in a gel-like material which contained at least some opal and in which were developed cracks resembling desiccation cracks. There is no positive evidence that all of the material was originally opal and that this changed to fine-grained quartz during the drying represented by the cracks, but this view seems not unlikely. The origin of the more coarsely crystalline quartz in the veinlets and its subsequent recrystallization, together with that of the older fine-grained quartz, are also not susceptible of definite proof, but it might well be the result of slow deposition from expelled liquid and subsequent growth induced by the continued presence of the liquid.

Dolomitization.—Dolomitization is one of the most widely distributed of the four types of alteration recognized. It does not affect, in general, the limestones near the quartz monzonite contact, but rather those at some distance from the intrusive. Thus, the Cambrian limestones in the Deep Creek Mountains and the northern part of Dutch Mountain have been locally converted to dolomite, as have the Ochre Mountain limestone on Dutch Mountain and the limestones of the Oquirrh formation in the vicinity of Twin Peaks. On the other hand, there has been some dolomitization of the Ochre Mountain limestone at the Western Utah Copper Co.'s mine at Gold Hill rather close to the quartz monzonite, but this seems to be of comparatively small extent.

The Cambrian limestones and to a smaller degree the Carboniferous limestones have been changed by the alteration from a dense blue limestone to a rather coarsely crystalline rock which weathers to shades of light brown to chocolate-brown. Blowpipe tests on some of these dolomites show that manganese as well as iron is present, and it is probable that the coloring on the weathered surfaces may be ascribed to this metal. The marked distinction in color between the unaltered limestone and the dolomite makes it possible to prove the dependence of the alteration upon lines of fracturing in the limestone beds. This is best shown in the Deep Creek Mountains, where the alteration is comparatively slight. Near the Garrison Monster mine, however, dolomitization of the Cambrian limestone has been so nearly complete that remnants of unaltered limestone are relatively rare.

The time of dolomitization with respect to the other phases of metamorphism is not definitely known, as dolomitized bodies are not in contact with the other types of altered rocks. Carbonate veins, containing dolomite of apparently similar composition to that replacing the limestone, are, however, rather abundant in the mineralized quartz monzonite and appear to represent the latest stages of the magmatic after effects.

ALTERATION OF THE QUARTZ MONZONITE

The quartz monzonite stock has been altered over much of its extent. Several different facies of alteration may be distinguished in it, but they are not spatially so distinct as those recognized in the metamorphosed sedimentary rocks, although it is believed that the two groups may be directly compared. The oldest facies contains garnet, diopside, orthoclase, and other silicates. In many places these minerals, as well as the original constituents of the quartz monzonite, are altered to sericite and chlorite with some quartz, and this grouping is considered to form the second facies. A stage in which fine-grained quartz was introduced appears to have been still later and apparently was essentially contemporaneous with the formation of jasperoids in the sedimentary rocks. The second of these three facies appears to occupy the largest area. In many specimens two or even all three may be observed in contact.

Diopside-orthoclase alteration.—The alteration that introduced diopside and orthoclase was of relatively small extent. Most of the exposures are found in a linear belt extending from the Reaper and Yellow Hammer claims, in Clifton Flat, to the U.S. mine. In this zone diopside, orthoclase, and other silicates are rather abundant and at a few places have almost completely replaced the original minerals of the quartz monzonite over large areas. Similarly altered rock is found in other localities but in the form of small isolated patches.

Orthoclase is the most abundant and wide-spread mineral in this group. In most localities it is associated with other minerals, but in several places it appears to occur alone. A short distance north of the Yellow Hammer mine irregular veinlets and splotches of pink orthoclase have replaced the quartz monzonite over a considerable area and constitute almost half of its volume. As seen in thin sections, the orthoclase is in the form of large crystals, much of it with a pseudopoikilitic habit due to the enclosure of incompletely replaced fragments of other minerals. Locally the orthoclase is replaced by white, finer-grained albite.

Diopside is the next most abundant member of the facies. It is similar to that found in the metamorphosed sedimentary rocks and replaces all the original minerals of the quartz monzonite. Its localization in the altered areas of the quartz monzonite shows clearly that it has been introduced after the consolidation of the intrusive. In many of the occurrences of this mineral it is either bordered or invaded along its cleavage lines by an amphibole near actinolite. The diopside is, in part at least, older than the orthoclase, for remnants of similar orientation may be found embedded in a single orthoclase crystal.

Titanite in euhedral crystals is also wide-spread and might almost be considered to characterize the facies as well as diopside or orthoclase. In some places it has formed as a swarm of tiny crystals, but in others it occurs as larger grains adjoining diopside areas.

Garnet was found only in the vicinity of the Frankie and Lucy L mines, where it is locally abundant. Its general absence contrasts with its wide-spread occurrence in the altered limestone that contains silicates. Scapolite, epidote, and black tourmaline were noted in small amounts. The epidote and tourmaline are also found away from the metamorphosed areas coating joints in the quartz monzonite. This habit of the tourmaline is especially striking in the bottom of the gulch northwest of United States mineral monument no. 11.

In all the areas that have suffered the diopside-orthoclase alteration, minerals characteristic of the two other groups have replaced the minerals of this group. The diopside appears to have been particularly susceptible to later alteration, and in many places it is almost completely altered to chlorite, calcite, or quartz or a mixture of these three minerals.

Sericitization and chloritization.—The most extensive area showing sericitization and chloritization lies east of and roughly parallel to the northward-sloping portion of Rodenhouse Wash, extending from hill 5675 on the north to a point about half a mile north of Goshute Spring on the south. On the north this area extends much farther westward and encloses the greater part of the relatively low-lying country west of the Climax mine. This area of intense alteration is situated immediately west of a series of barren quartz and quartz-carbonate veins that dip at a rather low angle to the west and are thought to mark a zone of reverse faulting in the quartz monzonite after its consolidation (pp. 89–90).

Evidence of this alteration is also prominently displayed in the quartz monzonite walls of the ore-bearing quartz veins, but in these the altered zone does not as a rule extend more than a few feet from the vein. The characteristic minerals are also developed in most of the exposures of the altered rock of the diopside-orthoclase phase.

In the Rodenhouse Wash area the igneous texture is largely and in places completely destroyed, and the resultant rock is a rather pale greenish-gray fine-grained aggregate of sericite and chlorite, cut by reticulating veinlets of quartz. The microscope shows that the dark minerals are the first to be attacked, and these are followed by plagioclase, orthoclase, and quartz in the order named. In the less altered portions the outline of the former feldspar crystals is preserved by an aggregate of matted sericite of slightly different grain size than that in the remainder of the rock, but as the alteration becomes more intense even this remnant of the old texture is lost. The altered wall rocks of the veins are similar in appearance and composition.

The relation between the sericite and chlorite is not clearly understood from the specimens studied. In the less altered rocks chlorite tends to be localized in the original dark minerals and sericite in the feldspars, but in the more highly altered rocks this is not true. From the several specimens in which the two minerals are in contact it is difficult to determine their relative age. In some places remnants of chlorite appear to be enclosed within masses of sericite and might therefore be thought to be earlier. In other places veinlets of quartz and chlorite cut across sericite areas and must be later. Finally, in several specimens the relations observed might be interpreted to indicate that either one or the other of the two minerals was formed first. These relations seem to be most easily explained by assuming that the two are essentially contemporaneous and that locally, depending upon the physico-chemical conditions, either mineral may have replaced the other.

Sericite is the more abundant of the two minerals. The proportion varies widely in different specimens, and in places either one may be present to the exclusion of the other. By a rough estimate, whose only value lies in indicating the order of magnitude, sericite is between 5 and 10 times as abundant as chlorite.

Introduced quartz and calcite are found in many of these altered rocks. Almost all of the quartz is clearly later than the chlorite and sericite, cutting across them as veinlets or replacing them in bulk. It is similar in appearance and habit to the jasperoidal alteration product next described.

Silicification.—Silicification of the quartz monzonite, corresponding to the formation of jasperoids in the sedimentary rocks, has occurred, for the most part, on a microscopic scale. The only place where it was found to have occurred on a large scale was underground in the Western Utah Copper Co.'s Gold Hill mine, where a rather large mass is exposed at several places along the western contact of the limestone with the quartz monzonite. The partial replacement of the quartz monzonite by microscopic quartz appears to have been rather wide-spread in the region between Lucky Day Knob and Gold Hill and is shown with particular abundance in specimens taken in the vicinity of ore bodies.

The silicified rock differs from the jasperoid texturally. It is almost invariably somewhat coarser grained, and only one of the specimens examined showed the successive generations of quartz that are so marked a feature of the jasperoids. Vugs are almost entirely lacking. The silicification produced either veinlets cutting the quartz monzonite or irregular masses of quartz that form a matrix around the remnants of unattacked minerals. In one specimen showing almost complete silicification the quartz grains instead of having their usual anhedral habit, are in the form of laths, which show in some places a subparallel orientation (pl. 9, *A*).

Sericite, chlorite, barite, and an iron-rich carbonate are in places associated with the quartz. The chlorite may be either green or colorless in thin section, but the colorless variety is the more characteristic. It is difficult to determine definitely whether or not the sericite and chlorite are invariably earlier than the quartz or are in part contemporaneous with it. Some of the specimens suggest strongly that small amounts of these minerals are of the same age as the quartz. Barite was recognized in only one specimen, as microscopic crystals within a veinlet of the fine-grained quartz. The carbonate, which is in part at least an ankerite (index of refraction of ω near 1.70), occurs as megascopic rhombs in the quartz or as veinlets cutting the quartz. Barite and ankerite were both found with quartz in the same veinlet and were presumably deposited at the same time. These minerals were not seen in quartz containing what was thought to be contemporaneous chlorite or sericite, however, and it is suggested that the silicification continued over a considerable period of time, in the early stages of which chlorite and sericite were deposited and in the later stages barite and ankerite.

COMPARISON OF THE ALTERATION OF THE SEDIMENTARY ROCKS AND THE QUARTZ MONZONITE

In comparing the results of the metamorphism of the sedimentary rocks and that of the quartz monzonite, three features may be noted that appear to bear upon the process—the phases of alteration bear definite time relations to one another; the phases recognized in the quartz monzonite overlap to a far greater extent than those in the sedimentary rocks; and phases that are prominent in the one may be absent or unimportant in the other.

The first of these observations has been emphasized in the descriptions of the individual phases, and the consistency with which all the specimens collected showed the same succession appears to warrant the generalization that the metamorphism was accomplished over a relatively long period of time, during which the conditions under which the alterations took place changed progressively in such a way that periodically groups of minerals already formed were no longer stable and were replaced by a new set.

The three phases that were distinguished in the alteration of the quartz monzonite not only overlap spatially to a marked degree, but there also appears to be a mineralogic overlap between the second and third phases. These two features are only rarely observed in the altered sedimentary rocks. The cause of this distinction is not entirely clear, but it seems most reasonable to infer that it is the result of an essentially continuous passage of the metamorphosing fluids through the major fractures in the quartz monzonite, from which they were derived, as opposed to a discontinuous flow through the outlying sediments.

The fact that phases present in the quartz monzonite may be essentially lacking in the sediments, or vice versa, is probably in large part the result of the different composition of these two kinds of rock. The lack in the igneous rock of a corresponding phase to the recrystallization in the sediments obviously cannot be explained in this way but is better interpreted as indicating that the quartz monzonite was still largely molten at the time of recrystallization. The silicate alteration of the sedimentary rocks was clearly very similar to the diopside-orthoclase alteration of the quartz monzonite—so similar, in fact, that it is almost impossible to distinguish the intrusive contact in places where this kind of alteration has taken place. There is, however, a distinction between them that appears to have a bearing on the later alteration—the absence of orthoclase in the altered limestones. This is clearly the result of the low alumina content of the unaltered limestone. Eskola [21] has shown that rocks in which the alumina content is too low to permit the development of feldspar commonly contain garnet. Conversely, the relative rarity of garnet in the quartz monzonite appears to show that it contained sufficient alumina to satisfy the K_2O content of the solutions causing metamorphism.

The wide-spread sericite-chlorite alteration of the quartz monzonite is for the most part lacking or only sparsely developed in the sediments. If this phase is considered to be the result of the hydration of older aluminous silicates of magnesium, iron, or potassium, it is apparent that the explanation may be found in the fact that such silicates are far more abundant

[21] Eskola, P., The mineral facies of rocks: Norsk. geol. Tidsskrift, vol. 6, pp. 143-194, 1920.

in the igneous rock than they are in either the altered or unaltered limestones or sandstones. The relation of dolomitization to composition is of course obvious.

The course of the metamorphism may be summarized as follows: Coincident with the intrusion of the quartz monzonite, the invaded sedimentary rocks were subjected to a wide-spread recrystallization and bleaching, which appears to have been induced by circulating fluids, probably propelled by the heat of the magma and certainly impeded in their progress by such relatively impermeable material as the fault breccia along the Ochre Mountain thrust. After the consolidation of the now exposed portions of the intrusive rock, solutions containing large quantities of silica, potash, iron, and magnesia and probably small quantities of alumina traveled along fractures and reacted with both the intrusive and the invaded rocks, forming a group of minerals characterized by diopside, orthoclase, and garnet. Smaller quantities of minerals containing the so-called "volatile constituents" of the magma, such as scapolite, tourmaline, and axinite, were also formed at this time, apparently somewhat later than the bulk of the other minerals. After the deposition of these minerals the alteration became essentially one of hydration, and large areas in the quartz monzonite were converted to rocks containing much chlorite and sericite. This phase is almost lacking in the sedimentary rocks, probably because of their composition. Still later the solutions, becoming cooler, appear to have lost their corrosive power and instead deposited silica, much of it apparently in a gelatinous form, which afterward largely recrystallized to quartz. The final stage in the metamorphism resulted in the dolomitization of limestone, at considerable distances from the intrusive mass but clearly related to fracturing. This phase appears to be related to veins of quartz and ferruginous dolomite that cut the quartz monzonite and are later than the other products of alteration.

ORE DEPOSITS

The ore deposits found within the Gold Hill quadrangle differ from those of many other mining districts in that they are not closely similar deposits, which may be described as a group. On the contrary, the greater number of the explored ore bodies differ from one another to a marked degree, both as to form and as to composition. Hence, a general treatment of the ore deposits must be in the nature of a series of descriptions of individual ore bodies. As another section of this report (pp. 119–168) contains detailed descriptions of the mines and prospects, the descriptive part of this section is rather more brief than might otherwise be considered desirable and is designed to show primarily the relations that exist between the several kinds of deposits rather than their individual characteristics. Readers desiring more information about a particular type of deposit are therefore referred to the detailed descriptions and also to the sections on superficial alteration and mineralogy (pp. 104–107, 110–118).

CLASSIFICATION

As the ore bodies within the quadrangle include representatives of several different kinds of deposits, which vary not only in mineralogy but also in form, it is desirable first of all to classify them in order that they may be described systematically. Three methods of classification have been used more or less generally—one based on the metal present, a second based on the form of the deposit, and a third that utilized the supposed temperature of formation of the deposit, often referred to as a "genetic" classification. The first of these is scarcely applicable to this area, for not only do many of the ore bodies contain minerals of several different metals, but several of the metals are found in utterly unlike kinds of deposits. Neither of the other two methods of classification is entirely satisfactory, because, if they are applied rigidly, they result either in the separation of rather closely related types of deposits or in the combination of unlike types. This difficulty is, of course, inherent in any system based on a single factor that attempts to classify objects that vary in several different ways. The following classification of the ore bodies found in the quadrangle is essentially a combination of the second and third methods noted above, with the primary emphasis placed upon form:

1. Pipelike deposits locally containing tungsten and molybdenum.
2. Veins:
   - (a) Veins characterized by silicate minerals in the gangue.
   - (b) Veins containing chiefly quartz and metallic sulphides.
   - (c) Veins containing chiefly carbonate minerals with or without quartz.
3. Replacement bodies:
   - (a) Arsenic minerals dominant.
   - (b) Copper-lead-silver minerals dominant.

The replacement bodies have furnished by far the greater part of the production recorded from the Clifton district. The pipelike deposits yielded small quantities of tungsten ores during the period of high tungsten prices; small quantities of tungsten and copper and moderate amounts of gold have been produced from the silicate veins; and a fair tonnage of lead-silver ore was obtained from the quartz veins in the earlier part of the district's existence.

PIPELIKE DEPOSITS

The ore bodies belonging to the first group are pegmatitic masses in the quartz monzonite that have a tubular or pipelike habit. The few deposits of this kind occur almost entirely in the nearly level stretch of country immediately north of the town of Clifton, but a few are present in other areas underlain by the intrusive rock.

The largest and best-known representative of the group is the tungsten-bearing pipe on the Reaper claim. This ore body had an elliptical cross section at the surface, with a long axis of nearly 60 feet and a short axis of about 30 feet. On the 50-foot level it was considerably smaller and had a circular outline, with a diameter of about 20 feet. On this level there are two apophyses from the pipe, one extending to the northwest and the other to the north-northeast. The pipelike habit persists only a short distance below this level, however, for on the bottom or 100-foot level the ore shoot has a lenticular shape, striking northeast. Smaller pipes were observed on the Centennial, Enterprise, and Doctor claims and on the property of the Yellow Hammer mine. In these the tubular form is clearly the result of localization of mineralization at the junction of two intersecting fractures, along both of which apophyses may extend for short distances away from the pipe. None of these pipes have been sufficiently developed to show whether or not the tubular habit changes downward to a veinlike habit, but it is perhaps significant that on all these claims there are veinlike masses of similar composition.

The walls of the pipes are not well defined, for not only are there numerous irregular projections of pegmatitic minerals from the pipe into the wall rocks, but in many places there are isolated occurrences of these minerals in the quartz monzonite adjacent to the pipe. The igneous rock itself is rather thoroughly altered for some distance from the ore bodies. Two kinds of alteration were recognized. One has resulted in the formation of a rock of striking appearance but was quantitatively of relatively little importance. It consisted in the development in the quartz monzonite of pink perthitic orthoclase and a green amphibole that is near actinolite in its optical properties. Both of these minerals are also found in the pipes, but there they are much more coarsely crystalline. This phase of alteration, however, was not everywhere closely related in space to the pipes but locally took the form of irregular replacements of the igneous rocks some distance away from the pipes. The second and more wide-spread kind of alteration produced sericite, chlorite, and calcite in the quartz monzonite adjacent to the ore body.

Both Butler [22] and Hess [23] have referred to these deposits as pegmatites, and, if variety of minerals and a large size for individual crystals are considered as characterizing pegmatites, these bodies may well be called by that name.

The two most abundant minerals in the pipes are orthoclase and amphibole. Cleavage faces of perthitic orthoclase may be more than a foot across. The mineral is pink, in contrast to the white albite that locally has replaced it. The amphibole is actinolite and occurs as sheafs of crystals as much as 4 feet in length. Much of it is partly altered to micaceous minerals, calcite, and quartz, but even in these the amphibole cleavage is preserved. Black tourmaline is also abundant but tends to be found near the borders of the pipes, where it is generally accompanied by clear glassy quartz. Smaller amounts of diopside, epidote, titanite, zircon, garnet, and scapolite have also been recognized among the silicate minerals forming the pipes.

Scheelite is the most abundant of the nonsilicate minerals. Very little scheelite could be found in the prospects at the time of this examination, but Butler, who examined the district before the active exploitation during the war, writes that on the Reaper claim "a body composed largely of scheelite 18 to 24 inches in thickness had been exposed for 4 or 5 feet along the strike and 3 or 4 feet below the outcrop. The scheelite occurs in large crystals, some of which are 4 inches long. One block of nearly pure scheelite on the dump was estimated to weigh fully 200 pounds." [24]

Apatite is also abundant in euhedral crystals that are commonly embedded in the actinolite, particularly near the base of the sheafs. Much of it at first glance resembles scheelite, but it lacks the cleavage commonly found in the tungsten mineral. Molybdenite occurs as small rosettes and is locally rather abundant. Chalcopyrite, pyrite, magnetite, and specularite may also be recognized in small amounts.[25] Gold is reported to occur in the pipes, and its presence is said to have led to the development of the pipe on the Reaper claim.

There is some question as to the propriety of calling these deposits pegmatites, for the evidence is clear that the minerals were introduced by a long series of replacements, first of the country rock and later of the earlier-formed replacing minerals. The localization of the pipes along intersecting fractures alone suggests an origin by replacement, and specimens taken at the borders confirm this view in that they show the minerals of the pipe embaying and replacing the minerals of the quartz monzonite. The fact that isolated patches of the introduced minerals are found in the walls of the pipes is also difficult to explain except by replacement.

The exact sequence in which the minerals forming the pipe were deposited cannot be ascertained from the specimens collected. A fair amount of information is available, however, and may be summarized as follows: Epidote and titanite were among the first minerals to form, as they have replaced the minerals of the quartz monzonite and have been replaced by other constit-

[22] Butler, B. S., Ore deposits of Utah: U.S. Geol. Survey Prof. Paper 111, pp. 476–477, 1920.

[23] Hess, F. L., Molybdenum deposits: U.S. Geol. Survey Bull. 761, p. 5, 1924.

[24] Butler, B. S., op. cit., p. 476.

[25] Photographs illustrating the occurrence of scheelite and molybdenite in deposits of this type in the Gold Hill area are included in two reports by F. L. Hess (Tungsten minerals and deposits: U.S. Geol. Survey Bull. 652, pls. 12, *A*; 16, *A*, *B*, 1907; Molybdenum deposits: U.S. Geol. Survey Bull. 761, pl. 5, *B*, 1924).

uents of the pipes. Zircon may be contemporaneous with them, and also possibly scheelite, of which Butler writes, "The scheelite was one of the earliest minerals to form. Much of it is in well-formed crystals, and little of it includes the other minerals." [26] The epidote and titanite are definitely earlier than diopside in a specimen from the Reaper claim, but this mineral is relatively rare. It is probable that the equally sparse garnet found in the pipes is also of this stage. The diopside in turn is replaced by actinolite along its cleavage planes (pl. 9, *B*). In other specimens actinolite appears to have formed immediately after epidote and titanite, without an intervening stage in which diopside was formed. Apatite and molybdenite are in many places associated with the sheafs of amphibole and are possibly of about the same age, although they generally appear to replace the amphibole (pl. 9, *C*), as they interrupt and embay individual crystals.

In all the specimens in which actinolite and orthoclase are in contact, orthoclase is clearly later, for it corrodes the amphibole and locally includes oriented remnants of it. Orthoclase in turn has been replaced by albite, in the few places that this mineral was recognized. The next mineral to form appears to have been tourmaline, with which is generally associated some glassy quartz that must have been developed somewhat later. The greater part of the tourmaline is dense black and rather coarsely crystalline, but locally this variety is replaced by a much finer grained blue tourmaline. The last stages in the formation of the pipe were the introduction of sericite, chlorite, calcite, and quartz. The sericite and chlorite are generally accompanied by either calcite or quartz or both, but these two minerals also continued to form for some time afterward. The sulphide minerals are associated with this group of minerals.

The pipes are associated with veinlike bodies of similar mineral composition, and the large pipe in the Reaper claim changes downward into a deposit of veinlike form. This relation of the pipes to veins may be a result of proximity to the upper surface of the intrusive, which acted to dam the solutions forming the pipe and caused them to spread beyond the fissure to which they were limited at greater depths in the intrusive. That this may be the explanation is indicated by the localization of the pipes in the region north of Clifton, where it is clear, from exposures in the surrounding hills, that the original, nearly flat top of the intrusion must have been only a short distance above the present surface.

VEINS WITH SILICATE MINERALS IN THE GANGUE

Three subclasses of the veins with silicate minerals in the gangue may be distinguished for purposes of description, but there are almost continuous gradations between them.

26 Butler, B. S., op. cit., p. [illegible]

The first subclass includes the lenticular or veinlike bodies that are associated with the tungsten-bearing pipes. They are mineralogically similar to the pipes, except that the size of individual crystals tends to be smaller and the content of scheelite is probably distinctly lower.

The second subclass is found both in the quartz monzonite and in the sedimentary rocks and is characterized by a general fine-grained habit of the silicate minerals and by the general dominance of copper over tungsten as the valuable metallic constituent. These veins are restricted to the region between the Lucy L mine on the north and the town of Clifton on the south.

These veins vary considerably in form, ranging from the rather small lenticular masses found in places on the Gold Bond claim and the Copper Bloom group to the persistent lode on the Frankie claim, which has been developed for several hundred feet. All of them, however, appear to have been localized by earlier fractures or narrow sheeted zones. Some of these fractures give evidence of having been reopened over a long period of time. Thus the vein on the Frankie claim is in a narrow dike of quartz monzonite which was intruded along a fault that was active at a period long prior to the intrusion. After the intrusion, fissuring along the same line permitted the introduction of the silicate minerals, which in turn were cut by closely spaced parallel fractures, in which copper minerals are concentrated.

Mineralogically these veins show a rather wide variation, and one vein may contain one or more minerals in abundance that are almost or entirely lacking in an adjacent vein. In general, epidote, titanite, and scheelite, which are thought to have been among the earliest minerals to form in the pipelike deposits, are relatively scarce in these veins. Garnet is particularly abundant, however, and with diopside appears to have been among the earliest minerals to form. Amphibole is distinctly later but is irregularly distributed, being very scarce in some of the deposits, particularly on the Gold Bond claim. Orthoclase also is of rare occurrence.

Tourmaline is wide-spread, and in some of the deposits, as in the Keno, Pole Star, and Copper Bloom claims, it was the only silicate mineral observed. Most of the tourmaline occurs as black bladed crystals, similar to those found in the pipes, and there is in addition some finer-grained blue tourmaline that is of somewhat later development. In the Gold Bond deposits specularite is widespread and is clearly later than tourmaline (pl. 10, *B*).

The next minerals to be formed are characterized by the presence of boron, chlorine, and fluorine and include danburite, humite, scapolite, and fluorite. These minerals are surprisingly abundant, the veinlike occurrences of danburite in the Gold Bond claim being nearly a foot across and similar masses of humite on the Calaveras claim being several inches thick

These minerals are clearly later than the other silicate minerals except sericite, and on the Gold Bond claim danburite and fluorite corrode and embay specularite (pl. 10, *A*).

The final stage in the mineralization consisted in the introduction of small amounts of sericite, calcite, quartz, and the metallic sulphides, which have all replaced the older silicate minerals. Chalcopyrite is by far the most abundant sulphide, and most of the prospecting on these deposits has been for copper. Gold is present in small quantities in all of them, and in a few properties it has been the sole element present in anything approaching economic amounts. Pyrite is wide-spread in small amounts, and locally bismuthinite is fairly abundant. Tetrahedrite was recognized on the Copper Bloom group, and grains of galena and sphalerite were recognized on the Lucy L and Gold Bond claims, respectively.

There is an obvious similarity in mineralogy and habit between the veins of this subclass and those of the first subclass. The chief differences between them appear to be a somewhat finer grain size, a general lack in deposits of the second subclass of the earlier-formed minerals in the first subclass, and a greater variety and abundance of sulphide minerals in the deposits of the second subclass. Similarly there is a rather close relationship between the veins of this subclass and those of the third subclass.

The veins of the third subclass have been exploited for their gold content. They are more widely distributed than those of the first two subclasses, although they appear to be considerably less abundant. They are restricted to limestone beds near the contact of the sedimentary rocks with the quartz monzonite. In all of them the gold ore is found in relatively small shoots that appear to be localized along minor structural features, such as linear igneous contacts, as in the Alvarado and the Rube mines, or along fractures parallel to the bedding, as in the Cane Springs and Midas mines.

The Cane Springs, Alvarado, Midas, and two smaller deposits are very similar in character and may be considered as a unit. The ore is found in limestone that has been almost completely altered to silicate minerals and resembles very closely similarly altered limestones that are wide-spread throughout the district. Zoisite and vesuvianite are relatively rare constituents of the rock and appear to have been the first minerals to form during the alteration. They were succeeded by equally small amounts of garnet and diopside. The bulk of the rock in all the mines, however, is made up of white bladed wollastonite which is invariably later than the other silicates. This in turn has been widely altered to spadaite (see pl. 8, *B*).

The last stage consisted of the introduction of the metallic sulphides with quartz and calcite. The observed relations between the quartz and calcite indicate either that there were several generations of each or that conditions of temperature and pressure varied so that first one and then the other might be deposited. Chalcopyrite is by far the most abundant sulphide, but the quantity found varies in the different mines. It is relatively abundant in the Cane Springs mine and rather scarce in the Alvarado. Pyrite, bornite, arsenopyrite, and galena have also been recognized in the ore specimens. Molybdenite has been reported from the upper levels of the Cane Springs mine, but its relations to the other sulphides are not known. It is extremely probable that the gold in the ores of these mines is essentially contemporaneous with the quartz, calcite, and sulphides, for all the specimens of ore that were examined contained some of these minerals. On the 200-foot level of the Alvarado mine several small pipes of ore were stoped that were not connected with the main shoot, and in these there were apparently practically none of the silicate minerals that form so large a proportion of the other ore shoots. The gangue in these places was composed almost entirely of quartz and calcite. Kemp has described ore from the Cane Springs mine in which gold was embedded in some of the silicate minerals,[27] and there may therefore be some occurrences of the mineral that are not related to the introduction of quartz. It seems very improbable, however, that the amount of such gold is very great.

The ore at the Rube mine is somewhat different from that described above. Most of it is composed of limestone, partly or completely replaced by quartz, sericite, calcite, and several metallic minerals, among which gold, pyrite, and galena are the most abundant, although chalcopyrite, spalerite, pyrrhotite, and arsenical boulangerite have also been recognized. Bismuth is shown by analysis of the ore, but no bismuth minerals were recognized in the specimens collected. One portion of the new ore shoot in the mine, however, was of radically different composition and appears to provide a connecting link between the Rube and the other deposits in this subclass. This part of the shoot contains as the earliest-formed minerals small quantities of zoisite, scapolite, and muscovite and rather large quantities of molybdenite. These have been replaced by green and colorless chlorite, which with calcite, makes up a large part of the rock. Pyrite is also abundant, particularly near the borders of this phase of the ore, but quartz is relatively rare.

The remaining deposit in this subclass is that on the property of the Wilson Consolidated Mining Co. Here a bed of limestone intercalated between sandstones contains a small shoot of ore locally rich in gold and bismuth. The bulk of the ore is composed of coarsely crystalline white calcite, undoubtedly derived from the original limestone, in which are veinlets and euhedral crystals of quartz (pl. 10, *D*). Locally small

[27] Kemp, J. F., Notes on Gold Hill and vicinity, Tooele County, western Utah: Econ. Geology, vol. 13, p. 258, 1918.

quantities of orthoclase and sericite are also found. Bismuthinite, scheelite, and native gold were the only hypogene metallic minerals recognized.

This class of veins with silicate minerals in the gangue present an almost continuous sequence from the pipelike deposits in which silicate minerals are dominant and quartz, carbonates, and sulphides are relatively rare to deposits like the Copper Bloom or Wilson Consolidated, in which the silicates have been reduced to a single variety, and the bulk of the ore is composed of quartz, carbonates, and sulphides. The transition is marked more or less definitely by a uniform decrease of the earlier-formed minerals and a comparable increase in the younger ones. In all the deposits there is a clear dependence of localization upon earlier-formed fractures. On the other hand, there is relatively little relation between the character of the ore and the character of the wall rock, except for the obvious restriction of wollastonite and other lime-rich silicates to deposits formed in limestone.

VEINS CONTAINING CHIEFLY QUARTZ AND METALLIC SULPHIDES

The veins characterized by quartz and metallic sulphides are found chiefly in the quartz monzonite, but some are known to occur in the sedimentary rocks. They have a wide distribution throughout the intrusive mass, showing no discernible tendency toward localization. The veins are found along fissures, many of which can be definitely proved to be minor faults, or, as in the Cyclone mine, along dikes. Most of the veins show a postmineral gouge along one or both walls. A general northerly strike and westerly dip are characteristic, but exceptions to both are not uncommon.

Sericite, chlorite, and quartz have been introduced into the quartz monzonite where it forms the wall rock of the veins, but it is in most places impossible to determine the amount of such alteration that may be attributed to vein formation, because of the mineralogically similar regional alteration of the igneous rock. There appears to have been essentially no alteration of the wall rock adjacent to the few veins that occur in the sedimentary rocks.

Like those of the preceding class, these veins are rather variable in mineral composition. The variations, however, are expressed in the metallic minerals present, and there appears to be a rather complete series showing the stages in the variation.

A subclass that appears to be most closely related to the veins described in the preceding section is typified by the bismuth-bearing gold quartz vein on the Lucy L group of claims. This deposit is a lenticular body of quartz containing bismuthinite and native gold, enclosed in quartz monzonite. The greater abundance of quartz and the absence of orthoclase definitely distinguish this ore from the gold-bismuth ore at the Wilson Consolidated mine, but there is obviously a rather close resemblance between them.

A second subclass contains arsenopyrite and quartz. Such veins are fairly abundant throughout the quartz monzonite area, but, except for the one on the Boston claim, they have been only slightly developed. The Boston vein contains also small quantities of other sulphides and in addition is reported to carry $14 to the ton in gold.

The most abundant veins in this class and about the only ones that have yielded any significant tonnage of ore are the quartz veins containing the sulphides of the base metals. The Cyclone, Success, and Southern Confederate veins are representative of this subclass. They are restricted to the quartz monzonite but are scattered over the greater part of its outcrop. Many of these veins may be traced for long distances along their strike, but ore shoots have proved to occur rather sparingly and to have rather small dimensions.

The ore contains arsenopyrite, pyrite, sphalerite, galena, chalcopyrite, arsenical tetrahedrite or antimonial tennantite, and aikinite, the lead-bismuth sulphide. These sulphides are rather erratically distributed throughout the ore shoot, one predominating in some places and another in others. In polished sections arsenopyrite is seen to have been the earliest sulphide to form, as it has in most places been thoroughly fractured and cemented by quartz and the other sulphides (pl. 10, *E*). Quartz is the only abundant gangue mineral, but fragments of altered wall rock are not uncommon constituents of the veins. Veinlets of an iron-rich carbonate cut both quartz and sulphides.

The final subclass of veins in this group has furnished small quantities of rather rich ore. They are quartz-tetrahedrite veins, in which the only metallic minerals are arsenical tetrahedrite, which is rich in silver, and small quantities of galena. One of these veins occurs in the quartz monzonite on the Undine claim, but the others are in sedimentary rocks, the bulk of them being found on the northern and northwestern slopes of Dutch Mountain. A variety of this subclass is represented by a tetrahedrite-galena vein on the Reaper claim south of the open cut. This contained barite in the gangue, in addition to quartz, and is thus a connecting link between these veins and those of the next class.

VEINS WITH CARBONATE OR SULPHATE MINERALS IN THE GANGUE

The veins that have carbonate or sulphate minerals in the gangue are of relatively little economic importance but are described here because they appear to represent the final stages in the mineralization of the area. They are rather widely distributed throughout the quartz monzonite and the adjacent sedimentary rocks. Many of the veins follow older structural features. Thus the quartz carbonate veins in Rodenhouse Wash are thought to occupy a zone of probable thrust faulting (pp. 89–90); and carbonate veins on the north and south sides of Montezuma Peak follow linear contacts of the quartz monzonite with the sediments, which in turn were determined by old faults. On the Monocco claim a carbonate vein has been introduced along an older lead-bearing fissure.

The veins with carbonates in the gangue show a considerable variety in composition, ranging from those in which the carbonate is relatively scarce and quartz predominant to those in which carbonates form the bulk of the rock and quartz is essentially absent. In many places the wall rocks of the veins in which carbonate minerals are in excess contain isolated crystals of the carbonate.

The most striking feature of these quartz-carbonate veins is their texture. Almost all of them show a banding that is locally parallel to the walls of the veins but in most places is rosettelike or colloform. In some specimens such curved banding clearly reflects the outlines of inclusions of altered quartz monzonite (pl. 10, *C*), but in many of them no inclusions can be found. Thin sections of the veins show remnants of different sizes of sericitized and chloritized quartz monzonite, replaced by several generations of quartz and carbonate. The carbonate is iron-bearing in almost all specimens, but the proportions of iron, magnesium, and calcium in the mineral appear to vary widely. For example, one specimen had indices of refraction indicating a content of more than 75 percent of $FeCO_3$, and, at the other extreme, the carbonate from a vein in Rodenhouse Wash had much less than 25 percent. Small quantities of sulphides occur in some of the veins, but their presence is unusual. They appear to be limited to veins that contain relatively small amounts of carbonate. An occurrence of a pocket of rich gold ore is reported in one of these veins on the Troy claim, but there appears to be some doubt as to the validity of the discovery. (See p. 151.)

Barite veins are not abundant and are limited to areas of Ochre Mountain limestone near the quartz monzonite contact. The two regions in which they were found in any quantity were on the southeast side of Ochre Mountain and on the northeast side of the large roof pendant north of Clifton. In both of these places they are more or less closely associated with a jasperoid resulting from alteration of the limestone. In the Ochre Mountain occurrence the veins are controlled by lines of faulting but in many places spread out from the fault and replace the limestone. The barite is coarsely crystalline and has a platy habit. Where pure it is creamy white, but most of it has a dull-gray color due to inclusions. These veins have been practically unexplored, but it seems probable that a moderate quantity of fairly pure material might be exposed by a small amount of work.

ARSENIC REPLACEMENT BODIES

The arsenic replacement bodies have been developed in only two mines in the quadrangle—the Gold Hill mine of the Western Utah Copper Co. and the Gold Hill mine of the United States Smelting, Refining & Mining Co. (locally known as the U.S. mine). The ore bodies in these mines are the largest ones in the Clifton district and have furnished a large part of the ore produced.

In both mines the deposits are found within the Ochre Mountain limestone in roof pendants enclosed in quartz monzonite. The preference for the unaltered limestone as a site of ore deposition is striking, for wherever there has been extensive formation of silicate minerals, or where more siliceous rocks, such as the Manning Canyon or Oquirrh formation or the quartz monzonite, abut against the ore body, there is an almost complete lack of arsenic mineralization. Two other factors appear to have played an important part in determining the localization of the deposits. One of these is the presence of a major fracture through which the ore-bearing solutions could have traveled across the strike of the beds, and the other is the occurrence of one or more fissures essentially parallel to the bedding. The second factor appears to be required by the fact that locally unmineralized limestone beds may be found adjacent to the ore bodies in both mines, and that, in the U.S. mine at least, the beds which have been replaced are cut by minor faults parallel to the bedding. The combination of these two factors produces an ore shoot with a roughly triangular plan, the base of the triangle being the crosscutting fracture and the altitude being represented by the fracture parallel to the bedding. It would seem that these features show that the ore solutions found it difficult to react with the limestone for more than a relatively short distance away from the fractures through which they could circulate freely.

Most of these arsenic-rich ore bodies are, in their unoxidized portions, made up of arsenopyrite. In a few places this sulphide has a bladed structure (pl. 11, *A*), and this habit is also shown by isolated crystals of the mineral in unaltered limestone adjacent to the ore. No gangue minerals contemporaneous with the arsenopyrite have been recognized in this material. Most of the massive arsenopyrite, however, lacks the bladed habit and is apparently textureless when seen underground. Polished specimens of this kind of ore show that it is the result of a thorough brecciation by which almost all trace of the original bladed habit was destroyed. Small amounts of pyrite appear to have been introduced during the brecciation, for in many places this mineral also is brecciated, but by no means to the extent of the arsenopyrite. Still later, quartz was introduced into the brecciated sulphides, accompanied by small quantities of sericite, sphalerite, galena, and chalcopyrite (pl. 11, *B*). The introduction of silica appears to have continued over a long period, and locally it has largely replaced the arsenopyrite, the interior of the sulphide fragments apparently being particularly susceptible (pl. 11, *C*). In the U.S.

with the introduced quartz is locally continuous with a jasperoid alteration product of the sedimentary rocks.

In both the Western Utah and U.S. mines the arsenic ore bodies are associated with ore shoots that are valuable chiefly for their lead-silver content and contain relatively small amounts of arsenic. Such ores are characteristically found either along the wall of the arsenic ore or, as in the U.S. mine, replacing the same limestone bed in which the arsenic ore occurs, but beyond the arsenic ore in a direction away from the major fracture through which the mineralizing solutions are thought to have traveled. Where the relations between the two types of ore have not been masked by subsequent alterations it is clear that the arsenopyrite ore bodies are invariably the older.

COPPER-LEAD-SILVER REPLACEMENT BODIES

Three subclasses of the replacement ore bodies containing copper, lead, and silver may be distinguished—those associated with the arsenic ore bodies, those in the Oquirrh formation, and those characterized by barite in the gangue.

The lead-silver replacement bodies associated with the arsenic ore bodies are restricted to the occurrences of Ochre Mountain limestone in the Western Utah and U.S. mines. They have in many places a peripheral position with respect to the arsenic ore and are generally more distant from the mineralizing fissure. The relation of these ore shoots to fractures parallel to the bedding is particularly well shown by the "lead fissure" on the tunnel level of the U.S. mine. In the lowest of the three ore bodies in the Western Utah mine, ore of this type away from the mineralizing fracture is restricted to a single limestone bed and is separated from arsenopyrite that has replaced a similar bed by several feet of garnet-diopside rock.

All these ores contain some arsenopyrite. This mineral is distinctly older than the other sulphides and undoubtedly represents material deposited on the fringes of the main arsenopyrite ore bodies. Pyrite was the next mineral to form and is locally found almost to the exclusion of the other sulphides. It is in general rather thoroughly fractured and replaced by the later sulphides and quartz. Sphalerite is widespread throughout the ores and is invariably later than pyrite. It contains in many places inclusions of chalcopyrite and pyrrhotite in the form of dots and discontinuous veinlets. Chalcopyrite may also be found in irregular areas of microscopic size bordering the sphalerite, but it is for the most part relatively rare in these ores. Pyrrhotite in large masses was recognized only on the 760- and 900-foot levels of the Western Utah mine. On the upper level it was comparatively scarce and appeared to be present only adjacent to the mineralizing fracture. On the 900-foot level, however, it was wide-spread and had replaced pyrite as the most abundant sulphide. This was the only place in the quadrangle where there appeared to have been a change in the hypogene mineralization with increasing depth.

Galena was the next sulphide mineral to form. Locally it contains inclusions of the copper-bismuth-lead sulphide, aikinite. Galena is not found in specimens from the U.S. mine that contain a mineral identified by M. N. Short, of the Geological Survey, as jamesonite, which, however, has the same relations to the other sulphides as galena. The two minerals appear to have been mutually exclusive, the formation of one or the other seemingly having depended upon the local concentration of antimony. Stibnite was also recognized in specimens from the dump of the U.S. mine.

The several sulphides are not uniformly distributed throughout these ore bodies. Pyrite or pyrrhotite is almost invariably by far the most abundant, but the proportions of the other sulphides vary widely from place to place. In the 234-foot level of the U.S. mine, for example, much of the sulphide ore shows a rude banding, caused by the separation of the sulphide minerals into individual layers.

Gangue minerals are scarce in these replacement ore bodies. Most of them are composed of almost solid sulphides with small amounts of interstitial quartz and less abundant calcite veinlets. Near the margins the replaced limestone also acts as a gangue mineral.

The factors localizing the ore shoots are the same as those that have been described as causing the distribution of the arsenopyrite ore bodies (p. 102).

The replacement ore bodies in the Oquirrh formation are more numerous than those of the preceding subclass, but are much less extensive. They are found in the limestone beds of the Oquirrh formation both near to the quartz monzonite contact, as at the Monocco and Silver King prospects, and at some distance from the contact, as on the Walla Walla and Mohawk claims.

These ore bodies occur in thin beds of limestone which are rather free from impurities and which are interbedded with sandstone and siliceous limestone. Mineralization extends outward into these beds, which, wherever these deposits are found, have dips less than 30°, from steeply dipping fractures that are themselves mineralized. The dimensions of such ore shoots are small, ore being rarely found more than 15 or 20 feet away from the mineralizing fracture, and at such distances it is not uncommon for only a portion of the favorable bed to be ore-bearing. The mineralizing fissure itself locally contains as much as 2 feet of ore, but the average thickness is less than 1 foot. In several places more than one favorable limestone bed is cut by a single fissure, and in that case all the limestones may be mineralized.

None of the prospects on deposits of this subclass have had sufficient work done to disclose the characteristics of the unoxidized ore. The oxidized ore in the fissures is almost invariably higher in copper and lower in lead than the ore from the replaced limestone beds, and it seems certain that this difference represents an original distinction. Small quantities of galena and chalcopyrite have been recognized in these ores and are the only remnants of the original introduction of sulphides. Analyses of the ore shipped to smelters show also small quantities of zinc, arsenic, and antimony, and it is probable that sulphides of these metals were also present originally. The gangue of the ore in addition to the replaced limestone consists of fine-grained quartz and iron oxides.

The third subclass of the copper-lead-silver replacement ore bodies is represented by the deposit at the Garrison Monster mine. Similar deposits occur at several nearby localities on the north side of Dutch Mountain. These ore bodies lie chiefly along minor reverse faults that generally dip at low angles and are essentially parallel to the major thrust faults that are so abundant in that region. The deposits occur exclusively in limestone or dolomite, but individual beds of this composition have had no apparent influence on the localization of the ore bodies. Ore shoots are distributed sporadically along the fissures. They are relatively small in lateral extent, none of them having a strike length of more than 50 feet, but in the Garrison Monster mine, at least, they persist for considerable distances down the dip. In that mine, the ore shoots coincide with troughs in the fissure zone.

Unoxidized ore is found only in the Garrison Monster mine on the tunnel level. There it consists of relatively small amounts of pyrite and sphalerite as residual remnants in galena. Like most of the sphalerite found elsewhere in the district, this mineral contains microscopic rounded inclusions of chalcopyrite. Associated with the galena in some places, particularly near the borders of galena crystals, are small areas of an antimonial tennantite. In addition to the limestone or dolomite wall rock, the gangue contains small amounts of fine-grained quartz and considerable quantities of barite. The barite appears to be in large part later than the sulphides (pl. 11, *D*).

SUPERFICIAL ALTERATION OF THE ORES

The fact that many ore deposits in unglaciated regions have been extensively altered at the surface is generally recognized. This alteration is the result of the reaction of oxygen-charged surface waters upon the suphide minerals in the ore body, producing, near the surface, minerals characterized by a relatively high oxygen and low sulphur content, and locally, at greater depths, concentrations of redeposited or "secondary" sulphides. In many places such concentrations of redeposited sulphides are of considerable value, and much has been written concerning the mechanism and results of the process.[28]

Several factors influence the character and extent of the alteration. Among these are the position of the ground-water table, the rate at which erosion of the region is progressing, the past climatic history, the recency of any differential uplift, and the physical character and mineral composition of the ores and their walls. The greater number of the ore bodies in the Gold Hill quadrangle have not been sufficiently developed to determine adequately the true importance of these factors, but from the evidence available it would appear that the last one has been the most influential. In none of the ore bodies so far developed has there been any significant amount of enrichment through the formation of secondary sulphides.

RELATION OF THE WATER TABLE TO SUPERFICIAL ALTERATION

Only four mines in the district have, so far as known, reached the ground-water table. These are the Western Utah mine at the 760-foot level, equivalent to an altitude of about 5,125 feet; the U.S. mine at the 234-foot level, altitude about 5,430 feet; and the Success and Cyclone mines, in whose shafts the water table stands at altitudes of 5,450 and 5,950 feet, respectively. The Climax shaft was filled with water at the time of examination, but it is not known whether this water represents ground water or simply filling of mine openings in relatively impermeable rock. The altitude of the water table thus varies considerably in the places where it has been determined, and these localities also show a comparable variation in the distance [illegible] the water table to the surface. The data seem to indicate, however, that the water surface not only has a higher absolute altitude but is nearer the existing surface in regions where the old erosion surface, discussed on page 61, shows a maximum amount of dissection.

In all four of these mines the bottom of essentially complete oxidation is higher than the surface of the present water table. In the Western Utah and U.S. mines the distance betweeen the two is about 100 feet, in the Cyclone mine from 30 to 35 feet, and in the Success mine 20 feet. Oxidation, however, may extend down to the ground-water level along fractured zones. The somewhat abrupt transition between rather completely oxidized ore and relatively unaltered sulphides some distance above the present water table points definitely to a recent wide-spread lowering of the ground-water level. The relation that appears to exist between the level and the old erosion surface suggests that such a lowering is the result o[illegible] [illegible]he normal faulting that is thought to have deformed the old surface. (See pp. 61–63.)

[28] Emmons, W. H., The enrichment of ore deposits U.S. Geol. Survey Bull. 625, 1917. Locke, Augustus, Leached outcrops as guides to copper ore, Baltimore, 1926.

RELATION OF THE PHYSICAL AND CHEMICAL CHARACTER OF THE ORES TO SUPERFICIAL ALTERATION

Alteration of the pipelike deposits and of veins with silicate minerals in the gangue.—The pipelike deposits and the greater number of the veins with silicate minerals in the gangue are alike in being relatively little affected by oxidation. This condition arises in part because the silicate minerals are resistant to alteration, in part because the low content of sulphides prevents the formation of much sulphuric acid, and in part because the toughness and compact texture of the individual minerals do not permit the formation of cracks and fissures through which surface waters may percolate and react with the ore minerals. In many places in these ores hypogene sulphide minerals are found at or near the surface, essentially unaltered. Even in specimens that show some alteration it is generally found that the core of the mineral grain has not been affected. The changes that have been noted in these deposits are the local alteration of scheelite to cuprotungstite,[29] molybdenite to powellite, pyrite to iron oxides, and chalcopyrite to copper pitch which in turn is veined by copper carbonates and chrysocolla. These minerals are locally accompanied by supergene silica in the form either of chalcedony or of opal. The general occurrence of copper pitch in place of the usual oxidation products of chalcopyrite may be explained by the scarcity of pyrite and a consequent deficit in the amount of sulphuric acid available during the alteration. In ores like those found on the Copper Bloom group of claims, in which the ratio of quartz and sulphides to silicate minerals is higher, the secondary copper sulphides covellite and chalcocite have replaced chalcopyrite. This feature appears to be explained chiefly by the greater abundance of pyrite but is probably also accented by the greater mobility of solutions in the more readily fractured quartz. The hypogene bismuth sulphide, bismuthinite, was recognized only in ores containing small quantities of silicate minerals in the gangue. It was everywhere pseudomorphously altered to a mineral of varying appearance and optical properties that is probably close to bismutite in composition. A small piece of native bismuth was found in an area of the supposed bismutite, which in turn was thought to be pseudomorphous after bismuthinite.

Alteration of the quartz-sulphide veins.—Of the veins with a quartz gangue, those containing mixed sulphides are almost completely altered at the surface. Galena is the only sulphide that has been found near the surface in these deposits, and it is generally surrounded by rims of varying thickness of anglesite and cerusite. The stable lead mineral in the oxidized zone, however, is plumbojarosite, and this mineral probably contains the bulk of the lead in the ore shipped from the oxidized parts of these veins. Much of it is arsenical and approaches beudantite in composition owing to the general occurrence of arsenopyrite in the ores. Jarosite, also arsenical, is likewise widely distributed. The oxidized ore also contains some zinc, probably in the form of calamine, and copper, chiefly as the basic carbonates and chrysocolla. Small quantities of descloizite, mimetite, and wulfenite are also present. The Cyclone mine was the only one in which the contact between the oxidized and unoxidized ore could be examined, and here there was no evidence of any appreciable accumulation of secondary sulphides at the contact. The copper content of the unoxidized ore is low in this mine, ranging from 0.5 to 1.7 percent, and is apparently balanced by a sufficient quantity of carbonate in the vein to prevent any downward transportation of copper. There is certainly no accumulation of secondary copper sulphides at the present water table in this mine.

Quartz veins containing arsenopyrite as the metallic mineral are not so thoroughly oxidized at the surface. Scorodite is widely distributed throughout these veins, and all stages in its replacement of arsenopyrite may be recognized, but the alteration is far from complete. This in part at least appears to be the result of the massive character of the sulphide, in which relatively few cracks unhealed by quartz may be distinguished. The quartz veins containing tetrahedrite and galena are still less altered. The sulphide content of these veins is extremely small, and pyrite is totally absent.

Alteration of the carbonate and sulphate veins.—The carbonate veins are affected by weathering chiefly in the elimination of carbon dioxide from the iron-rich carbonates at the surface. Most of these veins on weathered surfaces are colored various shades of brown by the residual iron oxides. The barite veins are essentially unaltered.

Alteration of the arsenic replacement bodies.—The arsenic replacement bodies in limestone provide the most spectacular results of superficial alteration. The outcrop at the Western Utah mine consists of the hydrated iron arsenate, scorodite, with some intermixed iron oxides, and originally had a length of about 300 feet and a width of nearly 200 feet. The ore shoot represented by this outcrop and the next lower one are both completely altered, and the third and lowest ore shoot is similarly affected for most of its developed extent. The upper portion of the ore shoot at the U.S. mine has also been converted to scorodite.

The scorodite varies considerably in appearance and texture. The greater part of it is a fine-grained dense brownish to greenish-brown rock with a conchoidal fracture in which are sporadic vugs lined with finely crystalline material (pl. 12, *B*). In several places, however, there are considerable amounts of white material, which also has a conchoidal fracture. With this locally is associated crystalline green scorodite (pl. 12, *A*). Thin sections show the relations of these differ-

[29] Hess, F. L., unpublished notes.

ent kinds of material to one another. The dense white material, in which remnants of arsenopyrite may locally be distinguished, is a metacolloidal substance which has a streaked or colloform habit and which is in part isotropic and in part has a fibrous crystallization. The refractive indices and birefringence of the nonisotropic portion are both somewhat lower than those of scorodite. In sharp contrast with the white metacolloid is fine-grained crystalline green scorodite. The textures shown by the metacolloid do not pass across the contact into the true scorodite, and the grain size of the scorodite increases away from the contact, reaching a maximum in the terminated crystals that line the vugs (pl. 12, *C*). Several specimens show that the green scorodite has formed at the expense of the metacolloid, and in a few places, as on the 150-foot level of the Western Utah mine, it has almost completely displaced the metacolloidal material.

Similar stages may be observed in the brown to greenish-brown ore, but in this there are abundant microscopic flakes of iron oxide that impose their color upon the material. If the oxidation of arsenopyrite to scorodite, neglecting intermediate steps, is considered as represented by the equation

$$FeAsS + 7O + 3H_2O = FeAsO_4.2H_2O + H_2SO_4$$

it is clear that there is no excess iron to form the iron oxide observed in the brown ore, and it is necessary to assume that sufficient pyrite must have been present in the original ore to provide the excess iron.

Locally the scorodite has been altered to a micaceous golden-brown mineral that appears to be arsenosiderite. This alteration involves the addition of lime, which is probably derived from the limestone wall rocks.

The white metacolloidal mineral in the specimens studied appears to have been developed essentially in place, but there is abundant evidence to prove that scorodite has formed in the wall rocks at some distance from the hypogene sulphides. Veinlets of scorodite cutting the silicate minerals in the wall rocks are not uncommon.

Alteration of the copper-lead-silver replacement bodies associated with the arsenic replacement bodies.—The oxidation of the copper-lead-silver replacement bodies associated with the arsenopyrite ore shoots has been distinctly influenced by the proximity of the arsenic ore. The bulk of such oxidized ore consists of mammillary, stalactitic, and powdery iron oxides, members of the jarosite group, and a varying quantity of scorodite, depending upon the distance from the arsenic ore shoot. The jarosite minerals include both jarosite and plumbojarosite, both of which contain the arsenate radicle locally, and in some places qualitative tests show that the sulphate radicle has been almost completely displaced by the arsenate radicle.

Together with this aggregation of minerals in the upper ore shoot of the Western Utah mine there was apparently a considerable amount of copper in the form of copper arsenates. The greater part of this ore has been stoped, and the relations and identities of the copper arsenates are not known. Small amounts of conichalcite were recognized in the lower ore bodies in the form of mammillary growths upon iron oxide and scorodite mixtures. Small quantities of olivenite and clinoclasite were also found in specimens studied by W. F. Foshag, of the National Museum. Zinc is present in the oxidized ores as the arsenate, adamite, which forms white prismatic minerals resting upon the iron oxides.

The lead-bearing minerals in the oxidized portions of these deposits are not disseminated through the mass but are generally restricted to rather narrow lenticular masses. A jarositelike mineral is the only one present in any quantity in such lenses, but in composition it appears to range from plumbojarosite that is nearly free from arsenate to a hydrous arsenate of lead and ferric iron that is nearly free from sulphate. Doubtless some of this corresponds to the mineral beudantite. Small quantities of a white crystalline substance found in this material at the surface proved to be the lead chloroarsenate, mimetite.

Associated with both the oxidized arsenic and copper-lead ore shoots are considerable quantities of clay minerals. In most specimens these are isotropic and have a low refringence and are probably halloysite. Some, however, are distinctly birefrigent and probably belong to the leverrierite group. Locally masses of black wad are embedded in the clay. The greater part of the clay occurs in the walls of the oxidized ore, but some of it is intermixed with both the iron oxides and the scorodite. It appears to represent the product of the reaction between the silicate minerals in the wall rocks and the sulphuric acid set free during alteration. Small quantities of opal and quartz are also found with the other oxidation products.

Several additional minerals are present in the Western Utah and U.S. mines where oxidation has extended downward to the present water table. Small quantities of secondary sulphides, of which marcasite is the most abundant, have developed in these places. Some chalcocite was recognized but in insufficient quantities to form a copper ore. The most surprising sulphide in this group is arsenopyrite, which apparently has not been previously recognized as a supergene sulphide. The mineral, whose identity was determined by W. T. Schaller, was found as a crystalline coating on a mixture of scorodite and iron oxides from the 760-foot level of the Western Utah mine. In addition to these sulphides gypsum is wide-spread at this horizon and locally has associated with it small quantities of native sulphur. The assemblage of minerals clearly indicates that, at this depth, the addition of oxygen that characterized the processes of alteration nearer the surface was no longer operative and was replaced by an abstraction of oxygen.

On the lower levels of the Western Utah mine also, though not associated with the secondary sulphides, there are considerable quantities of siderite that has replaced the limestone wall rocks. In appearance this material is not unlike the smithsonite ores of other western mining districts, but chemical tests show that its zinc content is extremely low.

Alteration of the replacement bodies in the Oquirrh formation.—The replacement bodies in the Oquirrh formation are almost completely oxidized. The copper ores in the fissures consist dominantly of dark-brown to black copper pitch, which contains remnants of chalcopyrite and is veined by malachite, azurite, and chrysocolla. The lead ores contain sparse remnants of galena, from which anglesite, cerusite, and plumbojarosite have been formed. Several specimens show that these minerals were formed in the order named, and each one at the expense of the preceding mineral. The process of alteration has apparently nearly reached completion, for plumbojarosite is the most abundant lead mineral in these deposits. In both lead and copper deposits secondary silica in the form of opal and chalcedony is present.

Alteration of replacement bodies containing barite.—The lead replacement bodies with barite in the gangue have also been altered in a similar way. At the Garrison Monster mine, however, the proportion of cerusite to plumbojarosite is relatively high.

AREAL RELATIONS OF THE ORE DEPOSITS

In many mining districts it has been observed that different types of ore deposits are arranged in concentric zones with respect to a central area, which is commonly occupied by an intrusive rock mass. The deposits of the successive zones are held to represent deposition at decreasing temperature away from the central area, and the mineralogic changes that are observed in them are considered to be the same as those found at different depths in a single vein, the deeper mineral facies in the vein being represented by a similar grouping in the inner zones on the surface. Emmons [30] has recently summarized the evidence for such a zonal distribution of ore. In view of the large number of different kinds of ore bodies occurring in the Gold Hill quadrangle, it is desirable to bring out in what respects the distribution of these deposits conforms to the ideal arrangement, and in what respects and for what reasons it appears to depart from a uniform zoning.

Influence of zoning on the distribution of the ore deposits.—Almost all the ore bodies characterized by silicate minerals in the gangue are concentrated in a relatively narrow zone extending from a point near the town of Clifton to the vicinity of the U.S. mine. This zone coincides with a belt of normal faulting that is considered to be closely related in age to the intrusion of the quartz monzonite, and it has been suggested that the belt represents the primary channel through which the igneous rock was intruded (pp. 88–89). Such a relation between the site of intrusion and the higher-temperature ore deposits seems to be good evidence that areal zoning has to that extent been operative.

Within this same zone, however, there are numerous representatives of other types of deposits, which clearly have been formed at lower temperatures. Thus on the Reaper claim, in addition to the tungsten-bearing pipe, there is a quartz vein containing tetrahedrite, galena, and barite and a quartz-carbonate vein, both less than 300 feet from the pipe. Similarly, in the areas outside of the zone, deposits of notably different mineralogy are found in close proximity. At the Western Utah mine, on Gold Hill, for example, a gold-bearing lode with silicate gangue, a quartz-tetrahedrite vein, and arsenic and lead-zinc replacement bodies in limestone are essentially in contact with one another.

There must therefore be some other factor than distance from the center of intrusion that has influenced the distribution of the ore deposits. It seems probable that this factor lies in the age relations between the mineralogic facies characterizing the different types of ore deposits. As has been noted, there is a demonstrable sequence for the several facies, the higher-temperature deposits being the oldest. The writer believes that to these differences in age is due the lack of zoning shown by the greater number of the deposits, and that in this district the time factor (resultant from such age differences) has been vastly more important in determining the distribution of ore bodies than the space or temperature factor that causes the zonal distribution. It is not improbable that the dominance of the time factor in this area is in large part the result of the repeated fracturing of the quartz monzonite (p. 89), which provided channels for the ore-depositing solutions in regions that might otherwise have been closed to them through sealing of the earlier-formed fractures by older, higher-temperature ore bodies.

It is obvious that if the time factor is as important as is thought, the period during which ore deposition took place must have been a long one, because it must have included time enough for the ore-bearing solutions traveling through the same stretch of quartz monzonite country rock to cool from the temperatures at which the tungsten-bearing pipes were deposited to those which permitted the carbonate veins to form.

The proposed relation between the recurrent fracturing in the quartz monzonite and the lack of a general zoning pattern in the distribution of the ore deposits

[30] Emmons, W. H., Primary downward changes in ore deposits: Am. Inst. Min. Eng. Trans., vol. 70, pp. 964–997, 1924; Relations of metalliferous lode systems to igneous intrusives: Idem, vol. 74, pp. 29–70, 1926; Relations of the disseminated

would imply that regions in which a zonal distribution of the ores is well defined have undergone essentially no fracturing during the period of ore deposition.

Both Hills [31] and Knopf [32] have described districts in which the distribution of the ore deposits is markedly at variance with that to be expected if there had been a simple zonal control. Both men came to closely similar conclusions, which may be summarized by the following quotation from Knopf:

> The principle that successive ore-forming differentiates ("distillates"), each with its own distinctive constituents and characteristics, are given off during successive stages of a progressively cooling magma will be found, it is here suggested, to be widely applicable in the study of ore deposition. As a modifying factor the principle of zonal distribution is recognized as having been operative in some districts, but of and by itself the principle of zonal variation in ore deposition is of very narrow application.

The writer prefers the view that recurrent fracturing in the intrusive rock is of more importance in changing the character of the ore bodies than distinctive composition of successive differentiates. The evidence for this opinion is given in the section on the origin of the ores.

Influence of the Ochre Mountain thrust on the distribution of the ore deposits.—A singular feature in the distribution of the ore deposits is the barrenness of the formations above the Ochre Mountain thrust. In several places roof pendants within the quartz monzonite or reentrants of sediments into the intrusive rock are made up largely of Ochre Mountain limestone lying above the thrust, with only small amounts of the overridden beds beneath. The beds below the thrust are intensely metamorphosed and contain various kinds of ore bodies, but the overlying beds are essentially unaltered and in almost all places contain no ore bodies whatever. This difference in behavior cannot be attributed to any lithologic features of the overlying beds, because the occurrences of Ochre Mountain limestone beneath the thrust contain numerous and locally large ore bodies. It seems probable that the barrenness of the rocks above the thrust may be attributed to the fact that the thrust plane prevented the continuation upward of fractures that were forming in the quartz monzonite and in the rocks below the thrust and localized the flow of the solutions that were causing metamorphism and ore deposition. As almost all these fractures appear to be genetically connected with the intrusive rock, it is likely that the zone of weakness represented by the thrust would deflect the fractures horizontally along itself and prevent their further upward extension.

[31] Hills, Loftus, The zinc-lead sulphide deposits of the Read-Rosebury district: Tasmania Geol. Survey Bull. 23, pp. 86-88, 1915.

[32] Knopf, Adolph, Geology and ore deposits of the Rochester district, Nev.: U.S. Geol. Survey Bull. 762, pp. 57-58, 1924.

GENESIS OF THE ORE DEPOSITS

The ore deposits within the quadrangle very clearly represent the final stages of the intrusion of the quartz monzonite stock. The evidence proving the close relationship between them lies in the obvious connection between metamorphism and the ore deposits—particularly the pipes and the veins with silicate gangue—and the dependence of the metamorphism in turn upon the quartz monzonite intrusion. The exposures within the quadrangle appear to provide a rather complete picture of the ever-changing results effected by the emanations given off by the solidifying intrusive.

At the start of this final stage of the igneous activity the emanations resulted in the formation of anhydrous silicate minerals with, locally, tungstates in the form of scheelite. The minerals formed show that all the common rock-forming elements were contained in the emanations and, as they developed by the replacement of either the wall rocks or the quartz monzonite, lead to the view that the material was simply a residuum of the rock magma made highly mobile by the concentration within it of the small quantities of volatile constituents originally contained in the magma. These constituents do not enter into the earlier-formed minerals, however, either because their concentration was not large enough to cause precipitation, or, more probably, because the temperature was too high to permit them to enter a stable solid phase.

This assemblage of minerals was succeeded by one in which the minerals formed are made up not only of the rock-forming elements but also of the volatile constituents. Amphiboles, tourmaline, axinite, apatite, scapolite, fluorite, humite, and danburite, for example, were formed during this period, in many places at the expense of the minerals of the first stage. In addition, iron oxides appear to have been formed at this time.

The initiation of a third period is marked by the appearance of quartz and the metallic sulphides. Chlorite and sericite are essentially contemporaneous with these minerals and show that the emanations still contained some of the rock-forming elements, even though many occurrences of these minerals suggest that in large part they have developed at the expense of earlier-formed silicate minerals. This period, like both of the preceding ones, may be subdivided into successive steps. Thus, bismuthinite and arsenopyrite appear to have been among the earliest sulphides to form. Galena and tetrahedrite, on the other hand, are among the last and appear to have been deposited near the end of the period.

The products of the final period are characterized by the almost complete absence of silicate minerals and metallic sulphides. During this period the emanations deposited silica (much of it probably in the form of a gelatinous substance that later recrystallized to quartz), barite, and carbonates. The carbonate minerals contain considerable quantities of iron and magnesium and indicate the persistence of these rock-forming elements as constituents of the igneous emanations.

Although the assemblages of these four periods are distinct mineralogically, they are by no means separated areally; in many places all four may be found in the same ore deposit, where they are intimately associated but clearly of different ages. This fact, together with the persistence of certain of the constituents, such as iron, magnesia, and silica, throughout the series, makes it highly improbable that there have been several emissions of distinctive composition from the magma, as postulated by Knopf and Hills (see p. 108), but indicates rather that metamorphism and ore deposition have been one continuous process. The abrupt changes in mineralogy shown by the deposits of the four periods appear to have been the result of a constantly decreasing temperature, by which new mineral groups became the stable phase in place of the older minerals that they replaced. This view requires that the different elements contained in the emanations should have widely different fields of stability. Thus, fluorine and boron could have been precipitated during only one of the four periods, but magnesium, iron, and silicon appear to have formed stable compounds throughout the process, although it is recognized that the compounds formed differ for each period.

Although it is probable that all cooling igneous emanations in general pass through successive periods more or less similar to those recognized at Gold Hill, it is obvious that the details of the process must differ considerably in different places. The individual minerals formed reflect not only the original composition of the emanations but also changing concentrations of the different phases contained in them, the rate of change in temperature, reaction with the wall rocks, and the presence or lack of equilibrium. The important feature, it would seem, is that the fluids that cause igneous metamorphism and ore deposition undergo a differentiation of the same or even a greater degree of complexity than that which has been determined for the igneous rocks themselves.

The chief modifying factor in the progress of ore deposition appears to have been the presence of recurrent fracturing in the rocks within which the ores were being deposited. The evidence indicating that fracturing continued over a long period after the intrusion of the quartz monzonite is presented on page 89, and to this cause may be attributed many of the present features of the ore deposits found in the quadrangle. This factor can be used to explain the preservation of the pipelike deposits through the abandonment of the mineralizing channel by reason of renewed fracturing; had this not occurred, the mineral assemblages of the early periods would probably have been in large part replaced by those of the later periods. On the other hand, a channel once sealed by deposition of material from the emanations may be reopened and again filled by minerals of a much later period, as illustrated by the late carbonate veins that cut ore deposits of an earlier stage.

It is possible that the existence of so many small ore deposits instead of a smaller number of large deposits is to be ascribed to recurrent fracturing. As renewal of fracturing may have caused the abandonment of old channels and the opening of new ones, it would appear that the process, if carried far enough, might easily result in so shortening the time during which ore deposition was operative at any one place that the bodies of ore thus formed would be so small and of so low a grade as to be of relatively little value.

FUTURE OF THE DISTRICT

At the time of the last field work by the writer (1927) the production of the district had decreased to a small part of that made in the years after the completion of the railroad from Wendover. The reasons for this decrease were in part economic and in part inherent in the ore deposits themselves, but the two reasons were of different importance for each class of ore body. The future possibilities of the district may therefore be most readily discussed by a separate consideration of each type of deposit.

Tungsten-bearing pipes and veins.—The production of tungsten from pipes and veins has been small and was made only during the war-time period of high prices. Although it is probable that similar deposits might be developed in the region between Clifton and the Lucy L mine—particularly at the upper contact of the quartz monzonite stock beneath the roof pendants that conceal much of the igneous rock in this region—it is doubtful if such deposits could be worked profitably at the prevailing prices for tungsten.

Veins with silicate minerals in the gangue.—Two main varieties of the veins having silicate minerals in the gangue have been prospected: in one, copper is the valuable metal; in the other, gold. The copper-bearing veins have been rather thoroughly prospected on the Frankie, Calaveras, Pole Star, and other claims, and several shipments of ore have been made from them. In general, however, the average copper content is too low and the ore bodies developed are too small for them to be worked profitably except when prices for copper are unusually high, and owing to the nearly complete extraction of these ores at the outcrop, where mining has been relatively cheap, it is doubtful if they will ever be of any importance.

A different conclusion may be drawn concerning the veins in which gold is the valuable constituent. At least four mines have worked ore deposits of this type—the Rube, Alvarado, Midas, and Cane Springs—and these have shown that the ore shoots, though small, contain sufficient gold to make properly conducted operations successful. The known deposits have a rather wide distribution in the sedimentary rocks near the quartz monzonite contact, but the outcrops of the ore deposits are relatively inconspicuous. It seems probable that careful prospecting in the sediments near the igneous contact may disclose other deposits of this class which contain either direct smelting ore similar to that at the Rube, or lower-grade milling ore. The tonnage of milling ore in a single one of these veins would probably be insufficient to warrant the erection of a mill, but it is probable that ore from several of them would justify the operation of one mill.

Quartz-sulphide veins.—A large number of the quartz-sulphide veins have been prospected more or less thoroughly and have furnished some small shipments of ore, valuable chiefly for the content of silver and lead. The work that has been done has shown rather conclusively that the ore shoots are too small for any operations except on the most modest scale, and future production from deposits of this type will very probably be confined to occasional carload lots extracted by lessees.

Carbonate-sulphate veins.—The carbonate veins have essentially no valuable metallic constituents and need not be further considered. If the demand for barite continues to increase, however, there is a possibility that deposits large enough to warrant mining operations may be developed. So little work has been done on the deposits containing barite, however, that it is difficult to predict their future importance.

Arsenic replacement bodies.—The two important arsenic replacement bodies—in the Western Utah and U.S. mines—have, with the lead-silver replacement bodies associated with them, provided a large part of the district's production. The shipments of arsenic ore from the two mines were made during the period from 1919 to 1925, when prices of white arsenic (As_2O_5) ranged from 7 to 20 cents a pound. Both mines still possess large reserves of arsenic ore, but the prevailing prices of 2 to 4 cents a pound for white arsenic since about 1925 have been too low to permit profitable operations. Should prices improve sufficiently, these mines would undoubtedly be able to provide a large quantity of ore. According to Clifford F. Rowley, manager, the Western Utah mine has 225,000 tons of proved ore, averaging 24 percent of arsenic. The quantity of arsenic ore developed in the U.S. mine was not ascertained but must be of about the same magnitude. Only a minor amount of exploration has been directed toward the development of new arsenic ore bodies, but it seems probable that, if due regard is given to the factors which were operative in localizing the two known deposits, additional ore bodies may be found in regions where the Ochre Mountain limestone beneath the Ochre Mountain thrust is adjacent to the quartz monzonite.

Copper-lead-silver replacement bodies.—The remarks made above concerning the quartz-sulphide veins are applicable also to the copper-lead-silver replacement bodies, for, except for the lead-silver ore associated with the arsenic ore deposits, the exploitation of these ore bodies has been, in general, disappointing. Some of the deposits, particularly those in the Garrison Monster mine, contain rather rich ore, but the ore shoots without exception are so small in cross section that the quantity of ore available is meager.

Summary.—A large tonnage of arsenic ore is developed in the quadrangle, and the possibilities of increasing the amount are thought to be good. Profitable exploitation of the ore, however, must wait until the price of arsenic is higher than that which has prevailed in recent years. It is also considered that careful prospecting may disclose additional deposits of gold ore which, though of small size, may repay the discoverer. Possibly the district contains barite deposits that may be worked at a profit if the demand for this material increases. The remaining types of deposits are thought to be too small or too low in grade to provide any great future production. Many of these deposits, however, offer opportunities to small groups of individuals who, working with little or no overhead expense, might extract several carloads of ore at a satisfactory profit.

MINERALS OF THE METAMORPHOSED ROCKS AND THE ORE DEPOSITS

In this section the minerals are described in the order followed by Dana.

NATIVE ELEMENTS

Graphite (C).—Found as small flakes in the altered limestone wall rock in the Alvarado mine, associated with muscovite, quartz, calcite, and spadaite (?). Opal and a clay mineral are also present, but are probably supergene.

Sulphur (S).—Small quantities of native sulphur were recognized in the Western Utah mine at ground-water level. Marcasite, gypsum, and iron oxides were the most abundant associated minerals.

Bismuth (Bi).—Small quantities of bismuth were found at the Wilson Consolidated and Lucy L mines. In the former a speck of native bismuth was embedded in bismuthinite; in the latter it was associated with bismutite.

Gold (Au).—Native gold is present in a number of the mines in the district, particularly those in which the gangue consists of silicate minerals. Previous observers have considered the gold to be contemporaneous with the silicate minerals, but the writer's observations indicate that it was introduced somewhat later and is more closely associated with quartz and sericite. Two varieties of gold were recognized in specimens from the Rube mine. One was in the form of microscopic specks widely distributed throughout the unoxidized ore. The other was coarser-grained and in the form of well-developed crystals and was observed in anglesite, cerusite, and other supergene minerals and also resting upon iron oxides. The second variety was clearly formed during the oxidation of the ore. There was, however, no appreciable enrichment during the oxidation, for the unoxidized ore has essentially the same content of gold as the oxidized ore.

Copper (Cu).—Mr. Tiffany, superintendent of the Western Utah mine in 1925, reported that some native copper had been found on the 760-foot level.

SULPHIDES, SELENIDES, TELLURIDES, ARSENIDES, AND ANTIMONIDES

Realgar (AsS).—Small quantities of realgar are reported to have occurred in the Western Utah mine, but it was not observed by the writer. The almost complete absence of realgar and orpiment from the ores of the district is rather surprising, in view of the abundance of arsenopyrite and the fact that the two iron-free arsenic sulphides are generally considered to be supergene alteration products.

Orpiment (As_2S_3).—Also said to have been found in small amounts in the Western Utah mine.

Stibnite (Sb_2S_3).—Stibnite is locally abundant on the 234-foot level of the U.S. mine. In one specimen, in which it was identified by W. T. Schaller, bladed crystals more than 1 inch long were associated with pyrite.

Bismuthinite (Bi_2S_3).—This hypogene bismuth sulphide was found in the ores from the Lucy L and Wilson Consolidated mines, as rounded blebs in both quartz and calcite. It is generally either partly or completely replaced by bismutite, which retains the pronounced cleavage of the older mineral.

Molybdenite (MoS_2).—Molybdenite is present in many of the ore deposits containing silicate minerals in the gangue and was also noted disseminated through altered quartz monzonite in the vicinity of the Reaper claim. It appears to have formed earlier than most of the other sulphides, for it is embayed and replaced by chlorite in specimens from the Rube mine. In this mine it is extremely abundant in one portion of the ore shoot. Because of its presence in several of the gold ore bodies the mineral is thought by some to be gold-bearing. This, however, is not borne out by an assay made by E. T. Erickson, of the Geological Survey, of a specimen containing 61.6 percent of MoS_2, in which the gold content was 0.26 ounce to the ton—much less than is found in the shipping ore. A second assay was made of material containing less molybdenite, which may be compared with the first as follows:

MoS_2 (percent)	Ash (percent)	Gold (ounce per ton)
20.4	79.6	0.52
61.6	38.4	.26

The gold content is thus almost exactly proportional to the ash content and bears no relation to the molybdenite content whatever.

Galena (PbS).—Galena is found in almost all the quartz-sulphide veins and limestone replacement bodies and is sparingly present in some of the veins with silicate minerals in the gangue. It has clearly formed later than arsenopyrite, pyrite, and sphalerite, but its relations to chalcopyrite are obscure, as in some places it appears to be later and in others to be veined by chalcopyrite. In several places it contains tiny inclusions of aikinite and tetrahedrite or tennanite. In specimens from the Garrison Monster mine it is replaced by barite (pl. 11, *D*). Alteration to anglesite, cerusite, and plumbojarosite has been wide-spread.

Chalcocite (Cu_2S).—Small quantities of chalcocite were found in several places as supergene replacements of the hypogene sulphides.

Sphalerite (ZnS).—The distribution of sphalerite is similar to that of galena. It was noted in quartz-tourmaline rock at the Gold Bond claim and is moderately abundant in the quartz-sulphide veins and in the limestone replacement deposits. It replaces arsenopyrite and pyrite and is generally replaced by quartz and the other sulphides. Tiny rounded inclusions of chalcopyrite and pyrrhotite are present in most of the specimens. In several of the mines sphalerite occurs in masses 1 inch or more across and has a nonmetallic appearance. The color is dark brown to black, and the cleavage is well marked. A thin section from the footwall of the Rube vein contained some dark sphalerite embedded in dolomite. Several quartz veinlets cut the section and in one place a veinlet impinges upon the sphalerite. Adjacent to the quartz the dark sulphide has been bleached to a colorless sphalerite whose index of refraction is slightly lower than that of the older darker sphalerite.

Covellite (CuS).—Covellite was recognized in a few specimens as a supergene alteration product of the hypogene sulphides, chalcopyrite, galena, and tetrahedrite.

Pyrrhotite (FeS_{1+}).—Pyrrhotite is abundant only on the 900-foot level of the Western Utah mine, where it appears to have taken the place of the pyrite that is found on the upper levels. It was also noted as inclusions in sphalerite in specimens from other mines.

Bornite (Cu_5FeS_4).—Bornite was noted in small quantities in ores from the Alvarado, Midas, and Cane Springs mines.

Chalcopyrite ($CuFeS_2$).—Chalcopyrite is found in small amounts in all the different types of ore deposits except the carbonate and sulphate veins. It occurs both interstitial to other sulphides and silicate minerals and as tiny rounded inclusions in sphalerite. Much of it has been altered to copper pitch, in which remnants of the sulphide are generally abundant.

Pyrite (FeS_2).—Pyrite is found both in many of the ore deposits and disseminated through the altered quartz monzonite. It was one of the earliest sulphides to form in the ore deposits. It is probably later than molybdenite and has definitely replaced arsenopyrite but has been replaced by all the other sulphides.

Marcasite (FeS_2).—Marcasite was noted in several specimens from the Western Utah mine that were collected at about the present ground-water level. It has replaced pyrite, from which it may be readily distinguished in polished specimens by reason of its anisotropism in polarized light.

Arsenopyrite (FeAsS).—Arsenopyrite occurs in very large quantities in the ores of the district, both in the quartz-sulphide veins and in the limestone replacement bodies, locally being present to the almost complete exclusion of the other sulphides. The arsenopyrite masses in the Western Utah and U.S. mines are probably the largest bodies of this mineral that have thus far been discovered. Where arsenopyrite has replaced limestone it appears to have formed originally as bladed radiating crystals (see pl. 11, *A*), but in most of the occurrences this habit has been destroyed by later fracturing and subsequent cementation and replacement by quartz, sericite, pyrite, and other sulphides. The arsenopyrite has been altered in many places to scorodite. Another mode of occurrence was noted on the 760-foot level of the Western Utah mine, at ground-water level, where tiny crystals of supergene arsenopyrite rest upon a mixture of iron oxides and scorodite.

Calaverite? ($AuTe_2$).—Kemp [33] has described a mineral from the Lucy L mine that "afforded the characteristic and unmistakable test for tellurium and sweated under the blowpipe little beads of gold. Traces of lead and antimony were also indicated. The mineral is a silvery, thin-bladed brittle variety and would suggest a telluride or stibnite to an observer."

SULPHOSALTS

Jamesonite ($4PbS.FeS.3Sb_2S_3$).—Identified by M. N. Short, of the Geological Survey, in several polished specimens of ore from the U.S. mine. In the sections it appears as a bladed

[33] Kemp, J. F., Notes on Gold Hill and vicinity, Tooele County, Utah: Econ. Geology, vol. 13, p. 260, 1918.

mineral with a galenalike color that has replaced arsenopyrite, pyrite, and sphalerite. No galena was found in the specimens containing jamesonite, and the two appear to have been incompatible.

Boulangerite ($Pb_5Sb_4S_{11}$).—Identified by Mr. Short in a specimen from the wall rock of the Rube mine. It was rather abundant as small particles in limestone. Microchemical tests by Mr. Short showed that it contained appreciable amounts of arsenic.

Aikinite ($2PbS.Cu_2S.Bi_2S_3$).—Small amounts of the bismuth-bearing sulphide aikinite were identified by Mr. Short in specimens from both the Cyclone and U.S. mines. It is associated with galena and appears to have formed relatively late in the sequence of sulphide minerals.

Tetrahedrite and tennantite ($5Cu_2S.2(Cu,Fe,Zn)S.2Sb_2S_3$; $5Cu_2S.2(Cu,Fe,Zn)S.2As_2S_3$).—Microchemical tests by Mr. Short showed that both tetrahedrite and tennantite are present in the ores of the district. Neither, however, is free from varying quantities of the other mineral, and it is probable that all gradations between the two end members could be found. No correlation could be made between the content of arsenic or antimony and the type of deposit in which the mineral was found, although the amount of material tested was not sufficient to make this conclusion a certainty. Small quantities of these two minerals were found in the veins having silicate minerals in the gangue, but they are most abundant in the quartz-sulphide veins and in the limestone replacement bodies, where they appear to be of nearly the same age as galena. Quartz veins containing tetrahedrite (or tennantite) as the chief sulphide are widely distributed, particularly in the vicinity of Royal Gulch. In these veins the minerals contain considerable amounts of silver, specimens from the Undine claim being said to run as high as 409 ounces to the ton.

HALOIDS

Fluorite (CaF_2).—Small amounts of purple and white fluorite are associated with danburite on the Gold Bond claim.

OXIDES

Quartz (SiO_2).—Quartz, as is usual, is the most abundant and widely distributed mineral in the ore deposits and was also introduced in considerable amounts in the metamorphism of both the sedimentary rocks and the quartz monzonite. It is relatively rare in the pipelike deposits; becomes more abundant in the veins with silicate minerals in the gangue (some of which contain only a few remnants of silicates surrounded by quartz); is the dominant constituent of the quartz-sulphide veins; and becomes progressively less abundant in the carbonate and sulphate veins. It is the chief gangue mineral, except for the replaced limestone, in the replacement deposits.

Much of the quartz found associated with the ore deposits characterized by silicate minerals is relatively coarse-grained and contains numerous fluid inclusions, within which are gas bubbles. This habit is also found in much of the quartz that has replaced the quartz monzonite. In the quartz-sulphide veins the grain size is also relatively large, but the fluid inclusions were not observed to be so abundant. Much of the quartz associated with the limestone replacement bodies and composing the jasperoids, however, is extremely fine-grained and apparently free of the fluid inclusions. This material locally is associated with contemporaneous opal and barite, and much of it has apparently resulted from the crystallization of a gel-like material. (See pp. 93–94.)

In several specimens there is good evidence for the presence of some supergene quartz. One from the Rube mine, for example, is made up of quartz molded on pyromorphite and containing euhedral crystals of plumbojarosite.

Chalcedony (SiO_2).—All the occurrences of chalcedony are

lected near the outcrops of different types of ore bodies and occurred both as veinlets and as cavity fillings. It is locally associated with both opal and quartz.

Opal ($SiO_2.nH_2O$).—Some opal that is definitely hypogene was noted in thin sections of the silicified wall rock in the U.S. mine. The opal occurred as irregular microscopic inclusions in fine-grained quartz. (See pl. 8, *C*.) All the other occurrences of this mineral, however, are probably supergene, and it is generally associated with chalcedony. Opal was locally abundant on the Undine claim and in the Alvarado mine, but elsewhere it was noted only in small quantities.

Hematite (Fe_2O_3).—The specular variety of hematite was found on the Reaper claim and in several of the veins with silicate gangue, notably on the Gold Bond claim, where it clearly replaced tourmaline (see pl. 10, *B*) and was replaced by danburite.

Hematite is undoubtedly present in the oxidized portion of many of the ore bodies, but no attempt was made to distinguish it from goethite, and the two have been grouped together and described as iron oxides throughout this report.

Spinel ($MgAl_2O_4$).—A green isotropic mineral of high relief, recognized in a thin section of altered rock from the Undine claim, was identified as spinel. It was partly replaced by muscovite.

Magnetite (Fe_3O_4).—Small quantities of magnetite were found in several deposits of different types. For the most part it has replaced calcite that appears to have formed relatively late, but on the Doctor claim it has replaced apatite and amphibole. In much of the altered quartz monzonite it is also abundant and has apparently formed as a result of the alteration. It is suggested that this mineral tends to form as a result of the attack of the later stages of mineralizing or metamorphosing solutions upon earlier-formed iron-bearing minerals. On the Undine claim there is a considerable amount of magnetite that has replaced limestone. This material was reported by the owner of the claim to carry 0.96 ounce of gold to the ton.

Rutile (TiO_2).—In several specimens of an altered quartz monzonite porphyry dike from the Western Utah mine the original biotite was found to be altered to chlorite, sericite, calcite, and an acicular mineral that has the habit of rutile.

Wad (amorphous brown manganese oxide of indefinite composition).—Small black nodular masses embedded in a clay mineral were found in the walls of the oxidized ore bodies of the Western Utah mine. The material gave off chlorine when dissolved in hydrochloric acid, left a large insoluble residue, and gave a strong test for manganese, all of which indicate that it is probably wad.

Copper pitch (amorphous cupric oxide of indefinite composition, usually containing silica and manganese).—Much of the chalcopyrite in the district has been altered to a dark-brown to black resinous-appearing substance that has been called copper pitch. Remnants of chalcopyrite are found in most of the material, and veinlets of chrysocolla and other oxidized copper minerals are generally associated with it. Some of this material from the Silver King claim was reported to contain 62 percent of copper and must therefore be composed largely of copper oxides.

CARBONATES

Calcite ($CaCO_3$).—Calcite is a wide-spread constituent of both the metamorphosed rocks and the ore deposits. Considerable quantities are found in the pipes and veins with silicate minerals in the gangue, in which it appears in general to be later than all the silicate minerals. Its relations to quartz are contradictory, as in some places it is earlier and in others later. Locally it is closely associated with either magnetite or specularite and appears to be roughly contemporaneous with them. In most of the limestone replacement ore bodies and in the quartz-sulphide

A peculiar habit of the calcite was observed in a thin section from [illegible] mine. A veinlet shown in the slide was composed of calcite crystals developed normal to the walls of the veinlet. These showed an extinction inclined to the direction of growth, however, and the crystals must therefore be elongated parallel to the rhomb faces rather than the prism faces.

Calcite is also wide-spread as a supergene mineral, and in several places it was observed associated with supergene opal or as well-formed crystals on iron oxides.

Dolomite ($(Ca,Mg)CO_3$) *and ankerite* ($CaCO_3(Mg,Fe,Mn)CO_3$).—Veinlets of pink carbonate cutting the quartz monzonite in the vicinity of the Midas and U.S. mines were found to have ω near 1.70 and are therefore ferrodolomite, or ankerite. Carbonates of similar appearance were also found cutting several of the quartz-sulphide veins. Very large quantities of dolomite were also formed in the limestones of the quadrangle, probably during the final stages of metamorphism. In most places these weather to shades of brown, indicating that they are ferruginous. Some of the dolomitized rock near the Garrison Monster mine weathered to a deep chocolate-brown, and blowpipe tests showed that this material contained also some manganese.

Siderite ($FeCO_3$).—Rather large quantities of siderite are found on the 700- and 760-foot levels of the Western Utah mine. The mineral resembles closely the "dry-bone ore" of many mining districts, but chemical tests show that it is almost pure siderite and contains less than 1 percent of zinc. This siderite has replaced the limestone beds immediately north of the lower ore body of the mine and is limited downward by the groundwater level. It is clearly supergene.

In several of the quartz-sulphide veins some hypogene siderite is present as thin veinlets cutting the sulphides. One of these veinlets in ore from the Copper Queen Midland prospect was tested microscopically and found to have ω near 1.83, indicating an $FeCO_3$ content of 75 percent. It is probable that there are all gradations between this material and the ferrodolomite found at the U.S. and Midas mines.

Large crystals of an iron-rich carbonate are also found in many of the carbonate veins. At the surface, however, these have largely weathered to iron oxides, but the preservation of the carbonate cleavage lines indicates their original nature.

Smithsonite ($ZnCO_3$).—Small quantities of smithsonite are present in the Garrison Monster mine, and probably it can also be found in the oxidized ores of some of the other limestone replacement ore bodies.

Cerusite ($PbCO_3$).—Small quantities of cerusite were found in almost all the mines containing lead ore. Most of the occurrences of this mineral are coarse-grained gray masses associated with galena but generally separated from it by a zone of anglesite. In the Garrison Monster mine, however, the mineral is in the form of the familiar "sand carbonate" and is unusually abundant. Locally small cream-colored terminated crystals of the mineral were observed. In almost all places the cerusite has been partly replaced by plumbojarosite.

Malachite ($CuCO_3.Cu(OH)_2$).—Veinlets and small crystals of malachite can be found in all the mines that have copper sulphides in the hypogene ore. It is generally associated with azurite, chrysocolla, and copper pitch.

Azurite ($2CuCO_3.Cu(OH)_2$).—Azurite is relatively rare, but small quantities of it were noted as an oxidation product of copper sulphides at several localities.

Bismutite ($Bi_2O_3.CO_2.H_2O$?).—The mineral referred to bismutite is a common constituent of the ores in the Wilson Consolidated, Lucy L, and Copper Bloom claims. It has formed as a result of the oxidation of bismuthinite. In places the material is pseudomorphous after the sulphide, preserving the old cleavage planes perfectly. This variety of the mineral is gray in color and is for the most part isotropic with an index of refraction greater than [illegible]. It is apparently not of homogeneous composition, for in thin section it is streaky and of variable color. The gray color is possibly due to the content of tiny bismuthinite remnants, because in specimens in which the mineral is not pseudomorphous but is localized along fractures of quartz or calcite it is granular in habit and is either green or yellow. Some of this material has a rather high birefringence. No optical distinction could be made between the yellow and green varieties, and it is possible that the green color may be caused by relatively small amounts of admixed malachite.

SILICATES

Orthoclase ($KAlSi_3O_8$).—Orthoclase feldspar is one of the most abundant silicate minerals that were formed during the metamorphism of the quartz monzonite and of the intruded sandstones and calcareous sandstones. In the vicinity of the Wilson Consolidated mine, for example, a sandstone bed in one place is almost completely converted to orthoclase; and near the Yellow Hammer mine the quartz monzonite in several places was found to contain as much as 50 percent of introduced orthoclase. The mineral is also present in large amounts in the pipelike deposits, where single crystal faces more than 1 foot across were observed, and in smaller quantities in many of the veins with silicate gangues. The color in most occurrences is pink.

The orthoclase is generally perthitic and locally has been replaced by rather coarse-grained white albite, particularly in the pipelike deposits, but this feature has also been observed in the metamorphosed quartz monzonite. The mineral appears to have been, except for albite, one of the last of the anhydrous silicates to form, as it has replaced garnet, diopside, epidote, and amphibole. In several localities it has been replaced by minerals characterized by the presence of mineralizers, such as tourmaline and danburite, and replacement by quartz and sericite has been very common.

Albite ($NaAlSi_3O_8$).—Noted in several specimens from the pipelike deposits and in the altered quartz monzonite, where it has replaced orthoclase. It is also present in the orthoclase in the form of perthitic inclusions.

Oligoclase (albite with 10 to 30 percent of $CaAl_2Si_2O_8$).—Small amounts of a fine-grained mineral identified as oligoclase were found in altered limestone at the Alvarado mine.

Diopside ($CaMg(SiO_3)_2$).—Diopside is an abundant constituent of both the metamorphosed quartz monzonite and the altered sedimentary rocks. Where the mineral is found in the igneous rock it may be readily distinguished in thin sections from the augite that is a sparse original constituent by the larger size of the crystals, their euhedral habit, and the fact that they have replaced all the original constituents. The mineral is particularly abundant in the altered limestones and sandstones, in some of which it is present to the almost complete exclusion of other minerals. It is relatively rare in the pipelike deposits but is abundant in many of the veins with silicate gangue. It is probable that in some occurrences the mineral is aluminous, as much of it has replaced garnet. It has also been observed as a replacement product of zoisite, epidote, and titanite. Locally the diopside has been replaced by amphibole, the alteration starting along the cleavage lines. Orthoclase has also replaced this pyroxene, and in the altered limestone wollastonite has developed at its expense.

Wollastonite ($CaSiO_3$).—Wollastonite is one of the most abundant silicates in the metamorphosed limestones. It occurs as bladed crystals that may be an inch or more in length, and locally it has almost completely replaced a thick limestone bed. It is generally associated with small quantities of garnet and diopside, both of which have been replaced by it. Wollastonite itself in many places has been altered to the mineral spadaite, particularly in the vicinity of the gold-bearing veins having silicate minerals in the gangue. The wollastonite can be readily distinguished optically from tremolite, which it closely resembles, by the fact that it has a transverse optic plane. A specimen from the Cane Springs mine gave the following optical data: α near 1.618, γ near 1.628, optically negative, rather small 2V and transverse optic plane.

Tremolite ($CaMg_3(SiO_3)_4$).—Tremolite was recognized microscopically in two specimens of hornfels from the Lucy L claim. These specimens were altered members of the Oquirrh formation. The mineral was not found in any of the specimens of altered Ochre Mountain limestone.

Actinolite ($Ca(Mg,Fe)_3(SiO_3)_4$) *and hornblende* (similar to actinolite but containing alumina, ferric oxide, and alkalies).—Monoclinic amphiboles are wide-spread both in the metamorphosed sedimentary and igneous rocks and in the pipes and the veins having silicate minerals in the gangue. In the altered rocks amphibole has generally replaced diopside and locally garnet, a common mode of occurrence being along the cleavage lines of the older pyroxene. This habit is also found in many of the silicate veins, and in both modes of occurrence the amphibole has been partly replaced by calcite, chlorite, sericite, and quartz. Orthoclase, tourmaline, apatite, humite, and scapolite have also replaced the amphiboles. In the pipelike deposits the mineral is a conspicuous constituent. Here it has a sheaf-like habit, and individual clusters of crystals more than 3 feet in length may be observed. Remnants of diopside have been found in these crystals, but it is uncertain to what extent these giant crystals have formed at the expense of a preexistent pyroxene. The same minerals have replaced the amphibole in the pipes as in the other occurrences.

There appears to exist a nearly continuous gradation between a strongly colored hornblende and a nearly colorless (in thin section) variety that is probably actinolite. The darker varieties are the older and in many specimens are altered along cleavage planes to the lighter and nonpleochroic actinolite. The large crystals found in the pipe on the Reaper claim seem to have a composition intermediate between pargasite and common hornblende, as is shown by the following optical data: α near 1.628, γ near 1.645; optically negative; 2V large; pleochroism, X = pale yellow-green, Y = deep green, Z = blue-green.

Garnet ($R''_3R'''_2(SiO_4)_3$).—Garnet is an abundant constituent both of the metamorphosed rocks and of many of the ore deposits. It appears to have been one of the first minerals to form during the postmagmatic stage of igneous activity and generally has been more or less completely replaced by younger minerals. There is a rather wide variety of composition represented by the specimens collected, as the indices of refraction range from 1.777 to 1.91. Most of the specimens tested, however have n near 1.88, indicating a dominance of the andradite molecule. The specimen (from the Lucy L mine) whose index was 1.91 was associated with titanite and is probably titaniferous.

Where the age relations of the different varieties could be determined, the garnet with the higher index of refraction was generally thought to be older. This variety also seemed to show fewer optical anomalies than the garnets of lower index. The birefringence of some of the garnets was close to 0.008, and those specimens that were tested were found to be optically positive. Twinning and zonal growth were also observed in many of the garnets, and skeleton crystals in calcite are rather abundant.

Scapolite group ($Ca_4Al_6Si_6O_{25}$–$Na_4Al_3Si_9O_{24}Cl$).—Minerals belonging to this group were recognized microscopically in specimens from the Rube, Doctor, and Gold Bond claims. In the specimen from the Rube the mineral is associated with calcite and chlorite. The birefringence is about 0.030, α being about 1.55, and γ near 1.58. This indicates a composition near the meionite end of the series. In the other two specimens the scapolite has replaced garnet and hornblende. The material from the Doctor claim shows a well-developed prismatic cleavage, has a small optic angle, is optically negative, and has α = 1.539 and γ = 1.549. In this occurrence, therefore, the composition is rather close to the marialite end member.

Vesuvianite (complex calcium-aluminum silicate containing OH and F).—Vesuvianite was noted in thin sections of the gold ore from the Midas and Cane Springs mines. In the Cane Springs specimen it occurred as large crystals in association with zoisite, from which it was distinguished by its uniaxial negative character. In this occurrence it was older than diopside and wollastonite, having been partly replaced by these minerals.

Zircon ($ZrSiO_4$).—Abundant crystals of zircon were noted under the microscope in several specimens of metamorphosed rocks and also in a specimen from the pipe on the Reaper claim. They showed the simple combination of prism and pyramid faces, were optically positive, and had a moderately strong birefringence.

Danburite ($CaB_2(SiO_4)_2$).—Flesh-colored massive danburite is abundant on the Gold Bond claim, where it was found in veins as irregular or lenticular masses that were more than 1 foot across. The mineral had replaced specularite and was itself partly replaced by calcite. The following optical data were determined by W. T. Schaller and E. P. Henderson: Orthorhombic, optically positive, 2E large, α = 1.627, β = 1.629, γ = 1.632.

Andalusite (Al_2SiO_5).—Andalusite was noted in several specimens taken from the Manning Canyon formation near the quartz monzonite stock. An extended description of the occurrence of the mineral near the Cane Springs mine has been given by Kemp.[34]

Zoisite ($Ca_2(AlOH)Al_2(SiO_4)_3$).—Greenish-brown zoisite was recognized in several specimens of altered limestone and also in the gold ores from the Cane Springs, Rube, and Bonnemort claims. It is locally associated with vesuvianite. Where it has formed in calcite, euhedral crystals a quarter of an inch in diameter may be found. In other specimens the mineral has formed at the expense of garnet and has itself been replaced by diopside, wollastonite, spadaite, and chlorite. The index of refraction near 1.72, low birefringence, biaxial positive character, parallel extinction, and small optic angle are characteristic.

Clinozoisite ($Ca_2(AlOH)Al_2(SiO_4)_3$).—Brownish-green radiating fibrous crystals of clinozoisite were found in a specimen of metamorphosed limestone near the Frankie claim.

Epidote ($HCa_2(Al,Fe)_3Si_3O_{13}$).—Two varieties of epidote were recognized in the specimens collected. A normal green epidote was found in the pipe on the Doctor claim and in the wall rock of the silicate vein on the Frankie claim. The other variety was in the form of black euhedral crystals 3 millimeters in maximum length in the tungsten-bearing ores on the Reaper, Yellow Hammer, and Lucy L claims and in the wall rock of the Gold Bond claim. The mineral had the following optical properties: Biaxial negative; 2V large; strong dispersion ($r > v$ on material from the Lucy L and $r < v$ on specimens from the Gold Bond); α near 1.745, γ near 1.772; twinned and strongly zoned; notably pleochroic, X = pale yellow to nearly colorless, Z = deep greenish brown to nearly opaque. The pleochroism is unlike that reported for other epidotes and is similar to that of allanite, but the indices are much too high for allanite. These crystals were among the first minerals to form in the deposits in which they are found, being associated with titanite and garnet. It is possible that the unusual properties of the mineral may be due to the presence of titanium, as the garnet in some of these deposits has properties suggesting that they also are titaniferous.

Axinite (a borosilicate of aluminum and calcium).—Axinite was found by Butler[35] at several localities. It was not recognized by the writer in any of the specimens collected by him,

[34] Kemp, J. F., Notes on Gold Hill and vicinity, Tooele County, Utah: Econ. Geology, vol. 13, pp. 254–257, 1918.

[35] Butler, B. S., Ore deposits of Utah: U.S. Geol. Survey Prof. Paper 111, p. 479, 1920.

but its presence in Butler's specimens was checked by optical determinations.

Humite group ($Mg(F,OH)_2.MgSiO_4$–$Mg(F,OH_2).Mg_7(SiO_4)_4$).—Considerable quantities of a pale flesh-colored mineral thought to be humite were found on the Calaveras and Frankie claims. The mineral has replaced garnet, tourmaline, orthoclase, and other silicates and appears to have been the last silicate to form. It has been extensively replaced by calcite and some quartz. A similar mineral was recognized in the altered wall rock of the lower ore body in the Western Utah mine. The following optical data were determined: Biaxial positive, large axial angle, parallel extinction, α near 1.619, γ near 1.652.

Calamine (H_2ZnSiO_5).—Small crystals of a mineral determined optically and chemically as calamine were found in the oxidized ore of the Garrison Monster mine. It was associated with clay minerals and iron oxides.

Tourmaline (complex silicate of boron and aluminum).—Tourmaline is of wide-spread occurrence in the district. It has been noted along joints in the quartz monzonite, as a constituent of the metamorphosed rocks (particularly in the Manning Canyon formation, in which it forms stubby black crystals as much as an inch in length), and as a common mineral in many of the ore deposits with silicate minerals in the gangue. It was formed relatively late, for the only minerals noted as having replaced it are danburite, specularite, quartz, sericite, and calcite. The tourmaline is generally found in sheafs of acicular crystals, which, on the Reaper claim, reach a length of several inches. In these occurrences the color of the mineral is a brilliant black, and under the microscope its indices were found to be $\epsilon=1.655$ and $\omega=1.695$, and the pleochroism pale yellow-green to almost opaque. In several places the black variety was replaced by a fine-grained aggregate of sericite, calcite, quartz, and blue tourmaline, in which the pleochroism was ω=pale blue-green and ϵ=colorless.

Muscovite ($H_2KAl_3(SiO_4)_3$).—Muscovite, particularly the fine-grained variety sericite, is widely distributed in both the altered sedimentary and igneous rocks and in all types of the ore deposits. The mineral formed relatively late and has replaced all the other silicate minerals. It is generally associated with chlorite, quartz, and calcite. It is probably also in part at least contemporaneous with many of the metallic minerals, although in the Western Utah mine it has clearly replaced arsenopyrite. It occurs with quartz in all the gold ores of the district and is present in the wall rocks of the quartz-sulphide veins. The more coarsely crystalline form known as muscovite was recognized in several of the ore deposits with silicate minerals in the gangue.

Biotite ($(H,K)_2(Mg,Fe)_2Al_2(SiO_4)_3$).—Biotite is an abundant constituent of the metamorphosed shales of the Manning Canyon formation and is associated with quartz and andalusite. It was also observed in small quantities associated with muscovite in the pipe on the Reaper claim and in vein material from the Gold Bond claim.

Chlorite group ($H_8Mg_5Al_2Si_3O_{18}$).—Two varieties of chlorite were distinguished. The more abundant variety is nearly black when viewed in the mass and is green and pleochroic under the microscope. Much of it is either isotropic or has an extremely low birefringence. This variety is a wide-spread constituent of the metamorphosed rocks, particularly the quartz monzonite, and is generally found in association with sericite and quartz, having replaced the older minerals. It is also abundant in many of the ore deposits that contain silicate minerals. The second variety is colorless in thin section and has an appreciable birefringence. Material from the Rube mine was biaxial positive and had the following indices of refraction: $\alpha=1.549$, $\gamma=1.553$. The relations of this variety to the green chlorite are not known, but it is probably somewhat later, as it is a constituent of jasperoid in several localities, particularly in the U.S. mine.

Jefferisite (complex magnesium-aluminum silicate).—The vermiculite known as jefferisite was found in several places in the low-lying region north and west of the town of Clifton, either in the limestone at the quartz monzonite contact or in some of the silicate veins near the contact. In the veins it was associated at several places with magnetite. The mineral occurred as dull-green plates that were as much as 1½ inches in diameter in the occurrences in limestone. β and γ were close to 1.575, and C. S. Ross determined 2V to be about 11°.

Talc ($H_2Mg_3(SiO_3)_4$.)—Talc was identified by C. S. Ross in a thin section of ore from the Rube mine, in which it was present as fibrous fine-grained patches associated with calcite in muscovite.

Spadaite ($MgO.SiO_2.2H_2O$).—The unusual mineral spadaite[34] was found to be relatively abundant in the gold ores of the Alvarado and Cane Springs mines and was also recognized in a specimen of ore from the Midas mine and in metamorphosed limestone near the Monocco claim. In all the occurrences it has replaced wollastonite (see pl. 8, *B*) and has itself been locally replaced by quartz. It occurs as a fine-grained aggregate of fibers and in mass has a yellowish or pinkish color. The following analysis was made on a specimen from the Cane Springs mine that was largely composed of this mineral:

Analysis of spadaite from Gold Hill, Utah

[W. T. Schaller, analyst]

Insoluble	8.68
SiO_2 soluble in Na_2CO_3	.41
SiO_2	43.28
Fe_2O_3	.22
FeO	.27
CaO	1.58
MgO	24.72
H_2O-	10.36
H_2O+	10.51
	100.03

Deducting from this the impurities—8.68 percent insoluble residue (diopside and garnet), 3.27 percent wollastonite (based on the CaO percentage), 0.41 percent opaline silica (soluble in 10 percent Na_2CO_3 solution), 10.36 percent water at 110°, and 0.22 percent Fe_2O_3 as limonite—and recalculating to 100 percent gives the following figures for the composition of the mineral, with which may be compared the analysis of the original material from Italy:

	Gold Hill	Italy
SiO_2	53.96	56.00
FeO	.35	.66
MgO	32.08	30.67
H_2O	13.64	11.34
Al_2O_3		.66
	100.03	99.33

Clay minerals (hydrated aluminum silicates).—Clay minerals are found in the vicinity of many of the oxidized ore deposits in the district. In many places they occur as a sort of casing to the oxidized ore, a relation that is well illustrated by the body of clay that surrounds the lower portion of the gold-bearing quartz lens on the Lucy L claim. These minerals are commonly associated with iron oxides, and in one place they enclose masses of the mineral wad. They have apparently been formed as a result of the reaction between the sulphuric acid generated by the oxidation of the sulphides in the ore body and the silicate minerals in the wall rocks. At least three varieties of clay minerals

[34] Schaller, W. T., and Nolan, T. B., An occurrence of spadaite at Gold Hill, Utah: Am. Mineralogist, vol. 16, pp. 231-236, 1931.

were recognized under the microscope, and in many places these may occur together. One variety has an index of refraction near 1.57 and a low birefringence—properties that correspond to those of the kaolinite group; another has indices lower than canada balsam and a distinctly higher birefringence than the first variety and is possibly related to beidellite. The third variety is isotropic, and different specimens have indices ranging from 1.51 to 1.55. This variety has been referred to as halloysite.

Nontronite ($Fe_2O_3.3SiO_2.2H_2O$).—Nontronite, which is isomorphous with the clay mineral beidellite, was found as a yellow-green powdery coating on ore specimens from several mines in the district.

Chrysocolla ($CuSiO_3.2H_2O$).—Chrysocolla was noted in specimens from several mines and prospects as thin veinlets cutting copper pitch or as coatings on ore or wall rock. In the Western Utah extension mine it was in turn coated by the arsenic-bearing conichalcite.

TITANOSILICATES

Titanite ($CaTiSiO_5$).—Titanite was found to be an abundant constituent of some of the specimens of metamorphosed quartz monzonite and was also found in the ore of several of the tungsten-bearing pipes and veins. It occurs as swarms of small euhedral crystals from 0.1 to 1 millimeter long and is in many places associated with epidote and diopside. The diopside has locally replaced the titanite, and danburite, specularite, and orthoclase have also been noted as being distinctly later.

PHOSPHATES, ARSENATES, VANADATES, AND ANTIMONATES

Apatite ($Ca_5(F,Cl)(PO_4)_3$).—Considerable quantities of a pale flesh-colored or yellowish apatite are present in the tungsten pipes north of Clifton. In these occurrences the mineral tends to have crystal outlines, and crystals nearly an inch across are not uncommon. It is normally embedded in amphibole and clearly has replaced that mineral. On the Doctor claim it has been replaced by magnetite. Flakes of iron oxide along irregular cracks in the mineral in places give it a distinctly pinkish color. On the Copper Bloom claim the ore contains numerous small crystals of yellow or greenish crystals of apatite that are about an eighth of an inch in diameter. These appear to have replaced tourmaline. The mineral has also been recognized microscopically in some of the gold-bismuth ore.

Pyromorphite ($Pb_5Cl(PO_4)_3$).—Pyromorphite was identified by E. P. Henderson in a thin section of oxidized ore from the Rube mine. It occurred both in large prismatic crystals and in massive aggregates coated by supergene quartz and was partly replaced by plumbojarosite.

Mimetite ($Pb_5Cl(AsO_4)_3$).—Creamy-white crystals of mimetite were identified chemically by Mr. Henderson in oxidized ore from the Western Utah mine. He also recognized the mineral in oxidized ore from the Red Jacket claim, but at this locality the color was greenish.

Olivenite ($Cu_2(OH)AsO_4$).—Deep olive-green olivenite was recognized by W. T. Schaller and W. F. Foshag and was also identified by the writer in oxidized ore from the Western Utah Extension mine, where it was coated or partly replaced by conichalcite. Under the microscope the mineral was seen to have a high birefringence and 2V near 90°. β is a little higher than 1.80.

Adamite ($Zn_2(OH)AsO_4$).—Adamite was identified chemically by Mr. Henderson in oxidized ore from the Western Utah mine. It occurred as tiny white prisms with scorodite and iron oxides. Under the microscope the indices were seen to be near 1.73. The mineral has a prismatic cleavage, parallel extinction, and is optically positive.

Descloizite ($(Pb,Zn)_2(OH)VO_4$).—Small crystals of descloizite were determined by W. T. Schaller in oxidized lead ore from the New Baltimore claim.

Clinoclasite ($Cu_3As_2O_8.3Cu(OH)_2$).—Clinoclasite was identified by W. F. Foshag in oxidized ore from the upper ore body of the Western Utah mine.

Arseniosiderite ($Ca_3Fe(AsO_4)_3.3Fe(OH)_3$).—Several specimens of arsenic ore from the Western Utah mine were found to contain considerable quantities of arseniosiderite. In some specimens it appears to have formed at the expense of massive scorodite; in several, however, it is not associated with scorodite but contains blebs of jarosite or is coated with beudantite and mimetite. The mineral is found in aggregates of fine-grained, rather fibrous crystals that have a lustrous pale greenish-brown color and a reddish streak. Specimens gave qualitative tests for calcium, iron, and the arsenate radicle. The following optical data were also determined: Indices of refraction between 1.82 and 1.88, birefringence moderate, slightly pleochroic in reddish browns.

Ferrisymplesite? ($3Fe_2O_3.2As_2O_5.16H_2O$).—A bright-yellow powdery mineral coating a mixture of quartz and arsenopyrite from the U.S. mine was submitted to W. T. Schaller for identification. He writes, "The yellow coating contains ferric iron and arsenate with some lime and sulphate (probably due to gypsum). There is no uranium present. Ammonia does not turn it red, like pharmacosiderite. It may be related to ferrisymplesite,[37] which has the formula $3Fe_2O_3.2As_2O_5.16H_2O$. Refractive indices 1.650±. Strong birefringence."

Scorodite ($FeAsO_4.2H_2O$).—Scorodite is by far the most abundant oxidation product of the large masses of arsenopyrite that occur in the district. The largest quantities of the mineral are found in the Western Utah mine, in which the upper and middle ore bodies are composed almost completely of this mineral and also the lower ore body down to the 700-foot level. The amount in the U.S. mine is considerably less, because here oxidation extends only locally below the adit level. Scorodite is also present in the oxidized portions of all the other ore bodies in which arsenopyrite is one of the hypogene sulphides. The material that has been called scorodite varies widely in color and appearance. (See pp. 105–106 and pl. 12, *A*, *B*.) Most of it is extremely fine grained and breaks with a conchoidal fracture. Thin sections of such specimens show that it is composed of an isotropic streaked mineral that may be either white or brownish. The isotropic mineral is in many places in sharp contact with crystalline scorodite, much of which, however, is so fine grained that it has an appearance not unlike that of the isotropic substance. In most places this crystalline scorodite contains an admixed iron oxide, and the color of the mixture is brown of various shades, depending upon the amount of iron present. Where the iron oxides are absent the scorodite is deep green. In a few places the size of grain increases and crystals as much as an eighth of an inch in diameter may be found. A specimen obtained just above the 150-foot level of the Western Utah mine was composed almost entirely of crystalline material from which the following optical data were determined: Biaxial positive, moderate 2V, dispersion $r>v$; indices, $\alpha=1.788$, $\beta=1.797$, $\gamma=1.818$. Foshag, Berman, and Doggett[38] have recently studied the crystalline scorodite from the Western Utah mine and give the following optical properties:

"The mineral is optically negative[39]; $2V=54°\pm5°$. $r>v$ (easily perceived in the interference figure but not sufficiently strong to measure on the Fedorow stage). The indices of refraction for yellow light, as determined by the Merwin dispersion method, are as follows: $\alpha=1.784\pm0.001$, $\beta=1.796\pm0.002$, $\gamma=1.814\pm0.001$. Dispersion $F-C=0.03\pm0.005$."

[37] Walker, T. L., and Parsons, A. L., The arsenate of cobalt, nickel, and iron observed in the silver-bearing veins at Cobalt, Ontario: Toronto Univ. Studies, Geol. ser., no. 17, p. 17, 1924.

[38] Foshag, W. F., Berman, Harry, and Doggett, R. A., Scorodite from Gold Hill, Tooele County, Utah: Am. Mineralogist, vol. 15, pp. 390–391, 1930.

[39] Obviously a misprint for positive.—T. B. N.

[illegible] analysis of the mineral is as follows:

Analysis of scorodite from Gold Hill, Utah (U.S.N.M. 94821)

Fe_2O_3	34. 13
Al_2O_3	None
FeO	. 84
CaO	. 38
MgO	. 01
As_2O_5	48. 42
P_2O_5	None
H_2O+	15. 73
H_2O-	. 23
Insoluble	. 42
	100. 14

Conichalcite ($(Cu,Ca)_3As_2O_8.(Cu,Ca)(OH)_2\frac{1}{2}H_2O$).—The basic copper arsenate conichalcite appears to be the most widespread of the several green copper arsenates found in the oxidized ores of the district. It was recognized in specimens from the Western Utah and Western Utah Extension mines, in both of which it occurs chiefly as a mammillary coating on scorodite, iron oxides, or other minerals. It was also observed in one specimen as a replacement product of the olivenite. The mineral has a distinctly fibrous habit and under the microscope was seen to be nonpleochroic, with parallel extinction, with the slow ray parallel to the elongation, and optically positive. It is either uniaxial or has a very small optic angle and has α (or ω) near 1.76 and γ (or ϵ) near 1.80.

Pharmacosiderite ($6FeAsO_4.2Fe(OH)_3.12H_2O$).—Heikes[40] writes that the ore of the Western Utah mine is a "cellular mass of scorodite and brownish oxidized mineral (pharmacosiderite?)."

Beudantite ($3Fe_2O_3.2PbO.2SO_3.As_2O_5.6H_2O$).—A jarositelike mineral containing lead and arsenic is present in large quantities in the district, particularly in the Western Utah mine. It is probable that there are all gradations between pure plumbojarosite and beudantite. The mineral is in all places very fine grained and appears to have been one of the most recent of the oxidation products to form. The color is generally yellow-brown, but one specimen was greenish. Under the microscope the mineral is seen to occur in well-formed crystals, either as flat hexagonal plates or as positive and negative rhombs combined with the basal face.

SULPHATES, CHROMATES, AND TELLURATES

Barite ($BaSO_4$).—Barite is present in small quantities in almost all the jasperoid masses. It has also been recognized in several of the quartz-tetrahedrite veins. The mineral is particularly abundant in the Garrison Monster mine, where it is found in the vein itself and in the limestone wall rock. At this place it is later than the sulphide minerals and locally has replaced them. Large quantities of barite are also present in the barite veins and limestone replacement bodies at several places in the quadrangle. In these the barite appears to have been the only mineral introduced.

Anglesite ($PbSO_4$).—Anglesite was noted in almost all the lead-bearing ore deposits of the quadrangle. It was developed as the first stage in the oxidation of galena and generally borders and veins the sulphide. It has itself been replaced by cerusite and plumbojarosite. In the Rube mine native gold was observed embedded in anglesite in several specimens.

Gypsum ($CaSO_4.2H_2O$).—Considerable quantities of crystalline gypsum were found at the ground-water level in both the U.S. and Western Utah mines.

Chalcanthite ($CuSO_4.5H_2O$).—Blue and greenish blue glassy crystals of chalcanthite half an inch in maximum length were found embedded in copper pitch on the bottom level of the Alvarado mine. The mineral was also recognized in the Cyclone mine, where it occurred on the walls of the drift and had obviously formed since the workings had been driven.

Siderotil ($FeSO_4.5H_2O$).—Siderotil is associated with chalcanthite and copper pitch in the Alvarado mine. It is a pale-green fibrous fine-grained mineral that occurs in areas of rectangular outline. These areas, however, are cut by numerous desiccation cracks, and the mineral is probably pseudomorphous after melanterite. It is soluble in water and gives qualitative tests for iron and sulphate. The indices of refraction are α near 1.52, γ near 1.54.

Jarosite ($K_2Fe_6(OH)_{12}(SO_4)_4$).—Because of the difficulty in distinguishing members of the jarosite and related groups from one another except by chemical tests, it is uncertain how widespread the occurrence of pure jarosite is in the oxidized ores of the district. Most of the specimens tested contained lead, but several were lead-free and gave flame tests for potassium, so that jarosite is definitely present in at least some of the ores. One specimen from the U.S. mine contained no lead but did contain arsenic, so that there is probably a series comparable to the plumbojarosite-beudantite series in the lead-free minerals.

Natrojarosite ($Na_2Fe_6(OH)_{12}(SO_4)_4$).—A specimen of a jarosite mineral from the Western Utah mine was found on testing to be free from lead and potassium and gave a strong flame test for sodium. It is probably natrojarosite.

Plumbojarosite ($PbFe_6(OH)_{12}(SO_4)_4$).—Plumbojarosite or gradations between it and its arsenic-bearing analog, beudantite, is probably the most abundant lead mineral in the oxidized ore of the district. It is found in all the lead-bearing veins and is clearly later than either anglesite or cerusite, and in many places it also veins and coats iron oxides. In the Rube mine the mineral is embedded in supergene quartz. Variations in the arsenic content may be found in the same mine. In the Western Utah mine, for example, a specimen from the south end of the open cut contained almost no arsenic, and another less than 100 feet away contained a considerable percentage of it. The mineral is found in various shades of brown and is always very fine-grained. At the Monocco mine lessees shoveled all run of mine ore through a screen and shipped the screenings, which were composed largely of plumbojarosite. Like beudantite, the mineral is seen under the microscope to be in the form of well-developed crystals, either as the common flat hexagonal plates or in crystals made up of combinations of rhomb faces and the base.

TUNGSTATES AND MOLYBDATES

Wolframite ($(Fe,Mn)WO_4$).—Hess found wolframite on the Keno claim, according to his unpublished notes.

Scheelite ($CaWO_4$).—Only small quantities of scheelite can now be found in the district, but it has been recognized in several of the pipes and veins having silicate minerals in the gangue. The numerous large crystals on the Reaper claim described by Butler[41] are no longer there, having been mined during the World War when the demand for tungsten was at its height. Similar deposits nearby have also been almost completely stripped of the visible scheelite. In the specimens collected by the writer from the Wilson Consolidated, Reaper, Centennial, Yellow Hammer, and Copper Bloom claims the scheelite appears as a dull-white or yellowish mineral of rather greasy appearance and in places is very similar to the apatite that also occurs in these deposits. The two may be readily distinguished

[40] Heikes, V. C., Arsenic in 1923: U.S. Geol. Survey Mineral Resources, 1923, pt. 1, p. 166, 1924.

[41] Butler, B. S., Ore deposits of Utah: U.S. Geol. Survey Prof. Paper 111, p. 476, 1920.

under the microscope, however, by reason of the high index of refraction of the scheelite, as well as its higher birefringence. In all the specimens studied the scheelite was seen to have formed relatively early, and it has been replaced in different specimens by amphibole, tourmaline, chlorite, sericite, quartz, and sulphides.

Cuprotungstite ($CuWO_4$).—Hess recognized cuprotungstite on the Keno claim, according to his unpublished notes.

Powellite ($Ca(Mo,W)O_4$).—Powellite was found as white porcelaneous pseudomorphs after molybdenite at several places on the Reaper claim.

Stolzite ($PbWO_4$).—The stolzite was questionably identified by Butler [43] in a specimen from the Wilson Consolidated mine.

Wulfenite ($PbMoO_4$).—Small brilliant orange-colored crystals of wulfenite are present in the oxidized ore of several of the quartz-sulphide veins north and northwest of Clifton, such as the vein on the Red Jacket claim, in which it is associated with mimetite.

MINES AND PROSPECTS

The mines and prospects in the quadrangle are included in the Clifton and Willow Springs mining districts. The Clifton district is by far the more productive of the two. Its outlines are not well defined but are approximately those of the area shown on plate 2. The boundary between the two districts has never been fixed, so far as known, but in practice the line of Overland Canyon is used to separate them. The Willow Springs district extends for some distance beyond the southern boundary of the quadrangle, but the prospects outside of the quadrangle were not examined during this survey.

The descriptions of individual mines and prospects in the Clifton district are arranged in the same order as that in which the different types of ore bodies were described. Several of the mines contain more than one type of deposit however, and for such mines, the more productive type was used to determine the position of the description.

It is probable that the names here used for some of the prospects no longer apply, because each year many of the unpatented claims are allowed to lapse by omission of the required assessment work. Many of these claims are then restaked under new names.

CLIFTON DISTRICT

HISTORY OF MINING AND PRODUCTION

The following account of the early history of the Clifton district is quoted from Heikes:[43]

The first discovery of mineral is said to have been made in 1858, but the hostility of the Indians retarded development until 1869, when the first mining operations were begun and the district was organized (on October 18). Huntley [44] reviews the conditions in November 1880 as follows:

"A smelter was built in 1871 and was moved in 1876 to a spot 6 miles distant by the St. Louis Consolidated Co. Probably 150 tons of bullion were produced. * * * About 50 claims, of over 500 located, are still worked occasionally. Little has been done since 1877."

The smelter built in 1871 is reported by an old resident [45] and mine owner of the district to have been a stack furnace operated with three blacksmith bellows. Three tons of lead bullion represented the results of the first operations. In 1872 Gilbertson & Berry's furnace was built at Clifton to treat the ores from the Gilbertson mine at Gold Hill. About 30 tons of lead bullion [46] shipped to Salt Lake averaged $93 in silver per ton. A few years later this furnace was moved to Gold Hill by J. W. Harker. The crude ore smelted carried about $4 in gold, 30 ounces of silver per ton, and 25 to 30 percent of lead.

Activity in mining did not again assume importance until 1892, when a mill was put in operation at Gold Hill. The ores treated were from the Cane Springs, Alvarado, and Gold Hill claims, which were credited with a total gold production of $207,986 from September 1892 to November 1895. Of this total probably half the ore and more than three-fifths of the gold came from the Alvarado mine. No complete record of the amount of ore handled exists, but a partial record shows 9,475 tons of ore milled from August 1892 to May 1894, assaying $14 per ton and yielding $97,393, or $10.28 per ton. At the same rate, the total ore worked was about 19,000 tons.[47] The gold produced was very pure, some of it 0.946 fine.

The Midas property is about 3 miles southeast of Clifton. In 1896 and prior to that year 95 tons of ore averaging $56 in gold and a trace in silver per ton were treated at the Cane Springs mill and shipped to the smelter. In 1902 a 40-ton cyanide mill was constructed and treated 622 tons with a reported saving of $15 per ton in gold. In 1904 the mill was operated again, but the results were unfavorable, and the property was practically abandoned.

In 1906 the Western Utah Copper Co. acquired the principal properties on Gold Hill, and during the succeeding 10 years this company confined its efforts to development work in anticipation of the construction of a branch line of the Western Pacific Railroad from Wendover. In this period there was no production from the district except for small lots from a few prospects.

Construction of the long awaited branch railroad was finally started in 1916 and completed in 1917; in that year the production of the district amounted to 33,960 tons of ore valued at $705,957. Over half of this came from the Western Utah Copper Co.'s Gold Hill mine. From this initial production shipments gradually declined, except for a slight rise in 1920, until in 1922 only 211 tons of ore was shipped. In 1923 and 1924, however, a demand for arsenic, which had been discovered in large quantities at the Gold Hill mine, caused a temporary revival. The collapse of the arsenic market in 1925 caused a curtailment of activities, and the production for the following year declined sharply. Since 1926 the production has been made up chiefly of small and intermittent shipments.

The following table shows the production of gold, silver, copper, lead, and zinc in the district from 1901 to 1932, the figures being obtained from the annual

[42] Butler, B. S., Ore deposits of Utah: U.S. Geol. Survey Prof. Paper 111, p. 482, 1920.

[43] Heikes, V. C., Ore deposits of Utah: U.S. Geol. Survey Prof. Paper 111, p. 475, 1920.

[44] Precious metals: Tenth Census U.S., vol. 13, p. 456, 1885.

[45] Dunyon, Isaac, Salt Lake City, personal interview.

[46] Fabian Bentham, Resources of Utah, 1872, p. 16, Salt Lake City, Utah, 1873.

[47] Daggett, Ellsworth, unpublished mining notes.

statistical reports by V. C. Heikes (1900–25) and C. N. Gerry (1926–32) in Mineral Resources of the United States. It is not complete for the years before 1914, but the omissions are probably of no great importance. There have been in addition small shipments of tungsten, bismuth, and molybdenum ore, but nothing is known as to their monetary value.

The production of arsenic ore is also uncertain, for most of it was shipped on the basis of a flat rate per ton. Rough estimates, however, indicate that the arsenic ore contained about 9,000 tons of metallic arsenic, which, when converted to As_2O_5, would have had a value of about $2,500,000, on the basis of the average prices during the years of production.

Gold, silver, copper, lead, and zinc produced in the Clifton district, 1901–32

Year	Ore (tons)	Gold (ounces)	Silver (ounces)	Copper (pounds)	Lead (pounds)	Zinc (pounds)	Value
1901	18		68		666		$69
1902	651	482. 20	641		6, 000		10, 554
1903			(a)				
1904	1, 660	969. 00	92				20, 085
1905			(a)				
1906			(a)				
1907			(a)				
1908			(a)				
1909			(a)				
1910			(a)				
1911			(a)				
1912			(a)				
1913			(a)				
1914	66	57. 25	146	5, 054			1, 936
1915	16	5. 21	149	1, 470	1, 924		530
1916	67	8. 90	645	10, 547	4, 782		3, 532
1917	33, 960	564. 31	161, 204	1, 894, 731	513, 929		705, 957
1918	19, 714	449. 56	97, 241	828, 658	1, 204, 472		396, 730
1919	14, 257	233. 89	53, 706	194, 476	778, 869		142, 439
1920	39, 656	77. 43	89, 578	92, 913	1, 010, 833		197, 204
1921	11, 627	266. 09	23, 208	3, 194	336, 292		44, 253
1922	211	278. 61	2, 974	4, 521	16, 524		10, 252
1923	13, 237	860. 60	41, 195	33, 040	291, 554		76, 836
1924	33, 094	511. 05	147, 786	3, 615	1, 840, 453		257, 290
1925	13, 721	808. 90	111, 372	54, 459	1, 960, 853		272, 339
1926	1, 382	1, 129. 20	13, 772	13, 826	267, 083	2, 243	55, 416
1927	526	926. 04	4, 413	2, 396	53, 701	14, 754	26, 286
1928	195	3. 24	1, 578	2, 995	50, 233		4, 355
1929	415	480. 27	1, 229	40, 001	1, 237		17, 703
1930	1, 009	77. 84	3, 704	47, 885	280, 480		23, 284
1931	2, 259	1, 142. 40	2, 384	22, 046	458, 723		43, 285
1932	2, 915	2, 361. 00	1, 207	6, 473	174, 084		

[a] Not recorded.

MINES AND PROSPECTS

PIPELIKE DEPOSITS

REAPER

The Reaper group of claims, owned by the Seminole Copper Co. and managed by the Wilson Brothers, of Salt Lake City, is about three-quarters of a mile west of north from Clifton. The group appears to have made the largest production of all the several tungsten prospects in the Clifton district, but the total amount is not known. It must have been very much less than 100 tons of 60 percent ore, for that figure represents the total production from Utah during the period 1914–18 and includes ore shipped from several other districts.

The ore body was developed by a vertical shaft 105 feet deep, from which were driven 2 levels, one at the bottom of the shaft and one 56 feet higher. The upper level was driven beneath the outcrop, from which the ore body was removed by means of an open stope to the surface (fig. 13). There are in addition several other shallow prospect holes on the property. Those adjacent to the main workings are shown in figure 14.

The country rock of the vicinity is quartz monzonite. Where unaltered, this appears to be normal mineralogically but of rather finer grain than the average specimens. Locally the rock has a distinctly pink color, due to the introduction of feldspar. A green pyroxene has also replaced the rock in some places. In a specimen of wall rock from the 100-foot level the original plagioclase of the quartz monzonite had been partly altered to albite and calcite, and the dark minerals had been completely replaced by calcite, sericite, and iron oxides. Some orthoclase has been introduced into the rock, giving it a distinctly pink color in the hand specimen, and in addition there are several areas of clear, glassy quartz and black tourmaline. Locally also veinlets of an iron-rich calcite with some fine-grained quartz cut the quartz monzonite. The quartz monzonite at this locality must have been about at the upper boundary of the stock, for at the higher altitudes to the northeast and southwest are sedimentary rocks whose contacts with the igneous rock are nearly horizontal.

Two thin basic dikes were found in this vicinity and are shown in figure 14. Neither was traced for any distance because of the poor surface exposures, but they appear to have had no influence upon the ore. A light-colored quartz carbonate vein is also exposed nearby. It strikes a little west of north and may be traced for several hundred feet by means of its conspicuous light-colored float.

The ore body was an irregular pipelike mass of pegmatite with a north-northeast trend and a nearly vertical dip. At the surface the mass had an elliptical shape with a long axis of nearly 60 feet and a short axis of about 30 feet. On the 50-foot level it was considerably smaller and had a circular outline about

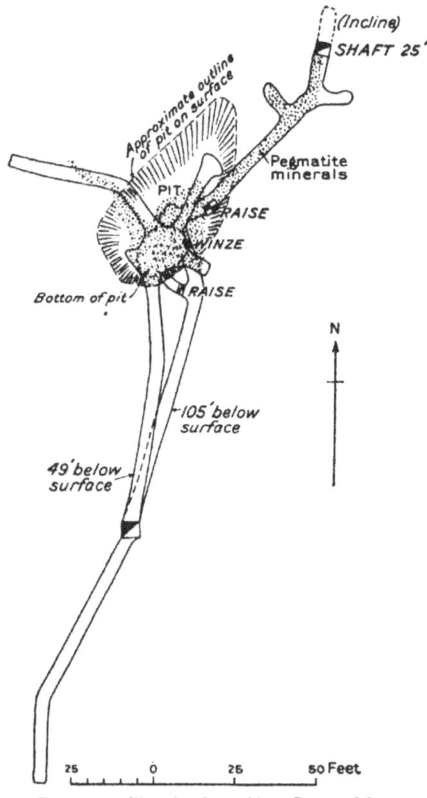

FIGURE 13.—Plan of main workings, Reaper claim.

20 feet in diameter, from which two apophyses extended, one to the northwest and one to the north-northeast. On the bottom level the pipelike character is not apparent, and the pegmatite minerals are found in a lenticular zone striking northeast. Near the north end of the lens a blunt apophysis extends to the northwest. The deposit thus shows on a small scale a form characteristic of many larger bodies of ore-bearing material, a pipelike shape at the surface, which contracts in size downward and eventually changes into a tabular form.

The walls of the pegmatite are not sharp and definite, as they simply mark the limit of replacement of quartz monzonite by the pegmatite minerals. In general the boundary between wall rock and ore body is not notably irregular, but locally bunches of pegmatite minerals may be found beyond this boundary and entirely within the quartz monzonite. The apophyses noted in the preceding paragraph represent accelerated replacement of the wall rock along preexistent fractures. On the 50-foot and 100-foot levels small discontinuous stringers of pegmatite minerals in the quartz monzonite are the only indications of the approach to the blunt south end of the pegmatite.

The two most abundant minerals in the pegmatite appear to have been green amphibole and pink orthoclase. The amphibole is found in sheafs as much as 4 feet in length. It has been locally replaced along the cleavage planes by chlorite, biotite, muscovite, calcite, or quartz. Orthoclase is also found in large crystals, single cleavage faces as much as a foot across being noted. It is later than the hornblende, which it has replaced. White albite is found with the orthoclase in some places. Apatite is surprisingly abundant. Much of it has a pink coloration due to films of iron oxide along fractures in the crystals, but a large proportion has a light cream color and closely resembles scheelite. Molybdenite and its oxidation product, powellite, are also found in many places. Black tourmaline, in many places accompanied by glassy quartz, occurs in considerable quantities around the edges of the pegmatite and is also present in bunches in the quartz monzonite wall rock.

Small aggregates of sulphides, now largely oxidized, are locally conspicuous within the pegmatite. They are especially abundant at the north end of the bottom level, where with quartz they form much of this part of the pegmatite lens. Chalcopyrite appears to have been the most abundant sulphide but is now represented by copper pitch and malachite. In addition to these minerals, epidote, titanite, diopside, and zircon were identified microscopically. Subhedral magnetite was also found, a specimen from the dump showing the mineral embedded in a white calcite.

Tungsten was present in the form of scheelite. Very little of this mineral can now be found either underground or on the dump. It is reported to have occurred abundantly in the stope from the 50-foot level to the surface, in the central portion of the pipe. Butler examined this property during its development and writes as follows [48] concerning the occurrence of the scheelite:

> Adjacent to the shaft [49] a body composed largely of scheelite 18 to 24 inches in thickness had been exposed for 4 or 5 feet along the strike and 3 or 4 feet below the outcrop. Deeper in the shaft other apparently smaller bodies of scheelite were exposed. The scheelite occurs in large crystals, some of which are 4 inches long. One block of nearly pure scheelite ore on the dump was estimated to weigh fully 200 pounds.

[48] Butler, B. S., Ore deposits of Utah: U.S. Geol. Survey Prof. Paper 111, p. 476, 1920.

[49] This shaft was in the part of the ore body removed during the stoping.—T. B. N.

The bodies of high-grade ore appear to occur as lenticular masses in the vein and suggest segregations of the scheelite through the pegmatite material of which the scheelite is an essential part. The scheelite was one of the earliest minerals to form. Much of it is in well-formed crystals and little of it includes the other minerals.

According to the Wilson brothers, who developed the deposit, the ore also contained some gold. No bismuth minerals were found during mining, however.

Pits 1 and 4 expose quartz veins that carry minor amounts of sulphides. Galena and tetrahedrite are the most abundant, but some chalcopyrite was observed. Malachite and other oxidized copper minerals are present, and some of the galena has been replaced by covellite. In specimens from pit 1 the quartz included irregular areas of barite and also a few euhedral crystals of this mineral.

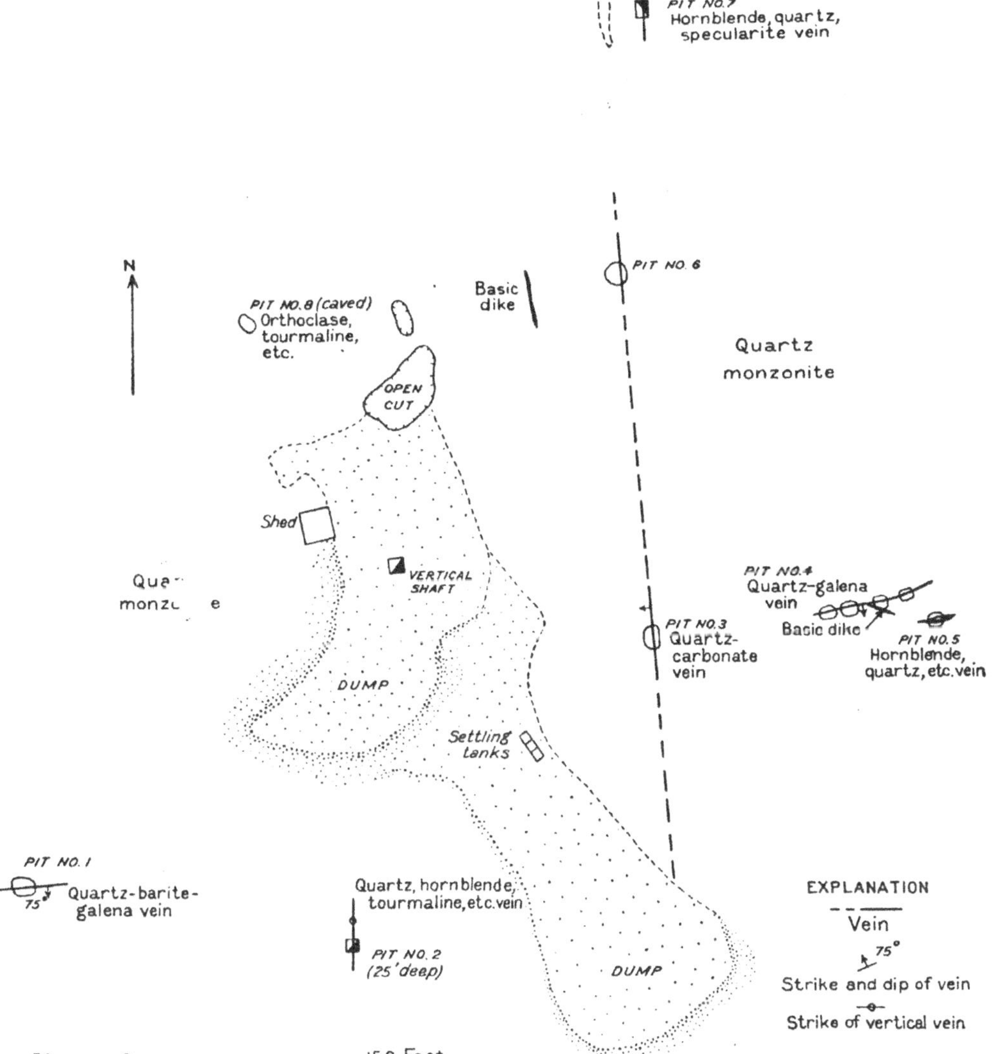

FIGURE 14.—Prospect pits and mineralization adjacent to Reaper open cut.

Rather similar pegmatites were present in pits 2, 5, 7, and 8 (fig. 14), but little or no scheelite has been found in them. In all but pit 8, which is caved, the pegmatites had a distinctly veinlike habit and thus resembled the relatively barren lower portion of the main ore body. Pit 7 showed in addition to the usual pegmatite minerals a considerable amount of specularite, and much of the quartz in this body had a purple

About 1,000 feet northwest of the main shaft, on the adjoining Rex claim, also owned by the Seminole Copper Co., there is a smaller body of pegmatite that is of similar character to the main body of the Reaper. Some scheelite has been found at this place. In the altered wall rock of this body there are moderate amounts of disseminated sulphides, of which those recognized were pyrite, chalcopyrite, bornite,

YELLOW HAMMER

The Yellow Hammer property includes three claims about three-quarters of a mile northwest of Clifton. The Reaper group adjoins it on the east, and the Centennial on the west. The claims are owned by the Western Utah Copper Co. The property is developed by several shallow workings and by a shaft that was inaccessible at the time of the survey. The only recorded production was made in 1917, when 1,646 pounds of scheelite that averaged 69.5 percent of WO_3 was shipped.

The claims are all in the quartz monzonite, but sedimentary rocks are found nearby in every direction except to the southeast. As in the adjoining Reaper, the present surface at the Yellow Hammer is thought to be very near the original upper surface of the intrusive. The quartz monzonite where unaltered shows no pecularities, biotite or biotite and hornblende being the dark minerals. In many places, however, it shows a rather striking alteration to a pink fine-grained rock with numerous green splotches. Orthoclase appears to be the most abundant mineral in the pink portions of the rock, and the green mineral is an amphibole that is similar to those found in the ore bodies. A specimen of the wall rock of one of the tungsten-bearing ore bodies showed none of this alteration, however. In this specimen calcite, sericite, and chlorite were moderately abundant, and in addition it contained small quantities of a brown pleochroic epidote resembling allanite and numerous small crystals of titanite.

The ore bodies that were seen on these claims are more tabular than pipelike and thus resemble the lower part of the Reaper deposit. The walls, like those of other deposits of this type, are not sharp. The veinlike or tabular habit seems to be controlled by a major fracture, along which the ore-depositing solutions entered and from which they extended for varying distances into the walls. In many of the deposits mineralization has extended along other fractures at angles to the main one. All the deposits that were examined are of small size, having a length of less than 25 feet and a width of less than 5 feet.

The minerals forming the ore bodies are similar to those of the Reaper. Green hornblende, in many places altered to quartz and calcite, pink orthoclase, black tourmaline, albite, apatite, chlorite, muscovite, quartz, and sulphides, more or less oxidized, are readily recognized. Scheelite is rather irregularly distributed in the deposits. It was observed in several places in the prospect about 400 feet south of the main shaft. It can be readily recognized by its good cleavage, dull-gray color, and greasy luster. In this deposit the long sheafs of hornblende show a strong tendency to occupy the central part of the ore body, and tourmaline is generally found near its borders.

Copper, chiefly in the form of copper pitch, chalcopyrite, and malachite, is locally abundant in most of the ore bodies. Custer[50] writes that "samples from the ore exposed gave 0.40 to 0.62 ounce gold, 1.40 to 3.80 ounces silver and 1.36 to 1.68 percent copper."

DOCTOR

The Doctor claim is just south of the junction of the branch road to the Yellow Hammer mine with the road from Clifton to Gold Hill, about three-quarters of a mile northwest of Clifton. It was owned in 1917 by Duncan MacVichie, of Salt Lake City, and, so far as known, still belongs to him. The developments consist of a shallow shaft, now inaccessible, and several surface cuts. A small amount of tungsten ore is reported to have been shipped from the claim.

The claim includes the contact between the quartz monzonite and poorly exposed sandstones and limestones of the Oquirrh formation. The two principal openings, however, are in the quartz monzonite about 50 feet east of the contact. In the more northerly one the ore seems to have occurred in a small pipelike body that has a diameter of about 5 feet and dips 65°–70° W. The walls of the pipe are poorly defined, and bunches of silicate minerals occur in the surrounding igneous rock. In the southern prospect the ore zone is more veinlike.

The ore was composed of scheelite, quartz, calcite, magnetite, and sulphide and silicate minerals. The silicates recognized include green crystalline epidote, pale-greenish scapolite, partly altered actinolite, abundant brownish-green garnet, black tourmaline, orthoclase, albite, chlorite, and sericite. The sulphide minerals occur chiefly with the quartz and include chalcopyrite, bornite, and pyrite. Copper pitch and malachite are plentiful as oxidation products. The sulphides are more abundant in the more southern of the two workings. No scheelite was observed by the writer, but Hess,[51] who examined the deposit in 1917, notes that "the scheelite is nearly white in pieces reaching more than 2 inches through. * * * A couple of hundred pounds of good ore is said to have been taken from the hole." He also notes the presence of bismuth in the deposit.

CENTENNIAL AND ENTERPRISE

The Centennial and Enterprise claims are about a mile northwest of Clifton, west of the Yellow Hammer mine and north of the road from Clifton to Gold Hill. The claims are reported to be owned by M. E. Jones, of Salt Lake City. The developments consist of several cuts and shallow shafts. Only one shipment from the property is recorded. This was made in 1917 and consisted of 47 tons of ore that assayed 0.05 ounce of gold and 1.6 ounces of silver to the ton and 5.4 percent of copper. Scheelite is found in some of the

[50] Custer, A. E., Deep Creek, Clifton mining district, Utah: Eng. and Min. Jour., vol. 103, p. 916, 1917.

[51] Hess, F. L., unpublished notes.

prospect holes, but it is not known whether [illegible] any tungsten [illegible] was shipped.

The claims cover the contact of the quartz monzonite with the Oquirrh formation. The trend of the contact here is irregular in detail, and both igneous and sedimentary rocks have been considerably metamorphosed. Just west of the Enterprise claim the sedimentary rocks have been replaced by jasperoid, and to the greater hardness of this rock is due hill 6455.

The ore lies close to the contact in both the sedimentary and the igneous rocks. The pit near the south end of the Enterprise claim is on a pipelike mass in the quartz monzonite, whose position seems to have been controlled by the intersection of two fractures, one striking N. 7° E. and dipping 70° E. and the other striking N. 60° W. and dipping south. Green amphibole, black tourmaline, apatite, calcite, quartz, and sulphide were recognized, in addition to much iron oxide and splotches of blue tourmaline, which together with sericite, quartz, and calcite is pseudomorphous after large crystals that were probably originally black tourmaline. In the prospect hole in quartz monzonite on the Enterprise claim the zone strikes N. 75° W. but apparently does not cross the contact into the sedimentary rocks. Black tourmaline is the most abundant mineral; green amphibole, jefferisite, quartz, muscovite, iron oxides, copper pitch, and malachite also occur.

In the prospect in the Oquirrh formation on the Centennial claim the copper minerals are found in belts on a band of silicate rock that strikes northeast. The silicate minerals appear to be chiefly diopside and green amphibole. Magnetite is unusually abundant here, and with it are crystals of the green micaceous mineral jefferisite. Copper is found as copper pitch, malachite, and chalcopyrite. In one specimen composed largely of porous green amphibole a poorly defined pinkish-gray patch proved to be chiefly scheelite.

VEINS WITH SILICATE MINERALS IN THE GANGUE

FRANKIE

The Frankie mine is immediately west of the Lucy L mine and north of the Calaveras claim. It is owned by the Woodman estate. In addition to a number of surface cuts and pits, it is developed by a tunnel, whose portal is at the 5,972-foot point shown on the map and from which several stopes extend upward to the surface. The mine was actively worked in 1917–19, during which 3,056 tons of ore was shipped that had an average content of 0.08 ounce of gold and 1.5 ounces of silver to the ton, 4.8 percent of copper, and 0.7 percent of lead. The lead ore seems to have been obtained from a different deposit than the copper ore and to have contained relatively more silver and less gold. The writer was informed that some scheelite was found on the property and that a small quantity of it was shipped.

The geologic relations at the Frankie are rather similar to those at the Calaveras, which adjoins it on the south. Metamorphosed limestones and sandstones of the Oquirrh formation cap the ridge above the mine workings and are limited on both the east and the west by dikelike masses of quartz monzonite. The dike on the east side is the narrower of the two, being from 200 to 500 feet across, and ends abruptly near the north end of the claim. On its east side it is intrusive into the Ochre Mountain limestone, and from the exposures to the north it is seen that this dike has followed the line of a normal fault separating the Ochre Mountain limestone from the Oquirrh formation. The outcrops of the Oquirrh formation in the region between the two masses of quartz monzonite are rather widely altered to garnet, diopside, clinozoisite, humite, and wollastonite. The quartz monzonite is also altered, a specimen taken from the southern pit at the contact with the sediments containing garnet, titanite, epidote, calcite, and chlorite as introduced minerals.

The ore is found in a zone 20 feet or less in width at the contact of the eastern dike of quartz monzonite with the Oquirrh formation. The zone strikes west of north and dips about 65° E. at the north but steepens to nearly 90° at the south. Ore has been found for a distance of over 250 feet along the contact, chiefly in the metamorphosed sedimentary rocks and to a small extent in the quartz monzonite.

The ore has a gangue of generally fine-grained silicate minerals. Black tourmaline and a green garnet are the most striking of these, possibly because in many places they occur, unlike the other silicates, in rather large, euhedral crystals. Diopside, amphibole, apatite, and humite also appear to be abundant, and calcite alone or with fine-grained quartz forms a matrix in much of the rock. The ore minerals are pyrite, bornite, and chalcopyrite with their oxidation products, chiefly copper pitch, chrysocolla, and malachite. The sulphides and to a less extent the silicate minerals show a pronounced tendency to occur in sheets parallel to the contact. This habit is probably the result of a preexistent sheeted zone parallel to the normal fault that apparently localized the dike of quartz monzonite. A moderate amount of the sulphide, however, is found in blebs within the silicate rock. Thin sections of such ore show that the sulphides are almost invariably embedded in the calcite matrix rather than intergrown with the silicates.

The copper content of the ore mined appears to have been rather constant throughout the stoped portion of the ore body. No scheelite was recognized in the field, and the average content of this mineral is not known but is presumably low. The deposit from which the lead ore was shipped was not examined during the survey.

CALAVERAS

The Calaveras claims, owned by the Western Utah Copper Co., are about 2 miles south of Gold Hill, south of the Frankie claim and west of the Gold Bond. The developments consist of 4 shallow pits on the ridge line southeast of summit 6266 and 2 tunnels on the slope west of the ridge. Some shipments of ore are reported from the claims, but their grade and quantity are not known.

The area covered by the claims includes part of a narrow band of the Oquirrh formation extending southward from the Frankie that is irregularly embayed by quartz monzonite. The igneous rock is a part of the dikelike mass that lies west of the main stock. Both sedimentary and igneous rocks have been extensively altered, and in many places it is extremely difficult to locate exactly the contact between them.

Ore bodies are exposed both in the quartz monzonite and in the sediments. Those in the igneous rock are small pipelike shoots composed largely of quartz. In the northernmost pit in the quartz monzonite black tourmaline is abundant, but in the southernmost pit this mineral appears to have been replaced by a very fine-grained aggregate of blue tourmaline, sericite, and quartz. Blebs of copper pitch, in which are locally remnants of sulphides, are scattered through these gangue minerals, as are coatings of chrysocolla, azurite, and malachite. The specimens collected from these shoots contain a considerable amount of supergene chalcedony.

The ore body in the sedimentary rocks strikes northeast and appears to be localized at the contact with the quartz monzonite. The gangue minerals are considerably more varied than in the quartz monzonite. Both a green and a reddish-brown garnet are abundant, together with a green amphibole, black tourmaline, orthoclase, and specularite. A flesh-colored fine-grained mineral that appears to have replaced all the gangue minerals just named was determined microscopically as humite. Quartz is not abundant. Pyrite and chalcopyrite are the most plentiful sulphides and in many places show comparatively little oxidation.

Custer[52] reports that samples from the property assayed 0.11 to 0.20 ounce of gold and 0.20 ounce of silver to the ton and 1.99 to 9 percent of copper.

POLE STAR COPPER CO.

The Pole Star Copper Co. formerly owned about 15 claims in the vicinity of Lucky Day Knob, about halfway between Clifton and Gold Hill. All but two of these were unpatented and have been abandoned. The two remaining claims are the Keno and the Pole Star, the former lying to the west of Lucky Day Knob and the latter to the east. The writer understands that the Western Utah Extension Copper Co. was under the same control.

A considerable amount of development work has been done on the property. The chief openings are an inclined shaft on the Keno claim about 500 feet west of Lucky Day Knob, an inclined shaft on the Pole Star claim on the eastern slope of the knob at an altitude of 6,075 feet, and two tunnels, one about 300 feet south of the latter shaft and another about 800 feet west-northwest of it. The recorded production from the company's claims amounts to shipments of 313 tons in 1917. These averaged 0.096 ounce of gold and 3.65 ounces of silver to the ton and 2.96 percent of copper.

Quartz monzonite underlies the greater part of the two claims. It has suffered a wide-spread but not especially intense alteration, during which sericite, chlorite, locally some orthoclase, and fine-grained quartz have been developed in the rock. Adjacent to the ore bodies sericite appears to be the most abundant of the introduced minerals. The summit of Lucky Day Knob is composed of Ochre Mountain limestone, and this formation is also found in several other places in the vicinity, suggesting strongly that the roof of the quartz monzonite stock was here close to the present surface.

On the Keno claim there are a few surface pits and an inclined shaft. The shaft is now caved, but it appears to have been sunk on the intersection of two veins, one striking about N. 30° W. and dipping 70° W. and the other striking nearly west. The quartz monzonite wall rock is intensely sericitized at the shaft. The gangue minerals of the two veins observed were green hornblende, black tourmaline, quartz, and muscovite. The ore consists of oxidized iron and copper minerals, the latter being chiefly malachite, azurite, chalcedony, and copper pitch. Except for small amounts of pyrite, no sulphides were found in the ore on the dump.

On the Pole Star claim the most thoroughly prospected vein strikes N. 40° W. and dips 35° SW. The wall rock is quartz monzonite that is thoroughly crushed and sericitized. At the inclined shaft the vein is from 3 to 5 feet wide, with local short spurs into the walls. Where the tunnel south of the shaft intersects the vein the thickness is somewhat less and is notably variable, pinches and swells alternating within short distances. The ore is similar to that on the Keno claim, tourmaline and quartz being the most abundant minerals. At the surface the oxidation of the ore minerals is complete, but on the tunnel level some sulphides still remain. F. L. Hess[53] during a visit to the property in 1917 recognized wolframite, scheelite, cuprotungstite, and ferberite (?) in this vein.

[52] Custer, A. E., Deep Creek, Clifton mining district, Utah: Eng. and Min. Jour., vol. 103, p. 916, 1917.

[53] Unpublished notes.

Published descriptions of the property[64] include assays that indicate the presence of local concentrations of copper-rich and silver-rich material; but the grade of the ore shipped seems to show that these concentrations must have had a rather slight extent.

COPPEROPOLIS (IDA LULL)

The Copperopolis or Ida Lull group of 6 patented and 20 unpatented claims lies on the southeast slope of Gold Hill, about three-quarters of a mile southeast of the portal of the Western Utah mine. The property in 1919 was owned by the Copperopolis Mining Co., 161 South Main Street, Salt Lake City. It is also known locally as the Bamberger mine, after its principal owners. Nearly 550 tons of ore was shipped from 1917 to 1919, the average metal content of which was 0.11 ounce of gold and 5.5 ounces of silver to the ton, 5.6 percent of copper, and 0.6 percent of lead.

The south end of the mass of sedimentary rocks that occurs as a roof pendant in the quartz monzonite and underlies Gold Hill is included within the boundaries of the group of claims. The jasperoid mass that was formed along the fault passing through the crest of Gold Hill makes up most of this portion of the pendant. The Ochre Mountain limestone, which to the north is extensively exposed west of the jasperoid, is almost completely lacking at the surface in this region, quartz monzonite being in contact with the jasperoid over most of the distance. The only known outcrop of the Ochre Mountain limestone in this vicinity is at the southern tip of the pendant, where there is a small mass of lime-silicate rock, to which the limestone has been altered. Other small masses of altered Ochre Mountain limestone are exposed in the adit tunnel, whose portal is at an altitude of 5,517 feet.

East of the jasperoid zone both the Manning Canyon formation and the Ochre Mountain limestone are exposed to the north. To the south, however, the Manning Canyon formation is cut out, owing to the more southeasterly strike of the jasperoid. The Ochre Mountain limestone outcrop is itself limited on the east by a westward-dipping fault that separates it from the quartz monzonite. The fault is well exhibited in a tunnel on the east side of the low knoll that marks the south end of the roof pendant.

The ore bodies occur in lime silicate rock formed as a result of the metamorphism of the Ochre Mountain limestone. Three separate shoots have been developed. The largest and the one from which the bulk of the ore shipped was obtained is on the west side of the small knoll at the southern tip of the roof pendant. The ore shoot was localized along a nearly vertical shear zone in garnet-diopside rock that was 2 or 3 feet wide and had a strike a few degrees east of north. The ore consisted of oxidized copper minerals and some blebs of the copper sulphides, chalcopyrite and bornite, in a matrix of silicate minerals.

Two smaller ore shoots were found in the adit tunnel (fig. 15). One of these was very near the portal, in what was apparently a small mass of altered Ochre Mountain limestone on the footwall side of the jasperoid zone. The dimensions of this shoot were small, and the ore has been completely stoped out. Carl Bailey, of Gold Hill, reports that some scheelite was found in this ore shoot. The other ore shoot occurred near the face of the tunnel along a narrow fracture zone that here forms the contact between the quartz monzonite and the altered limestone. An interior shaft has been sunk to an unknown depth on this shoot, and two small stopes extend upward. Not much ore is exposed at this locality on the tunnel level. A mass of nearly solid chalcocite more than 2 inches in diameter was found on the tunnel dump, but it is not known from which of the two ore shoots it was obtained.

NAPOLEON MINING CO.

The principal workings on the property of the Napoleon Mining Co. are about a mile north of the Western Utah mine, on the northwest slope of the small but prominent peak known locally as Calico Hill. The seven patented claims of the property have also been known as the Incas group and were at one time controlled by the Red Copper Queen Mining & Milling Co. Several small shipments of ore have been made from the property. Lots aggregating 135 tons that were shipped in 1917–18 averaged 0.11 ounce of gold and 2.6 ounces of silver to the ton and 6.4 percent of copper.

The ore occurs in a small body of Ochre Mountain limestone that on the west and south is irregularly embayed by the quartz monzonite and on the east is separated by a fault from beds belonging to the central facies of the Oquirrh formation. The limestone is for the most part bleached and recrystallized, but locally, particularly near the contact with the intrusive, it is altered to silicate minerals. In other places it has a pronounced pinkish-brown color due to the widespread presence of small quantities of iron oxides. Locally the iron oxides are concentrated into "iron blowouts." Such masses, however, are shown by several prospect pits to have relatively small dimensions.

The ore bodies have been developed by several shallow pits or short tunnels and also by two shafts, both of which are now inaccessible.

The ore shoots consist of small lenses of copper-bearing lime-silicate rock within a few feet of the quartz monzonite contact. The ore minerals are all oxidized copper compounds, chiefly copper pitch, malachite, and chrysocolla. No sulphide minerals were observed.

GOLD BOND

The Gold Bond claim is in Lucy L Gulch, about

[64] Custer, A. E., Deep Creek, Clifton mining district, Utah: Eng. and Min. Jour., vol. 103, p. 919, 1917. Higgins, W. C., Flourishing condition of Clifton mining

now reported to be owned by the Galinske brothers, of Sioux City, Iowa, but in 1917 it appears to have been the property of the Babcock Mining Co. One shipment, presumably of copper ore, is said to have been made from the property some time ago, but the amount and grade are not known. The developments on the claim consist of a tunnel, whose portal is 800 feet west of the cabin at an altitude of 6,053 feet, and several shallow pits. The claim appears to have been actively worked in 1917–18.

The country rock consists of altered quartz monzonite, in which the dark minerals have been replaced by calcite and chorite and much of the remainder of ularite are the most abundant minerals. The specularite has been locally altered to a reddish powdery oxide and in such places is generally associated with quartz or chalcedony. Coarsely crystalline glassy quartz is also found in parts of the vein, and much of the copper ore is associated with it. Diopside, amphibole, biotite, a white scapolite in part sericitized, orthoclase also locally sericitized, and purple and white fluorite are found less abundantly. Danburite, the calcium borosilicate, is surprisingly abundant in the vein but in many places has been partly replaced by calcite. In the pit on the vein southeast of the tunnel portal danburite makes up a large part

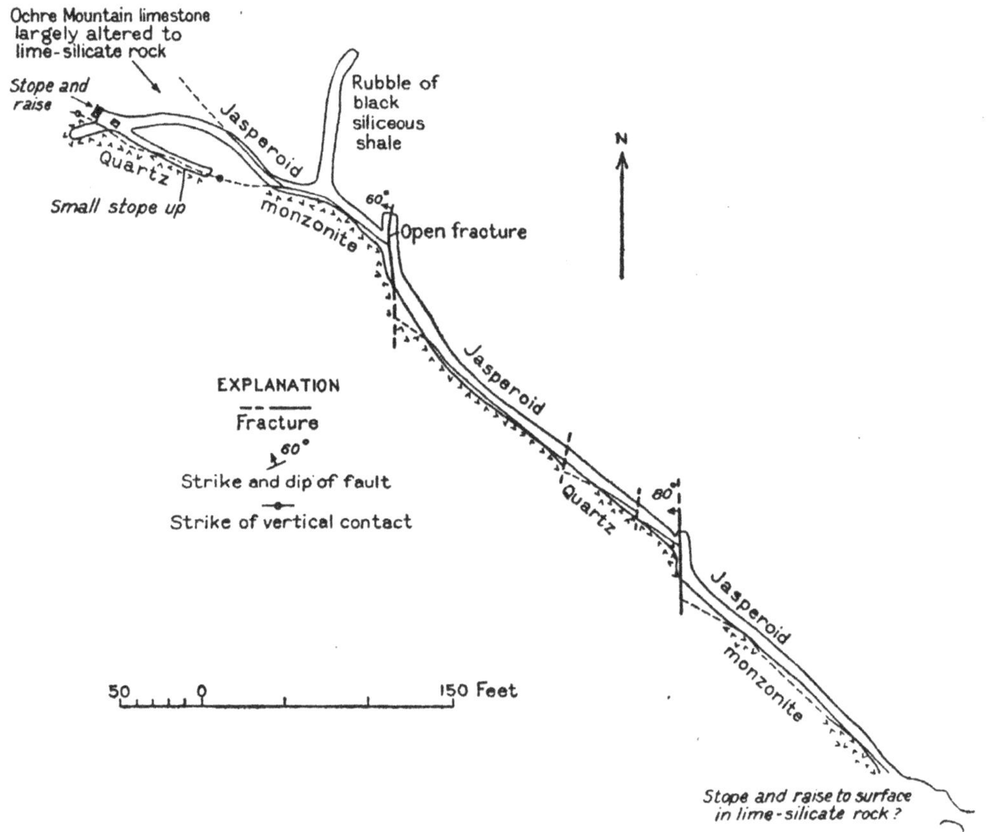

FIGURE 15.—Plan of adit tunnel, Copperopolis group.

the rock by a fine-grained mixture of quartz, orthoclase, and albite. The quartz monzonite is near the eastern edge of an irregular mass that lies west of the main stock. Ochre Mountain limestone underlies the eastern part of the claim.

The largest vein on the claim is exposed in the tunnel. It strikes N. 50° W. and dips 45° SW. The vein zone is about 5 feet wide, but this figure includes nearly 1 foot on each wall that is composed of quartz monzonite largely replaced by massive dark epidote and smaller amounts of other silicate minerals that are also found within the ore-bearing portion. In the central portion of the vein black tourmaline and specof the vein and has clearly replaced the other silicates and specularite. The ore minerals are copper pitch, in which are remnants of chalcopyrite, and other oxidized copper minerals, chiefly chrysocolla and malachite. Much of the copper pitch is found within quartz, but some of it is embedded in the silicates. It was reported that during the period of activity at this mine the ore taken out carried 2 to 4 percent of copper.[55] The writer's observations indicate that the distribution of the copper minerals in the vein is irregular.

[55] Schwalenberg, L. G., Mining in the Deep Creek region: Salt Lake Min. Rev., vol. 19, p. 43, January 15, 1918.

There are three other veins on the claim that have a similar strike. All three, however, appear to have a small horizontal extent and might better be described as pipelike. They carry ore of a similar type but show rather less diversity in the number of minerals present.

COPPER BLOOM

The Copper Bloom group of claims is about halfway between the towns of Clifton and Gold Hill, adjoining the Keno claim on the west and south. It is owned by the Copper Bloom Mining Co., in which the Wilson brothers, of Salt Lake City, are the guiding spirits. Shallow shafts and cuts constitute the developments, but, so far as known, there has been no production.

The quartz monzonite that forms the walls of the ore bodies is a part of the main Gold Hill stock. The area covered by the claims is near the western border of the stock, which is, in plan, highly irregular. Several roof pendants composed chiefly of Ochre Mountain limestone are found east and northeast of the claims within the quartz monzonite.

Four ore bodies have been exposed on the claims. In all of them black tourmaline with a sheaf-like habit and smaller amounts of coarsely crystalline quartz are the most abundant minerals. The two more westerly deposits are about 1,500 feet south of west of the old Keno shaft. One of these is a vein striking N. 45° E. and dipping about 65° SE. The vein filling consists of black tourmaline with some quartz. Abundant pulverulent iron oxide fills areas formerly occupied by sulphides. Some chalcedony veinlets and coatings of yellow-brown jarosite were also recognized. The iron oxide is said to be rather rich in gold, with the result that locally assays of $50 a ton have been obtained. Some bismuth is also reported from this vein, but none was recognized in the specimens collected. Nearby a shaft has been driven on a vein that strikes north and dips east. Black tourmaline and quartz are the most abundant minerals, as in the other deposit, but instead of the iron oxides there are splotches of copper pitch, which contain remnants of chalcopyrite and pyrite. In one specimen a pseudomorph of bismutite after bismuthinite has the same relations to the gangue as the copper pitch. Azurite, malachite, and a clay mineral that is probably beidellite occur in small quantities. Tungsten minerals and gold are reported also to be present. This vein is not persistent downward.

A few hundred feet east of these two veins a similar vein is exposed. This strikes N. 10° W. and dips 45° E. and is about 3 feet in width. Near the bottom of the shaft the vein is displaced about 2 feet by a westward-dipping normal fault. The vein filling consists chiefly of tourmaline and quartz, in which are local concentrations of muscovite. Unreplaced remnants of the bleached and altered quartz monzonite that forms the walls also occur within the vein. In this gangue are found patches of the ore minerals. Those observed include pyrite, chalcopyrite, tetrahedrite, and gold. Oxidation products are chalcocite, covellite, copper pitch, malachite, azurite, bismutite, and a dark-gray copper-bismuth mineral that is probably a very intimate mixture of bismutite and chrysocolla. Specimens rich in these ore minerals are reported to assay as high as 60 ounces to the ton in silver and $20 to the ton in gold.

Still farther east, about 500 feet south of the old Keno shaft, a fourth ore body has been prospected. This has a pipelike form, in contrast to the other deposits, and pitches steeply to the southeast. It is mineralogically similar to the vein deposits except that sulphide minerals are somewhat less abundant and that apatite and scheelite are both present, locally in considerable quantity. Apatite was found both as small cream-colored crystals and as large greenish masses that had replaced the tourmaline. Scheelite occurs as large greasy-appearing grayish crystals partly replaced by tourmaline. Bismuth minerals are reported to occur in this deposit, but none were recognized in the specimens collected.

VICTORY NO. 1

The Victory No. 1 claim, owned by the Hudsons, of Gold Hill, is about 1,500 feet southeast of the road fork at an altitude of 5,783 feet on the Lincoln Highway south of the town of Gold Hill. Several surface workings have been opened on the claim, but so far as known no ore has been shipped.

The claim is near the contact of a broad tongue of quartz monzonite from the main stock, with limestone and dolomite of the Oquirrh formation. The sedimentary rocks have been locally replaced by jasperoid. The ore body is a vein that strikes about N. 50° W. and dips vertically within the quartz monzonite, but at its intersection with the sedimentary rocks it changes its course to follow the contact. Quartz and black tourmaline with some cream-colored apatite are the most plentiful gangue minerals. Pyrite, chalcopyrite, and tetrahedrite occur in blebs and patches throughout the rock; the pyrite and chalcopyrite are more abundant in the tourmaline, and the tetrahedrite is localized in the quartz. "Limonite," azurite, malachite, chalcocite, and chrysocolla are oxidation products. No assays of the ore are available, but it is certain that the average grade is low.

MINNEHAHA

The Minnehaha group of 13 claims lies along Goshute Wash about a mile east of Montezuma Peak. The claims, of which three are patented, are owned by P. H. Robinson, of Gold Hill. Mr. Robinson reports that small shipments of ore were made from one of the patented claims, the Albert, in 1912 and 1925. These contained $1.60 in gold and 6 or 7 ounces of silver to the ton and from 5 to 16 percent of copper.

The claims cover a considerable distance along the contact between the quartz monzonite and the Oquirrh formation. The contact in this region dips to the east-southeast at a moderately low angle. The Oquirrh formation has been converted to jasperoid for as much as 50 feet above the contact. The ore is found in the jasperoid in sheetlike layers 5 to 10 feet above the contact. Over much of the distance the ore zone is essentially barren and consists of jasperoid very rich in iron oxides, much of it carrying 20 percent or more in iron. Locally, however, the material is cupriferous, and the most abundant copper mineral is a siliceous copper pitch, in which are not uncommonly remnants of chalcopyrite. Chrysocolla and the basic copper carbonates are locally conspicuous but are probably unimportant as ore minerals. One specimen from the Albert claim contained considerable arsenopyrite, but this mineral was not noted elsewhere. There has been considerable post-ore shearing in the vicinity, both along the ore horizon and at the underlying contact of the jasperoid with the quartz monzonite.

Another small copper prospect on the group is a short distance southwest of Mr. Robinson's house, within a small block of limestone surrounded by quartz monzonite. The limestone has been largely converted to lime-silicate rock, in which there has been a slight copper mineralization similar to that at the Frankie mine.

OZARK

The Ozark group of claims, about a mile southeast of Montezuma Peak, is reported to be owned by F. M. Johnson, of Wendover. A shipment of 12 tons of ore from this group in 1917 contained 0.11 ounce of gold and 5.1 ounces of silver to the ton and 3.2 percent of copper.

In the vicinity of the claims a small triangular plug of quartz monzonite, satellitic to the main stock, is intrusive into the Oquirrh formation. The sedimentary rocks here are composed of interbedded thin limestones and sandstones. The limestone beds in particular have been thoroughly altered in the vicinity of the workings, in part to silicate minerals and in part to jasperoid.

Two ore shoots are present on the property, both in the sedimentary rocks near the quartz monzonite contact. The larger one is a vein striking N. 20° W. and dipping 60° E. The hanging wall of the vein is a dark porphyry dike and the footwall a mass of jasperoid 25 feet in width. The ore mined contained abundant iron oxides and various copper minerals, of which copper pitch appears to have been the most plentiful. In the more westerly workings on the claim scorodite and arsenopyrite appear to be the only ore minerals present.

COPPER HILL

The Copper Hill group of unpatented claims is on the west and southwest side of hill 5852, a little less than 2 miles north of west from the town of Gold Hill. In 1926 it was owned by J. C. and H. V. Hicks, of Salt Lake City.

The ore shoots are in lime-silicate rock produced by the alteration of limestone beds in the Oquirrh formation. They occur near dikelike masses of quartz monzonite that were intruded in part along a northwestward-striking fault that brings the Manning Canyon formation into contact with the Oquirrh formation. The mineralization was rather scanty, copper pitch and other oxidized copper minerals being found locally in ore shoots of small dimensions.

ALVARADO

The Alvarado mine is about 1 mile east of the town of Gold Hill and half a mile northwest of the Western Utah Copper Co.'s Gold Hill mine. It is now owned by the Woodman Estate. The writer was informed that difficulty in securing united action by the large number of heirs to the estate has prevented recent attempts to work the mine. The mine workings consist of an inclined shaft about 250 feet deep and about 1,500 feet of tunnels, in addition to short raises and winzes (fig. 16). A shaft house and a bunk house, both in need of repair, are on the property, which adjoins the spur of the railroad to the Western Utah property.

The bulk of the production from the mine was made in the period from 1892 to 1895, during which it is supposed to have produced about $120,000 in gold. Since that time the mine has been idle for the most part, although several small shipments of ore have been made. One lot of 25 tons is reported by William Darnell to have been shipped in 1909 and another of 35 tons in 1916.

Since the field work for this report was completed some ore has been extracted from the mine by lessees. Toward the end of 1931 the Aurum Mining Corporation was reported to have obtained control of the property.

Two formations are recognized near the Alvarado mine—Ochre Mountain limestone and quartz monzonite. The thick beds of limestone are generally bleached to a dazzling white color and are coarsely crystalline. Locally silicate minerals have replaced the limestone; the most wide-spread is wollastonite in bladed crystals as much as an inch in length. One notable exposure of this mineral was found a short distance southeast of the shaft house. The beds strike rather uniformly a little west of north and dip steeply to the east.

The quartz monzonite is not notably different from the average for this formation. Biotite appears to be the most abundant of the primary dark minerals, but diopside, partly altered to hornblende, has been introduced into the rock in many places. In a specimen from the east end of the 200-foot level magnetite

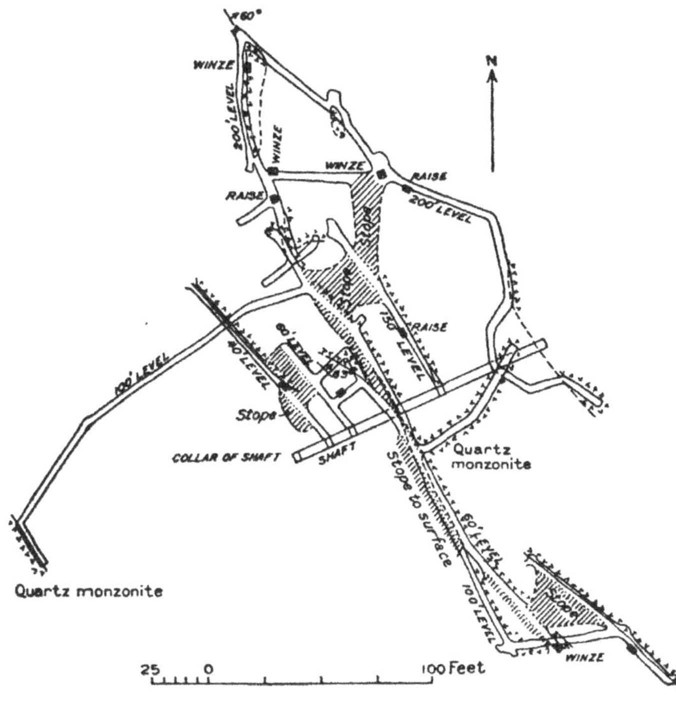

FIGURE 16.—Plan of Alvarado mine workings. Blank areas are limestone.

and smoky apatite are unusually abundant accessory minerals and quartz is relatively rare. Calcite and pyrite are secondary minerals in this place, as in several others.

The quartz monzonite is a part of the main stock, and its contact with the limestone beds, about 150 feet southwest of the shaft, is approximately parallel with their strike. This contact is also exposed on the 100-foot level, where the dip is steep to the northeast. A dike from the main body about 20 feet wide is also exposed at the surface. At the shaft the dike has a course that is approximately the same as that of the bedding and dips steeply to the northeast. It does not extend to the northwest much beyond the mine workings but may be traced with the same strike about 200 feet to the southeast. There the strike swings sharply to the south, and the width increases rapidly until a junction with the main body of the stock is effected.

Underground the dike is found to have some minor irregularities. On the 40- and 60-foot levels, for example, it cuts across the bedding of the limestone at a low angle, thereby terminating the main ore body. On the 100-foot level irregularities also appear. The hanging-wall crosscut just south of the shaft shows a minimum thickness of 60 feet for the dike, although only 20 feet was found at the surface. Further, near the shaft the contact of limestone and quartz monzonite on the 100-foot level is almost vertically beneath the contact on the 60-foot level, indicating that here the dike transgresses the dip of the beds. Finally, at the south end of the 100-foot level, a hanging-wall crosscut discloses 25 feet of limestone between walls of quartz monzonite. These features indicate that the dike branches at this altitude near the shaft, and that the southwesterly branch is a spur that extends upward so short a distance that it is not exposed on the 60-foot level (fig. 17). The block of limestone between the two branches apparently reaches a greater depth to the south than it does near the shaft.

The 200-foot level adds little to the knowledge of the dike except that its dip must flatten notably below the 150-foot level. The extension of the shaft below the 200-foot level, however, again cuts quartz monzonite and strongly suggests a reversal of dip, as shown in the section.

The bottom level also shows three other exposures of quartz monzonite in the workings northwest of the shaft. All of these are rather irregular lenticular masses with relatively small cross sections. The limestones surrounding these masses have undergone a rather extensive replacement by silica. Much of this is in the form of fine-grained quartz that has veined

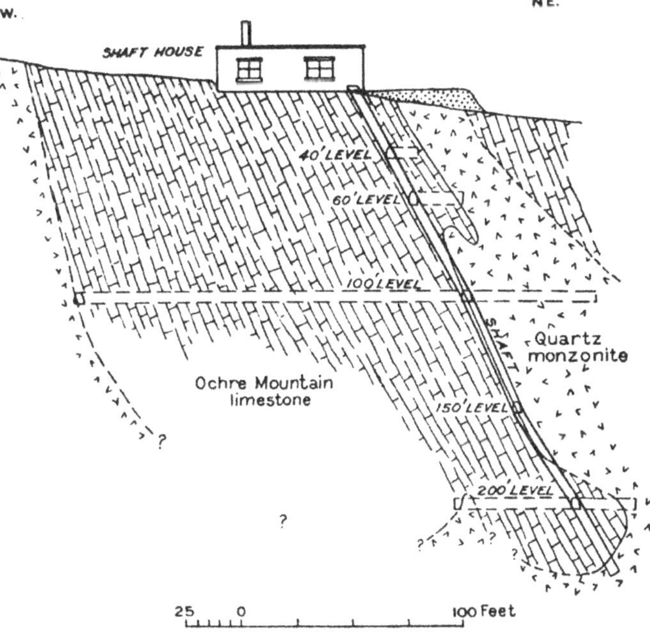

FIGURE 17.—Geologic cross section through Alvarado shaft.

or irregularly replaced the calcite, but locally thin lenses of chalcedony, which are bordered by quartz, are present. In many places the altered rock is colored a deep brown by specks of a finely disseminated mineral of that color. The several exposures of quartz monzonite on this level and the abundant silicification, together with the apparent reversal of dip of the dike indicated by the presence of the igneous rock in the bottom of the shaft, lead the writer to the belief that the limestone will be bottomed at no great distance below the level.

The ore bodies of the mine consist of irregular shoots, carrying a minable amount of gold in limestone that has been almost completely replaced by silicate minerals. Two chief ore bodies have been exploited.

One, which may be called the main ore body, is much larger than the other, here designated the footwall ore body. (See fig. 18.) It has been followed from the surface down to the 200-foot level and has been stoped over a width as great as 40 feet, with an average between 5 and 10 feet. The stope length reaches a maximum of about 120 feet on the 60-foot level and decreases considerably on the lower levels. The dike of quartz monzonite forms the hanging wall of this deposit almost throughout its extent, except for the portion below the 150-foot level, where limestone forms both walls. In this region the tabular form of the ore body is replaced by a roughly pipelike or cylindrical shape. On the upper levels the stopes indicate a pitch to the northwest. This may be the result, at least on the 60-foot level, of the transgression of the limestone bedding by the dike. Westward-dipping cross fractures, however, may also have influenced the pitch. The division of the ore body into two parts below the 60-foot level also appears to be the result of the position of the dike, as the unstoped region corresponds in position with the junction of the two branches of the dike that has interrupted the ore-bearing bed.

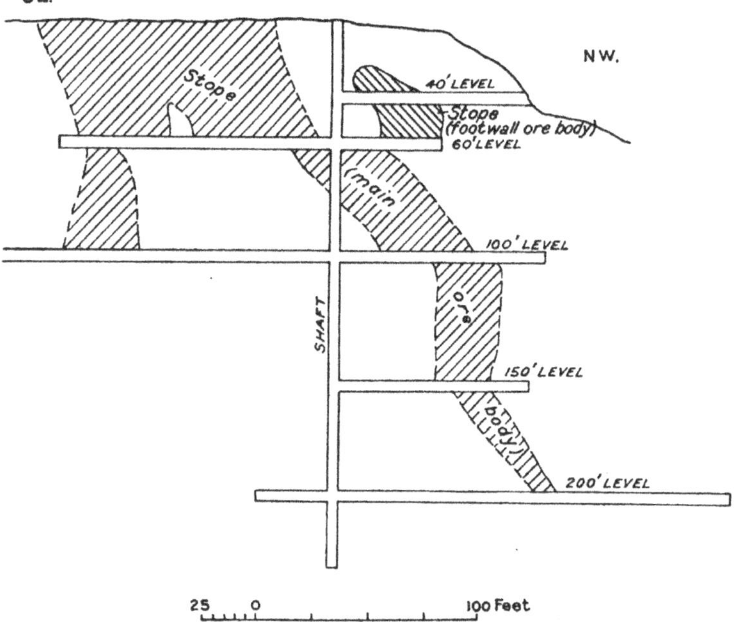

FIGURE 18.—Stope projection on plane through shaft, Alvarado mine.

The footwall ore body is comparatively small and was stoped only from the 60-foot level to a point a few feet above the 40-foot level. Its maximum stope length was about 30 feet. The northwestern part of this shoot had the dike of quartz monzonite for a hanging wall, but the remainder had limestone on both walls. A minor amount of stoping was done on the 60-foot level along the limestone and quartz monzonite contact in a way to connect the two ore bodies. It could not be ascertained, however, whether the material removed contained gold or whether the work was done in the expectation that the ore should be found along the contact.

In addition to these two main ore bodies there appear to have been several pipes of ore on the 200-foot level, for moderate amounts of stoping have been done from the several winzes and raises shown on the map. One of these pipes is entirely within a lenticular mass of quartz monzonite. The remainder are in the limestone.

A notable feature of most of the stoped areas is the general presence of cross fractures, striking somewhat east of north and dipping steeply, for the most part to the west. These are locally filled with wollastonite and other silicates, quartz, which is in part chalcedony, and oxidized iron and copper minerals. In most places the stope width appeared to reach a maximum where these cross fractures were intercepted. Similar fractures were found in the pipelike bodies on the 200-foot level. The writer feels that they have played a much more important part in localizing the ore shoots than the presence of the dike of quartz monzonite, for, as noted in a previous paragraph, most of the pipelike ore bodies and some parts of the tabular bodies may be found within walls of limestone.

Where quartz monzonite forms the hanging wall of the ore body the line between ore and waste is sharp and is found at the igneous contact. The limestone walls, however, are not sharp and appear to have been determined by assay, rather than by any obvious mineralogic change, for silicate replacement of limestone extended far beyond the limits that have been reached by the stoping.

The greater part of the ore mined consisted of silicate minerals that had replaced limestone, with which were associated considerable amounts of quartz, small amounts of sulphide minerals with their oxidation products, and native gold. The most widespread silicate mineral appears to be wollastonite, which in many places has been largely replaced by fine-grained fibrous spadaite. This alteration resulted in a massive, almost porcelaneous rock of a cream or pale-pink color. Smaller amounts of green diopside and brown garnet are also abundant, and Kemp[56] in addition mentions zoisite, vesuvianite, tremolite, and serpentine. The relations between the tremolite and serpentine as described by Kemp are similar to those noted between wollastonite and spadaite.

The silicate minerals have been replaced or cut by irregular areas or veinlets of quartz. Both megascopically crystalline and very fine-grained quartz have been recognized, and the latter is the younger. In addition, chalcedony is of frequent occurrence, but it seems in most places to be the result of weathering. Calcite veinlets of several ages with respect to the quartz are also abundant.

The sulphides recognized are pyrite, galena, chalcopyrite, bornite, and chalcocite. They are relatively rare in this mine but have been found both in the silicate rock and quartz veins. The occurrences in association with quartz are the more abundant. The most striking occurrence of sulphides is on the 200-foot level just south of the shaft. This exposure is not on either of the two chief ore bodies, and as it has not been stoped, presumably it is not rich in gold. This body has been thoroughly oxidized and now consists of brown resinous copper pitch with a few remnants of sulphides, which shows local alteration to iron oxides, a lighter-brown jarosite, blue crystalline chalcanthite, and a pale-greenish mineral that has the optic properties of siderotil, a hydrous iron sulphate.

Native gold is said to have been locally very abundant and to have been found in pieces "as large as a bean." William Darnell, who has worked in the mine, says that it was especially abundant in the spadaite areas, particularly where that mineral contained copper minerals or quartz veinlets. No gold was collected in the mine by the writer, but in specimens which he has seen the native gold is crystalline and is associated with oxidized copper and iron minerals and with chalcedony. The enclosing rock in these specimens was quartz and spadaite. Kemp[57] described native gold from this mine associated with zoisite, limonite, and malachite.

In the pipelike ore bodies on the 200-foot level the silicate minerals appear to be much less abundant. Small quantities of diopside and a very fine-grained mineral that is probably spadaite were recognized in the thin section studied, but the bulk of the rock is composed of calcite replaced by fine-grained quartz. No sulphides were noted in these pipes. Oxidation products are much more abundant near the ore bodies on this level than elsewhere, perhaps because of the greater abundance of easily replaced calcite.

The grade of the ore is reported to have been rather variable. No figures are available for the Alvarado mine alone. An examination of the assay records of the mill that treated ore from the Alvarado, Cane Springs, and Gold Hill mines, showed that the heads assayed from $4 to $35 a ton, of which about 80 percent was recovered. The average content during a period of slightly less than two years was $10.28 a ton. Bullion assays indicated a fineness of 0.750 to 0.850. Some of the gold, however, is reported to have been 0.950 fine.

CANE SPRINGS

The Cane Springs mine is about 2,000 feet southwest of the town of Gold Hill and 250 feet west of U.S. Mineral Monument No. 7. Like the Alvarado, it is owned by the Woodman Estate, and similar difficulties are reported to have been met in attempts to reopen the mine. The development consists of an inclined shaft 150 feet deep, two short winzes, and about 1,000 feet of drifts and crosscuts (fig. 19). A vertical shaft connects the most easterly workings with the surface but appears to have been little used.

In 1931 work was resumed at the Cane Springs mine by G. H. Short, of Salt Lake City, under a 3-year lease with an option to purchase the property. Toward the end of the year the Aurum Mining Corporation was organized to operate this lease together with one on the Alvarado. Development was actively prosecuted, and at the end of 1932 it was reported that 25 tons of ore a day was being mined, of an average grade of about $12 a ton.

The production of the Cane Springs mine is not accurately known. Its period of greatest activity appears to have been from 1892 to 1895, when the gold production was probably between $50,000 and $70,000. A shipment of 46 tons reported from the Cane Springs claim in 1914 contained 1.07 ounces of gold and 3 ounces of silver to the ton and 5.5 percent of copper.

The mine is in a rather narrow northwestward-striking belt of Ochre Mountain limestone. This is separated from the Oquirrh formation on the southwest by a normal fault of rather large throw, whose strike cuts that of the limestone at a small angle, with the result that individual beds are progressively cut out to the northwest, the uppermost one disappearing just southeast of the wash in which Cane Spring is located. The limestone is overlain by the Manning Canyon formation. Two small plugs of quartz monzonite cut the limestone belt, one about 1,000 feet northwest of the main shaft and the other, larger one a similar distance to the southeast. The main body of

[56] Kemp, J. F., Notes on Gold Hill and vicinity, Tooele County, Utah: Econ. Geology, vol. 13, pp. 258–259, 1918.

the quartz monzonite stock crops out only a slightly greater distance to the east.

The limestone is similar to that exposed at the Alvarado—massively bedded, bleached and recrystallized, and locally altered to silicate minerals. It has a rather constant northwest strike and dips 55°–65° NE. The Manning Canyon formation above is not well exposed but appears to have been rather generally metamorphosed to a dark andalusite hornfels. The only igneous rocks found in the mine are two dikes, each a foot or so thick. These occur along two fault planes, one exposed on the third level and the other on the fourth level. The dike rock is a dull brownish-gray fine-grained rock in which flecks of iron oxide are the only constituents readily recognizable. The microscope shows that it has been thoroughly altered and is now composed chiefly of fibrous pleochroic hornblende and sericite, together with smaller amounts of apatite, chlorite, calcite, and iron oxides. There is also a greenish isotropic mineral of high relief that is probably spinel. Rectangular areas of sericite apparently represent former feldspar phenocrysts.

The ore body is found in a thick bed of limestone that has been almost completely replaced by silicates, quartz, and sulphides. The walls appear in large part to have been assay walls, and the width stoped ranges from about a foot to 20 feet. Laterally the ore shoot passes into either a sheeted zone in metamorphosed limestone, as near the portal of the tunnel level, or a tight barren fissure within silicate minerals. The greatest stope length is on the first or tunnel level and amounts to about 125 feet.

Cross fractures are prominent within the ore shoots. These strike nearly east and dip steeply to the south. Mineralization similar to that of the ore body has occurred along these fractures and extended outward into the walls. One such fracture is excellently displayed in the winze connecting the third and fourth levels.

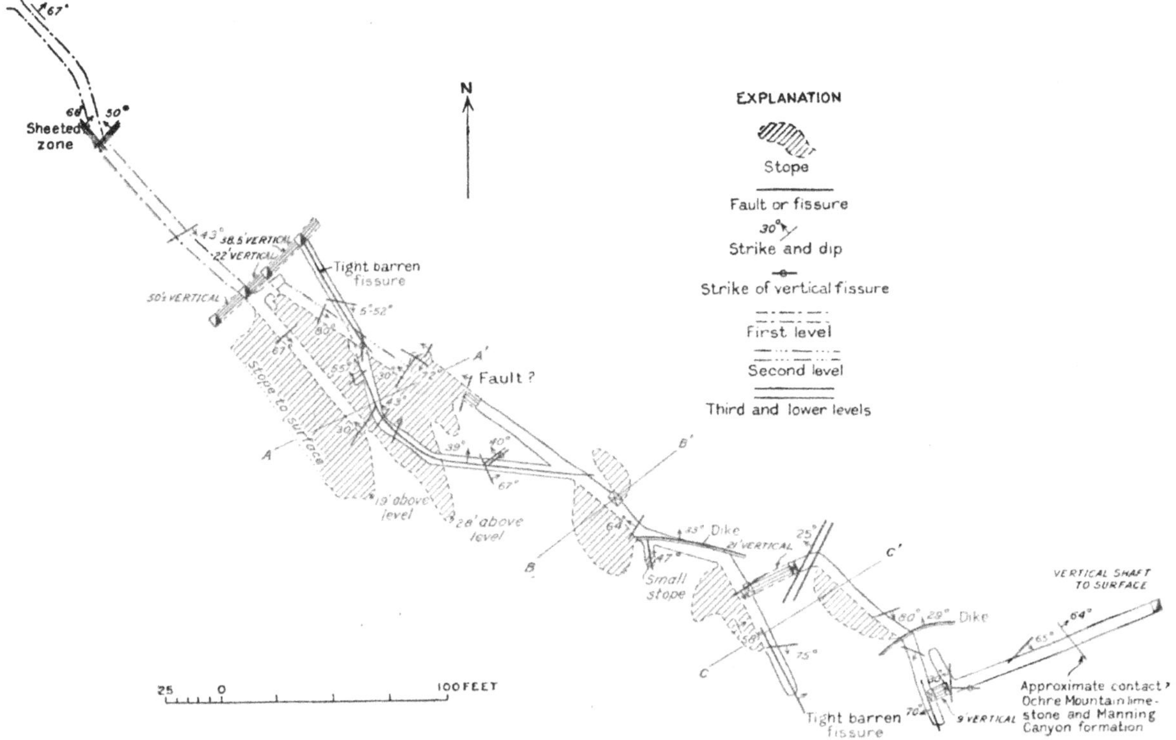

FIGURE 19.—Plan of Cane Springs mine workings. For sections on lines *A–A'*, *B–B'*, and *C–C'* see figure 20.

The continuity of the ore shoot is broken by six or seven low-angle faults (figs. 20 and 21). These have rather widely different strikes that range from north-northeast through east-west to north-northwest, considerable variations in strike being observed in a single fault. They are all alike, however, in having a low dip—25° to 35°—which always has a northerly element in its direction. The sections in figures 20 and 21 show an apparent gap in the ore above the third level, but it seems probable that this was actually stoped, for the ore shoot is shown by Billingsley[58] to be essentially continuous through this section. These workings if they are present, are probably now concealed by the

[58] Billingsley, Paul, Notes on Gold Hill and vicinity, Tooele County, Utah: Econ. Geology, vol. 13, p. 272, 1918.

filling at the bottom of the raise connecting the second and third levels.

The offsets of the ore shoot by the faults are not consistent among themselves. Some, particularly those on the higher levels, require reverse movement with a large horizontal component, but others show equally large offsets that require the normal type of movement, though also with horizontal components.

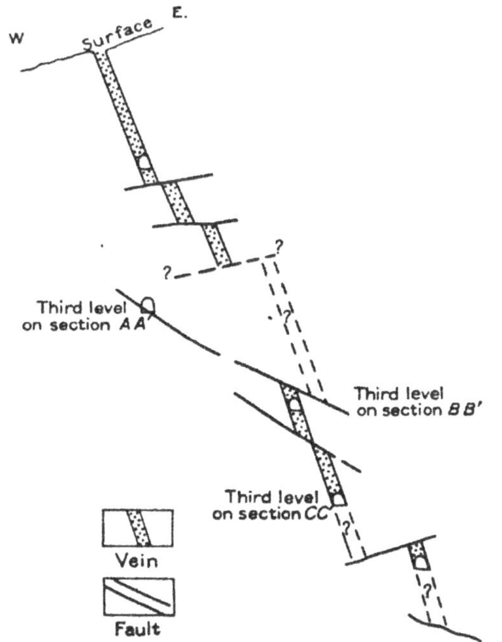

FIGURE 20.—Composite section along lines *A–A'*, *B–B'*, and *C–C'*, figure 19, through Cane Springs mine. Sections *B–B'* and *C–C'* have been shifted both vertically and horizontally relative to *A–A'* so that individual faults appear continuous.

These relations of the faults suggest that they were formed before ore deposition and that the apparent displacement of the ore by the faults is rather the result of a control of ore deposition by the faults. The reasons for this view are as follows:

The two dikes described in a preceding paragraph are intruded along the faults and thus are clearly younger. The dikes are themselves metamorphosed, and if it is held that faulting followed the deposition of the gold ore it becomes necessary to assume two periods of silicate metamorphism separated by an epoch of both reverse and normal faulting. This is difficult to accept in view of the fact that in other parts of the district mineralization has clearly followed dike formation.

The shapes of the portions of the ore shoot between faults offer some evidence. Although it is realized that the stoped areas had very different gold contents, a rough approximation to similarity in dimensions on both sides of a fault might be expected, but figure 21 shows that such a similarity is not present. Furthermore the extension of the stopes upward along the fault plane, as shown especially well by the stope above the end of the second level, suggests very strongly a greater age for the fault, which thus dammed and directed upward the incoming ore-forming material.

The apparent displacement of the ore shoots by the faults is difficult to accept on the theory that both reverse and normal faults, which are roughly parallel in attitude, could have formed in the interval between ore deposition and dike formation and be unrecognized elsewhere in the quadrangle. It is much more probable that the ore solutions entered along the closely related cross fractures and that deposition was controlled by preexisting faults, whose present attitudes may be quite different from their original ones.

The ore is similar to that of the Alvarado and Midas mines. Wollastonite, which is locally fibrous, is the most abundant silicate mineral and in many places has been altered to spadaite. Pinkish-brown garnet, green diopside, and greenish-brown vesuvianite and zoisite are also found. Fine-grained quartz and calcite cut the silicates in veinlets and more irregular masses. Sulphides and their oxidation products are relatively more abundant in the mine and consist of pyrite, chalcopyrite, bornite, chalcocite, covellite, and molybdenite. The molybdenite is reported to have been found very plentifully near the surface. These minerals occur in veinlets cutting the silicate minerals.

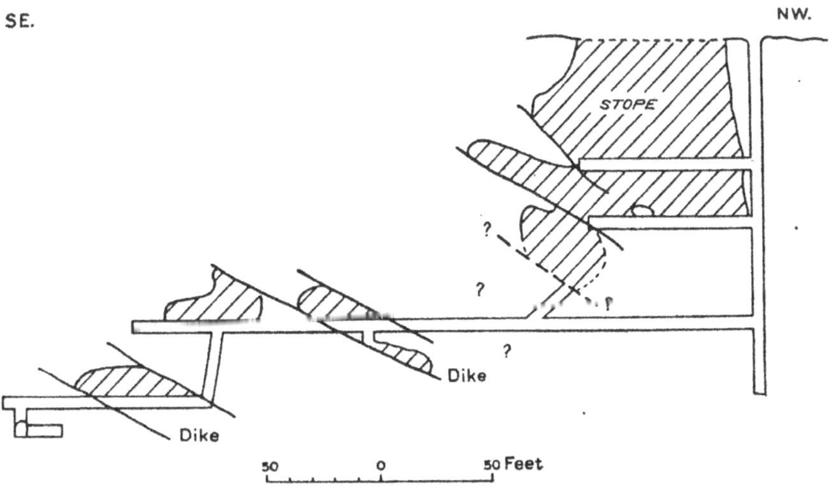

FIGURE 21.—Stope projection, Cane Springs mine.

No gold was observed in the specimens collected by the writer. William Darnell, who worked in the mine, informed the writer that the best ore was found near concentrations of copper minerals. Kemp,[59] however, has described the occurrence of native gold embedded in silicate minerals.

No data are now available as to the grade of the ores other than those quoted in the description of the Alvarado mine—namely, that the mill heads, on ore from the several mines, ranged from $4 to $35 in gold to the ton and the recovery averaged $10.28 a ton over a period of 2 years. It is said that the Cane Springs ore was somewhat more refractory than that from the other mines because of the higher content of sulphide minerals. Either for this reason or perhaps because of a generally lower grade, the stoping in this mine shows that only the most accessible material was mined.

MIDAS

The Midas mine is on the south side of Montezuma Peak, just east of Hopkins Gulch and a little more than a mile east-southeast of Mineral Monument No. 9. Four patented claims are owned by the Midas Gold Mining & Milling Co., of Salt Lake City, Utah. The mine developments consist of an adit tunnel in which about 1,100 feet of work has been done (fig. 22) and several stopes at the surface. It is said that the stopes were connected with the tunnel level by means of four raises, but it is not now possible to pass from one to the other. The tunnel is badly caved in several places. Water draining from it is piped to the location indicated by the spring symbol on the map and is utilized occasionally to water sheep. The ruins of a 40-ton cyanide mill are about 500 feet south of the tunnel portal.

Concerning the production Heikes [60] notes that "in 1896 and prior to that year 95 tons of ore averaging $56 in gold and a trace in silver per ton were treated at the Cane Springs mill and shipped to the smelter. In 1902 a 40-ton cyanide mill was constructed and treated 622 tons with a reported saving of $15 per ton in gold. In 1904 the mill was operated again, but the results were unfavorable, and the property was praccally abandoned."

The operations in 1904 resulted in the recovery of somewhat less than $20,000 in gold, and the grade appears to have been lower than that of the ore previously treated. The total production of the mine is about $35,000. So far as known no work has been done since 1904.

The mine workings are in metamorphosed sedimentary rocks belonging to the Manning Canyon and Oquirrh formations, which are cut by quartz monzonite. The Manning Canyon formation is exposed at the portal of the tunnel and for several hundred feet to the south and southwest. It is composed of black shale and dark sandy shale and quartzite. Biotite, andalusite, and tourmaline in microscopic crystals are present in many beds. The Oquirrh formation overlies the Manning Canyon formation southeast of the tunnel portal. North of the tunnel it is in contact with quartz monzonite at the surface, but the mine workings disclose the Manning Canyon formation beneath it. Sandstone beds form the bulk of the part of the formation here exposed. Interbedded with

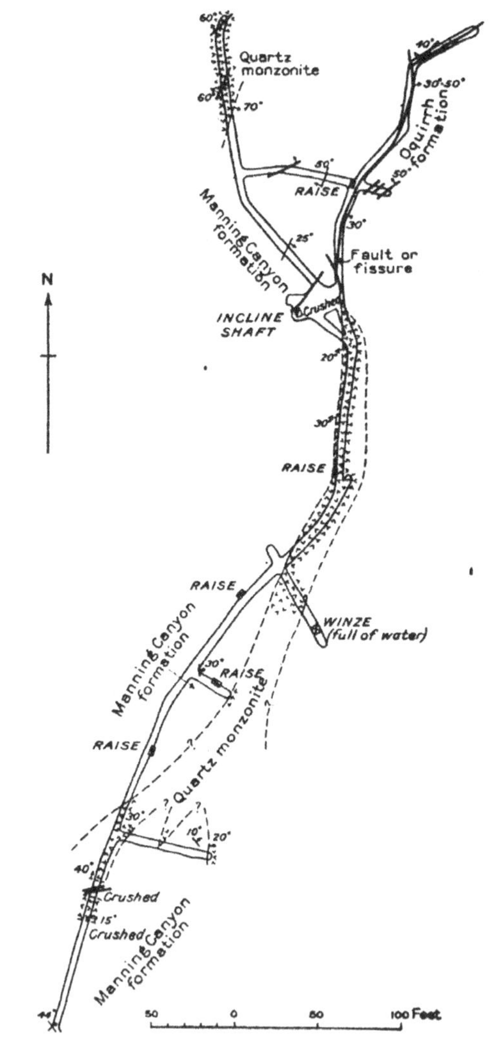

FIGURE 22.—Plan of tunnel level, Midas mine.

them are several beds of limestone. Both rocks are thoroughly bleached and contain varying amounts of silicate minerals, chiefly wollastonite, garnet, and diopside, as the result of metamorphism.

The beds have a rather general strike west of north and dip 30°–45° E. About 1,100 feet south of the tunnel portal the succession of beds exposed near the mine is terminated by an east-west transverse fault, whose throw is somewhat uncertain but appears to be more than a mile. Another fault exposed just north

[59] Kemp, J. F., Notes on Gold Hill and vicinity, Tooele County, Utah: Econ. Geology, vol. 13, pp. 257–258, 1918.

[60] Heikes, V. C., Ore deposits of Utah: U.S. Geol. Survey Prof. Paper 111, p. 475, 1920.

of the tunnel portal brings the Manning Canyon formation on the south into contact with the Oquirrh formation on the north. This fault may be traced up the hill to the east in a direction north of east until the crest is reached, where the course swings to east of north. The same fault is exposed in the tunnel along the hanging wall of a dike of quartz monzonite. Its strike is sinuous but averages a few degrees east of north. The dip is about 30° W., and this feature appears competent to explain the change in course on the surface. The throw is estimated to be about 200 feet, to judge from the position of the upper Manning Canyon contact on the two sides of the fault. The west side is downthrown.

Another fault is exposed in the tunnel at the interior inclined shaft. This strikes east of north and dips 30°–50° SE. It was not recognized on the surface. The relation of this fault to the one just described is not clear. It is probably cut by the westward-dipping fault, because it cannot be connected directly with the similar eastward-dipping fault in the eastern drift north of the shaft. However, if the two are the same, it indicates that there has been only a small displacement of a reverse character along the the westward-dipping fault, which directly opposes the stratigraphic evidence. On the other hand, the westward-dipping fault cannot be recognized to the north, either in the two drifts or in the crosscut connecting them. The writer suspects that the true relations between the two faults are that the eastward-dipping fault is younger than the bulk of the movement along the westward-dipping fault, but that there has been a slight renewed movement along the latter (for which there is some evidence, as noted below).

The quartz monzonite near the mine is at the southeastern tip of the triangular outcrop of this rock on the south side of Montezuma Peak. The contact at the mine trends roughly north and south but is irregular in detail. It is exposed underground near the north end of the tunnel workings and there dips 70° E. South of the tunnel a broad hook-shaped mass of the intrusive extends into the sedimentary rocks. An isolated mass of quartz monzonite crops out along the ridge east of the mine workings. On the surface its shape is that of a flattened triangle, whose base has a north-south direction and whose northwestern limb is the westward-dipping fault previously described. This mass is also exposed in several places in the tunnel, where the fault everywhere forms its hanging wall. To the north it apparently has a dikelike form, but to the south its lower boundary seems to be very irregular. (See fig. 22.) There has been some movement along the boundary fault after the emplacement of the quartz monzonite, as can be seen from the gouge along the fault, but the lack of displacement at the contact of the fault and the intrusive rock on the surface indicates that this movement must have been very small—far less than the 200-foot throw shown by the sedimentary rocks. Furthermore, at several other places in this region the quartz monzonite has utilized preexistent faults of similar strike and dip to this one during its intrusion. The evidence available therefore suggests strongly that the greater part of the movement along this fault preceded the intrusion.

The ore at the Midas mine was found in a bed of limestone that has been almost completely replaced by silicate minerals. The limestone is interbedded with the predominantly sandy beds that here make up the Oquirrh formation. The ore body in this bed is in the exposure of this formation on the hanging-wall side of the westward-dipping fault and cropped out on the east side of the gulch in which the tunnel is located, the contact with the main mass of monzonite being on the west side. The ore body had an average thickness of about 4 feet and was found in shoots for several hundred feet along the strike of the bed. A vertical depth of about 100 feet seems to have been the limit of the ore body, for it is not exposed on the tunnel level. Locally it is said that it was terminated above the level by a fault on whose footwall was found "granite", and it seems probable that the fault on the tunnel level is the one that terminated the ore. It was not possible, however, to examine the bottoms of the stopes to ascertain if this view is correct. If it is, it would appear that the reported effort to discover the faulted portion of the ore bed was foredoomed to failure, for, as shown above, the faulting preceded the intrusion of the quartz monzonite, which in turn is older than the ore. It would probably be more profitable to search for a new ore body in one of the limestone beds in the hanging wall of the fault.

The ore, like that of the Alvarado and Cane Springs mines, was composed chiefly of wollastonite, in part altered to spadaite, and less abundant diopside and garnet. Butler[61] also reports vesuvianite. Sulphides are not abundant and consist of pyrite and various sulphides of copper. Butler notes in addition arsenopyrite. No free gold was observed by the writer. The grade of the ore appears to have been somewhat higher than the average in the Alvarado and Cane Springs mines.

BONNEMORT

The Bonnemort claim is about 2,000 feet southeast of the U.S. mine and adjoins the Undine group on the northwest. It is owned by the Woodman Estate. Gold ore is reported to have been mined some years ago from the inclined shaft 350 feet west of hill 5901, but the amount and grade are unknown. The shaft is now considerably out of repair.

The country rock consists of sandstone and limestone belonging to the Oquirrh formation. These

[61] Butler, B. S., Ore deposits of Utah: U.S. Geol. Survey Prof. Paper 111, p. 479, 1920.

rocks make up the south end of the roof pendant of sedimentary rocks in which the U.S. mine is located. The sediments in the vicinity of the ore body are almost completely bleached and recrystallized, and many of the limestone beds have been altered to silicate minerals. In addition to the quartz monzonite on each side of the roof pendant, a dike of this rock occurs about 25 feet west of the inclined shaft. It strikes nearly due north over most of the exposure, but at the thicker south end it changes its strike abruptly to nearly due east. The portion of the dike with this strike does not extend far beyond the bend.

The ore body appears to be similar in several respects to that of the Cane Springs and Alvarado mines, but the inaccessibility of the workings prevents any close comparison. A bed of limestone more or less replaced by silicates was mined. This bed strikes N. 5° W. and dips 60° E. Gold is said to have occurred in thin seams within the bed as well as being disseminated through it. Factors such as cross fractures that may have localized the ore shoot could not be certainly recognized at the surface.

Specimens from the dump that were said to resemble the ore consisted of coarsely crystalline white calcite in which were scattered abundant laths of wollastonite or of dense greenish diopside. Brown zoisite was observed in a few specimens. Specks and patches of chalcocite and copper pitch with remnants of chalcopyrite were rather abundant in some specimens. Spadaite, which is so wide-spread at the Cane Springs, Alvarado, and Midas mines, was not recognized.

RUBE

The Rube mine, formerly owned by Leffler Palmer, of Gold Hill, is 1½ miles northeast of the town on the southeast side of Gold Hill Wash. The mine, which produces a high-grade direct-smelting gold ore, in 1927 was developed by a 150-foot inclined shaft from which two levels have been driven, in addition to a group of shallow workings east of the shaft. A small compressor and hoist engine were utilized. From April 1921 to July 1927, 22 shipments of gold ore that averaged more than 7 ounces of gold to the ton had been made.

In May 1932 the mine was sold to the Gold Hill Mines, Inc., and since then it has been actively worked. At the end of 1932 it was reported that 2 cars of ore a week were being shipped, the grade of which ranged from $12 to $30 a ton.

The wall rock shown by the mine workings is a white, massively bedded, finely crystalline limestone or dolomite, locally shattered and iron-stained. It is thought to be a portion of the Ochre Mountain limestone that is in part dolomitized. Comparatively little alteration to silicate minerals has occurred. The strike and dip of the bedding is difficult to determine. From several exposures the strike is rather confidently thought to be northwest and the dip is with considerably less assurance considered to be steep to the northeast.

About a quarter of a mile north of the shaft Prospect Mountain quartzite crops out with a nearly east-west strike and a moderate northerly dip. The contact between the quartzite and the Ochre Mountain limestone is a fault, the movement along which is thought to have been chiefly horizontal. The fault is cut and displaced by a later fault, which probably extends through the eastern part of the Rube No. 3 claim, although it is possible, as noted on page 80, that the offset is due to a northerly fault following Gold Hill Wash and concealed by the gravel in the floor of the wash.

Quartz monzonite crops out at the surface about 1,000 feet west of the shaft and at an equal distance to the south, but none has been found in the underground work. The outcrop west of the shaft is at the eastern edge of the body of igneous rock along the south side of Dutch Mountain; the other is at the north end of the main stock.

The only igneous rock found in the underground workings is a thin dike of hornblende andesite that forms the hanging wall of the ore bodies. This rock in most of the exposures is a dull brownish-gray rock composed of a paler fine-grained indeterminate matrix flecked with numerous areas of "limonite." It effervesces briskly with dilute hydrochloric acid, not only in the numerous veinlets of calcite that streak the rock but also in the matrix. At the bottom of the winze from the lower level of the western workings much fresher material is found. This is a fine-grained grayish-green rock of pepper and salt appearance. It is much jointed, with some calcite filling the joints, but the microscope shows that the hornblende and plagioclase that are the original minerals have been relatively little altered. The rock found on the upper levels, on the other hand, has been almost completely replaced by calcite.

The dike ranges in thickness from a few inches to 5 feet and has an average though variable strike of about east-west and dip of about 60° N. The hanging wall is generally a slickensided surface and the contact with the footwall sulphide-bearing dolomite is in many places a thin crushed zone or joint plane. Locally the andesite shows a faint banding parallel to these walls, but in other places small apophyses into the walls may be found.

Two small faults cut and offset the dike a few feet at the foot of the main shaft, and a third fault appears to terminate it about 110 feet east of the shaft on this level. The offsets along the two other faults and the presence of the dike in the eastern shallow workings indicate that the easterly continuation should be found south of the present workings.

The ore occurs chiefly in two pipelike shoots, known as the east and west ore bodies (figs. 23 and 24). The hanging wall of both these ore shoots is the hornblende andesite dike. The contact of the ore with the dike is in the eastern workings, a little ore has been found in the hanging wall of the dike.

The east ore body was the first to be discovered. The cross-sectional dimensions of this pipe average

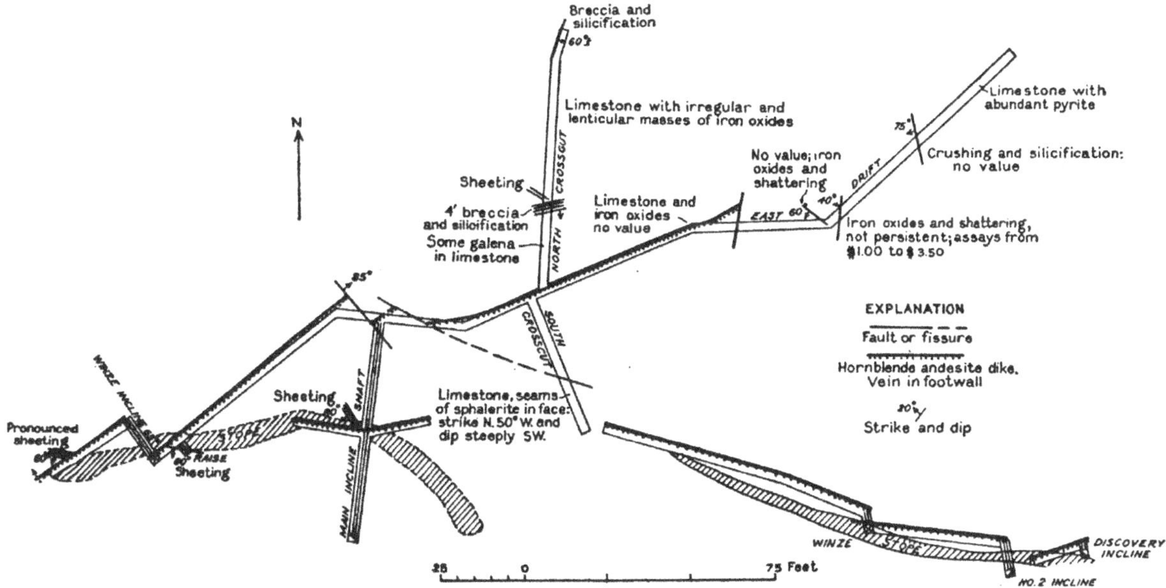

FIGURE 23.—Plan of mine workings, Rube mine. From map furnished by Leffler Palmer.

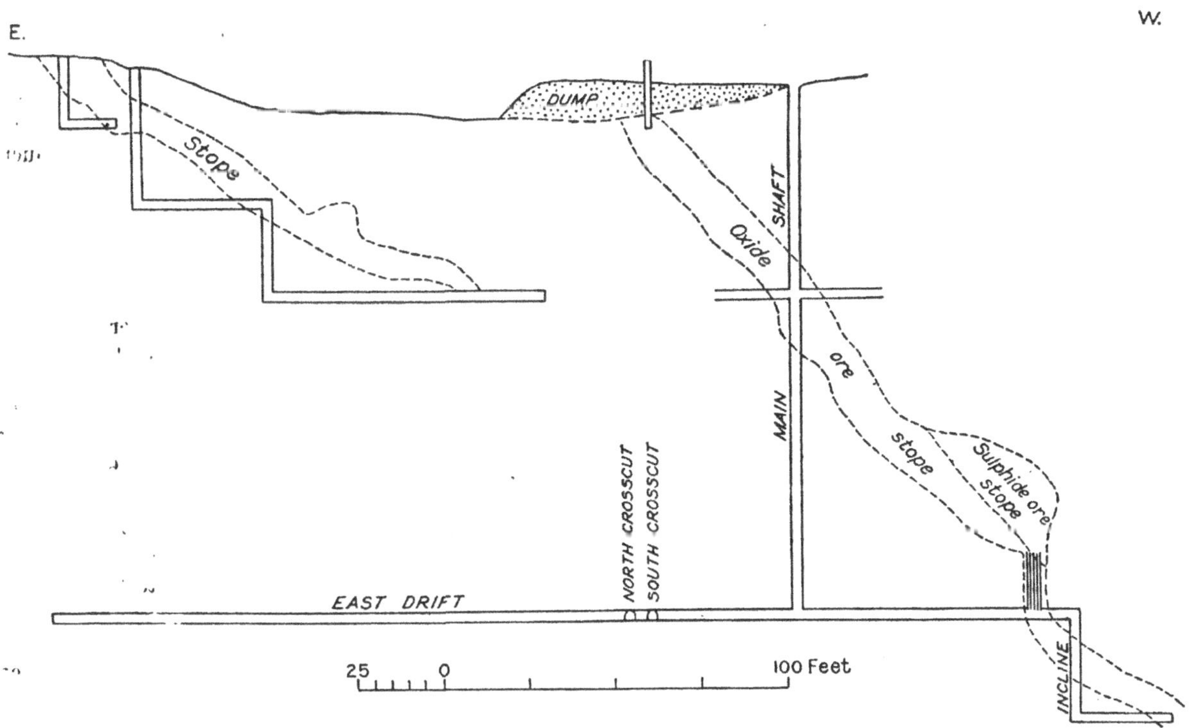

FIGURE 24.—Longitudinal section through Rube mine. Furnished by Leffler Palmer.

sharp. Sulphide-bearing dolomite forms the footwall of the ore bodies, and there is generally an abrupt contact between the two. Locally, as near the surface close to 3 feet in a direction normal to the andesite hanging wall and 15 feet parallel to it. The shoot rakes 35° W. and has been followed for a distance of

135 feet along the rake. The new or west shoot is somewhat larger in cross section than the eastern one and also extends to a greater depth, having been stoped for a distance of 230 feet down the rake, which averages about 45°. On the bottom level the rake is locally extremely variable, being 90° at the level and flattening to about 30° in the winze below. It is probably a coincidence that the flatter portion if projected upward would join the east ore body. Ore of good grade was still present in the lowest workings in 1927.

The hanging wall of the ore bodies is marked by a pronounced sheeted zone which in the western ore body strikes northwest and dips 60°–80° SW. Similar directions are shown by thin bands of sulphides in the footwall dolomites. The constant association of the sheeting and ore probably has a genetic significance, but there are several places where apparently similar jointing is not accompanied by a concentration of gold.

Northeast of the eastern workings there is a prominent outcrop of brecciated dolomite with quartz. This, like the main ore zone, has an approximate east-west strike. Both might be considered to have been formed at about the same time as the large transverse fault farther north and to represent sympathetic fractures.

The ore mined has several different facies. The most abundant variety so far has been a brownish fine-grained rock of siliceous appearance but having a notable content of calcite, as shown by its effervescence with dilute acid. Pseudomorphs of "limonite" after pyrite and of anglesite and cerusite after galena and veinlets of cerusite are abundant, and locally unaltered galena may be seen. Native gold in small partly crystalline aggregates is found in the iron and lead oxidation minerals and in one specimen was superposed on a "limonitic" coating. In a specimen of a heavy grayish-green fine-grained rock from the east ore body pyromorphite and plumbojarosite cemented by supergene quartz were found.

In thin sections quartz and calcite are found to be the most abundant minerals. The quartz grains are full of calcite inclusions and in most places contain numerous liquid inclusions, each with a tiny gas bubble. Calcite also occurs in larger grains and as veinlets cutting the rock. Its cleavages are usually deeply iron-stained. In a specimen of very rich ore from the east ore body sericite was abundant and was veined by anglesite and cerusite, as well as calcite. In this specimen the native gold was localized in the anglesite.

Ore of this type is seen to pass, in the lower portion of the western workings, into much less oxidized material. This is a blue-gray fine-grained rock locally splotched by brown oxidation products that in places shows a faint banding. Galena and less abundant pyrite are only partly altered, and locally native gold may be found either in galena or in the matrix, although most of it occurs in the supergene minerals. The banding is shown by the microscope to be due to varying proportions of calcite and quartz, which still form the bulk of the rock. Veinlets of coarser-grained clear calcite are abundant and in some places are closely associated with the gold and sulphides. In other places, however, the metallic minerals are without visible relation to the veinlets and appear as isolated areas in the matrix, surrounded by a rim of coarser-grained and clear calcite.

A third type of ore was found in the western ore body just above the second level, in the position marked "sulphide ore" on figure 24. The hanging-wall portion of this ore is composed chiefly of shattered crystalline pyrite that is cut by quartz and calcite veinlets containing small amounts of galena, chalcopyrite, and sphalerite. The remainder of this ore contains abundant molybdenite with some pyrite in a greenish or black fine-grained matrix, which the microscope shows to be composed of calcite, talc, slightly pleochroic muscovite, scapolite near meionite, zoisite, and two varieties of chlorite. This facies of the Rube ore appears to offer a sort of connecting link with the gold ore of the Alvarado, Midas, and Cane Springs mines.

Sulphide minerals are present in the footwall limestone or dolomite of the ore bodies. They are associated with relatively small quantities of quartz and sericite and locally contain some gold, although not enough to warrant mining at the time of examination. The metallic minerals recognized in the two specimens of this rock studied under the microscope include native gold, pyrite, pyrrhotite, deep-red and colorless sphalerite, galena, and arsenical boulangerite. Sphalerite is by far the most abundant.

The grade of the ore mined varies from place to place in the stopes. The carloads shipped up to June 1927 ranged in gold content from 2.83 to 24.42 ounces to the ton and averaged over 7 ounces. The silver content is generally lower and is roughly proportional to the lead content, ranging from 2 to 3 ounces to the ton for each percent of lead. One shipment from the east ore body carried more than 6 percent of arsenic. The presence of antimony and small quantities of bismuth and tellurium in the ore has been proved by analysis. One picked specimen, which the writer did not see, is reported by Mr. Palmer to have contained 7 percent of bismuth.

WILSON CONSOLIDATED

The Wilson Consolidated mine is on the northeast side of Clifton Flat, about 2,500 feet south-southwest of the prominent jasperoid hill at an altitude of 6,455 feet north of the road to Clifton and immediately west of hill 6266. The headquarters of the company is in Salt Lake City. Production from the property appears to be confined to several small shipments of high-grade ore in 1914 and 1917. Relatively little work has been done since 1917. The mine workings aggregate less than 500 feet, chiefly in the form of crosscuts and shallow winzes. The vertical range of the workings is about 75 feet (fig. 25).

The rocks exposed in the mine workings are metamorphosed sandstones and limestones belonging to the central facies of the Oquirrh formation. About 200 feet west of the portal of the tunnel these beds are separated from limestones thought to belong to the western facies of the same formation by a normal fault of unknown but probably considerable throw. The most pronounced effect of the metamorphism upon the sediments of the central facies is a nearly dip in the region southeast of the mine, however, is to the east, and it is thought that the westward dip may be a local feature peculiar to the zone bordering the large fault immediately to the west. Igneous rocks are almost lacking in the immediate vicinity of the mine. A dike of volcanic breccia was observed about 50 feet from the portal of the adit. This is thoroughly crushed and much altered, chiefly to chlorite with minor amounts of a clay mineral. Locally the texture has been preserved in some of the rock fragments, and there is little doubt that the dike is related to the outcrops of volcanic rocks that occur along the borders of Clifton Flat in this region.

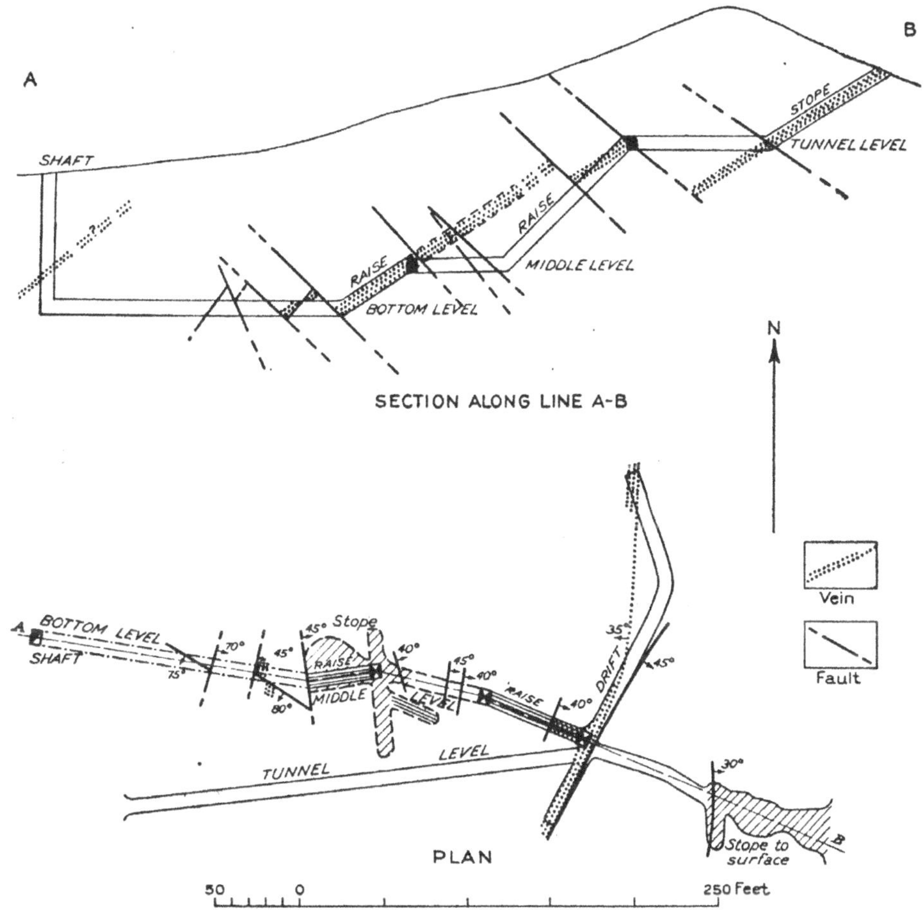

FIGURE 25.—Sketch plan and section of Wilson Consolidated mine.

complete bleaching to white or pale cream color. There has also been a marked mineralogic change in many of the rocks, and the resulting hornfels is in many places difficult to distinguish from bleached quartzite. In the two specimens of hornfels examined under the microscope diopside and orthoclase had been abundantly developed. Bedding can be distinguished with difficulty in this series, owing in part to the metamorphism and in part to the widespread shattering. So far as observed the bedding strikes a little west of

The bismuth-gold ore is found in what is locally known as a vein but what appears to be nothing more than a bed of coarsely crystalline bleached limestone. Like the barren wall rocks, it dips about 30° W. The contacts of the bed are sharp but show no signs of movement or replacement. The limestone has a maximum thickness of 6 feet at the south end of the drift on the tunnel level but is usually nearer 3 feet in thickness. The ore-bearing bed is cut by at least nine north-south normal faults. These dip 30°–70° E. and

that are shown in the tunnel level, the throw along the more easterly appears to be negligible and that along the more westerly to be about 25 feet. The throw along the fault that cuts off the limestone in the winze connecting the tunnel and middle level must be about 15 or 20 feet, as the three small faults exposed on the middle level displace the ore zone as it is exposed in the raise from the south drift on this level scarcely more than a foot apiece. The throw along the fault that terminates the ore at the bottom of the winze leading to the bottom level is easily determined as being close to 15 feet by reason of the exposure of the faulted segment in the crosscut to the west. This exposure of the ore zone is also cut by a fault striking north of west and dipping steeply to the south. The throw along it is about 5 feet. Both the fault and the ore zone are cut off a short distance to the west by another north-south fault dipping 45° E. The throw along this fault as well as along another a short distance to the west that has a similar strike but dips 70° E. is somewhat uncertain. If the southward-dipping fault which is exposed to the west of the more westerly of these two faults and which is cut off by it is the same as the fault of similar dip to the east, the combined throw along the two faults amounts to about 25 feet. On the other hand, the ore zone is reported to be reached in the shaft at a depth of 30 feet from the surface, and no faults were recognized between the shaft and the faults in question—facts which require a combined throw of about 50 feet. This figure is perhaps the closer to the truth, because to correlate the two southward-dipping faults would require horizontal movement along either or both of the north-south faults, and if this were admitted, the divergent figures for the vertical displacement could be readily explained.

The ore contains gold, bismuth, and a little tungsten. The chief gangue mineral is quartz, which is present either as euhedral crystals 1 millimeter or less in diameter, distributed through the limestone, or as veinlets of very fine grained allotriomorphic material. In one specimen from the south drift on the tunnel level the limestone is also cut by veinlets of orthoclase. This mineral was not found in any of the other ore specimens, however.

The ore minerals observed were native bismuth, bismuthinite, bismutite, and scheelite. Copper sulphides and a lead-tungsten mineral, probably stolzite, are also reported from this mine by Butler.[62] Bismuthinite and its oxidation product, bismutite, are by far the most abundant. The sulphide is found as rounded specks as much as a quarter of an inch in diameter embedded in the limestone. Much of the bismutite forms pseudomorphs after bismuthinite, as is shown by the preservation of cleavage lines, but a moderate amount is clearly transported, for it is found also in veinlets of supergene opal and chalcedony and along cleavage planes of the calcite matrix. Native bismuth was found in only one specimen, which was taken from the stope leading to the surface from the east end of the tunnel level. The mineral was found in the center of a grain of bismuthinite. Scheelite was also recognized in only one specimen, which was taken from the open cut about 50 feet south of the stope to the surface. Its occurrence is similar to that of the bismuthinite. Scheelite is reported to have been rather abundant in the raise from the south drift on the middle level. Native gold also occurs in the ores, but none was found in the specimens collected. The two stoped areas were mined chiefly for their gold content. Butler[63] notes that the gold is closely associated with bismuthinite, and in one of his specimens the writer observed gold adjacent to several copper minerals.

The grade of the ore is variable. The distribution of gold and scheelite is apparently limited to rather small shoots in the vein. No figures are available as to the grade of the scheelite-rich portions, but the shoots of gold ore seem to have averaged somewhat less than 1 ounce to the ton. Bismuth minerals, however, are rather widely distributed throughout the ore zone, although the amount is far from being constant. The only figures as to grade that are available apply to a shipment of 4.33 tons of concentrates that contained 12.43 percent of bismuth. This lot presumably came from the stope from the surface to the tunnel level. It contained about $9 a ton in gold. These figures are probably considerably higher than the average of the vein.

VEINS CONTAINING CHIEFLY QUARTZ AND METALLIC SULPHIDES

LUCY L

The Lucy L mine is in Lucy L Gulch about 2 miles south-southeast of the town of Gold Hill. It includes a group of seven patented claims that are owned by the Lucy L Mining Co. The Wilson Brothers, of Salt Lake City, have directed the past operations of the company. Exploration of the gold-quartz ore body had been effected prior to Kemp's visit in 1908, and the tungsten deposit on the property was being developed at the time of Butler's examination in 1912. The property was idle during the period of the writer's field work. It is developed by about 1,300 feet of workings from two adits (pl. 13), in addition to several shallow surface pits. No figures are available as to the production, but it is believed that a few small lots of gold ore and possibly one or more of tungsten ore have been shipped.

The most prominent formation in the vicinity of the Lucy L mine is the Ochre Mountain limestone. Massively bedded members of this formation make up

[62] Butler, B. S., Ore deposits of Utah: U.S. Geol. Survey Prof. Paper 111, p. 482, 1920.

[63] Butler, B. S., op. cit., p. 482.

the greater part of the hill (altitude 6,125 feet) on whose slopes the mine workings are found. The limestone is shattered and locally bleached but shows practically no development of silicate minerals. Strikes and dips are almost impossible to determine by reason of the thickness of the beds and the widespread shattering. Those that were obtained, however, suggest that minor warping or folding has been widespread.

Two other sedimentary formations are exposed on the lower slopes of the hill. One of these is the Manning Canyon formation, which crops out in the gulch on the south side of the hill and is also seen at the portal of the south tunnel. In the tunnel the formation is composed of badly crushed and crumpled black shale, with thin rusty sandy partings. On the surface southeast of the portal reddish quartzites are also found in the formation. About 20 feet from the portal the black shale is succeeded by a zone of intensely crushed shale in which are included blocks of Ochre Mountain limestone, and this in turn is followed by 60 feet of the massive limestone (pl. 13). A nearly vertical normal fault again exposes the breccia. These relations clearly require that the breccia zone represent a thrust fault, and on page 73 it was indicated that it is an eastern continuation of the Ochre Mountain thrust. The other formation is found on the eastern slope of the hill in and near the northern of the two tunnels. Here relatively thin bedded rocks crop out, which resemble closely the metamorphosed sandstones and limestones of the central facies of the Oquirrh formation that are exposed a short distance to the north. A specimen of a metamorphosed sandstone taken from a point near the tunnel portal was composed largely of quartz that was presumably recrystallized, as the grains were rimmed by fine dustlike material. Scattered throughout the quartz were smaller crystals of diopside and less abundant grains of orthoclase. Veinlets of tremolite cut the rock. Other beds, presumably with a higher original content of calcium carbonate, have been altered to garnet-diopside rock or to one composed chiefly of wollastonite. These beds are exposed throughout the greater part of the northern workings and must therefore underlie the Ochre Mountain limestone, which crops out at the surface. The contact between the two is not well exposed on the surface, but, in view of the presence of the thrust in the southern tunnel, it seems certain that this contact represents the same fault.

Quartz monzonite terminates the sedimentary rocks on the north and east, and small lenticular masses of the same rock occur on the south and west. The mine workings show that the quartz monzonite also underlies areas where sedimentary rocks are exposed at the surface, and it seems rather certain that igneous rock is present at no great depth beneath the whole hill. The upper surface of the quartz monzonite must be rather flat, although in detail it is very irregular

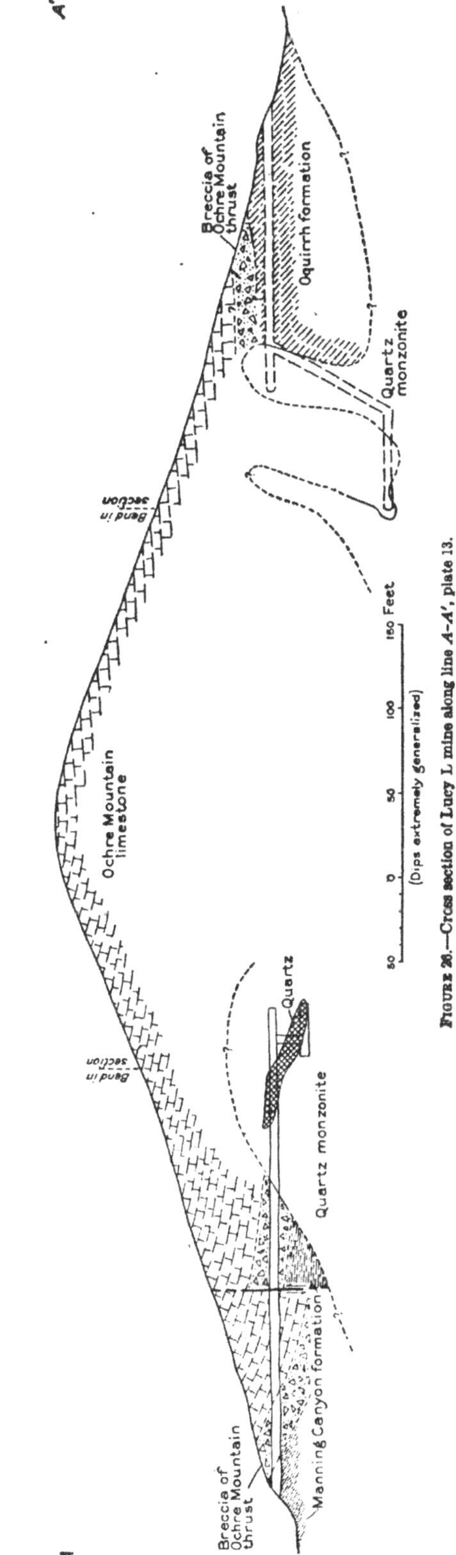

FIGURE 26.—Cross section of Lucy L mine along line A-A', plate 13.

(fig. 26). Two dikes are cut by the northern tunnels, for example, that do not appear at the surface, although

of the intrusive not much more than 100 feet below their apices. A specimen of relatively unaltered quartz monzonite taken from the western workings from the southern tunnel is of the normal type of biotite-quartz monzonite but shows some slight metamorphism by the presence of a few idiomorphic diopside crystals. Near the ore bodies the rock is as a rule considerably altered. A specimen from the southern tunnel workings about 75 feet east of the shaft has been largely replaced by garnet, diopside, and hornblende, and these minerals in turn have been partly altered to quartz, sericite, and calcite. Another specimen adjacent to the ore body on the bottom level of the southern workings has been bleached to a dull cream-colored rock in which the igneous texture can be recognized only locally. The dark minerals have been completely and the feldspars partly replaced by calcite, sericite, and quartz. Butler [64] noted that adjacent to the tungsten deposits on the southeastern slope of the hill diopside, a green hornblende, carbonate minerals, epidote, and a few crystals of allanite have been introduced. Underground the quartz monzonite locally includes blocks of the sedimentary formations. One of the Manning Canyon formation was observed in the long crosscut southeast of the shaft in the southern workings, and another, probably of the Oquirrh formation, which was found to be calcite-tremolite rock, was found at the extreme east end of these workings.

Two kinds of ore have been mined from the Lucy L property. These are gold-bismuth ore and tungsten-copper ore. The largest body of the gold-bismuth ore was found in the south workings about 225 feet from the portal of the tunnel and took the form of a lenticular mass of quartz 50 to 75 feet long and 10 feet in maximum thickness. The ore body has a crescent shape in horizontal section, with the concavity to the northwest. The dip is 40°–50° NW. Quartz monzonite forms both walls of the ore. On the tunnel level it is separated from the ore on the hanging-wall side by a well-defined slip and on the footwall side by a zone in which dark silicates are abundant. Both of these features are absent on the bottom level, where the quartz monzonite walls are thoroughly bleached. Locally minerals resembling kaolinite and halloysite have been developed in this rock as a result of weathering. On this level the dimensions of the ore body appear to be considerably smaller.

The ore is relatively simple mineralogically. It is composed almost entirely of quartz, which has been thoroughly shattered. The fracture planes in almost all places have been filled with a dark-brown iron oxide, with which yellow-brown jarosite is only locally associated. The microscope shows that the quartz has been formed at two stages. The earlier quartz is glassy and coarsely crystalline and tends to be euhedral. It forms the greater part of the ore body. The younger quartz is found chiefly in the interstices of the older crystals and is generally separated from them by a layer of chalcedony fibers. It is very fine grained. Locally this fine-grained material is found in relatively large areas where it has clearly replaced the older quartz. Sericite occurs in association with much of it.

The metallic minerals observed were bismuthinite and native bismuth (both largely oxidized to bismutite), pyrite (also oxidized), and native gold. Specimens containing these minerals were not abundant, but the impression was gained that they occur either in or near the areas of fine-grained quartz. All the gold seen was embedded in bismutite. Kemp [65] has described a gold telluride from this mine, but none was found by the writer. A copper mineral was also probably present in the primary ore, as a small amount of malachite was observed. The bismuth minerals and gold are of rare occurrence in the quartz body and appear to be limited to relatively small shoots that are roughly outlined by the stoped areas shown in plate 13. No figures are available as to the content of gold or bismuth in the shoots.

Gold-bearing rock is also reported to occur in two zones near the west end of the bottom level of the northern workings. (See pl. 13.) This is a shattered grayish-green rock in which large cleavage plates of calcite may be seen that are interrupted by dark minerals. There are a few pseudomorphs of "limonite" after pyrite and some copper stains. The microscope shows in addition to calcite, green hornblende, garnet, and apatite, together with numerous veinlets of fine-grained quartz. No gold was observed in the slide.

Tungsten-copper ore is found in a vein about 400 feet south of the north tunnel portal. The vein has a width of 4 feet or so and is exposed for a length of about 100 feet by a series of shallow pits in which it strikes about north and has a nearly vertical dip. The walls are both of quartz monzonite and are roughly parallel to the intrusive contact, which is less than 50 feet distant to the west. Some slickensides may be seen along the walls. The ore extended downward only about 15 feet. The eastern workings from the south tunnel underlie the northern extension of the vein about 100 feet below the surface but show no sign of similar mineralization.

The ore consists chiefly of dark silicates in a scant matrix of calcite. The calcite is coarsely crystalline and, though largely replaced by the silicates, is readily recognized by the reflection of light from the large but interrupted cleavage surfaces. Locally the calcite is relatively unreplaced, and in these areas the adjoining silicates show good crystal faces. Pyrite and chalcopyrite are more abundant in these calcite areas than in

[64] Butler, B. S., Ore deposits of Utah: U.S. Geol. Survey Prof. Paper 111, p. 477, 1920.

[65] Kemp, J. F., Notes on Gold Hill and vicinity, Tooele County, western Utah: Econ. Geology, vol. 13, p. 260, 1918.

the rock rich in silicates. The distinguishing feature of the ore is the presence of crystals of yellowish-gray scheelite, which may reach an inch in length.

The silicate minerals present include andradite garnet, diopside, epidote, titanite, green hornblende (partly altered to actinolite), and orthoclase. There appears to be a definite sequence in their formation, and the scheelite appears to belong to one of the early stages. Quartz and calcite veinlets with associated sericite and chlorite cut all the other minerals. In addition to the minerals cited, axinite and zoisite were noted in specimens collected in 1912 by Butler from this property.

Picked specimens of the ore are rich in scheelite or in chalcopyrite or its oxidation products, but the small extent of the deposit and the rather erratic distribution of the valuable minerals in it have prevented any recent development. It is thought that a small lot of tungsten ore was shipped some years ago from this property, but no data as to the grade were obtained.

A similar mineral assemblage but without any scheelite is exposed at the surface contact of the quartz monzonite by a prospect pit west of north from the tungsten workings and also within the sedimentary rocks in the northern tunnel. The copper present in these occurrences is far too low for them to be of value.

BOSTON

The Boston claim is south of the Lincoln Highway about 6,000 feet east-southeast of the summit of Gold Hill. It is said to be owned by the Boston-Utah Mining Co., whose headquarters are at Los Angeles, Calif. No shipments are known to have been made from the property.

Quartz monzonite forms the wall rock of the vein on the claim, which has been explored by several shallow surface cuts and by an inclined shaft of no great depth. To the north the vein strikes N. 40° W. and dips about 45° SW. Toward the south the strike swings to nearly due north and the dip steepens. The vein is offset for a few feet by several minor faults and is apparently terminated to the south by a larger one.

The vein filling is from 1 to 3 feet thick and consists of crushed quartz monzonite together with quartz, arsenopyrite, and oxidized minerals of iron, lead, and arsenic. Locally arsenopyrite and scorodite are present to the almost complete exclusion of the other minerals. At the surface the results of all stages of the alteration of the sulphide to scorodite may be observed. The arsenopyrite is reported by W. M. Lamb, of Gold Hill, to carry $14 in gold to the ton. Near the south end of the vein, at the inclined shaft, some lead-silver ore is said to occur. Specimens of plumbojarosite or the related arsenic compound may be seen on the dump and presumably were the source of the lead.

NEW YORK

The New York claim, on the southwest side of Dutch on the Ferber Road, is owned by Messrs. Bailey and Delmonico, of Gold Hill. In 1927 some assessment work was being done on the claim in developing a small mass of lead-arsenic ore that was found along a fault that separates the Pottsville portion of the Oquirrh formation from higher beds in that formation. The ore exposed was entirely oxidized and appeared to consist chiefly of scorodite. Assays of the ore were said by Mr. Bailey to show a content of $4.40 in gold and 12 ounces of silver to the ton and 8 to 9 percent of lead.

SILVER & GOLD MINING CO.

The Silver & Gold Mining Co., Inc., whose headquarters are in Spanish Fork, Utah, owns five claims about a mile northeast of the Western Utah mine and east of Calico Hill. So far as known no shipments have been made from the claims.

In 1926 the company was engaged in exploring a vein that cropped out in limestones and sandstones of the Oquirrh formation about 2,000 feet east of the summit of Calico Hill. The sedimentary rocks are very close to the northern contact of the quartz monzonite stock, and the igneous rock was cut at a shallow depth in the inclined shaft that was being sunk on the vein.

The vein occupies a fault fissure, the movement along which occurred before the mineralization. The throw along it amounts to about 10 feet, as is shown by the displacement of the quartz monzonite contact. The dip is about 55° W. at the surface but steepens to 65° after it enters the igneous rock. In the portion of the vein enclosed by sedimentary rocks the vein is as much as 4 feet in width and is almost completely oxidized. Quartz, scorodite, and oxidized minerals of iron and lead are the most prominent minerals in this portion. In the quartz monzonite the vein is much thinner (3 to 12 inches) and has been much less affected by oxidation. Pyrite, arsenopyrite, galena, and sphalerite were recognized in sulphide-bearing specimens from this part of the vein. The operators reported that the vein as exposed in June 1927 had an average content of $10 in gold and 3 ounces in silver to the ton. In places high gold assays were obtained.

MASCOT

The Mascot group of claims, in the quartz monzonite area north of Overland Canyon and west of Barney Reevey Gulch, is owned by Frank J. Guilmette, of Gold Hill. A small amount of development work has been done on several quartz-sulphide veins that strike about north and dip on the average 45° W. The metal present is chiefly arsenic, in the form of both arsenopyrite and scorodite, but locally there are small shoots of lead ore. On the Mascot No. 2 claim a small pegmatitic pipe is exposed, which is reported to contain small amounts of scheelite. The surface dimensions

MONTE DEL REY

The Monte del Rey group of four patented claims is in Hopkins Gulch a short distance northwest of the Midas mine. It is owned by P. H. Robinson, of Gold Hill. A long cross-cut tunnel has been driven westward in quartz monzonite from a point about 100 yards south of the spring to cut several veins that are exposed on the surface. The veins contain chiefly arsenic minerals but locally carry small quantities of lead minerals. No production is known from the group.

FORTUNA

The Fortuna group of three claims is in Hopkins Gulch about three-quarters of a mile northwest of the Midas mine. The claims are owned by Mrs. Emma C. Thompson, of Denver, Colo. Several surface cuts and pits have been made on a quartz-arsenopyrite vein in quartz monzonite similar to the other veins in this region. Locally it contains small quantities of lead minerals. No shipments have been made from the property.

BONANZA

The Bonanza group of claims, owned by Mrs. Emma C. Thompson, of Denver, Colo., covers most of the ridge north of the Cyclone mine. In 1926 it was under lease to Frank J. Guilmette, of Gold Hill. So far as known, no shipments have been made.

The ore is found as small shoots in a wide shear zone in quartz monzonite that has a general strike of about N. 20° E. and dips 65° W. The ore shoots, which are locally as much as 5 feet in width, contain chiefly arsenic ore, in the form of arsenopyrite and scorodite, but in some places a large proportion of the ore is composed of lead and zinc minerals. Mr. Guilmette was developing one such shoot in 1926.

The 170-foot tunnel on the claim exposes a dike of dark porphyry that has been cut by numerous minor faults.

CYCLONE

The Cyclone mine is about 1,600 feet south-southeast of U.S. Mineral Monument No. 9, in Barney Reevey Gulch, on the south side of Montezuma Peak. The mine takes its name from the Cyclone claim, which is one of the six claims owned by the Engineers Development Co., of Salt Lake City. This company acquired the claims in 1925 and since that time has established a camp and done a moderate amount of development work. The workings consist of an inclined shaft on the vein, from which, at a depth of 80 feet, a drift has been extended to the north more than 400 feet. Several raises extend upward from the drift, and the inclined shaft has been extended down the dip an unknown distance. The vein has also been explored by a tunnel whose portal is north of the shaft collar. Shipments of lead-silver ore are reported to have been made from

Only two formations are exposed in the vicinity of the mine. Quartz monzonite underlies most of the surface. It does not differ notably from exposures of this rock elsewhere. The quartz monzonite is cut by a dike of granite porphyry, a light greenish-gray rock that weathers in many places to shades of brown. This rock contains numerous phenocrysts of quartz 1 to 2 millimeters in diameter and less abundant phenocrysts of biotite and feldspar. The microscope shows that the feldspar phenocrysts include both orthoclase and albite. The groundmass of the rock is very finely crystalline and is made up of quartz, feldspar, and biotite. The dike strikes a little east of north and dips 50° W.

The quartz vein that contains the ore minerals follows the hanging wall of the granite porphyry dike. It is not continuous, stretches of quartz and sulphides alternating with stretches in which a foot or more of gouge takes the place of the vein. The alternation appears to be correlated with changes in the strike of the vein. In general, the portions with a nearly north-south strike are occupied by gouge, and those that strike east of north contain quartz and sulphides. Similar variations along the dip of the vein are exposed in the raises from the level. In at least one place the barren stretches may be correlated with a local steepening in the dip of the vein.

Gouge is also found on either wall of the quartz or on both. About 300 feet north of the shaft, for example, there is a few inches of gouge between the vein and the footwall granite porphyry and about a foot of gouge and crushed quartz monzonite on the hanging wall. The gouge contains fragments of quartz and sulphides and was reported to contain in one place 17 percent of arsenic.

Adjacent to the vein the granite porphyry has been considerably altered. The feldspar phenocrysts have been changed to a soft claylike mineral and the groundmass to a fine-grained aggregate of quartz and a little sericite. The quartz monzonite hanging wall, on the other hand, has been but little affected.

The drift from the inclined shaft has disclosed five shoots of quartz-sulphide ore. The most southerly of these is the longest, extending about 100 feet northward from the shaft. In the succeeding 200 feet to the north three small shoots are exposed, two of them having lengths of about 15 feet and one of 30 feet. The fifth shoot starts about 300 feet north of the shaft and has a length of about 60 feet. The thickness of the shoots reaches a maximum of about 3 feet, but the average thickness is between 18 inches and 2 feet.

The vein filling, as shown on the drift from the shaft consists of a mixture of quartz and sulphides in which the proportion of each varies, locally the one or the other predominating. The sulphides recognized are pyrite, arsenopyrite, galena, chalcopyrite, aikinite, and sphalerite. Small quantities of an iron-rich dolomite

phides are fine-grained and intermixed, but in a few places concentrations of a single mineral are found in which the grain size is considerably greater.

A series of 11 samples taken at 5-foot intervals along the southern ore shoot showed the following variations in content:

Gold (average) ..... ounces to the ton..	0. 03
Silver (average) .... do....	6
Lead .... percent..	0. 4–8. 2
Copper .... do....	0. 5–1. 7
Zinc .... do....	0. 5–3. 8
Arsenic .... do....	0. 5–7. 3

The ground-water level corresponds closely with the level of the drift, but there is comparatively little sign of oxidation in the vein at this horizon. The bottom of complete oxidation was found to be about 35 feet above the drift level in the shaft and about 30 feet above the level in a raise 300 feet north of the shaft. About 100 feet north of the shaft, at a point that corresponds with the position of a stream channel on the surface, the ore is partly oxidized and contains much greenish-blue chalcanthite. Near the surface yellow-brown powdery jarosite and plumbojarosite, both of which probably contain a little arsenic, are abundant.

SUCCESS

The Success mine is about 2 miles southeast of the Western Utah Copper Co.'s Gold Hill mine and 6,000 feet due west of bench mark 5060 on the Lincoln Highway. It is owned by W. F. Peters, of New York City, but in 1926 the property was being worked under lease by D. C. Scott, of Park City, Utah. In 1927 Messrs. Sevy & Wilkins, of Gold Hill, were lessees. Several shipments of lead-silver ore have been made from the property. In 1920 a lot of 94 tons of ore contained 0.06 ounce of gold and 32.3 ounces of silver to the ton, 1.55 percent of copper, and 8.96 percent of lead. Smaller shipments were also made in 1926 and 1927, but their grade is not known.

The country rock at the mine is quartz monzonite, which is rather thoroughly crushed and altered. Surface exposures of the rock near the mine are relatively few. In a specimen taken from the footwall of the vein all the original minerals of the rock, except quartz and the accessory minerals, have been almost completely replaced by sericite, calcite, and chlorite.

The ore is found in a quartz vein cutting the igneous rock. As exposed in the inclined shaft on the vein, the strike is northwest and the dip 30°–45° W. In the shaft the thickness of the vein ranges from a few inches to about 4 feet. There has been considerable movement after the formation of the vein, which has resulted in the presence of gouge on either or both walls. During the visits to the mine in both 1926 and 1927 the greater part of the workings from the shaft were inaccessible, but on one short drift on the vein north the vein were observed. The writer is informed that the vein was cut off at one place by an east-west fault and that the faulted segment was never found. Although the fault was not observed in the mine, the offsets of the dike east of the mine workings as shown in plate 2, suggest that there has been a relative shift to the east on the south side of the fault.

Oxidation of the ore minerals is complete at the surface, jarosite and plumbojarosite being abundant. Sulphides are found in the shaft about 90 feet below the collar (about 45 feet vertically), although the ground-water level is at 125 feet (about 65 feet vertically). The primary ore consists of white coarsely crystalline quartz, pyrite, arsenopyrite, galena, sphalerite, and tennantite. Polished sections show the presence also of thin veins of a carbonate mineral. As in other veins of this type in the district, both the ratio of the sulphides to the quartz and their relative proportions to one another vary considerably from place to place. Locally there are concentrations of cleavable black sphalerite that has a distinctly nonmetallic appearance when slightly weathered.

SPOTTED FAWN

The Spotted Fawn group of claims, now located under the name of the Silver Hill group, is in Spotted Fawn Canyon, on the east side of Dutch Mountain.

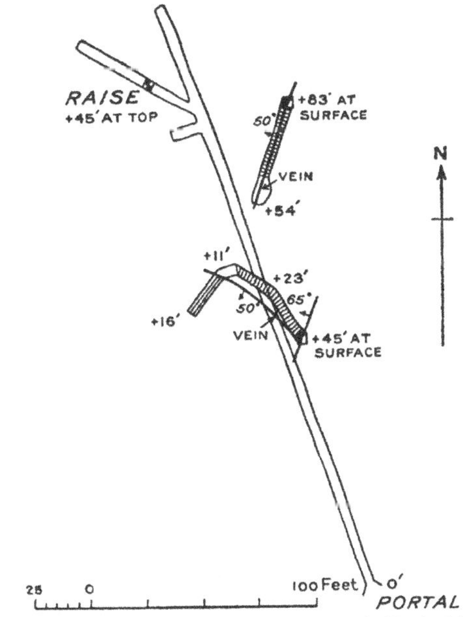

FIGURE 27.—Plan of tunnel and surface workings on north side of gulch, Spotted Fawn mine.

The Gold Hill Mines Co., of Salt Lake City, is the present owner. Shipments amounting to 78 tons were made from the property during 1901–17. These had an average content of 0.038 ounce of gold and 25.1 ounces of silver to the ton and 18.1 percent of lead. The main workings on the group are on the northeast side of the canyon, where a tunnel has been driven

also been done on the southwest side of the canyon, in another shallow shaft from which some short drifts have been driven. A well-built bunkhouse and a machine shop in which an air compressor is housed are situated just below the mine workings. These buildings may be reached by a wagon road following the bottom of the canyon. This road is passable by automobiles to a point within a quarter of a mile of the mine.

The mine workings are in much faulted Middle Cambrian rocks that lie a short distance beneath the Ochre Mountain thrust. The ore bodies on both sides of the gulch occur in thin-bedded limestones, locally dolomitized, but in the tunnel only the Busby quartzite was observed. South and east of the mine workings the contact between the limestone and the quartzite is a fault striking west of north that is a branch of the Spotted Fawn fault, the main branch of which lies about 500 feet west of the tunnel portal. The branch fault, however, cannot explain the presence of quartzite in the tunnel immediately beneath limestone exposed on the surface. To account for these relations (see p. 82) a nearly flat fault must intervene between the two. Such a fault is not readily recognized on the surface. The breccia exposed in the top 10 feet of the raise near the north end of the tunnel probably represents the fault breccia, and the fault must therefore dip gently to the south. Several nearly horizontal fractures that cut the quartzite beds exposed in the tunnel must be subsidiary to the major fault.

The ore is found along fissures striking east of north and dipping 50°–65° W. It consists of rather coarse-grained white quartz with some barite and local concentrations of galena in which are found small amounts of pyrite and other sulphides. Oxidation of the galena to anglesite and cerusite in most places has been rather complete, but unaltered sulphide nodules are not uncommon. The flat fault that must separate the quartzite from the limestone must also limit the ore downward, for no evidence of comparable mineralization was found in the tunnel. It was not ascertained whether the lack of ore in the tunnel was the result of movement along the fault subsequent to mineralization or whether the fault was formed earlier than the ore and the unfavorable character of the quartzite prevented any deposition of ore minerals.

WESTERN UTAH EXTENSION COPPER CO.

The group of 15 patented claims owned by the Western Utah Extension Copper Co. extends to the southeast from the open cut of the Western Utah Copper Co.

The ownership is reported to be the same as that of the Pole Star Copper Co. Superficial exploration has been carried on at several places on the group, but on only one claim, the Helmet, has any considerable amount of underground work been done. In 1917 and 1918 nearly 200 tons of ore was shipped from this claim. It had an average content of 0.026 ounce of gold and 5.4 ounces of silver to the ton and 4.08 per cent of copper. The property appears to have been idle since 1918.

The workings on the Helmet claim consist of a main tunnel and several higher levels, on all of which some stoping has been done. Nearly 1,000 feet of drifting has been done on the tunnel level (fig. 28), and from it two interior shafts have been sunk. The tunnel at an altitude of 5,751 feet is more than 250 feet lower than the summit of the east-west ridge beneath which it is driven.

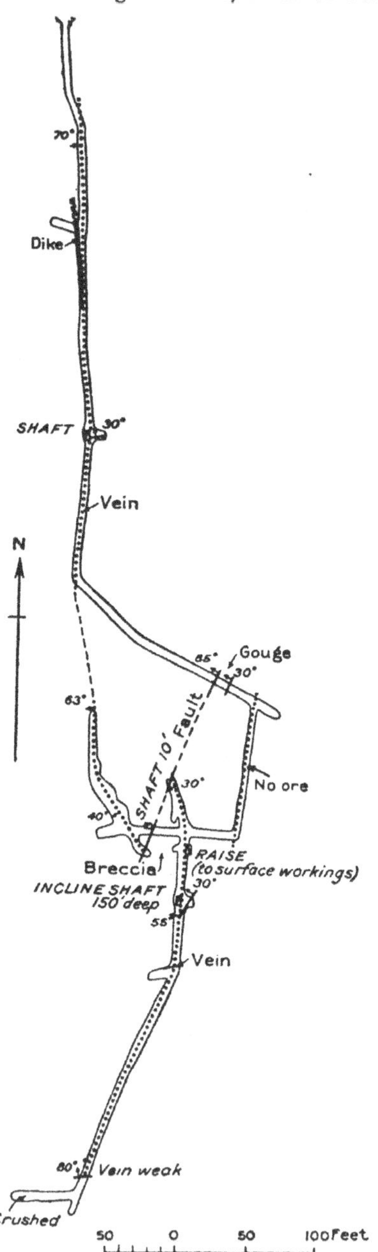

FIGURE 28.—Plan of tunnel level, Western Utah Extension Copper Co.

The claim is near the central part of the quartz monzonite stock, and this rock forms the walls of the ore. Both underground and on the surface a dark greenish-gray altered porphyry is exposed as a dike cutting the quartz monzonite. It is about 4 feet wide and strikes east of north.

The ore is found in a quartz vein that strikes approximately north and has a normal dip of 60°–70° W. The fissure occupied by the vein is clearly a fault fissure, for it cuts and displaces the porphyry. This is clearly shown in the tunnel about 150 feet from the portal, where the dike is present in the hanging wall of the vein but not in the footwall. The exposures of the dike on the surface indicate that the throw along the fissure is normal and amounts to about 50 feet.

The vein and the dike are cut by another fault about 500 feet south of the portal of the tunnel. This fault strikes about N. 20° W., dips to the west, and is marked by considerable brecciation. North of its intersection with the vein a crosscut shows 10 feet of gouge along the fault, the footwall of which dips 30° and the hanging wall about 85°. As the vein approaches the fault its strike swings to northwest and its dip flattens to 30°. The offset due to the fault on the tunnel level amounts to about 40 feet, the portion of the vein in the footwall of the fault being to the north. This implies either that the fault is reverse or that it is a normal fault with a large horizontal component.

The ore is almost completely oxidized from the surface to the tunnel level. It consists of quartz, altered quartz monzonite fragments, and various copper, iron, and arsenic minerals. The thickness of the vein ranges from a few inches to 3 feet, but in some of the thicker portions the ore minerals occupy only part of the vein. In a few places sulphide minerals had been preserved. Those recognized were arsenopyrite, pyrite, and sphalerite. The oxidized ore minerals appear to have been chiefly copper pitch and a deep-brown fine-grained scorodite. In many places, however, there are striking concentrations of blue-green chrysocolla, bright-green clinoclasite, and olive-green olivenite. The sulphide that was the source of these copper minerals was not recognized in the few specimens of unoxidized material that were collected.

At several places on this group of veins prospecting has disclosed veins in which arsenopyrite and scorodite are the most abundant constituents.

CLIMAX

The Climax group of 12 patented claims is in Rodenhouse Wash. The greater part of the work on the group has been done a short distance west of the prominent hill at an altitude of 5,675 feet on the north side of the wash. J. P. Gardner, of Sarasota, Fla., is reported to be the owner. The property has been idle for several years. A partly caved vertical shaft filled with water and the remains of a shaft house are about the only signs of former activity. Custer[66] reports that the shaft was 150 feet deep and that from it 250 feet of drifts and crosscuts had been driven. He further records the shipment of two cars of ore that contained 29 ounces of silver to the ton and 27 percent of lead.

Chloritized and sericitized quartz monzonite forms the wall rock of the ore bodies. East of the vertical shaft this rock is cut by prominent quartz and quartz carbonate veins that strike nearly north and dip at rather low angles to the west. So far as could be told the ore does not extend through or beyond them.

The vertical shaft is sunk on a vein striking N. 82° W. From the scant exposures on the surface and from small amounts of ore on the dump, the vein filling appears to have consisted of quartz, pyrite, arsenopyrite, galena, and sphalerite. The sphalerite appears to have been particularly abundant. These minerals are all cut by veinlets of a brown-weathering siderite.

SOUTHERN CONFEDERATE

The patented Southern Confederate claim, one of the oldest in the district, is on the high ridge southeast of the town of Clifton, the end of the wagon road at an altitude of 6,742 feet marking the present camp site on the claim. It is owned by the Southern Confederate Mining Co., Inc., of Salt Lake City, and in 1926 was under lease to T. E. Wessell. Much of the ore utilized by the old Clifton smelter is reported to have come from this property. Small shipments have been reported for the years 1918, 1919, and 1926. These shipments have averaged about 30 percent of lead and 30 ounces of silver to the ton. Small quantities of zinc, copper, and arsenic are also present.

The ore is found in a shear zone as much as 20 feet in width that strikes about N. 50° E. and dips 75°–80° SE. The wall rock is quartz monzonite altered to a dense greenish rock in which only small quartz grains can be recognized with the hand lens. The microscope shows that the alteration consisted of both sericitization and the introduction of fine-grained quartz and chlorite. In this ore zone lenses of lead ore as much as 2 feet in width and, exceptionally, 50 feet in strike length have been found. A shaft on the vein is said to reach a depth of 150 feet, but less than 50 feet of it is now accessible.

The ore minerals in these lenses consist almost entirely of the oxidized lead minerals anglesite, cerusite, and plumbojarosite, of which the anglesite is by far the most abundant. Unoxidized remnants of fine-grained galena are not uncommon, but no other sulphides were recognized. Limonite pseudomorphs after pyrite are found in many places in the wall rock. Coarsely crystalline quartz is the chief gangue mineral. Small quantities of azurite and malachite are distributed throughout the ore.

[66] Custer, A. E., Deep Creek, Clifton mining district, Utah: Eng. and Min. Jour., vol. 103, p. 920, 1917.

There is abundant evidence of movements along the vein since the ore was deposited. These have formed coarse breccias in the portions of the vein rich in quartz, and gouge walls to the ore shoots were noted in several places.

RED JACKET

The Red Jacket claim is immediately north of the Southern Confederate claim, less than half a mile southeast of Clifton. The owner of the claim is said to be R. W. Young, and in 1926 J. H. Allen and associates were at work under a lease and bond. Like the Southern Confederate, the Red Jacket is reported to have furnished ore to the old Clifton smelter. The only recent production known is that made by the lessees in 1926. The grade of the lead-silver ore shipped is not known.

As on the adjacent claim, the ore is found in a shear zone in altered quartz monzonite. The shear zone is about 4 feet wide, strikes northeast and dips steeply to the southeast. The workings on the vein are on the east side of the ridge line and consist of several tunnels and cuts on the vein. In one of the tunnels a winze was sunk on the vein and, at a depth of about 180 feet, is said to have struck an eastward-dipping fault that terminated the ore. This winze could not be examined at the time of this survey.

The ore is found in lenses in the shear zone and consists of coarse white quartz with galena and a little pyrite, together with oxidation products of the sulphides. Anglesite is the most abundant of these and forms the bulk of the ore. Other lead minerals present include cerusite, plumbojarosite, and, near the surface, rather considerable amounts of green crystalline mimetite. Small orange-colored crystals of wulfenite are also found in the oxidized ore.

COPPER QUEEN MIDLAND MINING CO.

The Copper Queen Midland Mining Co., whose headquarters are at Grantsville, Utah, owns a group of unpatented claims on the southwest side of Montezuma Peak, a short distance east of benchmark 5855, at the head of Overland Canyon. Prospecting has been done on several veins, chiefly by shallow cuts or pits. On one of the veins, however, a tunnel more than 600 feet long has been driven. Small shipments of ore were made from this group of claims in 1916, 1918, and 1919, which averaged 17.4 ounces of silver to the ton, 0.56 percent of copper, and 15.35 percent of lead.

The ore is found within the small triangular outcrop of quartz monzonite that lies to the west of and is connected with the larger intrusive mass on the south side of Montezuma Peak. The quartz monzonite contains both biotite and hornblende, in addition to the feldspars and quartz, and does not differ in any respect from the rock that forms the greater part of the main stock. Both the southern and northwestern borders of this small intrusive area are controlled by older faults and, because of this, three different sedimentary formations are in contact with the igneous rock—the Oquirrh formation on the northwest, the Manning Canyon formation on the east, and the Ochre Mountain limestone on the south.

The ore occurs in veins within the quartz monzonite that strike N. 15°–30° E. and dip 25°–40° W. Several of these veins have been developed, but the most persistent one appears to be that followed by the Midnight tunnel, whose portal is about 3,000 feet east of benchmark 5855. The vein is exposed throughout the length of the tunnel, a distance of 620 feet. The width of the vein ranges from 1 to 5 feet. As in other veins of this sort in the district, a moderate thickness of gouge is usually present on either the hanging wall or footwall, or both. In a few places nearly east-west, steeply dipping faults cut the vein and displace it for distances as great as 5 feet. In many places the quartz monzonite wall rock has been rather completely altered to sericite as much as 5 feet from the vein. Locally, however, the alteration was much less intense, and specimens taken less than a foot away may be essentially unaltered.

In the tunnel much of the ore is unoxidized and is seen to consist of white coarse-grained quartz, in which are fragments of sericitized wall rock, and a variable content of sulphides. Among these, arsenopyrite, pyrite, galena, sphalerite, and chalcopyrite have been recognized. The proportions and total quantity of these sulphides differ in different parts of the vein. Veinlets of a brown-weathering carbonate cut across the quartz and sulphides. Optical tests prove this to contain about 75 percent of the $FeCO_3$ molecule. In the surface workings oxidation of the sulphides has been nearly complete. In some places the oxidation products have migrated into fractures in the wall rocks, giving the appearance of spurs from the vein. Jarosite and plumbojarosite are among the most abundant of these later minerals.

CASH BOY (MAMMOTH)

The Cash Boy group of four claims is on the northeast slope of hill 5696, east of the Success mine. Two of the claims are owned by L. H. Sevy and C. H. Abercrombie, of Gold Hill, and the other two (comprising the old Mammoth claims, owned by J. P. Gardner) are under lease and bond to them. Some ore was being mined at the time of visit in 1926, and it is reported that several shipments had been made in the past. The only one of which there is record was made in 1915 and consisted of 4 tons, which contained 0.02 ounce of gold and 26 ounces of silver to the ton, 0.8 percent of copper, and 13 percent of lead.

Two shallow shafts 2,200 feet apart have been sunk on shear zones in quartz monzonite that contain shoots of lead-silver ore. At the northern shaft an ore shoot strikes N. 80° W. and dips 60° SW. At the southern shaft the strike of the ore is N. 50° W. and the dip 40°–60° S. It is not known if the two shear zones exposed in the shafts are connected, but the strikes recorded are similar to those shown by a continuous porphyry dike that crops out a few hundred feet west of both localities.

The ore shoots in the shear zones have relatively small dimensions and appear to be limited to regions in which abundant quartz has been introduced. At the surface the ore is completely oxidized, but in specimens on the dumps some sulphide minerals were observed. Galena, sphalerite, arsenopyrite, and pyrite were recognized in these specimens. The oxidized minerals include a lead-bearing jarositelike mineral, anglesite, cerusite, and locally considerable amounts of orange-colored wulfenite.

NEW BALTIMORE

The New Baltimore patented claim covers the slopes of hill 5625 in Rodenhouse Wash, about half a mile west of the Climax mine. It is owned by J. P. Gardner, of Sarasota, Fla., but in recent years has been worked in a small way under lease by Swan Moline. Several small shipments have been made since 1923. One of 22 tons in that year contained 0.02 ounce of gold and 53 ounces of silver to the ton and 47 percent of lead and is representative of the other shipments. The developments consist of shallow surface cuts and shafts.

The wall rock is the rather thoroughly altered quartz monzonite that is found over so much of the region drained by Rodenhouse Wash. Chlorite, sericite, calcite, and quartz have largely replaced the original minerals of the igneous rock, although in many places the alteration has preserved textures characteristic of the quartz monzonite, especially outlines of the old feldspar crystals. In one of the tunnels a dark altered porphyry was seen, but it could not be recognized on the surface.

The ore is found as thin lenses in an east-west zone of fissuring that dips almost vertically. The ore shoots in this zone range in thickness from a few inches to a foot or so and are succeeded by lower-grade material within short distances along the strike. Galena, showing relatively little alteration to anglesite, forms the greater part of the vein filling in the ore shoots. Near the surface it is found as rude nuggets coated with powdery calcite. Small amounts of pyrite, arsenopyrite, and quartz are present with the galena and have largely replaced it in the vein beyond the ore shoots. Locally the galena has been more completely oxidized, and in such places the ore consists of anglesite, cerusite, plumbojarosite, mimetite, and descloizite, together with small amounts of copper minerals. The fissure zone, together with the ore shoots, is cut in several places by north-south faults that dip to the west. The throw on all of them is small, but they are accompanied by a considerable amount of gouge. In one place an eastward-dipping fracture intersected the vein, and it is said to have contained some very rich ore.

BIRD

The Bird claim, which is unpatented, is owned by Ollie Young, of Clifton. It adjoins the Southern Confederate on the northeast and encloses the continuation of the fissure on that claim. A small lot of ore from the claim was included in a shipment by Young in 1926 that also contained ore from others of his properties.

The relations of the ore are the same as those in the Southern Confederate. A drift tunnel driven southwestward on the vein showed about 2 feet of ore in 1926.

SHAY

The Shay claims are near Goshute Spring, about a mile east of Montezuma Peak. In 1926 some prospecting was being done on a northeastward-striking vein in altered quartz monzonite that contained stringers of lead ore in a mixture of quartz and altered wall rock. The ore exposed was completely oxidized and was composed chiefly of a mineral resembling plumbojarosite. Numerous small orange-colored crystals of wulfenite were also observed in the ore.

GOLD HILL STANDARD MINING CO.

In 1926 the Gold Hill Standard Mining Co. owned 18 unpatented claims east of the town of Gold Hill. Several exploratory workings were being driven in that year on the Max No. 1 and Max No. 2 claims of the group, to expose a number of short linked veins in quartz monzonite that had a northwest strike and a dip of 30°–60° SW. The vein filling consisted of quartz, altered wall rock, galena and its oxidation products, and oxidized iron and arsenic minerals. The distribution of the several minerals is very erratic. In some places lenses of solid galena a foot wide and several feet long may be found, and in other places galena is entirely absent, and arsenopyrite and scorodite are the only metallic minerals present. Much of the galena has not been oxidized, but locally it has been converted to anglesite, plumbojarosite, and wulfenite. The galena-rich ore is said to contain 2 ounces of silver to each percent of lead.

GOLD BELT

The Gold Belt claim, owned by W. F. Cummings, of Gold Hill, covers the small outcrop of Prospect Mountain quartzite that occurs at bench mark 4293, on the edge of the Great Salt Lake Desert. The bedding at this locality strikes N. 30° E. and dips 30° SE. The ore has replaced a breccia zone striking N. 60° E. and dipping 50° SE. It consists of white coarsely crystalline quartz with local splotches of galena and minor amounts of other sulphides. It is only partly oxidized.

PAY ROCK

The Pay Rock group of three claims is on the south side of Spotted Fawn Canyon, a short distance west of its entrance. In 1926 it was owned by L. H. Sevy and C. H. Abercrombie, of Gold Hill. In that year work was being done on the ridge line a short distance west of summit 5729. Here a thin streak of cerusite and plumbojarosite was found along a brecciated bedding plane in the Prospect Mountain quartzite. Its width ranged from a fraction of an inch to several inches.

UNDINE

The Undine group of four unpatented claims and a fraction is half a mile southeast of the U.S. mine and half a mile north of the Lucy L. It is owned by W. M. Lamb, of Gold Hill. There are several relatively shallow workings on the claims that are grouped in two areas—north and northwest of hill 6081 and north and east of hill 5882. Three or four shipments of ore have been made from the group, but at the time of visit only assessment work was being done.

The rocks exposed on the claims are metamorphosed sandstones and limestones of the Oquirrh formation and quartz monzonite. The sedimentary rocks are found in relatively small and very irregular patches capping the higher summits. The igneous rock surrounds them and crops out in all the valley bottoms. These relations indicate that in this region the present surface approximates the original upper contact of the quartz monzonite. The sedimentary rocks are for the most part poorly exposed, but many of the limestone beds have clearly been replaced by silicate minerals. Garnet, wollastonite, amphibole, and a green muscovite were recognized in the field, and a careful study would doubtless show many others. Chlorite and sericite are abundant in places in the quartz monzonite. Weathering has been more intensive here than in many other places, and this in part accounts for the poor exposures. A large part of the outcrops of the sedimentary rocks and the nearby igneous rocks have been converted to a white powdery calcite that on casual inspection appears to be a clay mineral. Locally this is veined by dense reddish opal.

The most extensively explored ore body is that about 700 feet northeast of hill 6081. This is in a small patch of sediments at their contact with the quartz monzonite. The ore body is a nearly flat tabular mass and appears to be a bedded replacement deposit extending outward on both sides of a nearly vertical north-south fissure. Copper minerals, for the most part copper pitch and chrysocolla, are concentrated along the fissure, but away from it the limestone bed appears to have been replaced chiefly by magnetite, which is now partly oxidized to "limonite" and nontronite. A hand sample of the magnetite is reported by Mr. Lamb to have assayed 0.96 ounce of gold to the ton, and he believes that most of the gold in the two shipments made from this deposit was also contained in magnetite. One shipment, said to be a carload, he reports to have carried $8 a ton in gold and 7½ percent of copper and the other, of 12 tons, $9 a ton in gold and 8 percent of copper.

A different type of deposit is found to the southeast near the blacksmith shop, about 250 feet north of hill 6081. This is a thin quartz vein in quartz monzonite. It strikes N. 5° W. and is nearly vertical. The width varies, but the maximum observed was 14 inches. The vein appears to be moderately persistent along both strike and dip, as it has been followed to a depth of about 50 feet by two vertical shafts 50 feet apart, which did not reach its end. The vein filling consists of rather coarsely crystalline white quartz containing sporadic bodies of a black sulphide, which M. N. Short, of the Geological Survey, determined to be an arsenical tetrahedrite. Less common are patches of galena. The tetrahedrite is for the most part altered to green and blue oxidation products. Mr. Lamb states that a shipment of 3 tons returned $300 a ton, largely in silver, at a time when that metal was selling at $1 an ounce. Specimens of the sulphide alone were said by him to run as high as 409 ounces of silver to the ton.

Northwest of these deposits two veins have been prospected east of hill 5882. Both are in quartz monzonite just below the contact with the sediments. The more northerly vein strikes N. 15° W. and dips 55° W. It consists of sheared quartz monzonite impregnated with oxidized copper minerals, chiefly copper pitch and chrysocolla. Remnants of chalcopyrite may be seen in the copper pitch. The quartz monzonite in the hanging wall of the vein is iron-stained and streaked with white powdery calcite. A shipment thought to have been made from this prospect in 1918 yielded 0.03 ounce of gold and 5.8 ounces of silver to the ton, 3.05 percent of copper, and 1.02 percent of lead. The second vein, about 100 feet to the south, strikes N. 60° W. and dips about 70° SW. As exposed it is 2 to 3 feet in width and is filled by arsenopyrite, almost completely altered to green scorodite with a relatively small content of quartz. No other metallic minerals were observed.

The prospects north of hill 5882 lie along a jasperoid vein that follows a thin highly altered dike that cuts the sedimentary rocks. This vein is reported to carry about $1 a ton in gold.

REA

The workings on the Rea claim are on the floor of Accident Canyon just below the cabin at an altitude of 6,051 feet. In 1927 the claim was staked by Messrs. Parker & Hager, of Gold Hill, but at one time it was owned by the Brewer Gold & Copper Mining Co.

The small amount of development work is reported to have been done about 1900. No shipments are known to have been made from this claim.

The ore occurs along a fault between the Madison limestone and the Woodman formation. At the bottom of the canyon the fault strikes N. 55° E. and dips almost vertically, but a short distance up the side of the canyon where the Woodman formation is on both sides of the fault, the dip is much lower. (See pl. 7, *C*.) The ore consists of veinlets and irregular masses of quartz and coarsely crystalline calcite, which have replaced the wall rocks and with which is associated silver-bearing tetrahedrite. Material rich in this sulphide is said to have assayed 150 ounces of silver to the ton. Most of the ore now exposed is rather completely oxidized, malachite and azurite being the two most abundant secondary minerals.

CHRISTMAS MINING CO.

The Christmas group of 12 patented claims is near the eastern border of the quadrangle a little over 2 miles east-northeast of the Western Utah mine. So far as known, the company, whose headquarters is at Salt Lake City, has made only one shipment of ore, a lot of 11 tons produced in 1917 containing an average of 0.08 ounce of gold and 18.8 ounces of silver to the ton, 0.5 percent of copper, and 4.4 percent of lead.

The claims cover a series of outcrops of the Oquirrh formation that are irregularly embayed by quartz monzonite. To the north the exposures of the Oquirrh formation are terminated by the eastward extension of the Pool Canyon transverse fault, north of which is the Prospect Mountain quartzite. Much of the surface in the vicinity is covered by the gravel slopes that extend down to the Great Salt Lake Desert. The Oquirrh formation in this region consists of metamorphosed limestone and dolomite with some interbedded quartzite, which have been assigned to the central facies of the formation.

Several prospect pits have been sunk in the western part of the group on quartz stringers that follow shear zones. The quartz contains local concentrations of galena and tetrahedrite, and these two minerals are also found embedded in the wall rocks. Considerable quantities of barite are also present in the walls of some of the veins.

The main workings seem to have been about half a mile farther east, where a vertical shaft about 100 feet deep has been sunk in a small outcrop of the Oquirrh formation that is entirely surrounded by gravel. The shaft was sunk on a narrow quartz vein, in which galena and tetrahedrite are locally abundant. At the surface the ore appears to have been considerably oxidized.

VEINS WITH CARBONATE OR SULPHATE MINERALS IN THE GANGUE

TROY

The old Troy claim is on the east side of Rodenhouse Wash, about 2,000 feet south-southwest of the Climax mine. In 1926 it had been restaked by Perry Erickson and Amy Hicks under the name of Sam K. No. 1. The claim is underlain by quartz monzonite and covers the western part of a zone of quartz and quartz carbonate veins which are thought to mark a belt of reverse faulting in the quartz monzonite. (See pp. 89–90.)

One of these veins striking N. 75° W. and dipping 40° N., composed almost entirely of quartz in which are numerous fragments of altered quartz monzonite, has been rather extensively explored on the surface, as a result of the supposed discovery some years ago of a pocket of rich gold ore. Doubt as to the actual presence of gold in the vein was expressed by some of the older prospectors in the district, as the time of discovery coincided with a period in which "high-grading" was prevalent at the Cane Springs and Alvarado mines. No other occurrences of gold ore are known from either this vein or other similar veins. Small specks of a mineral thought to be chalcopyrite were observed in a few specimens of the ore.

IMMENSE

The Immense claim, owned by P. H. Robinson, encloses a large mass of jasperoid projecting into the quartz monzonite about 2,000 feet southwest of Minnehaha Spring. The jasperoid mass strikes nearly north and dips about 50° E. It appears to have been formed by a replacement of a projecting arm of the Oquirrh formation into the intrusive. No information was obtained regarding the presence of any valuable minerals in the jasperoid.

ARSENIC REPLACEMENT BODIES

GOLD HILL MINE OF WESTERN UTAH COPPER CO.

Location, history, and development.—The Gold Hill mine of the Western Utah Copper Co., sometimes called the Western Utah mine, has produced a large part of the copper, lead, and arsenic ore credited to the Clifton district. It comprises a group of nine claims and fractions, more or less overlapping, that cover the northwest slope of Gold Hill, about 1¼ miles east of the post office. Two of the claims were among the first staked in the district and appear to have made a small production of gold ore and oxidized silver-lead ore. It is said that some placer mining was done on the hill slope also. The activity at the Alvarado and Cane Springs mines in the early nineties resulted in renewed activity on these claims, and some gold ore from them was treated at the Cane Springs mill. Then followed a period of inactivity until 1906, when title to the group of claims was taken over by the Western Utah Copper Co., of which Duncan McVichie, of Salt Lake City, was the guiding spirit.

In the succeeding 10 years a considerable body of copper ore was developed above the 150-foot level and smaller bodies of lead-silver ore on a lower level. No ore was shipped in these years, however. Production began early in 1917, shortly after the completion of the Deep Creek Railroad, the construction of which was largely effected by those interested in this mining company.

Shortly thereafter control of the company passed to Frank G. Rowley, of Providence, R.I. After the first year lead surpassed copper in value in the ore shipped. The discovery that the ore contained a large percentage of arsenic resulted in the continued operation of the mine in the face of a decreasing content of silver, copper, and lead, and a considerable tonnage of arsenic ore was shipped from 1923 to 1925. Much of this ore was shipped at a flat rate per ton, without regard for its metal content other than arsenic. The drop in the price of arsenic early in 1925 resulted in the virtual shutdown of the mine and after a short period during which lead ore was shipped company work ceased and the production of the mine has since been confined to small shipments by lessees.

Production from Western Utah mine, 1917–29

[Figures furnished by C. N. Gerry, U.S. Bur. Mines]

	Ore (tons)	Gold (ounces)	Silver (ounces)	Copper (pounds)	Lead (pounds)
1917	32, 023	421. 00	150, 767	1, 715, 189	371, 418
1918	15, 893	233. 99	86, 716	420, 610	1, 062, 432
1919	13, 787	197. 33	49, 825	181, 786	652, 980
1920	39, 297	64. 70	83, 581	81, 928	958, 189
1921	11, 557	150. 24	22, 479	3, 172	329, 866
1922	74	1. 00	819	616	4, 178
1923	13, 049	7. 00	38, 487	28, 363	254, 854
1924	32, 780	82. 50	145, 034	3, 144	1, 753, 698
1925	12, 802	131. 60	107, 480	48, 101	1, 659, 613
1926	122	. 90	891	1, 681	22, 506
1927	76	1. 30	345	1, 033	5, 121
1928	145	. 72	792	480	42, 117
1929	[a] 33	1. 16	--------	2, 033	--------

[a] Dump ore.

The amount of arsenic recovered from the ores is not definitely known, but it appears to have been between 7,000 and 8,000 tons of metallic arsenic.

Two shafts, one vertical and one inclined, provide access to the deeper workings, on which the greater part of the mining was being done during the time of examination. Both of these have been sunk from the adit or 300-foot level, whose portal is at an altitude of 5,579 feet. The vertical shaft is near the portal and is 400 feet deep. From the bottom of it the 700-foot level has been driven. (See pl. 15.) This level is also cut by the inclined shaft, which is 700 feet farther south. From the inclined shaft the 400, 600, and 760 foot levels have also been driven. From the 760-foot level a winze about 150 feet deep has been sunk and a short drift, known as the 900-foot level, turned from it. Above the 300-foot level are several tunnels, designated on the mine maps as the 80-foot level, 150-foot level, etc. Only one of these, the 150-foot level, is at present extensive. The remainder have been largely destroyed by the caving operations in the glory hole that now marks the original outcrop.

Geology.—The geology in the vicinity of the mine is epitomized by plate 14, which is in brief a series of interconnected plans and longitudinal and cro sections.

The oldest of the formations shown in this diagra and also the most important economically is the Och Mountain limestone, which in most places forms th walls of the ore bodies. On the surface, north of th 300-foot level portal, the limestone is thick-bedde white, and recrystallized. South of the tunnel port and in most of the exposures underground much of th limestone has been either altered to silicate minera or partly replaced during the oxidation of the o minerals. White bladed wollastonite is the mo common of the silicate minerals, but a greenish-brow garnet is also widely distributed. In some plac diopside and zoisite are locally abundant. In man places, however, crystalline limestone may be foun in close proximity to the ores, and such specimens this as were tested proved to be remarkably free fro impurities. The limestone beds have a rather consta northwest strike. Near the surface they dip steepl to the east or even vertically, but on the lower leve of the mine the dip is 45° or less, because of the ap proach to a synclinal axis to the east. (See p. 77.

The next younger formation near the mine is th Manning Canyon formation, which occupies th eastern slope of the ridge beneath which lie the min workings. It is made up of dark quartzite and blac shale and is not exposed underground.

Between the Manning Canyon formation and the Ochre Mountain limestone there is a wide belt of jasperoid that has been called in previous reports quartzite or silicified limestone. It is reddish brown on weathered surfaces and forms the prominent jagged outcrops that make up the ridge line. Much of the rock has the appearance of a breccia, owing to the presence of several generations of quartz, each of which has a slightly different texture and color. Vugs lined with crystalline quartz are common, and in several places green chalcedony and plates of barite are present. In a few places fragments of limestone were found embedded in it. Thin sections show that the rock has a typical jasperoid texture, and this, together with the megascopic evidence, leaves little doubt that the rock is the result of replacement by silica along the limestone-shale contact. Butler [67] suggested that the contact was a fault, and the evidence indicating that it is one is mentioned on page 77. The thickness of the jasperoid is not exactly known. As shown on plate 14, it appears to be in excess of 100 feet, but this figure may be too large by reason of the difficulty in determining the exact location of the debris-covered contact with the Manning Canyon formation.

Underground the continuation of the surface exposure of the jasperoid is seen on the 300- and 700-foot

[67] Butler, B. S., The ore deposits of Utah: U.S. Geol. Survey Prof. Paper 111, p. 481, 1920.

levels. On both levels the rock was cut by the easterly crosscuts from the vertical shaft. On the 300-foot level only a small amount of the jasperoid was penetrated by the crosscut before a drift into the footwall limestones was started. On the 700-foot level, however, the contact of the jasperoid with the limestone was followed for several hundred feet. Here the contact is extremely sharp. The strike is N. 35°–55° W. and the dip 35°–45° E. The dip of the jasperoid, like that of the limestone beds, must decrease downward, for the average dip obtained by connecting the exposures on the 300-foot and 700-foot levels is 60° E., and at the surface the dip is even steeper.

Smaller masses of jasperoid are also found both on the surface and underground. On the surface a short spur from the main mass extends northwesterly from the mineral monument on peak 5901. On the 300-foot level similar material containing abundant residual calcite is found in the easterly crosscut north of the main ore body. This is directly beneath the spur on the surface and may be a continuation of it. Also on the 300-foot level typical jasperoid containing barite and some oxidized copper minerals has been developed at the contact between quartz monzonite and limestone near the end of the long combined drift and crosscut west of the ore body. Similar relations were observed on the 600-foot level. There appears to be a close relation between this contact jasperoid and the quartz-tetrahedrite veins in the limestone nearby. In these two places part of the jasperoid appears to have replaced quartz monzonite, rather than limestone.

Quartz monzonite occupies the largest area in the vicinity of the mine. It shows no unusual features here. Underground much of the rock is seen to be altered, rarely to jasperoid as noted above, or widely to a quartz-sericite-calcite aggregate, in which the outlines of the old crystals, particularly the feldspars, are commonly preserved.

The quartz monzonite is a part of the main Gold Hill stock and almost completely surrounds the block of sedimentary rocks in which the mine is located. North of the open cut it has a rather regular contact with the Ochre Mountain limestone, which strikes more northwesterly than the jasperoid, with the result that the width of the limestone outcrop increases to the north. South of the open cut, however, the igneous rock cuts off the limestone and at the surface is in contact with the jasperoid. The termination of the limestone is not the result of the convergence in strike of the jasperoid and the limestone and quartz monzonite contact but is rather accomplished by the penetration of the limestone by three blunt wedge-shaped dikes of the igneous rock.

The most westerly of these dikes is the widest at the surface and appears to widen rapidly downward. The dip of its eastern or hanging-wall side, however, is greater than the average dip of the jasperoid, so that limestone is exposed on the bottom levels of the mine directly beneath places on the surface where the intrusive is in contact with jasperoid. This same conclusion may be reached from the fact that limestone is found in the long Ida Lull tunnel, to the south.

The middle dike is about 30 feet wide at the surface and ends northward somewhere within the open cut. Near the surface it dips steeply to the east, but between the 300- and 400-foot levels it is nearly vertical, and below the 400-foot level it must reverse its dip and join the larger mass to the west.

The third dike is narrower than the other two. It ends bluntly on the northeast side of the open cut. A dike of similar width and position was recognized on the 300-foot level but was not traced confidently below it. On the 700-foot level a narrow dike that may be its continuation was found, but the gap between them was too great to warrant their connection on plate 14. If the two are actually the same, the dip must steepen to nearly vertical in the intervening distance.

The contact of the quartz monzonite with the east side of the sedimentary block is a westward-dipping fault. These relations are similar to those at the U.S. mine, but here the dip of the fault is so steep that there is no danger of its terminating the ore zone downward.

Another locality in which quartz monzonite is apparently exposed is in the south end of the 700-foot level in the hanging wall of the ore body, where a somewhat iron-stained rock of granitic appearance is found. A thin section of this rock showed that it was chiefly composed of a pale-green pleochroic amphibole and colorless humite, together with minor amounts of pleochroic apatite, titanite, iron oxides, and quartz. The rock is thus obviously a product of metamorphism, and it is not at all clear from the meager exposures whether or not it was originally a sedimentary or an igneous rock. Similar mineral assemblages have been found in other places in both sedimentary and igneous rocks.

A dike of quartz monzonite porphyry is exposed both on the surface and on the 150- and 300-foot levels. Megascopically, the rock is dull greenish gray or light green and at the surface is dotted with brown limonite pseudomorphs after pyrite. Rectangular phenocrysts of dull feldspar as much as a quarter of an inch long are abundant but in most places are not conspicuous because of the prevailing light color of the rock. Smaller, irregular phenocrysts of quartz and a few glistening areas of white mica can also be recognized. Under the microscope the rock is found to be considerably altered. The feldspar phenocrysts have been entirely replaced by calcite and sericite; the mica, which was originally biotite, has gone over to sericite and chlorite and is locally crowded with sagenite (rutile) needles that have the characteristic stellate arrangement; and the quartz phenocrysts show a slight veining by sericite. The groundmass is a finely crystalline aggregate of calcite, sericite, and quartz.

In the vicinity of the mine the dike in places is near the contact between the sedimentary rocks and the intrusive, and the exposures are in general rather poor. For these reasons, and possibly also because of the local enlargement of orthoclase crystals in the quartz monzonite itself, some of the previous observers have considered the dike to be a porphyritic marginal facies of the main intrusive. That it is a separate intrusion, however, is shown by the distinctive texture, linear trend, and independence of the sedimentary contact except near the mine. As the dike is followed to the south, it is found to be enclosed within the main intrusion, and three-quarters of a mile south of the open cut apophyses from the dike extend into the walls of quartz monzonite.

Near the mine the dike strikes nearly north and dips 45° or less to the west. Unlike the quartz monzonite, it is not susceptible to silicification and therefore appears to cut through the jasperoid without alteration (see pl. 14), although the jasperoid was undoubtedly formed at a later time.

Another dike was found at the south end of the 400-foot level, but it was not recognized elsewhere in the mine and is not shown on plate 14. It is a fine-grained pale-gray rock in which are scattered rectangular crystals of calcite 1 millimeter long and a few of quartz. A thin section showed that the matrix consisted of fine-grained quartz and feldspar partly replaced by calcite and sericite. The calcite crystals probably represent former feldspar phenocrysts. The rock is too much altered to permit determination of its original composition.

Ore bodies.—Three kinds of ore bodies are present in the mine—veins with silicate gangue, quartz-tetrahedrite veins, and large replacement deposits valuable chiefly for their arsenic content.

Veins with silicate gangue: In the central of the three limestone wedges extending southward from the open cut there are several prospect holes on an altered limestone bed paralleling the eastern contact. The ore is similar to that at the Alvarado and Cane Springs mines, consisting chiefly of silicate minerals, especially wollastonite, that have replaced the limestone, together with small amounts of oxidized copper minerals and native gold. It is reported that the earliest work in the district was done on this deposit. So far as known it was last worked in 1892–95, when some ore was milled at the then active Cane Springs mill. No information is available as to the grade of ore mined, but the amount must have been comparatively small.

Quartz-tetrahedrite veins: On the 150- and 300-foot levels a quartz vein containing copper minerals is found in the limestone immediately west of the arsenic ore bodies and a few feet east of the quartz monzonite contact. Both exposures strike a little east of north and dip to the east. If the two are the same, as seems probable, the vein must cut across the quartz monzonite porphyry dike, as shown in plate 14. A similar quartz vein at the surface near the west wall of the open cut is probably the upward extension of the exposures underground. The vein ranges in thickness from a foot or less to about 30 feet on the 300-foot level, but the average thickness and the one most commonly found is about 5 feet. On the 300-foot level the vein appears to terminate southward and its place to be taken by a zone of jasperoid in which copper minerals are disseminated. The contact between the two, however, is not exposed by the mine workings. Several small faults cross the vein on both levels and and offset it as much as 10 feet. The vein filling consists of coarsely crystalline white glassy quartz in which are numerous inclusions of altered wall rock. Disseminated through the quartz are specks and small blebs of pyrite and an arsenical tetrahedrite. The tetrahedrite in many places has been altered to a black sooty chalcocite, and films of chrysocolla, malachite, and azurite are found throughout the quartz. The quartz vein itself does not appear to have been mined at any place, but, to judge from the character of the two lower arsenic ore bodies, the higher copper content of the upper one (now represented by the open cut) must have been largely the result of oxidation and transportation of copper minerals originally present in this quartz-tetrahedrite vein.

Arsenic replacement ore bodies: Three distinct arsenic-rich ore bodies have been developed in the mine. The first of these to be explored extended from the surface to the 150-foot level, being terminated downward by the dike of quartz monzonite porphyry. The middle deposit was found beneath the dike on the 150-foot level and was followed downward to a few feet below the 400-foot level, where it appears to have been ended by the reversal in dip of the middle of the three wedges of quartz monzonite. The third ore body was found about 50 feet above the 600-foot level, below the quartz monzonite, and has been followed to the lowest workings.

The outlines of the upper ore body are roughly those of the open cut although, as shown on plate 14, there is a triangular cropping of gossan extending northward beyond the pit. At the surface the pit has a length of 300 feet and a width of nearly 200 feet, and these dimensions are probably only slightly greater than the ore-bearing zone.

The middle ore body on the 300-foot level is nearly circular, with a diameter of nearly 100 feet. On the 150-foot level the shape is similar but the dimensions are somewhat larger. On the 400-foot level, however, the circular form has changed to a tabular one, with a length of about 150 feet and a width of 10 to 30 feet.

The lower ore body on the 600-, 700-, and 760-foot levels has a pear-shaped section with the bulbous end to the south. The maximum length of this lower ore body is somewhat over 200 feet, and the maximum width in the enlarged southern portion is nearly 100 feet. On the 760-foot level there are two northerly prongs to the wider south end of the ore body, rather than a single one, as on the 600- and 700-foot levels. On this level, too, several faults displace the boundaries not more than 5 feet. A similar split in the ore body and minor faults are also indicated by the meager exposures on the 900-foot level. The apparent localization of these two phenomena on the two lower levels is probably due to the fact that the ore bodies on the higher levels are thoroughly oxidized, and during the process of oxidation sufficient quantities of material have migrated through the original walls to mask the former position effectually.

The location of the ore shoots is controlled by several factors. All the ore bodies when traced northward are found to be in beds of crystalline Ochre Mountain limestone. The easy replaceability of this rock makes it the most important single cause of ore localization. Obviously, anything that limits the limestone must also be considered as a factor. The quartz monzonite porphyry dike and the wedge of quartz monzonite that cut the limestone have clearly been unfavorable for ore deposition, as is shown by their lack of strong mineralization adjacent to the ore bodies. In a similar way the alteration of the limestone to lime-silicate rock has been a negative factor in ore deposition, for this rock also must have been essentially immune to attack by the ore-forming solutions. On the 760-foot level, for example, lime-silicate rock occupies the space between the two northern prongs of the ore body. It also forms the walls of the ore in several places on higher levels.

Two more direct factors in localizing the ore are suggested by the present exposures in the mine, but neither could be definitely proved because of the extensive surficial alteration. One is fissuring within and essentially parallel to a favorable limestone bed. This is illustrated on the 760-foot level by the occurrence of a pronounced sheeted zone that forms the footwall of the ore body and separates it from crystalline limestone. Unless a preliminary fracturing of the limestone were favorable or even necessary for ore deposition, there would appear to be no reason for the sharp contact observed between the barren, unfractured limestone and the ore. The other factor is largely hypothetical. Plate 14 shows that the ore bodies individually and as a group pitch to the southeast, and that on several levels, particularly the lower ones, the south ends of the ore shoots are blunt and much wider than the north ends. These features suggest that there is some sort of a controlling or limiting fracture at the south ends of the ore bodies that strikes about at right angles to the ore and dips to the south. A fracture of this description appears to limit the ore southward on the 760-foot level but could not be recognized on the higher levels, where the ore is so thoroughly oxidized. Billingsley has reported that the upper ore body, now inaccessible, was controlled by a northeasterly fracture that dips to the northwest.[68] This fracture obviously has not affected the two lower ore shoots, and this may mean that there is more than one cross fracture that controls the ore.

The three kinds of ore that have been mined from the large ore bodies—copper, lead-silver, and arsenic—have all been almost completely oxidized. Remnants of sulphides were found in several places on the 700-foot level, but the 760-foot level was the only one on which the relations of the sulphides to one another could be adequately studied. The west prong of the ore shoot on this level is composed almost entirely of arsenopyrite, and the east prong is made up of a mixture of sulphides in which pyrite greatly predominates and arsenopyrite is extremely rare. Farther south, partial oxidation masks the relations between the two types of ore, but there seems to be a gradual intermixture.

The arsenopyrite in the western prong has locally a radiating habit, but the great part of it is apparently massive and without crystal habit, a feature that polished sections show to be the result of a thorough brecciation on a small scale. Much of this ore contains little except the arsenopyrite. Near the hanging wall of the prong, however, euhedral crystals of arsenopyrite occur in a gangue of coarsely crystalline calcite; and near the south end of the ore body there is abundant fine-grained quartz, which has replaced both the calcite and arsenopyrite. The attack on the sulphide was most intense in the central portions of the crystals, and in many places the arsenopyrite remaining is simply a thin shell around a core of quartz.

In the eastern prong arsenopyrite is either absent or is found only as widely scattered crystals. Pyrite is by far the most abundant sulphide in this portion of the ore body. It is veined by varying but usually small amounts of pyrrhotite, sphalerite, chalcopyrite, and galena. Pyrrhotite is especially abundant in the ore on the 900-foot level. Calcite and quartz are sparse gangue minerals. At the south end of the ore body, where this assemblage of sulphides joins with the arsenopyrite ore, the arsenopyrite has been veined and replaced by them.

The oxidized arsenic ore above the 760-foot level consists chiefly of the hydrated ferric arsenate, scorodite, and iron oxides. Its appearance varies greatly from place to place, depending on the amount of iron oxides present and the presence or absence of crystallinity in the scorodite. If iron oxides are absent from the ore, the color may be either white or green. The white material is shown by the microscope to be amorphous or cryptocrystalline matter in which collo-

[68] Billingsley, Paul, Notes on Gold Hill and vicinity, Tooele County, Utah: Econ. Geology, vol. 13, p. 269, 1918.

form textures are well developed. This material grades rather sharply into fine-grained crystalline green scorodite. Increase in the size of the scorodite crystals does not appear to affect the color greatly. A brown color is characteristic of most of the ore and is caused by the presence of small flakes of iron oxide. There appear to be all gradations of mixtures between pure scorodite and pure iron oxide (goethite?). Although these two minerals are largely confined to the space once cocupied by sulphides, in many places the lime-silicate wall rock has been veined and impregnated by them.

In addition to these two minerals, arseniosiderite and jarosite were recognized in several specimens, and pharmacosiderite is reported to be locally present. The green copper arsenate, conichalcite, was found in the stopes above the 400- and 600-foot levels, and W. F. Foshag has identified the similar minerals, olivenite and clinoclasite. The zinc arsenate adamite was found in hairlike crystals in the open cut. Halloysite and another clay mineral of similar appearance but anisotropic occur throughout the ore, and manganese, probably entirely in the form of wad, is in many places associated with them.

The copper ore was found almost entirely in the upper ore body and has now been completely stoped. From the descriptions of Butler[69] and Billingsley[70] the ore probably consisted of copper arsenates and carbonates in a gangue of iron oxides and scorodite. The copper content of the ore was close to 3 percent.[71] The writer considers it probable that the bulk of this copper was derived from the quartz-tetrahedrite vein that is now exposed on the west side of the open cut. The reasons for this view are, first, that no similar concentrations of copper were found in either of the two lower ore bodies, although they are otherwise similar mineralogically, and second, that the quartz-tetrahedrite vein was not recognized below the 300-foot level.

Lead-silver ore has been found in a number of places from the surface down to the 760-foot level, as small lenses within the arsenic ore. There appears to be a strong tendency for such lenses to be situated either at the south ends of the ore shoots or near the hanging wall. A fine-grained powdery yellow-brown or greenish-brown material that appears to be made up of varying proportions of plumbojarosite and beudantite is the principal source of lead. Smaller quantities of mimetite, anglesite, and cerusite have also been found in the gangue of scorodite and iron oxides.

A rather unusual assemblage of minerals was found at the south end of the 760-foot level and also at the bottom of the two south winzes from the 700-foot level. At both of these places the bottom of the zone of surficial alteration is exhibited. In addition to minerals found both in the unaltered sulphide ore and in the completely oxidized ore, marcasite, chalcocite, supergene arsenopyrite in tiny crystals upon iron oxides, native sulphur, and abundant gypsum were recognized. Siderite appears to be rather widely developed at this horizon, not only at the two points cited but also north of the ore body on the 760-foot level. It closely resembles the smithsonite found in other western mining districts, but qualitative tests showed that it contained only a trace of zinc. Mr. Tiffany, who was in 1925 superintendent of the mine, informed the writer that small quantities of native copper, orpiment, and realgar had also been found at this level.

[69] Butler, B. S., The ore deposits of Utah: U.S. Geol. Survey Prof. Paper 111, p. 481, 1920.

[70] Billingsley, Paul, Notes on Gold Hill and vicinity, Tooele County, Utah: Econ. Geology, vol. 13, p. 266, 1918.

[71] Butler, B. S., op. cit., p. 481.

GOLD HILL MINE OF UNITED STATES SMELTING, REFINING & MINING CO.

Location and development.—The mine of the United States Smelting, Refining & Mining Co. is called by the company the Gold Hill mine but in the district is always spoken of as the U.S. mine to distinguish it from the Gold Hill mine of the Western Utah Copper Co. It is about 3,500 feet south of Gold Hill post office, east of the Lincoln Highway. The original claim, the Last Dollar, was developed by J. J. Gerster and in 1923 yielded a small shipment of copper ore.[72] In that year, however, a vertical shaft was sunk on the claim and passed through 42 feet of scorodite ore that contained from 2 to 15 percent of arsenic. The Grasselli Chemical Co. obtained an option on the claim, but a continuation of the shaft disclosed 30 feet of massive arsenopyrite, below which was found a mixture of arsenopyrite, galena, pyrite, and sphalerite in a quartz gangue.[72] The United States Smelting, Refining & Mining Co. about this time took over the option from the Grasselli Chemical Co. and continued the development work on the Last Dollar and adjacent claims. In 1924 this company mined about 10,000 tons of ore. Some of it averaged 38 percent of arsenic in carload lots, but the general average was 25.8 percent of arsenic, 30 percent of insoluble matter, 20 percent of iron, 12 percent of sulphur, 0.5 percent of lime, 0.4 percent of zinc, 0.02 percent of copper, and 0.86 percent of lead. Gold amounted to 0.03 ounce and silver 1.6 ounces to the ton. In addition several carloads were shipped that contained 10 to 16 ounces of silver to the ton and 6 to 13 percent of lead. These lots averaged 7 percent of arsenic.[73] In 1925 arsenic ore of similar composition was shipped during January and February, but the drop in the price of arsenic prevented any further shipments. In that year, in addition, a carload of lead ore was shipped that contained 10.8 percent of lead; and in 1926 lessees shipped 10 cars of similar ore reported to have averaged about 12 percent of lead and 15 ounces of silver to the ton.

[72] Heikes, V. C., U.S. Geol. Survey Mineral Resources, 1923, pt. 1, p. 167, 1927.

[73] Heikes, V. C., U.S. Bur. Mines Mineral Resources, 1924, pt. 1, p. 41, 1925.

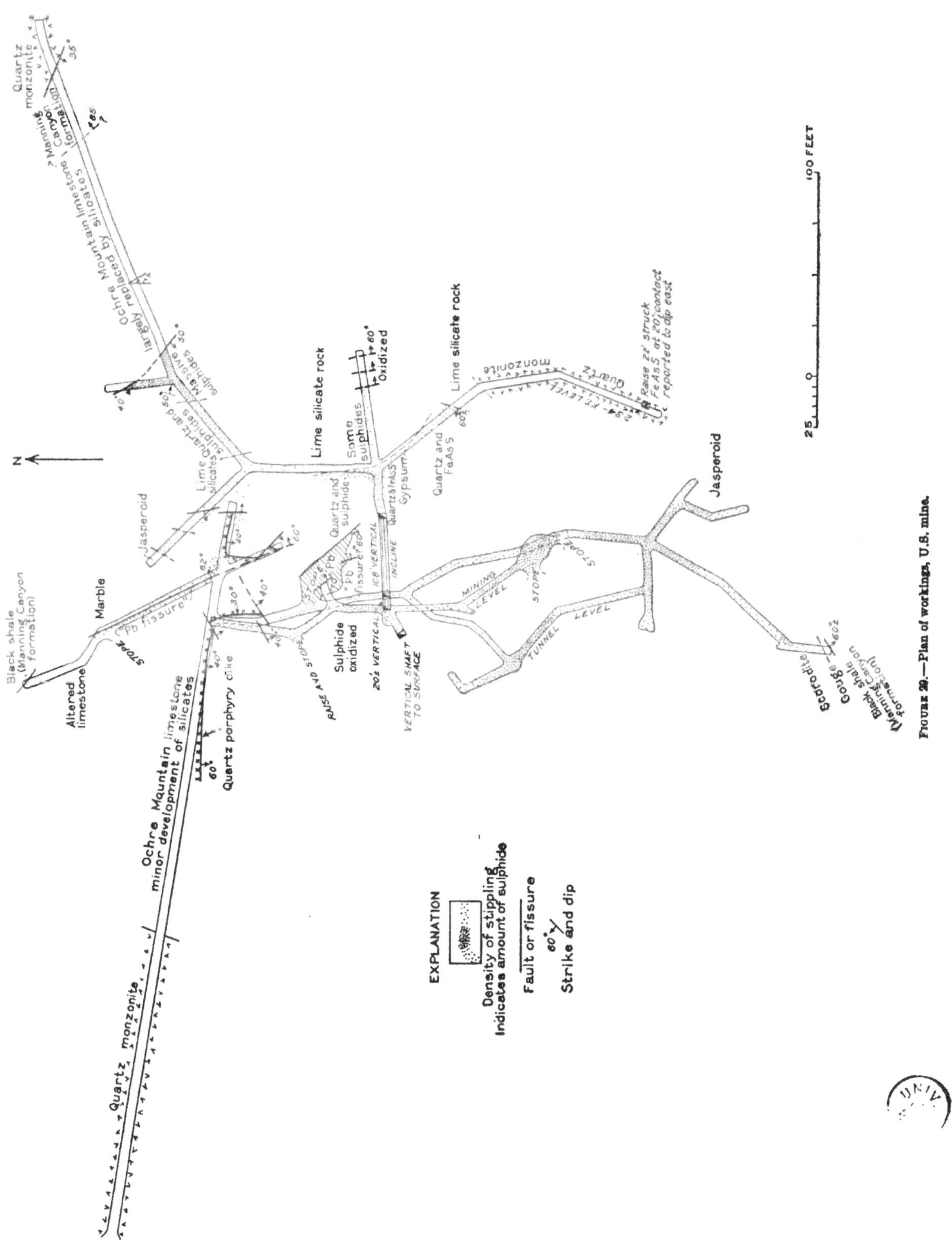

FIGURE 29.—Plan of workings, U.S. mine.

The principal workings at the mine (fig. 29) include a crosscut tunnel to the ore body, which is the chief means of access. This adit connects with about 800 feet of drifts and crosscuts that constitute the tunnel level. About 20 feet above this level is another series of workings known as the working level, but a larger part of it is no longer accessible owing to stoping. In the vertical shaft that extends from this level to the surface the original discovery was made. An inclined shaft extends downward from the working level and ends at the 234-foot level, on which nearly 700 feet of work had been done in 1927.

Geology.—Five formations are exposed in the vicinity of the mine. The oldest is the Ochre Mountain limestone, which crops out at the surface east of the portal of the adit and also to the north near benchmark 5416. It is a continuation of the outcrop in which the Cane Springs mine is located. Almost all the mine workings are in this limestone, although in most of them metamorphism and ore deposition have completely altered its original aspect. In the surface exposures as well as in the adit tunnel east of the quartz monzonite, the formation appears as a bleached and recrystallized coarse-grained limestone in which bedding planes are distinguished with difficulty. Silicate minerals are locally present in some beds. On the 234-foot level, east of the ore body, the limestone appears to have been almost completely replaced by pale-green garnet. In other places adjacent to the ore body, however, the limestone has been altered to a fine-grained pale-gray jasperoid. This rock at the surface weathers to a reddish-brown resistant rock that forms prominent outcrops.

The Ochre Mountain limestone is overlain by the Manning Canyon formation, consisting of black shale and dark quartzite. The beds of quartzite are the only ones that are exposed at the surface, and in places where the Ochre Mountain limestone has been silicified it is difficult to locate the contact between them exactly. Small patches of the formation are exposed underground that show the black shale characteristic of the formation. In the exposures of the contact between the Manning Canyon and the Ochre Mountain limestone at the north end of the tunnel level and at the 234-foot level there is evidence of faulting, but from the essential concordance between the two formations on the surface, the faulting is thought to have been relatively slight.

The Oquirrh formation is exposed south of the mine workings. It is made up of moderately thin bedded quartzites and limestones, some of the limestones silicified. It is not exposed underground. It is separated from the two preceding formations by a normal fault striking north of east. The beds that crop out just south of this fault must be near the base of the formation, for the fault is exposed at the south end of the tunnel level, and here the Manning Canyon formation is found in the hanging wall.

The next younger formation is the quartz monzonite. It underlies the gulch west of the adit portal and is part of a bulbous outcrop that is connected with the stock by a narrower mass extending to the south. The main mass of the stock is exposed about 850 feet east of the adit portal on the eastern slope of the ridge and also about an equal distance to the north. A narrow dike of similar character crops out along the road leading to the old vertical shaft and is approximately at the Ochre Mountain and Manning Canyon contact. The intrusive is also exposed at several places in the mine workings. In the adit it is found for a distance of 150 feet from the portal. This is a part of the body exposed in the gulch below the mine. At the contact with the Ochre Mountain limestone there has been a slight copper mineralization on the south side of the adit. On the 234-foot level quartz monzonite was struck about 60 feet south of the shaft crosscut and continued to the end of the drift. A raise near the end passed through the igneous rock in about 20 feet. The intrusive is also present in the northern workings. What appears to be the top of a dikelike mass was cut about 30 feet east of the massive sulphides, and at the end of this same crosscut another mass was found. The latter mass is separated from the sedimentary rocks by a fault with low southwesterly dip that is without doubt the same as one exposed at the surface east of the ridge above the mine workings. The quartz monzonite observed underground is all more or less altered. That on the tunnel level has been partly replaced by a later generation of orthoclase and quartz, and the dark minerals have been altered to actinolite, calcite, chlorite, and titanite. Moderate amounts of sericite are also found. On the bottom level dark silicates such as garnet and diopside have replaced the rock, and in the southern part of the level it is difficult to draw the contact with the metamorphosed limestone. The northern exposures are somewhat less altered but are badly crushed and contain veinlets of a pink ferruginous dolomite.

The youngest rock formation exposed is a quartz porphyry dike 2 feet thick that is seen in the adit. It has been highly altered and is now a soft pale-gray fine-grained rock in which are phenocrysts of quartz as much as a quarter of an inch in diameter and of feldspar that reach a length of nearly an inch. The microscope shows that the matrix is composed of laths that were probably at one time plagioclase crystals but are now made up of a fine-grained clay mineral. The interstices between the laths are composed of another clay mineral that has a lower index of refraction and a much lower birefringence. A little sericite and a few crystals of zircon and apatite are also present. This same dike appears to be exposed at the surface near the prospect hole 200 feet northeast of the adit portal.

The Ochre Mountain limestone and the Manning Canyon formation, being essentially conformable, both strike west of north and dip 60° E. They are separated from the Oquirrh formation to the south by a normal fault that strikes north of east and dips south. This fault also is exposed in the most southerly workings on the tunnel level, where the dip is seen to be 60°. It is of some economic importance in that it terminates on the south the beds of the Ochre Mountain limestone that contain the ore.

A fault that is of much greater economic importance however, is the one cut near the end of the most easterly workings on the 234-foot level. This separates the sedimentary rocks from the main mass of quartz monzonite exposed east of the mine. On the bottom level the fault, along which there is nearly 4 feet of gouge, strikes N. 65° W. and dips 35° SW., but the trace of the fault on the surface indicates that its average strike must be closer to N. 25° W. For the reasons given on page 76 in the discussion of the structure of this part of the quadrangle, the fault probably has normal relations. If this is so, the fault must terminate the ore-bearing portion of the Ochre Mountain limestone at a rather shallow depth below the 234-foot level. From its average strike and a dip of 35°, it should be found about 200 feet below the bottom of the inclined shaft. Furthermore, the fact that quartz monzonite forms the footwall of the fault at the surface indicates that the faulted portion of the limestone has been eroded away.

A similar fault is exposed on the 234-foot level about 150 feet in the hanging wall of the fault just described which cuts off the massive sulphide ore. This fault strikes N. 40° W. and dips 40° W. in the short drift and strikes N. 50° W. and dips 50° W. in the main crosscut. Projecting the Ochre Mountain and Manning Canyon contact that is exposed in the footwall of the fault, on the south end of the tunnel level, and the same contact exposed in the hanging wall, on the 234-foot level, indicates that the dip slip approximates 100 feet (fig. 30).

The fact that the several exposures of quartz monzonite on the 234-foot level are not represented at the surface raises a question as to the probable abundance of the intrusive rock on still lower levels. Quartz monzonite forms the footwall of the fault exposed in the northeasterly workings on the 234-foot level, and the low dip of the fault must cause a rapid encroachment upon the ore-bearing limestone in depth. In addition, the southeastern continuation of the block of sedimentary rocks in which the mine is located shows conclusively that it is a part of a roof pendant in the quartz monzonite and that it is underlain to the southeast at a shallow depth by the intrusive. The Western Utah mine at Gold Hill, however, proves that such pendants may locally have a very considerable depth in proportion to their width. Proximity to the bottom of a pendant, as at the Alvarado mine and in the country to the north, seems to be indicated by an abundance of small plugs and dikes of monzonite. In one sense the two exposures of intrusive rocks on the 234-foot level, neglecting that in the footwall of the eastern fault, could be interpreted as suggesting such proximity. On the other hand, they might be correlated with the dike on the surface that approximately follows the contact between the Ochre Mountain limestone and the Manning Canyon formation. This dike cannot be traced southward to the region of the mine workings, and its top is presumably below the surface

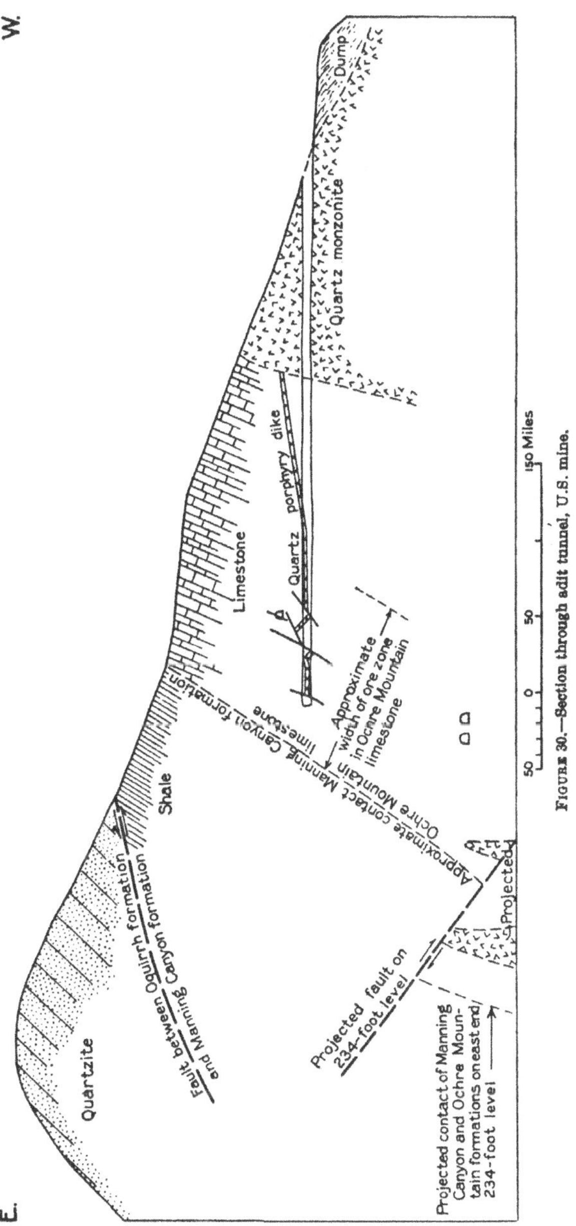

FIGURE 30.—Section through adit tunnel, U.S. mine.

in that direction. The more northerly of the two exposures underground might thus be interpreted as the top of the dike at that point, and the larger southerly exposure as a part of the dike that here extends more nearly to the surface but does not quite reach it. The only evidence in favor of this view is that the three are more or less in alinement, but considerably more extensive mine workings would be necessary to prove it. In figure 30 this interpretation has been accepted, and the dike is shown as being offset by the fault that terminates the sulphides, on the assumption that the fault is of the same age as that to the east which cuts the igneous rock.

Several small faults can be recognized on the tunnel level by reason of the displacement of the quartz porphyry dike. At least four faults cut the dike in the 25 feet between the two drifts that branch from the adit. The displacements are all small, and their algebraic sum is equal to zero, for the dike has the same position east of the fault zone as west of it (fig. 30). The largest throw appears to be along the so-called "lead fissure," and adjacent to it the dike changes its strike nearly 90°, becoming approximately parallel to the fault. Other fractures were recognized at different points underground, but the absence of any distinctive horizon in the beds cut by them prevented any estimate of their importance. To judge from surface exposures, however, their throws must be slight.

Ore body.—The ore body of the mine is a replacement deposit in a belt of Ochre Mountain limestone which is at least 100 feet wide and whose eastern boundary appears to be the contact with the Manning Canyon formation. The limits of the ore are not well defined except where quartz monzonite or a later fault is adjacent. On the tunnel level arsenic or lead-arsenic ore extends for more than 300 feet along the strike of this zone and for nearly 100 feet normal to the strike. The width appears to be at a maximum to the south and decreases to the width of the "lead fissure" at the north. On the 234-foot level the exposed mineralized area has considerably smaller dimensions. Nearly solid sulphides were cut for a distance of about 30 feet in the more northerly of the two east crosscuts and are terminated to the east by a fault. Disseminated sulphides, however, are found on this level over a strike length of about 175 feet and a width of nearly 100 feet. If the occurrence of sulphides cut in the raise at the south end of the level is considered, the strike length would be increased about 75 feet. On this level the apparent maximum width is much farther north than on the tunnel level.

The walls of the ore bodies are of different character in several parts of the mine. The fault on the 234-foot level is clearly later than the ore and is readily recognized. The quartz monzonite at the south end of the level is equally distinct. On the bottom level also a pale-greenish rock, which the microscope shows to be composed chiefly of garnet, is almost completely devoid of sulphides, except for thin veinlets and sparsely disseminated molybdenite. This rock may therefore be considered a well-defined wall rock, in that it has been distinctly unfavorable for the deposition of the sulphide ore. It is exposed on the east side of the drift for more than 50 feet north and south of the shaft and also makes up the stretch between the fault that terminates the nearly massive sulphides and the Manning Canyon formation.

In most places, however, the walls are gradational contacts between nearly solid masses of sulphide and fine-grained jasperoidlike quartz with a very minor content of metallic minerals. Much of the ore zone on the 234-foot level is occupied by such siliceous rock with only a moderate content of ore minerals. On the tunnel level similar rock separates areas of high-grade arsenic ore and in such places might be considered as in the nature of "horses" of low-grade material between the more valuable bodies. Microscopic study of the siliceous material shows that locally it contains considerable amounts of a colorless chlorite and also of opal which in most of the occurrences seems certainly to be contemporaneous with the quartz. On the north end of the tunnel level, particularly adjacent to the "lead fissure", silicification has been much less prevalent, and in the hanging wall of the stope at the north end crystalline marble is found adjacent to the ore. On figure 29 the intensity of the stippling indicates approximately the relative amount of the ore minerals to the gangue.

Ore.—Two classes of ore have been shipped from the mine—arsenic ore and lead-silver ore containing arsenic. On all the levels the arsenic ore is found to the south and the lead-bearing material to the north in the ore zone.

The hypogene arsenic ore mineral is arsenopyrite. The southern part of the ore body in the tunnel level is made up almost entirely of this mineral. Locally it occurs as long, slightly radiating bladed crystals that are generally found near the hanging wall, though some are within the ore body. For the most part masses of the arsenopyrite are almost structureless as viewed in the mine. Polished specimens of this kind of ore, however, disclose that it has been thoroughly brecciated and later cemented by quartz. The chief gangue mineral in the arsenic portion of the ore body is fine-grained quartz. This not only cements the fractured arsenopyrite but also forms rather linear bands within the ore body, like the jasperoidlike material that acts as the walls in many places. On the bottom level the portion of the ore body that contains chiefly arsenic has a much higher content of quartz than is found on the tunnel level. Small quantities of pyrite and even less abundant sphalerite are found in the arsenic ore. They normally occur near the edges of the ore body. Polished sections show that the sphalerite contains microscopic inclusions of chalcopyrite, jamesonite, and pyrrhotite.

The greater part of the arsenic ore on all three levels shows relatively little surficial alteration. Locally on the working and tunnel levels the sulphide is veined by thin seams of greenish massive scorodite, and in a few places small vugs filled with crystalline scorodite were found. On the bottom level the arsenopyrite appears to be essentially fresh, but the approximate coincidence of the level with the water table has caused it to be locally coated by gypsum, nontronite(?), and a yellow-green fine-grained mineral that appears to be an undescribed hydrous iron arsenate. In the hanging-wall crosscut from the shaft on this level a reddish-brown ooze that contained considerable quantities of arsenic was being deposited.

On the two upper levels about 25 feet north of the inclined shaft there is a rather sharp contact between nearly fresh sulphides and ore that is almost completely oxidized to scorodite. This is associated with an abundant white chalky-appearing mixture of opal and quartz. The occurrence of oxidized ore at this point is rather puzzling, because the vertical distance from the level to the surface here is somewhat greater than it is in the unoxidized area to the south. The explanation perhaps lies in the fact that there is much less of the relatively impervious jasperoid adjacent to the ore body here than there is to the south.

The lead ore on the tunnel level is thoroughly oxidized, and as a result its primary relations to the arsenic ore are not definitely known. The wide lead stope just north of the shaft immediately adjoins the scorodite portion of the arsenic ore, and in it, as well as in the small stopes on the working level above, both arsenic and lead minerals are found. A fine-grained pale-brown member of the jarosite group that is probably beudantite occurs in considerable quantities, in addition to varying quantities of cerusite, scorodite, and jarosite. In the large stope mentioned the ore appears to form a continuation of the wide body of rather poorly defined arsenic ore, and the arsenic content is relatively high. North of the stope the ore is limited to relatively narrow veinlike zones in which the arsenic content is probably somewhat lower, as some of the specimens of the jarosite minerals occurring to the north are found when treated to be nearly free of the arsenate radicle.

On the 234-foot level the massive sulphides terminated by the northwesterly normal fault probably represent the downward extension of the lead ore on the tunnel level. In polished specimens of this ore arsenopyrite, pyrite, sphalerite, chalcopyrite, galena, jamesonite, aikinite, and stibnite are the metallic minerals recognized and are set in a quartz or calcite gangue. Pyrite and arsenopyrite are the most abundant of the sulphides. Both are thoroughly fractured, and the angular fragments are cemented by quartz and the other sulphides. The arsenopyrite is the more thoroughly fractured of the two, and in some places angular and cracked fragments may be seen that are surrounded by unfractured pyrite. Sphalerite is the next most abundant sulphide. It appears to be essentially contemporaneous with the quartz and shows no sign of fracturing. It contains locally tiny dots and stringers of chalcopyrite, in addition to rounded remnants of the pyrite that it has replaced. Chalcopyrite was recognized only as small inclusions in the sphalerite. Jamesonite and galena are both somewhat later than the sphalerite, for they embay and vein it as well as the pyrite and arsenopyrite. They appear to be mutually exclusive, specimens that contain one being free from the other. Galena is readily recognized in polished sections by reason of its cleavage. It contains small inclusions of a darker-gray mineral that is aikinite, a copper-lead-bismuth sulphide. The relations between galena and jamesonite suggest that the formation of the one or the other was dependent on the local relative concentration of antimony with respect to lead at the time of ore formation.

The only gangue mineral in the massive sulphide ore is quartz in very small quantities. In the lower-grade ore to the west the sulphides, chiefly pyrite and arsenopyrite, have replaced coarsely crystalline calcite which the microscope shows to have suffered considerable deformation. Locally a white soft claylike mineral that has some of the optical properties of kaolinite veins and coats the lower-grade sulphide ore.

The relative proportions of the sulphides vary within the ore body. Pyrite or arsenopyrite or a mixture of the two generally predominates and in some places is present to the almost complete exclusion of the other sulphides. Sphalerite appears to be somewhat more widely distributed and more abundant than the lead-bearing sulphides. Near the eastern boundary of the high-grade sulphide mass differing proportions of sulphides have caused a rude banding that strikes nearly north and dips about 50° W.

There appear to be several factors that have controlled the ore deposition in this mine. The Ochre Mountain limestone is obviously the most important, in that it has provided an easily replaceable rock. The fault that terminates the limestone to the south and the quartz monzonite exposed on the bottom level both affect the continuity of the limestone. The relatively greater difficulty in the replacement of the formations thus brought into contact with the limestone may perhaps account for the large dimensions of the south end of the ore body. The alteration of the limestone to garnet and other silicate minerals is also unfavorable to ore deposition, as is clearly shown on the bottom level.

These factors are negative ones in that they limit the ore body. A more positive factor in its localization is thought to be a series of fractures or minor faults that are essentially parallel to the strike and dip of the limestone. The most evident of these is the so-called "lead fissure", which has faulted the quartz porphyry dike. Another parallel fracture that is closely related to the lead ore is exposed in the lead stope and at the north end of the working level. Its relation to the dike was not observed. These fractures were not observed in the arsenic-rich portion of the ore body, but the linear nature of the siliceous horses in the arsenic ore and the apparent gradation between arsenic and lead ore may indicate that similar fractures were utilized by the arsenic-bearing ore solutions.

The occurrence of the lead ores north of the arsenic ore is perhaps the result of the later introduction of the lead sulphides and the fact that the unreplaced rock to the north was more readily attacked than the nearly massive arsenopyrite.

OREGON

The Oregon group of 10 unpatented claims, owned by J. J. and Ada Gerster, of Gold Hill is west of benchmark 5416 on the Lincoln Highway, south of the town of Gold Hill. The workings consist of shallow pits and cuts, chiefly along or near a fault that separates the Ochre Mountain limestone from the Oquirrh formation. The fault strikes west of north and dips at a moderately low angle to the west. Along it the limestones have been crushed and thoroughly silicified and crop out as reddish-brown jasperoid. The footwall side of the fault line has been the site of two small intrusions of quartz monzonite in this vicinity. The work done has been in the nature of exploration for ores similar to those in the U.S. mine, to the east, or in the Cane Springs mine, to the northwest, both of which are in the same belt of Ochre Mountain limestone, rather than a development of any specific ore-bearing outcrops.

HERAT

The principal workings of the Herat mine are on the south side of the low hill about 1,000 feet northeast of Clifton. The mine was the scene of some of the earliest work in the district, and the inclined stack of an old smelter that treated the ores may still be seen extending up the side of the hill. In 1920 the owners of the mine were reported to be Messrs. Watson & Chandler, of Bingham, Utah.

The early production from the mine is not known. In recent years several shipments, mostly of slag and speiss from the smelter dump, have been made by lessees. One of 156 tons was made in 1920 and had an average content of 0.025 ounce of gold and 11.1 ounces of silver to the ton, 0.3 percent of copper, and 7.4 percent of lead. Another shipment of 47 tons in 1923 contained 0.021 ounce of gold and 16.0 ounces of silver to the ton, 0.15 percent of copper, and 11.4 percent of lead.

The mine workings are all in a mass of Ochre Mountain limestone that occurs as a blunt northward extending arm into quartz monzonite. The limestone near the mine has been rather thoroughly altered to lime-silicate rocks, and the detailed structure in the vicinity is not discernible.

The ore bodies appear to have replaced the limestone, but the original outlines of the ore bodies and their structural relations have been almost completely destroyed. Ore apparently cropped out both north and south of the road that runs along the south side of the hill, to judge from the old stopes and workings that are found there.

The ore that was seen in the old workings and on the dumps was thoroughly oxidized. In only one specimen were any sulphide areas noted, and these were all composed of arsenopyrite. The bulk of the ore now visible consists of brown and greenish scorodite, with which are large amounts of dark-brown to black massive iron oxides. Small quantities of plumbojarosite or its arsenic-bearing analog and minor amounts of other oxidized lead minerals are present. Vein quartz in small quantities was also found on the dumps. It resembles closely the quartz of the tetrahedrite-bearing veins, and the small copper content of the shipments may have been derived from this source.

The scanty evidence that is now available indicates that this deposit is in many respects similar to the oxidized portions of the arsenic-rich ore bodies in the Western Utah and U.S. mines. There is some doubt as to any future importance of the mine, however, for the contact of the quartz monzonite with the sedimentary rocks in this region has in most places a very low dip, and as the igneous rock is exposed at the surface only a short distance away, it probably cuts out the favorable limestones at no great depth.

COPPER-LEAD-SILVER REPLACEMENT BODIES

MONOCCO

The Monocco claim is about 1,000 feet west-northwest of Montezuma Peak and is reached by the northern branch of the central road leading eastward from Clifton Flat. The claim has been patented for many years and is now reported to be owned by the heirs of a Mr. Kimball. In recent years the claim has been worked by lessees. From 1917 to 1920 shipments amounted to 786 tons of copper and lead-silver ore, which had an average content of 0.002 ounce of gold and 3.52 ounces of silver to the ton, 10.17 percent of copper, and 0.88 percent of lead. In 1926 the claim was under lease to Richard Lyman, J. R. Driggs, and G. R. Steele. At the time of visit they had made a shipment of copper ore and one of lead-silver ore. The copper ore contained 0.01 ounce of gold and 3.6 ounces of silver to the ton, 11.1 percent of copper, 15.9 percent of iron, and 38.8 percent of insoluble matter. The lead-silver ore assayed 0.045 ounce of gold and 11.4 ounces of silver to the ton, 8.8 percent of lead, 1.0 percent of copper, 2.0 percent of zinc, 3.5 percent of arsenic, 0.5 percent of antimony, 3.0 percent of sulphur, 3.8 percent of lime, 2.5 percent of insoluble matter, and 25.6 percent of iron. Shallow cuts and tunnels are scattered over the surface of the claim, the only concentrated work being found in an incline 200 feet long on the southern slope of the ridge south

The workings are all in interbedded sandstone and limestone of the central facies of the Oquirrh formation. In the vicinity of the mine these beds strike N. 10°–20° W. and dip gently to the east. No igneous rocks are exposed on the claim, but the western contact of the quartz monzonite stock crops out about 1,500 feet to the north and a slightly greater distance to the east.

The ore is found both in fissures cutting the sedimentary rocks and as replacement deposits in rather pure limestone beds adjacent to the fissures. At least three fissures are exposed on the claim. They strike northeast and their dip ranges from 75° W. to nearly vertical. The thickness of ore in the fissures is generally less than 2 feet. Locally quartz-carbonate veins have been introduced along the older ore-bearing fissures. Eight ore-bearing limestone beds are cut by these fissures. Their average thickness is less than 3 feet, and in many places only a part of the limestone has been replaced by ore. Replacement has extended only a short distance away from the fissures, 15 feet being the maximum observed. Cherty limestone beds, sandstones, and limestone altered to silicates appear to have been unfavorable for ore deposition. At several places the ore beds are displaced a few feet by northwesterly faults that dip to the northeast.

The copper ore is found either in or very close to the fissures. It is almost completely oxidized and consists chiefly of copper pitch in which remnants of chalcopyrite may locally be observed. Chrysocolla, azurite, and malachite are less abundant sources of copper. The lead ore is found chiefly in the limestone beds, although small concentrations of unoxidized galena are not uncommon in the fissures. Plumbojarosite appears to be the most wide-spread lead mineral, but where superficial alteration has been less intense anglesite and cerusite are found, in places surrounding a core of galena. Fine-grained quartz and iron oxides are abundant gangue minerals, and in some places mammillary opal fills vugs in the ore.

SILVER KING

The Silver King group, which has also been known as the Mineral Hill, is on the western and northern slopes of Montezuma Peak. It is said to enclose about 200 acres of ground, which almost completely surrounds the Monocco claim. The owners of the claims are F. C. Little, of Moroni, Utah, and Ollie Young, of Clifton. Small shipments have been made from the group at different times. One shipment of 10 tons of ore containing 6 ounces of silver to the ton and 18 percent of copper prior to 1912 is reported by Dick,[74] and one of 64 tons in 1917 contained 9.3 ounces of silver to the ton and 8.1 percent of copper. Shipments of less than a ton that were valuable chiefly for their silver content were made in 1920 and 1921. In 1922 and 1923 shipments aggregating 132 tons had an average content of 0.035 ounce of gold and 18.1 ounces of silver to the ton, 2.77 percent of copper, and 5.19 percent of lead.

The greater part of the development on the group has been done a short distance west of the Monocco camp. Here the interbedded sandstones and limestones of the Oquirrh formation strike N. 40° W. and dip 20° NE. These beds are cut by three ore-bearing fissures that strike northeast and dip 85° NW. Ore is also found adjacent to the fissure in two thin limestone beds which are unusually free from impurities and which are separated from each other by 10 feet of thin-bedded cherty limestone, which has been partly replaced by wollastonite. An inclined shaft has been driven down the intersection of the strongest fissure with the higher of the limestone beds for about 200 feet, and from it have been extended several short drifts and stopes along the mineralized limestone. At the bottom of the shaft a fault striking N. 60° W. and dipping 30° SE. brings the ore bed into contact with cherty limestone similar to that in the footwall. If the two are the same, the throw along the fault cannot be much more than 5 feet.

The ore is almost completely oxidized. In the fissures a deep-brown to almost black copper pitch is the chief copper mineral. Some of the black pitch is said to assay 62 percent of copper. Chrysocolla, malachite, and azurite vein the copper pitch in most places. Comparatively little lead ore is found in the fissures. It occurs chiefly in the adjacent limestone bed and consists of cerusite, anglesite, and plumbojarosite. Although the limestone is about 2 feet thick, in many places the ore is present in only a part of the bed, the remainder being unmineralized.

Fine-grained quartz and iron oxides are the most abundant gangue minerals. In addition to being mixed with both copper and lead minerals, they also form a casing to the lead ore, extending beyond it in the replaced limestone bed.

Other parts of the group show similar copper and lead-silver deposits, though none so far developed are as extensive. A moderate amount of shallow work has been done on these other deposits, particularly on the Searchlight claim, which is north of the Monocco.

MOHAWK

The Mohawk group is on the eastern slope of hill 5852, about 1¾ miles west-northwest of the town of Gold Hill. In 1926 the claims were owned by Hicks & Hudson. Development work on these claims has been directed toward the exploration of lead replacement ore bodies in limestones of the Oquirrh formation. The limestone has been bleached and recrystallized to a white marble but shows almost no development of silicate minerals. The ore shoots are for the most part rather small and contain considerable quantities of quartz and iron oxides in addition to the

[74] Dick, J. C., unpublished mining report.

oxidized lead minerals. There are numerous minor faults on the property. A small dike of quartz monzonite crops out a short distance east of the workings.

WALLA WALLA

The Walla Walla claim is on the eastern slope of hill 5702 about a mile and a quarter west of Gold Hill. It is owned by Hicks & Hudson. The ore on the claim has replaced a limestone bed in the Oquirrh formation that strikes N. 20° W. and dips 30° W. A fissure striking N. 80° E. and dipping 65° N. appears to have afforded a channel for the mineralization. The limestone bed is about 3 feet thick but has not been completely replaced by the ore minerals. The ore consists of quartz, iron oxides, a mineral resembling plumbojarosite, and scorodite. Some unoxidized remnants of galena were also observed.

GARRISON MONSTER MINING CO.

The Garrison Monster group of 27 patented claims is on the northeastern tip of Dutch Mountain. The property is owned by J. P. Gardner, of Salt Lake City, but during the period of examination it was being worked by lessees. The first locations are reported to have been made in 1882. The earliest recorded production, however, was in 1917. In that year and the succeeding two years 700 tons of ore was shipped that averaged 0.004 ounce of gold and 2.38 ounces of silver to the ton, 0.63 percent of copper, and 15.33 percent of lead. Production began again in 1924, and from the end of that year until July 1927 about 35 carloads of ore were shipped. These shipments had a silver content that ranged from 1.16 to 6.2 ounces to the ton and a lead content from 6.70 to 40.40 percent.

An old camp, consisting of a bunk house and several smaller buildings, is 1¾ miles south-southwest of Garrison Monster siding on the Deep Creek Railroad and is reached by automobile along a road that branches from the Gold Hill-Wendover road a quarter of a mile north of the siding. The road branching from the main road south of the siding is passable by automobile only as far as the new camp near the tunnel portal at an altitude of 4,894 feet.

Activity on this group of claims has been concentrated at three places—the Uncle Sam claim, three-quarters of a mile southwest of the old camp in Royal Gulch; the New Year claim, at the old camp; and the Consolidated and adjacent claims, half a mile east of the old camp. The latter locality has provided almost the entire production credited to the company, and the tunnel at 4,894 feet, to the north, was driven with the idea of more fully developing the ore there exposed.

Consolidated claim.—The Consolidated claim is on the south side of the low hill (altitude 5,750+ feet) that has at times been known as Wilson Hill. The hill is separated from Dutch Mountain proper by a gulch eroded along a transverse fault. On the south side of the fault the Prospect Mountain quartzite is exposed. North of it are a series of nearly horizontal outcrops of formations that range in age from Middle Cambrian to Carboniferous. These are, for the most part, thrust plates related either to the Ochre Mountain thrust or to the transverse fault. (See structure sec. *A–A′*, pl. 2.)

The lowest outcrop in the vicinity of the claim consists of thin-bedded limestones and shales of Middle Cambrian age. In many places the limestones of this group have been altered to dolomite. The portions thus changed have lost all of their original texture and weather to a deep-brown color. Next above is a plate of Upper Cambrian dolomite. This rock is normally deep bluish black and is thick-bedded, but in a few places individual beds have been bleached to a cream color. A 10-foot zone of thin-bedded limestone is interbedded with the dolomite near the mine workings. This plate is about 300 feet thick on the south side of Wilson Hill but is more than 500 feet thick on the north side. Both upper and lower contacts are faults, as is shown not only by the stratigraphy but also by the striking discordance between the bedding of the formations on both sides of the two faults and between the bedding planes and the contacts. The contact between the dolomite and the underlying limestones is well exposed at several places on the east side of the hill at an altitude of about 5,300 feet and is made conspicuous by the contortions in the thin-bedded limestones. The upper fault is not as striking, but close observation readily reveals its presence on the south side of the hill a short distance higher up the slope from the line of prospect holes on the ore.

Overlying the dolomite is a plate of variable but small thickness, composed of interbedded brown-weathering sandstone and blue limestone. Its lithology and fossil content are those of the upper portion of the Woodman formation. It in turn is overlain by 100 feet or more of fossiliferous Madison limestone, the contact between the two being obviously a thrust fault. This fault is well exposed near the southwest shoulder of Wilson Hill at an altitude of about 5,650 feet. The limestone is overlain conformably by about 50 feet of reddish-brown sandstones and sandy shales that are characteristic of the basal portion of the Woodman formation.

Igneous rocks are not abundant near the mine. The most prominent is an exposure of thoroughly altered porphyry in which the "porphyry incline", or main shaft, is driven. This is a white, irregularly iron-stained rock in which a few quartz phenocrysts can be seen. Under the microscope a few laths of sericite after biotite are shown to be present, together with accessory apatite and zircon. The remainder of the rock is a fine-grained aggregate of quartz. The dike is exposed at intervals for more than 500 feet to the west. Another series of exposures of a porphyry is

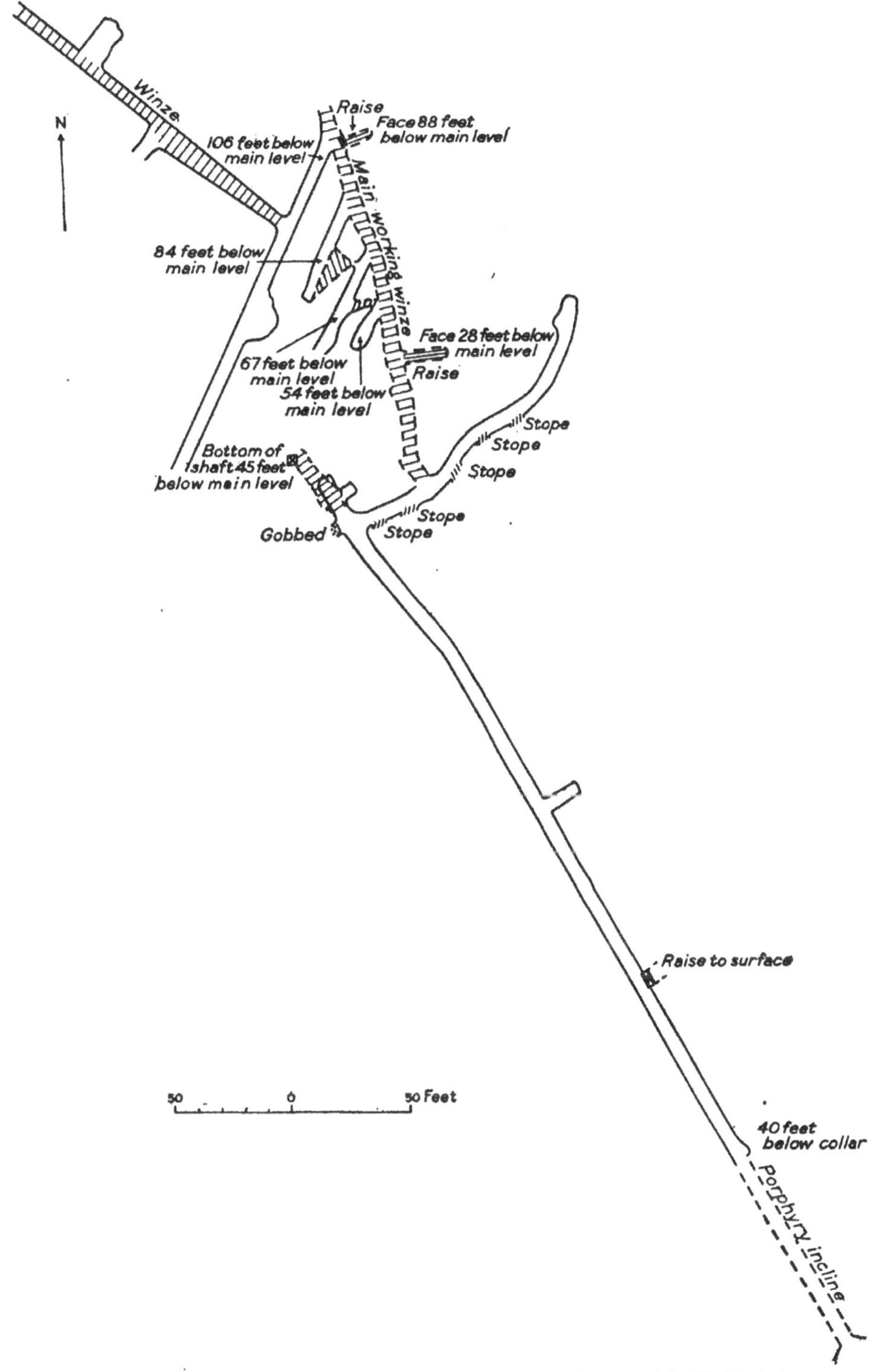

FIGURE 31.—Mine workings on Consolidated claim, Garrison Monster mine. From sketch furnished by the lessees.

present higher on Wilson Hill, along the thrust fault that separates the Madison limestone from the Woodman formation.

In addition to the thrusts that separate the several plates, other faults occur in the vicinity of the mine. In the long tunnel, for example, two steep reverse faults can be recognized at distances of 685 and 800 feet from the portal, by reason of the repetition of exposures of the Middle Cambrian limestone. In other places minor faults are made apparent by offsets of particular beds or contacts.

The ore appears to be localized in still another minor fault, for the wall rock is thoroughly brecciated, and its northeast strike and low northwest dip make large angles with the strike and dip of the adjacent sedimentary rocks. The fault fissure at the surface crops out within the plate of Upper Cambrian dolomite, about 75 feet below its upper limit. Several prospect holes along it show that it has a strike length of about 1,000 feet. The average strike as shown by these workings is east-northeast, but notable variations from this direction are shown by the mine workings (fig. 31). The dip is also somewhat variable but averages close to 30°, as shown not only by direct measurements on the vein but also by the point of intersection of the vein in the long tunnel. The fault is clearly later than the thrust between the Upper and Middle Cambrian, for the ore occurring in the tunnel has partly dolomitized Middle Cambrian limestones as its wall rock.

In the main workings from the porphyry incline the ore is thoroughly oxidized. Gray sandy cerusite and yellow-brown powdery plumbojarosite are by far the most abundant lead-bearing minerals. They occur, in many places relatively free from impurities, in lenticular masses as much as 3 feet in width and 10 to 20 feet along the strike. Such occurrences have a casing of banded reddish-brown iron oxides, in which are masses of a white clay mineral that appears to be largely halloysite. Smaller quantities of calamine, malachite, plumbojarosite, and other oxidized minerals are also included. The walls of the vein are composed of a thoroughly brecciated and bleached dolomite, in which there is locally a considerable amount of barite, and also isolated crystals of galena and limonite pseudomorphs after pyrite. In several places oxidation of the dolomite has converted the normally dense rock to a sandy aggregate of dolomite grains that closely resembles the sand carbonate (cerusite) found in the mine. The difference in weight of the two minerals, however, provides a ready means of distinguishing them. The rather scant exposures in these workings suggest that the shoots or concentrations of lead minerals may be correlated with synclinal warps in the vein.

The continuation of the vein struck in the long tunnel nearly 1,000 feet from the portal shows very little oxidation. It consists of a zone of dolomitized limestone 5 feet or more in width that is impregnated with sulphides and white barite. Galena is by far the most abundant sulphide. Small quantities of pyrite may also be recognized in hand specimens, but the microscope is required to prove the presence of small quantities of sphalerite and tennantite. Another galena-bearing zone was struck about 150 feet nearer the portal.

The exposures of the ore zones in the tunnel are much less veinlike than in the porphyry incline workings. This may be the result of the change in wall rock, for the thinner-bedded Middle Cambrian would probably not fracture as cleanly as the higher dolomites. The change might also be due to the fact that the exposed ore shoots on the higher levels pitch to the west and would at this altitude lie some distance westward along the strike of the ore zone.

New Year claim.—On the New Year claim, a short distance west of the old camp, a long tunnel has been driven to the south with the expectation not only of tapping several small veins on the hillside but also of eventually reaching the vein on the Uncle Sam claim, in Royal Gulch. The tunnel is now largely caved and could not be examined, but the writer was informed that nothing of consequence was found in it.

Uncle Sam claim.—The workings on the Uncle Sam claim are about 1,500 feet southeast of the cabin in Royal Gulch, on the northeast side of the gulch. As shown on plate 2, the structure in this vicinity is extremely complex. A number of thin and discontinuous thrust plates are exposed beneath the Ochre Mountain thrust.

The ore on the Uncle Sam claim was found in a vein essentially parallel to the bedding of the Madison limestone that forms one of these thrust plates. The ore mineral exposed at the surface is plumbojarosite, and the gangue is composed of barite and the limestone. A chute extending down to the gulch bottom seems to indicate that some shipments have been made from this claim, but the quantity and grade are not known.

EVANS

The Evans group of 21 claims, all of which are said to be patented, covers a large part of Royal Gulch other than that enclosed within the boundaries of the Garrison Monster property. Shallow pits, shafts, and tunnels are located at various places on the property, but so far as known there have been no shipments of ore.

The workings are concentrated for the most part either in the "window" of pre-Carboniferous rocks exposed in the gulch beneath the Ochre Mountain thrust or in the Madison limestone immediately above the thrust. The geologic structure in this region is unusually complex. (See pp. 81–82). The ore bodies developed include both galena-barite replacement deposits in limestone, similar to those on the adjoining Garrison Monster property, and quartz-tetrahedrite veins like those on the Undine and Rea claims. The replacement bodies are for the most part in the Madison limestone, and the quartz-tetrahedrite veins in the pre-Carboniferous dolomites.

WILLOW SPRINGS DISTRICT

HISTORY AND PRODUCTION

The Willow Springs district was organized May 21, 1891. Only a few claims in the district are within the Gold Hill quadrangle, and most of these, except for those of the Sunday group and the Dewey group, are unsurveyed. The production from the part of the district here considered appears to have been limited to a few small shipments of high-grade ore.

PROSPECTS

DEWEY

The Dewey group of five patented claims is on the north side of Sevy Canyon about half a mile west-southwest of South Peak, which is on the ridge line of the Deep Creek Mountains. Swan Moline, of Gold Hill, reports that a shipment of 800 to 900 pounds of ore was made from the property between 1890 and 1900 and yielded about $1,800, the valuable metal being silver.

The country rock in this vicinity is the upper portion of the Laketown dolomite, of Silurian age. A strike fault of low westward dip cuts the dolomite and has resulted in considerable brecciation. The fault has caused a repetition of beds in the dolomite and is therefore of the reverse variety. The throw was not determined but probably amounts to a few hundred feet.

The dolomite breccia along the fault has been cemented and partly replaced by fine-grained quartz across a width that is locally as great as 20 feet. In places the quartz is vuggy, and the vugs are lined with terminated quartz crystals. In the lower portion of the zone there is abundant coarsely crystalline white dolomite in the breccia. Several small prospect pits and stopes have been opened in this quartz-rich zone, and this material apparently constituted the ore. The only signs of mineralization other than the quartz are a few copper stains and small quantities of iron oxides. It is probable, in view of the copper stains and the high silver content of the ore shipped, that the valuable mineral was tetrahedrite and that the deposit is related to the quartz-tetrahedrite veins in the Clifton district.

SUNDAY

The Sunday group of 16 claims is in Bagley Gulch, on the south side of North Pass Canyon. The claims, some of which were being surveyed for patent in 1926, are owned by the Bullion-Bagley Mining Co. of Salt Lake City. A camp had been established at the point marked "7058" on the topographic map, within a short distance of which the prospecting activities of the company were concentrated.

The Abercrombie formation underlies the surface in the vicinity of the claims, and almost all of the prospecting has been done in the dolomitized massive limestones of that formation. The group of claims is about halfway between two northwestward-striking transverse faults, and the minor faults and fractures in the region, including those followed by the veins, are apparently related to them, as they have parallel strikes.

Prospecting has been done at several places on the group of claims. What appears to be the most promising deposit is a quartz vein exposed a short distance north of the camp. The vein is from 1 to 3½ feet wide, strikes N. 65° W. and has a dip that ranges from vertical to about 80° S. The vein filling consists of coarsely crystalline white quartz that contains numerous vugs lined with terminated quartz crystals. In this are local concentrations of galena and tetrahedrite with their oxidation products. Some of this sulphide-bearing ore is reported to contain as much as 1,700 ounces of silver to the ton, but so far as known no shipments have been made.

South of the camp a shallow shaft has been sunk to explore several "watercourses" in the limestone that are filled with barren iron oxides. No valuable minerals had been found in this material at the time of examination.

LEAD CARBONATE

The Lead Carbonate claim is in the south fork of Dry Canyon, at an altitude of about 7,200 feet. The present ownership of the claim and whether or not it is patented are unknown. The ruins of small buildings below the workings indicate the site of the former camp. The claim was worked in 1917 by W. J. McLaughlin, of Salt Lake City.

The workings are all in mottled limestones that are dolomitized here and there in the vicinity of the claim. The beds at this point strike a few degrees east of north and dip 35°–40° W. A large transverse fault, striking east, is exposed about a quarter of a mile north of the ore shoot.

The ore has replaced one of the limestone beds and is localized in a shoot that has a strike length of about 10 feet and a width of 2 to 3 feet. It appears to pitch to the southwest. An inclined shaft has been driven on the shoot, and a tunnel, whose portal is 40 feet below the outcrop, extends toward its projected position in depth. No transverse mineralizing fracture, such as was observed at other replacement bodies of this type, was recognized at the surface.

The ore appears to have been completely oxidized at the surface, but some specimens of relatively unaltered ore, presumably from the lower part of the ore shoot, were found on the dump. They showed veinlets and blebs of galena and tetrahedrite embedded in limestone or dolomitized limestone that contained a considerable amount of quartz, much of which was in the form of terminated crystals as much as a quarter of an inch in length. At the surface much of the carbonate has been leached out, leaving a skeleton of quartz, with which are associated various oxidized lead, copper, and iron minerals.

One shipment of 8 tons of ore was made from the claim in 1917. This contained 18 ounces of silver to the ton and 37 percent of lead. It is probable that some other small shipments have also been made.

SILVER

The unpatented Silver claim, which in 1926 was the property of Alvin Trippe, is on the south side of Dry Canyon a short distance east of summit 8182, at an altitude of about 8,000 feet.

The ore is found in fissures cutting dolomitized limestone in the lower part of the Abercrombie formation. The fissures strike about N. 70° W. and dip very steeply to the northeast. They are from 2 to 6 inches in width and are filled with quartz, fragments of wall rock, and oxidized copper, lead, and iron minerals. The wall rock shows minor amounts of silicification away from the fissures. Only a relatively small amount of shallow work has been done on the claim, and apparently no ore has been shipped.

OTHER PROSPECTS

There are several other prospects in the part of the Willow Springs district that is included within the quadrangle, particularly near the mouth of Dry Canyon. These do not differ in any important respect from the prospects already described, and as the names of the claims could not be ascertained they are not described here. The name of the claim upon which is located the shaft shown on the map near summit 6954, on the north side of North Pass Canyon, is also unknown. The shaft is an incline sunk on a few parallel joints that strike N. 85° E. and dip 75° S. No valuable minerals were observed in the shaft or on the dump.

INDEX

A

	Page
Abercrombie formation, age and correlation of	10
distribution of	8
fossils of	10
lithology of	8-9
section of	9
thickness of	9
Abstract of report	VII-VIII
Accessibility of the area	1
Acknowledgments for aid	4
Actinolite, occurrence of	114
Adamite, occurrence of	116
Aikinite, occurrence of	112
Ajax limestone, correlation of	15
Albert claim, features of	127-128
Albite, occurrence of	113
Alkali basalt, partial analysis of	52
petrography of	52
Alteration of ores, relation of physical and chemical character to superficial	105-107
relation of water table to superficial	104
Alvarado mine, features of	128-131
Amphibole, apatite and molybdenite in	pl. 9
Andalusite, occurrence of	114
Andesite, biotite and hornblende, petrography of	50
Anglesite, occurrence of	117
Apatite, occurrence of	116
Aplite dikes, features of	48
Arseniosiderite, occurrence of	116
Arsenopyrite, occurrence of	111
Axinite, occurrence of	114
Azurite, occurrence of	113

B

Bamberger mine, features of	125
Bar Creek, anticline west of	87-88
concealed thrust fault west of	88
faulting west of	88
minor faulting east of	86-87
minor folds west of	87-88
Bar Creek fault, relations of	56, 87
Barite, occurrence of	117
Beudantite, occurrence of	117
Bighorn dolomite, correlation of	17
Biotite, occurrence of	115
Bird claim, features of	149
Bismuthinite, occurrence of	111
Bismuth, occurrence of	110
Bismutite, occurrence of	113
Blood Canyon, normal faulting in	70
Blood Canyon fault, direction and amount of movement along	69
relations of	59, 67
Blood Mountain, minor structural features on	68-69
Bluebird dolomite, correlation of	11
Bonanza claims, features of	144
Bonnemort claim, features of	135-136
Bonneville beach and spit, view of	pl. 4
Bornite, occurrence of	111
Boston claim, features of	143
Boulangerite, occurrence of	112
Bowman limestone, correlation of	10
Brazer limestone, correlation of	28, 30
Burling, L. D., fossils collected by	27
Busby quartzite, age and correlation of	8
distribution of	7-8
lithology of	8
thickness of	8

C

Cabin shale, age and correlation of	7
distribution of	6
lithology of	6-7
thickness of	7

35311-35——12

	Page
Calamine, occurrence of	115
Calaveras claims, features of	124
Calaverite?, occurrence of	111
Calcite, occurrence of	112-113
Cambrian beds, unconformity at top of upper	14-15
Cambrian system, formations of	4-15
Cane Springs mine, features of	131-134
Carbonate-sulphate veins, alteration of	105
features of	101-102
mines and prospects in	151
outlook for mining	110
Carboniferous beds, unconformity at base of	21-22
Carboniferous system, formations of	23-42
formations of, correlations of	41-42
Cash Boy claims, features of	148-149
Centennial claim, features of	122-123
Cerusite, occurrence of	113
Chalcanthite, occurrence of	117
Chalcedony, occurrence of	112
Chalcocite, occurrence of	111
Chalcopyrite, occurrence of	111
Chisholm shale, correlation of	10
Chlorite group, occurrence of	115
Chloritization, alteration of quartz monzonite by	95
Chokecherry dolomite, age and correlation of	15-16
distribution of	15
fossils of	15
lithology of	15
thickness of	15
Christiansen and Sheridan Gulches, minor structural features between	69
Christmas Mining Co., claims of	151
Chrysocolla, occurrence of	116
Claron limestone, correlation of	43
Clay and gravel, older, occurrence and character of	54
Clay minerals, occurrence of	115-116
Clifton district, history of mining in	118
mines and prospects in	119-166
production of	118-119
Clifton Flat, major anticline south of	70
minor faults west and southwest of	70
view of, from the southwest	pl. 4
Climate, data on	2-3
Climax claims, features of	147
Clinoclasite, occurrence of	116
Clinozoisite, occurrence of	114
Cole Canyon dolomite, correlation of	12
Conichalcite, occurrence of	117
Consolidated claim, features of	164-166
Copper Bloom claims, features of	127
Copper Hill claims, features of	128
Copper, occurrence of	111
Copperopolis claims, features of	125
Copper pitch, occurrence of	112
Copper Queen Midland Mining Co., claims of	148
Covellite, occurrence of	111
Cuprotungstite, occurrence of	118
Cyclone mine, features of	144-145
polished section showing arsenopyrite fragments cemented by other sulphides and quartz from	pl. 10

D

Dagmar limestone, correlation of	10
Danburite, occurrence of	114
Deep Creek Mountain block, mutual relations of structural features of	69
structure of	66-69
Deep Creek Mountains, fault along east base of	56
fault along east base of, relations of	68
structure of	55
Deformation of the beds, progressive variation in character of	60-61
Descloizite, occurrence of	116
Deseret limestone, correlation of	28
Devonian system, formations of	18-21
Dewey claims, features of	167

Page

Dikes, porphyry, appearance of 46
porphyry, distribution and size of 46
microscopic features of 46-47
relations of, to one another 47-48
relations of, to other rocks 47
Diopside, occurrence of 113
Diopside-orthoclase alteration, features of 94-95
Doctor claim, features of 122
Dolomite, occurrence of 113
Dolomitic formations, origin of the pre-Carboniferous 22-23
Dolomitization, features of 94
Dry Canyon and Sevy Canyon faults, minor faults between 67
Dry Canyon fault, relations of 58, 66
minor faults south of 66
Dutch Mountain block, structural features of, mutual relations of 85
structure of 78-85
Dutch Mountain, fault along west side of 85
faults on 56
relations of recumbent anticline to structural features on 86
view of, from the southeast pl. 4
Dutch Mountain thrust, features of 54
relations of 84

E

Ely Springs formation, correlation of 17
Enterprise claim, features of 122-123
Eocene (?), unconformity at base of 42
Erosion surface, dissected postmature pl. 6
Epidote, occurrence of 114
Evans claims, features of 166

F

Fairchild, J. G., chemical analyses by 50, 51, 52
Faulting, late normal, characteristics of 63
late normal, relation of, to present topography 61-63
Faults in Gold Hill quadrangle, map showing pl. 3 (in pocket)
Ferrisymplesite?, occurrence of 116
Field work 3-4
Fish Haven dolomite, age and correlation of 16-17
distribution of 16
fossils of 17
lithology of 16
thickness of 16
Fluorite, occurrence of 112
Fortuna claims, features of 144
Frankie mine, features of 123
Fusselman limestone, correlation of 18

G

Galena, occurrence of 111
Garden City limestone, correlation of 15
Gardner dolomite, correlation of 27
Garrison Monster fault, probable conjugate faulting related to 83-84
relations of 59
Garrison Monster fault zone, nature and amount of movement along 83
relations of 82-83
Garrison Monster mine, thin section from, showing barite replacing sulphides pl. 11
Garrison Monster Mining Co., claims of 164-166
Geologic formations, age of 4
Geologic map and sections of Gold Hill and vicinity pl. 2 (in pocket)
Geologic map and sections of Gold Hill quadrangle, Utah pl. 1 (in pocket)
Gerster formation, age and correlation of 40-41
distribution of 39
fossils of 40-41
lithology of 39
thickness of 39-40
Girty, G. H., fossils identified by 26, 28-29, 30-31, 32, 33
quoted 26, 32, 35-36, 39, 42
Gold Belt claims, features of 149-150
Gold Bond claim, features of 125-127
replacement of minerals in specimens from pl. 10
Gold Hill mine of United States Smelting, Refining & Mining Co. *See* U. S. mine.
Gold Hill mine of Western Utah Copper Co., block diagram of pl. 14
geology of 152-154
level map of pl. 15
location, history, and development of 151-152
ore bodies of 154-156
Gold Hill, northeasterly faults west and northwest of 77
Gold Hill Standard Mining Co., claims of 149
Gold, occurrence of 111
Grampian limestone, correlation of 16
Graphite, occurrence of 110
Gravel and clay, older, occurrence and character of 54
younger, occurrence and character of 54

Page

"Great Blue" limestone, correlation of 30
Guilmette formation, age and correlation of 21
distribution of 20
fossils of 21
lithology of 20-21
section of 20-21
thickness of 21
Gypsum, occurrence of 117

H

Hartmann limestone, correlation of 10
Heikes, V. C., quoted 118
Hematite, occurrence of 112
Herat mine, features of 162
Herat shale member of Ochre Mountain limestone, lithology of 30
Herkimer limestone, correlation of 10
Hicks formation, age and correlation of 14
distribution of 14
fossils of 14
lithology of 14
pisolitic dolomite from pl. 5
section of 14
thickness of 14
Highland Peak limestone, correlation of 10
Hornblende, occurrence of 114
Humbug formation, correlation of 28
Humite, occurrence of 115

I

Ida Lull claims, features of 125
Igneous metamorphism, features of 91-97
Igneous rocks, older, age of 48
older, general features of 43
younger, distribution and relations of 49
petrography of 49-53
Immense claim, features of 151
Incas group of claims, features of 125

J

Jamesonite 111-112
Jarosite, occurrence of 117
Jasperoid, alteration to 93-94
calcite cleavage lines in pl. 8
Jefferisite, occurrence of 115

K

Keno claim, features of 124-125
Kirk, Edwin, fossils identified by 15, 17, 18, 20, 21
quoted 21
Knopf, Adolph, quoted 108

L

Lake Bonneville beds, occurrence and character of 54-55
Laketown dolomite, age and correlation of 18
distribution of 17
fossils of 18
lithology of 17
"marble cake" dolomite near base of pl. 5
thickness of 17-18
Lamb dolomite, age and correlation of 13
distribution of 12-13
lithology of 13
thickness of 13
Langston (?) formation, correlation of 8
Latite, biotite and hornblende, petrography of 50
biotite-augite, analysis of 50
hypersthene-augite, analysis of 51
petrography of 50-51
Lead Carbonate claim, features of 167-168
Lincoln Highway, minor thrust east of bench mark 5684 on 69-70
Location of the area 1
Lone Mountain limestone, correlation of 17, 18
Lucy L mine, features of 140-143
plan of workings of pl. 13

M

Madison limestone, age and correlation of 26-27
distribution of 24-25
fossils of 26-27
lithology of 25-26
variable dip of fault between, and Woodman formation pl. 7
Magnetite, occurrence of 112
Malachite, occurrence of 113
Mammoth claims, features of 148-149

Page

Manning Canyon formation, age and correlation of 32-33
distribution of 31-32
fossils of 33
lithology of 32
plunging minor anticline in pl. 7
thickness of 32
Marcasite, occurrence of 111
Mascot claim, features of 143
Mendha formation, correlation of 13, 14
Midas mine, features of 134-135
Mimetite, occurrence of 116
Mineral Hill claims, features of 163
Minerals, list of, in metamorphosed rocks and ore deposits 110-118
Mines and prospects 118-168
Mining, outlook for 109-110
Minnehaha claims, features of 127-128
Mississippian beds, contact of, with Pennsylvanian beds 33
Mohawk claims, features of 163-164
Molybdenite, occurrence of 111
Monocco claim, features of 162-163
Monte del Rey claims, features of 144
Montoya limestone, correlation of 17
Muscovite, occurrence of 115

N

Napoleon Mining Co., property of 125
Natrojarosite, occurrence of 117
Nevada limestone, correlation of 21
New Baltimore claim, features of 149
New Year claim, features of 166
New York claim, features of 143
Nontronite, occurrence of 116
North Pass Canyon, plunging anticline in 67
thrust plates on north side of 67-68
North Pass thrust, features of 57-58
relations of 70
warping of 71
North Pass transverse fault, relations of 67
Northwestern block, mutual relations of structural features of 88
structure of 85-88

O

Ochre Mountain, crumpling beneath nearly flat fault on west side of pl. 7
faults of first cycle on 55
minor thrusts and fold on south side of 75
normal faults on 75
northward-dipping transverse faults on 74
slopes of pl. 6
southward-dipping transverse faults on 74-75
transverse fault on south side of 71-72
Ochre Mountain block, mutual relations of structural features of 77-78
structure of 72-78
transverse fault at northern border of 77
Ochre Mountain limestone, age and correlation of 30-31
distribution of 29
fossils of 30-31
lithology of 29-30
thickness of 30
wollastonite replacing garnet in metamorphosed pl. 8
Ochre Mountain thrust, appearance of 79-80
exposures of, east of Lincoln Highway 73
features of 57-58, 59
folding in rocks beneath 81
folding of 80
influence of, on distribution of ore deposits 108
magnitude of 74, 80
main outcrop of 72-73
minor structural features in rocks above 84-85
northwesterly normal faults east of main outcrop of 76-77
relations of 71
along north edge of Dutch Mountain 79
between Pool Canyon and Garrison Monster mine 78-79
in Pool Canyon 78
near Garrison Monster mine 79
south of Pool Canyon 78
thrust plates associated with 79
south of Pool Canyon fault, faulting below 81
warping of 71
"window" west of main outcrop of 73
Ochre Springs, transverse fault north of 76
Oligoclase, occurrence of 113
Olivenite, occurrence of 116
Opal, occurrence of 112
Opex dolomite, correlation of 13
Ophir shale, correlation of 7

Page

Opohonga limestone, correlation of 15
Oquirrh formation, age and correlation of 35-39
alteration of replacement bodies in 107
chert-pebble conglomerate with oolitic matrix from pl. 5
distribution of 33
fossils of 36-39
lithology of 34-35
thickness of 35
Ordovician beds, unconformity at base of Upper 16
unconformity at top of Upper 17
Ordovician system, formations of 15-17
Ore deposits, areal relations of 107-108
classification of 97
genesis of 108-109
influence of zoning on distribution of 107-108
Oregon claims, features of 162
Orpiment, occurrence of 111
Orthoclase, occurrence of 113
Overland Canyon, faults east of 69
normal faults north of 71
transverse fault north of 70-71
Ozark claims, features of 128

P

Pay Rock claims, features of 150
Pharmacosiderite, occurrence of 117
Physical features of the area 1-2
Pine Canyon limestone, correlation of 27
Pioche shale, correlation of 7
Pipelike deposits, alteration of 105
features of 97-99
mines and prospects in 119-123
Pliocene(?) sediments, occurrence and character of 48-49
Plumbojarosite, occurrence of 117
Pogonip limestone, correlation of 16
Pole Star Copper Co., claims of 124-125
Pool Canyon transverse fault, features of 57, 58, 80
relation of, to North Pass thrust 80-81
Powellite, occurrence of 118
Pre-Carboniferous sedimentary rocks in eastern Nevada and western Utah, correlation of 28
Prospect Mountain quartzite, age and correlation of 6
distribution of 4-5
lithology of 5
section of 6
shale members of 6
thickness of 6
Pyrite, occurrence of 111
Pyroclastic rocks, petrography of 52-53
Pyromorphite 116
Pyrrhotite, occurrence of 111

Q

Quartz carbonate vein east of Clifton, specimen from pl. 10
Quartz monzonite, alteration of 94-96
areal extent of 43-44
chemical analysis of 44
comparison of alteration of, with alteration of sedimentary rocks 96-97
factors influencing the localization of 45-46
petrographic and chemical character of 44-45
silicified, elongated quartz grains in pl. 9
structural features not related to emplacement or cooling of 89-91
structural features related to solidification of 89
Quartz monzonite block, faults related to emplacement of 88-89
structure of 88-91
Quartz, occurrence of 112
Quartz-sulphide veins, alteration of 105
features of 101
mines and prospects in 140-151
outlook for mining 110

R

Rea claim, features of 150-151
Realgar, occurrence of 111
Reaper claims, features of 119-121
specimen from tungsten-bearing pipe on pl. 9
Red Jacket claim, features of 148
Reeside, J. B., Jr., fossils identified by 43
Replacement bodies, arsenic, alteration of 105-106
arsenic, features of 102-103
mines and prospects in 151-162
outlook for mining 110
barite, alteration of 107
copper-lead-silver, alteration of 106-107

Page
Replacement bodies, copper-lead-silver, features of 103–104
mines and prospects in 162–166
outlook for mining 110
Resser, C. E., fossils identified by 10, 14
Rhyolite, partial analysis of 51
Rhyolite, petrography of 51
Royal Gulch, "window" in 79
"window" in, faults in 81–82
Rube mine, features of 136–138
Rutile, occurrence of 112

S

Sam K. No. 1 claim, features of 151
Scapolite group, occurrence of 114
Scheelite, occurrence of 117–118
Scorodite, crystalline, forming from metacolloid pl. 12
occurrence of 116–117
Searchlight claim, work on 163
Secret Canyon shale, correlation of 14
Sedimentary rocks, alteration of 91–94
comparison of alteration of, with alteration of quartz monzonite 96–97
recrystallization of 91–92
Sericitization, alteration of quartz monzonite by 95
Sevy Canyon, structure in, south of Blood Canyon fault 67
transverse fault in, relations of 66–67
Sevy dolomite, age and correlation of 19
distribution of 18
lithology of 18–19
thickness of 19
Shay claims, features of 149
Siderite, occurrence of 113
Siderotil, occurrence of 117
Silicate-gangue veins, alteration of 105
features of 99–101
mines and prospects in 123–138
outlook for mining 109–110
Silicate minerals, alteration to 92–93
Silicification, alteration of quartz monzonite by 95–96
Silurian beds, unconformity at top of 18
Silurian system 17–18
Silver & Gold Mining Co., Inc., claims of, features of 143
Silver claim, features of 168
Silver King claims, features of 163
Simonson dolomite, age and correlation of 20
distribution of 19
fossils of 20
laminated pl. 5
lithology of 19
section of 19
thickness of 20
Smithsonite, occurrence of 113
Southern Confederate claim, features of 147–148
Spadaite, occurrence of 115
wollastonite replaced by pl. 8
Sphalerite, occurrence of 111
Spinel, occurrence of 112
Spotted Fawn claims, features of 145–146
Spotted Fawn fault, faults beneath thrust north of 82
minor faults between Pool Canyon fault and 82
relations of 56
Spotted Fawn normal-fault zone, features of 81
Stibnite, occurrence of 111
Stolzite, occurrence of 118
Structural cycles, stages of 55–61
Structural features, age of 63–64
correlation of 65
local descriptions of 64–91
Success mine, features of 145
Sulphur, occurrence of 110
Sunday claims, features of 167

T

Talc, occurrence of 115
Tank Wash fault, relations of 56, 86
Tennantite, occurrence of 112
Tertiary system, formations of 42–43
Tetrahedrite, occurrence of 112
Teutonic limestone, correlation of 10
Tintic quartzite, correlation of 6
Titanite, occurrence of 116
Tourmaline, occurrence of 115
Trachyte, partial analysis of 51
petrography of 51
Trail Gulch fault, relations of 56, 84
Tremolite, occurrence of 114
Triassic limestones, Lower, occurrence and fossils of 42
Trippe limestone, age and correlation of 12
distribution of 11
laminated pl. 5
lithology of 11–12
section of 12
thickness of 12
Troy claim, features of 151
Tungsten, outlook for mining 109
Twin Peaks, recumbent anticline on 56, 86

U

Uiyabi Canyon block, structural features of 69–72
Uiyabi Canyon, minor folds in 70
Uncle Sam claim, features of 166
Undine claims, features of 150
U. S. mine, bladed arsenopyrite from Tunnel level of pl. 11
faults near 76
geology of 158–160
jasperoid from, with inclusions of opal in quartz pl. 8
location and development of 156–158
ore of 160–162
polished section from, showing brecciated arsenopyrite veined by pyrite, quartz, sphalerite, and galena pl. 11
structural features east of 75–76

V

Vegetation 3
Vesuvianite, occurrence of 114
Victoria quartzite, correlation of 27
Victory No. 1 claim, features of 127
Volcanic rocks, age of 53
alteration of 53

W

Wad, occurrence of 112
Walla Walla claim, features of 164
Wells, R. C., chemical analysis by 44
Western Utah Extension Copper Co., claims of 146–147
Western Utah mine, polished section from, showing replacement of arsenopyrite fragments by quartz and sericite pl. 11
specimens of scorodite from pl. 12
structural features in vicinity of 77
White Sage formation, age and correlation of 43
distribution of 42
fossils of 43
lithology of 42–43
thickness of 43
unconformity above 43
Willow Springs district, history and productions of 167
prospects of 167–168
Wilson Consolidated mine, features of 138–140
quartz and orthoclase replacing calcite in pl. 10
Wolframite, occurrence of 117
Wollastonite, occurrence of 113–114
Woodman formation, age and correlation of 28–29
distribution of 27
fossils of 28–29
lithology of 27
minor thrust in, north of Garrison Monster new camp pl. 7
section of 28
thickness of 28
Wulfenite, occurrence of 118

Y

Yellow Hammer claims, features of 122
Yellow Hill limestone, correlation of 16
Young Peak dolomite, age and correlation of 11
distribution of 10
lithology of 10–11
mottled pl. 5

Z

Zircon, occurrence of 114
Zoisite, occurrence of 114

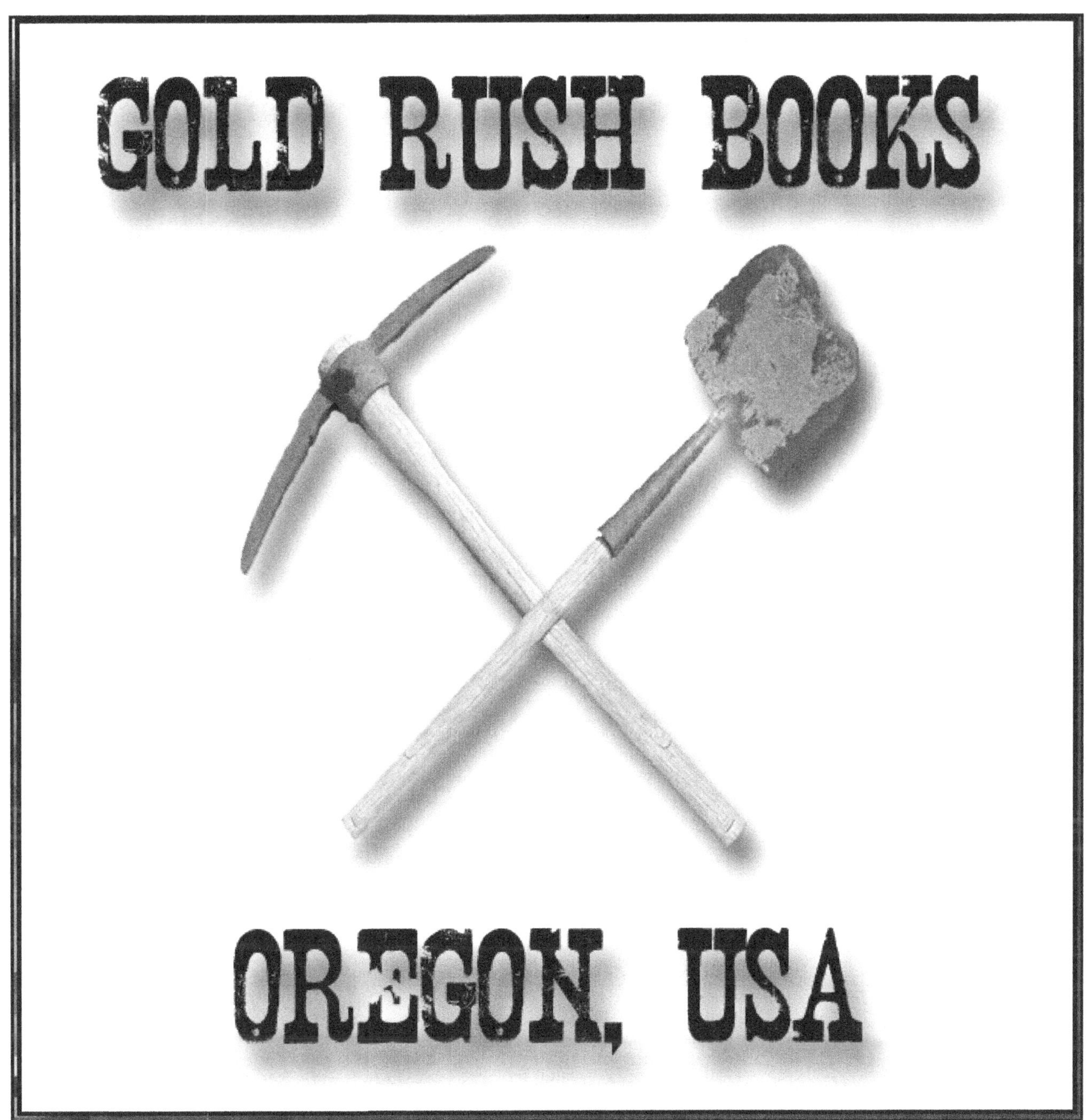
GOLD RUSH BOOKS
OREGON, USA

Books On Mining

Visit: www.goldminingbooks.com to order your copies or ask your favorite book seller to offer them.

Mining Books by Kerby Jackson

<u>Gold Dust: Stories From Oregon's Mining Years</u> - Oregon mining historian and prospector, Kerby Jackson, brings you a treasure trove of seventeen stories on Southern Oregon's rich history of gold prospecting, the prospectors and their discoveries, and the breathtaking areas they settled in and made homes. **5″ X 8″, 98 ppgs. Retail Price: $11.99**

<u>The Golden Trail: More Stories From Oregon's Mining Years</u> - In his follow-up to "Gold Dust: Stories of Oregon's Mining Years", this time around, Jackson brings us twelve tales from Oregon's Gold Rush, including the story about the first gold strike on Canyon Creek in Grant County, about the old timers who found gold by the pail full at the Victor Mine near Galice, how Iradel Bray discovered a rich ledge of gold on the Coquille River during the height of the Rogue River War, a tale of two elderly miners on the hunt for a lost mine in the Cascade Mountains, details about the discovery of the famous Armstrong Nugget and others. **5″ X 8″, 70 ppgs. Retail Price: $10.99**

Oregon Mining Books

<u>Geology and Mineral Resources of Josephine County, Oregon</u> - Unavailable since the 1970's, this important publication was originally compiled by the Oregon Department of Geology and Mineral Industries and includes important details on the economic geology and mineral resources of this important mining area in South Western Oregon. Included are notes on the history, geology and development of important mines, as well as insights into the mining of gold, copper, nickel, limestone, chromium and other minerals found in large quantities in Josephine County, Oregon. **8.5″ X 11″, 54 ppgs. Retail Price: $9.99**

<u>Mines and Prospects of the Mount Reuben Mining District</u> - Unavailable since 1947, this important publication was originally compiled by geologist Elton Youngberg of the Oregon Department of Geology and Mineral Industries and includes detailed descriptions, histories and the geology of the Mount Reuben Mining District in Josephine County, Oregon. Included are notes on the history, geology, development and assay statistics, as well as underground maps of all the major mines and prospects in the vicinity of this much neglected mining district. **8.5″ X 11″, 48 ppgs. Retail Price: $9.99**

<u>The Granite Mining District</u> - Notes on the history, geology and development of important mines in the well known Granite Mining District which is located in Grant County, Oregon. Some of the mines discussed include the Ajax, Blue Ribbon, Buffalo, Continental, Cougar-Independence, Magnolia, New York, Standard and the Tillicum. Also included are many rare maps pertaining to the mines in the area. **8.5″ X 11″, 48 ppgs. Retail Price: $9.99**

<u>Ore Deposits of the Takilma and Waldo Mining Districts of Josephine County, Oregon</u> - The Waldo and Takilma mining districts are most notable for the fact that the earliest large scale mining of placer gold and copper in Oregon took place in these two areas. Included are details about some of the earliest large gold mines in the state such as the Llano de Oro, High Gravel, Cameron, Platerica, Deep Gravel and others, as well as copper mines such as the famous Queen of Bronze mine, the Waldo, Lily and Cowboy mines. This volume also includes six maps and 20 original illustrations. **8.5″ X 11″, 74 ppgs. Retail Price: $9.99**

<u>Metal Mines of Douglas, Coos and Curry Counties, Oregon</u> - Oregon mining historian Kerby Jackson introduces us to a classic work on Oregon's mining history in this important re-issue of Bulletin 14C Volume 1, otherwise known as the Douglas, Coos & Curry Counties, Oregon Metal Mines Handbook. Unavailable since 1940, this important publication was originally compiled by the Oregon Department of Geology and Mineral Industries includes detailed descriptions, histories and the geology of over 250 metallic mineral mines and prospects in this rugged area of South West Oregon. **8.5″ X 11″, 158 ppgs. Retail Price: $19.99**

Metal Mines of Jackson County, Oregon - Unavailable since 1943, this important publication was originally compiled by the Oregon Department of Geology and Mineral Industries includes detailed descriptions, histories and the geology of over 450 metallic mineral mines and prospects in Jackson County, Oregon. Included are such famous gold mining areas as Gold Hill, Jacksonville, Sterling and the Upper Applegate. **8.5″ X 11″, 220 ppgs. Retail Price: $24.99**

Metal Mines of Josephine County, Oregon - Oregon mining historian Kerby Jackson introduces us to a classic work on Oregon's mining history in this important re-issue of Bulletin 14C, otherwise known as the Josephine County, Oregon Metal Mines Handbook. Unavailable since 1952, this important publication was originally compiled by the Oregon Department of Geology and Mineral Industries includes detailed descriptions, histories and the geology of over 500 metallic mineral mines and prospects in Josephine County, Oregon. **8.5″ X 11″, 250 ppgs. Retail Price: $24.99**

Metal Mines of North East Oregon - Oregon mining historian Kerby Jackson introduces us to a classic work on Oregon's mining history in this important re-issue of Bulletin 14A and 14B, otherwise known as the North East Oregon Metal Mines Handbook. Unavailable since 1941, this important publication was originally compiled by the Oregon Department of Geology and Mineral Industries and includes detailed descriptions, histories and the geology of over 750 metallic mineral mines and prospects in North Eastern Oregon. **8.5″ X 11″, 310 ppgs. Retail Price: $29.99**

Metal Mines of North West Oregon - Oregon mining historian Kerby Jackson introduces us to a classic work on Oregon's mining history in this important re-issue of Bulletin 14D, otherwise known as the North West Oregon Metal Mines Handbook. Unavailable since 1951, this important publication was originally compiled by the Oregon Department of Geology and Mineral Industries and includes detailed descriptions, histories and the geology of over 250 metallic mineral mines and prospects in North Western Oregon. **8.5″ X 11″, 182 ppgs. Retail Price: $19.99**

Mines and Prospects of Oregon - Mining historian Kerby Jackson introduces us to a classic mining work by the Oregon Bureau of Mines in this important re-issue of The Handbook of Mines and Prospects of Oregon. Unavailable since 1916, this publication includes important insights into hundreds of gold, silver, copper, coal, limestone and other mines that operated in the State of Oregon around the turn of the 19th Century. Included are not only geological details on early mines throughout Oregon, but also insights into their history, production, locations and in some cases, also included are rare maps of their underground workings. **8.5″ X 11″, 314 ppgs. Retail Price: $24.99**

Lode Gold of the Klamath Mountains of Northern California and South West Oregon
(See California Mining Books)

Mineral Resources of South West Oregon - Unavailable since 1914, this publication includes important insights into dozens of mines that once operated in South West Oregon, including the famous gold fields of Josephine and Jackson Counties, as well as the Coal Mines of Coos County. Included are not only geological details on early mines throughout South West Oregon, but also insights into their history, production and locations. **8.5″ X 11″, 154 ppgs. Retail Price: $11.99**

Chromite Mining in The Klamath Mountains of California and Oregon
(See California Mining Books)

Southern Oregon Mineral Wealth - Unavailable since 1904, this rare publication provides a unique snapshot into the mines that were operating in the area at the time. Included are not only geological details on early mines throughout South West Oregon, but also insights into their history, production and locations. Some of the mining areas include Grave Creek, Greenback, Wolf Creek, Jump Off Joe Creek, Granite Hill, Galice, Mount Reuben, Gold Hill, Galls Creek, Kane Creek, Sardine Creek, Birdseye Creek, Evans Creek, Foots Creek, Jacksonville, Ashland, the Applegate River, Waldo, Kerby and the Illinois River, Althouse and Sucker Creek, as well as insights into local copper mining and other topics. **8.5″ X 11″, 64 ppgs. Retail Price: $8.99**

Geology and Ore Deposits of the Takilma and Waldo Mining Districts - Unavailable since the 1933, this publication was originally compiled by the United States Geological Survey and includes details on gold and copper mining in the Takilma and Waldo Districts of Josephine County, Oregon. The Waldo and Takilma mining districts are most notable for the fact that the earliest large scale mining of placer gold and copper in Oregon took place in these two areas. Included in this report are details about some of the earliest large gold mines in the state such as the Llano de Oro, High Gravel, Cameron, Platerica, Deep Gravel and others, as well as copper mines such as the famous Queen of Bronze mine, the Waldo, Lily and Cowboy mines. In addition to geological examinations, insights are also provided into the production, day to day operations and early histories of these mines, as well as calculations of known mineral reserves in the area. This volume also includes six maps and 20 original illustrations. **8.5″ X 11″, 74 ppgs. Retail Price: $9.99**

Gold Mines of Oregon - Oregon mining historian Kerby Jackson introduces us to a classic work on Oregon's mining history in this important re-issue of Bulletin 61, otherwise known as "Gold and Silver In Oregon". Unavailable since 1968, this important publication was originally compiled by geologists Howard C. Brooks and Len Ramp of the Oregon Department of Geology and Mineral Industries and includes detailed descriptions, histories and the geology of over 450 gold mines Oregon. Included are notes on the history, geology and gold production statistics of all the major mining areas in Oregon including the Klamath Mountains, the Blue Mountains and the North Cascades. While gold is where you find it, as every miner knows, the path to success is to prospect for gold where it was previously found. **8.5" X 11", 344 ppgs. Retail Price: $24.99**

Mines and Mineral Resources of Curry County Oregon - Originally published in 1916, this important publication on Oregon Mining has not been available for nearly a century. Included are rare insights into the history, production and locations of dozens of gold mines in Curry County, Oregon, as well as detailed information on important Oregon mining districts in that area such as those at Agness, Bald Face Creek, Mule Creek, Boulder Creek, China Diggings, Collier Creek, Elk River, Gold Beach, Rock Creek, Sixes River and elsewhere. Particular attention is especially paid to the famous beach gold deposits of this portion of the Oregon Coast. **8.5" X 11", 140 ppgs. Retail Price: $11.99**

Chromite Mining in South West Oregon - Originally published in 1961, this important publication on Oregon Mining has not been available for nearly a century. Included are rare insights into the history, production and locations of nearly 300 chromite mines in South Western Oregon. **8.5" X 11", 184 ppgs. Retail Price: $14.99**

Mineral Resources of Douglas County Oregon - Originally published in 1972, this important publication on Oregon Mining has not been available for nearly forty years. Included are rare insights into the geology, history, production and locations of numerous gold mines and other mining properties in Douglas County, Oregon. **8.5" X 11", 124 ppgs. Retail Price: $11.99**

Mineral Resources of Coos County Oregon - Originally published in 1972, this important publication on Oregon Mining has not been available for nearly forty years. Included are rare insights into the geology, history, production and locations of numerous gold mines and other mining properties in Coos County, Oregon. **8.5" X 11", 100 ppgs. Retail Price: $11.99**

Mineral Resources of Lane County Oregon - Originally published in 1938, this important publication on Oregon Mining has not been available for nearly seventy five years. Included are extremely rare insights into the geology and mines of Lane County, Oregon, in particular in the Bohemia, Blue River, Oakridge, Black Butte and Winberry Mining Districts. **8.5" X 11", 82 ppgs. Retail Price: $9.99**

Mineral Resources of the Upper Chetco River of Oregon: Including the Kalmiopsis Wilderness - Originally published in 1975, this important publication on Oregon Mining has not been available for nearly forty years. Withdrawn under the 1872 Mining Act since 1984, real insight into the minerals resources and mines of the Upper Chetco River has long been unavailable due to the remoteness of the area. Despite this, the decades of battle between property owners and environmental extremists over the last private mining inholding in the area has continued to pique the interest of those interested in mining and other forms of natural resource use. Gold mining began in the area in the 1850's and has a rich history in this geographic area, even if the facts surrounding it are little known. Included are twenty two rare photographs, as well as insights into the Becca and Morning Mine, the Emmly Mine (also known as Emily Camp), the Frazier Mine, the Golden Dream or Higgins Mine, Hustis Mine, Peck Mine and others. **8.5" X 11", 64 ppgs. Retail Price: $8.99**

Gold Dredging in Oregon - Originally published in 1939, this important publication on Oregon Mining has not been available for nearly seventy five years. Included are extremely rare insights into the history and day to day operations of the dragline and bucketline gold dredges that once worked the placer gold fields of South West and North East Oregon in decades gone by. Also included are details into the areas that were worked by gold dredges in Josephine, Jackson, Baker and Grant counties, as well as the economic factors that impacted this mining method. This volume also offers a unique look into the values of river bottom land in relation to both farming and mining, in how farm lands were mined, re-soiled and reclamated after the dredges worked them. Featured are hard to find maps of the gold dredge fields, as well as rare photographs from a bygone era. **8.5" X 11", 86 ppgs. Retail Price: $8.99**

Quick Silver Mining in Oregon - Originally published in 1963, this important publication on Oregon Mining has not been available for over fifty years. This publication includes details into the history and production of Elemental Mercury or Quicksilver in the State of Oregon. **8.5" X 11", 238 ppgs. Retail Price: $15.99**

Mines of the Greenhorn Mining District of Grant County Oregon - Originally published in 1948, this important publication on Oregon Mining has not been available for over sixty five years. In this publication are rare insights into the mines of the famous Greenhorn Mining District of Grant County, Oregon, especially the famous Morning Mine. Also included are details on the Tempest, Tiger, Bi-Metallic, Windsor, Psyche, Big Johnny, Snow Creek, Banzette and Paramount Mines, as well as prospects in the vicinities in the famous mining areas of Mormon Basin, Vinegar Basin and Desolation Creek. Included are hard to find mine maps and dozens of rare photographs from the bygone era of Grant County's rich mining history. **8.5" X 11", 72 ppgs. Retail Price: $9.99**

<u>Geology of the Wallowa Mountains of Oregon: Part I (Volume 1)</u> - Originally published in 1938, this important publication on Oregon Mining has not been available for nearly seventy five years. Included are details on the geology of this unique portion of North Eastern Oregon. This is the first part of a two book series on the area. Accompanying the text are rare photographs and historic maps.**8.5″ X 11″, 92 ppgs. Retail Price: $9.99**

<u>Geology of the Wallowa Mountains of Oregon: Part II (Volume 2)</u> - Originally published in 1938, this important publication on Oregon Mining has not been available for nearly seventy five years. Included are details on the geology of this unique portion of North Eastern Oregon. This is the first part of a two book series on the area. Accompanying the text are rare photographs and historic maps.**8.5″ X 11″, 94 ppgs. Retail Price: $9.99**

<u>Field Identification of Minerals For Oregon Prospectors</u> - Originally published in 1940, this important publication on Oregon Mining has not been available for nearly seventy five years. Included in this volume is an easy system for testing and identifying a wide range of minerals that might be found by prospectors, geologists and rockhounds in the State of Oregon, as well as in other locales. Topics include how to put together your own field testing kit and how to conduct rudimentary tests in the field. This volume is written in a clear and concise way to make it useful even for beginners. **8.5″ X 11″, 158 ppgs. Retail Price: $14.99**

<u>The Bohemia Mining District of Oregon</u> - Originally published in 1900, this important publication on Oregon Mining has not been available for over a century. Included in this volume are important insights into the famous Bohemia Mining District of Oregon, including the histories and locations of important gold mines in the area such as the Ophir Mine, Clarence, Acturas, Peek-a-boo, White Swan, Combination Mine, the Musick Mine, The California, White Ghost, The Mystery, Wall Street, Vesuvius, Story, Lizzie Bullock, Delta, Elsie Dora, Golden Slipper, Broadway, Champion Mine, Knott, Noonday, Helena, White Wings, Riverside and others. Also included are notes on the nearby Blue River Mining District. **8.5″ X 11″, 58 ppgs. Retail Price: $9.99**

<u>The Gold Fields of Eastern Oregon</u> - Unavailable since 1900, this publication was originally compiled by the Baker City Chamber of Commerce Offering important insights into the gold mining history of Eastern Oregon, "The Gold Fields of Eastern Oregon" sheds a rare light on many of the gold mines that were operating at the turn of the 19th Century in Baker County and Grant County in North Eastern Oregon. Some of the areas featured include the Cable Cove District, Baisely-Elhorn, Granite, Red Boy, Bonanza, Susanville, Sparta, Virtue, Vaughn, Sumpter, Burnt River, Rye Valley and other mining districts. Included is basic information on not only many gold mines that are well known to those interested in Eastern Oregon mining history, but also many mines and prospects which have been mostly lost to the passage of time. Accompanying are numerous rare photos **8.5″ X 11″, 78 ppgs. Retail Price: $10.99**

<u>Gold Mining in Eastern Oregon</u> - Originally published in 1938, this important publication on Oregon Mining has not been available for over a century. Included in this volume are important insights into the famous mining districts of Eastern Oregon during the late 1930's. Particular attention is given to those gold mines with milling and concentrating facilities in the Greenhorn, Red Boy, Alamo, Bonanza, Granite, Cable Cove, Cracker Creek, Virtue, Keating, Medical Springs, Sanger, Sparta, Chicken Creek, Mormon Basin, Connor Creek, Cornucopia and the Bull Run Mining Districts. Some of the mines featured include the Ben Harrison, North Pole-Columbia, Highland Maxwell, Baisley-Elkhorn, White Swan, Balm Creek, Twin Baby, Gem of Sparta, New Deal, Gleason, Gifford-Johnson, Cornucopia, Record, Bull Run, Orion and others. Of particular interest are the mill flow sheets and descriptions of milling operations of these mines. **8.5″ X 11″, 68 ppgs. Retail Price: $8.99**

<u>The Gold Belt of the Blue Mountains of Oregon</u> - Originally published in 1901, this important publication on Oregon Mining has not been available for over a century. Included in this volume are rare insights into the gold deposits of the Blue Mountains of North East Oregon, including the history of their early discovery and early production. Extensive details are offered on this important mining area's mineralogy and economic geology, as well as insights into nearby gold placers, silver deposits and copper deposits. Featured are the Elkhorn and Rock Creek mining districts, the Pocahontas district, Auburn and Minersville districts, Sumpter and Cracker Creek, Cable Cove, the Camp Carson district, Granite, Alamo, Greenhorn, Robinsonville, the Upper Burnt River Valley and Bonanza districts, Susanville, Quartzburg, Canyon Creek, Virtue, the Copper Butte district, the North Powder River, Sparta, Eagle Creek, Cornucopia, Pine Creek, Lower Powder River, the Upper Snake River Canyon, Rye Valley, Lower Burnt River Valley, Mormon Basin, the Malheur and Clarks Creek districts, Sutton Creek and others. Of particular interest are important details on numerous gold mines and prospects in these mining districts, including their locations, histories, geology and other important information, as well as information on silver, copper and fire opal deposits. **8.5″ X 11″, 250 ppgs. Retail Price: $24.99**

Mining in the Cascades Range of Oregon - Originally published in 1938, this important publication on Oregon Mining has not been available for over seventy five years. Included in this volume are rare insights into the gold mines and other types of metal mines in the Cascades Mountain Range of Oregon. Some of the important mining areas covered include the famous Bohemia Mining District, the North Santiam Mining District, Quartzville Mining District, Blue River Mining District, Fall Creek Mining District, Oakridge District, Zinc District, Buzzard-Al Sarena District, Grand Cove, Climax District and Barron Mining District. Of particular interest are important details on over 100 mines and prospects in these mining districts, including their locations, histories, geology and other important information. **8.5″ X 11″, 170 ppgs. Retail Price: $14.99**

Beach Gold Placers of the Oregon Coast - Originally published in 1934, this important publication on Oregon Mining has not been available for over 80 years. Included in this volume are rare insights into the beach gold deposits of the State of Oregon, including their locations, occurance, composition and geology. Of particular interest is information on placer platinum in Oregon's rich beach deposits. Also included are the locations and other information on some famous Oregon beach mines, including the Pioneer, Eagle, Chickamin, Iowa and beach placer mines north of the mouth of the Rogue River. **8.5″ X 11″, 60 ppgs. Retail Price: $8.99**

Idaho Mining Books

Gold in Idaho - Unavailable since the 1940's, this publication was originally compiled by the Idaho Bureau of Mines and includes details on gold mining in Idaho. Included is not only raw data on gold production in Idaho, but also valuable insight into where gold may be found in Idaho, as well as practical information on the gold bearing rocks and other geological features that will assist those looking for placer and lode gold in the State of Idaho. This volume also includes thirteen gold maps that greatly enhance the practical usability of the information contained in this small book detailing where to find gold in Idaho. **8.5″ X 11″, 72 ppgs. Retail Price: $9.99**

Geology of the Couer D'Alene Mining District of Idaho - Unavailable since 1961, this publication was originally compiled by the Idaho Bureau of Mines and Geology and includes details on the mining of gold, silver and other minerals in the famous Coeur D'Alene Mining District in Northern Idaho. Included are details on the early history of the Coeur D'Alene Mining District, local tectonic settings, ore deposit features, information on the mineral belts of the Osburn Fault, as well as detailed information on the famous Bunker Hill Mine, the Dayrock Mine, Galena Mine, Lucky Friday Mine and the infamous Sunshine Mine. This volume also includes sixteen hard to find maps. **8.5″ X 11″, 70 ppgs. Retail Price: $9.99**

The Gold Camps and Silver Cities of Idaho - Originally published in 1963, this important publication on Idaho Mining has not been available for nearly fifty years. Included are rare insights into the history of Idaho's Gold Rush, as well as the mad craze for silver in the Idaho Panhandle. Documented in fine detail are the early mining excitements at Boise Basin, at South Boise, in the Owyhees, at Deadwood, Long Valley, Stanley Basin and Robinson Bar, at Atlanta, on the famous Boise River, Volcano, Little Smokey, Banner, Boise Ridge, Hailey, Leesburg, Lemhi, Pearl, at South Mountain, Shoup and Ulysses, Yellow Jacket and Loon Creek. The story follows with the appearance of Chinese miners at the new mining camps on the Snake River, Black Pine, Yankee Fork, Bay Horse, Clayton, Heath, Seven Devils, Gibbonsville, Vienna and Sawtooth City. Also included are special sections on the Idaho Lead and Silver mines of the late 1800's, as well as the mining discoveries of the early 1900's that paved the way for Idaho's modern mining and mineral industry. Lavishly illustrated with rare historic photos, this volume provides a one of a kind documentary into Idaho's mining history that is sure to be enjoyed by not only modern miners and prospectors who still scour the hills in search of nature's treasures, but also those enjoy history and tromping through overgrown ghost towns and long abandoned mining camps. **8.5″ X 11″, 186 ppgs. Retail Price: $14.99**

Ore Deposits and Mining in North Western Custer County Idaho - Unavailable since 1913, this important publication was originally published by the Us Department of the Interior and has been unavailable for a century. Included are fine details on the geology, geography, gold placers and gold and silver bearing quartz veins of the mining region of North West Custer County, Idaho. Of particular interest is a rare look at the mines and prospects of the region, including those such as the Ramshorn Mine, SkyLark, Riverview, Excelsior, Beardsley, Pacific, Hoosier, Silver Brick, Forest Rose and dozens of others in the Bay Horse Mining District. Also covered are the mines of the Yankee Fork District such as the Lucky Boy, Badger, Black, Enterprise, Charles Dickens, Morrison, Golden Sunbeam, Montana, Golden Gate and others, as well as those in the Loon Mining District. **8.5″ X 11″, 126 ppgs. Retail Price: $12.99**

Gold Rush To Idaho - Unavailable since 1963, this important publication was originally published by the Idaho Bureau of Mines and has been unavailable for 50 years. "Gold Rush To Idaho" revisits the earliest years of the discovery of gold in Idaho Territory and introduces us to the conditions that the pioneer [illegible] through the wilderness of Idaho's mountains and discovered the precious yellow metal at Oro Fino and Pierce. Subsequent rushes followed at [illegible], Newsome, Clearwater Station, Florence, Warrens and elsewhere. Of particular interest is a rare look at the hardships that the first miners in Idaho met with during their day to day existences and their attempts to bring law and order to their mining camps. **8.5" X 11", 88 ppgs. Retail Price: $9.99**

The Geology and Mines of Northern Idaho and North Western Montana - Unavailable since 1909, this important publication was originally published by the Us Department of the Interior and has been unavailable for a century. Included are fine details on the geology and geography of the mining regions of Northern Idaho and North Western Montana. Of particular interest is a rare look at the mines and prospects of the region, including those in the Pine Creek Mining District, Lake Pend Oreille district, Troy Mining District, Sylvanite District, Cabinet Mining District, Prospect Mining District and the Missoula Valley. Some of the mines featured include the Iron Mountain, Silver Butte, Snowshoe, Grouse Mountain Mine and others. **8.5" X 11", 142 ppgs. Retail Price: $12.99**

Mining in the Alturas Quadrangle of Blaine County Idaho - Unavailable since 1922, this important publication was originally published by the Idaho Bureau of Mines and has been unavailable for ninety years. Topics include the geology, rock formations and the formation of ore deposits in this important mining area of Idaho. Of particular focus is information on the local geology, quartz veins and ore deposits of this portion of Idaho. Included are hard to find details, including the descriptions and locations of numerous gold and silver mines in the area including the Silver King, Pilgrim, Columbia, Lone Jack, Sunbeam, Pride of the West, Lucky Boy, Scotia, Atlanta, Beaver-Bidwell and others mines and prospects. **8.5" X 11", 56 ppgs. Retail Price: $8.99**

Mining in Lemhi County Idaho - Originally published in 1913, this important book on Idaho Mining has not been available to miners for over a century. Included are rare insights into hundreds of gold, silver, copper and other mines in this famous Idaho mining area. Details include the locations, geology, history, production and other facts of the mines of this region, not only gold and silver hardrock mines, but also gold placer mines, lead-silver deposits, copper mines, cobalt-nickel deposits, tungsten and tin mines . It is lavishly illustrated with hard to find photos of the period and rare mining maps. Some of the vicinities featured include the Nicholia Mining District, Spring Mountain District, Texas District, Blue Wing District, Junction District, McDevitt District, Pratt Creek, Eldorado District, Kirtley Creek, Carmen Creek, Gibbonsville, Indian Creek, Mineral Hill District, Mackinaw, Eureka District, Blackbird District, YellowJacket District, Gravel Range District, Junction District, Parker Mountain and other mining districts. **8.5" X 11", 226 ppgs. Retail Price: $19.99**

Utah Mining Books

Fluorite in Utah - Unavailable since 1954, this publication was originally compiled by the USGS, State of Utah and U.S. Atomic Energy Commission and details the mining of fluorspar, also known as fluorite in the State of Utah. Included are details on the geology and history of fluorspar (fluorite) mining in Utah, including details on where this unique gem mineral may be found in the State of Utah. **8.5" X 11", 60 ppgs. Retail Price: $8.99**

California Mining Books

The Tertiary Gravels of the Sierra Nevada of California - Mining historian Kerby Jackson introduces us to a classic mining work by Waldemar Lindgren in this important re-issue of The Tertiary Gravels of the Sierra Nevada of California. Unavailable since 1911, this publication includes details on the gold bearing ancient river channels of the famous Sierra Nevada region of California. **8.5" X 11", 282 ppgs. Retail Price: $19.99**

The Mother Lode Mining Region of California - Unavailable since 1900, this publication includes details on the gold mines of California's famous Mother Lode gold mining area. Included are details on the geology, history and important gold mines of the region, as well as insights into historic mining methods, mine timbering, mining machinery, mining bell signals and other details on how these mines operated. Also included are insights into the gold mines of the California Mother Lode that were in operation during the first sixty years of California's mining history. **8.5" X 11", 176 ppgs. Retail Price: $14.99**

Lode Gold of the Klamath Mountains of Northern California and South West Oregon - Unavailable since 1971, this publication was originally compiled by Preston E. Hotz and includes details on the lode mining districts of Oregon and California's Klamath Mountains. Included are details on the geology, history and important lode mines of the French Gulch, Deadwood, Whiskeytown, Shasta, Redding, Muletown, South Fork, Old Diggings, Dog Creek (Delta), Bully Choop (Indian Creek), Harrison Gulch, Hayfork, Minersville, Trinity Center, Canyon Creek, East Fork, New River, Denny, Liberty (Black Bear), Cecilville, Callahan, Yreka, Fort Jones and Happy Camp mining districts in California, as well as the Ashland, Rogue River, Applegate, Illinois River, Takilma, Greenback, Galice, Silver Peak, Myrtle Creek and Mule Creek districts of South Western Oregon. Also included are insights into the mineralization and other characteristics of this important mining region. **8.5" X 11", 100 ppgs. Retail Price: $10.99**

Mines and Mineral Resources of Shasta County, Siskiyou County, Trinity County: California - Unavailable since 1915, this publication was originally compiled by the California State Mining Bureau and includes details on the gold mines of this area of Northern California. Also included are insights into the mineralization and other characteristics of this important mining region, as well as the location of historic gold mines. **8.5" X 11", 204 ppgs. Retail Price: $19.99**

Geology of the Yreka Quadrangle, Siskiyou County, California - Unavailable since 1977, this publication was originally compiled by Preston E. Hotz and includes details on the geology of the Yreka Quadrangle of Siskiyou County, California. Also included are insights into the mineralization and other characteristics of this important mining region. **8.5" X 11", 78 ppgs. Retail Price: $7.99**

Mines of San Diego and Imperial Counties, California - Originally published in 1914, this important publication on California Mining has not been available for a century. This publication includes important information on the early gold mines of San Diego and Imperial County, which were some of the first gold fields mined in California by early Spanish and Mexican miners before the 49ers came on the scene. Included are not only details on early mining methods in the area, production statistics and geological information, but also the location of the early gold mines that helped make California "The Golden State". Also included are details on the mining of other minerals such as silver, lead, zinc, manganese, tungsten, vanadium, asbestos, barite, borax, cement, clay, dolomite, fluospar, gem stones, graphite, marble, salines, petroleum, stronium, talc and others. **8.5" X 11", 116 ppgs. Retail Price: $12.99**

Mines of Sierra County, California - Unavailable since 1920, this publication was originally compiled by the California State Mining Bureau and includes details on the gold mines of Sierra County, California. Also included are insights into the mineralization and other characteristics of this important mining region, as well as the location of historic gold mines. **8.5" X 11", 156 ppgs. Retail Price: $19.99**

Mines of Plumas County, California - Unavailable since 1918, this publication was originally compiled by the California State Mining Bureau and includes details on the gold mines of Plumas County, California. Also included are insights into the mineralization and other characteristics of this important mining region, as well as the location of historic gold mines. **8.5" X 11", 200 ppgs. Retail Price: $19.99**

Mines of El Dorado, Placer, Sacramento and Yuba Counties, California - Originally published in 1917, this important publication on California Mining has not been available for nearly a century. This publication includes important information on the early gold mines of El Dorado County, Placer County, Sacramento County and Yuba County, which were some of the first gold fields mined by the Forty-Niners during the California Gold Rush. Included are not only details on early mining methods in the area, production statistics and geological information, but also the location of the early gold mines that helped make California "The Golden State". Also included are insights into the early mining of chrome, copper and other minerals in this important mining area. **8.5" X 11", 204 ppgs. Retail Price: $19.99**

Mines of Los Angeles, Orange and Riverside Counties, California - Originally published in 1917, this important publication on California Mining has not been available for nearly a century. This publication includes important information on the early gold mines of Los Angeles County, Orange County and Riverside County, which were some of the first gold fields mined in California by early Spanish and Mexican miners before the 49ers came on the scene. Included are not only details on early mining methods in the area, production statistics and geological information, but also the location of the early gold mines that helped make California "The Golden State". **8.5" X 11", 146 ppgs. Retail Price: $12.99**

Mines of San Bernadino and Tulare Counties, California - Originally published in 1917, this important publication on California Mining has not been available for nearly a century. This publication includes important information on the early gold mines of San Bernadino and Tulare County, which were some of the first gold fields mined in California by early Spanish and Mexican miners before the 49ers came on the scene. Included are not only details on early mining methods in the area, production statistics and geological information, but also the location of the early gold mines that helped make California "The Golden State". Also included are details on the mining of other minerals such as copper, iron, lead, zinc, manganese, tungsten, vanadium, asbestos, barite, borax, cement, clay, dolomite, fluospar, gem stones, graphite, marble, salines, petroleum, stronium, talc and others. **8.5" X 11", 200 ppgs. Retail Price: $19.99**

Chromite Mining in The Klamath Mountains of California and Oregon - Unavailable since 1919, this publication was originally compiled by J.S. Diller of the United States Department of Geological Survey and includes details on the chromite mines of this area of Northern California and Southern Oregon. Also included are insights into the mineralization and other characteristics of this important mining region, as well as the location of historic mines. Also included are insights into chromite mining in Eastern Oregon and Montana. **8.5" X 11", 98 ppgs. Retail Price: $9.99**

Mines and Mining in Amador, Calaveras and Tuolumne Counties, California - Unavailable since 1915, this publication was originally compiled by William Tucker and includes details on the mines and mineral resources of this important California mining area. Included are details on the geology, history and important gold mines of the region, as well as insights into other local mineral resources such as asbestos, clay, copper, talc, limestone and others. Also included are insights into the mineralization and other characteristics of this important portion of California's Mother Lode mining region. **8.5″ X 11″, 198 ppgs. Retail Price: $14.99**

The Cerro Gordo Mining District of Inyo County California - Unavailable since 1963, this publication was originally compiled by the United States Department of Interior. Included are insights into the mineralization and other characteristics of this important mining region of Southern California. Topics include the mining of gold and silver in this important mining district in Inyo County, California, including details on the history, production and locations of the Cerro Gordo Mine, the Morning Star Mine, Estelle Tunnel, Charles Lease Tunnel, Ignacio, Hart, Crosscut Tunnel, Sunset, Upper Newtown, Newtown, Ella, Perseverance, Newsboy, Belmont and other silver and gold mines in the Cerro Gordo Mining District. This volume also includes important insights into the fossil record, geologic formations, faults and other aspects of economic geology in this California mining district. **8.5″ X 11″, 104 ppgs. Retail Price: $10.99**

Mining in Butte, Lassen, Modoc, Sutter and Tehama Counties of California - Unavailable since 1917, this publication was originally compiled by the United States Department of Interior. Included are insights into the mineralization and other characteristics of this important mining region of California. Topics include the mining of asbestos, chromite, gold, diamonds and manganese in Butte County, the mining of gold and copper in the Hayden Hill and Diamond Mountain mining districts of Lassen County, the mining of coal, salt, copper and gold in the High Grade and Winters mining districts of Modoc County, gold mining in Sutter County and the mining of gold, chromite, manganese and copper in Tehama County. This volume also includes the production records and locations of numerous mines in this important mining region. **8.5″ X 11″, 114 ppgs. Retail Price: $11.99**

Mines of Trinity County California - Originally published in 1965, this important publication on California Mining has not been available for nearly fifty years. This publication includes important information on mines and mining in Trinity County, California, as well insights into the mineralization and geology of this important mining area in Northern California. Included are extensive details on hardrock and placer gold mines and prospects, including charts showing the locations of these historic mines.. **8.5″ X 11″, 144 ppgs. Retail Price: $12.99**

Mines of Kern County California - Originally published in 1962, this important publication on California Mining has not been available for nearly fifty years. This publication includes important information on mines and mining in Kern County, California, as well insights into the mineralization and geology of this important mining area in California. Included are extensive details on hardrock and placer gold mines and prospects, including charts showing the locations of these historic mines. **8.5″ X 11″, 398 ppgs. Retail Price: $24.99**

Mines of Calaveras County California - Originally published in 1962, this important publication on California Mining has not been available for nearly fifty years. This publication includes important information on mines and mining in Calaveras County, California, as well insights into the mineralization and geology of this important mining area in Northern California. Included are extensive details on hardrock and placer gold mines and prospects, including charts showing the locations of these historic mines. **8.5″ X 11″, 236 ppgs. Retail Price: $19.99**

Lode Gold Mining in Grass Valley California - Unavailable since 1940, this publication was originally compiled by the United States Department of Interior. Included are insights into the gold mineralization and other characteristics of this important mining region of Nevada County, California. This volume also includes important insights into the geologic formations, faults and other aspects of economic geology in this California mining district. Of particular interest are the fine details on many hardrock gold mines in the area, including their locations, histories, development and mineralization. Some of the mines featured include the Gold Hill Mine, Massachusetts Hill, Boundary, Peabody, Golden Center, North Star, Omaha, Lone Jack, Homeward Bound, Hartery, Wisconsin, Allison Ranch, Phoenix, Kate Hayes, W.Y.O.D., Empire, Rich Hill, Daisy Hill, Orleans, Sultana, Centennial, Conlin, Ben Franklin, Crown Point and many others. **8.5″ X 11″, 148 ppgs. Retail Price: $12.99**

Lode Mining in the Alleghany District of Sierra County California - Unavailable since 1913, this publication was originally compiled by the United States Department of Interior. Included are insights into the mineralization and other characteristics of this important mining region of Sierra County. Included are details on the history, production and locations of numerous hardrock gold mines in this famous California area, including the Tightner Mine, Minnie D., Osceola, Eldorado, Twenty One, Sherman, Kenton, Oriental, Rainbow, Plumbago, Irelan, Gold Canyon, North Fork, Federal, Kate Hardy and others. This volume also includes important insights into the fossil record, geologic formations, faults and other aspects of economic geology in this California mining district. **8.5″ X 11″, 48 ppgs. Retail Price: $7.99**

Six Months In The Gold Mines During The California Gold Rush - Unavailable since 1850, this important work is a first hand account of one "49'ers" personal experience during the great California Gold Rush, shedding important light on one of the most exciting periods in the history of not only California, but also the world. Compiled from journals written between 1847 and 1849 by E. Gould Buffum, a native of New York, "Six Months In The Gold Mines During The California Gold Rush" offers a rare look into the day to day lives of the people who came to California to work in her gold mines when the state was still a great frontier. **8.5" X 11", 290 ppgs. Retail Price: $19.99**

Quartz Mines of the Grass Valley Mining District of California - Unavailable since 1867, this important publication has not been available since those days. This rare publication offers a short dissertation on the early hardrock mines in this important mining district in the California Mother Lode region between the 1850's and 1860's. Also included are hard to find details on the mineralization and locations of these mines, as well as how they were operated in those day. **8.5" X 11", 44 ppgs. Retail Price: $8.99**

Alaska Mining Books

Ore Deposits of the Willow Creek Mining District, Alaska - Unavailable since 1954, this hard to find publication includes valuable insights into the Willow Creek Mining District near Hatcher Pass in Alaska. The publication includes insights into the history, geology and locations of the well known mines in the area, including the Gold Cord, Independence, Fern, Mabel, Lonesome, Snowbird, Schroff-O'Neil, High Grade, Marion Twin, Thorpe, Webfoot, Kelly-Willow, Lane, Holland and others. **8.5" X 11", 96 ppgs. Retail Price: $9.99**

The Juneau Gold Belt of Alaska - Unavailable since 1906, this hard to find publication includes valuable insights into the gold mines around Juneau, Alaska. The publication includes important details into the history, geology and locations of the well known gold mines and prospects in the area, including those around Windham Bay, Holkham Bay, Port Snettisham, on Grindstone and Rhine Creeks, Gold Creek, Douglas Island, Salmon Creek, Lemon Creek, Nugget Creek, from the Mendenhall River to Berners Bay, McGinnis Creek, Montana Creek, Peterson Creek, Windfall Creek, the Eagle River, Yankee Basin, Yankee Curve, Kowee Creek and elsewhere. Not only are gold placer mines included, but also hardrock gold mines. **8.5" X 11", 224 ppgs. Retail Price: $19.99**

Arizona Mining Books

Mines and Mining in Northern Yuma County Arizona - Originally published in 1911, this important publication on Arizona Mining has not been available for over a hundred years. Included are rare insights into the gold, silver, copper and quicksilver mines of Yuma County, Arizona together with hard to find maps and photographs. Some of the mines and mining districts featured include the Planet Copper Mine, Mineral Hill, the Clara Consolidated Mine, Viati Mine, Copper Basin prospect, Bowman Mine, Quartz King, Billy Mack, Carnation, the Wardwell and Osbourne, Valensuella Copper, the Mariquita, Colonial Mine, the French American, the New York-Plomosa, Guadalupe, Lead Camp, Mudersbach Copper Camp, Yellow Bird, the Arizona Northern (Salome Strike), Bonanza (Harqua Hala), Golden Eagle, Hercules, Socorro and others. **8.5" X 11", 144 ppgs. Retail Price: $11.99**

The Aravaipa and Stanley Mining Districts of Graham County Arizona - Originally published in 1925, this important publication on Arizona Mining has not been available for nearly ninety years. Included are rare insights into the gold and silver mines of these two important mining districts, together with hard to find maps. **8.5" X 11", 140 ppgs. Retail Price: $11.99**

Gold in the Gold Basin and Lost Basin Mining Districts of Mohave County, Arizona - This volume contains rare insights into the geology and gold mineralization of the Gold Basin and Lost Basin Mining Districts of Mohave County, Arizona that will be of benefit to miners and prospectors. Also included is a significant body of information on the gold mines and prospects of this portion of Arizona. This volume is lavishly illustrated with rare photos and mining maps. **8.5" X 11", 188 ppgs. Retail Price: $19.99**

Mines of the Jerome and Bradshaw Mountains of Arizona - This important publication on Arizona Mining has not been available for ninety years. This volume contains rare insights into the geology and ore deposits of the Jerome and Bradshaw Mountains of Arizona that will be of benefit to miners and prospectors who work those areas. Included is a significant body of information on the mines and prospects of the Verde, Black Hills, Cherry Creek, Prescott, Walker, Groom Creek, Hassayampa, Bigbug, Turkey Creek, Agua Fria, Black Canyon, Peck, Tiger, Pine Grove, Bradshaw, Tintop, Humbug and Castle Creek Mining Districts. This volume is lavishly illustrated with rare photos and mining maps. **8.5" X 11", 218 ppgs. Retail Price: $19.99**

The Ajo Mining District of Pima County Arizona - This important publication on Arizona Mining has not been available for nearly seventy years. This volume contains rare insights into the geology and mineralization of the Ajo Mining District in Pima County, Arizona and in particular the famous New Cornelia Mine. **8.5" X 11", 126 ppgs. Retail Price: $11.99**

Mining in the Santa Rita and Patagonia Mountains of Arizona - Originally published in 1915, this important publication on Arizona Mining has not been available for nearly a century. Included are rare insights into hundreds of gold, silver, copper and other mines in this famous Arizona mining area. Details include the locations, geology, history, production and other facts of the mines of this region. **8.5" X 11", 394 ppgs. Retail [illegible]**

Mining in the Bisbee Quadrangle of Arizona - Originally published in 1906, this important publication on Arizona Mining has not been available for nearly a century. Included are rare insights into hundreds of gold, silver, copper and other mines in this famous Arizona mining area. Details include the locations, geology, history, production and other facts of the mines of this important mining region. **8.5" X 11", 188 ppgs. Retail Price: $14.99**

Montana Mining Books

A History of Butte Montana: The World's Greatest Mining Camp - First published in 1900 by H.C. Freeman, this important publication sheds a bright light on one of the most important mining areas in the history of The West. Together with his insights, as well as rare photographs of the periods, Harry Freeman describes Butte and its vicinity from its early beginnings, right up to its flush years when copper flowed from its mines like a river. At the time of publication, Butte, Montana was known worldwide as "The Richest Mining Spot On Earth" and produced not only vast amounts of copper, but also silver, gold and other metals from its mines. Freeman illustrates, with great detail, the most important mines in the vicinity of Butte, providing rare details on their owners, their history and most importantly, how the mines operated and how their treasures were extracted. Of particular interest are the dozens of rare photographs that depict mines such as the famous Anaconda, the Silver Bow, the Smoke House, Moose, Paulin, Buffalo, Little Minah, the Mountain Consolidated, West Greyrock, Cora, the Green Mountain, Diamond, Bell, Parnell, the Neversweat, Nipper, Original and many others. **8.5" X 11", 142 ppgs. Retail Price: $12.99**

The Butte Mining District of Montana - This important publication on Montana Mining has not been available for over a century. Included are rare insights into the gold, copper and silver mines of Butte, Montana together with hard to find maps and photographs. Some of the topics include the early history of gold, silver and copper mining in the Butte area, insight into the geology of its mining areas, the local distribution of gold, silver and copper ores, as well their composition and how to identify them. Also included are detailed facts about the mines in the Butte Mining District, including the famous Anaconda Mine, Gagnon, Parrot, Blue Vein, Moscow, Poulin, Stella, Buffalo, Green Mountain, Wake Up Jim, the Diamond-Bell Group, Mountain Consolidated, East Greyrock, West Greyrock, Snowball, Corra, Speculator, Adirondack, Miners Union, the Jessie-Edith May Group, Otisco, Iduna, Colorado, Lizzie, Cambers, Anderson, Hesperus, Preferencia and dozens of others. **8.5" X 11", 298 ppgs. Retail Price: $24.99**

Mines of the Helena Mining Region of Montana - This important publication on Montana Mining has not been available for over a century. Included are rare insights into the gold, copper and silver mines of the vicinity of Helena, Montana, including the Marysville Mining District, Elliston Mining District, Rimini Mining District, Helena Mining District, Clancy Mining District, Wickes Mining District, Boulder and Basin Mining Districts and the Elkhorn Mining District. Some of the topics include the early history of gold, silver and copper mining in the Helena area, insight into the geology of its mining areas, the local distribution of gold, silver and copper ores, as well their composition and how to identify them. Also included are detailed facts, history, geology and locations of over one hundred gold, silver and copper mines in the area . **8.5" X 11", 162 ppgs, Retail Price: $14.99**

Mines and Geology of the Garnet Range of Montana - This important publication on Montana Mining has not been available for over a century. Included are rare insights into the gold, copper and silver mines of the vicinity of this important mining area of Montana. Some of the topics include the early history of gold, silver and copper mining in the Garnet Mountains, insight into the geology of its mining areas, the local distribution of gold, silver and copper ores, as well their composition and how to identify them. Also included are detailed facts, history, geology and locations of numerous gold, silver and copper mines in the area . **8.5" X 11", 100 ppgs, Retail Price: $11.99**

Mines and Geology of the Philipsburg Quadrangle of Montana - This important publication on Montana Mining has not been available for over a century. Included are rare insights into the gold, copper and silver mines of the vicinity of this important mining area of Montana. Some of the topics include the early history of gold, silver and copper mining in the Philipsburg Quadrangle, insight into the geology of its mining areas, the local distribution of gold, silver and copper ores, as well their composition and how to identify them. Also included are detailed facts, history, geology and locations of over one hundred gold, silver and copper mines in the area **8.5" X 11", 290 ppgs, Retail Price: $24.99**

Geology of the Marysville Mining District of Montana - Included are rare insights into the mining geology of the Marysville Mining District. Some of the topics include the early history of gold, silver and copper mining in the area, insight into the geology of its mining areas, the local distribution of gold, silver and copper ores, as well their composition and how to identify them. Also included are detailed facts, history, geology and locations of gold, silver and copper mines in the area **8.5" X 11", 198 ppgs, Retail Price: $19.99**

The Geology and Mines of Northern Idaho and North Western Montana

See listing under Idaho.

Nevada Mining Books

The Bull Frog Mining District of Nevada - Unavailable since 1910, this publication was originally compiled by the United States Department of Interior. This volume also includes important insights into the geologic formations, faults and other aspects of economic geology in this Nevada mining district. Of particular interest are the fine details on many mines in the area, including their locations, histories, development and mineralization. Some of the mines featured include the National Bank Mine, Providence, Gibraltor, Tramps, Denver, Original Bullfrog, Gold Bar, Mayflower, Homestake-King and other mines and prospects. **8.5" X 11", 152 ppgs, Retail Price: $14.99**

History of the Comstock Lode - Unavailable since 1876, this publication was originally released by John Wiley & Sons. This volume also includes important insights into the famous Comstock Lode of Nevada that represented the first major silver discovery in the United States. During its spectacular run, the Comstock produced over 192 million ounces of silver and 8.2 million ounces of gold. Not only did the Comstock result in one of the largest mining rushes in history and yield immense fortunes for its owners, but it made important contributions to the development of the State of Nevada, as well as neighboring California. Included here are important details on not only the early development and history of the Comstock, but also rare early insight into its mines, ore and its geology.**8.5" X 11", 244 ppgs, Retail Price: $19.99**

Colorado Mining Books

Ores of The Leadville Mining District - Unavailable since 1926, this publication was originally compiled by the United States Department of Interior. This volume also includes important insights into the ores and mineralization of the Leadville Mining District in Colorado. Topics include historic ore prospecting methods, local geology, insights into ore veins and stockworks, the local trend and distribution of ore channels, reverse faults, shattered rock above replacement ore bodies, mineral enrichment in oxidized and sulphide zones and more. **8.5" X 11", 66 ppgs, Retail Price: $8.99**

Mining in Colorado - Unavailable since 1926, this publication was originally compiled by the United States Department of Interior. This volume also includes important insights into the mining history of Colorado from its early beginnings in the 1850's right up to the mid 1920's. Not only is Colorado's gold mining heritage included, but also its silver, copper, lead and zinc mining industry. Each mining area is treated separately, detailing the development of Colorado's mines on a county by county basis. **8.5" X 11", 284 ppgs, Retail Price: $19.99**

Gold Mining in Gilpin County Colorado - Unavailable since 1876, this publication was originally compiled by the Register Steam Printing House of Central City, Colorado. A rare glimpse at the gold mining history and early mines of Gilpin County, Colorado from their first discovery in the 1850's up to the "flush years" of the mid 1870's. Of particular interest is the history of the discovery of gold in Gilpin County and details about the men who made those first strikes. Special focus is given to the early gold mines and first mining districts of the area, many of which are not detailed in other books on Colorado's gold mining history. **8.5" X 11", 156 ppgs, Retail Price: $12.99**

Mining in the Gold Brick Mining District of Colorado - Important insights into the history of the Gold Brick Mining District, as well as its local geography and economic geology. Also included are the histories and locations of historic mines in this important Colorado Mining District, including the Cortland, Carter, Raymond, Gold Links, Sacramento, Bassick, Sandy Hook, Chronicle, Grand Prize, Chloride, Granite Mountain, Lucille, Gray Mountain, Hilltop, Maggie Mitchell, Silver Islet, Revenue, Roosevelt, Carbonate King and others. In addition to hardrock mining, are also included are details on gold placer mining in this portion of Colorado. **8.5" X 11", 140 ppgs, Retail Price: $12.99**

Washington Mining Books

The Republic Mining District of Washington - Unavailable since 1910, this important publication was originally published by the Washington Geologic Survey and has been unavailable for a century. Topics include the geology, rock formations and the formation of ore deposits in this important mining area of Washington State. Also included are hard to find details on the geology, history and locations of dozens of mines in the area. Some of the mines featured include the New Republic Mine, Ben Hur, Morning Glory, the South Republic Mine, Quilp, Surprise, Black Tail, Lone Pine, San Poil, Mountain Lion, Tom Thumb, Elcaliph and many others. **8.5" X 11", 94 ppgs, Retail Price: $10.99**

The Myers Creek and Nighthawk Mining Districts of Washington - Unavailable since 1911, this important publication was originally published by the Washington Geologic Survey and has been unavailable for a century. Topics include the geology, rock formations and the formation of ore deposits in these important mining areas of Washington State. Also included are hard to find details on the geology, history and locations of dozens of mines in the area. Some of the mines featured include the [illegible] Mine, Monterey, Nip and Tuck, Myers Creek, Number Nine, Neutral, Rainbow, Aztec, Crystal Butte, Apex, Butcher Boy, Molson, Mad River, Olentangy, Delate, Kelsey, Golden Chariot, Okanogan, Ohio, Forty-Ninth Parallel, Nighthawk, Favorite, Little Chopaka, Summit, Number One, California, Peerless, Caaba, Prize Group, Ruby, Mountain Sheep, Golden Zone, Rich Bar, Similkameen, Kimberly, Triune, Hiawatha, Trinity, Hornsilver, Maquae, Bellevue, Bullfrog, Palmer Lake, Ivanhoe, Copper World and many others. **8.5" X 11", 136 ppgs, Retail Price: $12.99**

The Blewett Mining District of Washington - Unavailable since 1911, this important publication was originally published by the Washington Geologic Survey and has been unavailable for a century. Topics include the geology, rock formations and the formation of ore deposits in this important mining area of Washington State. Also included are hard to find details on the geology, history and locations of dozens of mines in the area. Some of the mines featured include the Washington Meteor, Alta Vista, Pole Pick, Blinn, North Star, Golden Eagle, Tip Top, Wilder, Golden Guinea, Lucky Queen, Blue Bell, Prospect, Homestake, Lone Rock, Johnson, and others. **8.5" X 11", 134 ppgs, Retail Price: $12.99**

Silver Mining In Washington - Unavailable since 1955, this important publication was originally published by the Washington Geologic Survey. Featured are the hard to find locations and details pertaining to Washington's silver mines. **8.5" X 11", 180 ppgs, Retail Price: $15.99**

The Mines of Snohomish County Washington - Unavailable since 1942, this important publication was originally published by the Washington Geologic Survey and has been unavailable for seventy years. Featured are details on a large number of gold, silver, copper, lead and other metallic mineral mines. Included are the locations of each historic mine, along with information on the commodity produced. **8.5" X 11", 98 ppgs, Retail Price: $10.99**

The Mines of Chelan County Washington - Unavailable since 1943, this important publication was originally published by the Washington Geologic Survey and has been unavailable for seventy years. Featured are details on a large number of gold, silver, copper, lead and other metallic mineral mines. Included are the locations of each historic mine, along with information on the commodity. **8.5" X 11", 88 ppgs, Retail Price: $9.99**

Metal Mines of Washington - Unavailable since 1921, this important publication was originally published by the Washington Geologic Survey and has been unavailable for nearly ninety years. Widely considered a masterpiece on the Washington Mining Industry, "Metal Mines of Washington" sheds light on the important details of Washington's early mining years. Featured are details on hundreds of gold, silver, copper, lead and other metallic mineral mines. Included are hard to find details on the mineral resources of this state, as well as the locations of historic mines. Lavishly illustrated with maps and historic photos and complete with a glossary to explain any technical terms found in the text, this is one of the most important works on mining in the State of Washington. No prospector or miner should be without it if they are interested in mining in Washington. **8.5" X 11", 396 ppgs, Retail Price: $24.99**

Gem Stones In Washington - Unavailable since 1949, this important publication was originally published by the Washington Geologic Survey and has been unavailable since first published. Included are details on where to find naturally occurring gem stones in the State of Washington, including quartz crystal, amethyst, smoky quartz, milky quartz, agates, bloodstone, carnelian, chert, flint, jasper, onyx, petrified wood, opal, fire opal, hyalite and others. **8.5" X 11", 54 ppgs, Retail Price: $8.99**

The Covada Mining District of Washington - Unavailable since 1913, this important publication was originally published by the Washington Geologic Survey and has been unavailable for a century. Topics include the geology, rock formations and the formation of ore deposits in this important mining area of Washington State. Also included are hard to find details on the geology, history and locations of dozens of mines in the area. Some of the mines featured include the Admiral, Advance, Algonkian, Big Bug, Big Chief, Big Joker, Black Hawk, Black Tail, Black Thorn, Captain, Cherokee Strip, Colorado, Dan Patch, Dead Shot, Etta, Good Ore, Greasy Run, Great Scott, Idora, IXL, Jay Bird, Kentucky Bell, King Solomon, Laurel, Laura S, Little Jay, Meteor, Neglected, Northern Light, Old Nell, Plymouth Rock, Polaris, Quandary, Reserve, Shoo Fly, Silver Plume, Three Pines, Vernie, White Rose and dozens of others. **8.5" X 11", 114 ppgs, Retail Price: $10.99**

The Index Mining District of Washington - Unavailable since 1912, this important publication was originally published by the Washington Geologic Survey and has been unavailable for a century. Topics include the geology, rock formations and the formation of ore deposits in this important mining area of Washington State. Also included are hard to find details on the geology, history and locations of dozens of mines in the area. Some of the mines featured include the Sunset, Non-Pareil, Ethel Consolidated, Kittaning, Merchant, Homestead, Co-operative, Lost Creek, Uncle Sam, Calumet, Florence-Rae, Bitter Creek, Index Peacock, Gunn Peak, Helena, North Star, Buckeye. Copper Bell, Red Cross and others. **8.5" X 11", 114 ppgs, Retail Price: $11.99**

Mining & Mineral Resources of Stevens County Washington - Unavailable since 1920, this important publication was originally published by the Washington Geologic Survey and has been unavailable for a century. Topics include the geology, rock formations and the formation of ore deposits in these important mining areas of Washington State. Also included are hard to find details on the geology, history and locations of hundreds of mines in the area. **8.5" X 11", 372 ppgs, Retail Price: $24.99**

The Mines and Geology of the Loomis Quadrangle Okanogan County, Washington - Unavailable since 1972, this important publication was originally published by the Washington Geologic Survey and has been unavailable for a century. Topics include the geology, rock formations and the formation of ore deposits in this important mining area of Washington State. Also included are hard to find details on the geology, history and locations of dozens of gold, copper, silver and other mines in the area. **8.5" X 11", 150 ppgs, Retail Price: $12.99**

The Conconully Mining District of Okanogan County Washington - Unavailable since 1973, this important publication was originally published by the Washington Geologic Survey and has been unavailable for a century. Topics include the geology, rock formations and the formation of ore deposits in this important mining area of Washington State, which also includes Salmon Creek, Blue Lake and Galena. Also included are hard to find details on the geology, mining history and locations of dozens of mines in the area. Some of the mines include Arlington, Fourth of July, Sonny Boy, First Thought, Last Chance, War Eagle-Peacock, Wheeler, Mohawk, Lone Star, Woo Loo Moo Loo, Keystone, Hughes, Plant-Callahan, Johnny Boy, Leuena, Gubser, John Arthur, Tough Nut, Homestake, Key and many others **8.5" X 11", 68 ppgs, Retail Price: $8.99**

Wyoming Mining Books

Mining in the Laramie Basin of Wyoming - Unavailable since 1909, this publication was originally compiled by the United States Department of Interior. Also included are insights into the mineralization and other characteristics of this important mining region, especially in regards to coal, limestone, gypsum, bentonite clay, cement, sand, clay and copper. **8.5" X 11", 104 ppgs, Retail Price: $11.99**

New Mexico Mining Books

The Mogollon Mining District of New Mexico - Unavailable since 1927, this important publication was originally published by the US Department of Interior and has been unavailable for 80 years. Topics include the geology, rock formations and the formation of ore deposits in this important mining area in New Mexico. Of particular focus is information on the history and production of the ore deposits in this area, their form and structure, vein filling, their paragenesis, origins and ore shoots, as well as oxidation and supergene enrichment. Also included are hard to find details, including the descriptions and locations of numerous gold, silver and other types of mines, including the Eureka, Pacific, South Alpine, Great Western, Enterprise, Buffalo, Mountain View, Floride, Gold Dust, Last Chance, Deadwood, Confidence, Maud S., Deep Down, Little Fanney, Trilby, Johnson, Alberta, Comet, Golden Eagle, Cooney, Queen, the Iron Crown, Eberle, Clifton, Andrew Jackson mine, Mascot and others. **8.5" X 11", 144 ppgs, Retail Price: $12.99**

The Percha Mining District of Kingston New Mexico - Unavailable since 1883, this important publication was originally published by the Kingston Tribune and has been unavailable for over one hundred and thirty five years. Having been written during the earliest years of gold and silver mining in the Percha Mining District, unlike other books on the subject, this work offers the unique perspective of having actually been written while the early mining history of this area was still being made. In fact, the work was written so early in the development of this area that many of the notable mines in the Percha District were less than a few years old and were still being operated by their original discoverers with the same enthusiasm as when they were first located. Included are hard to find details on the very earliest gold and silver mines of this important mining district near Kingston in Sierra County, New Mexico. **8.5" X 11", 68 ppgs, Retail Price: $9.99**

East Coast Mining Books

The Gold Fields of the Southern Appalachians - Unavailable since 1895, this important publication was originally published by the US Department of Interior and has been unavailable for nearly 120 years. Topics include the geology, rock formations and the formation of ore deposits in this important mining area of the American South. Of particular focus is information on the history and statistics of the ore deposits in this area, their form and structure and veins. Also included are details on the placer gold deposits of the region. The gold fields of the Georgian Belt, Carolinian Belt and the South Mountain Mining District of North Carolina are all treated in descriptive detail. Included are hard to find details, including the descriptions and locations of numerous gold mines in Georgia, North Carolina and elsewhere in the American South. Also included are details on the gold belts of the British Maritime Provinces and the Green Mountains. **8.5" X 11", 104 ppgs, Retail Price: $9.99**

Gold Rush Tales Series

<u>Millions in Siskiyou County Gold</u> - In this first volume of the "Gold Rush Tales" series, leading mining historian and editor Kerby Jackson, introduces us to the story of how millions of dollars worth of gold was discovered in Siskiyou County during the California Gold Rush. Lavishly illustrated with photos from the 19th Century, this hard to find information was first published in 1897 and sheds important light onto the gold rush era in Siskiyou County, California and the experiences of the men who dug for the gold and actually found it. **8.5" X 11", 82 ppgs, Retail Price: $9.99**

<u>The California Rand in the Days of '49</u> - In this second volume of the "Gold Rush Tales" series, leading mining historian and editor Kerby Jackson, introduces us to four tales from the California Gold Rush. Lavishly illustrated with photos from the 19th Century, this hard to find information was first published in 1890's and includes the stories of "California's Rand", details about Chinese miners, how one early miner named Baker struck it rich and also the story of Alphonzo Bowers, who invented the first hydraulic gold dredge. **8.5" X 11", 54 ppgs, Retail Price: $9.99**

More Mining Books

<u>Prospecting and Developing A Small Mine</u> - Topics covered include the classification of varying ores, how to take a proper ore sample, the proper reduction of ore samples, alluvial sampling, how to understand geology as it is applied to prospecting and mining, prospecting procedures, methods of ore treatment, the application of drilling and blasting in a small mine and other topics that the small scale miner will find of benefit. **8.5" X 11", 112 ppgs, Retail Price: $11.99**

<u>Timbering For Small Underground Mines</u> - Topics covered include the selection of caps and posts, the treatment of mine timbers, how to install mine timbers, repairing damaged timbers, use of drift supports, headboards, squeeze sets, ore chute construction, mine cribbing, square set timbering methods, the use of steel and concrete sets and other topics that the small underground miner will find of benefit. This volume also includes twenty eight illustrations depicting the proper construction of mine timbering and support systems that greatly enhance the practical usability of the information contained in this small book. **8.5" X 11", 88 ppgs. Retail Price: $10.99**

<u>Timbering and Mining</u> - A classic mining publication on Hard Rock Mining by W.H. Storms. Unavailable since 1909, this rare publication provides an in depth look at American methods of underground mine timbering and mining methods. Topics include the selection and preservation of mine timbers, drifting and drift sets, driving in running ground, structural steel in mine workings, timbering drifts in gravel mines, timbering methods for driving shafts, positioning drill holes in shafts, timbering stations at shafts, drainage, mining large ore bodies by means of open cuts or by the "Glory Hole" system, stoping out ore in flat or low lying veins, use of the "Caving System", stoping in swelling ground, how to stope out large ore bodies, Square Set timbering on the Comstock and its modifications by California miners, the construction of ore chutes, stoping ore bodies by use of the "Block System", how to work dangerous ground, information on the "Delprat System" of stoping without mine timbers, construction and use of headframes and much more. This volume provides a reference into not only practical methods of mining and timbering that may be employed in narrow vein mining by small miners today, but also rare insights into how mines were being worked at the turn of the 19th Century. **8.5" X 11", 288 ppgs. Retail Price: $24.99**

<u>A Study of Ore Deposits For The Practical Miner</u> - Mining historian Kerby Jackson introduces us to a classic mining publication on ore deposits by J.P. Wallace. First published in 1908, it has been unavailable for over a century. Included are important insights into the properties of minerals and their identification, on the occurrence and origin of gold, on gold alloys, insights into gold bearing sulfides such as pyrites and arsenopyrites, on gold bearing vanadium, gold and silver tellurides, lead and mercury tellurides, on silver ores, platinum and iridium, mercury ores, copper ores, lead ores, zinc ores, iron ores, chromium ores, manganese ores, nickel ores, tin ores, tungsten ores and others. Also included are facts regarding rock forming minerals, their composition and occurrences, on igneous, sedimentary, metamorphic and intrusive rocks, as well as how they are geologically disturbed by dikes, flows and faults, as well as the effects of these geologic actions and why they are important to the miner. Written specifically with the common miner and prospector in mind, the book will help to unlock the earth's hidden wealth for you and is written in a simple and concise language that anyone can understand. **8.5" X 11", 366 ppgs. Retail Price: $24.99**

<u>Mine Drainage</u> - Unavailable since 1896, this rare publication provides an in depth look at American methods of underground mine drainage and mining pump systems. This volume provides a reference into not only practical methods of mining drainage that may be employed in narrow vein mining by small miners today, but also rare insights into how mines were being worked at the turn of the 19th Century. **8.5" X 11", 218 ppgs. Retail Price: $24.99**

Fire Assaying Gold, Silver and Lead Ores - Unavailable since 1907, this important publication was originally published by the Mining and Scientific Press and was designed to introduce miners and prospectors of gold, silver and lead to the art of fire assaying. Topics include the fire assaying of ores and products containing gold, silver and lead; the sampling and preparation of ore for an assay; care of the assay office, assay furnaces; crucibles and scorifiers; assay balances; metallic ores; scorification assays; cupelling; parting' crucible assays, the roasting of ores and more. This classic provides a time honored method of assaying put forward in a clear, concise and easy to understand language that will make it a benefit to even beginners. **8.5" X 11", 96 ppgs. Retail Price: $11.99**

Methods of Mine Timbering - Originally published in 1896, this important publication on mining engineering has not been available for nearly a century. Included are rare insights into historical methods of timbering structural support that were used in underground metal mines during the California that still have a practical application for the small scale hardrock miner of today. **8.5" X 11", 94 ppgs. Retail Price: $10.99**

The Enrichment of Copper Sulfide Ores - First published in 1913, it has been unavailable for over a century. Topics include the definition and types of ore enrichment, the oxidation of copper ores, the precipitation of metallic sulfides. Also included are the results of dozens of lab experiments pertaining to the enrichment of sulfide ores that will be of interest to the practical hard rock mine operator in his efforts to release the metallic bounty from his mine's ore. **8.5" X 11", 92 ppgs. Retail Price: $9.99**

A Study of Magmatic Sulfide Ores - Unavailable since 1914, this rare publication provides an in depth look at magmatic sulfide ores. Some of the topics included are the definition and classification of magmatic ores, descriptions of some magmatic sulfide ore deposits known at the time of publication including copper and nickel bearing pyrrohitic ore bodies, chalcopyrite-bornite deposits, pyritic deposits, magnetite-ileminite deposits, chromite deposits and magmatic iron ore deposits. Also included are details on how to recognize these types of ore deposits while prospecting for valuable hardrock minerals. **8.5" X 11", 138 ppgs. Retail Price: $11.99**

The Cyanide Process of Gold Recovery - Unavailable since 1894 and released under the name "The Cyanide Process: Its Practical Application and Economical Results", this rare publication provides an in depth look at the early use of cyanide leaching for gold recovery from hardrock mine ores. This volume provides a reference into the early development and use of cyanide leaching to recover gold. **8.5" X 11", 162 ppgs. Retail Price: $14.99**

California Gold Milling Practices - Unavailable since 1895 and released under the name "California Gold Practices", this rare publication provides an in depth look at early methods of milling used to reduce gold ores in California during the late 19th century. This volume provides a reference into the early development and use of milling equipment during the earliest years of the California Gold Rush up to the age of the Industrial Revolution. Much of the information still applies today and will be of use to small scale miners engaging in hardrock mining. **8.5" X 11", 104 ppgs. Retail Price: $10.99**

Leaching Gold and Silver Ores With The Plattner and Kiss Processes - Mining historian Kerby Jackson introduces us to a classic mining publication on the evaluation and examination of mines and prospects by C.H. Aaron. First published in 1881, it has been unavailable for over a century and sheds important light on the leaching of gold and silver ores with the Plattner and Kiss processes. **8.5" X 11", 204 ppgs. Retail Price: $15.99**

The Metallurgy of Lead and the Desilverization of Base Bullion - First published in 1896, it has been unavailable for over a century and sheds important light on the the recovery of silver from lead based ores. Some of the topics include the properties of lead and some of its compounds, lead ores such as galenite, anglesite, cerussite and others, the distribution of lead ores throughout the United States and the sampling and assaying of lead ores. Also covered is the metallurgical treatment of lead ores, as well as the desilverization of lead by the Pattinson Process and the Parkes Process. Hofman's text has long been considered one of the most important early works on the recovery of silver from lead based ores. **8.5" X 11", 452 ppgs. Retail Price: $29.99**

Ore Sampling For Small Scale Miners - First published in 1916, it has been unavailable for over a century and sheds important light on historic methods of ore sampling in hardrock mines. Topics include how to take correct ore samples and the conditions that affect sampling, such as their subdivision and uniformity. Particular detail is given to methods of hand sampling ore bodies by grab sample, pipe sample and coning, as well as sampling by mechanical methods. Also given are insights into the screening, drying and grinding processes to achieve the most consistent sample results and much more. **8.5" X 11", 124 ppgs. Retail Price: $12.99**

The Extraction of Silver, Copper and Tin from Ores - First published in 1896, it has been unavailable for over a century and sheds important light on how historic miners recovered silver, copper and tin from their mining operations. The book is split into three sections, including a discussion on the [illegible] of silver ores, the mining and treatment of copper [illegible] practiced at [illegible], Spain and the smelting of tin as it was practiced by metallurgists at [illegible], Singapore. Also included is an overview and analysis of these historic metal recovery methods that will be of benefit to those interested in the extraction of silver, copper and tin from small mines. **8.5″ X 11″, 118 ppgs. Retail Price: $14.99**

The Roasting of Gold and Silver Ores - First published in 1880, it has been unavailable for over a century and sheds important light on how historic miners recovered gold and silver rom their mining operations. Topics include details on the most important silver and free milling gold ores, methods of desulphurization of ores, methods of deoxidation, the chlorination of ores, methods and details on roasting gold and silver ores, notes on furnaces and more. Also included are details on numerous methods of gold and silver recovery, including the Ottokar Hofman's Process, the Patera Process, Kiss Process, Augustin Process, Ziervogel Process and others. **8.5″ X 11″, 178 ppgs. Retail Price: $19.99**

The Examination of Mines and Prospects - First published in 1912, it has been unavailable for over a century and sheds important light on how to examine and evaluate hardrock mines, prospects and lode mining claims. Sections include Mining Examinations, Structural Geology, Structural Features of Ore Deposits, Primary Ores and their Distribution, Types of Primary Ore Deposits, Primary Ore Shoots, The Primary Alteration of Wall Rocks, Alterations by Surface Agencies, Residual Ores and their Distribution, Secondary Ores and Ore Shoots and Vein Outcrops. This hard to find information is a must for those who are interested in owning a mine or who already own a lode mining claim and wish to succeed at quartz mining. **8.5″ X 11″, 250 ppgs. Retail Price: $19.99**

Made in the USA
Las Vegas, NV
04 December 2023

82069077R00111